Between Jaffa & Tel Aviv, 1870–1930

Between Jaffa & Tel Aviv, 1870–1930

A MEMOIR

Yosef Eliyahu Chelouche

Edited and with an introduction by
Michelle U. Campos *and* Or Aleksandrowicz
Translated by Marty Friedlander
Translation edited by Evyatar (Tari) Chelouche

BRANDEIS UNIVERSITY PRESS Waltham, Massachusetts

Brandeis University Press
© 2025 by Michelle U. Campos and Or Aleksandrowicz
All rights reserved
Manufactured in the United States of America
Designed by Richard Hendel
Typeset in Bulmer types by Passumpsic Publishing

For permission to reproduce any of the material in this book,
contact Brandeis University Press, 415 South Street, Waltham MA 02453,
or visit brandeisuniversitypress.com

Originally published as *Parashat Hayay, 1870–1930* (Tel Aviv: Stroud, 1931).
Also published as *Parashat Hayay, 1870–1930* (Tel Aviv: Babel, 2005).

Library of Congress Cataloging-in-Publication Data
available at https://catalog.loc.gov/
978-1-68458-256-3 (paper)
978-1-68458-301-0 (cloth)
978-1-68458-255-6 (ebook)

5 4 3 2 1

FRONTISPIECE
Yosef Eliyahu Chelouche, 1870–1934.
Chelouche Family Collection.

This publication has been made possible with support from the Judaica Stiftung, Geneva, Switzerland, established by Nahum Goldmann. Special thanks to Guido Goldman and the Robert D. Farber University Archives and Special Collections Department, Brandeis Library.

The translation of the original Hebrew text was made possible thanks to the generous donations of Dalia and Merrill Berman, Nava and Menachem Kfir, Dafna and Avi Bahir, Yair and Tessa Chelouche, and Gadi Chelouche.

CONTENTS

List of Illustrations *ix*
Acknowledgments *xi*
Note on Transliteration and Citation *xiii*
Editors' Introduction *1*
Preface *77*

I

1 : Days of My Infancy, Childhood, and Youth *85*
2 : The Kidnapping of Yosef *99*
3 : My Earliest Life Experiences; The First Pioneers *118*
4 : My School Days in Beirut *126*
5 : My Engagement, and My Father-in-Law Rabbi Avraham Moyal *137*
6 : My Wedding, and My Entry into the World of Commerce *149*
7 : In the Days of the Turkish Regime *171*
8 : Visits to Our Home by Famous People *181*
9 : Between Building and Destruction *186*
10 : Founding of Tel Aviv and Construction of the Gymnasium *196*
11 : New Company and the Shield Association *218*
12 : The Silicate Initiative, My Dream — and Those for Whom It Came True *232*

II

13 : Beginning of the World War *241*
14 : The Days of Ottomanization and the Cruel Expulsion of the Foreign Subjects *259*

15 : The Final Days in Power of Baha al-Din and the
Audience with Djemal Pasha *273*
16 : Days of Hunger in the Land *291*
17 : The Expulsion of Jaffa and Tel Aviv *301*
18 : A Terrifying Night in Deserted Jaffa and More . . . *308*
19 : The Entry of the English into Petah Tikva, and Their Departure *320*
20 : And They Journeyed and Encamped in the Village of Qalqilya *325*
21 : From Qalqilya to Kafr Jammal *336*
22 : Informers, the Turkish Government, and Kindly Arabs *352*
23 : Imprisoned in Tulkarm, and Once Again in Kafr Jammal *363*
24 : The Arrival of the Redeemers and Conquerors of Our Country *379*
25 : Following the Balfour Declaration, Days of Light and Shadow *393*
26 : Bloody Clashes in Jaffa, May 1921 *403*
27 : The Neighborly Relations That Broke Down *412*
28 : My Work on Behalf of Building and Expanding Tel Aviv *422*
29 : The Bloody Riots of August 1929, and Their Aftermath *432*
Epilogue *442*

Appendix: Family Tree of Yosef Eliyahu Chelouche *451*
Bibliography *455*
Index *469*

ILLUSTRATIONS

FIGURES

Figure I.1	Jaffa from the Mediterranean Sea, ca. 1890	12
Figure I.2	Jaffa's town walls and main gate from the northeast, 1860	18
Figure I.3	Theodor Sandel's map of Jaffa and its environs, 1880	20
Figure I.4	Jaffa's vegetable and fruit market square near the Jerusalem Gate, ca. 1890	21
Figure I.5	Jaffa's verdant groves to the northeast of the city, ca. 1900	24
Figure I.6	The first house built by Aharon Chelouche in the 1880s outside Jaffa's city core, ca. 1921	29
Figure I.7	The Chelouche family in Neve Tzedek, ca. 1900	31
Figure I.8	Jaffa's train station, ca. 1896	32
Figure I.9	The clock tower square in Jaffa, ca. 1921	33
Figure I.10	The Ottoman government house (*saraya*) in Jaffa, ca. 1898–1901	34
Figure I.11	Bustrus Street in modern Jaffa, ca. 1921	35
Figure I.12	Chelouche Brothers' factory advertisement, early 1920s	36
Figure I.13	Herzl Street in Tel Aviv, 1911	40
Figure I.14	Residents of Tel Aviv in front of a "Diligence" carriage on Herzl Street, ca. 1911	41
Figure I.15	Aerial photograph of northern Jaffa, 12 January 1918	49
Figure I.16	Yosef Eliyahu Chelouche's funeral procession, 24 July 1934	59
Figure I.17	Yosef Eliyahu Chelouche, late 1920s	76
Figure 1.1	Aharon Chelouche (father of Yosef Eliyahu), late nineteenth century	84

Figure 4.1	Yosef Eliyahu Chelouche wearing an Ottoman fez and Western suit, 1886	132
Figure 9.1	Yosef Eliyahu, his wife, Freha, and their children, 1907	194
Figure 10.1	The members of the first Tel Aviv municipal council, 1911	206
Figure 10.2	The founders of Tel Aviv, 1929 celebration gathering	216
Figure 16.1	Yosef Eliyahu Chelouche during his service on the Wheat Committee, 1917	292
Figure 20.1	Yosef Eliyahu Chelouche and Me'ir Dizengoff, late 1920s	334
Figure 25.1	Aharon Chelouche shortly before his death in 1920	397
Figure 27.1	Members of the Jaffa municipal council, early 1920s	413
Figure 27.2	Members of the Jaffa municipal council (seated), early 1920s	414
Figure 28.1	Members of the Tel Aviv municipal council, early 1920s	423
Figure 29.1	Members of the Chelouche family in their home in Tel Aviv, ca. 1927	433
Figure 29.2	Yosef Eliyahu Chelouche, late 1920s	440

MAPS

Map 1.1	Yosef Eliyahu Chelouche's residences in Jaffa and Tel Aviv, 1870–1934	82
Map 17.1	The Chelouche family's travels after their expulsion from Jaffa in April 1917	307

ACKNOWLEDGMENTS

This book would not have been possible without the generous support and participation of many members of the extended Chelouche family. First of all, Tari (Evyatar) Chelouche and Tomer Chelouche were indefatigable visionaries and vital partners in the project, from start to finish. Their deep knowledge of Chelouche family history, Jaffa's built landscape, and their lasting family networks were invaluable. Tari also painstakingly reviewed and corrected the translation, contributed his rich knowledge of Biblical Hebrew, and shared the fruit of his personal research on various aspects of the Chelouche family history.

The translation of the original Hebrew text was made possible thanks to the generous donations of Dalia and Merrill Berman, Nava and Menachem Kfir, Dafna and Avi Bahir, Yair and Tessa Chelouche, and Gadi Chelouche.

The Chelouche family papers are held in the Central Zionist Archives in Jerusalem. We thank the archivists for their assistance in accessing and digitizing materials. While the collection is extensive, particularly with regard to some aspects of Yosef Eliyahu Chelouche's public life, there is unfortunately very little documentation available about his businesses and his personal life. Where possible, we drew on the published memoirs and the valuable oral histories of other Chelouche family members. Despite their generous contributions to the project at various levels, the Chelouche family from the outset supported this as a scholarly and not a hagiographic project; we sincerely thank them for their trust.

While preparing the memoir for an international audience, we attempted to more fully document, corroborate, and contextualize some of the episodes in Yosef Eliyahu Chelouche's life history as well as some of the people with whom he interacted. Unfortunately, this proved particularly difficult when it came to Ottoman and Palestinian sources and figures. The vast Ottoman archives did not yield as much information as we had hoped about the administration of the Jaffa district or about the period of World War I in Palestine, especially regarding the expulsions of civilians from Jaffa. On the other hand, local Palestinian sources such as the registries of the Islamic (*shariʻa*) courts and the sole surviving registries of the civil (*nizami*) courts were rich depositories of local life in late Ottoman Jaffa. However, the court records are so extensive, and are not digitized, indexed, or searchable, so we were only able to scratch the surface. We thank Ahmad Mahmoud for his valuable research assistance in finding some Chelouche cases in the Jaffa *shariʻa* courts, and we thank Büşra İyibaş for her important research assistance in the Ottoman imperial archives.

Penn State University's History Department and Program in Jewish Studies provided generous research funding to help with this project; Michelle Campos thanks in particular the former Head of History Michael Kulikowski for his enthusiastic support at the beginning of the project. Or Aleskandrowicz acknowledges the support of the Azrieli Fund for Advanced Studies.

At Brandeis University Press, Sylvia Fried has been a supportive and extraordinarily patient believer in the importance of Yosef Eliyahu's life story; we thank her for the curiosity, generosity, and unstinting faith that she extended to our project, as well as for her incisive editorial feedback. Eugene Sheppard has been an instrumental facilitator, reader, and supporter; we thank him for all of this as well as for his capacious vision of "European Jewish history" that stretches across the Mediterranean. We also thank Jonathan Decter and Yuval Evri for their critical support and feedback on earlier versions of the introduction. Many thanks also to the talented team that helped bring this book to life: Karen Levy for her skillful copyediting; Ashley Burns and Katie Smith for their herculean efforts with the complex production process; and Maxine Rosenfeld for her help making sure that Yosef Eliyahu Chelouche gains the broad international readership he so richly deserves. We can think of no better home for his story than with Brandeis University Press, not least of all due to its continued commitment to "social justice, wide cultural representation, and intellectual integrity," all the more important in these challenging times.

NOTE ON TRANSLITERATION AND CITATION

Personal names have been transliterated according to the conventions of the language of origin, with the exception of cases where the individual was known to write his/her name in a particular manner. For this reason, we have adopted Djemal Pasha's chosen transliteration of his first name instead of Cemal (contemporary Turkish) or Jamal (Arabic). Place-names are written in the commonly adopted Anglicized form. Administrative terms are given in both Arabic and Turkish forms.

Words in Hebrew have been transliterated according to Brandeis University Press's simplified Hebrew transliteration system. Arabic and Turkish words have been transliterated according to the *IJMES* convention, unless the word has become commonly known in English. We have used ' for the Arabic and Hebrew letter *ayin* regardless of its placement, and ' for *alef/alif*, but only when used in the middle of a word or name (in Hebrew) or when it indicates a *hamza* (in Arabic).

In order to facilitate the reader experience, we have elected to cite our sources only when taking direct quotes, specific figures, or original arguments from them; otherwise, readers are directed to look at the full bibliography for the general and specialized scholarship upon which we relied.

EDITORS' INTRODUCTION

When Yosef Eliyahu Chelouche (1870–1934) published his Hebrew-language memoir, *Parashat Hayay* (The story of my life), in Tel Aviv in honor of his sixtieth birthday, he sent dozens of copies to family members, friends, colleagues, and acquaintances.[1] Most copies were sent within Mandatory Palestine, crisscrossing the town of Tel Aviv as well as to Jerusalem, Tiberias, and Safed, but a few books were shipped farther afield, including one to a nephew in Grenoble, France, and another to a family friend studying law in London. Among those with whom Chelouche shared his life story we find rabbis, teachers, bankers, clerks, government officials, journalists, and authors, including the two most luminary Hebrew-language writers of the day, Haim Nachman Bialik and Shai Agnon.[2] Chelouche also took care to donate copies to the libraries of the B'nai B'rith Jewish fraternal organization in Jerusalem and the Alliance Israélite Universelle (AIU) school in Beirut.[3]

If Chelouche's numerous gifts were aimed at ensuring that his memoir gain a broad readership, it proved to be a sound strategy, and within weeks trickles of praise began to arrive in the author's mailbox. A journalist in Jerusalem enjoyed the book so much that he passed it on to his wife to read. A farmer in the Jewish agricultural colony of Binyamina shared that after a long day in the fields, he could not resist picking up *Parashat Hayay* to "feed his soul." Perhaps most flattering given Chelouche's insecurities about his amateur writing style, the poet Bialik warmly complimented Chelouche that his memoir "reads like a novel."[4]

These private letters were soon joined by laudatory reviews published throughout the spring and summer of 1931 in the Hebrew, Yiddish, and English press in Palestine and Europe.[5] As those readers and reviewers quickly discovered, *Parashat Hayay* was a riveting narrative. The reviewer in the English-language *Palestine Bulletin* effusively reported that the memoir was written "as if [Chelouche] were sitting in a Jaffa café and were telling the story of bygone days to a group of old friends gathered round"; he confessed that he devoured the memoir in one sitting.

Beyond its dramatic readability, *Parashat Hayay* was also recognized as a singularly important eyewitness account of more than fifty years in Palestine.[6] This momentous period included the last decades of the four-hundred-year-long Ottoman rule over the country, the beginning of Zionist settlement, the tumultuous years of World War I, and the rocky first decade of the British Mandatory regime. Moreover, Yosef Eliyahu Chelouche was much more than just a distant narrator or passive observer; as he recounted on the pages of his memoir, he was very much an active agent of change. By the time Chelouche finally became a celebrated memoirist he was already a successful entrepreneur and building contractor, affluent landowner, generous philanthropist, respected community leader, retired public official, and provocative public commentator.

Intersecting many of these roles was Chelouche's position as an experienced "practical Zionist": he spent the second half of his life helping to found, settle, build up, and manage Tel Aviv, the first so-called Hebrew settlement established on the northeastern outskirts of Jaffa that quickly became the cultural and ideological center of the modern Zionist enterprise.[7] However, in contrast to the vast majority of the first founders of Tel Aviv and the local Zionist leadership who were European immigrants to the country, Yosef Eliyahu Chelouche was a native-born Sephardi ("Oriental" or "Eastern") Jew.[8] This simple fact meant that Chelouche brought a unique life experience and perspective, one that also made his memoir "exotic" in the eyes of many readers in his day.[9]

Chelouche was a "native son" of Palestine who spoke and wrote Levantine Arabic fluently and was fully integrated into the Ottoman modernizing *effendi* class (educated "gentlemen" who had political, economic, and/or social capital).[10] His nativeness not only informed his individual biography, cultural orientation, and social networks, as his memoir richly details, but it also shaped his political worldview to a certain extent, both in terms of his understanding of intra-Jewish relations and in terms of his outlook on Jewish-Arab relations in Palestine.

As *Parashat Hayay* recaptured this late Ottoman landscape and society it also—and more crucially—provided an alternative vision of Jewish-Arab relations, one that showed the *ordinariness* of native relations in Palestine under a very different political and social order. By retelling stories of his relationships with neighboring Palestinian Arabs in their dynamic and lived contexts and over his lifetime, Chelouche placed Jewish-Arab relations in a fuller, more three-dimensional context than the dominant and narrow one that by the 1930s focused solely on politics and violence. Instead, his account of his personal relations with Palestinian Arabs veered between partnership and rivalry, trust and betrayal, respect and hatred, generosity and anger—in fact, the ordinary span of human relationships, not at all unlike his description of his relationships with his fellow Jews.

By now, the story of Palestine in the early twentieth century has been told many times from the perspectives of British officials, Zionist and Palestinian nationalist leaders, and even—although far less frequently—ordinary Arabs and Jews on the ground.[11] In recent years, specialist historians and other scholars have turned to Chelouche's original Hebrew memoir as their guide to understanding turn-of-the-century Palestine, particularly in considering the limitations of the dominant binaries of "Arab" and "Jew," "native" and "foreigner," "Zionist" and "anti-Zionist."[12] As we will see, Chelouche inhabited the seam line in many ways, upending standard categories and assumptions about identity and belonging. However, Chelouche's memoir is much more than the potential—or the limitation—of its politics. *Parashat Hayay* is also a unique and fascinating mixture of ethnography, *bildungsroman*, wartime testimony, political and social homily, and an original, albeit partial, mirror onto the searing transformation of a country, a community, and an individual.

This English translation of *Parashat Hayay* allows nonspecialists for the first time to delve into this world from the unique lens as a Jew of Middle Eastern heritage who was locally born and raised, as someone deeply embedded in Palestinian society but also wholeheartedly active in the Eretz Israel (Land of Israel) Zionist movement, as an Arabic- and Hebrew-speaking bilingual, and as a resident, builder, defender, and critic of both Jaffa and Tel Aviv. We follow Chelouche from childhood to near the end of his life, through his friendships and business relationships and rivalries and favors, and against the backdrop of urban and commercial development, wartime imperial collapse, nascent nationalist conflict, and imperial and colonial rule. Along the way, readers are confronted with important questions about the meaning of culture, identity, intra- and intercommunal conflict, the tensions between political and social belonging, and changing expectations and relations between Jews and Arabs in Palestine.

In order to better appreciate Chelouche's unique perspective, we must first delve into the world in which his memoir was written and which it sought to depict and, ultimately, to change.

LATE OTTOMAN JAFFA

Jaffa is a port city on the eastern shores of the Mediterranean Sea with a recorded history of more than four millennia: it is mentioned in ancient Egyptian papyri and in biblical scriptures, in Greek mythologies and Roman chronicles, and in Byzantine, Islamic, and Crusader accounts.[13] Over the course of its history, Jaffa went through numerous periods of massive building and devastating destruction; this did not end after the town and its surrounding region, Palestine, became part of the Ottoman Empire in the early sixteenth century.[14] Modern Western accounts often depict Jaffa as a neglected and backward corner of the empire, but in fact, Jaffa underwent tremendous transformation and dynamic development during the four hundred years of Ottoman rule, and as we shall see, especially in its last half century during Chelouche's lifetime.

Almost immediately after the Ottoman conquest, Jaffa's port was fortified and its citadel was rebuilt and manned by Ottoman troops, an attempted defense against sea-born pirates as well as Bedouin nomads on land. Recently uncovered Ottoman ledgers from the seventeenth century detailing soldiers' salaries and Jaffa fortress expenses offer a glimpse at some of the ways in which the Ottomans invested in the region and sought to buttress their expanded borders.[15] After an initial period of stability and growth, however, by the late eighteenth century, the Ottoman Empire was experiencing the stresses of imperial rule, confronting crises of decentralization sparked by opportunistic challenges from local military and political rulers.

In this period, Jaffa suffered several major assaults launched from neighboring Egypt to its west, the worst of which was the short-lived but brutal Napoleonic invasion in the spring of 1799, in which approximately four thousand men, women, and children of Jaffa were massacred and large portions of the town were destroyed. After the French withdrawal from the region and the reassertion of nominal Ottoman control, some of the earliest entries preserved in the Jaffa Islamic (*shari'a*) court registers include edicts from Istanbul urging local officials to rebuild the town. As a result, in the 1800–1810s Jaffa experienced an unprecedented project of urban renewal under the acting governor Muhammad Amin

Agha Abu Nabbut. Abu Nabbut not only repaired the town walls but also built a Great Mosque on the ruins of the mosque destroyed by Napoleon's forces, together with a school of religious learning (*madrasa*), a manuscript library (*kutuphane*), and public drinking fountains (*sabils*). Dozens of stores, houses, cafes, warehouses, and workshops were built nearby and dedicated to Abu Nabbut's religious endowment (*waqf*) to fund these public works projects in the town.

This building boom not only shifted the town's built-up center to the northeast, land that had previously been gardens, barren fields, or recent ruins, but it also led to the development of a more sophisticated local economy with the addition of seven specialized markets. Already a central node in the travel of goods, people, and ideas across the sea as well as across the overland caravan routes, Jaffa supplied the regional and international trade of grains, olives, soap, and other products from the interior towns of Nablus and Ramle. The town's main gate (known today as the "Jerusalem Gate" or "Abu Nabbut Gate") connected the central bazaar and the adjacent Great Mosque to the roads leading to Jerusalem (to the east), Nablus (to the north), and Gaza (to the south). To support movement and commerce between those towns, public wells and drinking fountains were constructed on the roads to Jerusalem and Ramle. In addition, migrant laborers and investors from Egypt and elsewhere who were attracted to the town's growth began to settle in the area.

In one of his last acts before he was deposed and exiled, Abu Nabbut built a seawall on Jaffa's western edge to add to its maritime defenses. Despite this recent fortification, however, Jaffa was once again invaded in the 1830s, this time by Egyptian forces directed by the son of its ambitious governor, Mehmet Ali (known in Arabic as Muhammad 'Ali). By that point Jaffa had eclipsed Acre to become the second-most important port on the Eastern Mediterranean coast following Beirut. After a decade-long occupation, the Ottomans reestablished their control over southern Palestine in the early 1840s, but this occurred alongside a growing European presence and pressure as Western powers began to vie for greater influence in the region. Western consulates were established in Jerusalem in that decade, followed in the next decades by the establishment of vice-consulates in Jaffa. In dozens of cases, Western navies sent ships to patrol the Jaffa coastline, an obvious attempt to intimidate local Ottoman officials and to assert their primacy as key players in the region.

They did so because the Western powers had dual direct interests in Jaffa: trade and pilgrims. France was an early trading partner with the Palestinian coastal town already in the eighteenth century, one of the reasons for Napoleon's invasion; by the mid-nineteenth century, other countries like England, the Austro-Hungarian Empire, the German states (and later, unified Germany), and the Russian Empire had joined its customer base, spurred on by favorable (or exploitative, depending on your perspective) trading treaties with the Ottoman government as well as by a growing desire for the goods produced locally. The most important exports for Jaffa in the midcentury were still grains (wheat, barley, and sorghum), sesame, olive oil, and soap, as well as fruits and vegetables like oranges, lemons, figs, and pomegranates. Periodically, Ottoman officials attempted to control and subordinate the foreign export of Jaffa's goods to their own imperial needs, such as by issuing export bans on its grains during times of famine or grain shortage within the empire.

However, these export controls were always short-lived, and Jaffa's international trade grew rapidly in the second half of the nineteenth century. In 1857, Jaffa's exports were valued at almost 15 million piastres; twenty-five years later, in 1882, the value of Jaffa's exports had more than tripled to over 37 million piastres.[16] It was in this period when Jaffa's local citrus industry—and particularly its large and growing orange orchards—took an increasingly larger share in the number and value of the town's exports, becoming Jaffa's main export commodity by the end of the century. This constant increase in the flow of trade over several decades made Jaffa an attractive location for investment and commerce, so much so that the district's commercial court was eventually moved from Jerusalem to Jaffa. While a comprehensive economic history of late Ottoman Jaffa remains to be written, numerous surviving primary source documents—including Islamic (*shari'a*), commercial (*ticari*), and civil (*nizami*) court records, Ottoman agricultural bank (*ziraat bankası*) account ledgers, chamber of commerce (*ticaret odası*) reports, consular files, and more—further attest to the rapid growth and increasingly sophisticated development of the local economy.

The town's economic growth was not only a result of commercial trade, but it was also tied to its central role in the pilgrimage and tourism industry to the Holy Land. Long a necessary stop for pilgrims from all points west on their way to Jerusalem, traffic to Jaffa increased dramatically with the rise of steamship travel in the 1850s. In the 1860s, Ottoman officials began a public works project to construct a macadam (crushed stone) carriage road between Jaffa and Jerusalem to ease the passage between the two towns. Able-bodied Jaffan men were either conscripted into labor battalions forced to build and maintain the road or they bought their way out of them. By the early 1870s, Jaffa reportedly hosted over forty thousand visitors to and through the town annually, more than double the size of its resident population.

All of this is to say that in the second half of the nineteenth century, Jaffa was very much a boom town, and this economic dynamism attracted a steady arrival of new migrants. As one newspaper account noted in the early 1880s regarding the town's rapid growth and transformation: "[Jaffa] can almost compete with the large cities in Turkey [sic] on the Mediterranean."[17] Although admittedly not yet at the level of the much larger major Ottoman port cities of Salonica, Izmir, Alexandria, or even Beirut, Jaffa was indeed an exciting town on the rise, promising substantial rewards to enterprising young men.

THE CHELOUCHES AND BARUKHS ARRIVE IN JAFFA

When Yosef Eliyahu Chelouche's parents Aharon and Sara (née Barukh) arrived as children in the 1840s together with their families, Jaffa was only beginning to settle into the political and military stability and economic growth that it would enjoy for decades. In both cases, the families' precise origins are somewhat murky, although it is certain that they originated either in or just beyond the western and eastern borders of the Ottoman Empire.

Chelouche family lore and Yosef Eliyahu's memoir claim that the family originated in Oran, Algeria; however, archival sources prove definitively that this is untrue.[18] The earliest record of the family in Palestine, in the 1849 Montefiore register,[19] did not list their origin, but in the subsequent 1855 register the family was listed as originating in Fez, Morocco, which is supported by Jewish communal records in that city. Claims to Oranian origins first appeared in the 1866 Montefiore register. It is certainly possible that coastal Oran was the final point of departure for the Chelouche family from North Africa, as it was a site of significant regional migration and rising western Mediterranean commercial traffic; it was also the closest major Mediterranean port to Fez. In fact, more than half of the Maghrebi Jews arriving in Palestine in the 1830s reported they were from Oran.[20] However, even if they had departed from Oran, the family's stay there could only have been temporary. As we will see shortly, the difference between claiming Moroccan versus Algerian origins would have tangible repercussions for the Chelouche family.

The Barukh family's origins are even more opaque in the surviving records. The family is first listed as originating in Iran in the 1855 Montefiore register, but then in the 1866 register they are listed as originating in Baghdad; however, later mentions of the men of the family in the Jaffa *shari'a* court registers describe them as "Iranian." To be sure, the border zones in Mesopotamia were not terribly stable at the time, having changed hands several times between the Ottoman and Safavid and then Qajar empires, with the most recent war between them ending in 1820. Moreover, Jewish families often spanned both imperial geographies as they intermarried, traded, and traveled between the two empires, so it is certainly possible that the Barukhs had footing in both Iran and Baghdad. However, due to the geopolitical tensions with the Qajar dynasty, the Ottoman government repeatedly cracked down on Iranian migrants in its territories, which would have made Ottoman Baghdad a safer, legal point of origin for the family to claim.

In other words, practical, legal, and diplomatic concerns led both the Chelouches and the Barukhs to obfuscate their precise origins on the western and eastern edges of the Ottoman world. Family lore also does not shed light on the reasons for the families' relocation to Palestine. As with most cases of migration, there must have been a strong combination of push and pull factors that led them to move thousands of miles away into an unknown—albeit spiritually and liturgically familiar—land. Both families surely undertook lengthy and dangerous journeys to arrive in Palestine.

For the Chelouche family, the 1830s was a period of extreme violence and upheaval in North Africa due to the recent French occupation of Algeria and the subsequent chaotic influx of refugees and overall military uncertainty in neighboring Morocco. At least two hundred North African Jewish families immigrated to Palestine in this decade, many of them settling in the northern port towns of Haifa and Acre—as the Chelouches initially planned to when they set sail in the early 1840s, before they relocated down the coast—or in other northern towns in the Galilee, particularly the holy cities of Tiberias and Safed, which were long associated with Jewish mysticism, or Kabbalah. Hundreds more

North African Jewish families would follow this path in the subsequent decades, spurred on by continued political and economic instability, general insecurity in addition to occasional anti-Jewish violence, as well as visions of religious piety and messianic redemption in the Holy Land.

The journey from North Africa across the Mediterranean was fraught with dangers at that time: the untamed sea, which downed ships on a regular basis, but also piracy and maritime lawlessness. For centuries, Mediterranean pirates had attacked passing ships for captives, who they then enslaved for their labor in the ship galleys or ransomed for cash or goods. In fact, uncontrolled piracy had been one of the pretexts for the French invasion and occupation of Algeria in 1830, although it continued unabated off the Mediterranean and Aegean coasts for decades even after.

The journey across the Mediterranean was also long, despite the recent invention of steamships, and ships would have anchored at various stops—from North Africa across to Marseille or Trieste, back to Alexandria, and then to Beirut or Acre. (Direct ship service from Alexandria to Jaffa would not begin until the late 1840s, after the Chelouches were already settled in the town.) Maritime passengers had to contend with generally low sanitary conditions on ships, the irregular supply of food and drinking water, and broader health dangers like the spread of plague and disease, lack of access to medical treatment, and the threat of theft or of insufficient funds for the remainder of the journey.

In his memoir, Yosef Eliyahu relays few details about the family's first arrival in the north of Palestine off the coast of Acre other than to report that tragedy struck the family, as the two young uncles he was later named after (Yosef and Eliyahu) were reportedly lost in the waves. One family account claims that after landing near Acre, the Chelouches went to Nablus and Jerusalem before settling in Jaffa, although there is insufficient historical evidence offered for this itinerary.[21] In the absence of other details about the journey, the searing memory of the family's bitter loss along the way was passed on for generations.

Let us now turn to the Barukh family's probable journey, which took place only a few years after the Chelouches'. Whether they originated in Iraq or in Iran, it is likely that they, too, sought more political stability and safety by moving further west into more firmly Ottoman-controlled lands. In the early 1830s, the Ottomans reasserted their central control over the Mamluks in the Mesopotamian region, but the timing was unfortunate, as Ottoman troops and officials arrived in Baghdad at the same time as flood, plague, and famine. Pacification of Kurdish and other tribes as well as of Shi'ites rebelling against Sunni Ottoman control in the south plus state-led development and control took several more decades for the Ottomans to implement in the region.

If, on the other hand, the family originated across the border in Iran, they would have contended with even less political stability and security. There were ancient and established Jewish communities in a number of Iranian towns, perhaps most prominently in Shiraz. However, the Qajar dynasty was decentralized and highly dependent on tribal loyalties outside of the capital. In addition, the particular emphasis in Shi'ism on the impurity of Jews and other non-Muslims meant that Jewish communities in nineteenth-century Iran were at times subject to the extremism of religious and political figures. In contrast, despite the local upheavals in early 1840 around the Damascus blood libel,[22] the Ottoman Empire had publicly proclaimed the equality and protection of its non-Muslim communities in a famous 1839 imperial rescript. Although not without problems, Jews in the reform-era Ottoman Empire certainly had more protections and stability than ever before in the region.

It is not difficult to understand, then, why the Barukhs might have embarked on the westward journey, although migration from this eastern region to Palestine was far less frequent in this period, with barely three dozen Jewish families from Iraq and two dozen from Iran listed in the Montefiore registers. This might have to do with the fact that while only about one-third of the distance to Palestine as the crow flies, the Barukhs' journey would have been much more treacherous and much less comfortable than the (admittedly dangerous and uncomfortable) sea crossing undertaken by the Chelouches.

Assuming they came from or near Baghdad, as the family later claimed, for their safety the Barukhs would have had to join a caravan heading westward toward Damascus, perhaps — depending on the season and rainfall — traveling for part of the journey along the Tigris River before riding on camels on uneven roads and through the desert and camping along the way. In that period, the journey between Baghdad and Damascus alone took at least thirty days, and its success depended heavily on the alliances, securities, and services that the caravan received from tribes along the route.

It is likely that the Barukh family paused for some months in Damascus, as one of the son's later entries in the Montefiore registers state that he was born there.[23] From Damascus, the family might have continued westward to Beirut and then taken a ship down the coast to Jaffa; alternatively, they might have gone by land on the *hajj* caravan route through southern Syria, through the plains and the mountains known today as the Golan Heights, before cutting their way across northern Palestine and down to coastal Jaffa.

The initial overlap with the stations of the caravan and *hajj* route would have provided shelter and services for the travelers, but the remainder of this route through the interior would have been more perilous given the lack of security between towns and villages on the poorly guarded roads. Despite the potential dangers, however, this interior route would have been attractive for those who sought to stop in some of the holy cities in Palestine, as this route could have taken them past Tiberias and Safed and possibly through Jerusalem. In addition, at least one family account claims that an uncle of Sara, Yosef Eliyahu's mother, lived in Nablus, which he might have chosen for settlement if the family had traversed the interior route.[24]

If we take the family lore at face value, then, it is entirely possible that neither the Barukhs nor the Chelouches first entered Palestine through the Jaffa port, but rather ended up in the town by the late 1840s after a series of stops in other Palestinian towns. However, given its utter importance to all future traffic to Palestine as well as considering the fact that Yosef Eliyahu himself traveled through the port numerous times, let us briefly explore what that arrival would have been like in the second half of the nineteenth century.

Passengers approaching the Jaffa coastline were met with their first glimpse of the town, as described in a later account by Iskandar 'Awad, the Jaffa hotelier whom Yosef Eliyahu mentions in his memoir as a family friend: "Jaffa stands on a symmetrical hill of rock, which rises from the low, sandy coast, and presents a beautiful and picturesque appearance from the sea."[25] Because Jaffa did not have a deep water port, ships anchored about a kilometer off the coast, and smaller boats were dispatched to meet them to help unload passengers and goods. In the winter, when the ocean was stormy, ships would have to wait until conditions improved enough to permit the transfer; in many cases, they were turned away from the port and rerouted back to Acre or Beirut, only to attempt again another day. At times when the transfer to the smaller

FIGURE I.1. *Jaffa from the Mediterranean Sea, ca. 1890. Due to the rocky terrain near the port, ships anchored one kilometer off the coastline and passengers and goods were transferred to smaller boats. Matson Collection, Library of Congress, Prints & Photographs Division, LC-DIG-ppmsca-02680.*

boats was attempted, stormy seas or unfortunately timed waves could claim the lives of passengers, crates of merchandise or luggage, or even those of Jaffa's experienced and intrepid boatmen.

On various occasions, Ottoman officials dynamited the large rocks off the port to try to facilitate the smaller boats' safe passage, but numerous proposals to construct a proper deep-water port for Jaffa, including later pressure from Jaffa's municipal council, urban elite, and newspaper editors, failed to bear fruit. Once safely through the rocky reef to the port, passengers and goods were unloaded at the Jaffa customs house. After the Ottomans began using quarantine stations in the 1840s to stem the spread of plague and contagion, Jaffa's boat passengers would have had to pass a cursory health and luggage inspection before being allowed to enter the town.

Settling Down

At the time of the arrival of the Chelouche and Barukh families in the early 1840s, Jaffa had only recently survived the Egyptian invasion, rebellions in the countryside, plagues, and the aftershocks of a deadly earthquake in the north. The Ottoman government was only just reasserting its control, and it was still in the beginning stages of implementing a decades-long series of imperial reforms throughout the province. At the time, Jaffa was welcoming migrants from many backgrounds—laborers, peasants, merchants, and families from Egypt, greater Syria, and North Africa. Over the coming decades, they would benefit from the increased political stability and modernization brought by the Ottoman state as well as the economic boom taking place in Jaffa, and also from the closer attentions of Western powers to the Holy Land. Likewise, the extended Chelouche family's success would be intimately intertwined with the opportunities of mid-century Jaffa.

In the 1840s, there were reportedly only a few dozen Jewish families living in the port town of Jaffa, but up to ten thousand Jews in all of Palestine, most of them concentrated in the holy cities of Jerusalem, Tiberias, Safed, and Hebron.[26] Half of Jaffa's Jews came from North Africa, like the Chelouches, primarily from Algeria and Morocco; most of the rest came from other Ottoman cities like Istanbul and Damascus, or from other Palestinian towns. In contrast, only a handful of Jaffa's Jews came from other places, such as Gibraltar, Iran, and Ukraine. Upon their arrival in Jaffa, the Chelouches, Barukhs, and other Jewish families would have stayed at the Jewish hostel established for pilgrims decades prior, located in the al-Qal'a neighborhood in the northwest of the town, while they looked for more permanent lodging, prayed in the town's only synagogue, tapped into the community's limited resources, and charted out their integration into the town.

When the Viennese Jewish traveler Ludwig August Frankl visited Jaffa the following decade in the mid-1850s, he reported that the small Jewish community was "poor," with only four members who were property owners and the bulk of the community making its living from crafts and manual labor. Indeed, the Montefiore registers from that same period show a community of migrants struggling to make their way. These are also virtually the only surviving records of the Barukh and Chelouche families' first decades in Palestine; taken together, they illustrate the Chelouches' remarkable upward mobility within their first decades in the country.

In the 1855 Montefiore register, the Barukhs were one of only two wealthy Jewish families in town, reporting assets of 10,000 *quruş*; Sara's father, Haim, was listed as a banker and an oil merchant. A few other men in the community were recorded as affluent bankers, merchants, and moneylenders, with assets ranging from 1,000 to 10,000 *quruş*, but there were far more peddlers, tailors, servants, and people living off charity in circumstances that ranged from modest to precarious.

By this point, Aharon Chelouche's father, Avraham, had died, leaving his mother, Simha, and the fifteen-year-old Aharon to care for the family, which included his younger brother Yosef. Unlike most other widows who were listed as being without a profession and living entirely off of communal or family charity, Simha worked as a seamstress. Young Aharon was listed as a silver- and goldsmith, a trade in which he must have already been apprenticed for several years, reportedly learning the craft from a brother-in-law.[27] Although Aharon and Yosef's older sister Rika was not linked to the family in the registers, other sources reveal that she was married to Nissim Carsenty, an Oranian immigrant of stable means, and she already had a young child of her own; another sister, Hana, was married to one of the few Ashkenazi men in Jaffa at the time, Alter Louria, the silversmith who, according to family accounts, had trained Aharon; this was one of the earliest "mixed" marriages between Jaffa's Sephardi and Ashkenazi Jews.

Unfortunately, there is no indication at this time of where in the town the Barukhs, Chelouches, or other Jewish families recorded in the Montefiore registers were living. However, property sales recorded in the Islamic (*shari'a*) court registers of Jaffa show that Jews were leaving the neighborhood around the Jewish hostel and were beginning to spread throughout the town. Ottomans of all religions were permitted to own property already, but it was only in the aftermath of the 1858 land law that foreigners residing in the empire were also allowed to purchase and register private property. In December 1859, for example, a Jewish woman named Sara purchased a house from the Muslim property owner Saleh al-Basir al-'Akki in the al-Fallahin neighborhood in the southeast of Jaffa.[28] Curiously, though, neither Sara nor a single one of the Jewish male witnesses who appeared in court on her behalf are traceable in the Montefiore registers, underscoring the incomplete nature and the (at most) partial portrait of Jewish life that the registers represent.

Sara's property purchase was a harbinger of more prosperous times for the Jewish community in Jaffa as they began to root themselves in the urban landscape. In the following decade, in the 1866 Montefiore register, Aharon Chelouche reappears as an established family man with a wife and young child of his own—Avraham Haim, Yosef Eliyahu's older brother. He proved himself to be industrious and talented in his trade, and his assets placed him in the top 15 percent of Jaffa's Jewish community; this was a remarkable rise for an orphan boy who not only managed to become prosperous but also gained the hand of the daughter of one of Jaffa's wealthier Jewish families. As the patriarch of his own family, Aharon Chelouche was a generous philanthropist and active member in the Jewish community, contributing his resources as well as his time to religious, educational, and social institutions. In fact, Aharon was well-off enough to support a prayer room in his home as well as to commission a Torah scroll in that same year.

Over the subsequent decades of Jaffa's development and growth, the Chelouches and other native "Eastern" Jews became crucial protagonists in the daily life of the land. Court records show that Jews owned property and lived in various neighborhoods, such as the important neighborhood of Sheikh Ibrahim, adjacent to the town's markets, as well as the prestigious neighborhood of al-Naqib, where numerous notables and merchants lived. Retracing their activities and contributions to Jaffa's history is a laborious task that will require extensive additional historical research into the Ottoman and Arabic language sources. What is already obvious, however, is that the history of Jaffa's Jews cannot continue to be told as if it took place in a bubble, isolated from the rest of Jaffa's social, economic, and political life.

As he aged, Aharon became a member of the local elite, an urban notable[29] in a position of prestige and respectability based on his economic success as a silversmith and money changer, his longevity in the town as a pillar of the tiny but growing Jewish community, and his multi-nodal contacts in Ottoman and Palestinian Arab society. Aharon counted among his friends and allies local Ottoman officials and Palestinian Arab mayors, merchants, rural notables, and workers. Archival traces of Aharon Chelouche appear in the registers of the Jaffa Islamic (*shari'a*) and commercial (*ticari*) courts, as well as in the French and Spanish consular archives, underscoring his active presence in the town's commercial life.

Some of these transactions had to do with Aharon Chelouche's land investments, about which Yosef Eliyahu writes in his memoir, but others were about his business dealings with his fellow residents. In early 1878, for example, "Khawaja[30] Aharon the silversmith son of Ibrahim Chelouche the Jew" issued a power of attorney to a Haim [name illegible] to conduct the sale of his shares in a property.[31] In another case, the Muslim woman 'Aisha daughter of 'Abdullah al-Hilu sold some jewelry she had inherited, valued at almost 1,500 piastres, to Aharon Chelouche to settle her debts.[32]

At the same time that he was embedded in the local Ottoman economy and society, like many Jews from North Africa, Aharon benefited from his fabricated claims to French nationality. This is where the distinction between his origins in either Algeria or in Morocco mattered: the first would have entitled him to French protection, whereas the latter did not.[33] In the second half of the nineteenth century, European protégés and foreign nationals received significant privileges in the Ottoman Empire, including tax and conscription exemptions, but more importantly they received the interest and protection of consular officials and the right to use consular or mixed courts. Yosef Eliyahu's memoir details his father's friendship with the French vice-consul in Jaffa, and Aharon's French protection was consistently invoked in his court appearances, per the custom of identifying the nationality, religion, and residence of legal parties. In this regard, Aharon Chelouche instrumentally navigated between "localness" and "foreignness," a position of rootedness and relative prestige and protection in the late Ottoman landscape, made possible particularly in the globalizing economy of the growing port town.

YOSEF ELIYAHU CHELOUCHE'S BIRTH AND CHILDHOOD IN A CHANGING URBAN LANDSCAPE

By the time of Yosef Eliyahu Chelouche's birth in 1870, Jaffa's population had grown to between six thousand and eight thousand residents, 70 percent of whom were Muslim, with the rest evenly split between Jews and Christians. An 1871 Ottoman government yearbook entry on Jaffa provides a snapshot of a vibrant provincial town: there were over five hundred shops and stores in the town's markets, soap factories, bakeries, ironworks, public drinking fountains, governmental and religious schools, a hospital, bathhouses, a telegraph and post office, and over a dozen mosques, churches, and synagogues. The built-up area of the walled town was no larger than 32 acres, but its vast hinterland of cultivated citrus groves and vineyards to its east and south extended over more than 1,850 acres to the east and south of the town walls.

The decade of Yosef Eliyahu's birth marked a gradual yet unprecedented change in the spatial transformation of Jaffa, as the town walls were partially dismantled and new commercial and residential buildings were constructed along the main roads extending from the town's center. This change can be attributed to the growing political stability and economic activity in Palestine, as well as to the increased effectiveness of local governance in the town itself. As part of broader empire-wide reforms, in 1871 the Ottomans reorganized the administrative structure of southern Palestine and approved the establishment of a local municipal council (*meclis-i beledi*, also known as *al-baladiyya* in Arabic) in Jaffa.

The council's first action was to order the opening of another gate in the town walls, perceived as a pressing necessity since the historic Jerusalem Gate had become so "crowded with donkeys, camels and lazy Arabs, that one has difficulty in forcing his way through," as was colorfully—if offensively—described in an 1868 travel book.[34] A Hebrew-language newspaper report of the municipality's decision stated that the new gate would be reserved for animal traffic, while the original gate would remain for human traffic alone.[35] The town's main market square and main street were paved in 1875, making it easier for wagon and carriage wheels as well as cutting down on the dust and dirt of the unpaved roads.

As the number of new buildings continued to grow in the 1870s, new plots had to be found for construction. A few years prior, Ottoman officials in Istanbul had been informed that the need for housing had outgrown the town, and permission was granted to build outside of Jaffa's walls.[36] In late 1879, Conrad Schick, a German missionary, architect, and archaeologist who had lived in Palestine for over thirty years, described the demolition of Jaffa's walls, the filling up of the modest ditch around them, and the construction of "a number of large new houses and stores, even palatial buildings," yet also noted that "in the gardens of Jaffa there is a large number of new houses, and to the south and to the north of the city complete Arab quarters were built, most of them by settlers from Egypt."[37] That is to say, by the 1870s urban Jaffa had outgrown the town walls and informal settlements (*sakanat*) had already sprouted up around the town, in many cases to accommodate the migrants arriving for Jaffa's expanded opportunities.

FIGURE I.2. *Jaffa's town walls and main gate from the northeast. This panoramic view was stitched together from the oldest surviving photographs of the town, three photos taken by the Frenchman Louis Vignes in 1860. Vignes placed his camera outside the town's main gate at that time, next to a small*

This short description by Schick is supported by a beautifully detailed map prepared between 1878 and 1879 by Theodor Sandel, a German architect who lived in Jaffa's small Templer colony along the road to Nablus.[38] Sandel's map, which was first published in 1880 in the key journal of German Holy Land studies, provides an astonishing depiction of the geography of Jaffa and its environs, the type of agricultural lands surrounding its historic core, the town's intricate street network, names of important landmarks, and places of residence of notable public figures. Some of these prominent residents appear in Chelouche's memoir as business partners, landowners, allies, and rivals. The map's importance lies not only in its superb skill and wealth of information, but also in its uniqueness: it is the best, most, detailed, and most accurate modern mapping of late Ottoman Jaffa's built-up area and its agricultural hinterland.[39]

Sandel's map also offers a clear spatial illustration of the ethnic, religious, and cultural diversity of Jaffa in the late 1870s that was more tersely

bastion and leading to the town's main mosque (right). The town walls are surrounded by a shallow defensive ditch that, during the 1870s, began to be filled with new structures. National Library of France (BnF), RESERVE EI-68-BOITE FOL B - n. 34–36.

recorded in the Ottoman yearbook and that we encounter in Chelouche's memoir.[40] The main entrance to the town (in the northeast corner) led directly to the Great Mosque and was surrounded by a busy tapestry of bazaars and commercial streets, one of which was described by Sandel as a "Jewish bazaar" while another was given the name "Arab bazaar." The building that Sandel called the "Jewish bazaar" was a large commercial and residential complex built in 1878 by three affluent Maghrebi Jewish businessmen, Maimon 'Amiel, his son-in-law Aharon Moyal, and Shlomo Abushadid. The building had more than four dozen storefronts on the ground floor connected through covered passageways, with residential apartments on the upper floor. Aharon Chelouche's workshop was located in that building, facing the town's main commercial street that went all the way to the port; the Chelouche family also lived in an apartment upstairs for a few years.[41] (See Figure I.4.)

At the southwest corner of the 'Amiel/Moyal bazaar, Sandel marked the main commercial street as the "Arab bazaar." This area is where

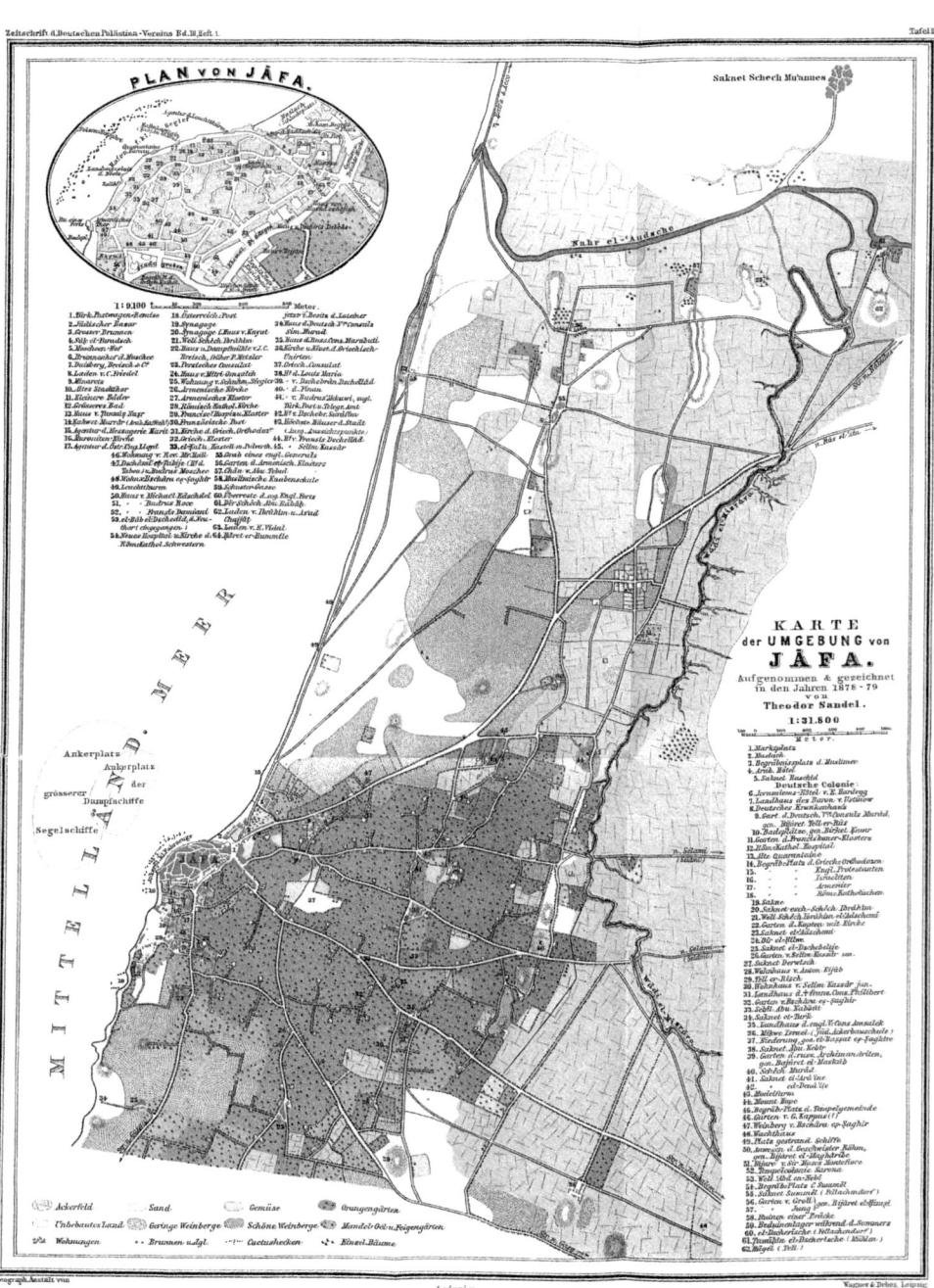

FIGURE I.3. *Theodor Sandel's map of Jaffa and its environs, Zeitschrift des Deutschen Palästina-Vereins, 1880.*

FIGURE I.4. *Jaffa's vegetable and fruit market square, near the Jerusalem Gate and in front of the Maimon 'Amiel-Aharon Moyal building, ca. 1890. Aharon Chelouche's shop was located in that building, next to the city's main commercial street. According to Yosef Eliyahu's account, the Chelouche family lived in that building from 1883–1887. Photo by Maison Bonfils, Rijksmuseum Photograph Collection, RP-F-F01089-B.*

various specialized markets were located, including the clothing market and the spice market. Here, too, we find stores and warehouses belonging to other Maghrebi Jews in the town, such as the store belonging to the Jewish merchant E. Vidal and a warehouse (*khan*) belonging to the Jewish family Abutbul (Abu Teboul in Sandel's rendering).[42] Nearby was the Suq al-Khawajat (*Khawajas*'s market), where the money changers (*sarrafs*) set up their shops. The *shariʿa* court records list dozens of cases involving money changers, and from them we see that there was a significant overrepresentation of North African Jews in this profession in Jaffa. Aharon Chelouche was himself involved in money changing in addition to his silversmith craft, as Yosef Eliyahu recounts in his memoirs, and so were many of their relatives and friends and other members of the Maghrebi Jewish community.[43]

The house in which Yosef Eliyahu Chelouche was born was a five-minute walk to the northwest, along one of the main shopping streets that connected the northern part of the town to the bazaar area on its eastern side. Although Sandel only identified one of the town's neighborhoods on his map, al-Rumeila (er-Rummile), the Chelouche home was in the adjacent neighborhood of Sheikh Ibrahim, site of the shrine to the Muslim saint as well as two bathhouses, an important public service at a time when most homes did not have private baths. When Sandel drew his map, the family had already moved out to a building adjacent to the town's historic citadel (Qal'a), and the building had already been taken over by the Ottoman administration and transformed into the town's government house (*saraya*, Ara.; *seray*, Tur.), as Chelouche describes in his memoir; atypical of most of Jaffa's historic core,[44] it still stands today.

In addition to the local bazaars, Sandel's map further showed the importance of international trade and connections for the port town by marking the location of branches of the Austrian, French, and Ottoman postal services, as well as the offices of agents of the Austro-Hungarian Lloyd and Messageries Maritimes shipping companies. Scattered throughout Jaffa's dense urban core were also a considerable number of Christian religious establishments, including Armenian, Greek Catholic, Greek Orthodox, Maronite, and Roman Catholic churches and monasteries. Sandel documented these thoroughly, while in comparison, he identified only three smaller mosques besides the Great Mosque at the main town gate, and only two synagogues, one of them the synagogue in al-Qal'a next to Jaffa's historic citadel that was already then occupied by Franciscan monks; a decade later, the citadel was rebuilt as a Catholic church that still maintains its status as one of Jaffa's most prominent landmarks.[45]

Sandel's personal background and his assumption of his European audience's interests likely led him to more thoroughly document the European and Christian presence in Jaffa, but his mapping is nevertheless helpful in its reflection of the heterogeneous nature of this growing town and its openness to external influences. At the same time, Sandel's map also raises important questions about which elements of the urban landscape were invisible to his foreign eye, and what a contemporary mapping of Jaffa might look like if done instead by one of its local residents. *Parashat Hayay* narratively takes us through many of the everyday spaces and places in Chelouche's Jaffa, but there are many absences in the text as well, not least due to the passage of time and memory.

Sandel's map is also telling in the way it can be read as a blueprint for the expansion of Jaffa's built-up area. According to this, Jaffa's immediate hinterland to the east was rich in hundreds of citrus groves, as well as scattered orchards of almond, olive, and fig trees. These vast and productive agricultural lands were located south of the Nablus road and east of the Gaza road, extending more than two kilometers south of the town itself. North of the Nablus road, the landscape abruptly changed into a long strip of sand dunes that stretched between the coast and the road branching out north to the village of Summeil, with some fertile areas of "melons, Indian corn, grapes, and other produce" farmed by Bedouins.[46] (This is the area where Yosef Eliyahu was taken when he was briefly kidnapped, as he recounts in chapter 2.) East of this road, the area was fertile with agricultural fields, probably of seasonal vegetable crops. To the south of the town, along the narrow and elevated strip of land between the road to Gaza and the Mediterranean Sea, the area was rich with what Sandel described as "fine vineyards."

It is worth lingering for a moment on this visual reminder of the close relationship between Jaffa the town and its agricultural hinterland. There are accounts of marriages, festivals, and other celebrations that took place in the groves outside of the town, as Jaffans reveled in their fertile backyard. As marked on Sandel's map, wealthy urban dwellers had large homes in the groves where they retreated for holidays. (Although Yosef Eliyahu does not mention it in his memoir, one of his grandchildren, Aharon Chelouche, recalled his childhood holidays spent at the family's orchard north of town, which was full of subtropical trees and plants.[47]) Westerners, too, marveled at the beauty surrounding Jaffa. As one Western traveler reported, "The gardens of fruit-bearing trees are the glory of Jaffa. There are endless groves of oranges and lemons, apricots, pomegranates, figs, and olives, with mulberry and acacia trees, the stately palm towering above them all."[48] Even the Cook's travel guide, which had archly labeled Jaffa the town as "the reverse of beautiful," was extravagant in its appreciation of Jaffa's hinterland: "For miles round the scene is one of luxuriant beauty. . . . The traveler must by no means omit

FIGURE I.5. *Jaffa's verdant groves to the northeast of the city, ca. 1900. The photograph was taken from the small Templer Colony located several hundred meters northeast of Jaffa's main mosque. Also seen to the right are the buildings of the main new commercial street (Bustrus-'Awad Street) of Jaffa's northern expansion, built during the 1880s and 1890s. Matson Collection, Library of Congress, Prints & Photographs Division, LC-DIG-matpc-06521.*

to visit here; the aroma in the evening and early morning is delicious, and every sweet scent should be courted in Palestine."[49] Cook's called the fruits of Jaffa "exquisite," "luxurious," and "perfection."

Since citrus was one of Jaffa's primary sources of wealth at this point, the expansion of the town's built-up area was initially directed to the agriculturally inhospitable sand dunes along the coast, especially to the north of the town, and then to the economically less lucrative vegetable fields and vineyards. Though some signs for this future expansion trend were already present in the late 1870s, it was only during the second half of the 1880s that steady development, both to the north and to the south of the town, began to take place.

As the Sandel map illustrates, corroborating textual sources, in the 1870s the area around Jaffa was already flowing if not with the proverbial "milk and honey," then certainly it was bursting with oranges and grapes. There were already relatively few uncultivated areas in the greater Jaffa area, and those were primarily the coastal sand dunes to the north of the town. Furthermore, we see on Sandel's map the Jewish institutions that assumed an outsized role in the Jewish community's historiography and collective memory about this early settlement period, such as the Montefiore orchard, detailed by Chelouche in chapter 2, and the Mikve Israel agricultural school established by the French Jewish philanthropic association the Alliance Israélite Universelle. As important as they were as markers of the early development of Jewish agricultural institutions in Palestine, they were established against an already highly developed and fertile agricultural backdrop, and their relative insignificance against the greater Jaffa landscape comes into sharp detail in Sandel's map.

Overall, then, this is the physical landscape and the economically dynamic environment and moment in which Yosef Eliyahu Chelouche's *Parashat Hayay* opens. Chelouche offers a loving description of the everyday hum of activity in the town's prayer rooms and workshops, its alleys and courtyards. Here, Yosef Eliyahu attempted to give depth and connection to the Ottoman Jaffa of his childhood and youth. The Jaffa of Chelouche's childhood is small and intimate, privileged and protected, albeit occasionally frightening. In addition to the snapshots of routine daily life, Chelouche recounted extraordinary moments such as Bedouin raids, his own harrowing if blessedly short-lived kidnapping, tragic shipwrecks, and plague. The events he narrated also reveal how much the fortunes of Jaffa were tied up with regional and global trade and commerce, foreign exchange and currency.

The center of the Chelouche family's life was undoubtedly the small and tight-knit Maghrebi and Sephardi Jewish community in Jaffa, but they were by no means isolated. As we come to understand through Chelouche's account of his childhood, the Jewish community was connected to, dependent on, in competition with, and deeply entwined with their Muslim and Christian neighbors. As Sandel's map suggests, Jaffa's Jewish families came into everyday contact with their Muslim and Christian neighbors as they physically inhabited the same spaces, living in close proximity and passing each other on the streets. Further, Jaffa's Jews had significant contact and connections with Jaffans of other religions with whom they entered into partnerships, bought and sold goods, and entrusted their families' business and financial fortunes. Chelouche cites several examples of these ties, the various court registers document dozens if not hundreds of others, and still more remain to be uncovered in future historical research.[50]

A few anecdotes from the Hebrew-language press in the 1870s can give us an additional perspective on Jaffan Jews' relationship with their neighbors in the period of Yosef Eliyahu's childhood.[51] In one example, we find that Jewish rituals could be considered a good luck charm for the local non-Jewish population, and folk practices and superstitions transcended religious lines. In an article published the year of Yosef Eliyahu's birth, a correspondent in Jaffa relayed that a Muslim woman who had tragically lost a number of infants at birth had promised to circumcise her newborn son if he survived; she made good on her promise and her entire family undertook the joyous procession to the synagogue, where a North African rabbi circumcised the Muslim baby.[52] Another newspaper report of the arrival of three new Torah scrolls for Jaffa's synagogues gifted by the congregation of a respected Moroccan rabbi relays that members of the Jewish community went on a public procession throughout the town with the scrolls, singing religious songs and praising the sultan. The correspondent noted that the town's deputy governor and the English and Spanish vice-consuls accompanied them, which his readers surely interpreted as both a sign of respect and a guarantee of their safety throughout the town.[53]

To be sure, the Hebrew press also recorded tragic and dangerous incidents concerning Jews in 1870s Jaffa, but the context of these accounts is important. Some accounts were clearly depicted as incidents that could, and did, happen to anyone of any religion, rather than being depicted as a specifically Jewish fate. For example, the account of a Jewish merchant from Damascus en route to Jaffa who died when his horse fell into the al-Auja river, two hours north of the town, and the case of a Jewish merchant from Jerusalem en route to Alexandria whose boat sank off the coast of Jaffa were signs of the general dangers of travel and the fragility of life in an unpredictable world.[54] Both men had their last rites and burials taken care of by the local Jewish community.

Other examples concerning Jews and the justice system were published either as warnings to keep behavior in line or as homilies providing happy endings with Jewish protagonists finding vindication. For example, a newspaper report from May 1872 relayed that the Jews of Jaffa were stunned to discover the guards (*kawass*) of the Ottoman deputy governor (*kaymakam*) arriving at the synagogue to arrest a parishioner. Their target was a young Jew from Alexandria who had recently moved to the town, who the night before had gotten drunk, allegedly insulted Islam, and fought with others at the tavern before fleeing to the synagogue. The report made clear that the young man had not only violated common sense and legal and social norms, but he had also recklessly and selfishly endangered his fellow Jews who hastened to distance themselves from his actions. In contrast, a happier ending met the Jewish woman who was robbed on a boat arriving in Jaffa and had the quick wits to surreptitiously "tag" her robber with a string tied to his clothing; he was successfully identified and apprehended the following day and her stolen money was returned to her.[55]

It is noteworthy that in all of these published accounts, the mobility of Jews to and through Jaffa features prominently, while the stability of a Jewish community in Jaffa is a vital resource, there to bury the dead, shun the criminals, educate the ignorant, or welcome and aid the migrants. While there is no evidence that Aharon Chelouche traveled much after his initial immigration to Jaffa as a child, his three sons all experienced the mobility of the era and of their class, moving around the Jaffa region, the wider Levant, and the globe for their education, business, and leisure.

In the mid-1880s, after his childhood years of primary religious education with respected North African rabbis in Jaffa, Yosef Eliyahu, like his brothers Avraham Haim and Ya'akov, was sent to a Jewish boarding school in Beirut along with other affluent Jewish boys from his town and from around the region. As Yosef Eliyahu writes in his memoir, he viewed this experience as formative in preparing him for life as an educated (indeed, "enlightened"), modern young man. This meant expanding his spoken Palestinian Arabic and religious Hebrew to include commercial and literary Arabic, French, and some secular studies, but it also meant shedding the traditional Middle Eastern cloak for a Western-style suit and fez, the marker of a modern Ottoman gentleman (*effendi*). Moreover, his years in Beirut corresponded with the intellectual and creative ferment of the *nahda*, or the Arab enlightenment, centered there, although Chelouche never used that term. However, his Jewish school's pedagogy very clearly and deliberately engaged modern Arabic language and literature as a key touchstone for its young Levantine students, whom it was preparing for elite leadership in their hometowns.

By his own account, Yosef Eliyahu's years in Beirut were the most stimulating and influential in his young life, but much to his devastation, he was forced to end his studies prematurely after he was betrothed to Freha/Simha Moyal,[56] the daughter of a wealthy Maghrebi Jewish family back in Jaffa. Although their lifelong marriage seems to have been a contented one, nearly half a century later Chelouche never forgot his bitter disappointment at being sent home from Beirut unable to complete his studies and his modern transformation. However, Chelouche's experiences led him to prioritize modern education for his six sons, first at Francophone institutions in Jaffa and later at the modern Herzliya Hebrew Gymnasium. Five of his six sons went abroad to Beirut, Cairo, France, and England for their studies, further cementing their position in the modernizing Levantine elite.[57] In these respects, Chelouche's autobiography is a revealing look at a Jewish family undergoing the transition from traditional religious education and craftsmanship to modern secular studies, white-collar professionalism, and a Mediterranean/Levantine Westernization.

FIRST STEPS OUTSIDE THE TOWN WALLS: BUILDING MODERN JAFFA

During Chelouche's lifetime, his hometown of Jaffa expanded more than a hundredfold, from the thirty-two acres of Jaffa's historic core to over five thousand acres that were eventually divided between the city of Jaffa and the township of Tel Aviv. Chelouche's memoir provides rare firsthand observations about some of these events, starting with the story of the first house built by his father outside Jaffa's historic core, in the sandy area to the north of the town. He described his father Aharon as a visionary pioneer of land acquisitions in the vast uncultivated areas north of the town who, in 1883, decided to build a house one kilometer north of Jaffa's Great Mosque past the northernmost built-up area of Saknat al-Rashid. According to Yosef Eliyahu, this was done to prevent ownership disputes that had already affected other vacant lands he owned in the area.[58] The house, built next to a road that branched out from the northern coastal route and connected it to the village of Summeil, was left unoccupied until "many families" decided to move to the mostly vacant lands to the north of the town. This coincided with

FIGURE I.6. *The first house built by Aharon Chelouche in the 1880s outside Jaffa's city core. The house stood in an area named Manshiya in Arabic and Neve Shalom in Hebrew. Photograph by Frank Scholten, ca. 1921. Leiden University Libraries, NINO F Scholten Jaffa 10: 46.*

Chelouche's wedding in 1887, and his description of the ceremonies reflected the then-isolated location of the house, which forced the urbanite guests to travel by seven horse-drawn carriages to reach it.

The Chelouches' first *extramuros* house appears to have been in the "new neighborhood of Manshiya," as it was called in the Islamic court registers from around that time, the area that Chelouche refers to as Neve Shalom (Oasis of Peace).[59] In its early stages of growth, Manshiya was, in local terms, the first modern urban (in contrast to suburban) expansion of Jaffa. Contrary to recent studies that mistakenly describe Manshiya as an organically developed village,[60] Manshiya's urban landscape consisted mostly of relatively spacious, two-story residential buildings built along a grid-like street network. This new area of settlement was clearly a mixed area with both Muslim and Jewish residents, as one of the court registries listed a Zabida Hanim, daughter of al-Hajj Ahmad Muneimna (?), as a property owner in the area as well.[61] Another property sale records that the eastern edge of the property belonging to the Muslim woman Bahiya al-Nabulsi bordered the house rented by a Jewish man, Simhon.[62]

Over the following years, the Jewish population in Manshiya grew, both as renters and as property owners. At least three Jewish residents of the neighborhood endowed their private property as religious endowments (*hekdesh* in Hebrew or *waqf* in Arabic) to benefit the Ashkenazi Jewish community to which they belonged. For example, Levi and his wife Miriam endowed their house for "the poor of the Ashkenazi rite"; Shlomo endowed a house for the students of the Ashkenazi Talmud Torah; and the Austrian subject Haim endowed a house and land for a Jewish hospital to be established in the neighborhood that would benefit both Ashkenazi and Sephardi Jews, which was known as Sha'ar Zion (Gate of Zion).[63]

At around the same time in the late 1880s, a bit further to the north of Manshiya/Neve Shalom, the first fully organized and exclusively Jewish settlement, a neighborhood called Neve Tzedek (Oasis of Justice), was built. Here, more than a kilometer northeast of Jaffa's Great Mosque, near the road to Nablus, the Jerusalemite brothers Shim'on and El'azar Rokach established a private Jewish association for housing. Aharon Chelouche was one of the neighborhood's founders and the owner of the land on which it was built; in 1892, he and his family moved from their house in Manshiya to a new and larger house near the new Jewish neighborhood in Neve Tzedek.

As per the custom of the time, Aharon's grown sons lived in the family home with their own families; this family home, which still stands today, was captured in a photograph of Aharon and his three sons, Avraham Haim, Yosef Eliyahu, and Ya'akov, standing at the entrance. The home was large and impressive, if modestly adorned on the exterior. The first floor had seven large rooms, each with windows to the outdoors, surrounding the large central chamber. A second, smaller, floor was added probably during the first decade of the twentieth century to accommodate the sons' expanding families.

Despite the pioneering reputation it later gained over the years, however, at the time Neve Tzedek was actually a humble building enterprise of eight row houses consisting of forty-eight small apartments. Its historic significance lies not in its size but rather in the model it set for future Jewish organized building initiatives in northern Jaffa that ensued during the 1890s and 1900s following an influx of Jewish immigrants to Palestine. Many of these new neighborhoods were built on lands owned by Aharon Chelouche or some other prominent local Jewish figures

FIGURE I.7. *The Chelouche family home in Neve Tzedek, with Aharon (seated) and his three sons, ca. 1900. Chelouche Family Collection.*

like Haim Amzalak and Yosef Moyal, men who featured prominently in Yosef Eliyahu Chelouche's memoir and who appeared regularly in the Islamic court records. Nevertheless, Jewish landowners were not the only investors in the new and rapidly developing economic field of local real estate; a rare mapping from August 1913 of land ownership in the yet unbuilt parts of northern Jaffa registered a number of Arab owners and one European owner, men named Badrani, Bamiya, Da'das, Fouda, Friedel, Hamdan, Mashharawi, and Shahin.[64]

Coinciding with these small-scale housing initiatives, the area to the north of the old town was rapidly developing to become the new commercial center of Jaffa. This development, too, was carried out in a sporadic nature, driven by private entrepreneurs and apparently without a master plan. Although Jaffa's built-up area was expanding southward, too, this emerging northern quarter was far more urbanized than the

FIGURE I.8. *Jaffa's train station, ca. 1896. Inaugurated in 1892, the Jaffa–Jerusalem railroad shortened a twelve-hour overnight journey to four hours. This photo is taken from the south of the station looking northeast; the Chelouche family home in Neve Zedek is visible in the upper right quadrant. Photo by Bonfils, Shay Farkash Private Collection.*

main development on Jaffa's southern part, which consisted mainly of private houses. In 1892, with the opening of Jaffa's train station to the north of the town just past the Muslim cemetery, this area's importance as a commercial focal point was further strengthened. The station connected Jaffa to Jerusalem in what was the first railway connection in Palestine, opening up new opportunities for travel and trade in both cities.

The area adjacent to the main gate was the launching point for new expansion going north of the town. This was already a site of extensive private building and investment, including the warehouses and apartment complexes owned by the North African Jewish Abutbul, 'Amiel, and Moyal families, as mentioned earlier. Throughout the 1890s, this area also became the site of significant government investment: the Ottoman telegraph and post office were already located there, but then the new government house (*saraya*) was built in this area in 1897, as was the army barracks and jailhouse (*kishle*). A sultanic clock tower was erected

FIGURE I.9. *The clock tower square; to the right of the tower is the new Ottoman government house (*saraya*). Photo by Frank Scholten, ca. 1921. Leiden University Libraries, NINO F Scholten Jaffa 08: 90.*

by the city's commercial elite in the square in 1900–1903 in honor of Sultan Abdul Hamid II's silver jubilee, and it stood as a symbol of the modern development and power of the empire as well as of the affluence of the town and the loyalty of its merchants; from then on, this area was known as "clock tower square" (*meidan al-se'ah*). Intra- and intercity carriages were stationed there as a sort of taxi stand or bus station.

Just north of clock tower square was the heart of the new commercial area of modern Jaffa, Bustrus and 'Awad streets, named after the Christian partners Najib Bustrus and Iskandar 'Awad (the western segment closest to the square was called 'Awad Street, while the eastern segment was known as Bustrus Street). An advertisement in the Hebrew press from this period described the street as "large and luxurious," a marked change from the narrow alleys of the old city.[65] The Howard Hotel (the anglicized version of the proprietor's name, 'Awad) and the kosher

FIGURE I.10. *The Ottoman government house (saraya), the seat of administrative power in Jaffa. Photo by Maison Bonfils, ca. 1898–1901. Jacob Wahrmann Archive, National Library of Israel, Bonfils and Zangaki Album, Album 7, ARC. 4* 1858 2.1 07.*

Palestine Hotel anchored this area, and they both bragged about their views of the sea to the west, the lush orchards to the east, and the colorful markets and Bedouin caravans directly below and to the north. Half of the Howard Hotel was rented out as commercial spaces, and dozens of stores and businesses were established in this new, bustling area.

Although these modern new areas were lauded as a sign of progress and desirable urban development, one case in the Islamic court records the complexities of the changing urban landscape, the busyness of this new area, and the dangers of unchecked urban growth: in early May 1895, a horseman riding recklessly fast through 'Awad Street accidentally trampled a Jewish man with his horse; after two days of anxious waiting,

FIGURE I.11. *Bustrus Street in modern Jaffa. Photograph by Frank Scholten, ca. 1921. Leiden University Libraries, NINO F Scholten Jaffa 09: 03.*

the man perished and the rider was arrested for involuntary manslaughter.[66] Carriages were also potential dangers for the town's pedestrians.

The substantial increase in building activities in modern Jaffa was directly reflected in the professional career that Yosef Eliyahu Chelouche carved out for himself starting in the early 1890s. It began with the opening of a shop selling building materials and household hardware on 'Awad Street, where it stood for almost forty years, followed by successful attempts to set up workshops for manufacturing suitcases, glue, and eventually cement floor tiles. In the way Chelouche described it, because of a chance encounter with an Armenian architect who was hired by his father to survey some of his properties, he became interested in the actual construction of buildings and began designing and constructing small houses based only on practical experience. In the early 1900s, he began receiving larger commissions, including several public buildings.

FIGURE I.12. *Chelouche Brothers' factory advertisement illustrating the floor tiles, columns, and balusters that they specialized in, early 1920s. Design by Marco Eini. Zvi Pomrock Collection.*

At the same time, his floor tiles workshop grew to become a small-scale factory under the name of Chelouche Frères, owned by Chelouche and his elder brother Avraham Haim and located next to Aharon Chelouche's house near Neve Tzedek.[67] The factory was probably the first to produce a variety of precast concrete elements in Palestine, including stairs, pipes, balustrades, window trims, balcony supports, and eventually concrete building blocks, a technology that had been invented only a decade earlier in the United States. The Chelouche Frères firm was also active in the fast-growing business of importing Portland cement, a material that was then used not only for the manufacturing of the precast concrete elements but also for on-site casting of floors, balconies, and roof slabs in the newly constructed buildings.

Chelouche's choice to enter the building profession can be understood in two contexts: first, as part of the Ottoman modernist and developmentalist agenda that was already well underway in the region and throughout the empire. The imperial state was preoccupied with development in the last decades of Abdul Hamid II's rule: thousands of new state buildings were built throughout the empire, such as schools, hospitals, municipal buildings, police buildings, and other markers of a centralizing state pushing itself into more spheres of everyday urban life.[68] In fact, photographs of these modern state buildings were collected into an album for the sultan as visual proof of his efforts to push the empire into a new era. In addition, private capital played a key role in the urban development of the cities of the empire like Beirut, where Chelouche had spent two years, and he doubtless had a clear image of what a modern Ottoman city could look like. Promoting Jaffa's development and modernization was in one sense the act of a loyal son who wanted to see his city grow and prosper, as well as of an astute businessman who sought self-sufficiency and economic independence.

On the other hand, the second context we must consider is that Chelouche turned to building at the same time as the nascent "practical Zionist" project of "building the land" was getting underway. By the 1890s, up to two thousand Jews were arriving in Palestine every year, a development that elicited increasing alarm among Ottoman officials as well as Palestinian elites. The Ottoman government had repeatedly attempted to restrict non-Ottoman Jewish immigration to the country starting already in the previous decade, limiting their sojourn to only three months, ostensibly more than enough time to conduct religious pilgrimage and return home. State regulations also sought to ban land sales to foreign Jews, although this, like the immigration ban, was at best only inconsistently applied due to local corruption, slippery registration practices that placed properties intended for the settlement of foreign Jewish immigrants in the legal name of Ottoman Jews, and the pressure of European powers.

Above all, the Ottoman state's attempts to tighten control over European Jewish immigration and land purchases were due to its internal and external problems. It did not want to permit the mass settlement of foreign nationals who brought with them the meddling power of their foreign consuls and states, nor did it want to encourage the separatist ideology that it was warned Zionism entailed. Problems elsewhere in the empire with ethnoreligious separatism and Great Power interventions (in the Balkans and Greek territories with respect to Orthodox Christians, as well as in eastern Anatolia with respect to Armenians, in particular) made the Ottoman state vigilant against the creation of a new and wholly unwelcome Ottoman "Jewish problem."

For their part, some Arab Palestinian notables, intellectuals, and even peasants began to express concern about the palpable changes underfoot in the country. In addition to the visible presence of boatloads of immigrants, almost a dozen Jewish colonies had been established in the greater Jaffa area in the 1880s–1890s. This period was also one of broader unrest with regard to land registration and taxation, and local petitions to the central government in Istanbul also protested unchecked Jewish immigration, questionable land registration practices, and the eviction of tenant farmers from properties sold for Jewish settlements.

In several notable cases, physical clashes broke out between new Jewish colonists and local Palestinian villagers. Although some were isolated cases of theft or murder solved through negotiations and reparations, others portended much more serious conflicts over land ownership and the rights to lease and work the land. Hand in hand were less legal but nonetheless growing feelings of embedded resentment and fear, extraterritorial arrogance and privilege, and competing claims over rootedness and foreignness. In Jaffa, a small-scale riot broke out in March 1908 against a group of Russian Jewish immigrants, although Chelouche neglects to mention it in his memoir.

Given these developments, by the first decade of the twentieth century, the population of Jaffa had doubled over the preceding thirty years, to somewhere around seventeen thousand Ottoman residents. The Muslim population of the city had declined slightly to around 65 percent, with the remainder still divided between Christians and Jews.[69] Immigrant and native-born Jews, like other population groups in the city, were just one agent of economic growth and expansion in the city. Of the sixteen new neighborhoods and residential compounds built in Jaffa from 1880–1909, eleven were Jewish, although these were of varying sizes, ranging from a few houses to several dozen. However, as Margalit Chelouche-Havatzelet, the daughter of Yosef Eliyahu Chelouche's brother Ya'akov, recorded in her memoir, these all-Jewish neighborhoods like Neve Tzedek, where she grew up, were still deeply integrated into and dependent on Jaffa, only one to two kilometers away. The men of the neighborhood were craftsmen who traveled daily to the commercial center for work, by foot or by donkey.

In the decades that followed, as practical Zionism primarily sought to carry out a project of separatist development for Jews, the tension for native Jews like Chelouche between civic and local commitments and religious and, increasingly, national commitments would grow. Nothing brought these tensions into sharper relief than Chelouche's participation in building Tel Aviv alongside his hometown of Jaffa.

TEL AVIV: THE "JAFFA OF THE JEWS"

Beyond all his professional activities in the field of construction, Chelouche became involved in a local Jewish housing association that —unlike previous projects—had bold cultural ambitions. Founded in the summer of 1906, the Ahuzat Bayit association was a first conscious attempt to establish a "Hebrew city" in Palestine, at first as a separatist entity within Jaffa's municipal territory. Chelouche, one of its founding members, was heavily involved in the construction of the neighborhood, which began in 1909 and was soon renamed "Tel Aviv." According to his own account, Chelouche became the building contractor of about half of the new development's houses and of its only public building, the Herzliya Hebrew Gymnasium.

The creation of Tel Aviv was strongly related to what can be described as the "Hebrew cultural project" and its realization in Palestine. One of the key objectives of Zionism, as a national movement for the creation of a Jewish homeland in Eretz Israel (the Hebrew name for the Land of Israel), was the creation of a new Hebrew culture distinct from diasporic Jewish culture. The Land of Israel, so it was believed, was the only place in which Jews could transform themselves into "Hebrews," revive their national identity, and create an autonomous modern nation. In cultural terms, this shift mandated the creation of an entirely new cultural repertoire in which each aspect of individual and communal life had to be reinvented to conform to the Hebrew ideal. This also included the creation of new, "Hebrew" forms of settlement, in which the physical environment would support the metaphysical transformation of the Jewish people.

At the time of the establishment of Tel Aviv, there were at least five thousand Jews living in Jaffa, a significant increase within a few short decades. The fact that most of them lived, worked, and shopped alongside and in close proximity to Arabs was an issue of growing concern to Zionist ideologues, for whom Jaffa represented the worst possible symbol on practical, cultural, economic, ideological, and geopolitical levels. Some European Zionists admired the autonomous Templer colonies in Palestine and also fretted about the Jews contributing to the Arab economy through rented apartments. Arthur Ruppin, the key World Zionist Organization (WZO) functionary in Jaffa and himself a recent immigrant from Germany, connected civilizational, economic, and national aims in the need to establish a separate, modern Jewish neighborhood. In his view: "The narrow streets [of Jaffa], the dirt and quality of the hideous neighborhood buildings, are a disgrace to the Jews, deterring many respectable people from settling in the country. The construction of good, salutary homes for middle class Jews in Jaffa is of the greatest importance. I do not believe I exaggerate when I say that a properly built Jewish quarter is the most important step in the Jewish economic conquest of Jaffa."[70]

FIGURE I.13. *Herzl Street in Tel Aviv, with the Hebrew Gymnasium in the center. Photo by Abraham Soskin, 1911. Betsy Frenkel Collection, Amsterdam Jewish Museum, F000520.*

Tel Aviv was thus conceived and developed as a "Hebrew city," which affected not only the daily life in the neighborhood but also some of its spatial and architectural characteristics. The most conspicuous of all was the selection of a Hebrew school instead of a synagogue as the neighborhood's main public building. To emphasize its cultural significance, the building was designed in a "Hebrew" architectural style at the focal point of the neighborhood's main street and could be clearly seen from the nearby trains traveling between Jaffa and Jerusalem. In addition, the planners envisioned that the built environment would promote a "healthy atmosphere and in hygienic conditions . . . with a small garden and courtyard" for each home.[71] To create a distinctive "Hebrew" atmosphere, indeed a "Jaffa of the Jews," Tel Aviv was purposefully built as spatially detached from Jaffa's northern urban fabric. In reality, though, this detachment was more symbolic than effective since the new neighborhood was located only about 1.5 kilometers from Jaffa's main square at that time, just outside the Great Mosque, and still heavily relied on the economic activity of Jaffa, its mother-city.

FIGURE I.14. *Residents of Tel Aviv in front of a "Diligence" carriage, on Herzl Street, ca. 1911. Yosef Eliyahu Chelouche's house is visible in the foreground at the corner of Herzl Street and Rothschild Boulevard. Photo by Abraham Soskin. Betsy Frenkel Collection, Amsterdam Jewish Museum, F000520.*

However, it is clear from the founding documents that Tel Aviv's visionaries hoped it would be a model of "Jewish urban colonization" that might spread to other cities in Palestine. As one 1909 Russian-language handbook explained, "[Ahuzat Bayit seeks] to constitute, in our own country, as soon as possible, not only an economic force but a political one. There is no doubt that we will not be able to own the country if we do not own the land. . . . The development of a Jewish urban community is without a doubt the most important stage in the bolstering of our position in the country."[72]

In fact, from the outset, the sale of Ahuzat Bayit was fraught with legal, administrative, and political complexities and presaged the conflicts that would emerge around future land sales for Jewish settlement. The Sephardi lawyer handling the sale for Ahuzat Bayit, David Moyal, relied on his linguistic, legal, and political acumen to overcome the various hurdles in place to finalize the sale. Likewise, Yosef Eliyahu Chelouche would be called on repeatedly to serve as an intermediary to the Ottoman government, the Jaffa municipality, and other local institutions on behalf of Tel Aviv. His knowledge of Arabic and his status as a native son were no doubt key considerations, for other than himself and his brother Ya'akov, there were very few Sephardi Jews among the more than five dozen founders of Tel Aviv, although more began moving to the neighborhood after its founding.[73]

As a committed builder and land purchaser, Chelouche was undoubtedly an active "practical Zionist." However, Chelouche also relays in his memoir that he was skeptical of some aspects of the early Zionist project, such as the "Hebrew labor" (*'avoda 'ivrit*) demands of members of the socialist Zionist immigrant wave in the years before World War I, which pressured Jewish employers to hire only Jewish rather than Arab laborers, farmers, and guards. Not only were the Jewish immigrant workers that Chelouche was pressured to hire more expensive and troublesome than his Arab workers, but in Chelouche's view they also lacked their knowledge, expertise, and experience, leading in at least one instance to the collapse of a building under construction. (Chelouche was keen to be exonerated of responsibility for the collapse at the time and insisted on retelling his side of the story decades later in the memoir.) Surviving letters show that the Ahuzat Bayit committee warned Chelouche more than once about his Arab laborers, threatening to fine him if he continued to employ them on the Sabbath. Chelouche's opposition to Hebrew labor was seemingly professional and financial; if he shared the concerns of other political moderates at the time that "Hebrew labor" would damage Jewish-Arab relations, he did not express them in his writings. In fact, throughout his memoir, Chelouche failed to recognize the political impact of his activities on behalf of the Zionist movement, even when confronted by Palestinian critics.

For some of Jaffa's Arab residents, this proximity and overt ideological mission rendered Tel Aviv as a visible outpost of European culture and proof of the refusal of immigrant Jews to integrate into the country. The Arabic press in Palestine that emerged after the 1908 Ottoman revolution and upended the heavy censorship in the empire strongly critiqued what they saw as the unwelcome signs of Jewish autonomy found in Tel Aviv. Specifically, local Palestinian observers noted with concern that immigrant Jews did not want to live as neighbors with Palestinian

Arabs, nor did they want to learn the majority language of the land and assimilate with the local society. In addition, in a prominent incident in early 1914 that Chelouche also recounted in his memoir, the anti-Zionist newspaper *Falastin* published an article stating that residents of Tel Aviv had arrested Arabs who wandered into the neighborhood and had imprisoned them in the Hebrew Gymnasium. The accusation was so severe—and the agitation of the Jaffa populace so destabilizing—that Ottoman officials investigated the report, ultimately finding it without basis.[74]

Without a doubt, Chelouche considered his role in building Tel Aviv to be among his most important contributions to the Jewish community of Palestine and to the project of Jewish revival, and as a result, *Parashat Hayay* focuses on this public role. Unfortunately, Yosef Eliyahu shies away from much personal reflection in these years; he does not describe the home he built in Tel Aviv, nor does he share much with his readers of his family life as an adult. Instead, we must try to fill in the outlines with other sources. Thanks to the memoir of one of Yosef Eliyahu's grandchildren, Aharon, the son of his eldest son Moshe, we have a more domestic picture to complement Yosef Eliyahu Chelouche's public persona in these years. (Aharon's rich description starts in the 1920s, but some elements would certainly have been in place a decade earlier.)

Yosef Eliyahu and his younger brother Ya'akov built adjoining houses in Tel Aviv, located on Rothschild Boulevard at the corner with Herzl Street, the main street in Tel Aviv. The house that Chelouche designed and built was grand, the picture of comfort, affluence, and respectability: four large rooms, high ceilings, strategically placed windows, and fine craftsmanship.[75] There were Western bourgeois elements like the Czech crystal glasses in various colors and heavy Russian silverware, the markers of a Jewish home like a separate set of dishes for Passover and ritual objects like candles for the Sabbath, and signs of a Levantine home like the large coffeepots and water pipes (*nargileh*) and the stockpiles of olive oil and Nabulsi soap. The family's menu reflected their North African origins and Palestinian environment: vegetables stuffed with rice and meat, couscous, *bamia* with lamb or chicken, *kubbe* with burghul and pine nuts, *sofrito*, *hamin*, various soups, North African–style spicy fish, fried *kashkaval* cheese, homemade *laban* and *labaneh*, and Sephardi and Levantine savories and sweets like *burekas*, *ka'ak*, marzipan, and baklava. On special occasions, the family would eat pigeon stuffed with rice, taking them from the dozens of pigeons caged on the rooftop of the family home.

Chelouche writes little about his wife, Freha Simha, perhaps in accordance with the customs of family modesty, but their grandson Aharon described her as a talented and hardworking woman who, despite her wealthy family origins, cooked and cleaned for her growing family almost entirely on her own. She was highly respected and sought after as a healer, and her folk traditions and medicinal practices were so effective that one recipe was allegedly copied by one of the certified doctors in Jaffa and was formulated into commercially successful throat lozenges. Due to her noble birth in the Moyal family, Freha was treated with great honor in the synagogue and among the women of the community, although it appears she was also the victim of the petty jealousies of other women, including some of her own sisters-in-law.

According to their grandson, much of Yosef Eliyahu and Freha Chelouche's social life revolved around the synagogue attached to Aharon Chelouche's home in Neve Tzedek, to which they continued to walk for the Sabbath services until the end of their lives. During the long services there was plenty of time for men and women to separately circulate to discuss business, politics, and community gossip. We have clues in Yosef Eliyahu's memoir that his fellow Sephardi Jews remained his closest, most intimate friends, and Yosef Eliyahu, his brothers, and his sons were active in numerous Sephardi religious, political, and social organizations. To be sure, Chelouche's move to Tel Aviv brought him into regular contact and circulation with Ashkenazi Jews and the organized Zionist movement, and as he writes, the informal council of Tel Aviv kept him busy, as they met nightly after dinner to discuss the neighborhood's affairs. In addition, Yosef Eliyahu's regular visits to the family store on Bustrus Street and the commercial and political contacts and relationships he had in Jaffa continued. Those Jaffan elite circles proved lifesaving during the crucial years of World War I.

WORLD WAR I AND THE END OF EMPIRE

As war broke out in the summer of 1914, and especially after the Ottomans joined the side of Germany and the Austro-Hungarian Empire in late October, Chelouche's memoir shifts gears dramatically to recount his attempts to navigate safety for himself, his family, and his community. Early on, Yosef Eliyahu and his family felt pressured to give up their

French protection and adopt Ottoman citizenship, as a public campaign was carried out among the Jewish communities in Palestine in the summer and fall urging foreign Jews to "become Ottoman."[76] The immediate impetus for this Ottomanization campaign was the abrogation of the extraterritorial privileges that the capitulations had given foreign citizens in Ottoman lands and the looming threat of deportation of "enemy aliens" in an empire at war. Over several months in the fall of 1914, thousands of foreign Jews long-resident in Palestine registered as Ottoman citizens for the first time, finally convinced by the stick of Ottoman threats more than the carrot of Ottoman incentives.

In his retelling, Chelouche immediately used his government and elite connections to rescue dozens of Jewish youths from conscription in the Ottoman army. When the Ottomans finally expelled "enemy foreign nationals" who refused to take Ottoman nationality beginning in December 1914, this also included Yosef Eliyahu's third son, Me'ir, who was forbidden reentry to Jaffa upon his return from school in Cairo after he refused to forfeit his French protection. As Chelouche poignantly described in his memoirs, over seven hundred foreign nationals, five hundred of whom resided in Tel Aviv, were expelled on 17 December, without warning and virtually overnight.[77] Various eyewitnesses reported that Ottoman police and gendarmerie marched through primarily Jewish neighborhoods arresting those who could not prove their citizenship and took them directly to the port. Foreign consular archives, particularly those of the neutral Spanish government that took over concern for the affairs of the shuttered consulates of enemy states, further detail the panicked attempts that foreign Jewish residents made to entrust their possessions and inventories to neighbors or to the consul himself.[78]

After the December 1914 expulsion, another list from 1915 shows that over seven hundred Jews still remained in Tel Aviv and thousands more remained in greater Jaffa. In those early years of the war, Chelouche tells us that Jews and Palestinian Arabs in Jaffa cooperated against the machinations of exploitative local Ottoman officials, coordinated efforts to distribute grain and other much-needed resources, but also tensely and jealously watched to ensure that the responsibilities—and costs—of war were distributed evenly. Merchants and suppliers such as Chelouche were forced to "contribute" goods and money to the Ottoman war effort, and able-bodied non-Muslims were conscripted into the humiliating and backbreaking labor battalions. In addition, Ottoman officials clamped down on perceived nationalist movements, including Zionism and Arab nationalism; while Chelouche himself was arrested several times and faced temporary internal deportation due to his Zionist connections, as he describes in his memoir, other Zionist officials and Arab nationalists were deported from Palestine or, in the latter case, publicly executed.

When Ottoman prospects in the war diminished in March 1917 as British troops shelled nearby Gaza, the Ottoman command ordered the mass evacuation of civilians from Jaffa and Tel Aviv, an order that applied to Muslims, Christians, and Jews. One historian estimates that ten thousand people were expelled from Jaffa at this time, about one-third of them Jews.[79] According to one of Yosef Eliyahu's grandchildren, the family received offers of refuge in the orchard villas outside of Jaffa belonging to unnamed family friends, but they turned them down in order to keep their large party of three dozen family members together.[80] As a result, the Chelouches spent a year and a half in rented shelters in various villages and towns in central and northern Palestine, first in the Jewish settlement of Petah Tikva, then in the Palestinian town of Qalqilya, and finally in the Palestinian village of Kafr Jammal, forty kilometers northeast of Tel Aviv. As Chelouche recounts in his memoir, over this difficult period the family experienced poverty, homelessness, humiliation, imprisonment, and the death of the family matriarch, Yosef Eliyahu's beloved mother Sara.

And yet, during the war years Yosef Eliyahu also nimbly engaged in trade and investment, successfully found respectable refuge for his large entourage, and emerged as a selfless and resourceful community leader in a time of profound crisis. Moreover, as he took care to document for his readers, Chelouche's life, well-being, and honor were spared numerous times by local Palestinian contacts—former employees and partners, former neighbors and urban notables, friendly government clerks and officials, sympathetic army officers, and even concerned strangers. Chelouche's detailed description of his family's internal expulsion is an invaluable addition to the bottom-up histories of World War I in the Ottoman Middle East and in Palestine, offering a unique perspective on the impact of the war on the local populations as well as the difficult experiences of a Jewish family in Palestine.[81]

THE ARRIVAL OF THE BRITISH AND THE SEPARATION OF TEL AVIV FROM JAFFA

In sharp contrast to the detailed and rich focus on the years before and during World War I, *Parashat Hayay* presents an abbreviated and grim picture of the last fifteen years of Chelouche's life spent under British rule. Although the British conquered Jaffa already in November 1917, the Chelouches were stuck on the Ottoman side of the front until the British successfully occupied the rest of Palestine in late 1918. British troops were initially met with optimism and relief, as Chelouche recounts, and a sense of salvation from the brutal martial law and wartime suffering. The Chelouche family returned to their home in Tel Aviv and tried to pick up the pieces of their old, comfortable life. However, this optimism was to be short-lived. Across the region, Arabs confronted their own dashed hopes for independence as the British and French powers installed themselves in deeply unpopular Mandatory regimes, in some cases facing significant rebellions and uprisings that they crushed with massive military brutality and diplomatic indifference.[82] In Palestine, the Mandatory regime embedded the pro-Zionist Balfour Declaration within its charter and policy, and this, together with the political disempowerment of the native Palestinian population, set up a combustible formula.[83]

The postwar population of Jaffa was around forty-eight thousand people, the second largest city in the country after Jerusalem. Of the town's residents, there were an equal number of Muslims and Jews, around twenty thousand, with the remainder Christians; 75 percent of Jaffa's Jews (fifteen thousand) resided in Tel Aviv and the Jewish neighborhoods to the north of Jaffa's city center, and they were a considerable and growing bloc. Soon after the British military occupation, calls for an official separation from the Jaffa municipality began to surface among the residents of Tel Aviv. It did not take much before these calls were formulated into an official request for limited independence, submitted by Me'ir Dizengoff, the head of the Tel Aviv committee, to Herbert Samuel, the first British High Commissioner to Palestine and himself a committed Zionist, during the latter's first visit to Jaffa on 28 July 1920, less than a month after assuming his office. The request was extremely exceptional, especially since Tel Aviv's territory was relatively small compared to the other new urban expansions of Jaffa.

The British authorities took kindly to a separation between Jaffa and

Tel Aviv, which was officially explicated by Dizengoff as a wish emanating from the heavy taxation imposed on Tel Aviv's residents, who were obliged to pay taxes to both the Jaffa municipality and the Tel Aviv committee; the desire to receive a loan for the development of the neighborhood, which was not possible due to its informal status; and the intention to register the neighborhood properties under the name of the genuine owners of the houses, which was prohibited by the still-binding Ottoman land laws. The British positive reaction to the request could be attributed to their sympathy for Zionism as well as to their stated belief that Jews and Arabs were inherently distinct and should be separate. However, historical evidence sheds little light on the possible reasons behind the assent of Jaffa's mayor, 'Asim Bek al-Sa'id, to Tel Aviv's separation request, especially considering the fact that it effectively blocked the future development of Jaffa to the north.

A final version of the official separation ordinance was formulated in early April 1921, approved by Herbert Samuel on 11 May and published on 1 June. Tel Aviv was then granted an official status of a township and received a considerable degree of independence, especially in the domains of planning and taxation, although it formally continued to belong to the Jaffa municipality until 1934, when it officially gained the status of an independent municipality.

Ten days before the ordinance was approved, on 1 May 1921, a violent riot broke out in Jaffa. The events, which British officials concluded were triggered spontaneously by a May Day procession of a small group of Communist Jews in the main shopping street of Manshiya/Neve Shalom, lasted three days, spreading to other parts of central Palestine. In Jaffa, 43 Jews were killed by Arab rioters and 134 more were wounded; 14 Arab Jaffans were killed during the event, most of them by British troops attempting to regain control. Most of the Jewish victims were murdered in the 'Ajami and Manshiya neighborhoods in Jaffa, the latter not far from Tel Aviv.[84] The approval of the separation ordinance had no apparent causal relation to the attacks; nevertheless, the leaders of Tel Aviv started using the attacks as supporting post-factum evidence for an allegedly inevitable need to divide Jaffa's urban area into two disparate entities, "Hebrew" and "Arab."[85]

The newly drawn border between Jaffa and Tel Aviv took shape in light of the "Hebrew city" concept. The expanded territory of Tel Aviv now consisted of parts of the older Jewish neighborhoods of northern

FIGURE I.15. *Aerial photograph of northern Jaffa by the German Air Force, with the future municipal border between Jaffa and Tel Aviv overlaid in a dotted line, 12 January 1918. Bayerisches Hauptstaatsarchiv, München, via Younes and Soraya Nazarian Library, University of Haifa, 990009566050402791.*

Jaffa, following the wish to include within the "Hebrew city" as many Jews as possible, while leaving out ethnically mixed areas. A direct outcome of this principle of division was the winding nature of the boundary line; this act had its most radical effect on the ethnically mixed Manshiya/Neve Shalom quarter, where the line was drawn along two of its main commercial streets, Suq al-Yahud (The Jewish Market) and Rehov Haitlizim (The Butchers' Street), leaving thousands of Jewish residents who were living in houses owned by Arabs or in houses adjacent to Arab houses in Jaffa's territory. A similar logic of division was applied to the area of Harat al-Tanak which was left within Jaffa's borders because of its ethnically mixed nature, despite an initial intention to include it within the borders of Tel Aviv due to future planning considerations.

The immediate effect of the new status of Tel Aviv on Jaffa's urban development was the division of planning powers between the Jaffa municipality and the new township of Tel Aviv. In 1925, Patrick Geddes, the renowned Scottish town planner, was invited to come to Tel Aviv to produce the first master plan for the city, which was by then not more than a chance agglomerate of small neighborhoods. Although his plan was limited only to the territories then under Tel Aviv's powers, Geddes opened his town planning report with a statement that questioned the spatial independence of Tel Aviv: "With all respect to the ethnic distinctiveness and the civic individuality of Tel Aviv, as Township, its geographic, social and even fundamental economic situation is determined by its position as Northern Jaffa.... The old town, the modern Township, must increasingly work and grow together.... The more efficient and well developed can be Greater Jaffa, the better for all its component quarters and townships, and for their related districts also."[86] Yet Geddes's naïve advice could not have had a lesser impact on his clients. Ever since the establishment of Tel Aviv, Jaffa was destined to perpetually serve as its negative mirror image. The leaders of Tel Aviv were constantly trying to differentiate it from Jaffa as much as possible, both by emphasizing its Hebrew character (which contrasted the "Arab" nature of Jaffa) and by claiming a modern character for its built form, allegedly contrasting the "traditional" and "Oriental" character of the spatial organization of the mother-city. Geddes's plan, which restricted itself only to Tel Aviv's town planning area, was therefore no more than a tool for creating a distinct spatial order that should have shifted Tel Aviv's center of gravity up north, as far away as possible from old Jaffa and even from the old urban center of northern Jaffa in the Manshiya/Neve Shalom quarter.

In this regard, the drawing of the border between Jaffa and Tel Aviv was intended to enforce an allegedly spatial homogeneity upon a heterogeneous urban fabric that had gradually evolved over more than three decades. At the same time, the much more homogenous urban fabric of Manshiya/Neve Shalom had been divided "on paper" because of the different ethnic identities of its property owners. The new border thus had no roots in the self-organization of the urban activities, nor did it have any conspicuous physical elements to be attached to or existing cognitive divisions to follow. Moreover, as with many urban boundaries, the new border lacked physical manifestations, making it impossible to discern only by looking where Jaffa ended and where Tel Aviv began.

Nevertheless, as a cultural tool for shaping a common cognitive division of urban space, the new boundary proved to be more than effective, since it provided Tel Aviv with a clear territorial definition that was an essential component in realizing the cultural ideal of a "Hebrew city."

DEEPENING SEPARATION AND SEPHARDI STEPSONS

The separation of Tel Aviv from Jaffa is but one aspect of the broader separation that took place during the 1920s in Palestine. Historians have called the autonomous Zionist institutions established with British approval and operating with wide latitude as a Jewish "state in the making," which included an executive branch (the Jewish Agency), a legislative branch (the National Council, or *Va'ad le'umi*), and a judicial branch (the Hebrew courts, *Batei mishpat hashalom*). In addition, throughout the 1920s, Jewish schools expanded their outreach, the Hebrew press grew significantly, and social and cultural life flourished—all as part of a distinct "Hebrew" cultural and national project. Earlier ideological commitments to creating an autonomous and discrete Jewish society led to attempts to separate the Jewish economy from Palestinian Arabs—first through "Hebrew labor," then through the purchase of only "Hebrew products," and finally through "Hebrew transportation," the establishment of separate bus lines servicing Jewish neighborhoods. While it is not accurate to say that Jewish society in Mandatory Palestine was completely separate from Palestinian Arab society, there were certainly many forces attempting to make it so.

For his part, Yosef Eliyahu Chelouche spent years on the "quiet work" of Jewish-Arab relations. As Chelouche recounts in chapter 28, he served alongside Palestinian Arabs on Jaffa's municipal committees, although many other details of his activities attempting to better Jewish-Arab relations in the 1920s are left out from his memoir. For example, other sources reveal that he was among the founding members who established a joint bank for commerce and industry.[87] In addition, the Tel Aviv township, and Mayor Dizengoff himself, also turned to Chelouche on numerous occasions to ask for his help. In 1926, for example, the township asked Chelouche to smooth over relations with a Palestinian notable, Ragheb al-Imam, whose property bordering Tel Aviv to the north had been disturbed by the township's road work.[88] Again in 1931, Dizengoff turned to Chelouche directly to consult with him about a new initiative by the Jaffa mayor to form a Jewish-Arab sailors union.[89] These instances were only a couple whose documentation survive, but they suggest there is much more that Chelouche could have covered.

For their part, Palestinian Arabs saw their own political ambitions repeatedly shut down by the British, who were willing to recognize their "civil" and "religious" rights while relegating them to the status of a political minority. Palestinian nationalists organized into political organizations like the Muslim-Christian Associations, and they submitted hundreds of petitions to the Mandate authorities and League of Nations with their demands to end the support for the Balfour Declaration and to alter the terms of the mandate. Nationalists also periodically instituted national strikes against the Mandate and called for boycotts against conducting business with Jews throughout this period. With the steep and rapid Jewish immigration and land purchases of the 1920s, both peasant landlessness and urban migration grew, further contributing to the structural instability of colonial rule and a growing nationalist clash on the ground.

This wave of Jewish immigration in the 1920s was sparked by unrest and anti-Semitism in eastern and central Europe, where the postwar minorities protections did little to provide Jews with safety and equal protection in their home countries. British immigration policy in Palestine facilitated this flow of immigrants, and within the first decade of British rule, the Jewish community more than doubled from 84,000 (11 percent of the country) to 175,000 (almost 17 percent of the population). While this population growth had direct effects on Jewish-Arab relations, it also had an important impact on intra-Jewish relations and on Yosef Eliyahu Chelouche's public persona.

After decades in private business and as a behind-the-scenes community leader, Yosef Eliyahu Chelouche emerged in the 1920s as a public voice publishing dozens of opinion pieces and open letters in the Hebrew press, almost exclusively in the Jerusalem newspaper *Do'ar hayom* (Daily Mail).[90] As his grandson Aharon related, Chelouche often published his essays anonymously. Some of his writing drew on his business acumen: during the economic crisis of 1926–1927, for example, Chelouche advocated personal austerity and prudishly chastised his readers for wasting money at the theater and on other unnecessary leisure activities. He also was antagonistic to the socialist and Communist ideas swirling around the Jewish community in Palestine, and he saw himself as firmly aligned with the interests of private capitalists.

However, most of Chelouche's writing in these years was directed at the debates around ethnic representation in the Jewish councils in Palestine and within the World Zionist Organization. Chelouche's writing on this topic was a rebuke against the tidal change in intra-Jewish hierarchies that had taken place in the aftermath of World War I. Whereas in the Ottoman era Sephardim had served as the official representatives and elites of the Jewish community as a result of their nativeness, less than two years after the arrival of British troops in Palestine a Sephardi community leader complained at a public event in Jerusalem that suddenly Ashkenazim were the "favored sons" and Sephardim the "stepsons" in the new British Palestine.[91] Nativeness was now a liability, and it was Europeanness that bestowed the privileges of access, authority, and legitimacy.

In response to this turn of events, throughout the 1920s prominent Sephardi communal leaders struggled to be included in the new Zionist institutions created under the Mandate, and when that failed, they turned to establish political institutions of their own.[92] Chelouche and his adult sons were active in organizing a variety of Sephardi communal, political, and cultural institutions that worked to demand a larger role in Zionist institutions and decision-making bodies as well as to make a more prominent imprint on Jewish society.[93] Their record was mixed: Chelouche was a founding member of the World Federation of Sephardi Jews that was established at the Fourteenth Zionist Congress in Vienna in 1925, but he later complained bitterly that they were virtually ignored by the Zionist Executive.[94]

In Chelouche's view, the ascension of foreign Ashkenazi Jews to the leadership of the Jewish community in Palestine and the process of native Jewish marginalization was unfair and unrepresentative: Sephardim were more than one-third of the Jewish population but held a miniscule number of public roles. Thus, when the Mandatory government proposed legislation to standardize the constitution of the Jewish representative body known as the Knesset Israel in the summer of 1927, many Sephardi leaders objected and feared they would be absorbed by the Ashkenazi-dominated organizations and left without a voice. Chelouche and the Tel Aviv–Jaffa branch of the Sephardi Union were in favor of joining, but they shared the concerns of other Sephardi organizations that wanted to ensure their institutional and legal autonomy and demanded a Sephardi quota within the Knesset Israel. Chelouche also deeply resented the criticism voiced by Zionist leaders in the press that Sephardi demands for representation quotas were divisive, underscoring that his own family was "mixed" (since all his children had married Ashkenazi Jews) and that it was Ashkenazi organizations and parties themselves that worked against Jewish unity.[95]

Against this backdrop of intra-Jewish ethnic tensions and competition, Chelouche published an "open letter to the Sephardim and the Eastern ethnicities" in which he urged them to demand their rights from the Jewish Agency and other central Zionist organizations.[96] In his eyes, not only did Sephardi Jews have a "right to exist in the land," but moreover they had "the fullest right," since they had remained residents in the country throughout history (presumably, in contrast to Ashkenazi Jews, who largely had not).

In addition to these political battles, Chelouche struggled against the symbolic erasure of Sephardi Jews from the cultural institutions and collective memory of the new "Hebrew" community. One episode in particular represents the deeply personal stakes for Yosef Eliyahu Chelouche. In early 1927, after a Sephardi beauty was crowned as Queen Esther for the annual Purim pageant held in Tel Aviv to great acclaim, an anonymous column published in *Haaretz* newspaper criticized the ethnic aspect of her selection and approval.[97] The author, who chose the pen name "Mezeg Tov" (Good Spirit), wrote, "From now on, there's no point in the Sephardim complaining against the Ashkenazim who allegedly oppress the rights of the other communities.... From now on, all differences are canceled.... There's no Ashkenazim and no Sephardim, only beauty in the world." Then Mezeg Tov sarcastically advised the Yemenite community to prepare their campaign to win the pageant the following year—and he placed the "Bukharans, Kurds, and all the other communities" on notice for future pageants, even predicting that one day, "an Arab woman will stand for election."

The ridicule and scorn oozing from the column wounded Yosef Eliyahu Chelouche greatly, not least because it was his own niece, Riquetta (Rivka) Chelouche, who had been crowned as Queen Esther. In response, Chelouche sent his own anonymous letter (signed plainly "Yehudi/Jew") to the editor of the Sephardi-friendly *Do'ar hayom* requesting publication. In it, he called out the anonymous letter writer for his "hatred" and divisiveness and reminded him that Queen Esther was originally Persian ("that is to say, Oriental").⁹⁸ Rather than the "good spirit" that the anonymous author claimed to possess, Chelouche retorted that it would have been more fitting for him to sign his name "bad spirit."

Like his father Aharon, Chelouche deeply longed for a united Jewish people, but as long as that reality had not yet arrived, he would continue to assert his Sephardi credentials. In many ways, *Parashat Hayay* was Yosef Eliyahu Chelouche's more complete answer to his feelings of being erased and marginalized by the Zionist establishment in British Palestine. As Chelouche's proud recounting of his and other prominent Sephardi families' early, active involvement in "building the Hebrew national home"⁹⁹ makes clear, the Zionist enterprise would never have gotten off the ground without their agile and critical intervention. As he reminds his readers, when the first Zionist dreamers, philanthropists, and functionaries arrived in Palestine from Europe in the first decade of Yosef Eliyahu's life, they were met by a small but tight-knit Sephardi community that—while initially skeptical of the Russian Zionists' Jewishness—eventually aided the Zionist project by drawing on their nativeness in instrumental ways, primarily in purchasing and registering land and mediating between local government officials, landowners, and tribal leaders. It is no coincidence, then, that among the recipients of Chelouche's gifted memoir was Samuel (Shmu'el) Tolkowsky, the Belgian agronomist and Zionist official who immigrated to Palestine in the years before World War I and who published two prominent books on the Zionist colonization of Palestine and the history of Jaffa, neither of which even mentioned Sephardi Jews.¹⁰⁰

When Chelouche began drafting his memoir at some point in the mid-1920s, he was encouraged by his acquaintance Moshe David Gaon, a Sarajevo-born journalist, teacher, and amateur historian who at the time was compiling an encyclopedia of prominent Sephardi families.¹⁰¹ In this decade of intense ethnic competition within the Jewish community, one of Chelouche's key aims in penning his memoir was to restore Sephardi Jews to the limelight as agents and leaders in the most important aspects of the Zionist project. Chelouche finished his first draft of his memoir in 1928, but he was not able to publish it before the outbreak of the bloody August 1929 riots that resulted in hundreds of dead and injured Jews and Arabs throughout the country.

Violence Tears the Seams of Brotherhood

The riots had been sparked in Jerusalem by a clash over the Western Wall, revered by Jews as a retaining wall of King Solomon's Temple and by Muslims as the wall on which the prophet Muhammad had tethered his horse, al-Burak, on a night holy in Islamic tradition. The merging of the religious and political symbolism of the wall was part of the deeper conflict developing under British rule between the Palestinian nationalist and Zionist movements over rights to the land and its future. Yosef Eliyahu was in Lebanon at a spa with his convalescing wife at the time of the 1929 riots, but he received alarmed telegrams sent from his adult sons back home in Jaffa. The viciousness of the riots, in which Jewish women and children were slaughtered in their homes, and the political reckoning that took place in their aftermath, shook Chelouche deeply. Although Chelouche does not offer extensive political thinking in his memoir, his contemporary writings shed light on how he attempted to understand and navigate this changed political climate.

Almost exactly one year prior to the riots, in the aftermath of the first incidents of violence at the Western Wall, Chelouche had written an open "Letter to my Arab brothers" that was published in the Damascene newspaper *Alif Baa'*, edited by the Jaffan intellectual and former editor of *Falastin*, Yusuf al-'Issa, who was in exile. In that piece, Chelouche appealed to historic ties of Jewish-Muslim brotherhood, talked up the benefits of Zionism, and attempted to revive the idea of a homeland shared between Arabs and Jews. Chelouche also emphasized the biblical connection of Jews to Palestine and chastised his presumedly pious readers for opposing divine will that had brought them back.

Chelouche developed these themes later in an anonymous essay submitted to *Falastin* in early 1930, in which he criticized its published account of a speech by the Lebanese-American intellectual Amin al-Rihani, who had evidently criticized the Zionist movement on Arabist nationalist grounds.[102] Chelouche characterized (the Christian) al-Rihani's speech as religious incitement and nationalist distortion, and instead emphasized the shared friendship and brotherhood that had tied Jews and Muslims together from ancient times as common sons of Shem, the son of Noah, through the trials of the Crusades and the Christian Reconquista of al-Andalus. As he argued, Christians like al-Rihani (and, presumably, Chelouche's anti-Zionist rivals in Jaffa) should stay out of Jewish-Muslim relations. Chelouche was certain that, left to their own devices, they would fulfill the maxim of the king of Iraq, Faysal, whom he quoted as saying: [the Land of Israel] will not advance only with Muslims but without Jews, just as the Land of Israel will not advance only with Jews but without Muslims.[103] It is not known whether Chelouche published more pieces in the Arabic press (and, in fact, neither original text has yet been located), but his efforts to mediate between his neighbors, friends, and colleagues preoccupied him dearly near the end of his life.

By the time *Parashat Hayay* finally appeared in print in 1931, Chelouche had added three more chapters on the recent events, including a searing epilogue in which he critiqued official Zionist policy and argued that the Jewish community needed to dramatically change course in its relations with Palestinian Arabs. In Chelouche's view, Jews in Palestine could not (and should not) rely on the British bayonet to subdue the Palestinian Arabs, but instead, they needed to build bridges on their own. Moreover, Chelouche asserted, it was only "native sons" like himself, rather than the immigrant and foreign leadership of the Zionist movement that had risen to power in recent years, who could steer the course toward mutual understanding and peace in the land. He wrote:

> The relations with our neighbors in this country must now be the main thrust of our activities. This is the biggest issue of all, which must be the focus of all of our attention.... This is something that we natives of the land understood a long time ago, even before the British occupation, and right after it. But our managers, who steered the storm-tossed ship of the *yishuv* over our heads and without our knowledge, who did so from Berlin before the war and from London after the war, who had no interest in taking into consideration our own opinions. For we natives of the land thought differently, and they always tried to silence our correct voice on this issue, like "a voice ring[ing] out in the desert."[104]
>
> ... And although this work has become so much more difficult since the days of the Balfour Declaration and the bloody events that ensued, it is nevertheless incumbent upon the native sons of this land, those who are most familiar with the issue, to carry out the task tactfully and quietly. (pp. 443, 447)

Chelouche picked up this criticism again in a piece he published in response to the Seventeenth Zionist Congress, which had met in February 1931 in Basel.[105] Against the backdrop of general criticisms of the leadership of Chaim Weizmann and the Zionist Executive, Chelouche harshly criticized the Congress's decision to establish a new department dedicated to "relations with the neighbors" while ignoring the person he considered the most suitable expert for the position, the Orientalist and native Jew, Avraham Shalom Yahuda, who at that time was a professor of Semitic languages in Madrid. Chelouche cited Yahuda's fluency in Arabic and Hebrew, his deep knowledge of the Qur'an and Arabic literature, and the esteem in which he was held by Palestinian notables and Muslim intellectuals as his chief qualifications for the position. As Chelouche saw it, only a native Jew like Yahuda understood the true pain of all sides and could rise above petty politics and self-interest to improve Jewish-Arab relations. The refusal of the Zionist Congress to select him for the task revealed, to Chelouche's mind, the indifference with which they treated the position.

THE DEATH AND AFTERLIFE OF YOSEF ELIYAHU CHELOUCHE

On 23 July 1934, Yosef Eliyahu Chelouche passed away suddenly after a short illness, only months after the death of his beloved wife. The Hebrew press immediately published the news of his passing and extensively covered his funeral, which took place the following day. These accounts described how the funeral procession was led by an honor guard of police officers from Tel Aviv escorted by three police officers sent by the Jaffa municipality.[106] The crowd of mourners passed by his home, where the Sephardi chief rabbi (and his lifelong friend) Me'ir Ben Zion 'Uziel[107] gave a eulogy, then proceeded to the Ben Zkenim synagogue, where another eulogy was delivered by Yitzhak 'Abadi,[108] then to the city hall, where a third eulogy was given by Israel Rokach,[109] and finally to the Trumpeldor cemetery, where the final eulogy was delivered by Rabbi Korkidi.[110] Photographs of the funeral show a large crowd, many of the mourners wearing straw hats to protect them against the blazing summer sun, with a few fezzes visible. Male family members wore satin black and white funeral sashes that are still preserved in the family archive in Jerusalem.

The published eulogies praised Chelouche's life work as well as his loyalty to the Jewish community and to Zionist settlement. Reading through the condolence cards sent to the family, one encounters the towering superlatives that were meant to convey the depth of the loss: "his death is a

FIGURE I.16. *Yosef Eliyahu Chelouche's funeral procession on Allenby Street, Tel Aviv, 24 July 1934. Source:* R. Yosef Eliyahu Chelouche Z"L: A memorial book to mark the first anniversary of his death, *1935.*

huge loss to our public," "he will never be forgotten in the history of the Hebrew community of the land."[111] In addition to the many condolences sent in Hebrew, there are no small number in other languages: French, English, German, and a handful in Arabic. The king of Bulgaria, King Boris, even sent a condolence card to the family, as Yosef Eliyahu's eldest son, Moshe, was the Bulgarian consul in Jaffa at the time.[112]

The Jaffa newspaper *Falastin* published a short death notice on page six, in its regular local news column, under the headline "The passing of a notable."[113] The editor acknowledged Yosef Eliyahu Chelouche's long-standing ties and family position in Jaffa (*'a'ilat Chelouche al-ma'arufa qadiman fi Yafa*), although he did not list any of Chelouche's individual accomplishments. After relaying the time and place of the funeral procession, *Falastin* wished Chelouche's many friends "patience and solace."

Among the cards sent by Jaffan mourners, some were written in French, testament to a shared Levantine urban cosmopolitanism of bygone days.[114] In the remaining letters from Palestinian mourners in handwritten Arabic we find two of particular historical importance: the first, written on the official stationery of the Jaffa municipality, was sent by Mayor 'Asim Bek al-Sa'id, addressed to Chelouche's eldest son, Moshe (Musa). Al-Sa'id apologized that his "tooth illness" had prevented him from attending the funeral and mourning with the family in person, as Yosef Eliyahu was held "in the depths of my heart with pure love and respect." Another letter arrived from 'Umar al-Bitar, the former city council member and mayor of Jaffa,[115] who also wrote of his "deep sadness and sharp sorrow" at the death of his "dear friend" while also mentioning he had received the sad news at his "sickbed."[116]

What do we make of these letters of mourning by prominent Palestinian politicians, neither of whom attended Chelouche's funeral, nor did they mention stopping by the family home to console the mourners sitting shiva? As a former member of the Jaffa municipality, Yosef Eliyahu had worked alongside both men for years. In addition, Chelouche and 'Umar al-Bitar had previously worked closely together during World War I, and al-Bitar had visited him at his home before. Both men appear in Chelouche's memoir as two out of the three municipal council members who sat by idly during the 1921 riots, and al-Bitar is identified as the one who verbally threatened Chelouche in the heat of their argument about who was to blame for the riots. As al-Bitar reportedly said, "If you weren't Yosef Chelouche, the son of Aharon Chelouche, a man who is highly respected by all of us, I would kill you right now" (p. 407).

With those threatening words, al-Bitar honored Chelouche's embeddedness in a multigenerational social network, while at the same time reminding him of its conditionality. In times of tension, Chelouche's perceived greater loyalty to Tel Aviv over Jaffa was seen as a violation of the earlier social ties he held. Even still, for years after that tense exchange, Yosef Eliyahu's grandson Aharon wrote that al-Bitar was a frequent guest in Chelouche's sitting room, where he would drink coffee, smoke *nargileh*, and talk for hours with Chelouche. According to Aharon, the two men parted ways irreparably only in 1932, when a photograph of al-Bitar leading an anti-Zionist demonstration in Jaffa was published in the newspaper *Falastin*.

While we know little about Chelouche's relationship with al-Sa'id,

Jewish leaders in Tel Aviv reportedly saw al-Sa'id as "easygoing, moderate, welcoming, and open to discussion,"[117] and as a result, they had encouraged Jewish voters to support his candidacy for mayor of Jaffa in the 1927 elections. Al-Sa'id reportedly had good relations with Me'ir Dizengoff, the longtime mayor of Tel Aviv and Chelouche's close colleague, and while he did not attend Dizengoff's seventieth birthday celebrations due to the boycott called for by the Arab executive, al-Sa'id did send him a private telegram of congratulations.

It is not clear, then, how we should judge the strength of Chelouche's interpersonal ties at the end of his life—from the careful absence of public expressions or the warmly expressed private ones? Despite the absence of these two prominent men, the apparent presence of other Arab mourners at Chelouche's funeral entered into the closing eulogy in the memorial book published after Chelouche's death, and it is worth quoting at length, for it captures both the sense of loss at Chelouche's death and the sense of the end of an era in Jewish-Arab relations:

> One by one they are leaving us—they, *natives of the Near East* who were connecting us to some degree to our Arab neighbors in grave hours of this painful land of ours. Dr. Abushadid [passed] approximately two years ago, Yitzhak Elyashar, a year ago, Yehoshu'a Abrevaya, the representative of the philanthropist [Baron Edmond de Rothschild] in Tel Aviv, only a few months ago, and the last one in importance and brilliance, R. Yosef Eliyahu Chelouche, who left us last week.
>
> Only he who participated in their funerals, only he who saw the large numbers of non-Jews there, can understand the great loss to our national home [that has occurred] with the death of public men like these, who were concerned every day of their lives that the remaining thin threads that enabled relations of friendship and brotherhood between us and our neighbors would not be completely severed in the future.
>
> They were, the four of them, the moral heirs of their great predecessors who paved the way before them up until the Balfour Declaration, men such as the esteemed Nissim Behar, whose bones we brought back to our land two years ago, Eliyahu Sapir, who died as the associate director of the Anglo Palestine Bank, and also Albert Antébi, the great friend of Djemal Pasha,[118] whom we recognize that

if they had been still living among us today then the Hebrew *yishuv* might have been protected from many disasters—public, territorial, spiritual. . . .

Who will fill their place?

Who among the young generation can follow in their footsteps to be the connecting line between the three pillars of the land—Christians, Muslims, and Jews?

Maybe one more in the city and possibly two in the whole country. . . .

The hour has come to face this truth and correct it before we miss the opportunity.[119]

The author of these lines, I. B., closed with a demand that Tel Aviv commemorate these men with street names—as he advocated, not small, hidden alleys but instead with streets as visible and as honorable as the large and distinguished streets commemorating the contribution of Ashkenazi Zionist figures.[120] In fact, it took years before Yosef Eliyahu Chelouche was finally commemorated in the city he helped build and on whose behalf he advocated for years—but Yosef Eliyahu (Chelouche) Street is a rather small residential side street, not far from the large and prominent Dizengoff Street.[121]

Indeed, Chelouche's memory largely disappeared from public life in the decades after his death until his memoir was republished in 2005 by one of his great-grandsons, Or Aleksandrowicz, coeditor of this translation.[122] The publication of that edition made a deep impression and was widely covered in the Hebrew press. The review in the leading Israeli newspaper *Haaretz* featured a breathless headline: "Hebrew and Arab, Zionist and Palestinian, Tel Avivan and Jaffan—once there was such a man." The unstated premise for the newspaper's contemporary Israeli readers, of course, was that these terms were inherently incompatible, underscored once again by the spectacular failure of the 1993 Oslo Accords and in the aftermath of the violence of the Second Intifada. At the time, it seemed that readers saw Chelouche as a tool for repopulating a world and a worldview in which the duality of Jew-and-Arab (or "Arab Jew")[123] was possible, albeit at times (and increasingly) uneasily so.

However, rather than turning to overly romanticized views of the past "roads not taken," this is an opportune moment to reevaluate the historical significance of Yosef Eliyahu Chelouche's *Parashat Hayay*. Recent studies have focused renewed attention on native Jews like Chelouche and their role in the history of Palestine and in the Middle East more broadly. If earlier scholarship sought to harness these Jews firmly to the Zionist and state-building project, a recent generation of scholarship instead has tackled their contributions to Arabic literature and thought, popular culture, and politics, with new questions raised about the cultural outlook and identity of the "Arab Jew." Some of this work shows quite clearly the deep connections between Sephardi/Mizrahi Jews in Palestine with the rest of the region as country of origin, inspiration, and dominant cultural milieu. Other studies focus more directly on the political and social roles that these individuals and communities played in the history of Palestine and in the course of the Jewish-Arab conflict. In these renderings, native Jews were alternately important—if handcuffed—mediators between European Zionists and Palestinian Arabs, or they represent a "road not taken" in the history of the country, or they index a turning point in the conflict over Palestine.

More recent scholarship, however, has suggested that we might consider the role of these native Jews somewhat more critically, with attention paid to their structural roles in the conflict over Palestine and in dialogue with settler colonial studies. As one provocative article has argued, the history of native Jews like Chelouche cannot ignore the political, economic, social, and ideological processes by which the "native" became a "settler" in Palestine, central to the Zionist project that displaced Palestinians even if at times discursively critical of it. Chelouche's *Parashat Hayay* suggests the complexity of this position. On the one hand, Chelouche was a pious Jew and an unapologetic Zionist, and in his articles designated for the Arabic press he repeatedly wrote about the divine commandments that gave Palestine to the Jews and the divine hand that had guided the issuance of the Balfour Declaration. For those who seek in historical figures a different path, it is difficult to read Chelouche's positions as conciliatory or compromising from a Palestinian perspective. In fact, in his memoir, his language toward Palestinian nationalists was dismissive and scathing, at times virtually indistinguishable from that of the Ashkenazi Zionist leadership he criticized.

At the same time, for much of his life, Chelouche saw his Zionist activities in apolitical terms, as congruent with local development and modernization and Jewish regeneration, and he repeatedly criticized the more exclusionary aspects of the Zionist movement. In the years before

World War I, Chelouche was involved with a group of Jaffa intellectuals and businessmen who advocated Palestine as a "shared homeland" between Jews and Arabs, and even after the Balfour Declaration he continued to work for the improvement of his birth town, Jaffa, and for better relations between it and Tel Aviv, his new home. Chelouche's vision of Zionism sought to incorporate and work with Palestinian Arabs, not to ignore them or separate from them. The question remains, of course, whether it was realistic from the outset to assume that Palestinians would sideline their political critique of Zionism in order to benefit from it economically; tragically, it does not appear that Chelouche truly engaged with this question.

Readers of *Parashat Hayay* are left to grapple with these complexities, their possibilities, and their limitations, considering the broad poles of "understanding" and "misunderstanding," "insider" and "outsider," agency and marginalization, and mediation and collaboration that are so vividly expressed through one man's life experiences and memories. It is precisely Chelouche's delicate position—on the seam lines between Jaffa and Tel Aviv, Arab and Jew, and even "native" and "settler" —that makes *Parashat Hayay* such a compelling and important text almost a century later. The drama—and tragedy—of *Parashat Hayay* thus emerges from Chelouche's positioning between his fellow Jews, his most intimate community of believers, and his Palestinian Muslim and Christian neighbors, whose language he shared but whose critique of and experiences with Zionism he ignored; between Arab Jaffa, the city of his birth and youth, and Hebrew Tel Aviv, the city he helped build and in which he died.

NOTES

1. Yosef Eliyahu Chelouche, *Parashat Hayay, 1870–1930* (The story of my life) (Tel Aviv: Stroud, 1931).

2. Central Zionist Archives (hereafter CZA) A488/693.

3. The B'nai B'rith was established in the United States in the early 1840s as a fraternal and humanitarian organization; its Jerusalem lodge was established in 1888. The AIU was a French Jewish philanthropic organization established in 1860 with the aim of bringing "emancipation and social regeneration" to Middle Eastern Jewry.

4. Chelouche's preface is full of self-deprecating apologies over his amateur style —but this was also part of his developed public persona as a humble and plainspoken man. Letters in CZA A488/693; Shimon Cohen, 2 May 1931.

5. The memoir was reviewed in "Hatihat hayim yishuvit," *Do'ar hayom*, 3 March 1931; "Parashat hayai," *Ha'olam*, 11 August 1931; "Parashat hayay (Mein Lebens-

weg)," *Der Moment*, 30 April 1931; "Hag hayovel hashishim," *Miginzei Yerushalayim*, May 1931; "Chelouche," *Palestine Bulletin*, 25 June 1931; "Parashat Hayai," *Hahed*, August 1931; "Bahayim uvasifrut," *Der Tag*, 12 February 1931; "Basifrut uvaomanut," *Davar*, 24 April 1931; "Fonum eretzisraeldigen buchertisch," *Heint*, 28 August 1931. In addition to these detailed reviews, other papers simply announced its publication: "Yatzu leor," *Haaretz*, 27 March 1931; "Yediot," *Ktuvim*, 31 March 1931.

6. This was one of the first native-born Jewish memoirs published in Palestine. The first, *Zikhronot leben Yerushalayim* (Memories of a Jerusalemite), Yehoshu'a Yellin's memoir detailing Jewish life in Jerusalem in the second half of the nineteenth century, was published in Jerusalem in 1923. One ungenerous reviewer who only focused on the Zionist chapters of *Parashat Hayay* (incorrectly) claimed that previously published accounts by various Zionist functionaries had already covered that material.

7. Practical Zionism was preoccupied with implementing Zionist settlement and establishing Zionist institutions in Palestine, as opposed to other strands of Zionism that were focused on international diplomacy or promoting a cultural or spiritual Zionism without any material aspects.

8. We use "Sephardi" (plural, Sephardim) as an umbrella term for all communities of Middle Eastern Jews then present in Palestine—Sephardim (Ladino-speaking Jews who moved to Ottoman lands after the Iberian expulsions of 1492 as well as Arabized—*mist'arab*—Jews in Egypt and the Eastern Mediterranean/Mashriq), Ma'aravim/Maghrebim (North African Jews, many of whom also had Iberian origins but who spoke Arabic, Judeo-Arabic, or Haketia), Persians, Mesopotamians, Yemenites, etc. These various ethnic groups had their own organizational trajectories and at times competing interests, but there were also strategic shared interests and a shared sense of collectivity at various moments in time. The Chelouche family belonged to Maghrebi as well as Sephardi and Mizrahi institutions in Jaffa.

9. This was the term used in a Yiddish language review; the same reviewer referred to Chelouche as a "Frenk," an arguably derogatory—if commonplace—Ashkenazi term for Middle Eastern Jews at the time. "Word of the Day Frenkim: Our Very Own F Word," *Haaretz*, 13 August 2013.

10. Chelouche referred to himself in his memoir and other writings as "native" (*yelid haaretz*).

11. Most memoirs from this period are either out of print or untranslated from the original Arabic or Hebrew. For a list of recently published and English-language memoirs, see the bibliography.

12. See the bibliography for a list of secondary scholarship relying on or analyzing Chelouche's memoir.

13. We label Jaffa a "town" before the 1870s when it expanded outside the walls, after which we call it a "city." This terminology reflects to a certain degree the Ottoman distinction between *kasaba* (town) and *belede/şehir* (city), but also recognizes the growing demographics of Jaffa in the second half of the nineteenth century, discussed in this section.

14. For several hundred years Jaffa and southern Palestine were part of the provinces of Sidon and Damascus. Starting in 1871, southern Palestine became its own

district (*mutasarrifiyya*, Ar., *mutasariflık*, Tur.) with its own governor (*mutasarrıf*) based in Jerusalem directly answerable to Istanbul. Jaffa had its own deputy governor (*kaymakam*). The center and northern areas of Palestine were part of the governorate (*vilayet*) of Beirut, although there were repeated proposals to alter these administrative boundaries before World War I.

15. After the Ottomans' loss in World War I, thousands of archival documents from the Ottoman Ministry of Finance were sold as scrap paper and carted off to Sofia, Bulgaria. Once they were identified as having historical value, they were rescued and incorporated into the Bulgarian National Library's Oriental Studies collection. Scholars have not yet exploited this rich trove of historical documents, which promise to shed light on the early modern empire's southern territories, although the Open Jerusalem project has digitized an index of some of those documents.

16. This data is supplied by Western consular officials, who could have received information from the local customs house.

17. *Havatzelet*, 10 November 1881.

18. Rabbi Netan'el Avital, a researcher of Moroccan Jewish communities, recently uncovered the marriage contract (*ketubah*) of Yosef Eliyahu's grandparents, Avraham Chelouche from Meknes and Simha née Hacohen Alkalatz from Fez, dated 5 October 1826. A copy was issued in 1848 to Avraham upon his return visit to Fez. Evyatar Chelouche, *Descendants of Aharon Chelouche Family Newsletter* 16 (April 2020).

19. The British Jewish philanthropist Sir Moses Montefiore sponsored a series of five population registries of Jews in Palestine that corresponded with five of his seven visits to the country. These cannot be properly understood as a state-sponsored census, because registration was completely voluntary, but Montefiore did link registration to personal charity and communal investments.

20. Ben-Ya'akov, "Mifkadei Montefiore," 134.

21. The 1848 copy of the parental marriage contract that was retrieved in Fez supports the claim that the rest of the family was in Jerusalem during Avraham's journey, but by the following year they were firmly ensconced in Jaffa.

22. In the spring of 1840, a Catholic friar in Damascus falsely accused members of the Jewish community of murdering a missing monk and his servant. The event sparked a localized riot and international attention over the fate of the Jewish communities in Ottoman lands.

23. However, the Montefiore registers have numerous inconsistencies regarding birthplace and birth year, so this detail is far from certain.

24. There is no evidence of the uncle in the Nablus registers, although one of Sara's brothers, Avraham, did live in Nablus for some time during the mid-1860s.

25. Howard, *Howard's Guide to Jerusalem and Vicinity with Map of Palestine*, 5.

26. According to the 1839 Montefiore register, there were just under forty Jewish families present in Jaffa at the time, virtually all of whom were Sephardi immigrants from North Africa or other Ottoman cities and towns. Within a decade, that number had doubled. The Montefiore register is problematic and undoubtedly not exhaustive, but it provides a sense of the relative scale of Jewish migration. Other population figures for the nineteenth century are estimates only.

27. However, the historical details are murky, and the dates do not really match up; Louria is also not identifiable in the Montefiore registers.

28. December 1859–January 1860 (Jumada al-thani 1276), p. 9. Jaffa Shari'a Court Register.

29. The "politics of notables" has been primarily considered the purview of Muslims, although as Chelouche's memoir reveals, non-Muslim elites were also able to accumulate and expend social, economic, and political capital.

30. *Khawaja* was an honorific used for non-Muslim or European "gentlemen."

31. 18 January 1878 (14 Muharram 1295), Document 182, p. 48. Jaffa Shari'a Court Register, defter 299.

32. 29 June 1899 (19 Safar 1317), Document 648, p. 475. Jaffa Shari'a Court Register, defter 349.

33. There is some evidence that French consular officials looked the other way when giving nationality or protégé status to Moroccan Jews like Chelouche. It was in their interest to expand their influence with larger numbers of protégés.

34. Quoted in Porter, *A Handbook for Travellers in Syria and Palestine*, 272.

35. *Havatzelet*, 20 October 1871.

36. BOA, MVL 771/4, 20 June 1864 (15 Muharram 1281). The document also refers to the need to open a new gate in the city walls. Another document a few months later reiterated this need. BOA, A.MKT.MHM. 308/19, 4 August 1864 (1 Rabi'a awwal 1281).

37. Schick, "Fortschritte der Civilisation in Palästina in den letzten 25 Jahren," *Österreichische Monatsschrift für den Orient*, 64.

38. Sandel, "Karte der Umgebung von Jafa." The Templers (after *Tempelgesellschaft* — Temple Society) were a movement of German Protestants who sought to live "authentic Christian lives" in the Holy Land. They established seven colonies between the late 1860s and 1900s.

39. Contemporary mapping of the central coastal plain of Palestine, including Jaffa and its environs, was prepared in 1878 by Charles Claude Reignier Conder and Horacio Herbert Kitchener on behalf of the British Palestine Exploration Fund. Their map was far less detailed and accurate than Sandel's and, therefore, cannot be regarded as a proper urban mapping of the town or its surrounding area.

40. This ethnic and religious diversity of Jaffa is also captured in the *shari'a* court registers as well as the local Arabic press.

41. The Chelouches were related to two of the three partners in the building: Aharon Chelouche's nephew married 'Amiel's daughter, as described by Yosef Eliyahu in chapter 1 of his memoir, and Yosef Eliyahu married the granddaughter of Aharon Moyal, as described in chapters 5 and 6.

42. The young widower Shlomo Abutbul arrived in Jaffa in 1864 from Marrakech with his young son, Moshe. Shlomo was a money changer with significant economic resources, and his brother Abraham Abutbul is also listed in the 1875 register as of equal wealth. In the *shari'a* court registers the brothers are listed as joint owners of a house in the Sheikh Ibrahim neighborhood.

43. For example, Yosef Eliyahu's maternal grandfather Haim Barukh and his maternal uncles Daniel and Yehezkel Barukh were involved in money changing; his

father-in-law Avraham Moyal was a money changer, as were other members of his wife's family.

44. Part of Jaffa's historic core was destroyed in a British air bombing in June 1936 in their effort to crush the Palestinian revolt; a more comprehensive destruction of historic Jaffa was carried out in 1950–1951 by the Tel Aviv municipality.

45. Compared to the Ottoman yearbook, this is an undercounting of Muslim and Jewish institutions and an overcounting of Christian institutions; the yearbook lists four smaller mosques and three synagogues and only two monasteries and three churches. *Sâlnâme-yi vilâyet-i Sûriye*, vol. defa' 3 (1287/88 [1871/72]), 160.

46. Howard, *Howard's Guide to Jerusalem*, 13.

47. The family orchard was located near the village of Jerisha on the eastern bank of the Musrara River. In the early nineteenth century the majority of Jaffa's citrus orchards were located this far north, near the al-Auja River, before the growth in trade led orchard owners to expand their holdings southward to Jaffa; in the period between 1850–1880 the land used as citrus orchards quadrupled in size.

48. Norman Macleod, *Half Hours in the Holy Land: Travels in Egypt, Palestine, Syria* (London: William Isbister, 1885).

49. *Cook's Tourists' Handbook*, 72–73.

50. In contrast to the extensive scholarly work done by Amnon Cohen and his collaborators in uncovering the presence of Jews in the Jerusalem *shari'a* courts in the sixteenth to nineteenth centuries, no comparable study has yet been carried out on Jaffa. Two books on the history of Jaffa that rely extensively on *shari'a* court registers mention numerous cases involving Jews, but they are listed only incidentally rather than meriting close analysis. Our sampling of five different *shari'a* court registers from the 1850s to the 1900s has identified over 130 court cases where at least one party was Jewish, on matters ranging from divorce and guardianship of orphans, to business loans, partnerships, and property sales. In addition, our survey of the one surviving year of the register of the Jaffa Court of First Instance (1900–1901) has yielded over one hundred cases involving Jews as at least one party in various commercial cases. There are dozens of court notebooks from Jaffa that have survived in the Israel State Archives, but the Arabic and Ottoman Turkish paleography and quality of the microfilms makes them difficult to read at times. Much more research should be conducted in the future.

51. There were two Hebrew language newspapers published in the 1860s and 1870s: *HaLevanon*, which was published from 1863–1867 in Jerusalem and then afterward in Europe, and *Havatzelet*, published in Jerusalem. After *HaLevanon* moved to Paris it retained a local correspondent in Jaffa. No Arabic-language newspapers were permitted to be published in Palestine until after the 1908 Ottoman revolution.

52. *Havatzelet*, 25 November 1870. Other similar stories of the circumcision of Muslim boys by Jewish circumcisers appeared in the press, as well as in the notebooks of one of the town's circumcisers, Me'ir Hamburger.

53. *Havatzelet*, 6 January 1871. The article does not name these consular officials, but it is possible they were the two Sephardi Jews who filled those offices in the second half of the nineteenth century. Haim Amzalak was an unsalaried honorary

British vice-consul from 1872–1902, which is to say a year after the event in question. Yosef Moyal was the Spanish vice-consul, but his dates of service are unknown.

54. *Havatzelet*, 19 December 1871 and 16 May 1873.

55. *Havatzelet*, 10 May 1872 and 3 January 1873.

56. Although Farha is the standard Arabic version of Simha, Freha is the Moroccan Jewish pronunciation.

57. His oldest son, Moshe, studied at the AIU and then St. Joseph's (Frères School) in Jaffa before being sent abroad to study commerce in Marseille. Me'ir studied at St. Joseph's in Jaffa, then in Cairo, and finally law in Paris. Avner was the first son to study at the Herzliya Hebrew Gymnasium. Zadoc studied at the AIU and then in England. Hillel studied architecture and urban planning in Paris. Yoram studied at the Herzliya Hebrew Gymnasium, then in Beirut and in France.

58. It is difficult to trace these property disputes in the court registers. A surviving case of inheritance from Tanus Nasr's estate indicates that he and Avraham Moyal, Yosef Moyal's elder brother and the father-in-law of Yosef Eliyahu, were partners on a property south of Jaffa, in Saknat al-'Ajami (Avraham Moyal died in 1885, presumably meaning this property reverted to his heirs). In contrast, the disputed properties were reportedly in the north. 4 April 1898 (12 Dhu al-Q'ada 1315), Document 32, pp. 164–65. Jaffa Shari'a Court Register, defter 349.

59. "Neve Shalom" was originally used by the Jewish entrepreneur Zerah Barnett to describe a small housing compound he built around 1890 in the center of Manshiya, not very far from Aharon Chelouche's house. It was soon used by Jews to describe the entire development in the northern part of Jaffa, though most of the area had nothing to do with Barnett's initiative. In the years before World War I, the *shari'a* courts referred to a "Jewish Manshiya" (Manshiyya al-Yahud [*sic*]), according to LeVine, *Overthrowing Geography*, 70, although it is unclear what the boundaries of that area were.

60. LeVine, *Overthrowing Geography*, 51; Hatuka and Kallus, "Loose Ends," 28, 31.

61. Bawwab, *Mawsu'at Yafa al-jamila*, 568. 7 April 1890 (16 Sha'aban 1307).

62. August/September 1904 (Jumada al-akhira 1322), document 239, pp. 163–65. Jaffa Shari'a Court Register, defter 322.

63. These three cases are summarized in Tawarneh, but without dates. This last endowment was made by Haim Shmerling, an Austro-Hungarian immigrant who was one of the administrators of Sha'ar Zion hospital; a Hebrew document certifying its status as an endowment dates to 1899. Aharon Chelouche regularly made donations to the hospital, according to donor lists from the 1890s.

64. Aleksandrowicz, "Paper boundaries."

65. Advertisement for the Kaminitz Hotel, *Havatzelet*, 3 August 1894.

66. 4 May 1895 (9 Dhu al-Qada 1312), cited in Bawwab.

67. Chelouche does not give many details on this aspect of his business, but cement tile factories existed in Beirut as of the 1880s, which is where he brought a master craftsman from when he later transitioned into mosaic tiles. In September 1909, a Beirut industrialist and businessman, Nejuib 'Araman, ordered a cement press for a customer in Jaffa looking to establish a cement tile factory, possibly a competitor.

68. Yosef Eliyahu reported that together with two partners, they helped build two government buildings around the turn of the century, the customs house and the quarantine station.

69. *Luach Eretz Israel*, cited in Ram, *Hayishuv haYehudi beYafo*, 85. However, most population figures for the nineteenth century are notoriously unreliable.

70. Quoted in Katz, *Zionism and Urban Settlement*, 14.

71. Quoted in LeVine, *Overthrowing Geography*, 62.

72. Quoted in Katz, *Zionism and Urban Settlement*, 11.

73. Nearly 90 percent of Tel Aviv's founders were Ashkenazi Jews, the vast majority recent immigrants to the country. Other Sephardi founders included the Beirut-born Shlomo Abulafia, also a graduate of Beirut's Tif'eret Israel School and an Arabic teacher in Jaffa, who died before his house was built; Shmu'el Tajer, who emigrated from Ottoman Sofia and sold Western furniture and shoes; the Jerusalem-born David Mizrahi, who supplied the Ottoman army with materials; Yosef Nissim Mizrahi; Nissim Korkidi, a native of Bergama who grew up in Jerusalem before moving to Jaffa and Tel Aviv and becoming cantor at the Sephardi synagogue; and Ben Zion Rizo Levy, who was born in Jaffa and was married to a niece of Yosef Eliyahu Chelouche.

74. The initial report was published in *Falastin*, 18 February 1914. The Ottoman investigation that exonerated Tel Aviv is in BOA, DH.EUM.EMN. 113/15, 9 March 1914 (H 11/4/1332). However, Emanuel Beška found that residents of Jaffa continued to petition the government about this affair and other related credible acts of detention and violence in Tel Aviv. Beška, *From Ambivalence to Hostility*, 103–4.

75. By 1925, when Aharon Chelouche was a child, two additional floors were added to the house as well as an additional wing; this expansion was designed by Yehuda Stempler, a trained architect.

76. This public Ottomanization campaign had begun already in 1908, as Jewish communal leaders sought to increase the number of Jewish voters to the Ottoman parliament and in local elections; it had some limited success at that stage.

77. These numbers are based on lists kept in the Central Zionist Archives.

78. One source claimed that over eleven thousand foreign Jews were expelled from Palestine during the entire war, although this number is unsubstantiated and would represent an unrealistically large proportion of the total Jewish community.

79. To our knowledge, only one account from a Christian family has survived, although other evidence from the Ottoman archives mentions Christians and Muslims expelled from Jaffa. Chelouche himself discusses meeting Muslim Jaffan exiles while in other towns and villages in Palestine, underscoring that this was not a specifically Jewish punishment.

80. Chelouche-Havatzelet, *Zikhronot leveit saba*.

81. The few extant wartime memoirs from civilian Jews in Palestine have not yet been translated into English; some memoirs of Palestinian Jewish soldiers stationed elsewhere have been translated.

82. In particular, French policy in Syria and British policy in Iraq relied on repression and violence almost immediately; the British pursued imperial force and repression in Palestine in the 1930s.

83. The Balfour Declaration was initially a private letter between the British foreign minister Lord James Balfour and Lord Lionel Walter Rothschild (a British Jewish community leader and firm Zionist) on 2 November 1917, in which Balfour conveyed His Majesty's government's support for a "national home for the Jewish people" in Palestine. It is considered the foundational document for international diplomatic support of the Zionist movement, and after the war it was integrated into the Mandate for Palestine issued by the League of Nations.

84. Great Britain Colonial Office, *Palestine: Disturbances in May, 1921*, 22–26. Riots also spread to three neighboring colonies, Rehovot, Petah Tikva, Hadera, and the village of Yahudiya.

85. "On the Situation [in Hebrew]." *Yediʻot Tel Aviv* (Tel Aviv News) 1, no. 2 (1921): 3–6.

86. Geddes, "Town Planning Report Tel Aviv," 1.

87. *Doʼar hayom*, "Organization of the City," 9 January 1921, 21 January 1921. Chelouche was the only native Jew selected by the British to serve on the committees; *Doʼar hayom*, 8 July 1923.

88. 29 October 1926. CZA A488/128.

89. 22 July 1931. CZA A488/185. This was also covered in the press in *Davar*, 20 July 1931; *Doʼar hayom*, 20 July 1931.

90. Chelouche received some fan mail in support of his public writing. CZA A488/110, see letters from Aron Jacob Levy, 29 April 1027 (Jaffa) and Z. Glouzka, 17 May 1928 (Alexandria). *Doʼar hayom* was criticized as a vehicle of trashy "yellow journalism," but it was the only newspaper in the early Mandate period that gave significant voice to Sephardi concerns and authors. (Specifically Sephardi organs included *Haherut* in the pre-Mandate period and *Hed haMizrach* in the 1940s.)

91. Quoted in Michelle U. Campos, "Mizrah Umaarav (East and West): A Sephardi Cultural and Political Project in Post-Ottoman Jerusalem," *Journal of Modern Jewish Studies* 16, no. 2 (2017).

92. In the fall of 1919, Chelouche joined other Sephardi leaders to establish the Organization of Sephardi Jews (*Histadrut haYehudim haSfaradim*) to organize Sephardi efforts in the national project. See *Doʼar hayom*, 4 November 1919. Later this was a platform to demand increased political representation on the Vaʻad Leʼumi and in the Zionist Commission, which essentially functioned as the legislative and executive branches (respectively) of the Jewish community at the time. For their part, European Zionist leaders continuously denied the need for specifically ethnic institutions or representation in Palestine, as they claimed they represented all Jews.

93. Chelouche and his younger brother Yaʻakov were both elected to the Asefat hanivharim in the summer of 1920, but there is little documentation of his activity there. *Doʼar hayom*, 4 July 1920. His eldest son Moshe was a founding member of the Sephardi-Mizrahi Workers Organization and later headed the Flag of Zion (*Degel Zion*) Sephardic youth movement, and his son Avner was a founding member of the Youth of the East (*Zeʻirei haMizrach*).

94. Letter from Yosef Eliyahu Chelouche to *Haaretz*, 22 May 1928. CZA A488/119.

95. "Haemet hamara," *Doʼar hayom*, 1 May 1928.

96. "Kri'a leahi haSfaradim vele'edot haMizrahiot bee"I," *Do'ar hayom*, 22 November 1927.

97. *Haaretz*, 24 January 1927.

98. The response appeared in *Do'ar hayom*, 2 February 1927.

99. This was the language used by Chelouche and his reviewers, but it is an anachronism when applied to the 1880s.

100. Samuel Tolkowsky, *The Gateway of Palestine*; Samuel Tolkowsky, *The Jewish Colonisation in Palestine*. Chelouche also sent copies of his memoir to other Zionist officials and chroniclers, including Alter Druyanov, who admitted he "learned a few things," and Z. D. Levontin.

101. Gaon and Chelouche exchanged letters about their respective projects, and it appears Chelouche shared an early draft with Gaon.

102. The Hebrew title was "Hegiu miyam ad nefesh," 13 February 1930. It's unclear whether Chelouche's essay was ever printed in *Falastin*, and only the Hebrew translation is extant. It seems Chelouche chose to write under a pen name ("A Jew with an open heart") so as to not increase the likelihood of being censored by the editor, 'Issa al-'Issa, with whom he had a tumultuous relationship. The manuscript version is in CZA A488/140.

103. This must date to the period 1918–1920, when Faysal and Weizmann held a series of official and unofficial meetings.

104. Isaiah 40:3. Chelouche frequently drew on biblical phrases, imagery, and parallels in his memoir. We use the JPS 2023 revised translation for biblical quotes.

105. "After the 17th Zionist Congress," *Do'ar hayom*, 31 July 1931. The manuscript version is in CZA A488/140.

106. In the photo there are three officers on horseback and three officers on foot behind them. A. Elmaliach and Y. A. 'Abadi, *R. Yosef Eliyahu Chelouche*.

107. 'Uziel (1880–1953), from a prominent Jerusalemite rabbinical family, was a religious teacher, scholar, chief rabbi of Jaffa and Salonica, and chief rabbi of Palestine. He served in numerous communal and public offices over decades.

108. 'Abadi (1897–1969) was a journalist, translator, and public official in Jerusalem, as well as a Sephardi activist in the 1920s.

109. Rokach (1897–1959), born to a prominent Ashkenazi family in Jaffa, was a Swiss-trained engineer who in the 1920s served alongside Chelouche on the Tel Aviv council.

110. Nissim Korkidi (1872–1937) was born in Bergama (Anatolia) to a rabbinical family that migrated to Jerusalem in his childhood, around 1880. A businessman, cantor, and community leader, Korkidi served in the Jaffa municipality before World War I; he was also a Tel Aviv neighbor of the Chelouches.

111. Letter from Ya'akov Me'ir, 24 July 1934, CZA A488/683; letter from the General Council (*Va'ad Le'umi*) of the Jews of Palestine, 25 July 1934, CZA A488/683.

112. Elmaliach and 'Abadi, *R. Yosef Eliyahu Chelouche*, 67.

113. *Falastin*, 24 July 1934.

114. CZA A488/684, letter from Anis Jaber, vice-consul of Persia, 24 July 1934; letter from Saleem Barakat, 27 July 1934.

115. ʻUmar al-Bitar (1880–1948) was council member from 1905–1908 and mayor from 1908–?. He was chairman of the local Muslim-Christian Association from 1921–1938 and served as mayor again from 1941–1945.

116. CZA A488/684, letter from ʻAsem Bek al-Saʻid, 2 August 1934; undated letter from ʻUmar al-Bitar.

117. Goren, "Relations between Tel Aviv and Jaffa," 5.

118. As Chelouche notes in the memoir, despite his presumably "close" ties to Djemal Pasha, the non-Zionist Antébi was expelled from Palestine along with other Zionist leaders. He died in exile in Istanbul.

119. The author was likely Itamar Ben-Avi, the editor of *Do'ar hayom* newspaper, where Chelouche published many of his editorials. Elmaliach and ʻAbadi, *R. Yosef Eliyahu Chelouche*.

120. That same year the Tel Aviv council approved naming the major boulevard in the north in honor of the seventy-third birthday of Meʼir Dizengoff, contradicting its own policy of not naming streets after living persons.

121. There is also a (Aharon) Chelouche Street in the Neve Tzedek neighborhood, where the Chelouche family home still stands. Although this area has undergone gentrification and historic preservation in recent decades, for many years it was considered a slum.

122. Or Aleksandrowicz researched and edited this new, corrected, and annotated edition based on the original memoir. Yosef Eliyahu Chelouche, *Parashat Hayay (1870–1930)* (Tel Aviv: Babel, 2005).

123. A critical engagement with this term (translated from the Arabic, *al-yahud al-ʻarab*) dates back to Albert Memmi's discussion in 1974 in a series of articles compiled as *Jews and Arabs*.

Between Jaffa & Tel Aviv, 1870–1930

FIGURE I.17. *Yosef Eliyahu Chelouche, late 1920s. Photo by Nahman Gamzu. Chelouche Family Collection.*

PREFACE

In this memoir, I have recorded, from time to time, all the events of great significance—both to the public in general and to those near and dear to me in particular.

The story of my life and my memories as a native of the land, beginning some sixty years ago to the present day, aside from their connection with my own personal history, also bring to light the living chain history of the Hebrew *yishuv*[1] in Jaffa from its earliest days. This includes the era of the foundation and construction of the first Hebrew neighborhoods in Jaffa a full half-century ago, of which my father, of blessed memory, was among the first builders and founders, and of Neve Shalom and Neve Tzedek, as well as other neighborhoods; and also of the founding of the Ahuzat Bayit company a quarter-century ago with the goal of founding and building Tel Aviv, which I, too, was honored to be among the original founders and builders.

I have endeavored to the best of my ability to record my memories so that they may be preserved for my descendants, as well as for those individuals interested in the history and development of the Hebrew *yishuv* in Jaffa. They also shed light on the good relations that existed between us and our Arab neighbors over the course of several decades, until the arrival of the "redeemers" of our country, the English.

I have approached this task not as a professional writer, but as a man of the *yishuv*, as one of the people,[2] as a native of the land,[3] who in his

---

1. In the original, Chelouche writes "hayishuv ha'ivri." We have kept his original formulation for two reasons. First, translating "Hebrew" as "Jewish" would erase the ideological-cultural project of creating Hebrews out of Jews that was critical to the Zionist movement. Second, translating "yishuv" as either "community" or "settlement," as is often done, is inaccurate and incomplete—it was decidedly more than a community in the religious sense, and more than just a physical settlement in the ideological sense.

2. In the original, Chelouche writes "'am," which refers to the Jewish people as a collective. The basic tenet of Zionism is that the Jewish people comprise not only a religious collective, but a national one as well.

3. Chelouche writes "yelid haaretz." The nativeness of Chelouche is central to his worldview.

childhood was honored to be an eyewitness to the history of the new Hebrew *yishuv* in Jaffa at its founding, and as an active participant in its construction and development over a long period of several decades.

That is to say, I approached this endeavor not as someone who is knowledgeable about and familiar with literary matters. Most certainly, there are places here and there where I should have gone into greater detail, but instead I condensed it, and vice versa, and in this or that chapter I may have failed to mention this or that fact. The reader, if he is being meticulous and strict toward the author, will most certainly find much room for criticism. The only thing that can be raised raise in my defense is that my intention, which was undoubtedly good, has been to relate as far as possible only in an objective and nonpartisan manner the truth of my life story and my faithful memories, about friendships and people I have encountered over my lifetime, people with whom I have conducted business dealings and other matters, and all of this I have related in good faith and with the full weight of responsibility.

Despite my literary weakness, I have endeavored to express in some manner, even if not the most linguistically pleasing, then at least to the extent of my abilities and the progression of my thoughts and feelings on the existence of my people in my land and its future, for "worry in a man's heart weighs it down."[4]

In my memoirs I have charted, chapter by chapter, my lifelong efforts in which I devoted my blood, sweat, and tears in an effort to build myself up and live a worthwhile life, improving the world by laboring and working hard, creating, and building—undertakings for which I have made great efforts and strained under the sun throughout my life on this earth for the benefit of our people and our land, in keeping with my point of view and understanding.

I have endeavored in my memoirs to not emerge as a social critic, as I feel that I am neither skilled nor suited to fill that role. Only the love and rebirth of my people and my land have pulsed in my heart and brought me to relay to the next generation that which befell the previous generation, from our recent past from which there is much to be learned, to study and observe the primary issue that we have encountered in the course of settling our land, namely the complex relations between Jews

---

4. Proverbs 12:25. The full verse reads: "If there is anxiety in someone's mind, let them quash it, and turn it into joy with a good word."

and Arabs today, as well as other matters in the life of the people and the country, as well as in my personal life.

The history of human life is a single progression of events and upheavals. Although there are differences between one period and the other, when over the course of time these changes do take place, be it for better or for worse, the essence of life is the same on this earth then as now.

Each and every one of us, no matter what he has gone through in life, whatever it is that he has done, if it is of any value and of any status, then it is desirable and proper—and very worthwhile—to not throw the past into the abyss of oblivion and instead it should be recorded in a book, and all the more so if the story of his life is tightly linked to the life of his people and his country and if it is pertinent to the general public.

In this history of my life, I have endeavored in simple, plain words to relay my life story, the most significant events and changes that have transpired and that I have experienced. More than anything else, it is my fervent desire to show the path to my sons after me so that they will not forget the actions of their father and also will know how to fulfill their own national duty to their people and their land. What's more, the mere act of reading the memoir of any person, from his dawning day to his old age, is of great educational value.

This sort of book is reflective of an epoch that has passed, a period of dreaming and yearning, of big, beautiful hopes, some of which have been actualized and transformed into living reality, some of which have not been actualized, and others that will take a little while longer for them to strike roots in the soil of reality.

The heart of the faithful reader who accompanies the author of this memoir through the course of his life, chapter after chapter, will shudder along with him at every expression of sorrow and sadness experienced by the author, and will rejoice alongside him at every event of happiness and joy. These changes in emotions in the life of the individual and of the collective make a deep impression on our hearts. And when you present the reader with a description of the journey through life of one man, one of the people, and you describe his life and his activities in family and in public, this leads the good reader to a state of deep reflection and self-examination.

Days pass, years pass, summer ends, winter arrives, day and night invariably come and go, and in the end, it is the destiny of every man to die. Even if he does good throughout his days, endeavoring to rise to a more sublime, beneficial, and beautiful level, he is not exempt from the evils that surrounded him and embittered his life. A person of some sensitivity may conclude that this is the fate of every human being, and that fate is fate, so there is no point trying to change it because "man was born to struggle."[5] It is the command of the generations, and we must surrender.

However, so long as there remains a spark of life in our souls, so long as our strength has not failed us, we must strive with all our heart and soul and effort to give a purposeful wholeness to our lives: to work and build, to act and create things of value for the benefit of the nation and of humankind. Each of us in accordance with the ability and the capability and the talents of each individual, for the sake of improving his life and the lives of the public, and for the general good. For you are born against your will and you exist against your will and you must die against your will, and it is not possible for an individual to escape, to flee to some place of refuge somewhere else in the world, to evade this eternal generational edict.

Therefore, in the course of a human being's journey on this earth, throughout his life, from the day he is born to the day he dies, he should work tirelessly, take action, create, build, improve, and perform as many goodly acts as possible for his people and his country and for the sake of all human society.

And this is my last will and testament, my personal will to the members of my family and to all my relatives and friends: a person should conduct his life in moderation and with integrity, with good behavior and a pleasant demeanor toward each and every human being. He should come to the aid of the wretched, the downtrodden, and the embittered, supporting them as much as he is able, and performing acts of benevolence for all mankind. Bear in mind the words of King David from the psalms: "Which of you are eager for life and desire years of good fortune? Guard your tongue from evil, and your lips from deceitful speech. Shun evil, and do good; seek peace, and pursue it!"[6]

I have set these words before me as a straight path to follow throughout my poor and difficult life in the course of my public service, [which I carried out] due to faith, and not for the sake of receiving a reward. My

---

5. Job 5:7: "For people are born to [do] mischief, just as sparks fly upward."
6. Psalms 34:13–15. The JPS translation of "shalom" is "amity."

forefathers' merits and actions have enabled me to have the good fortune to witness with my own eyes the rebirth of my people and my land, and the establishment of the first Hebrew city in our land and in the entire world, Tel Aviv. May I yet live to see the building of the Hebrew national home, speedily and in the near future, and may I bear witness to the solace of Zion and Jerusalem.

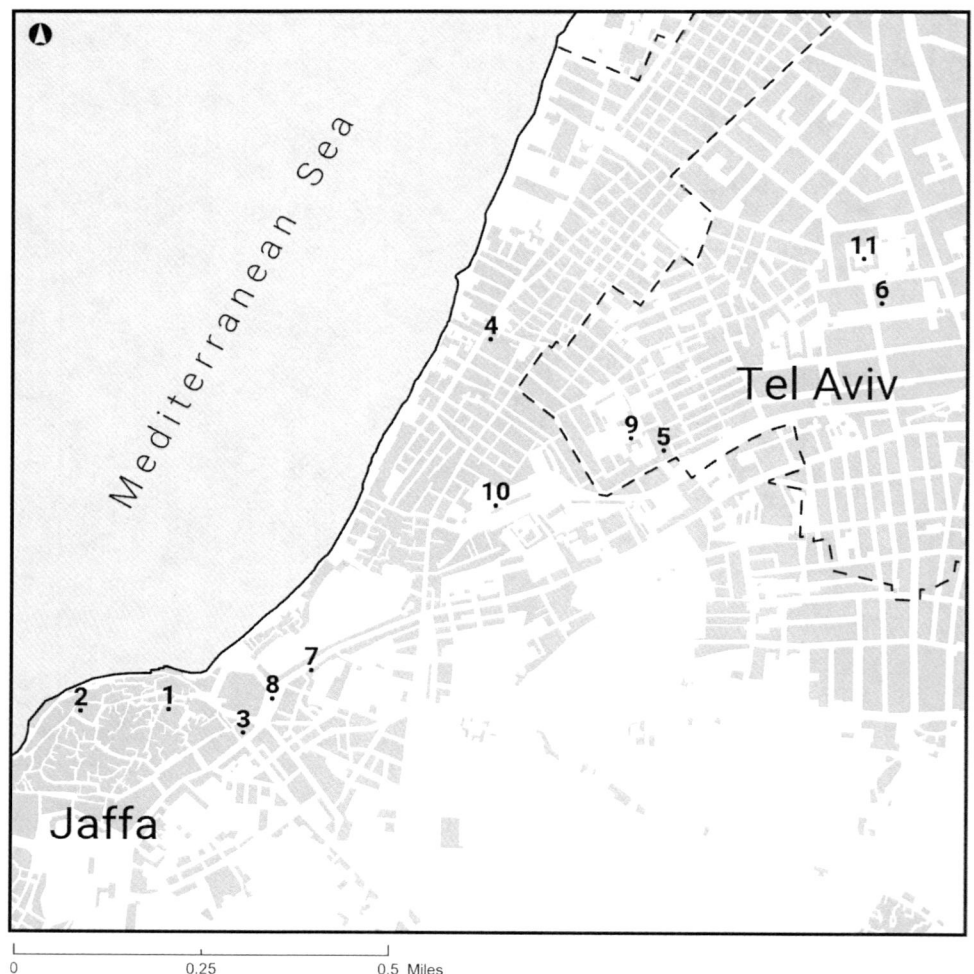

MAP 1.1. Yosef Eliyahu Chelouche's residences in Jaffa and Tel Aviv, 1870–1934. The numbers indicate, respectively: Yosef Eliyahu Chelouche's birthplace (1); Chelouche family residence near the old citadel, now Saint Peter's Church (2); Maimon 'Amiel-Aharon Moyal building near Jaffa's main gate, where the Chelouche family resided 1883–1887 (3); the first family house built by Aharon Chelouche, where the family settled in 1887 (4); the second family house built by Aharon Chelouche, where the family settled in 1892 (5); Yosef Eliyahu Chelouche's house in Tel Aviv, built in 1910 (6); Yosef Eliyahu Chelouche's hardware store on Howard Street (7); Jaffa's clock tower square (8); the girls' school in Neve Tzedek, built by Yosef Eliyahu Chelouche (9); Jaffa's train station (10); Herzliya Gymnasium in Tel Aviv, built by Yosef Eliyahu Chelouche (11). The dashed black line indicates the municipal boundary between Jaffa and Tel Aviv, delineated after the latter was granted township status by the British administration in June 1921.

Map by Or Aleksandrowicz, based on cartographic data from the 1930 and 1935 maps of Jaffa and Tel Aviv prepared by the Survey of Palestine.

I

FIGURE 1.1. *Aharon Chelouche (father of Yosef Eliyahu), late nineteenth century. Photo by Da'ud Sabanji. Chelouche Family Collection.*

CHAPTER 1 *Days of My Infancy, Childhood, and Youth*

My birth, without a definitive date | My father's house in old Jaffa | My first education | At Talmud Torah in Jaffa | My first journey to Jerusalem via donkey | My father's house | Headquarters of the early Jewish yishuv *in Jaffa | My mother, who hosts and serves religious scholars | The coin uproar | Our first tract of land in Jaffa | Neve Shalom | Rabbi Shlomo Bohbut, the new rabbi*

In the year 1870 I was born in old Jaffa to my parents, the late Rabbi Aharon Chelouche,[7] who was born in Oran in Algeria,[8] and the late Sara of the Barukh Matzliah family of Baghdad.[9] To my regret, I was unable to find in the books belonging to my late father of blessed memory any mention of the day or month in which I was born.

The place where my mother gave birth to me is still preserved in my memory, just as it was handed down to me by my parents and family: it is in old Jaffa. The building now serves as a soap factory owned by the Christian by the name of Hanna Damiani.[10] At the time my father was living in this house, it was three stories high and had a multitude of

7. Aharon Chelouche (1829?–1920) arrived in Palestine as a child, possibly in 1842 or 1844, but certainly by 1849, when he was registered in that year's Montefiore register along with his parents, Avraham and Simha née Alkalatz, and his brother Yosef.

8. As discussed in the introduction, existing evidence indicates that the family originated in Fez and not in Oran.

9. Sara, the daughter of Haim Barukh and Rahel, arrived in Jaffa in 1848 as a toddler. The Barukh family first appears in the 1849 Montefiore register. It is unclear whether Matzliah was the maiden name of Rahel, Sara's mother.

10. A prosperous landowner and merchant in Jaffa, Damiani was a descendant of a prominent Roman Catholic family in the city whose members had served as European vice-consuls and honorary consuls for almost a century, until the 1850s. In the 1880s, Damiani was contracted by the chief rabbi in Istanbul to protect Jewish pilgrims arriving in Jaffa, which included housing them in a guesthouse. Damiani purchased the soap factory in 1890, and he appears in a British list of soap manufacturers in 1920.

rooms, which he subdivided into different apartments in order to give an opportunity to other Jewish families to live together with him. He dedicated a spacious room to serve as a prayer room, and our family lived in the two remaining rooms, which is where I spent my childhood years. When the population began to expand, the Turkish[11] government selected this building, made some changes to it, and designated it as "government house," in which all of its services and affairs were concentrated. The bottom floor served as a jail and to this very day the building is known as the old government house [al-saraya al-'atiqa].[12]

In 1875, I began to understand, as much as a child at my tender young age could, the surroundings in which I lived. My parents raised me in the lap of the Torah and Jewish ethics, and they aspired to instill in their children a spirit of love and affection for Israelite tradition and for all of our nation's spiritual assets. Each and every day I attended a small Jewish school called a Talmud Torah,[13] which operated under the supervision of my own late father. To this day, the figure of my late teacher, Rabbi Ya'akov Bouskila, is well preserved in my memory.[14] The Talmud Torah was divided into a few separate rooms, with different subjects taught in each one. In one room the children read scriptures and in another they prayed, and another, where I studied, was designated for children ages four to five.

I remember that late one morning in the year 1876, my late father walked into my Talmud Torah classroom without prior notice, just as the teacher was instructing us in the alphabet. The rabbi was surprised, and all the older children murmured and whispered to one another: "The treasurer [gabbai] has come to test us." My father was asked to take a seat, and the teacher and his assistant began to silence the children

---

11. Throughout his memoir, Chelouche refers to the Ottomans as "Turks." We have retained the original despite its historical anachronism.

12. The building still stands and currently houses the Museum of Jaffa History.

13. The Talmud Torah employed three rabbis, who taught different age levels and subject matter. In the lowest level children learned the Hebrew alphabet and simple prayers, then prayers and scriptures, then scriptures and the Talmud. In the 1875 Montefiore register, the Talmud Torah was listed as having seventy-five students, at which time Montefiore's clerks noted that the school was running at a deficit and was in need of repairs.

14. According to the Montefiore register, Ya'akov Bouskila arrived from Rabat as a child in 1844.

who were making noise, saying: "Hush, children, sit down, this is the treasurer." Among the youngest children absolute silence and attention prevailed. Once it was quiet, my father asked the rabbi about my diligence and devotion to my studies, but he was not satisfied with the answer of the teacher alone, and instead he went on to test me himself. My father-teacher and the rabbi rejoiced in my excellence, and to this day I hold on to the sacred words that my late father expressed: "Because you are diligent in your studies and because the rabbi has testified to that fact, I am going to take you with me to Jerusalem today." And at that very moment, I got up and went home with my father.

When I arrived home, the household was filled with my entire family, who would travel to Jerusalem. Everything was already prepared, even the baskets containing provisions for the journey. Everyone was waiting just for me in order to dress me in traveling clothes. Because I did not know the reason for this journey, they enlightened me and explained that we were traveling to the wedding of my cousin, the late Yehuda Carsenty,[15] the father of Nissim[16] and Barukh[17] Carsenty, who was then marrying the daughter of Señor Maimon 'Amiel.[18]

---

15. Yehuda Carsenty (1855–1892/3) was the son of the late Nissim Carsenty, a well-to-do tobacco merchant originally from Oran, Algeria, and Rika (Rivka) Chelouche, Yosef Eliyahu's paternal aunt. Both parents had died by the time of the 1875 Montefiore register, when Yehuda and his sisters were listed as orphans. Yehuda studied in the school of the Alliance Israélite Universelle (hereafter, AIU) and completed his commercial training in France. He later imported lumber for building supplies, setting up his warehouse in the Suq al-Salahi; he also assisted other Jews in land purchases in and around Jaffa.

16. Nissim Carsenty (1879–1932) studied at Zaki Cohen's school in Beirut. Upon his return to Jaffa, he continued his studies at the local AIU school, after which he was sent to Paris to train at the École Normale Israélite Orientale (ENIO), the AIU teachers' college. Nissim served as a teacher of French and Arabic in Damascus, Jerusalem, Rishon LeZion, and Alexandria before returning to teach at the Hebrew Gymnasium in Tel Aviv.

17. Barukh Carsenty (1883–1963) studied in the local Talmud Torah until he too went to Beirut to study at Zaki Cohen's school. After returning to Jaffa, he continued his studies at the local AIU school and then at Mikve Israel. He worked in commerce and lived in Alexandria from 1907–1920, after which he returned to Jaffa.

18. The bride was named Haya. Maimon 'Amiel was a wealthy merchant from Rabat who immigrated to Jaffa around 1873–1874 before later moving to Jerusalem. 'Amiel invested in real estate, and at the time of his death his will included his

In those days there were not yet any automobiles in Palestine, nor were there trains nor were there even horse-drawn carriages to be found, so all the traveling was done on the back of donkeys and camels. As a six-year-old boy, there was no end to my delight in traveling to another city about which I had heard a great deal, and I also had a strong desire to ride on a donkey, as was the norm at the time of my childhood.

The journey lasted almost twenty-four hours. We departed Jaffa at around noon and arrived in Jerusalem on the afternoon of the second day. All day and night, traveling, then stopping to rest. I remember how during our journey they passed me from one donkey to another, at first with my father, then with my mother, or with my brother, but for the most part I was barely aware of what took place during the journey, because I fell asleep. But I remember well the moment when we arrived in Jerusalem and they stationed us in front of the first entrance that is today called Bab al-Khalil.[19] It was the first and only structure that we saw, because in those days there was not a single building outside of the walls of the city. The sight of the wall around the city came as a shock to my tiny soul and entering inside was like entering a closed-up, sealed city.

Near the entrance to the city, we got down from the donkeys and my parents began rummaging through the saddlebags until they found what they were searching for. And as I looked on with amazement at being dismounted from the donkey, suddenly each of us was given a piece of onion along with a glass of water, and we were forced to chew the bitter onion and then drink down the water. It was said that this was a requirement to enter Jerusalem, for otherwise he who enters the city is liable to come down with malaria because the water in Jerusalem is rainwater and not spring water.[20]

---

share of twenty-eight shops in the Jaffa market. In Jerusalem, 'Amiel purchased land and built housing and a synagogue for the Maghrebi community, first in the walled city and then outside the city walls near Mamilla cemetery. Upon 'Amiel's and his own son Eliyahu's deaths, his minor grandson Avraham 'Amiel was placed under the guardianship of Aharon Chelouche. Note that Chelouche uses the Sephardi honorific "Señor" for wealthy and important notables in the community.

19. Literally, "Hebron Gate," though it is more commonly known in English as Jaffa Gate. This was the main entrance to the city from the west on the Jaffa road, which also connected to the road heading south toward Hebron.

20. Cisterns collected rainwater throughout the city; by the late nineteenth cen-

Against my will, I chewed the piece of onion and then drank a lot of water, after which we entered the city. The city was overflowing with people, all the roads and alleys were crowded with men and women, donkeys and flocks of sheep who were all together. Human voices mixed with the braying of the donkeys and the racket of the herd. Amidst all the noise, we climbed from one alley to the next, our legs pounding on the stones and rocks of Jerusalem until we finally arrived at the special home of the in-laws. Due to fatigue and also the eating of the onion, which evidently had a negative effect on me, I fainted and fell asleep, such that I have no memory of what happened to me in Jerusalem. Only upon our return to Jaffa was I informed that I had been ill and was at death's door throughout my stay in Jerusalem.

My father's home was a meeting place for Torah sages and scholars, and it was always open to all Jewish travelers, a place where one could find rest and spiritual sustenance. After the government requisitioned the building in which my parents and other Jewish families lived, they were compelled to find another apartment. For about two years they suffered wandering from one apartment to another, until my late father could no longer bear the wretched reality and rented a large and suitable house on the higher slopes of old Jaffa that belonged to a Christian named George Saliba,[21] for himself and for some other Jews with whom he was accustomed to living together, for my father's sole ambition was to gather the few Jews in one area for Torah study and for prayers.

The house was at that time deep inside the old city, on a lot higher up than the rest of the city. Where it once stood, there is at present a French church known as *al-qala'a* [the French fortress].[22] It was a three-story building built on uncultivated land, on a large tract on which a few trees had been planted. My father dedicated the ground-floor rooms as reception for guests, leaving only two rooms for his private work that led out to the wide square. The middle floor was the most spacious with six large rooms and a spacious balcony enclosed in glass. Our family

---

tury, residents received instruction from public health officials on how to keep their cisterns clean to limit the risk of cholera, but outbreaks were still common.

21. This likely refers to George Saliba Slim, from a Christian landowning family.

22. This is the Franciscan Church of St. Peter, originally constructed in the mid-seventeenth century over the ruins of a medieval fortress, only to be destroyed again in the late eighteenth century. The edifice that Chelouche is referring to was constructed in the 1890s.

occupied some of these rooms, but my father left the second half unoccupied for the sake of a suitable future tenant. On the third floor, he set aside two large rooms, one for a synagogue and the other for religious studies, where sages arrived every day from three o'clock in the afternoon to read together until the afternoon and evening prayers.[23] At night, they would get together for the *tikun hatzot* [midnight] prayers, which began two hours before dawn, and would then study until after the morning prayers were complete.

My late mother rose early, even before the sages would arrive to reflect on the Torah, and she prepared the lanterns and the coffee to drink. In her eyes this was a great commandment and was very dear to her, as she truly enjoyed sitting in her corner and taking pleasure in the sweet melodic sounds of the Torah sages and at the same time serving them tea, coffee, water, and so on. The rest of this apartment was set aside as the living quarters of the beadle of the synagogue, the late Habib Sabbah,[24] and his family. He was a decent and God-fearing man, who volunteered to serve as beadle, a position in which he served the community before God. In the area around my father's home lived a near majority of the Jews who lived in Jaffa at that time.[25]

In the month of Elul[26] 1878 (that month remains in my memory because it was the season of *selichot*[27]), something happened that caused a tumult in the city and was known as *dawshat al-bishlik*.[28] As natives of the country know, the coins that were in use at the time were the *bish-*

---

23. The historian Hanna Ram describes community life as divided up into various *kehilot* (congregations), each centering around a strong and wealthy personality who distributed religious services to his clientele. The "*kehila* of Aharon Chelouche" was one such congregation.

24. Sabbah arrived in 1867 from Essaouira, Morocco, along with his wife. He is listed in the Montefiore register as serving as beadle of a burial society for which Aharon Chelouche is listed as scribe.

25. According to the 1875 Montefiore register, there were approximately two hundred Jewish families living in Jaffa at that time, the majority of whom were from North Africa.

26. Elul is the twelfth and final month of the Jewish lunar calendar, which falls between August and September.

27. The penitential prayers recited throughout the month leading up to Rosh Hashanah, the Jewish new year.

28. Literally, "the uproar of the *bishlik*" (*beşlik* in Turkish).

lik, which was worth 2.5 Turkish piastres, and the *wuzari*,[29] which was worth five Turkish piastres. There was a significant difference between the two coins—the *bishlik* contained a slight amount of silver, whereas the *wuzari*, which was worth twice as much as the *bishlik*, actually contained five times the amount of silver as the *bishlik*.[30] My father, who was a silversmith, knew how to differentiate between these two coins.

One morning, a large Bedouin[31] caravan entered the city, having traveled some distance and bringing both types of currency, the *bishlik* and the *wuzari*, in extremely large quantities. The members in the caravan scattered around the city to purchase all sorts of merchandise and load the goods onto their camels. That day, the volume of commercial transactions in the Jaffa marketplace increased significantly. The whole city rejoiced and celebrated. There was not a single merchant, major or minor, who did not profit, and in practically a single day the shops were emptied of all their wares, fabrics, and other merchandise. In exchange for payment in the two aforementioned types of coins, all of the purchased merchandise was loaded and transported that very evening to the distant desert.

The next morning, when the merchants rose from their night's slumber and their state of inebriation, they went to the money changers to exchange the coins for gold because, at the time, there were not any banks in the country, not even in the capital city of Jerusalem.

In the first few hours of that day, everything went smoothly. The merchants converted the coins into gold, which they received from the money changers at the cost of a few coins. When the number of individuals

---

29. Piastres were known by the Turkish name *quruş*, while the *wuzari* seems to be the local equivalent of the *altılık*.

30. According to numismatic reports, the *altılık* contained twice as much silver as the *beşlik*. However, metallic dilution and currency debasement was very common, as was fluctuation in the currency exchange rates.

31. Nomadic, seminomadic, and sedentary Bedouin tribes lived in the area surrounding the al-'Auja River north of Jaffa as well as to its south in Gaza and beyond in the Negev desert, the Sinai desert, and Transjordan. Bedouin tribes supplied livestock and goods to the city markets; they also could threaten the security of the *hajj* and intercity travelers. Ottoman efforts to tax, conscript, and even count Bedouins were frequently unsuccessful. Starting in the 1880s, Bedouins fell into disputes with new Jewish agricultural settlements over land tenancy, grazing, and watering rights.

changing money increased, the gold-exchange rate increased from one moment to the next, but on the other hand, the price of the *wuzari* and especially of the *bishlik* dropped.

My late father, who was a silversmith by vocation and was well known in the city as being one of the leading silversmiths as well as a large-scale money changer,[32] began to receive clientele from all sides, but he, being a rational person who could foresee what was happening, had realized already the previous day that all this hasty buying and selling of sacks of coins as if they were sacks of grain was somewhat dubious, and that the matter called for a practical solution. He immediately conducted examinations on the two types of coins by melting them, and he discovered that the *wuzari* coins contained a greater amount of silver than the *bishlik*, and so he resolved to purchase only the *wuzari*s without making any exchanges. His response to the merchants was that he did not have any gold.

Already that same day, the shopkeepers offered their coins to the money changers at half the going rate, but there were no takers, because all of the money changers had used up nearly all of the inventory of gold in their possession already that morning. The small-scale money changers began approaching the larger money changers, among them my late father and two Christians, but all of them responded in the negative. On the third day, when the value of the two coins dropped to a new low of no more than a few piastres, my late father began purchasing only *wuzari*s, as they contained more silver for casting than the *bishlik*s. These purchases were not made directly through the merchants or the other money changers but were made covertly by middlemen—individuals whom my father knew to be trustworthy—and he supplied them with silver and gold and instructed them to purchase only *wuzari*s at his set price. He ordered them to bring the coins to his home clandestinely, without anyone noticing.

That same day and the following day, these emissaries purchased large quantities of *wuzari*s and moved them to our home in secret, with-

32. In his discussion of Jewish money changers (*sarraf*s) in Jaffa, al-Tarawnah lists one Khawaja Harun bin Ibrahim al-Yahudi al-sarraf (literally, "the Jewish money changer Aharon son of Abraham") recorded in the Islamic (*shari'a*) court registers, very possibly referring to Aharon Chelouche. Aharon Chelouche was more definitively identified as a silversmith in the court registers decades later, in 1899. Al-Tarawnah, *Qada' Yafa*, 390, 474.

out even any of the neighbors knowing about it. Given the large number of purchases, my father was forced to send two clerks to our home in order to receive the purchases from each middleman in exchange for a receipt. The volume of activity increased to the extent that my father had to send another few clerks over to help count the money. When my father realized that the clerks could not keep up with counting all the coins, he hit on a unique solution—instead of counting the money, the coins would be weighed—since his examinations had proven that the difference between the number and the weight was minimal, and this was particularly true once the price dropped. Every so often, my father would set a new price for the middlemen, and this entire episode continued for approximately a week. In our house there was not a single empty closet or empty space that was not filled up, including underneath the couches and beds. When Father came home with strong, brand-new gunnysacks, he looked around the house to find places to hide the rest of the money, but he could not find any.

As the reader already knows, in the house in which my parents lived at the time (in which the French church is now located), alongside the ground-floor rooms that served to receive guests my father had two rooms and a balcony that led out to a large square. These rooms were dedicated to his work casting silver and gold, which would be turned into jewelry in time of need. In the courtyard there was a large pit with a furnace and all the tools needed for casting gold or silver. Once a month, my father would cast a set amount of gold or silver and send it to London to the famous firm of Samuel Montagu;[33] in exchange, he received gold coins through the banks in either Constantinople[34] or Beirut, as per the commercial arrangement at the time. And since my father could not find room to hide the rest of the *wuzari*s, he directed his workers to melt them down and turn them into pure silver.

The work was carried out with great urgency. The most skilled craftsmen were brought over from the store and began to build—in a corner of the large city square that was practically hidden from view—a large

---

33. The Liverpool-born Montagu (1832–1911) established a bullion brokerage firm in 1853. He was an active supporter of the Hibbat Zion (Love of Zion) movement that was related to the Hovevei Zion movement discussed in chapter 3.

34. The capital of the Ottoman Empire until its dissolution, Constantinople (also called Istanbul) was called "Kushta" in Hebrew.

furnace with three chimney flues whose air was conducted into the furnace through pipes. A day after the furnace, which was made of mud, had dried, they started melting down the metals throughout the day until midnight, with the help of lanterns, and in a few days all the *wuzaris* that were hidden in the house were melted. All newly purchased coins were brought directly to the workshop to be melted down. *Wuzaris* disappeared from the market and the middlemen paid more than double the normal price for the slight quantity that still remained, and then the purchasing ended. Once the large merchants found out the secret they tried to follow in my father's footsteps, but by then they had already missed the opportunity.

Two weeks later, even before the city had a chance to recover from the first uproar, a new and even more riotous commotion erupted. The same Bedouins returned with other Bedouins, their camels and donkeys loaded with lots of *bishliks* and relatively few *wuzaris*, to buy merchandise. The merchants and shopkeepers whose shops had been emptied of goods and who were left with very little gold in exchange for the *wuzaris* that they sold at a huge loss, and the *bishliks* that sat like a stone that no one could overturn, refused to sell their goods to the Bedouins. But the latter, faced with a hunger that beset them and their livestock, pounced on the shops and simply stole whatever they could put their hands on, in broad daylight. The entire city was in a tumult, fear-stricken residents shuttered themselves in their homes, and the city streets went deadly still.

The government gathered what remained of its strength and, seeing that these Bedouins had committed these actions as a result of the hunger that beset both them and their livestock and was driving them out of their minds, the authorities provided the Bedouins and their livestock with food and other basic provisions; the caravan loosened its grip on the city and went on its way.

After three days of quiet and a state of depression that descended on the city, when the government official came out and declared that calm has been reestablished in the city and the authorities were prepared to defend the peace of the residents, shops reopened and city life got back on course, but barely so, due to the deep crisis that had assailed the city and the lack of both merchandise and money, a situation that persisted for nearly an entire year.

In those days, a trustworthy clerk named Ya'akov Barukhi'el,[35] may peace be upon him, served in my father's shop and assisted him in all of his business dealings out of love and dedication. My father was fond of him, as well, and found him to be a man who walked with God, and who was very honest in all his dealings. One day, an Arab named Hassan Stughum[36] approached him and proposed that he negotiate with my father to purchase his vineyard outside the city at a low price. He set up a time to meet Barukhi'el early the following day, before dawn. The Arab would come to his home, and they would then go together to see the vineyard, on the condition that if he liked the vineyard, he would then propose the deal to my father.

The following day, the clerk was late coming to work, and my father impatiently awaited his arrival, since none of the workers could begin their tasks because the gold and silver inventory was under Barukhi'el's lock and key, and it was he who distributed it among them and gave directions on how it was to be used. His absence was, then, deeply felt, but as all the workers were standing around with nothing to do, Barukhi'el entered the shop, pried open the crates, distributed the material among the workers, and work commenced.

My father, who was unhappy about the holdup in the work, did not voice any complaint, as he assumed that the cause had to do with a family matter. All through the afternoon my father and the clerk did not exchange a single word about it, as each one of them was then caught up in his own work, the one composing letters and receiving visitors, the other giving instructions to workers.

Toward the end of the day, as my father was sitting alone in his office, the clerk walked in and explained the reason for his lateness. He had gone to see the Arab's vineyard and had decided that it was worthwhile for him to recommend it to my father to purchase, for a price that he himself had finalized with the Arab—400 *mejidi*s.[37] The vineyard had an annual income of approximately 60 *mejidi*s, and it also had a

---

35. The Montefiore register lists a child named Ya'akov Barukhi'el who lived in Jerusalem with his family in the 1850s, but it is not certain that this is the same individual.

36. Due to the Hebrew transliteration, it is unclear what his last name really was in Arabic, and no information has been found about him.

37. In 1881, the *mejidi* was worth around twenty piastres.

spring-water well and a small, insubstantial, mud-brick house, and the loyal clerk urged my father to buy it.

Without even seeing the vineyard and the tract of land, my father immediately agreed to the purchase, as he had full faith in the integrity of his clerk. Within a few days the transaction was finalized, whereupon my father received the *kushan* [title deed]. This was the first land that my father bought in the sand dunes of Jaffa, today on which you may find the homes of Rabbi Zerah Barnett[38] and his synagogues in Neve Shalom. Thanks to the trusted clerk Barukhi'el, the notion of redeeming the land struck deep roots in my father's heart and with all of his heart and soul he began to devote himself to the purchase of tracts of land from foreigners.[39] He began to buy up vineyard after vineyard, large tracts of land, some of them on his own, some in partnership with the late Señor Haim Amzalak,[40] and some with Amzalak and Yosef Moyal.[41] Several Hebrew neighborhoods now stand on these tracts of land, including Neve Tzedek; Neve Shalom; parts of Mahane Yehuda; parts of Mahane Yosef; the Aharon neighborhood (named after my late father); and the Yemenite place of residence called Mahane Israel (Karton), excluding the entire section along the shoreline that borders the neighborhood of Mahane Yosef and the Yemenite residence up to the Feingold houses.

This entire area is called by the Arabs [*al-*]*ard al-munaza'a biha*, meaning "the disputed land." This area actually belonged to us, in partnership with Amzalak and Moyal, but at that time there was a well-

38. Lithuanian-born Zerah Barnett (1843–1935) immigrated to Palestine in 1872 and helped establish the settlement of Petah Tikva; after many years back and forth between London and Palestine, in 1891 Barnett moved to Jaffa.

39. "Zarim." In this case, Chelouche is referring to non-Jews.

40. Haim Amzalak (1828–1916), born in Gibraltar to a Moroccan family, immigrated to Palestine as a child in 1834. He was successful in business, served as honorary British vice-consul in Jaffa for thirty years (1872–1902), and helped facilitate the purchase of land for Zionist settlement. A copy of the contract for the sale of land co-owned by Chelouche and Amzalak is found in Ram, *Hayishuv haYehudi beYafo*, p. 25 of the appendix.

41. Yosef Moyal (1843–1914) was born in Rabat to Sa'ada née 'Amiel and Aharon, a wealthy landowner and merchant; the family immigrated to Palestine before 1860. Yosef became a wealthy merchant in his own right and served as vice-consul for Spain and Persia; he eventually adopted Ottoman nationality, after which he received the honorific title *bek* in recognition of his economic and social status and contributions to the state.

known Christian, a man of dubious reputation who was capable of physical violence, a man who was a danger to society and who struck fear and terror into many, including government officials. He forcibly conquered the entire aforementioned area by building a temporary structure and a guard station. Lawsuits ensued and continued without end, due to the fact that the defendant had a great deal of power, and the judges saw this.

Despite this, a worthless verdict was handed down that on the one hand recognized our rights but on the other hand, out of the judges' fear of him, also recognized his rights, and the lawsuit dragged on for years. Expenses increased from one day to the next due to the high number of trips taken to Beirut, which is where the chief tribunal was located,[42] until my father and Amzalak simply gave up, choosing not to invest any more blood in it, and transferred their rights to the late Yosef Moyal, who was not willing to concede his ownership of the land in question. The lawsuit between the late Moyal and the Christian, whose name was Tanus Nasr,[43] continued for thirty years, and in the meantime both of them died.

Throughout this parcel of land, various owners seized plots of land and built simple buildings of tin sheets and wood, according to contracts that they made at first with the Christian and subsequently, with the late Moyal. Each plot of land, measuring five hundred cubits, was sold for five napoleons on a first come, first served basis.[44]

Today there are also respectable buildings built on this strip of land, but their owners do not possess titles issued in their names, and no one knows when the government will be able to recognize their ownership on this land, because to this day it is known to the government in the official land registry [*tabu*] books by the name "the land that is the subject of dispute between Tanus Nasr and Yosef Moyal."

In 1879, the committee representing the Jewish community in Jaffa

---

42. Chelouche is likely referring to the appeals' court, which was in Beirut. Jaffa had several local courts for everyday legal matters, as did Jerusalem.

43. Chelouche misspelled his last name as Nassar. One of Tanus Nasr's land purchases north of the city is registered in the Jaffa *shari'a* courts, and he was prominent enough to merit his house being marked on Sandel's map. According to another court register entry, Nasr was a *dragoman* (translator) for the French consulate in Jaffa. Bawwab, *Mawsu'at Yafa al-jamila*, 597, 946.

44. In 1881, one French gold napoleon was worth between 90 and 106 Ottoman piastres.

came to understand that there was a critical need to expand the Talmud Torah building and to open a higher level for the study of the Talmud, *Shulhan Arukh*, and Jewish law, due to the fact that in the existing Talmud Torah they only taught the children prayers, Bible, *Law for Israel*,[45] and very little religious law. Once the decision was made, the community invited a new rabbi, Rabbi Shlomo Bohbut,[46] the father of Rabbi Shabtai Bohbut,[47] who admirably serves as the rabbi of the city of Beirut. An apartment was rented especially for the rabbi, and thirty or so students from the age of ten years and older were selected from among the most talented in Jaffa to learn Torah from the rabbi. I was the only one of the pupils who was not yet ten years old, but due to the fact that they found me to be diligent and industrious in my studies, I was accepted into the new level.

Time passed, and the new Talmud Torah was organized in good fashion. Its pupils would tease those children who remained behind in the old Talmud Torah, because the new rabbi would treat his pupils lovingly and show them abundant affection so that they would grow close to him. But after a while, the situation changed for the worse, and the rabbi began to display his strength and bravery—when it was called for, he would beat the children mercilessly. The children complained but without success, and they would accept their punishment with love. As for myself, the rabbi never beat me, because I studied faithfully and I was always diligent in my studies, and that is how I spent about one and half years in this level.

---

45. This is a compendium of Jewish texts for daily and weekly study.

46. Shlomo Bohbut (1823–1900) was born in Rabat and immigrated to Jaffa as a child. He wrote the religious treatise *Kohelet Shlomo*.

47. Shabtai Bohbut (1870–1948) was born in Jaffa but moved to Jerusalem and later Istanbul for rabbinical study. Bohbut served in the rabbinical court of Jaffa, and he spent the war years in Syria. In 1923–1924 he became the chief rabbi of Beirut, an office he filled until his death.

CHAPTER 2 *The Kidnapping of Yosef*

*In my father's office | The Maghrebi Arab who followed me |
On the road behind Jaffa | My adventures and my suffering | Stolen
from my parents | Between life and death | Rabbi Israel Simhon | The
orchard of Sir Moses Montefiore | The lost donkey | What is done in my
parents' home | The Ottoman governor of Jaffa and the foreign consuls
share my father's sorrow | The governor's help in my search | Jaffa
city is noisy and on alert | Religious sages pray for my rescue |
My return to my parents' home | The government assists in
the search for the abductor | The kidnapper's end*

On the fourth day of the month of Tammuz 1880,[48] I left the Talmud Torah on foot and headed home for lunch, as was my custom. My mother and sister and the servant were busy washing the linens and would not permit me to enter the house, as it was dirty from all the wash water. So my mother told me to head down to my father's office for a while and then return together with him in half an hour. As I missed seeing the workers on the job and watching them cast molten metals into gold and silver jewelry, I did not hesitate long and obeyed my mother.

Before entering the workroom, I passed through my father's office and found him there conversing with a Maghrebi Arab,[49] who spoke in a Maghrebi dialect that is common in Morocco, which I barely understood. Seeing me there, my father asked what I was doing in his office at

---

48. The fourth month of the Jewish lunar calendar, Tammuz falls between June and July.

49. Muslim immigrants from Morocco, Algeria, Tunisia, and Libya (the Maghreb) arrived in Jaffa in the mid-nineteenth century after the French colonization of Algeria, as well as continuously en route to or from the Muslim pilgrimage (*hajj*) in Mecca. They are mentioned in the Islamic (*shari'a*) court records in Jaffa as working in agriculture, as orchard and village guards, as teachers, and as laborers and merchants in the city markets. By the early twentieth century, Maghrebis reportedly "had a particularly bad reputation and were considered extraordinarily violent" in the Arabic press. Quoted in Dierauff, *Translating Late Ottoman Modernity in Palestine*, 139. The Moroccan dialect (Darija) is significantly distinct from Levantine Arabic.

this time of day, and I explained the reason. My father smiled and then asked if I had brought him the keys that he had told me to bring him earlier that morning. I apologized as I had forgotten. At hearing this, my father ordered me as a punishment to go home immediately and bring him the keys. Of course, I obeyed my father and left in order to carry out his order without any grudge in my heart against him, because I knew that my father had good intentions to accustom me to be quick in all of my actions.

As I walked home through the alleys of the city, I felt that someone was following me and calling out my name. I looked back and recognized the Maghrebi Arab who had been sitting and talking with my father. He told me that my father had asked that I go with him to someplace nearby to receive from him a certain amount of gold that was meant for my father. I could barely understand his Maghrebi dialect, and it was only through the signs that he made invoking my father's name and the fact that I had just now seen him with my own eyes sitting and talking with my father that I believed him and followed.

The Maghrebi began leading me through the roads of old Jaffa, places where I had never been despite being a native of the city, and by way of these twisted roads and narrow alleys he led me out of the city—onto the 'Ajami Road, which at the time was uncultivated land without any buildings at all. From there he led me along paths and lanes, through vineyards and orchards, until we reached the sand dunes behind Mikve Israel.[50]

That day was one of the stultifying days of the month of Tammuz and the heat wave was in full force, and that tiring walk, in particular for a soft and delicate child, affected me badly. I was almost sorry that I had listened to the Maghrebi, but the hope that I would soon be going back to my father and bringing him the gold lifted my spirit and gave me strength. I was dressed like a native of the land, with a silk caftan (called a *kumbaz* in Arabic) and on top a thin black coat. On my feet I wore respectable shoes, as befitting a schoolboy.

When we arrived at a wide-open space without seeing a single other mortal being, the Maghrebi turned to me and said: "Now we must go somewhere where there are people, and I do not wish for them to recognize me, so I must wear a disguise. Therefore, you must take off your

---

50. Mikve Israel was the agricultural school for Jews established in 1870 by the French philanthropic society, the Alliance Israélite Universelle.

clothes and pass them to me." I immediately took off my overcoat, and my shoes and socks, and all I had left on was the silk caftan that now made me unrecognizable. He put the rest into the saddlebag that he carried on his shoulder, telling me that if we met anyone alone the way, I was to say that I was his son 'Ali and that he was my father, Muhammad.

I agreed to lie only because I could not understand his intentions or interests. It had been clear to me that the man I was accompanying was a Jew, as in my innocence I thought that every Maghrebi was a Jew, but now I was surprised to realize I had been wrong. When, due to the extreme heat and the rough terrain, he raised up his sleeves to wipe off the profuse sweat pouring down his face, I discovered tattoos in several places on his flesh. I was shocked, as only that week I had learned from my rabbi the "laws of scratches"—that it was absolutely forbidden for a Jew to make any scratch on his flesh.[51]

I began to suspect the man I was accompanying and in order to test him, seeing that the sun was about to set, I asked him where we were going to be praying the *minkha* [afternoon] prayer. The Maghrebi, who had no way of comprehending the intent of my words, began stuttering in his language, which was incomprehensible to me. I asked him if we were going home before the evening prayers or if he would let me know where we were to pray, and once again the Maghrebi was confused. He began to blabber the word *'arvit* [evening prayer], without knowing exactly how to pronounce it or understand its meaning.

Instantly, I came to the clear realization that I had fallen into a trap, and that here I was in the hands of a stranger, in a desolate desert where I had never been before. My hunger bothered me greatly. But yet, as all of my senses were focused on consideration of my fate, I forgot my hunger completely. My thoughts focused on the dreadful situation in which I found myself. In my imagination, different thoughts and reflections came to mind that shocked my gentle soul, until it was clear to me that I had been kidnapped from my parents for some purpose and no one would be able to find this forlorn place to save my life, especially when the last rays of the sun were now setting; I settled into a state of despair that profoundly depressed me. I began to internalize this dismal reality in all its dreadfulness, thinking, how was it possible that my father would

---

51. Originating in Leviticus 19:29, the regulation against tattoos also appears in the *Shulhan Arukh*, which is probably where Yosef Eliyahu studied it.

trust me, a ten-year-old boy, to bring him a quantity of gold along this long route; was it feasible for a boy to master these desert routes?

From the depths of my despair and bitterness, I approached one of the native trees, glued myself to it with my entire shaking body, and resolved that I would walk no further. Live or die, I would hold steadfast onto this one idea: I would go no further. My escort approached me and said: "You are probably tired, rest for a while and then we will continue on our way, for we are close to the destination where the gold is." I responded angrily that I would not move. At first, he tried to pacify me and pointed to a distant hill that was supposedly our destination, but I remained mutinous; I would not walk any further. I sat down and became deaf and mute, not exchanging any words with him whether for good or ill. The Maghrebi then spoke harshly to me: "I am the one who took you out of your father's arms, and I must return you with the gold."

I could not hold in my feelings, my spirit was restless, and I told him, crying: "No, you are a liar, my father did not hand me over to you, you have deceived me, because how would he ever send me with you on a difficult route like this, when I have never ever been allowed to leave the city? My feet are swollen from all the thorns that I have pulled out from them, and I cannot walk with you—here I will either live or I will die." When he saw that my decision was so resolute, he grabbed me by the scruff of my neck with both hands and forced my head down into the sand, until I could taste my own strangling.

My eyes, which were full of flowing tears, and my face, which was wet from them, filled with dust, and my life was in danger. I moaned, "Leave me alone and I will walk, because I am dying." He left me alone, and I stood up to my full height, astounded and confused, a human being who was suspended between life and death. My mouth, nose, and eyes were filled with sand, and I started cleaning them with my hand and my cloak. I cleaned and I cried until little by little, I was able to open my eyelashes and the light grew brighter; my tears, which were flowing like water, rescued me.

The sun set and in the twilight I saw in the distance three people on horseback, getting closer to us. I recognized them as Greek Christians among the notables of the land, two of whom I even knew by name; one was called Dmitri and the other was Onayudo.[52] I thought of shouting

---

52. It has not been possible to identify either of these men.

and calling to them for help, falling down at their feet and begging them from the bottom of my soul to rescue me and bring me to my father. But then I changed my mind, as I was afraid that they might be indifferent to my plea for help and would not answer my request, and then my escort's hatred toward me would grow, and who knows if he might not just kill me on the road. So I refrained from putting my thoughts into action and trailed behind the Maghrebi like a lamb to the slaughter.

Half an hour later, the moon was high in the sky, its light turning the desolate desert silver. After the daytime heat wave, the mountain breeze began to blow, and it restored my spirits. I took deep breaths in order to slightly ease my state of torment. And as I walked behind my tormentor without any hope, a man riding on a donkey appeared in front of us, traveling east to west, while our route was south to north. It was there at the junction that we encountered this old man, who appeared to me like the Prophet Elijah—angel and redeemer and savior. It was the late Israel Simhon,[53] peace be upon him.

When the old man saw me, he yelled, "Where are you going at this time of night?" I grabbed onto his hand: "Take me with you." Without a moment's hesitation, he got down from his donkey, grabbed me in his strong arms, sat me down on his donkey, and started speaking with the Maghrebi. Based on the conversation, the old man understood the whole deception and he separated from the Maghrebi when the latter asked that he deliver me to my father and tell him that he would bring him the goods the following day. Rabbi Simhon, whose facial expression and the splendor of his erect posture and the courage of his heart all testified to his bravery, and who never set out on the road without being armed with a pistol and clubs, scared the Maghrebi, who did not put up any opposition to Rabbi Simhon, who took me with him.

Riding alongside Rabbi Simhon, I settled down a little and my frayed nerves calmed down somewhat. Nevertheless, my heart did not cease to beat against my chest and every few moments I looked back in fear, lest the villain be following us. Due to my intense joy at having been redeemed from my abductor, I forgot to demand the return of my coat, shoes, and socks, which remained in his saddlebag. Now I would ride

---

53. Of Moroccan origin, Israel Simhon (d. 1895) worked in the Montefiore orchard for twenty-seven years until 1894, when the orchard was leased and turned over to the management of the Mikve Israel school.

home with Rabbi Simhon barefoot and coatless. I was very ashamed that I would have to enter the city in this state of dress, but I took comfort in the fact that at night no one would recognize me.

Exactly how the old man found his way to the road on which I was being led by the Maghrebi is quite interesting in and of itself. In the same period the great Sir Moses Montefiore,[54] a native of England, visited the Land of Israel many times and performed many acts of benevolence for the Jews of the country. His last visit was in 1875, when he stayed at the home of Señor Haim Amzalak, who at the time served as the consul of England in our city. During this visit,[55] he purchased a plot of land outside the city walls of Jaffa, on the boundary of the Germans' property, and once the *kushan*s were issued, Montefiore asked the late Señor Amzalak to introduce him to some of the notables of the city of Jaffa in order to consult with them. Señor Amzalak complied with the request and provided Montefiore with the names of several of the city's notables, who were then invited to meet the baron[56] and were presented by Señor Amzalak, each one by name. His Honor the Baron received them cordially and shook their hands with abundant affection. Among these invitees was also my esteemed father.

The gathering was held at the home of Señor Amzalak, which to this day remains in the same condition, without any changes, in the old city. His Honor the Baron spoke before the gathered men and informed them that he had purchased a property and intended to plant an orchard on it, but he needed a brave individual who would live on the land. Montefiore was ready to build a house for that man and also dig him a well. He

---

54. Sir Moses Montefiore (1784–1885) was a Sephardi British banker and philanthropist. He undertook seven visits to the Holy Land in his lifetime, during which he donated extensive sums to fund five registries of the Jewish communities in the region as well as to support the establishment of new residential compounds and neighborhoods outside the city walls of Jerusalem. Montefiore was a baronet and served as president of the Board of Deputies of British Jews for thirty-nine years.

55. Ram writes that this took place during Montefiore's fifth visit in 1866. However, Amnon Cohen has translated the original purchase from the Islamic court registers on 19 August 1855.

56. Chelouche calls him "sar" and "kvod hasar," a generic honorific, which we have replaced with his correct title. In contemporary sources, Montefiore was regularly referred to as "hanadiv" (the patron), due to his expansive philanthropy in the Land of Israel.

would leave the budget for planting with Señor Amzalak, and he was prepared to continue paying until the orchard began to bear fruit. When the time came that the orchard bore fruit, its income would be divided into three parts: one part would be dedicated to the poor of the city; the second part for the expenses of the orchard, its improvement, and expansion; and the third part for the caretaker.

The baron had two requests to make of the notables: (a) that they recommend two honest, fair-minded, heroic, courageous individuals, and (b) that two of the notables be appointed as managers of the property, who would be in close and constant contact with the caretaker. All of the required expenses would be disbursed by the baron's proxy, Señor Amzalak. Following some debate, the assembly chose as the two managers Rabbi Yehuda Halevi[57] and my respected late father, and as the two individuals who would be engaged in planting the orchard, Rabbi Ya'akov Shimol[58] and Rabbi Israel Simhon. Rabbi Ya'akov Shimol was physically weak and turned down the position, so Rabbi Israel Simhon was left as the sole caretaker of the Montefiore orchard, which is situated next to the Sarona German colony[59] on the Petah Tikva road, and which is now known as the Montefiore neighborhood.

As the caretaker of the Montefiore orchard, Rabbi Israel Simhon lived on the site permanently. Every so often, he would go down to the city to purchase whatever was needed for the orchard as well as foodstuffs for his family. He told our family and many residents of the city that on the day that I was kidnapped by the Maghrebi, Rabbi Simhon prepared himself to go down to the city. He fed his donkey and prepared his pistol and his clubs, without which he never went out on the roads,

57. Yehuda Halevi (1783–1879) was born in Sarajevo and taught in Ragusa (Dubrovnik), from whence he immigrated to Jerusalem in 1835; he later served as a rabbi, judge, and teacher in Jaffa. There is evidence that he first purchased the orchard in 1853 before reselling it to Montefiore.

58. Ya'akov Shimol (or Ben-Shimol, per Ram) arrived in Jaffa from Tetouan in 1844 and worked as a shoemaker. Shimol also founded the Jewish burial society (*hevra kadisha*) and aid to the needy (*gmilut hasadim*) in town.

59. The German colony of Sarona was established in 1871 four miles northeast of Jaffa, on land that housed a Greek monastery. The German Templer society had been established a decade prior with the conviction that German evangelists should actively work to bring about the spiritual and political regeneration of the Holy Land through immigration and occupation.

not only because of the threat of robbers but also out of fear of rabid animals among the wolves and foxes, which on more than one occasion attacked him; thanks to his weapons, he was saved from them.

When Rabbi Simhon arrived at the gate that faces the northern side of the city, he noticed a large pile of small buckets, which would normally hang side by side on an iron chain mounted on a large wheel placed atop the well. When the horse that was tethered to a bar fastened to the wheel was led around the well in circles, these little buckets would circulate, creating a sort of ring-shaped pump that raised a great deal of water from the well. All these buckets had been arranged in a corner of the courtyard, one on top of the other, awaiting some needed repairs, but now Rabbi Simhon found them scattered on the ground in disarray and was puzzled by it.

He immediately dismounted his donkey, which was already loaded with the weapons, and began to rearrange the buckets. In the meantime, the donkey disappeared because the gate on the northern side was wide open. Rearranging the buckets took about two hours. When Rabbi Simhon finished his task, he began to contemplate whether it was still worthwhile for him to go down to the city or not, since it was already late in the day, before sunset. As he was contemplating, he noticed that the donkey was missing. He began looking for it and upon his entry into the orchard, he noticed some tracks and proceeded to follow them.

When he arrived at the wide-open northern gate he stood there, baffled. He never opened this gate except for on those days when the soil was being tilled, in order to dispose of the weeds and other rubbish, and also on days when they would bring in the manure. He thought long and hard about it but could not find an answer to the riddle. As is known, the hour was growing late. The laborers had finished their day's work and returned to their homes. That day, the gardener's wife had taken ill and he had taken her to her relatives living in one of the nearby villages, leaving behind his children, the oldest of whom was a ten-year-old girl. Rabbi Simhon turned to her and asked if she knew who opened the northern gate and why. The girl related that her father had to open the gate because he was transporting her sick mother on a donkey, since she was unable to walk even to the entrance gate. He had ordered his daughter to shut the gate, but she forgot to do so.

Rabbi Simhon again began to search for the donkey; now it was clear to him that it had walked out through the open gate, so he followed in its footsteps. He looked all around—but no donkey. He encountered an Arab and asked him if he had seen a donkey, and the man replied that he had seen a donkey not far away, grazing on the grass, without anyone watching over it. Rabbi Simhon rushed to the spot, which was past the Salama lands,[60] but the donkey was not there. Out of exhaustion he entered one of the villages where he had some acquaintances and told them about the donkey that had disappeared. A neighbor who was listening to the conversation informed him that just moments ago he had encountered a man walking and holding a donkey and that the man was declaring out loud that he had found a donkey walking alone through a field hauling tools on its back. They went to this man and found the donkey tied to his tent. Rabbi Simhon took the donkey, thanked the man, and headed back toward the orchard.

Night settled and spread over the Salama countryside, which is known for its hills and peaks, and its rivers and streams that run dry in the summertime. Rabbi Simhon, going up and down the hills in the darkness, lost his way. After much hard going, he arrived at the main road, which is where he found me and rescued me from the hands of the Arab. Rabbi Simhon at first thought to take me to the orchard, but when he imagined to himself the state of mind of my family, which was without doubt filled with sorrow and despair for the son who was now lost to it, he took me straight to the city.

Whenever I reflect on what I went through, I always am amazed at the wondrous chain of events and the numerous miracles that led to the loss of the donkey and the search for it mounted by Rabbi Simhon, all so that he would be able to rescue me from my abductor and return me to my parents.

My father, who had waited in his office for me and for the keys and who saw that I was late in returning, left his business and went home approximately one hour past noon. Arriving at home, he asked: "Has Yosef

60. Salama was located five kilometers east of Jaffa. Much of its land was planted with citrus groves and grains. After the 1947 UN partition resolution, Salama was the site of several military skirmishes between villagers, Hagana (Jewish militia) forces, and Arab militias; in late April 1948, Salama was finally occupied by the Hagana. Its villagers had fled the fighting and were not allowed to return, despite a request in early May to "accept Jewish protection." By late May, 135 Jewish immigrant and refugee families were settled there, and the village was renamed Kfar Shalem. Morris, *The Birth of the Palestinian Refugee Problem Revisited*, 96, 126, 217, 343, 384.

Eliyahu eaten?" and was embarrassed when he heard that I had not returned home yet. My father thought that I surely resented being told to bring him the keys and that I had returned to the Talmud Torah without eating lunch, and he immediately sent the beadle there. In the meantime, my father sat down at the table and requested his lunch, but the storm in his soul bothered him a great deal, and due to his worry over me, he could not put anything in his mouth.

The long wait was hard on my father, until the beadle returned and reported that Yosef Eliyahu was not at the Talmud Torah and no one had any knowledge of his whereabouts since he left for lunch. My father was extremely sorrowful, his heart tightened in pain, and given the intense grief he did not taste a thing. He went back to the shop and asked the clerks and workers if perhaps anyone had seen me, but in vain, as no one knew anything about me. My father immediately ordered all the workers to scatter about the city and search for me. Hour after hour passed without news about Yosef Eliyahu.

In those days, the *kaymakam*[61] was in the daily habit of sitting in my father's office, since he was very fond of him, drinking coffee, smoking *narghileh* [water pipe], and chatting with him. When he walked into my father's office at the usual time, he found my father in a state of agitation without his usual expression. Out of grief over his son Yosef Eliyahu, my father did not receive him with his usual welcome. When the *kaymakam* asked my father the reason for his distress, my late father burst into tears and told him about his tragedy.

The *kaymakam* was extremely distressed to hear of the woeful incident and comforted my father, saying that he would help him find his lost son. He immediately had a word with the soldier standing by the door, ordering him to summon the town crier (a man with a strong voice whose job it was to make the rounds of the city streets to inform residents of government edicts). A few minutes later, the crier arrived and the *kaymakam* ordered him to announce throughout the city that anyone who sees me should return me to my father, and he provided him

---

61. The *kaymakam*, or deputy governor, was the foremost Ottoman official of the Jaffa district, which was part of the Jerusalem province (*mutasarrifiyya*, Ara.; *mutasarrıflık*, Tur.) headed by the provincial governor (*mutasarrıf*). Like the *mutasarrıf* in Jerusalem, district *kaymakam*s could have cooperative or antagonistic relationships with local elites.

with all of the details of my clothing, my physical appearance, etc. The crier, who had been given his orders directly by the city governor, immediately began to make the rounds of all the alleys and streets of the city and made the announcement. But it was all in vain; there was no sound, and no answer.

While the *kaymakam* sat and spoke comforting words to my father, an Arab came in and informed the *kaymakam* that at noon he saw me talking with a Maghrebi in a nearby alley. When my father heard the Arab's report, he jumped out of his seat as if bitten by a snake. The catastrophic episode, which had until then been somewhat murky in his eyes, gradually began to grow much clearer and he cried out: "Yes, that Maghrebi left my office just a few moments after I sent my son home to bring the keys."

His suspicions began to take root in his heart—that wicked Maghrebi was the one who abducted his son. The rumor spread through the city that I had been abducted by a sorcerer, and all of the residents began to search for their children and kept them at home. The *kaymakam* issued orders to announce the request for volunteers to accompany the Ottoman soldiers in the area and the villages to search for the Maghrebi. Many heroic Arab residents volunteered for the task, for two reasons: one, to ascertain whether there really was such a kidnapper who abducts young children from the clutches of their parents, and two, out of their love for my father. Group after group arrived at the government office in order to take horses and set out accompanied by the soldiers. Many others went out on their own to search for me, with the authorities' permission, through the remote alleys and dim lanes. But the boy was nowhere to be found.

My father was accustomed to leaving his office every day at three o'clock in the afternoon to go home, wash his face, hands, and feet, take off his city clothes, and then go—now dressed in his house clothes—straight up to the *Beit Midrash*[62] that was located directly above our apartment next door to the synagogue. There he would convene with the elders of the community who came there regularly to study and to pray. For the most part, the same rabbis and scholars were at the *Beit Midrash* each day, and they were joined by travelers passing through

---

62. "House of Study": a room for Torah study.

Jaffa who would be hosted in our home. I can still remember the names of these rabbis:[63] the eminent rabbi and kabbalist[64] Eliyahu Mani,[65] the father of the judge Malki'el Mani,[66] who used to stay with us due to the condition of his health; the eminent rabbi Shlomo Bohbut, father of Rabbi Bohbut, who is the chief rabbi of Beirut; the eminent rabbi Mercado Me'ir,[67] father of the chief rabbi of the Land of Israel, the Rishon LeZion Rabbi Ya'akov Me'ir;[68] the eminent rabbi Ya'akov Simhon,[69] the father of the late rabbi Yosef ben Simhon;[70] the eminent rabbi Me'ir Hamburger,[71] the father-in-law of the man who was the English military

63. When Chelouche refers to men as "rabbis" (literally, "masters"), this was meant as a title of respect for their piety and religious learning rather than necessarily an indication of their professional ordination or occupation in the rabbinate. Here he seems to distinguish the men who were engaged full time as rabbis and religious officials with the term *harav hagaon* (the eminent [or exalted] rabbi).

64. Literally, *mekubal*. The mystical tradition of Kabbalah was prominent among Sephardi religious figures, and from the sixteenth century on, Safed, in northern Palestine, became a key site for Kabbalah pilgrimage and study.

65. Rabbi Eliyahu Mani (1824–1899) immigrated to Palestine from Baghdad in 1855–1856 and settled in Hebron, where he led the small Jewish community for decades. He was the author of several works of religious scholarship.

66. Yitzhak Malki'el Mani (1860–1932) was a lawyer and communal leader. In addition to his Jewish religious learning, Mani also reportedly studied the Qur'an, Islamic law, and tribal customs (*'urf*).

67. Mercado Me'ir (d. 1896) was born in Rhodes to a Sephardic family migrating from Yanina to Jerusalem. He was a religious scholar and a wealthy merchant in Jerusalem, and he supported numerous Jewish philanthropic efforts.

68. Rishon LeZion (literally, "First in Zion," the Hebrew title for the preeminent rabbi in Jerusalem) was drawn from a verse in the book of Isaiah. The Ottoman title was *hahambaşı*. Ya'akov Me'ir (1856–1939) served as chief rabbi in Jerusalem and Salonica over a number of years. His initial election as chief rabbi in Jerusalem in 1906 led to a yearslong internal struggle over the direction of the rabbinate, known as *el pleyto* (the argument). Me'ir was considered the candidate of the reformers and youth of the community, while the conservatives supported his rival.

69. Rabbi Ya'akov Simhon (ca. 1830–1893/4) immigrated to Jaffa from Fez in 1863.

70. Yosef Simhon (1859–1919) was a rabbinical scholar and a Hebrew and Talmud teacher at the Alliance Israélite Universelle school in Jaffa for thirty years.

71. Me'ir Hamburger (1836–1913) immigrated to Jaffa in 1857 from the Austro-Hungarian Empire. His family was one of the earliest Ashkenazi families to settle in Jaffa, but because the Ashkenazim could not yet form a quorum of ten Jewish men (*minyan*) required for collective prayer, he reportedly prayed at Sephardi syn-

commander in Alexandria, David Blattner Bek;[72] Rabbi Yitzhak Assouline;[73] Rabbi Mas'ud Hacohen;[74] Rabbi Moshe Tzeruya;[75] and other rabbis whose names I cannot recall.

Together with these rabbis and scholars, my father would delve into Torah study and debate matters of Jewish law until the *minkha* prayer. As soon as the prayers ended, they would again sit around the table and continue to study as before until the *'arvit* prayer. Two hours before dawn, they would get up for the *tikun hatzot* and read until dawn, when they would recite the *shaharit* [dawn prayers].

On the day of my kidnapping, my father did not go as usual to study in the *Beit Midrash*. All the assistance of the authorities and residents was in vain. At five o'clock in the afternoon, my father left his office and all the notables who had come to visit him and personally went out in search of his son, as he believed that his son was not outside the city but was being hidden inside the city. Because of that, he asked for permission from the authorities to search the homes accompanied by the *mukhtar*.[76] He began entering the homes of suspected Arabs. He entered the courtyards and opened up the wells, yelling into them "Yosef

---

agogues in the Sephardi custom and served as their secretary for European correspondence. Hamburger worked as a money changer in addition to his work as a ritual circumciser (*mohel*) to Jaffa's Jews and Muslims. Although Hamburger does not have an individual entry in the Montefiore registers, he does appear as serving in the Sephardi Talmud Torah and Bikur Holim (Care for the Sick) in 1866.

72. We have been unable to find additional information on his adulthood, but as a child Blattner lived with his widowed mother Roiza and had three older brothers in Jaffa. The family originated in Poland; David's age suggests that he was born in Jaffa around 1857.

73. Yitzhak Assouline (1837–1912) emigrated from Morocco to Jaffa in 1861 and served as a ritual slaughterer (*shochet*) in the city for many years.

74. Mas'ud Hacohen arrived in Jaffa in 1844 from Tlemcen, Algeria. He was a merchant and served as treasurer for the synagogue.

75. Moshe Tzeruya immigrated to Jaffa from Tetouan, Morocco, in 1856. A merchant by trade, he also served as treasurer of the Sephardi philanthropic burial society.

76. *Mukhtar*s were communal, neighborhood, and village officials with specific obligations in the Ottoman administrative system, such as registering residents for the census, appearing as a witness in court, and in general serving as an intermediary between the government and the population under their jurisdiction. There were neighborhood *mukhtar*s as well as *mukhtar*s for the non-Muslim communities.

Eliyahu" — but there was no answer. After two hours of searching, he returned exhausted to his shop and then, without any news about his son, he went home depressed. At home, an atmosphere of mourning reigned; the family was in a state of grief and their Jewish neighbors cried along with them. [My father] went to the synagogue, put on his *tallit* and *tefillin*,[77] opened the doors of the holy ark, and prayed to God, weeping bitterly.

The rabbis and scholars sat in the study hall next door to the synagogue immersed in Torah. They were surprised that my father did not come as usual to sit and enjoy studying in their presence, but they had already heard from the beadle that I was missing. They assumed it was not that serious and that he would surely find me. My late brother Avraham Haim[78] suffered tremendously from his sorrow over me and from his fear that, Heaven forbid, our father might go crazy from the agony. He kept careful watch over my father's comings and goings and went to the shop to ask for Father, but he was not there. He also asked at our home, which was completely filled with people: he was not there, either. He went up to the *Beit Midrash*, where he found all the rabbis studying, but Father was not among them.

He stood and thought to himself, where could my father have gone? He made up his mind and entered the synagogue, thinking that he might find him there. How astounded he was to see Father sitting on the floor in front of the holy ark, crying bitterly! He also began to cry, going downstairs to summon my mother, who returned with my father's mother and all the other female relatives. When they saw the terrifying scene, they too burst into wails, to the point when the sound could be heard in the rabbis' room.

When the rabbis came to the synagogue, my mother turned to them with a bitter cry: "Great rabbis, pray for my son Yosef Eliyahu, save him with your prayers." The rabbis were overwhelmed with compassion and stood together by the open holy ark, around Father, and the eminent rabbi Eliyahu Mani began to recite some of the Yom Kippur liturgical poems — A Prayer to David, A Prayer to Habakuk the Prophet, A Prayer

---

77. The prayer shawl and phylacteries worn by Jewish men during prayer.

78. Avraham Haim Chelouche (1867–1925) was a grain merchant for many years before establishing the Chelouche Frères company together with Yosef Eliyahu and Ya'akov.

to Moses, and others. And in this manner, they continued with prayers and heartbreaking supplications for several hours.

At the same exact time as my entire family was sinking into a general mood of worry and gloom over my fate, I was riding with Rabbi Israel Simhon toward the city. When we reached the broad square through which those who enter Jaffa from the entire country pass and on which the government house and the clock tower now stand, back when Suq al-Deir [the Market of the Monastery] and all the other present-day buildings aside from a few vegetable and bakery stalls were not yet built, we found the residents of the city standing around in groups talking about the tragedy that had befallen my father and asking every person arriving in Jaffa from elsewhere in the country if they had not seen me on the road. Various Arabs from the villages and the city approached us and asked if we had seen so-and-so along the road.

One of the groups recognized me, and instantly the cry rang out across the city that I had been found. I was lifted off the donkey and led to the *kaymakam*, who was sitting next to a coffee house with a few government officials awaiting an outcome. The *kaymakam*, upon seeing in the moonlight the older man who was leading me, erupted in rage directed at him, but the old man shouted: "It is I who rescued the boy! I am Israel Simhon." Everyone drew closer to see me, forming a crowd in front of the *qadi*[79] and the *kaymakam*, while I was very embarrassed, as I was barefoot and undressed. The *kaymakam* took me by the hand and accompanied by the government officials, led me home, with everyone in the city following right behind.

Our family, which had been told the good news about my arrival by a few others who ran ahead, came out to receive me, followed by the neighbors, and so we met, one camp opposite the other camp. My father approached me, hugged and kissed me, and burst into tears: "Is it you, my son?" He grasped me tight in his two pure hands and walked with me, taking long strides in order to reach our home as soon as possible. For a few moments, he scrutinized me in the light of the lamps; it was like a dream for him, and he could not believe that it was real. Rabbi Simhon approached my father, hugged and kissed him, and joined in our rejoicing.

---

79. The *qadi* was the judge in the Islamic court (*al-mahkama al-shari'a*), among the most important provincial government positions.

They brought me into the house, plucked the thorns from my feet, and made me coffee with milk to drink. Since I was tired, weak, and agitated, they asked the crowd to disperse so as to permit me to calm down and relax. Gradually, the residents went back to their homes, clasping my parents' hands and sharing their feelings at my family's rejoicing. Out of exhaustion, I fell asleep in my father's bed without having eaten a thing. I awakened before dawn, looked around, and saw that there was no one in my parents' room. I entered the dining room, which I found lit, the table as usual filled with platters of cakes and cheeses, fruits and liquors, and the beadle took them to the *Beit Midrash*.

I wrapped myself in a coat and walked upstairs to sit with the rabbis because I could not go back to sleep, and the terrible scenes and nightmares would not allow my eyelids to close. As I stood at the entrance, I saw the rabbis sitting there as usual reading, and among them was my father in his regular clothes and not his house clothes. I then realized that my father had been keeping watch all night. My late mother was sitting, as was her custom, next to the stove, preparing coffee and tea, and Rabbi Simhon, who had brought me home, was sitting and reading with them.

When I entered the rabbis received me lovingly, and each of them in turn embraced me and blessed me. I drank tea and ate with them. Some of the rabbis asked me to tell them about the events, but my late father did not permit me to respond because he was concerned for my health and feared that I would become agitated. I sat in the company of the rabbis until I fell asleep, at which point I was moved back into my bed. For days and nights, I was overcome by a powerful sleep of which I could not be cured, but then I would wake up in a panic, shaking and agitated. My family realized that I was suffering from anxiety, as I became alarmed by the faintest noise, and they began to treat me.

The happiness in our home grew, and every day, visitors, friends, and acquaintances came to see me and to congratulate my parents. On Friday night people from the other synagogue came to pray at our synagogue, and the prayers went on until after midnight. In our home, refreshments were set out for the numerous people who came to visit and dine at our table. This chapter of great commotion and tumult in our home persisted for over two months. From all over the area, both Jewish and non-Jewish friends came to express to my parents their feelings of joy. And so it was that my father was busy every day welcoming guests and my mother was busy and preoccupied with running the house, cooking and preparing coffee and tea, serving fruits and sweets, in addition to her usual everyday work. My parents also tired of retelling this entire terrifying tale from start to finish to everyone who asked. It always shocked the listener and cast upon him at first a spirit of grief and sadness that culminated in rejoicing and happiness.

The day after my arrival, the *kaymakam* issued strict orders to all the villages around the city, to the *sheikh*s and *mukhtar*s, to search for the Maghrebi who abducted me. On several occasions, the soldiers made patrols of the surrounding area and the province, but they returned as they had gone. Each day, the *kaymakam* came into my father's shop and informed him of the steps he had taken to catch the kidnapper.

One day, the Christian Arab Teodor George[80] came over. He was the man who had related to the *kaymakam* that he had seen me on the day of my abduction speaking with the Maghrebi. He informed my father that only he could find the kidnapper, since the villain's face was inscribed in his memory. My father relayed this to the *kaymakam*, who then agreed to the Arab's conditions, providing him with a horse and dressing him in a soldier's uniform, and sent him on his mission. A few days later, the *kaymakam* summoned my father and confidentially told him that the spy who had been dispatched had succeeded in his task, and the abductor was at this moment lying in his own vomit in a coffee house outside the city. My father would have to accompany the *kaymakam* to see if it was really the kidnapper in order to imprison and punish him, but if it was not, then they would free him. My father immediately rushed home in order to bring me with him to identify the abductor, but I myself was panic-stricken with terrible fear, and I refused to go.

My father was to go alone and identify him. When he confirmed to the authorities that the man was indeed the kidnapper, they sent soldiers who arrested him in iron chains and put him in jail. The following day, the *kaymakam* informed my father that the kidnapper could not be put on trial until I myself appeared and identified him. My father and some friends implored me to go and see the prisoner, but I was determined —I would not go.

In the end, the *kaymakam* came to our house accompanied by Señor Haim Amzalak, the consul of England, and Yosef Bek Moyal, the consul of Persia, together with my father. Since I was confined [at home] I had

---

80. We have been unable to locate information about him.

been walking around in my house clothes, but I was immediately dressed in other clothes and presented to the guests; I kissed their hands, as was the custom. The *kaymakam* immediately seated me next to him, but out of embarrassment I responded to his questions curtly and with great difficulty. The *kaymakam* calmed me down, telling me I had nothing to be afraid of by seeing the villain, who was bound in iron chains, and that I only had to look at him from above, at a distance, and to testify whether this prisoner was my abductor. Given the endless entreaties and my own embarrassment, I consented—against my will—and went in the company of the entire respectable entourage, holding onto my father's hand tightly, lest he leave me.

We went up to the *saraya* and the *kaymakam* asked me to look down below, as he commanded the soldiers to face the prisoner in my direction. After once glance at him I yelled out loudly: "Yes, that's my kidnapper!" In the blink of an eye, the *kaymakam* took a pitcher of water that was next to him and told me to throw it at my kidnapper, but out of fear and panic I refused. When the *kaymakam* saw the intense emotional state I was in, he himself threw the pitcher at the head of the prisoner, who was wounded by the powerful blow.[81]

The Maghrebi kidnapper was sentenced to life in prison. A year and a half later, he developed a terminal illness while in prison and begged for death. The *qadi* summoned my late father and informed him that the prisoner was about to die and if my father had mercy on him and permitted him to be freed from prison, on condition that he be expelled from the city and forbidden to ever set foot in Jaffa again, then there was hope that he might live. "We know," said the *qadi*, "that you are among the leaders of the Jewish religion here, a fair and honest man, and surely you will agree to save a man's life from 'descending to the pit.'"[82] My father agreed without hesitation. The kidnapper was sent to Nablus under heavy guard, and the authorities there were ordered not to allow him to leave the city for the rest of his life.

    81. It is unclear what Chelouche is referring to here, as to our knowledge this was not a known custom in Ottoman criminal procedure.

    82. Job 33:24: "Redeem him from descending to the pit, for I have obtained his ransom." Chelouche is referring to the Maghrebi's illness as the fitting "ransom" for his crime, and his father therefore agreed to spare him from further punishment in accordance with the biblical verse. Many thanks to Evyatar (Tari) Chelouche for the interpretation and reference.

With this, the episode—which had terrified all of the residents of Jaffa, who were concerned with the fate of my family and were amazed to hear about the miracles through which I was rescued and returned to my parents—came to an end. For a long time afterward walking through the streets of Jaffa, I was pointed out as the protagonist of the event. After the torment I had undergone, I was like a person reborn who sees light for the first time. Even now, decades later, older residents of Jaffa can retell the whole affair without skipping a single detail.

For what purpose I was kidnapped was a riddle whose answer remains unclear to this very day. Numerous rumors rooted in groundless superstition spread throughout Jaffa. Nevertheless, so as to illustrate their mythological nature, it may be worth noting that there were some people who naively believed that the Maghrebi kidnapped me for riches. According to a popular legend, every child bearing the mark of a greenish vein between the eyes is likely to enrich the man who kidnaps him and takes him to the desert, digs a pit in the desolate surroundings, and orders him to pile up the gold that would start to appear out of the ground in great abundance; once the gold stream stops, the man puts the boy into the grave and seals it with sand.

However, this is but a fable, woven with the threads of the Oriental imagination. The naked truth has never been revealed from its deep abyss to this very day.

CHAPTER 3 *My Earliest Life Experiences; The First Pioneers*

*My work as a goldsmith | "The Yosef Eliyahu Invention" |
The first visit by the first pioneers from Russia and Romania |
Their goal to establish a Hebrew colony | The first Bilu pioneers,
headed by Israel Belkind | Their visit to Father's home |
My longings to study and be educated.*

Once the echo of the episode began to subside, my father sent me back to study at the Talmud Torah of Rabbi Shlomo Bohbut, where I continued to study for approximately two more years. My older brother Avraham Haim was enrolled at a German school in the German colony, which was known as Al-Amrikan.[83]

After two years had passed, my father found out that a Jewish school called Tif'eret Israel had been established in Beirut by the late Zaki Cohen.[84] He quickly wrote to ascertain the conditions of the school, and once this was clarified, he sent my brother Avraham Haim to be ed-

---

83. Literally, "the Americans." There had previously been an American colony established by Protestants in 1866, but it was abandoned only a year later, and its real estate holdings were sold to German settlers who established the Templer colony of Jaffa.

84. Yitzhak Zaki Cohen (1829–1904), born in Aleppo, established the city's first modern school for Jews in 1874, also known in Arabic as al-Madrasa al-wataniyya al-Isra'iliyya (The National Israelite School). Cohen's 1881 visit to Jerusalem merited a long feature article on the school published in the Hebrew newspaper *Havatzelet*, in which the author praised the school's spacious and well-appointed building, its curricular offerings, and its leading place among Beirut's schools as confirmed by the Ottoman reformer and former governor of Syria, Midhat Pasha, who visited the school twice. *Havatzelet* assured its readers that "the student who completes his studies in this school will emerge from it knowledgeable about our religion, literate in numbers, and conversant in the most honorable languages that qualify him to go before people and to be a respectable member of human society." *Havatzelet*, 22 September 1881. Tif'eret Israel placed a heavy emphasis on Arabic literacy, and its original school plays were covered in the local Arabic press. Tuition and boarding

ucated in Beirut.[85] During this period, my own rabbi became ill and the doctors forbade him from teaching, meaning that I was to remain idle without any further learning. So that I would not be left with nothing to occupy my time, my father took me with him to sit in his office.

In those days my heart was drawn to silversmithing, and I used to observe the work of each craftsman with appreciation and great curiosity. I immersed myself in the profession, and as my love for it grew more intense, I plucked up the courage to request materials so that I could create from them different items according to my desires and understanding. My father acceded to my request and instructed the supervisor in charge of materials to give me silver rather than gold so as to first test my work and see the results. They cleared a special place for me to work, and I began as an actual craftsman to shape the material, which I broke and ruined, then repaired and broke again, until I became accustomed to working without asking for help from one of the workers. All my passion was focused on creating a beautiful piece of jewelry by myself and presenting it to Father and the workers.

I began to be diligent in my work. I would wake up early in the morning, pray, quickly grab a bite to eat, and rush to my father's shop, because every night, lying in bed, I was fully focused, body and soul, on inventing new designs for my work. In the morning, I sought to bring them to fruition, lest I forget, Heaven forbid, some tiny detail that would present an obstacle in my path. As time passed, my father discovered talent in me, not only for fashioning the same ordinary everyday items, but also for inventing new designs. Those same pieces of jewelry that I designed made a great impression on my father, and I remember that many of the goldsmiths were interested in these pieces and were amazed at the way they were produced.

One day, my father instructed the supervisor of materials to give me a piece of gold so that I could make out of it a piece of jewelry according to my wisdom and creativity. I succeeded to produce the piece of jewelry,

---

fees were twenty Ottoman lira for the eleven-month academic calendar, with another lira for laundry services. The school had fifteen teachers for ninety students.

85. Avraham Chelouche is listed among the students with outstanding results in the series of public examinations held at the beginning of the school year in 1882. One of the exam days had a public audience of five hundred in attendance. *Havatzelet*, 13 September 1882.

and it was named after me: "the Yosef Eliyahu Invention." Gradually I turned into a craftsman and sold my handiwork, and all my earnings were allocated to me as per my father's directive. Out of my passion to earn money on my own, both my industriousness and my savings grew, since I had no need for expenses, as my parents took care of me out of love. They raised and educated me as best they could.

In the beginning of the summer of 1882, the first pioneers from Russia and Romania, who arrived as emissaries and individuals to scout out the land with the aim of establishing a Hebrew colony in the Land of Israel, paid a visit to my father's home. At Father's home they sought advice on all their first steps in settling the Land of Israel. I remember the most important among them, such as Yitzhak Moshe Brenner, the head of the committee for Yesud Hama'ala of Jews in Romania, and the elderly Zvi Levontin, Z. D. Levontin, and Freiman, who were among the first pioneers settling the Land of Israel.[86] That year they founded the Pioneers of Yesud Hama'ala association, and they purchased a plot of land from 'Ayun Kara,[87] on which they built the colony Rishon LeZion.[88]

I remember that when they arrived in the country, they first entered our home at the hour when we were in the house of prayer. Some Jews in the community escorted them and led them to our synagogue. From the beginning the encounter was strange, as they remained standing and surveying the crowd of worshippers. Then a few of them drew closer and kissed the ark and looked at what was written on the ornamental curtain. Nevertheless, despite this, the members of our community viewed them with suspicion, as they thought they were like the English missionar-

---

86. Brenner was a wealthy merchant from Romania. Zvi Levontin (1832–1898) was a wealthy Russian merchant who put up most of the money to purchase the land. His nephew Zalman David Levontin (1856–1940) became an important Zionist official, managing first the Jewish Colonial Trust and then the Anglo-Palestine Bank in Jaffa, which he headed for over twenty years. Ya'akov Peretz Freiman (1851–1920) was a Warsaw businessman who immigrated to and emigrated from Palestine several times before ultimately returning to Poland.

87. This was the name of the original Palestinian village lands and remained the name by which Ottoman officials referred to the settlement.

88. Rishon LeZion (literally, "First to Zion") was the second Jewish agricultural settlement established in the nineteenth century, after Petah Tikva. Yosef Navon, a Sephardi Jew from Jerusalem, facilitated the land purchase, and Haim Amzalak (sometimes spelled Amzaleg) registered the land in his name.

ies,[89] who were in the practice of coming and hunting for souls, and only for the sake of appearances would they honor our holy ark.

When the prayers ended, members of the delegation approached my father and introduced themselves as Jews, saying that they wished to speak with him. My late father immediately rose to his feet and, along with a few other elders of the community, walked down to our house accompanied by the guests. They escorted them to the spacious balcony that was adjacent to two large rooms that had been prepared for a decent and suitable tenant who was appropriate to live together with our family. At my father's command, chairs and a table were brought, and coffee and sweets were set out in accordance with the customs of hospitality.

In the eyes of our elders, it was a wonder to see people wearing elegant European clothing with hats on their heads; some of them wore glasses and all were speaking in Hebrew, which was well understood in our community. Were they really Jews or English missionaries? This was the talk of the day throughout our Jewish center. My father was overjoyed when he spoke with these pioneers of Hovevei Zion[90] for a few hours and he understood that this was a group of notable Jews from Russia who came to tour the land in order to purchase a plot and to settle on it.

How happy he was to hear that their goal was to research if there was a possibility for Jewish families to settle on the land and find serenity in the land of our forefathers. My late father responded with utmost pleasure to their request for his help and that he arrange an office for them among the Jews. Without thinking for long and trembling with joy, my father offered them these two rooms, including the balcony, at their disposal. The guests very much appreciated my father's sentiments and out of their great pleasure at this first success, they offered him some money, but my father was firm: Your movement devoted to the revival of the Jewish *yishuv* in the Land of Israel is very dear to me.

My father furnished the rooms in which these first pioneers lived,

---

89. The London Society for the Promotion of Christianity among the Jews, also known as the London Jews' Society, established a mission in Jaffa in 1844, six years after it first began proselytizing in Jerusalem. Missionary activity in Palestine was a source of deep anxiety among the small Jewish communities, as they offered resources (education, food, housing) to impoverished community members in exchange for their conversion.

90. Literally, "Lovers of Zion." This organization was established in Russia in 1881, and many of its members arrived in Palestine as settlers in the 1880s–1890s.

which included the respectable gentlemen: Brenner, Levontin, and Freiman (and three other people whose names I regrettably cannot recall). All the gatherings were held in our house, which is where the important Zionist work was conducted. On holidays and on the Sabbath, some of them would dine with us, while others traveled to Jerusalem to celebrate the holidays. The tables were always filled with papers and notebooks and rubber stamps, and most were disorganized. They spent about three months in our house before parting from us with affection and admiration. But my family and many members of our community were left with a strange impression: these Jews, pioneers of such an important Jewish movement, whose actions were respectable and sincere, who related to both young and old from our community with the utmost courtesy, who gave generously to all downtrodden and bitter souls and shared their fate, why did they not fulfill the desire of our Father in Heaven and put on tefillin?

Their minds could not rest over this issue, and it was expressed in doubts and negative speculations: perhaps in truth these people were not really Jews, but instead they were, Heaven forbid, deceivers? This thought lived on long after their departure, until other people arrived in the country to bring to fruition the idea of Jewish settlement in the Land of Israel, the representatives of Hovevei Zion and also from the Bilu association,[91] and the farmers from Ruzhany who were brought by Brill,[92] the editor of *HaLevanon*, who like the former group were also hosted in our home for a short while, and then continued on to the 'Ekron colony and to Gedera, which was established by Hovevei Zion in 1884 with much help from Y. M. Pines.[93]

91. Named after an acronym of a biblical verse (Isaiah 2:5: *Beit Ya'akov lechu venelcha* — O House of Jacob, come, let us walk), the Bilu members arrived from Russia in 1882 and established the settlement of Gedera two years later.

92. Yehi'el Brill (1836–1886) was a journalist and publisher. Born in Russia, he spent several periods in Palestine in between years in Europe. He published his early experiences with Zionist settlement in 1883 in the book *Yesud kama'ala*. The "farmers from Ruzhany" that Chelouche refers to was a group of Jewish farmer immigrants from Belarus who established the settlement of 'Ekron (later, Mazkeret Batya) in 1883.

93. Yehi'el Michal Pines (1843–1913) was a scholar, journalist, and intellectual who moved to Jerusalem in 1878 to work for Montefiore's foundation supporting the Jewish community. As a member of the executive committee of Hovevei Zion, Pines supported their purchase of lands on which to establish the colony of Gedera.

From the first group of the Russian Jewish pioneers who came as the first of the Bilu in 1882, I remember the late Israel Belkind.[94] The Biluim stayed in Jaffa for a few days, paying a few visits to our home and our community, and then went on to Mikve Israel and sometime after that to Rishon LeZion to work there as laborers until they became farmers, some of them in Rishon LeZion and some in Gedera.

Before Passover 1885, my late brother Avraham Haim arrived in Jaffa to spend his school holidays at our home. Arriving at the port, he made his way home, bathed, dressed in European clothing, and then went to see our father. He kissed us and all the workers, and he also shook hands with the translator for the French consul, the late Mitri Jellat,[95] who was present at the time and spoke with him in French. At that moment, I was filled with envy of my brother.

I began thinking of my own future and my own purpose in life; my emotions turned upside down at that hour and I became another person. My soul wondered: Would I ever learn other languages? How much longer would I wear this Arab clothing, and will it become for me an inheritance and tradition, in place of the European clothing that my brother wears? How would I find my place among people of stature, and in which language would I speak with them? Although these were the musings of a youth of fifteen, only a childish jealousy that had stolen its way into my heart and gave me no rest, their influence on the course of my future development and education was great.

Together with his son-in-law David Yellin, Pines published a translation of Ottoman land laws into Hebrew in 1887.

94. Minsk-born Belkind (1861–1929) was a founder of the Bilu movement, a journalist, and an educator.

95. Translators (singular known as *dragoman*, a corruption of the Turkish term *tercüman*) had extraordinary influence in the late Ottoman Empire as they were the key intermediaries between consular officials and local government officers and the local population. Because fluency in a Western language was required, many *dragomen* were Christians who were commonly taught European languages in schools. The Catholic Gelat (also written as Jellad, Jellat, and Gélat) family had decades of consular service; Hanna Carlo Gélat was listed as a French *dragoman* in the 1850s until his death in 1871. Later, a "Martin Gelat," likely the Gallicization of Mitri Gelat, is listed as a French consular *dragoman*. France Ministry of Foreign Affairs, Nantes Archives, CADN/294PO/B/3-b. Martin Gelat was the director of the Messageries Maritimes and the French post during World War I, according to 'Issa al-'Issa.

I felt inertia at work. My mind was overcome with thoughts of my future. I did not reveal to my parents a single thing that was in my heart. In those days I walked around like a shadow, wondering how I might cast off this heavy stone and convey to my father my desire and ambition, even while knowing the three difficult obstacles that stood in my way, which would prevent my father from complying with my request: one, that he discovered my talent for working with gold and silver and began to rely on me; two, Father's situation did not permit him to cover the tuition expenses up front for both me and my brother; and three, my grandmother, my father's mother, who loved me very much, was very attached to me and clung to me with all the strength of her love, and at night I would sleep in her bosom, because I was named "Yosef Eliyahu" after her two sons who drowned in the sea at Haifa as they were arriving in the Land of Israel from Morocco, one of whom was named "Yosef," the other one "Eliyahu." She would not be capable of parting from me.

These hurdles were altogether obvious to me, and I knew that I could not overcome them easily. Nevertheless, due to my overwhelming urge to study and to become someone in life, I began to search for means to prepare the groundwork for accomplishing my goal. These thoughts of my purpose in life, which were hidden in my heart, gave me no rest. I was repulsed by work, I lost all my appetite, and I could not sleep. In those days, I spent a great deal of time sitting alone in the synagogue, immersing myself in the holy books. In the afternoons, I visited the *Beit Midrash* to hear Torah lessons given by the rabbis. This situation continued for about two weeks, until my parents sensed my depressed spirit and tried to persuade me to reveal to them what was troubling my heart. But I remained silent and did not say a word.

One day my late father, who could not come to terms with the fact that his son was in a state of sorrow whose source was unknown to him, ushered me into a separate room after prayers and, passing his pure hands over my forehead, asked me the meaning of the monumental change that he saw in me. It was hard for me to speak, but the kind words of my father, who assured me that he would fulfill any wish if only I would tell him what I desired, shocked me, and I broke down in tears. Out of great love for my father, which grew even stronger in my heart, and my unwillingness to cause him any distress, I revealed to him all that was hidden in my heart, and about the obstacles that were liable to prevent me from realizing my most sacred aspirations.

My father embraced me, and with tears in his eyes from love and happiness, he explained to me that while these were difficult obstacles, a solution could be found. He promised me that in half a year, when my late brother Avraham would complete his studies, he would send me in his place. I kissed his hands and left my father's presence, happy and satisfied that my aspirations in life would be fulfilled.

CHAPTER 4 *My School Days in Beirut*

The Tif 'eret Israel School | Order and discipline at the school | My fellow students | Barukh Cohen, a Karaite Jew from Egypt | Reuven Yehezkel Sasson, from Baghdad | Days and nights spent immersed in study | The headmaster's lesson on ethics | A holiday spent at my father's home | Boredom and idleness | Back to the books | Vacation is over | Again in Beirut | Honors bestowed by the school | I return to Jaffa | The late headmaster Zaki Cohen and the fate of his school

In this chapter, in which I offer a detailed description of the Tif'eret Israel School, which was established and superbly administered by the late, great Zaki Cohen, I consider it my duty to linger and to explain in detail the exemplary manner in which the school was organized and run, which could serve as a model even today. The virtues of this school — at which I had the pleasure of spending some time and which helped to produce many significant alumni, most of whom now serve in senior positions throughout the East and the West — may be attributed to the fact that its directors went to the greatest possible effort to implant and inculcate among the pupils a fierce passion for Torah and wisdom, and to nurture in them perpetual diligence.

After Passover 1886, I began preparing for the voyage to Beirut, where I would study and continue my education; my parents were fully committed to this endeavor. Based on the list provided by the school, they prepared on my behalf clothes and provisions for the journey. Aside from that, they granted me pocket money for my regular expenditures abroad. My late father entrusted me with a check made out to one of the banks in Beirut to cover the school tuition fees, to be paid in advance.

Following my difficult parting from my parents, and especially from my paternal grandmother, who out of grief at my departure took ill and passed away, I sailed on the Egyptian ship the *Khedivate*, together with the late Yosef Moyal, who was accompanying his two sons to Beirut.[96]

---

96. This would have been Moyal's two oldest sons, Shim'on and David. Shim'on

I stopped in the office of the headmaster of the Tif'eret Israel School together with Mr. Yosef Moyal, and I placed in his hands my father's letter and the check, along with my possessions. The headmaster ushered us into the teachers' room and introduced us to them. That same day, examinations were being held for the new students in order to place each pupil in the correct grade[97] according to his level of understanding and knowledge.

Of course, my turn also came, and I was found to be diligent and industrious, and very proficient in Hebrew and religious studies, according to the level expected at that school. However, since I was behind in my knowledge of Arabic and French and was then a youth of fifteen years, the teachers disagreed among themselves about which grade to assign me to. Due to my poor knowledge of foreign languages, I agreed to sit with pupils younger than me, but the teachers comforted me, saying that if I was diligent about my studies, I would be able to move up to a higher grade even in midyear.

The order and discipline in the school, the cleanliness, and the consummate safeguarding of the pupils' health had a strong effect on me. At six o'clock in the morning all the pupils woke up, bathed, and dressed, and then went all together to a large and spacious hall, where they sat on benches, each one at his desk. Inside his closed drawer were his books and writing instruments. They took out their books and notebooks and then prepared their assignments that the teachers had assigned the previous day. When the bell rang, the pupils walked upstairs to the synagogue. The cantor stood in front of the pillar and prayed, and the pupils followed him.

(1866–1915) studied at Zaki Cohen's school for two years, where he reportedly excelled in Arabic and French. He later trained as a doctor at St. Joseph's University in Beirut. At some point Shim'on moved to Cairo, where he studied informally at al-Azhar and became an admirer of the Egyptian reformer 'Abdallah Nadim, after whom he named his eldest son. While in Cairo, Shim'on translated parts of the Talmud into Arabic. After 1908, Shim'on returned to Jaffa, where he became active in journalistic circles, eventually starting a short-lived newspaper *Sawt al-'Uthmaniyya* (Voice of Ottomanism). His wife, Esther Azhari, was a prolific Arabic-language journalist in her own right. David (1880–1953) subsequently earned a law degree in Paris in 1904. He became a key figure in land purchases for the Zionist movement.

97. We have chosen the term *grade* to reflect the linear progression of the school curriculum, although since the youth in Tif'eret Israel enrolled after their primary education, it does not reflect the typical age levels in the American grade system.

At the end of the prayers, the pupils entered the dining hall and from there to the wide courtyard, which was planted with trees and a landscaped garden, to rest and regain their energy for lessons, to converse and amuse themselves, each pupil according to his temperament. After ten minutes the pupils entered a large hall and took dictation of several sentences in Hebrew, French, and Arabic, each language in its own special notebook. Three expert teachers came in and checked the passages, correcting the mistakes and taking note of how much each pupil had progressed from the day before. The teacher awarded progress with a good score and lack of progress with a bad score. Once the pupil received his score, he entered his classroom and continued to write in the three notebooks—three entire pages in the three languages.

The headmaster visited each class starting from the first grade on, going from one pupil to the next and checking his compositions and scores. If they excelled, he praised them in front of the other pupils, and if not, then he criticized them so that they would make an effort to excel in their studies and be regarded among the good pupils. At half past nine, the bell announced the first recess; after a twenty-minute rest, the pupils reentered the large hall. Each pupil prepared his books for French and then entered his classroom. The teacher tested his pupils' grasp of the previous day's material, wrote down his comments, and gave new lessons. At twelve, the pupils went straight to the dining hall, each one at his assigned seat, and ate lunch. Then the older pupils would take turns delivering sermons to the students from the raised stage, alternating between French and Arabic, but on the Sabbath the sermon was given solely in Hebrew by the headmaster, Mr. Zaki Cohen himself.

At the end of the meal, one of the pupils would take a turn in leading the blessing after meals, with everyone following him. For about half an hour, the pupils relaxed in the schoolyard and garden, playing and amusing themselves, and at the sound of the bell the pupils would come in to prepare their lessons in Arabic. Following the first afternoon recess, the pupils would prepare their lessons in Hebrew until half past three, at which time the regular school day ended, and the pupils entered the synagogue to recite the *minkha* prayer. From there, they would go to the large hall, take out their books, and then, in exemplary silence, they would prepare their general assignments until six o'clock, and then the pupils would return to the synagogue to pray the *'arvit*. Following prayers, they would go out for a full hour to the lit courtyard, and when the bell rang, everyone would head upstairs to sleep. Two attendants were awake all night, making the rounds of the pupils' beds to ensure their well-being. The following day would see a repeat of the same schedule and the same routine.

Prompted by my interest in being as diligent as possible in my studies, I made a friend who was my age, whose fluency in French and Arabic surpassed my own; he had spent a full year at the school prior to my own arrival but was not as zealous as myself about catching up to the rest of the class since he was the son of a wealthy Karaite family from Egypt.[98] His name was Barukh Cohen. He sat next to me throughout my studies, and he also walked next to me in line, since we were the same age and were of equal height.

I was never without a book in my hand, neither at mealtimes nor during the rest and relaxation hour. My psychological need to advance in my studies intensified from one day to the next. I was resolved that I would not spend any more time than I had to in this grade, which was inappropriate for my age. With the utmost industriousness, I began reading and studying books until I knew them perfectly, and as a result of my hard work I advanced to sit in the front row of the class. It had only been five weeks, but I felt that I had expanded my knowledge; my eyes opened to see a new world that captured my attention.

When I realized that the teachers were not keeping their promise and were not moving me up to the next grade, I went to see the headmaster and I informed him of my desire; he listened to me but remained silent. He called in the head proctor and asked that he consult on the matter with my teachers and with teachers of the grade I was interested in entering. An hour later, during the morning recess, I was called to the headmaster's office, where I found the head proctor and the teachers. They began to test me, and my answers were well received. I received a new book list and then went to the person responsible for the books and writing instruments, where I signed an invoice presented to me in my late father's name. I received all that I needed and that same day I

---

98. Karaite Judaism emerged in the late eighth to ninth centuries as a rejection of rabbinical Judaism and its codifications in the Mishna and Talmud. Karaism remained important in Egypt through the mid-twentieth century, with its own synagogues, schools, and Arabic language newspapers, although the community numbered only between four and five thousand in the 1930s–1940s. We have been unable to find information about this person.

moved to the new grade. In that grade, I also made a new friend—a boy my age, better than the first—who, like me, aspired to advance in his studies. We became familiar with each other and our mutual affection increased from one day to the next. This friend was Reuven Yehezkel Sasson Salih,[99] who now serves as the minister of finance in Baghdad.

I studied a great deal in my new grade, day and night, with the help of my new friend. The two of us would learn our assignments by heart together. Two months later, we advanced to the third grade, together. What helped us a great deal was the fact that both of us knew Hebrew better than the other pupils, and we could devote our regular Hebrew study hours to studying French and Arabic. When we realized that the exam season was growing near and that we would not manage to accomplish the study of both languages, we decided to dedicate ourselves more to Arabic, as we considered it more critical for our futures, as it was the language of the country.

But our most fervent wish was to be on an equal footing with the others even in French. We came up with the idea of asking the proctors to permit us to continue studying at night, without saying a word about it to the headmaster. And in spite of all the difficulty, namely that each of us slept in a different room with other roommates and that we had to be careful that no other pupil would find out about it, we would wake early every morning, wash up and get dressed, walk over to a hallway between the toilet and the bathroom, which was well lit and was far enough away from the bedrooms that no one would notice us, and then we would study.

The combined effect of all these efforts was that we did very well on the examinations on the two languages but were left tired and gaunt. Being closely connected, we decided to stay together in Beirut despite the custom among natives of the Land of Israel to travel back home for the break and holidays, since the brief vacation would not allow my friend to travel to distant Baghdad and back. I decided not to go see my parents and to stay with my friend Reuven and prepare ourselves for fourth grade. Nevertheless, whatever we were thinking did not come

99. Sir Sassoon Hezkel (1860–1932) was indeed the first finance minister of modern Iraq, from 1920–1925, after which he served in the Iraqi parliament until his death. But he was born in 1860 and, according to biographies, never studied in Beirut. He was the only Jewish finance minister of Iraq, so something is incorrect in Chelouche's account.

to pass. Three days or so before the school break, Mr. Ya'akov Yosef Tawil,[100] an important gold and gemstone merchant in Beirut, came to speak with the headmaster. He had commercial contacts with my father and asked to see me. When I went into the headmaster's office, he informed me of my parents' wish that I head home for the school break.

When I expressed to him my decision to remain in Beirut with my friend in order to prepare for fourth grade, the headmaster jumped up from his seat and called out, politely:

> Is it your idea to complete all your studies all at once? I know what you've been up to, studying during mealtimes and rest hours and bedtime. We have discreetly punished the proctors, although I have not interfered with your deeds, as I admire your pure desire to advance to a level of studies that is appropriate to your age. However, there is a long future ahead of you. Now you have become gaunt and thin, and what will your parents say? That we are not serving enough food at school?
>
> After all, you know what is written in the books of our prophets: "For now I would be lying in repose, asleep and at rest,"[101] "In this vein have those who revere God been talking to one another,"[102] and "Let the lowly eat and be satisfied."[103] From the Hebrew letters of these three biblical phrases we arrive at the number eight—eight hours of sleep and eight hours of study and eight hours of eating and resting. It was on this basis that I founded my school. The teacher passed on to me your request that you receive a new book list, but to my regret, I cannot fulfill your request, because we are to a large extent replacing and changing the syllabus in the new school term, and we ourselves do not yet know which books you will need in fourth grade, which is why I ordered them not to give you any list.

He began to praise me in the presence of Mr. Tawil, making note of my diligence and good behavior and stating that not a single demerit had been recorded against me during my time at the school. But the headmaster also reprimanded me, telling me not to make matters worse

---

100. A man with the family name Tawil was elected to the Beirut communal council in 1909, but we were unable to find out further information about him.
101. Job 3:13.
102. Malachi 3:16.
103. Psalms 22:27.

FIGURE 4.1. *Yosef Eliyahu Chelouche wearing the Ottoman fez and Western suit of a young* effendi, *age sixteen (1886). Chelouche Family Collection.*

and to go easy on myself and my health, for he would regret sending me home to my parents with my face looking so fatigued and irritable. He implored me not to remain at school but to travel home, to rest and then return with renewed vigor. I quickly relayed the news to my friend Reuven Yehezkel and the following day bade him farewell, against my will and with great sorrow.

I arrived in Jaffa two days before Rosh Hashanah and was received with much love by my parents, who looked at me and saw a completely different person, albeit one who was thin and gaunt. I was terribly saddened by the death of my beloved grandmother, in whose bosom I used to fall asleep. My parents comforted me, but a heavy grief took root in my heart. I spent most of my vacation days at home. Not having any of the new books with me, I studied the old ones, and when I had enough of them, I rested completely and slept a great deal.

When the inactivity grew oppressive, I pleaded with my late brother Avraham Haim to search for the books I needed for fourth grade. He found some of them among his books and I diligently began working my way through them. Even he, being a manager, asked me not to do it, saying I would be better off resting after all my hard work. But after he confidently informed me that they would not be changing the syllabus at the school—that it had only been a pretext employed by the headmaster to force me to relax—I realized that I should be preparing for fourth grade. The new books were unfamiliar and difficult for me, but my late brother complied with my entreaties and taught me different sections every evening, even though he was busy all day long at the office or was conducting correspondence.

The days after the High Holidays and the beginning of the school year finally arrived. My parents had new winter clothes made for me and before I parted from them, they had me photographed. This picture of me is a memento of the days of my youth, and I include it here.

A few days later, I was back in Beirut with my Baghdadi friend, who had been extremely bored without me. I showed him the new books I had received from my brother, and he was especially pleased to see them, saying, "These really are the books required for the fourth grade, but you're still missing a few." I asked him how he knew all this. He replied that during the holidays he had been invited to celebrate at the homes of acquaintances. At one home he saw the Arabic teacher, who told him that the school would not be replacing the syllabus in the upcoming term; the headmaster, out of his desire for Pupil Chelouche to rest from his schoolwork, made it up as a pretext. The next day, my friend received his new books, and I got the ones I was still missing, and we entered the fourth grade.

We planned out our schedule so we could be diligent about our studies without breaking the school rules. We did not study at night, and during the short recesses we rested like the other pupils. But we petitioned the school administration to release us from Hebrew-language class, due to the fact that we knew the language better than all the other pupils. After numerous pleas the administration accepted our request, and this helped us quite a bit in our progress. Our fluency in Arabic far surpassed our fluency in French, for two reasons: one, Arabic was the native language of our countries, and two, the Arabic teacher explained and elucidated his lessons very well, whereas the French teacher taught in a more superficial fashion.

In order to develop a passion for learning in the pupil, even the laziest, the school introduced special measures that I have not seen even in our modern schools today.

As I have written above, the pupils entered the large hall every morning and then prepared the lessons the teachers assigned to them. The teacher would test the pupils and mark down each one's score. After the tests, he would remove a notebook from his cabinet in which the names of the pupils are recorded, and next to each pupil's name he would note the score, whether good or bad. All the other teachers in every subject would do the same, and even the chief proctor would give grades on each pupil's behavior.

On Fridays, a designated official would review all the grades, collect all of the lists from all of the teachers, and record on a chart the names of the outstanding pupils and their scores on each subject. Another chart outlined with black lines would mark the names of the indolent and slower pupils, and both charts were hung up in the great hall. Hung on a separate chart were the silver medals of honor, a Star of David drawn on each and every one of them with the imprinting of the words "Tif'eret Israel." Affixed to these medals were ribbons in different shades, such as: for Hebrew, blue; for Arabic, green; for good leadership, white; etc.

Classes ended in the afternoon, when the pupils would bathe and dress in honor of the Sabbath. At three o'clock we would file into the great hall, where we would be greeted by the headmaster. The proctors called up each pupil by name to approach the headmaster; if he was among the outstanding pupils, he would be pinned with a medal of honor, shake the headmaster's hand, and return to his seat. And at the same time, the indolent pupil would be standing across from him on the left side.

For the most part, my Baghdadi friend and I would wear every day of the week about five or six medals of honor, and sometimes even seven, because the pupil was permitted to keep the medal all week long and then only on Friday morning return it to the school official responsible for tabulating the scores and the grade lists. Aside from that, each pupil had a special uniform with the school insignia on it, which he was obliged to have made before beginning his studies. This garment was made according to a uniform design, with copper buttons and a blue hat —the same color as the uniform—that was wrapped with a gold ribbon on which "Tif'eret Israel" was written. The uniforms were worn only on Sabbath days, Sunday afternoons for two hours, and Wednesday afternoons for two hours, for the purpose of taking an excursion outside of school grounds, as well as on the ceremonial occasions to welcome government officials. Outstanding pupils were obligated to wear the medals of honor on their chest whenever they wore their uniforms. Conversely, indolent pupils were forbidden to wear their uniforms that week, and instead they had to wear their normal clothes so that they would stand out to onlookers, who would easily differentiate between the good and the bad pupils. Through these methods, the remedial pupils decreased in number, and even they progressed in their studies.

In late 1887, when the school year ended, my Baghdadi friend and I successfully passed the tests. At a ceremony led by the headmaster, the teachers and visiting dignitaries distributed gifts to the pupils—books with elegant bindings that had the pupil's name printed on it along with the subject in which he had excelled, book after book for each subject. Next to a large table on which the gift books were placed sat the headmaster. One of the dignitaries who had been honored by the headmaster walked up to the table to distribute the gifts and then read aloud from each book the name of the pupil and the specific subject for which he had been awarded the gift. The pupil would approach with reverence, accept his gift, and shake their hands. I recall that my Baghdadi friend and I were honored with seven books, while each of the other pupils received between two and four.

Two days after receiving the books, the school staged a historical play about the Hasmonean period, which was attended by all the pupils and teachers, as well as their families who lived in Beirut. As I sat and watched the play, the headmaster received a telegram sent by my father requesting that I be sent to Jaffa with the Moyal children aboard the *Khedivate* ship for the Passover holiday. We sailed to Jaffa the following day, the Moyal boys and me, along with my possessions, including the gifts and the certificate I had received from the school. I was welcomed at my parents' home with great joy. My father boasted to his visitors about my progress in my studies, and he would sometimes also show his guests the books I had been honored to receive.

The school existed for a mere ten years, and many lamented its closure. The late Zaki Cohen, seeing that so many young people from neighboring countries and even from Europe were streaming to his school, wished with all his soul to improve the school and raise it to the highest standards like he envisioned. But while he had good intentions, to our sorrow he failed in his journey. He purchased a plot of land on a hilltop outside Beirut, investing a great deal of money in it, going into debt for several thousand pounds.

Ultimately, the high interest rate proved his undoing. Despite his many doubts and deep sorrow over his necessary parting from his spiritual child, which he had nurtured with so much faith and devotion, he was compelled to close his school, which caused him a great deal of anguish. He was forced to sell the building at a low price in order to settle his debts, and then he and his family left Beirut penniless and relocated to Egypt. The people in Egypt held the late Zaki Cohen in high esteem and showed him great deference. They appointed his four sons to respectable positions that provided a dignified livelihood to the family. Their father, however, remained in his house shut up in his rooms, studying Torah and mourning his school until his dying day. May these few words serve as a memorial to his exalted soul.

CHAPTER 5 *My Engagement, and My Father-in-Law Rabbi Avraham Moyal*

My engagement at age seventeen | My fair bride Freha Simha | An internal emotional war | Between school and marriage | The night of my engagement | My visit to the home of my father-in-law | With the bride | Relations between me and my bride | Signing the marital conditions without reading what I signed | My father-in-law Avraham Moyal | His pedigree | The first representative of Hovevei Zion from Russia in the Land of Israel | His purchase of land for Hovevei Zion | Receiving kushans *despite the government ban | Assembling the huts in Jaffa | Transferring the huts to the land without a government permit | His proud stand before the pasha in Jerusalem | The buildings are left in place | Continuation of my studies | The beginning of the Jewish* yishuv *outside of old Jaffa*

On one of the intermediate days of Passover, when the Maghrebi rabbi of Jerusalem, Moshe Malka,[104] was our guest in our home, my father praised me in front of the rabbi during the lunch meal and showed him the books I had been awarded by the school administration. Upon hearing these words of praise, the rabbi smiled and said: "The hour has come to seek a bride from a good family for your son." My parents gave their consent and began talking among themselves using abbreviated phrases such that I could not understand the conversation. At five o'clock that afternoon, Rabbi Malka came back to my parents' house and entered into a secret conversation with them. I had the feeling they were talking about me, and everyone was showing signs of agreement and joy at the rabbi's comments.

When I went to my room and began leafing through a book, my dear

104. Malka (d. 1900) immigrated to Palestine from Meknes as a youth. He was a respected rabbi and the author of several religious texts; he also served as an emissary and fundraiser for the Maghrebi community in Jerusalem.

late mother walked in and began kissing me, saying: "We have decided to arrange a match for you with a gentle bride, the daughter of an honorable family, Miss Freha, daughter of the late Señor Avraham Moyal,[105] with whom you are acquainted." I listened to the words of my mother but did not know how to respond to them, for I was struck dumb, and nothing came out of my mouth. I looked down at the ground, utterly silent, sinking deep into my thoughts. When my mother left me, I was left alone, in doubt and in wonder. I was only seventeen, I had just now begun to study, and already my parents were talking seriously about an arranged marriage for me. Nevertheless, I understood well that it was absolutely forbidden for me to dare interfere in my parents' affairs by expressing any opinion on the matter. In those days, young men even older than I did not dare speak with their parents about marriage, but rather trusted them to decide the matter without even asking their opinion. So how could I, a youngster of seventeen, express an opinion to my parents?

I must confess the truth that on the one hand I was happy to be marrying a girl from a good family with a good pedigree, a pretty young woman about whom I had heard good things and with whom I was personally acquainted, albeit from a distance. And so it was that I felt an immediate emotional attachment to her. On the other hand, I had a great desire to complete my studies, and I began to be tormented by an internal emotional struggle. It was hard for me to believe my parents had agreed to marry me off even before I had completed my studies. At the time, it was common practice that a certain amount of time would pass between the engagement and the wedding, and I had no doubt that by the time of my wedding, I would have the opportunity to realize my aspirations and complete my schooling. That thought calmed me and sparked a sort of joy in me, although it remained concealed deep inside me, and I never revealed a thing, not only to my parents—with whom I could not speak about this matter—but even to those to whom I might have been able to bare my conscience.

On the Friday of the intermediate days of Passover, I sensed an un-

---

105. Avraham Moyal (1850–1885) was born in Rabat and immigrated to Jaffa as a child. As Chelouche describes more fully later in this chapter, Moyal aided the Hovevei Zion with their various land settlement projects. Moyal's wife (Chelouche's mother-in-law) was Zimbul, the daughter of Rabbi Yosef Bin-Nun, who had arrived in Palestine from Yenişehir in the 1820s.

usual commotion in our house. My father's shop clerk was coming and going, bringing in various drinks and fruits and sweets, and also bracelets of varying styles so that my mother could choose a pair. I realized that something out of the ordinary was happening because in the kitchen, too, they were not cooking the usual Sabbath fare, but rather larger, more generous amounts. On Friday evening, when the whole family reclined around the table, and after the wine was sanctified and I had shaken the hands of my parents and Rabbi Malka, who was dining with us, the rabbi turned to me and said: "And so, I have selected for you an industrious, beautiful, respectable bride, the daughter of an upright, noble family, Freha al-'aziza,[106] whom you surely know." I blushed with embarrassment and felt goosebumps going up and down my body, and a cold sweat covered my forehead. I remained silent in my seat. From the family's discussion, I understood that according to my parents' request, Rabbi Malka had taken up the matter with the bride's family, who expressed their satisfaction with this match and set the night of the engagement for this Saturday night.

On Saturday night, on the fourth day of the intermediate days of Passover 1887, as I was starting the seventeenth year of my life, I became engaged to my bride, Miss Freha (Simha) Moyal, who is now my wife and the mother of my children, in whose pleasant company I have lived to this very day and with whom I hope to live henceforth.

On the night of our engagement, once I had finished arranging my clothes and my hairdo, suited to the honor of the day, I walked escorted by my entire family to the home of the future in-laws.[107] On the way there, I felt a shiver and a tremor course through my entire body, and a shaking in my limbs. When we entered the in-laws' house, I struggled to brace myself, but I could not control my strong emotions; my body trembled, and my hands were clammy and cold. The parlor was full of men, while the women sat in the other room. They seated the bride next to me, and she remained in her seat until the completion of the "conditions" ceremony.

I was instructed to kiss the hands of her parents and of my parents; she was instructed to kiss my parents' hands and then those of her par-

---

106. Freha the precious.

107. Dar (House of) Moyal was in the Sheikh Ibrahim neighborhood. Bawwab, *Mawsu'at Yafa al-jamila*, 322. Today this is 29 Hatzorfim Street.

ents. However, we were not permitted any physical contact nor even a simple exchange of words. The sum total of contact between me and my bride was only a stolen glance from time to time, which resulted in both of us turning red with embarrassment and emotion, because we were young and inexperienced and did not yet understand life very well.

And so it was, without understanding how or why, the "conditions" that linked our two young souls were signed.[108] On the bride's side they were signed by the late Señor Aharon[109] and the elderly Yosef Moyal, the bride's uncle, and on the other side by my late father and myself, which I signed without reading or knowing what was written in them.

As I write about my engagement and my connection with my wife Freha Simha, daughter of Señor Avraham Moyal, I cannot fail to devote a few lines to her family and her father's home.

The family of Avraham Moyal was a well-to-do family with origins in Morocco who now lived in Jaffa. The head of the family was the elderly late Rabbi Aharon Moyal, who had four sons, the second one being Rabbi Avraham Moyal, father of Shmu'el[110] and my betrothed.

Throughout his life, Señor Avraham Moyal was beloved by all the residents for the good deeds that he performed in the land and for the outstanding noble measures and contributions in which he excelled. He aided tradesmen without means to become established and live in dignity in the land of the forefathers, so they would not leave the Land of Israel and wander to other countries. He opened warehouses and shops for their goods and provided them with the push and the material and moral capacity to advance in their businesses. I still remember three tradesmen whom the late Avraham Moyal aided and helped stabi-

---

108. The marriage contract lays out the financial terms of the marriage.

109. Aharon Moyal (1813–1897/1898) was born to a commercially successful rabbinical family in Rabat. His wife Sa'ada was from the 'Amiel family. After their immigration to Palestine before 1860, Moyal became active in business and land purchases. The family is listed in the 1866 Montefiore census as Amoyal, having arrived in 1854 and owning 40,000 *quruş*, making him by far one of the wealthiest members of the Jewish community at the time. Aharon gained French nationality and appeared in the 1869 *shari'a* registers as working in foreign currency exchange.

110. Shmu'el Moyal (1879–1947), Yosef Eliyahu Chelouche's only brother-in-law from his wife, also studied in Beirut and became a teacher upon his return to Jaffa. Later he lived in an apartment in the Moyal-'Amiel building together with his widowed mother and unmarried sister, adjacent to his uncle David Moyal.

lize their positions. They are: Me'ir Alchemister,[111] owner of the Gold Star pharmacy; Moshe Goldberg,[112] who owned a large clothing store; and the Biton family, for whom he opened an etrog shop. He himself engaged in banking services and financial contacts abroad. Notable citizens of the city would pay him visits each and every day, and he had great influence on the Turkish government.

One of his most important activities that can serve as a symbol and model was the loyal service he rendered to the Hovevei Zion society from Odessa, which he did without any intention of personal gain. As their representative, he purchased estates and land tracts on their behalf. He was compelled to hire a special secretary for correspondence between himself and Hovevei Zion, because his own Solitreo script[113] was unknown to the people from Russia, just as their script was unknown to him. For the purposes of keeping the books and accounts, he hired at a monthly salary paid by Hovevei Zion the late El'azar Rokach,[114] brother of the well-known public figure, the late Shim'on Rokach.[115]

He [Avraham Moyal] purchased many land holdings on behalf of Hovevei Zion, including the colony near Qastina, known as Be'er Tuvia. Thanks to his influence with the government, he received *kushan*s, despite the fact that at the time there was a ban on Jews possessing land, particularly outside of the city and in large tracts of land.[116] Following the purchase of the Qastina–Be'er Tuvia land, Mr. Moyal saw to building several houses and cowsheds on it, but the government did not see

---

111. Alchemister (1854–1931) was born in Ukraine and immigrated to Jerusalem in 1875/1876. He was a pharmacist at the Misgav Ladach hospital before moving to Rishon LeZion to serve as pharmacist there. After some years he moved to Jaffa and worked as a pharmacist.

112. Goldberg (1863–?) was born in Russia and was one of the founders of a joint Ashkenazi-Sephardi Jewish craftsman society; he later joined the Masonic lodges Barkai/Shafaq and Port de Solomon's Temple.

113. This was the distinctive cursive style used by Sephardi Jews, which differed from the Rashi block script familiar to Ashkenazi Jews.

114. El'azar Rokach (1854–1914) was a journalist and newspaper editor from a prominent Hasidic family in Jerusalem.

115. Shim'on Rokach (1863–1922) was a tax farmer, a leader in the tiny Ashkenazi Jewish community in Jaffa, a citrus farmer, and a founder of Neve Tzedek neighborhood.

116. Ottoman land policy fluctuated from 1881–1914, with intermittent efforts to clamp down on foreign Zionist land purchases.

fit to permit the construction of any kind of building.[117] The obstacle was raised by the pasha in Jerusalem, and Mr. Moyal went there to meet with him and ask for his help. But the pasha held his ground, saying that he was not permitted to authorize the construction of any buildings, as he held in his hands a telegram from Constantinople that ordered him to forbid Jews to possess the land and build on it. Mr. Moyal asked the pasha: "Didn't we already purchase the land and have in our possession a *kushan*, so how is that you will not allow us to build houses on it and live in them?" "That is the fault of the *kaymakam* in Jaffa," replied the pasha, "who authorized all of this and thus he bears the responsibility."

Mr. Moyal was not satisfied with the pasha's answer, and asked a second time: "But after all, the land now belongs to us, we have paid the peasants what it is worth, so how is it that the government will not permit us now to settle on the land, work the land, and make it arable?" Nevertheless, the pasha would not budge: "I will under no means authorize it." When Mr. Moyal realized that his appeals would not bear fruit, and that his pleas were in vain, he returned to Jaffa. He contemplated the matter, considering what to do next. He had already informed Hovevei Zion about the purchase of the land, and they had asked him to build homes and cowsheds on it for the few families who were ready to immigrate to the land and settle it.

He decided to order a large quantity of lumber and placed it in the city square that belonged to his father, on which today are built the *tabu* [property registry] office, the courthouse for land, Banco di Roma, and the Ottoman Bank, although at the time, there were no buildings at all on this piece of land. He then hired carpenters to build five huts, and they raised them on the property, complete with roof tiles, hooks, locks, etc. As soon as the families arrived in the country, he dismantled the huts and loaded them onto camels, together with the roof tiles, and the families rode right behind them, along with several workers and Moyal's own men. Within a few days they assembled the huts, arranged in two rows, and each family moved into their home.

117. Since Moyal died in 1885 and this settlement was founded only in 1887, it is probable that Chelouche mistakenly attributed the story to Qastina; the settlement to which the structures were sent was actually 'Ekron, a colony with whose founding Moyal was deeply involved in 1884.

After two weeks, a telegram was received by the Jaffa *kaymakam* from the pasha, instructing him to send Mr. Moyal to Jerusalem immediately. When Moyal arrived in Jerusalem and stood before the pasha, the latter became enraged and shouted: "How dare you do such a thing, building without government permit?" "But I did not build," Mr. Moyal responded. "I only assembled huts, and for that one does not require a permit." "Nevertheless," the pasha angrily yelled, "you are liable to be prosecuted in a criminal case for violating the laws of the state. Aside from that, you will have to demolish the huts immediately."

Mr. Moyal then rose from his seat and said to the pasha, with great emotion: "I have nothing to add to what I have already said to you. If the government disagrees with what I've done, you can appeal to the French consul, for I am his subject," he said, and turned to leave.[118] But the pasha detained him and said: "My mind is now at rest. Believe me that from the start my wish was actually to help you, but the orders I received from Constantinople prevented me from doing so, and because you did something contrary to the wishes of the government, I became responsible, which is why I spoke harshly to you. However, since you are a French subject, the responsibility does not fall on me after all. As far as you are concerned, it is now clear to me that you acted wisely, as you had no other choice." And Mr. Moyal parted from the pasha with affection.

It was in this manner that Mr. Moyal worked for the benefit of his brethren, without submitting to the will of high officials or people in power, whenever the affairs of his people and his land required him to do so. It was only thanks to his remarkable energy, talents, and thorough understanding of the ways of the land that he significantly assisted in the development and blossoming of the Jewish *yishuv* in the Land of Israel.

Moyal's important and invaluable work on behalf of Hovevei Zion and their first steps was acknowledged and highly appreciated by the leaders of Hovevei Zion in Russia, Y. L. Pinsker and M. L. Lilienblum.[119] And

---

118. The issue of foreign subjects and protégés residing in Ottoman lands — and more specifically, the intervention of foreign consular officials on their behalf — was a chronic headache for Ottoman provincial officials as well as the central government.

119. Yehuda Leib (Leon) Pinsker (1821–1891) was a physician who became a prominent Zionist intellectual in Odessa after the 1881 pogroms, when he published a widely read call for Jewish "auto-emancipation." He was a founder and leader of Hovevei Zion. Moshe Leib Lilienblum (1843–1910) was a Russian intellectual of the *Haskala* (Jewish "Enlightenment") who joined the Hovevei Zion and served as its secretary.

in the literature of Hovevei Zion from that period, they expressed more than once their deep gratitude to this estimable man of his people, who worked tirelessly for the sake of establishing and expanding Hovevei Zion's first Hebrew colonies in the Land of Israel.

But not many years passed before Hovevei Zion suffered a great setback with Moyal's sudden death. He had been Hovevei Zion's general supervisor and stood at the head of its work in the land. He was known for his outstanding talent in the administration of the colonies and he gave Hovevei Zion hope for numerous actions and good outcomes in the matters of the *yishuv*, for he himself was a fervent Hovev Zion—a Lover of Zion—devoted to the idea with all of his heart and with all of his power, who made every effort to improve the lot of the farmers and who stood by them in their hour of need.

Following Moyal's sudden death, all of Hovevei Zion's activities in the Land of Israel might have been lost had another man not been found to fill the gap at this difficult time, himself an accomplished man with many talents, who acceded to their request to take upon himself the administration of Hovevei Zion affairs in the Land of Israel immediately after Moyal's death. While this man was not as impassioned and devoted a Lover of Zion as Avraham Moyal, he did possess some important virtues. That man was Shmu'el Hirsch,[120] the director of Mikve Israel and the primary agent for handling the affairs of Baron Edmond de Rothschild[121] in the Land of Israel during the latter's first steps in the settlement of the land.

We have mentioned only a miniscule share of the tremendous work performed by Avraham Moyal for the benefit of settlement of the Land of Israel, and whoever writes the chronicles of the *yishuv* will most certainly need to devote a substantial and beautiful chapter to him.

Following my engagement, my sole desire was to clarify the date that had been set for my wedding, for I innocently enough believed that my parents had it postponed for a long enough period that I would be able to complete my education. Similarly, I was interested in finding out the

120. Hirsch (1845–1925), born in Alsace, taught in several AIU schools in the region before serving as the director of the AIU agricultural school, Mikve Israel, from 1879–1891.

121. Rothschild (1845–1934) was a member of the prominent Rothschild banking family based in Paris. He helped finance the early colony Rishon LeZion and other early Zionist endeavors.

amount of dowry I would be given. Many days passed and I was too embarrassed to ask any of my family members about it, even though for me, knowing this information had become vital. But from family discussions, over time everything that had been unclear to me was clarified. I knew that my wedding date would be no later than the Sukkot holiday, and that the dowry I would be getting was a sum of 200 gold napoleons and 4,000 francs in cash, proper garments for the bride, and furniture for the room in which I would live following my marriage.

On the other hand, my honorable father had committed to seeing to my living expenses in his home for no less than five years. I was in complete agreement with all of this except for the date of the wedding. I was especially sad that I would not be able to attend the seventh grade, because one needed a full two years to accomplish that goal. But what could I do, since not only was I forbidden to oppose my parents but even to voice a single word that might reveal my private opinion on the matter? And I had only two weeks left until my return to school. I found myself in a difficult life struggle.

On the one hand, my soul had been drawn together with that of my future wife, and I aspired to see her at the very least before my return to school, although in those days such a thing was absolutely forbidden. As for me, given my immaturity, I was embarrassed to meet with my betrothed, a girl of fifteen, but the feelings that I had for her compelled me to try and see her without her noticing me, as she stood at the window of her home or as she passed by on her way somewhere. But over these two weeks, I managed to see her face only twice: once when she was walking up the stairs of her home and another time in the market, while she was buying silk thread, but of course, each time we were both embarrassed and did not exchange a single word.

Following the engagement, my late brother Avraham Haim accompanied me to the home of my future in-laws to kiss their hands, as was the custom then, and they seated the bride next to me. They offered us fruits and sweets, but given my extreme shyness I cannot even remember if I tasted them, because I was in a state of distress. I was so happy to be sitting next to my bride, but on the other hand I was overcome by immense sluggishness and was unable to maintain control over my excited soul or my embarrassment.

On the day that I traveled to Beirut, I was ushered over to my in-laws' home a second time, to bid farewell to them and to my bride. I shook everyone's hands and kissed the hands of the older people, all but that of my bride. I also did not say goodbye to her, for even that was forbidden at the time; none of those present encouraged me to do so, but both of us felt in our hearts and in our pure consciences the nature of this farewell that linked us together for eternity. I sailed [from] there on a Russian ship and arrived safely at school.

Already on the first day of school, my Baghdadi friend and I worried about our studies. We heard that the administration decided to open a new accounting course in Arabic, for the sixth and seventh grades. But we were only at the beginning of fifth grade, and wouldn't be able to take the course, which we considered critical for both of us but for me in particular, as I had no more than six months left in school. We consulted with others, and then decided to go to the headmaster to ask him to let us take the Arabic-language course with the sixth-grade pupils even though we were in the fifth. With great difficulty, after we passed several tests, the headmaster finally gave his consent, especially once he found out that I was already engaged and was to be married half a year later. We were given the list of books and notebooks and began to study. I was particularly interested in learning accounting.

Our studies were difficult that term, and despite our lack of desire to violate the school rules, we were obliged, in order to catch up with the other pupils in our grade, to influence the dormitory attendant and the proctor to move my friend's bed from his room to mine, and to place his bed next to mine. All the dormitory rooms were lit up by candle wicks in glasses that were filled mostly with water and partly with oil, which floated to the top of the glass. The candle in our room would shed its light in the corner across from our beds, but we convinced the attendant to move it to the corner near our beds, arguing that if the headmaster asked about it, they should answer him that the change was needed because the draft blowing in from the window was extinguishing the flame.

Our routine was to wait for the other children to fall asleep, at which point we would start to study, learning our lessons by the dim light of the candle. Whenever we sensed footsteps near our room, we hid the books lest someone notice what we were doing. Before dawn we would review and fall asleep again, until the attendants woke us at the regular time in exchange for the set payment that they would collect from us. Thanks to these arrangements, we succeeded in catching up to the rest of our grade and we completed the accounting course together with the sixth grade.

The only thing is that the faint light in which we conducted our studies seriously damaged my eyesight, which remains weak to this day.

When the term ended, we sat for examinations and passed them successfully. It was very difficult for me to part from my Baghdadi friend, who was like a brother to me in love and affection. We broke down in tears when we realized that we would not meet again, spending time with one another in the safe shelter of the school. I returned home safely aboard a Turkish ship that weathered stormy sea conditions. I found my family rejoicing and happy, preparing to celebrate my wedding fifteen days later, but only I was missing, as they still had to buy me new clothes in my size and prepare me for the wedding day.

By the year 1883, the city of Jaffa began to develop. Some Jews built themselves houses outside the city, throughout the area where the Neve Shalom neighborhood is today. We changed our residence from a building called Dar al-Qal'a to a building belonging to Señor Maimon 'Amiel, which was connected to the Aharon Moyal building, and in which we lived for a few years.[122] Day by day several new buildings were added outside the city, and my esteemed father, who owned many plots of land, feared that Tanus Nasr, who had forcibly taken some of the land that we owned in partnership with Moyal and Amzalak, would touch the rest of the land. In order to put an end to the machinations of this good-for-nothing, my father decided to construct a building that would prove that the land on which it was built had an owner.

In 1883, he began building his first house outside the city. At first, he considered building only two rooms and all the conveniences, but subsequently, during the planning and construction process, he gradually enlarged the building, which over time became a decent five-room house with a spacious yard surrounded by a well-arranged fenced garden.[123] At the same time when others also built new buildings in the same area and the new *yishuv* outside of the city was beginning to take form, my father decided to construct a second story and renovate the

---

122. This building was in the commercial center of town, right above the Money Changers' Market (*Suq al-Sarrafin*).

123. This building, which stood at the heart of the Manshiya/Neve Shalom neighborhood, became part of the Manshiya police headquarters in the 1930s. On 1 May 1948, it was detonated to the ground by members of the Etzel Jewish militia as a part of their military operation to occupy Jaffa, two weeks before the end of the British Mandate of Palestine.

house so that we could live there on our own, for two reasons: one, the light was pure and healthy, and two, to motivate other Jews to purchase land, build houses on it, and settle in them.

In late 1886, construction of the house was completed, but my late father did not properly improve it because the building was some distance from the city and the family did not agree to live in it. Time passed, the house was improved but was not rented out; my father hired a watchman to guard the property and also work in the garden, while more buildings were being built to the extent that many families moved to live outside the city. In 1887, the year that I got engaged and the date of my wedding, which was set for Sukkot, my father decided that the time had come to move into the new house. It was improved and painted such that it became the most beautiful house in the whole area, and the rooms were furnished. We moved in two weeks before my wedding. On the top floor, [my father] set up rooms for my brother and me, and for guests, as well as a reception hall and a spacious balcony for "Sukkat Shlomo."[124] And on the lower floor, he arranged rooms for the rest of the family and for guests, aside from a large room for the synagogue.

From the day we built this first house, the Jewish *yishuv* began to leave old Jaffa, emerging from the city's narrow confines into the great and deserted space that awaited the arrival of loyal builder-sons who would come to revive it, make it fertile, and settle it with Jews whose sole ambition was to hold on to a piece of land in the land of the forefathers.

---

124. He is referring to the *sukkah* constructed during the Feast of the Tabernacles, a commemoration of the exodus from Egypt when families are instructed to eat outdoors under a temporary wooden hut. There is a typo in the original.

CHAPTER 6 *My Wedding, and My Entry into the World of Commerce*

I receive the dowry | The wedding | My work in commerce and industry | My store and the Hebrew colonies | The establishment of Neve Tzedek | My experience with architectural planning | Dedicating myself to the construction trade | I become a father | Antiquities of our land | Sinking of the Russian ship Chikhachev *in Jaffa | My father's efforts to rescue the passengers | The Russian consul Timofeev | Ze'ev Tiomkin thanks my father for his significant help in rescuing the pioneers*

About three days before the scheduled day of my wedding, the future in-laws invited us to their home in order to see the garments that had been tailored for my fiancée, the gifts, and the furniture. At the time, it was the norm to prove to the guests that the bride's parents had meticulously fulfilled their promises and met all the conditions of the engagement. We sat down and were treated to fruits and sweets.

An emissary called my father and me over to the elderly Señor Aharon Moyal, of blessed memory. He received us warmly and we had a pleasant conversation. Then he opened the iron safe and removed from it a cache of gold coins. He grabbed my hand and opened it, ordering me to count. He started to count into my hand 400 half-napoleons. When he was finished, he put the coins in a sack, tied it up well, and placed it in my possession. I kissed his hands and then we went to sit down with the other guests. The garments were sealed into trunks and porters were called in to convey them to our home, in order to arrange them in a special room that had been selected as our apartment. We then gave our farewells until we met again on the wedding day.

My late cousin Yehuda Carsenty was very pleased with the match and wanted to arrange a beautiful wedding for us. However, there was some difficulty due to the fact that there was an obligation to hold the wedding ceremony at the home of the bride and from there go to the groom's house, which was outside the city. Back then, due to the relative barrenness, the distance between the two seemed greater than it actually was. In those days, horse-drawn carriages were not yet available in Jaffa. Only the late Alexander 'Awad,[125] who opened a large tourist hotel, had acquired seven carriages, one for himself and six for tourists staying at his hotel. The late Yehuda Carsenty paid 'Awad a visit and invited him to the wedding; he requested that he rent him the wagons in order to convey guests from the bride's home to the groom's home. The late Alexander 'Awad, who knew well the Moyal and Chelouche families as respected members of the Jewish community in Jaffa, and being the generous-hearted man that he was, sent the seven carriages on the appointed day and at the appointed hour, with the carriages and the horses decorated with greenery and flowers.

The finest and most respected residents of the city, Jews and non-Jews, came to the wedding at the bride's home. As per custom, when the ceremony ended at the bride's home, we were conveyed in carriages to our own home, located today at the far end of Neve Shalom, across from the Feingold Houses, a house that now belongs to Mr. Ben-Zion Amzalak.[126] The celebration at our home continued all week long, with guests visiting us each and every day, both from our family's side and their family's side. Thus, I set out into the field of life, bearing the yoke of a family, a youth of seventeen years, and my wife, may she live a long life, who was fifteen years old.

Being a young man without a profession, after my wedding I began to ponder the difficult life question of how I might establish myself in a business that would enable me to meet the needs of my family. While I had gained some expertise in silversmithing and goldsmithing, I derived no spiritual satisfaction from it as I did not aspire to be a tradesman, but rather my ambition was to learn and to pursue my education. To my great sorrow, I did not have a chance to complete my studies, as my mar-

---

125. Iskandar 'Awad (Alexander Howard in English) was a prominent Maronite Christian, Thomas Cooke agent, and hotelier with modern tourist hotels in Jaffa as well as Jerusalem; he was decorated by several foreign governments.

126. Amzalak (1865–1934) was born in Jerusalem and moved to Jaffa to work in the ready-made clothing business. He was a nephew of Haim Amzalak, whose daughter, Luna Bulissa, he married. Both Amzalaks were occasional business partners with Aharon Chelouche. ISA, Jaffa Court of First Instance, 11 April 1900.

riage firmly separated me from the school I longed to attend and from my efforts to persevere in my studies.

My parents grew concerned about me and my future, as especially did my late cousin Yehuda Carsenty, who loved me very much, and who lived in our home for two months after my wedding. When we would recline around the table discussing various subjects, the conversation would come around to the issue of my future. The late Carsenty expressed his opinion that since construction in Jaffa was with each passing day becoming more extensive, particularly in the Neve Shalom neighborhood, and since construction materials and all of the things required for buildings, such as locks, hooks, paint, and nails, could only be found in Jaffa in the shop of the German merchant named Aberle,[127] who was growing wealthy from the sale of these items, he therefore proposed to my father that they open a similar store for Yosef Eliyahu, for the sale of construction materials. My father agreed to this suggestion, which he found to be quite timely, even though it was not yet clear to him how to turn the idea into reality.

The late Carsenty promised to learn in detail the conditions of this commerce, to ascertain the suppliers from which it was possible to order these goods, and to find out which of them we should contact. Knowing that it would take him a great deal of time to conduct the correspondence with foreign countries, he requested from my father to seat me in his office next to his desk, and that I work as a money changer until his proposal for opening the business could be realized. He justified his opinion that it was not good for me to be inactive, whereas for the time being it was important to learn the currency exchange rates and to acquire an understanding of and knowledge in accounting.

In 1887, I became a money changer,[128] and my place of business was my father's office. At the time, currencies of different countries were

127. The Templer Paul Aberle (1842–1922) had a shop for iron products in Jerusalem and Jaffa; this became the largest German commercial enterprise in Palestine.

128. According to the Jaffa *shariʿa* court registers, this was a very common profession for North African Jews in the 1880s–1890s. In addition to his father's position in the field, Yosef Eliyahu's maternal grandfather and uncles were also listed as working as money changers, as were his wife's father and grandfather. Al-Bawwab lists dozens of Jewish money changers from the court registers while using very distasteful and derogatory language in discussing their role in this industry.

used in the city, in silver, in gold, and in paper notes, and the understanding of this business enriched those who possessed it.

I was very undecided when it came to developing my new business. For anything too difficult I consulted with my esteemed late father and also frequently sought the advice of money changers in the same market. They always complained that I was buying foreign currencies at a high price, which left me with only a modest profit, whereas I could be making a higher profit, because the other money changers were not making do with less, as I did. I told my father about their complaints toward me, and he exhorted me not to follow the example of others by asking for greater than the value of said currency according to that day's exchange rate, "because that would be considered theft. The blessing in commerce is only through honesty and trust. You won't stay in this business for long, since this is a temporary occupation, but you must pursue it until we can order construction materials for you from abroad."

I listened to my father's advice and followed the path that he charted for me, and as time passed, I felt that I was successful in my endeavors, as the number of people wanting to do business with me increased from one day to the next. Similarly, the big money changers talked among themselves about the young money changer whose business was growing with each passing day. I conducted my business with honesty and trust, with the help of God, who guided me along his righteous path.

Three months later, the late Yehuda Carsenty came and informed my father that there was a French Christian man, a broker and shipping agent named Barrellet,[129] who had catalogs from various suppliers abroad that sold construction materials. He was willing to make every possible accommodation, but he himself did not know which construction materials would be needed in Jaffa. In order to learn exactly which materials were needed in the city, the late Carsenty found a man who had worked the previous year for Aberle, the German merchant who was proficient in this area of commerce. Carsenty offered the man a sum of money to review the catalogs and prepare a detailed list, in accordance with which he would order the merchandise from Mr. Barrellet. When the clerk was finished, my father, Carsenty, the clerk, and I all went to Mr. Barrellet and discussed with him the quality of the merchandise, the

---

129. Marius Barrellet also served for some years as the agent of the Crédit Lyonnais bank.

conditions, and the date by which the goods would be received. The late Carsenty proposed to Mr. Barrellet that, given the fact that the merchandise would arrive three or four months later, it would be desirable if the owner of the goods could work in his office as a clerk, not for any remuneration, but solely so that he could master the ways of commerce. Mr. Barrellet agreed to this proposal, and we parted on good terms.

A few days later, we changed all the coins we had in the register into gold napoleons and found that the net profit was 60 gold napoleons. I was not too happy with the profit, which I thought was meager given all the hard work, the slow counting and recounting every day and every hour, painstakingly calculating and thoughtfully deliberating on how to run the business. I thought that I must have made a mistake in my calculation, so I recounted several times, but I arrived at the same amount. Only my father was content with this profit, and he explained that money changing cannot be any more profitable than this.

In late 1888, I began working as a clerk for Barrellet, without salary, in order to learn the business of commerce from him. He sat me down with his experienced clerk As'ad 'Araktinji,[130] whom he asked to instruct me in each of the tasks that he performed.

Under 'Araktinji's tutelage, I plumbed the depths of office work. I faithfully carried out all the tasks assigned to me. Sometimes he would send me to the *gumruk* [customs house], since over time I learned the office's affairs at the customs house, until they finally appointed me to handle them regularly. I would board the ship and register goods according to their serial numbers and the certificates of trade that were marked on every trunk or package. Barrellet, the director, would occasionally observe me from a distance and was satisfied with my work that I carried out with precision and dedication. He expressed his great affection for me in every case and opportunity. I recall that in January 1889, on the New Year of the Christians, Barrellet's store was closed, and all the Christian clerks, wearing their holiday best, went to visit the director and shake his hand. I joined them, dressed in my Sabbath clothes, to express my good wishes. On that day he presented me with a gift, a green silk box from which he took out a gold chain that he then placed on my

130. The Greek Orthodox 'Araktinji family was prominent in business and trade, and was related through marriage to the Beiruti family, about whom Chelouche also writes. As'ad 'Araktinji (1872–1934) joined the Freemason lodge Barkai/Shafaq, where his brother Cesar was the grand master.

chest. I thanked him with a warm handshake and remained with him to celebrate the holiday at his home.

Three months later, when the merchandise finally arrived from abroad, and with it the various bills, my father and my cousin began to think practically about opening a shop for me. They opened the store in the new building that Iskandar 'Awad had just completed, adjacent to the main entrance to his hotel. My store was located in this building for thirty-nine years, and it was only in the middle of 1923 that my son Avner relocated my store to Tel Aviv.[131]

My initial steps in the business world were no bed of roses. This was a hard business, not only for me but for experienced merchants as well. However, I placed my trust in God and began to engage in commerce. I hired an assistant, and for the accounting and correspondence I appointed the late Yitzhak Barukh, the son of my uncle Yehezkel Barukh,[132] who at the time was a well-regarded Arabic-language accountant. I issued the invoices in French myself.

Once a few months had passed, I felt that the business had a chance of stabilizing my situation and ensuring my livelihood, although it is also true that there were no buyers for some of the inventory that I had purchased, and I was astonished that Mr. Najib Sabbagh[133] had suggested ordering it. Did he deceive us, or did he simply not know, and had professed to possess expertise in a profession in which he had none? What's more, I was aware that all the merchandise I had ordered through Barrellet, who was a subject of France, came from French factories whose wares may have been of high quality, but were also high in cost, while at the same time the goods that were imported from Germany may have been more plain but were also less expensive. And, of course, in order to import them one was forced to order them solely via a German broker, and in the entire city of Jaffa there was only one broker, a cousin of Aberle, who happened to sell the same goods in his own store. This competition with him meant that he would not be especially interested in ordering these goods for me.

131. This was on 'Awad Street (today's Razi'el Street), the new commercial center of modern Jaffa.

132. The elder Barukh was listed as a scribe in the 1875 Montefiore register, and he was also listed as a money changer in the *shari'a* court.

133. We have been unable to find information about him, other than that the Sabbagh family were Greek Catholics.

Nevertheless, I began to look around for different ways to build up my business. On a few occasions I traveled to Jerusalem, where I bought some goods from the father of Perlman,[134] a man who served as a sort of rabbi to his community and who charged me reasonable prices for all the goods I needed. I placed my trust in him and regularly bought from him, without my having to travel, but rather through an exchange of letters. Over time, I came to understand that there was a broker in Jerusalem named Singer,[135] who also had connections with Germany, and that everyone in the country ordered through him, including Aberle from Jaffa. I discerned that fact during my stay in the hotel in Jerusalem, from a man who worked for Singer.

The following day, I made my way to Mr. Singer's office, which I found to be a tumult of human activity, with several rooms filled with clerks occupied by their work. I started looking for the office manager and found my way to one room where an important-looking person sat by a desk on which the documents were neatly arranged. I spoke with him in French, and he responded in German and pointed at the adjacent room, toward a man who was not as good-looking as him and on whose desk the papers were scattered about in disorder. I walked up to him and struck up a conversation. I told him the story of my business, starting with the day I opened my store. I felt that he was sympathetic toward the simple and innocent style of my words. I informed him of my interest in ordering merchandise from Germany through him, and that since I was young and still lacked experience in the practices of commerce, I was trusting him to set reasonable and inexpensive prices for me so that I would remain one of his regular customers.

Mr. Singer called over one of his clerks and ordered him to arrange with me the order that I needed, but I addressed him directly and simply and said: "I am not interested in having a clerk do the work without you being present." He looked at me and smiled: "Look at the stack of letters

---

134. Elimelekh Perlman immigrated to Jerusalem in 1845 as a young child. A prominent member of the Hasidic community, he owned an iron and building materials shop in Jerusalem for decades. Both of his sons, Shlomo and Barukh, worked in the same business with him, so it is unclear to whom Chelouche is referring.

135. Albert Singer had offices in Jerusalem and Jaffa. Among its imports was a specialization in clay roof tiles imported from Marseille. The firm was mentioned in the *Konstantinopler Handelsblatt* v. 9 (3 February 1904) and it was a dues-paying member of the Jerusalem chamber of commerce upon its founding in 1908.

on my desk. I still must respond to them today, and my time is limited. Nevertheless," he added, after some thought, "come back to me today at two o'clock and I myself will arrange everything for you." I thanked him with a warm handshake and then made my way back to my hotel, to finalize the list of goods I required.

It was quite difficult for me to wait until two o'clock. I sat and pondered impatiently which goods I ought to choose and to order, and my mind was spinning like a wheel. I tried to take a nap in my bed for a half hour or so, but could not fall asleep, as by now it was already noon and I had to go down to the reception room. Before long, it was already half past one. I left the hotel and headed over to Mr. Singer's office. He received me warmly, took out his pocket watch, and smiled: "You arrived at a quarter to two, but what's a quarter of an hour between me and you?" We both laughed. I handed him the list of items I wished to order, and he then opened the catalogs in front of me and began to explain which goods I should order and which I should not, and similarly, their prices and quality. From the [quoted] prices, I realized that old man Perlman was calculating a price for me that was double what it cost him. I could see that Mr. Singer was an honest and goodhearted man. I trusted him, and based on his explanations, I arranged my order. He promised to write to the factory and ask them, in light of the fact that I was a new merchant and was placing a large order, that they grant me a discount. Indeed, that is what happened. Sometime later, a positive response was received from them.

The days I spent getting to know Mr. Singer and his goods brought me much satisfaction. We maintained a continuous correspondence. Within two years, I had become a more prominent merchant in this trade than Aberle. I treated all my customers with honesty and fairness and received every person with warmth. And in this manner the number of my customers proliferated, until over time I began receiving orders from the Hebrew colonies—Petah Tikva, Rishon LeZion, and Rehovot. Thanks to my good interpersonal relations, I was appointed by Mr. Hazan,[136] the manager of Rishon LeZion, to be his general contractor for the provision of construction materials. I also became the sole supplier of build-

---

136. Haim Hazan (1864–?), also referred to as Haim David, was a native of Tetouan who immigrated to Palestine in 1882. He was an AIU-educated agronomist who first served as a teacher at Mikve Israel before being employed as an administrator at both Petah Tikva and Rishon LeZion.

ing materials to Rehovot, by the appointment of its managers Messrs. Goldin[137] and Lewin-Epstein.[138] I made no profit on the vast majority of floor tiles that I supplied to this colony, which I purchased from others. Mr. Lewin-Epstein took note of all my hard and dedicated work, and when he came in to settle the bill, he added a commission of 2.5 percent for my efforts, which amounted to a total of seventy-five napoleons. That is how business was conducted at the time—with faith, honesty, and justice.

In 1891, I became a father when my eldest son was born; I named him Moshe.[139] His circumcision was celebrated with all due pomp and glory. The family event was attended—aside from our own relatives and respected members of the Jaffa community—by the senior rabbis from Jerusalem, including Rabbi Panijel,[140] Rabbi Elyashar,[141] Rabbi Malka, and other upstanding members of the Jewish community of Jerusalem.

Coincidentally, a Christian priest from the Assyrian community in Jerusalem also celebrated this family occasion with us; it might be worthwhile recounting the circumstances that happened to bring him to our home.

With the grading of the plot alongside our first house in Neve Shalom that flattened the hill toward the valley, over the course of the excavation they discovered an ancient marble floor ornamented with inscriptions

137. Shlomo Goldin (1860–1923) was the treasurer of Rehovot.

138. Eliyahu Ze'ev haLevi Lewin-Epstein (1863–1932) was a prominent Lithuanian-born Zionist and early advocate of agricultural colonization, helping to establish Rehovot in 1890. He later moved to the US and became prominent in the American Zionist movement; after 1919 he was a member of the Zionist Commission.

139. Moshe Chelouche (1891–1968) studied at the AIU and Frères School in Jaffa, and at the École Supérieure de Commerce in Marseille. He was active in the family business in the 1910s and 1920s, after which he dedicated himself to public service in community and municipal affairs. Moshe became a prominent public figure in Tel Aviv in the 1930s–1950s, promoting numerous economic and cultural initiatives, including the founding of the Palestine Symphony Orchestra, the Tel Aviv Museum of Art, and what would later become Tel Aviv University.

140. Rabbi Raphael Me'ir Panijel (1804–1893) became the chief rabbi of Jerusalem in 1880 until his death in 1893, after which he was succeeded by his son-in-law, Ya'akov Sha'ul Elyashar.

141. Rabbi Ya'akov Sha'ul Elyashar (1817–1906) was the head of the Jerusalem rabbinical court beginning in 1869, and in 1893 he became the chief rabbi of Jerusalem. He authored numerous religious texts.

in an ancient language. When my late father wanted to know the meaning of the inscriptions, he invited the high priest of the Samaritans from Nablus, who explained the important content of the inscriptions. News of the discovery spread among all those who were interested in the country's antiquities, and the Assyrian patriarch and his entourage came from Jerusalem to see the antiquities. It just so happened to be the day of the circumcision, and so the patriarch took part, along with the rabbis from Jerusalem, in the ceremony marking my son Moshe's entry into the covenant of our patriarch Abraham.

Sometime later following the birth of my son Moshe, the Samaritan Ya'aqub Shalabi[142] came from Nablus to visit us. He had already been to Europe several times, handling transactions related to antiquities of the Samaritan community, and he purchased the marble floor with the inscription from us for the sum of sixty napoleons and shipped it to Europe, where, we later heard, he resold it for a much higher amount. But now, as I recall this fact, my heart fills with sadness that we Jews, as well, without properly appreciating the importance of the antiquities of our own land remaining in our land, also assisted in moving them abroad to the museums of other peoples and other countries, from which they will no longer return to this land of ours from which they were taken.

In early 1893, I traveled to Beirut. There were two objectives to this trip, one spiritual, the other material. One, I had a strong yearning to see the school I had attended, to visit with the headmaster and the teachers, and two, I wished to visit a few stores that sold the same sort of goods as mine, and to carry out thorough research on costs and the opportunities to order quantities of goods that would net a decent profit. When I arrived in Beirut, I experienced deep dismay on the spiritual side: I learned that my school had closed. The building had been sold to a Christian man, and the family of the late Zaki Cohen had moved to Egypt. I was very upset to hear the news. To this very day, whenever my thoughts revert to that time, it weighs heavily on my heart. How great

142. It appears that Chelouche was deceived by this man as a British consular report from 1884 states that Shalabi was allegedly excommunicated from the Samaritan community for falsely collecting funds ostensibly on their behalf, refusing to attend the funeral of a rabbi, and other forms of "dishonesty." Great Britain National Archives, letter from William Khayat (acting consul, Jerusalem) to ambassador in Constantinople, 5 September 1884. (Open Jerusalem Project.)

was my anguish to see how the teachers had to become merchants, having lost their jobs teaching at the school that had been such a part of their souls, all because of the unfairness of life.

During my visit in Beirut, I felt a psychological need and could not restrain myself. I could not leave the city without at least seeing the site of the school where I was educated, to see it, even from outside its walls.

I hired a carriage and rode out to the large field on which the school was located. I circled around the house that is so powerfully linked to the memories of my youth that are so dear to me.

I circled the building, immersed in my thoughts and memories of my youth. My behavior was noticed by a stranger who had been watching me, as if I were an undercover policeman making a study of the building for some nefarious motive. As I was walking in this manner behind the wall of the building that had been my school, I suddenly heard a voice shouting from one of the windows of the building:

"Mister, what are you doing here? Why are you walking around here like that?"

In a broken voice, I responded to the shouted challenge, which had roused me as if from a dream from the memories of my teenage years: "Nothing . . . It's only that . . . I'm just walking around the area, that's all . . ."

Apparently, my answer did not satisfy the person in the window, whose suspicion of me was now even greater, suspicion of this strange man who was loitering in the area seemingly without purpose. A few moments later, he hurriedly descended the steps, as if frightened, with various allegations and questions. What was I doing here, walking around seemingly without purpose?

At that point I revealed to the man—the owner of the building who had purchased the school that I had attended—that the building had been the school where I studied, and since I was visiting the city of Beirut, my childhood memories had been aroused and I could not restrain myself from paying a visit to the place that was nothing short of sacred to me.

When the man was apprised of the secret behind my strange visit around his home, he respectfully invited me in. He showed me around the building, including its entrances as well as my own classroom. He treated me with great honor and friendliness, served me all sorts of delicacies, and asked me to stay as an overnight guest in my classroom. He also introduced me to his family—as a man who views the memories of his youth and his school years as nothing less than sacred.

When I parted from him, he made a comment that I remember to this day. "Anyone who has such a strong emotional attachment to the school he attended so many years later, such a person is due full respect. He is a man of valor, and he will succeed in life."

I paid visits to various stores in the city, where I saw different goods, their nature and quality, and I came to the realization that some of them could be ordered directly from Beirut, at a much lower cost than from the factories. I placed two orders with two different merchants as a trial run and then went to eat at a restaurant on the same street. Across the street from the restaurant was a Greek fellow who had a luggage factory. Each day that I went there, I would watch with great interest how the luggage was produced, until it ultimately kindled in me a strong desire to set up a similar factory in Jaffa as well. I purchased the raw materials required for this type of work, in modest quantities, in order to conduct a trial run. I chose not to hire someone with expertise in luggage manufacturing to come to Jaffa, as I feared that if he came to a city where no such industry existed, he would have control over me and might even end up competing with me, so I was satisfied with my own observations and decided to go it alone. I shipped the merchandise that I had ordered to Jaffa, along with the raw materials for the luggage industry.

Upon my arrival back in Jaffa, I arranged the merchandise and set the prices. I took on another assistant, in addition to my cousin Yitzhak Barukh, as I wanted to free myself to work on manufacturing the leather suitcases and trunks. With that in mind, I cleared out one of the cellars of our house in Neve Tzedek. I brought in the wood and cardboard and the rest of the required materials. As a trial, I secretly made a single suitcase so no one would see it, and once it was finished, I brought it up to the house to show my family. Everyone was very surprised by the suitcase, doubting that I had even made it myself, except for my father, who was certain that I had, saying: "I know well my son Yosef Eliyahu, who by the age of seven to eight years already had so much talent and wisdom."

I ordered more raw materials and got down to work. I took in Yosef Louria, the brother of my brother-in-law Zvi Yesh'ayahu Louria,[143] as an

---

143. Both Yosef and Zvi Yesh'ayahu (sometimes also referred to as Yesh'ayahu

assistant. I taught him all the work, until he became an expert at it. When I put the suitcases up for sale, the delighted customers fought over them, because they were so nice looking; no one believed they were made in the Land of Israel. I saw that business was going well and did what I could to improve the manufacturing process. I ordered types of rubber that are closer in look and feel to leather, so that the luggage would be more durable. I added on more workers, besides Yosef Louria, who was by then a master craftsman. The new workers considered the labor to be a respectable livelihood. The goods were ordinarily available and found only in my store. They were high quality and nice looking and sold in large quantities. Over time, I expanded the workshop even more so and transferred management of the factory over to my trusted workers, thus freeing me to seek new entrepreneurial experiences.

Back then, hoes and plows in Jaffa were handmade by local blacksmiths, without standard measure or weight, and no two tools were of the same shape or quality. I purchased one of each type, drew sketches of them, and sent them to the firm of Wirminghaus & Funcke in Germany. I asked if it was possible to manufacture these hoes and plows, with all of them of uniform size and shape. I received a positive response a few months later, including a price quote that was half of what they cost in the Land of Israel. I sent a telegram and placed a small first order, as a trial run.

When the merchandise arrived, I displayed it at the entrance to my store, and everyone who passed by was curious and asked how much they were and were astonished that I was asking the same price that the Arab blacksmiths were taking. Hoes are needed for work in the orchards, and as I came to understand, this task alone called for thousands of such tools, while I had only two hundred in stock. When Iskandar Rock,[144] a wealthy resident of Jaffa who owned many orchards, heard about these hoes, he made his way to my store and bought out the entire stock, to the

---

Aba Zvi) were the grandsons of Chana, one of Aharon Chelouche's sisters. Yesh'ayahu and his bride, Sultana, the sister of Yosef Eliyahu, were thus related, a not uncommon practice at the time. Yosef reportedly moved to Sidon (Lebanon) and married a Muslim woman there; nothing more is known of his fate. Another Louria sibling reportedly converted to Islam and moved to Damascus. Some family members adopted the spelling "Louria" at the beginning of the twentieth century.

144. The scion of a prominent Roman Catholic family that traces its roots in Jaffa to the Crusades, Rock was a member of the Jaffa municipality in the 1890s.

last one. I then sent a telegram and ordered two thousand of each type, asking them to ship the goods as quickly as possible. But many other merchants jumped on the same idea and ordered the same merchandise from another supplier. Competition ensued. Among these merchants were Perlman, Rokach, 'Akkawi,[145] 'Araktinji, and Hana Banat.[146] When I saw the situation, I went back to searching for new initiatives.

I began to consider the glue industry. I learned from an Arab that there was such an industry in Damascus, and that one of the men who had worked in the profession now lived in Jaffa. I asked him to locate the man for me, and the Arab sent him over. When the worker came in, I asked him all about the work procedures, but I soon realized that his knowledge was minimal. Nevertheless, I felt that given my own faculties, with some effort I would be able to establish such an industry. I told the man to collect the remainders of animal hides, and I got down to work, to carry out my first attempt at glue-making. The glue was not very good; I had the feeling that it lacked something but did not know what.

After spending some time thinking about it, I concluded that I would have to build a special oven in which the glue could form, without cooking all the hides in a plain metal oven. I would build a special hut and would install grills and boards in it for the purpose of drying out the glue. I thought about it and realized that the most suitable location was a building situated far outside the city (the building is situated nowadays across the street from the Eden silent movie theater), where my uncle Avraham Barukh[147] lived, and if the business succeeded then he too could earn a living from it, as I would send him round the villages to collect in sacks the remnants of animal hides. I built the drying hut, I installed the grills and boards, and I also built the oven. At the start, I waited until the winter came, when making glue was more successful. Early that winter, I sent my uncle to villages, and he brought back sacks

---

145. The Sandel map (discussed in the introduction) lists the home of a Budrus (Butrus) 'Akkawi, suggesting the family's commercial success and social prominence. In the post–World War I period, Elias 'Akkawi (spelled "Akaoui") had a hardware store in Jaffa, although it is not known whether this was the individual Chelouche was referring to or a descendant.

146. In the post–World War I period, Banat was a merchant still dealing with construction materials.

147. Avraham Barukh was Chelouche's youngest maternal uncle. No information has been found about him.

filled with large quantities of animal skin remnants, thus requiring me to build a larger oven. The product was popular in Jaffa and in every city in the country and generated respectable profits. This business continued for several years, until, due to my excessive love and passion for new inventions, I began dreaming of building a factory for floor tiles.

I set up the floor tile factory in a large and spacious shed, which is now being used as a warehouse, on an expansive plaza behind our house in Neve Tzedek, bordering on the Girls' School. Originally, I made plain tiles of different sorts and shades, until I ordered more up-to-date machines and brought in a master craftsman from Beirut, and then we began making mosaic floor tiles. Our products consistently improved and drew a great deal of attention in the commercial market, and they are manufactured to this very day. The factory, which was relocated to a stone building on the same plaza and that is known as Chelouche Frères, at present manufactures all sorts of construction tools, balusters, rails, steps, pipes, etc.

My late father, who aspired wholeheartedly to expand the Jewish *yishuv* in Jaffa, spoke at length with some of the local leaders at the time, all of whom have now passed away—Reuven Blattner,[148] Dr. [M.] Stein,[149] Shim'on Rokach—regarding the establishment of a Jewish neighborhood on our land to enable any Jew to build a home of his own. He offered the land for free, but the late Blattner objected to the proposal to distribute the land for free, suggesting instead that it be sold very cheaply, for a piastre or even half a piastre per [square] cubit, just so the public would not become accustomed to receiving donations. He set up a committee of four members, including Messrs. Blattner, Stein, Rokach, and my blessed father, and eventually, Mr. Israel Perlquart,[150] as well.

The highest spot on our property was allocated for the construction of new residences, and a purchase price of twenty *para*s per cubit was

---

148. Robert (Reuven) Blattner, who arrived in Palestine from Poland in 1846, was a merchant. In 1867 he was considered a candidate for the vice-consulate of Austria-Hungary, but his candidacy was vetoed by the consul in Jerusalem, because he considered the family, who ran a hostel, "not respectable enough" to represent a European power. Blattner eventually became an honorary vice-consul of Denmark.

149. Dr. Marc Stein (1855–?) arrived in Jaffa from Russia. He was a member of the Barkai/Shafaq Masonic lodge.

150. Perlquart was a merchant who came from a Jerusalemite family.

set, with the total amount to be paid off in installments. They compiled bylaws and named the new neighborhood Neve Tzedek.[151] The sum of half a *mejidi* per week was collected from each member, going toward the construction of eight residences each year. Each residence comprised two rooms and a kitchen. The residences were sold in a lottery, and the winner would purchase it and the lot and would be the owner in perpetuity. I recollect that my father was owed a total of approximately one hundred gold napoleons for the land, based on a calculation of twenty *para*s per cubit, which was to be repaid bit by bit each year. But my father refused to accept any money for the land, preferring that it go toward the construction of a synagogue, as a sign of gratitude and joy over the Holy One Blessed Be He enabling him to realize the ambition of establishing a Jewish neighborhood and expanding the Hebrew *yishuv*.

At that time, my late father contracted with an Armenian architect, the only architect in our city, named Qarqash, who carried out a general survey of our land and drew up plans, both for the land that was exclusively owned by us and also that which was held in partnership with Amzalak and Moyal. I spent a little time with the architect each day, in order to point out to him the borders between us and the neighbors, and I found myself very much attracted to this type of work. I studied each and every detail of the architectural plan, until I at some point made an attempt to sketch a plan on my own, which turned out well.

I recall that when the architect came in to pick up his wages from my father, he said to him: "According to the conditions of our contract, you were to pay me for architectural planning and measuring of the tracts of land, but it turned out that I also tutored your son, who has accompanied me through all the stages of the work. And if you send him to school to study, I can assure you that he would turn out to be a good architect." In fact, even the scant knowledge I acquired in architectural theory would end up being quite beneficial to me and especially to the Hebrew *yishuv*, to which I began devoting myself with all my might and energy, for the construction of new buildings.

In 1896, I began to dream of the construction of buildings in order to further expand the Jewish *yishuv*. I considered the fact that we had land, construction materials, and even building plans that I could create myself. So how could we sit by idly, without taking part in the field

---

151. "Oasis of Justice." The name comes from Jeremiah 31:23.

of construction? After a while, it was no longer merely a dream—it was reality. Each and every day, I would draw up plans of different sorts and then adapt them to this, that, or another plot of land, until my father and brother began to devote their full attention to the construction work as well. I began by building the two apartments opposite our home, and the floor tile factory.

About two years later, we arranged a land swap with one of the founders of the neighborhood, the late Mr. Stein; we gave him land in Neve Shalom near the railway station and received in exchange the building in Neve Tzedek that then served as a machine factory. I demolished the building and built in its place two housing units that remain on the site to this day. My passion for construction became all-consuming. I built myself a cabinet with instruments for surveying the land that we and our partners owned. Drafting my father's surveys was my responsibility in addition to managing the sale and purchase of land, but I would sell lots from our landholdings to private individuals only in consultation with my late brother, Mr. Avraham Haim of blessed memory.

Over time, I became an architect, albeit not a certified one. I maintained a large supply of ready-to-build architectural plans at home, which I had prepared myself; I ordered catalogs for the construction of various buildings from abroad, as well as land survey instruments that I imported from Europe. I committed myself to determine, in advance, the measurements of every plot of land I sold, and to transfer it to the owner with its boundaries already marked off on every side. The buyer would consult with me on the type of construction and the specific plan to use and then proceeded to build in accordance with my comments, and eventually even those people who were building homes not on our land would come to me to discuss their building plans. Because I was engaged all day long in my many business enterprises, people would come to see me at my home at night. I would hear what they had to say, offer them advice, sketch plans, and give them an estimate of how much, based on my experience and expertise, it would cost them to build. So it was that every fiber of my being was devoted to construction projects, out of an ideal of helping to expand the *yishuv* in Jaffa. I carried out these projects from a place of love, and because I was always drawn to work and hated idleness.

I was a young man, and I did not yet have the right to intervene in public affairs. They were overseen solely by the elders and notables of the community, who handled matters of charity and acts of benevolence with the utmost dedication. And yet my heart was also drawn to doing good for all the destitute and embittered individuals, because nearly all of the meetings of the community council[152] took place at our home or at our synagogue, and at times they permitted us to be present and to listen to them talking and discussing. All of this planted within me a love for acts of benevolence.

In any event, I used to help carry out the orders of the council, along with a few other young men my age. One instance in particular in which we young people played an important role is firmly etched in my memory. One winter day in 1891, word spread throughout the city that a Russian ship had gotten stuck in the rocks off the ʿAjami seashore and could not be freed.[153] All of Jaffa congregated on the spot to watch the spectacle unfold, particularly those who had never seen a sinking ship and for whom it was like one of the natural wonders. From afar, it seemed as if the ship was sitting on dry land due to its close proximity to the beach. The sea was very stormy, and the ship teetered with the crashing waves. As we got closer to the scene of the incident, we saw that the eastern side of the boat facing the old city was rising higher, while the western side that faced the sea was dipping lower. The waves were rising full of sea foam, arcing above the ship, and then crashing down on it with the fury of a white vein . . .

A heartbreaking scene was taking place on the ship itself, with all the passengers crowded together in one place on the deck of the ship, on the side that was rising up above the surface of the sea that faced the city. The ship was about two hundred meters from shore. We beheld the fate of the assembled passengers, whose hands gripped the sides of the ship and grabbed onto the ropes, filled with fear and a terror cast upon them by the sea, which swirled with terrible violence, lest they be swept away into the depths. The waves drenched their clothes, and they shouted and called for help.

We heard from the Arabs that it was a Russian ship called the

152. Here Chelouche uses the term *vaʿad haʿedah*, making clear that this was the Maghrebi community council. Other than a few short-lived efforts to unify, the various Jewish ethnic groups in Jaffa remained fragmented and separate in their communal organization until right before World War I.

153. Jaffa lacked a deep-water port and its harbor was full of large rocks, so ships had to anchor offshore and disembark passengers and goods via smaller boats.

Chikhachev,[154] and that it carried Jewish passengers who had come to the Land of Israel with intent to settle here. When we heard that, our hearts filled with deep compassion, and we immediately returned to the city to apprise the community council of what was going on, including my father, who at the time was chairman of the council. We broke down in tears as we described the passengers' fate. My father immediately summoned a few members of the community council, Rabbi Nissim Hanokh Cohen, Yosef Moshe,[155] and the beadle of the synagogue, and they brought donkeys and rode down to the shore, while many Jews native to the land followed behind them. At the shore, my father witnessed a shocking image: a huge crowd of city residents standing on the seashore watching the ship slowly sinking. Soldiers stood at the ready, awaiting any order that might be given, as a collective scream of the women and children on the deck of the ship rose heavenward. My father asked the soldiers what they were guarding, and they replied that at midnight the *kaymakam* had issued an order to guard the ship and all the property on it, and to ensure that no one got near it until the Russian consul and the *kaymakam* arrived on-site.

My father, who could not bear to witness the fate of the people aboard the ship, their suffering and torment, could not understand how the government could allow itself to simply wait without making any effort to rescue the miserable wretches on the ship. He started reprimanding the soldiers for their failure to act, but the officer in charge responded that he could not do anything without orders. The ship's agent, Gabriel Samoury,[156] also announced that no one had permission to do

154. This occurred in February 1891. Dispatch Nr 294 dated 23 February 1891, from the French consul in Jerusalem Charles Ledoulx to the French minister of foreign affairs Alexandre Ribot. French Consulate General Archives, Archives of the Ministry of Foreign Affairs of France, La Courneuve (Open Jerusalem Project). The event was covered in the Jerusalem newspaper *Haor*, but several details differed from Chelouche's account. According to the paper, the *kaymakam* took a proactive role, there were some fatalities, the passengers included Christians and Jews, and some of the cargo was successfully recovered. Aharon Chelouche was not mentioned among the Jews who played a leading role in the recovery efforts. *Haor*, 27 February 1891.

155. Moshe and Cohen were members of several Sephardi community councils. Cohen also served on the mixed Sephardi-Ashkenazi community council but quit over the conflict relating to ritual slaughter.

156. Samoury was a member of the Barkai/Shafaq Masonic lodge in Jaffa, as was another relative, 'Issa Samoury.

anything without receiving special orders from the Russian consul and the *kaymakam*.

None of this gave any satisfaction to my dejected father, who commissioned some boatmen to put up a few tents, lay down straw mats, and set up chairs and pitchers of water, etc., to be ready for use by the passengers when they got off the ship. He sent the younger ones among us to the city to bring a samovar, tea and sugar, wine and cognac, to be available in order to help them recuperate. Once my father had arranged all the assistance that was needed to receive the immigrants on the shore before they could be brought either home or to their hostels, he began to gather advice on how they might be rescued.

Small boats could not approach the ship because the sea was too stormy. The only remedy, according to the advice of those who were knowledgeable, was for a boatman to climb aboard the ship and with the help of the sailors on board the ship, throw ropes overboard, one end of which would be tied to the ship, with the other end tied to a thinner rope that would be grabbed by swimmers who would grab onto it and be pulled ashore. The boatmen on the shore would hold fast onto these ropes and tie them to a high place, safe and secure. When the ropes were tied and tightened, a chair could then be tied to these two ropes, with a thin rope tied on from beneath the chair, with one end tied to the ship and the other held fast by the sailors on the shore. One by one, people would be seated in the chair, tied into it very securely, and the sailors on the seashore would use the thinner rope to pull the chair to the shore.

It was only in this manner that they might save the passengers, who were likely to sink into the depths of the sea. If it were possible to wait until the following day, perhaps by then the sea would have exhausted its rage and the passengers would be able to get off the ship and come to shore on the small boats. My father was amazed at the delay of the *kaymakam*. Although he might have been able to rush him to hurry to the shore as quickly as possible, what could he do without the Russian consul's presence? The consul was an irritable and angry man, and who knows if these poor people's lives might be lost because of him.

Perplexed about how to proceed, my father ran around from place to place, unable to ease his stormy soul. He rushed over to the tents to see if everything was ready to receive the stricken travelers. He requested from a manufacturer of beds, sheets, and blankets to bring all of these goods to the tents, just in case the immigrants would have to sleep there due to their fatigue and hardship.

Noon came and went, and the Russian consul still had not arrived. My father observed the ship through binoculars, saw the agony on the faces of the passengers, and could not restrain his emotions any longer. He immediately rode to the city to the English consul, Señor Haim Amzalak, told him all about the incident, and asked him to immediately pay a visit to his colleague the Russian consul and urge him to arrange the rescue of the miserable passengers. Señor Amzalak immediately complied with my father's request and went to see the Russian consul, declaring that he himself was willing to help the Russian consul bring them ashore.

The Russian consul thanked him for his generosity and said that he wanted to wait another few hours, as perhaps by then the sea would calm down. In the meantime, the captain of the sailors announced that the sea would be no less stormy today, and that by tomorrow none of the passengers would be alive. The two consuls immediately rode to the shore in the company of local government officials and met with the boatmen to gather advice, with the participation of a few merchants, my father among them, who were among the city's most respected citizens. They discussed the matter and realized that there was no other way to rescue the passengers than to carry out the plan that the boatman had already explained to my father. Immediately they tied the ropes and began to bring the passengers off the ship and onto the shore, one by one, and we led them into the tents to rest and recuperate. Among them were many ill and elderly people who were broken and shattered, but not a single soul was lost. We immediately sent the sickest to the city, either to our own home or to the homes of others.

Simultaneously, in the afternoon hours, the head of the Hovevei Zion council, Mr. Tiomkin, arrived at the shore from the Gedera colony.[157] He was a handsome man with long, curly hair that went to his neck. He saw how we cared for these Jews, and then he approached them and inquired as to their well-being. Upon hearing that there had been no

157. Gedera was located over thirty kilometers south of Jaffa. (Vladimir) Ze'ev Tiomkin (1861–1927) was a member of several Russian Zionist organizations. He was prominently mentioned in the newspaper accounts as responsible for taking care of the ship's survivors, although Chelouche maintains that he arrived after all the initial arrangements had been made.

tragedies, he walked up to my father, shook his hand with affection and admiration, and said: "'See, the Guardian of Israel neither slumbers nor sleeps!'"[158] Our exiled brethren will find loyal brothers here, people with feeling and love, who will extend a helping hand as they become established in the land, who will not let them fall in their times of trouble." He praised my father and the members of the council, and he began transferring some of the passengers to the colonies, while the ill were sent to a recuperation site.

The following day, people went to see what had befallen the ship that was emptied of its passengers, and they found that in order to save the ship, the sailors had thrown all of the goods loaded on it into the sea. Hundreds of packages of cotton had been thrown into the sea, and boatmen were now positioned on the shore to collect them. However, the stormy sea was scattering them in every direction, and they were swept away by the waves, which spat them out in the Yarkon River. That year, not a single Arab lacked cotton, as all benefited from the deserted property, and they also sold large quantities of it to Jews at low prices.

In the end, they could not save the ship, and it was broken up into pieces and sold as scrap metal.

The passengers established themselves in the colonies, where many of them are now farmers who own estates and land and are settled in the land, enjoying their lives here, seeing their children and grandchildren also working in farming and in commerce in the Land of Israel.

---

158. Psalms 121:4.

CHAPTER 7 *In the Days of the Turkish Regime*

Building the railway from Jaffa to Jerusalem |
The good relations between the government and my father |
My desire to be a public figure | A brazen attempt at robbery |
Protection by the government | Days of my illness |
The cholera epidemic in Jaffa

In 1893–1894, a French company headed by a respectable and honest gentleman by the name of Bonnafous[159] came to the country and began to build the railway from Jaffa to Jerusalem. The concession was granted by the Turkish regime in Constantinople to a Jew named Yosef Bek Navon, a native of Jerusalem, who in turn sold it to the French company.[160]

Work continued for several years. The tracks, laid by workers brought in from Egypt, began at the edge of the Neve Tzedek neighborhood. Workers were compelled to dig a ditch deep in the ground so that the tracks could be laid on a straight stretch of land.

One year after the ditch was excavated, we built our big house, which is currently the home of the mixed school for boys and girls and our synagogue.[161] Our entire family lived in this house, including me and my brother, who had been married for about ten years, and afterward, with

---

159. Jean Louis Bonnafous (1840–1913) was a trained engineer with extensive experience in public works in France, after which he was awarded with the Legion of Honor. In the 1880s, he transferred to work on the railway in Brazil and then the Panama Canal before joining the railroad in Jaffa in 1890; he became director in 1895.

160. Navon (1858–1934) was a businessman from an elite Sephardi family in Jerusalem. He was granted the railroad concession by the Ottoman Ministry of Trade and Public Works in 1888. BOA, A-DVN-MKL/30-13, 23 October 1888. Construction began on the railroad in 1890, and the line was officially opened in 1892.

161. The building, now known as the House of Aharon Chelouche, is at 32 Chelouche Street in Neve Tzedek. It was the second home that Aharon Chelouche built for his family outside the walls of Jaffa. The first home was built on land that was part of the Neve Shalom/Manshiya neighborhood.

our father's permission, each of us lived with his family in a separate home. Only my father and his daughter[162] remained in the house until the outbreak of the World War.

When the railway company began its work, we signed an agreement with the company, together with the late Valero[163] from Jerusalem, to serve as its agents. At that time, great value was placed on small denominations of currency. In order to get change for a single lira, people would pay a commission of between five and six piastres. We therefore stipulated in the agreement that all the sums coming into their registers would be transferred to us each day, and we would repay them once every two weeks in silver, gold, and piastres, as per their demands. At the end of each month, we would repay in gold, in order to cover their clerks' salaries. After these two payments we would then carry out a general audit and would repay the remainder by means of a check sent to Paris. This arrangement continued for eight years.

Each year, on the occasion of his visit to the country, Monsieur Bonnafous, the head of the Palestinian railway company, would pay a visit to my late father and show him much affection and esteem. On one occasion, Bonnafous told him that the Crédit Lyonnais bank had been battling with him for some time to give it the concession, but that due to my father's honesty, he would not agree to leave him. As a token of his satisfaction and an expression of his admiration, he gave my father, his sons, and two of his clerks written certificates permitting them to travel for free in the first-class car.

In addition, as a sign of appreciation for my father's work, he complied with his request to build the bridge over the ditch that would serve as a conduit for traffic between Jaffa and Neve Tzedek to this very day.[164]

It was well known that my late father was engaged in banking affairs.

162. Luna Chelouche (1883–1915), who never married.
163. Haim Aharon Valero (1845–1923) was a prominent banker, landowner, and businessman in Jerusalem. His father, Ya'akov, immigrated to Jerusalem in the 1830s from Istanbul, and while he initially was registered as a poor ritual slaughterer, he later cofounded what is often referred to as the first bank in the city. The Valeros became one of the city's wealthiest Jewish families.
164. The bridge is known today as the Chelouche Bridge, and linked Neve Tzedek with Walhalla, the adjacent German (Templer) neighborhood.

My brother Ya'akov,[165] who had completed his studies, specialized in correspondence, accounting ledgers, and fluency in Hebrew, French, and Arabic. He was appointed as my father's chief assistant and was entrusted with managing our financial links with Beirut, Constantinople, and cities in Europe. He also handled correspondence between us and the central government in Turkey. When the government was in need of money, we would send it a check amounting to hundreds of Turkish pounds with the condition that within two weeks the same amount would be repaid to us from the local government account, without any additional fee. The special advantage that we got from this arrangement was that all local government officials, senior and junior alike, deferred to us at the hour of need. Whenever something happened and a Jew came and complained to my father and asked for his help concerning some injustice that had been committed against him, my father would simply write to clerk A or B, whereupon the matter would be resolved and peace and quiet would be restored.

This ability to rush to the aid of any Jew in trouble gave my father a sense of spiritual contentment more precious to him than any material gain. After a while, my father did not even have to rely on written communication but made do by dispatching one of his clerks or sons to the authorities or even to the *kaymakam* himself, at which point all would be settled peaceably. Usually, my father would choose me for this emissarial service, because by my nature, I was drawn to acts of benevolence. From that time onward, my passion to become a public figure only grew. As time went by, they would no longer trouble my father but would approach me directly, and I would handle the matter on my own. When something exceptionally important occurred, my father would be compelled to write a letter or personally visit the *kaymakam* in order to attempt to cancel the decree.

The relationship between us and the Turkish government lasted many years, and we would periodically send these checks to the central government. But over time the clerk responsible for local government finances began to delay the repayment, at times more than two weeks past the due date. When my father began to feel that the arrangement

---

165. Ya'akov Chelouche (1880–1944) worked at the Anglo-Palestine Bank beginning in 1903 until his death.

crossed all limits with no set date for repayment, and that the day of remittance seemed to depend on the whim of said clerk, he refused to send any more checks.

Aside from the delayed repayments, which were causing us material damage, my father also began to notice that the coins coming into the local government accounts as *verko*[166] and other taxes included about 10 percent that were smudged and worn. According to Turkish law, these coins could not be refused, especially not those received from the government, and it was mandatory to honor their value as legal tender. In deference to the law, my father was silent about this matter. Over time, however, it was discovered that the same government official in charge of finances had also become a merchant and was now covertly buying worn-out coins at reduced prices and then transferring them to us at full face value, for the quantity of worn-out coins had increased noticeably. Moreover, after a while, my father received nearly all his payments from the local government in the form of worn-out coins.

When he realized that he would no longer be able to continue issuing checks to the government under these conditions, he explained the reason for his refusal to the *kaymakam*, who then investigated and interrogated the financial official. The latter claimed that the public was paying with worn-out coins and that according to the law he could not refuse to accept them. The *kaymakam* then informed the pasha in Jerusalem of the situation, and not more than a few days passed until the government's town crier went through the streets of the city, announcing that henceforth the government would not accept worn-out coins and that anyone who dared to do so would be punished and imprisoned.

It was at that precise time that the government was preparing to receive from my father two checks for large amounts of money, but because my father refused to issue them under the previous conditions, the *kaymakam* invited my father to meet him at the telegraph office. At that same hour the pasha in Jerusalem sent a telegram, and the *kaymakam* translated his words. The Pasha declared his consent to my father's requested changes, assuring him that there would be no more delays in repayment. He asked my father to give the government two checks that would be payable at banks in Constantinople, on condition that on the very same day we would be paid the 150,000 piastres in small-

---

166. This was the purchase tax levied on real estate transactions.

denomination coins that were in the government coffers, not only from Jaffa but also from Nablus, Gaza, and the rest of the district, all in accordance with the governmental directives issued by the pasha. At my father's request, all of this was put in writing, with the *kaymakam*'s confirmation, after which my father gave the two checks to the government.

On that same Friday when my father gave the *kaymakam* the two checks per the pasha's request, my father was supposed to receive a total of 150,000 Turkish liras in small-denomination coins. My late father was not accustomed to working on Friday afternoons, and dealing with transferring the money and arranging for its safe storage would require several hours of work. My father was afraid to leave the money in his office, for fear that over the course of two nights and the full day between them [the Sabbath], thieves—who had already attempted to steal from his office once before—might succeed in their attempts this time. Because of that, he hurried to the *kaymakam* and informed him of his decision to accept the money on Sunday instead, and then he then went home, as usual, to bathe and get dressed for the Sabbath.

That Friday night, something happened in our large house in Neve Tzedek—the building that subsequently served for many years as the Tahkemoni School—that shook us to the core of our being. Our entire family lived there, in a building that stood isolated on the sand dunes, distant from the other, smaller houses that were scattered here and there. At around midnight, my father heard something taking place around the house, and he intermittently sensed irregular movement. He got out of bed, as he was accustomed to rising before dawn every day to study Torah, but now his senses were on edge, trying to figure out from which side the movement was coming.

Suddenly he heard a powerful movement and a pounding on the front door. He went to the door and called out loudly: "Who is it?" But there was no answer. The pounding continued, and then the sounds of axes striking at the door grew increasingly louder, until they were on the verge of shattering the door. My father shouted loudly: "Who dares come in the middle of the night and disturb our rest?" There was no sound, no answer—aside from the noise made by these invisible rogues who continued their work. The sound of my father's cries frightened everyone in our house; we watched him holding back the door with all his might, pressing his body up against it. My brother Avraham and I rushed to find our two pistols of different calibers, and out of sheer panic we mixed up the bullets when loading them. From one of the houses nearby we heard the voice of our elderly neighbor Mordekhai Cohen, may peace be upon him, shouting with all his might: "Mr. Chelouche, there are many robbers surrounding your house."

In the meantime, the robbers had tied up our watchman and one of them remained there standing guard over him. All the women of the house were shouting through the windows, and our pistols could not fire because we had loaded them with the wrong caliber bullets. People started to make their way over from Neve Shalom, and the robbers, hearing them coming, fled in the direction of the bridge. When we heard the voices of Jews from Neve Shalom we opened the door and they all entered along with our elderly neighbor Mordekhai Cohen. He told us how he shouted for help as loud as he could in order to save us from the robbers.

The entire crowd stayed with us until morning. At daybreak, we found outside of the house lying here and there iron tools and various signs. After morning prayers, my brother Avraham and I went to the *kaymakam* and told him all about the incident. He immediately came to our house along with the heads of the police and the legal investigator, and they drafted a protocol of the investigation based on our testimony. The *kaymakam* suspected the clerks at the telegraph office, who were fully aware of the nature of the negotiations between my father and the pasha and thought that my father would for certain receive the money that same day, and hence dispatched the robbers. The government made extensive efforts to discover the trail of the robbers, but all their efforts were in vain, and the guilty parties were never found.

Each evening, the *kaymakam* would send a detachment of fifteen soldiers to our yard to protect our home from any attack by robbers. They stood guard by our house for about two months, until it became too much of a financial burden on us. My father was compelled to pay for their upkeep and many expenses, until the weight of taking care of them led us to ask the *kaymakam* to release them.

In 1896, I grew quite tired of all the hassle involved in buying and selling land, and particularly from the drawing up of blueprints that took up all my time, night and day. I was also fatigued by the public activities I was so dedicated to with all my heart that I did not even set aside time for myself to eat or to rest. I felt a limpness in my bones. I felt drunk — but not from wine. Even though I did not smoke at night, my head was in a daze day and night, and my brain was in pain.

I consulted with doctors who prescribed new medications that did not help. There were a few occasions when I fell into bed and lay there for weeks on end in a state of general exhaustion. My businesses were increasingly left in the hands of clerks who were not as dedicated to them as I, and they began to decline from one day to the next. This situation continued until the year 1900, without my seeing any change for the better in my health, despite the extensive and dedicated care provided by the local physicians.

About two months before the start of 1900, two friends of mine, Shmu'el Moyal and Moshe Matalon,[167] decided to travel to Paris to see the commercial exposition there, and they proposed that I accompany them to be examined by the best physicians in Paris. After I consulted with my family, I decided to make the trip, and on 12 January we arrived in Paris safely. I was exhilarated by everything I saw at the exposition, by its beauty and abundant richness. Days of rest passed, and I imagined that my health had been restored.

But then one day as I was sitting with my friends at a cafe in thrilling Paris, the illness from which I had suffered in Jaffa reappeared. I began to seek out the underlying reasons for my disease, but my effort was in vain. I consulted with various doctors, but to no effect—until one day, I heard of a specialist who lived far from the city. I went to his clinic, and he diagnosed my disease. He prescribed the required medications for me, and since they were not available in the Land of Israel, he instructed me to buy three doses, so that I would be able to take the medicine again should the disease recur. Indeed, these medications had a positive effect on me, and I was restored to good health.

After recuperating and recovering my strength, I traveled on to visit the cities of Germany. I paid visits to factories, including a few with which I already had a business relationship, and studied their methods of commerce and industry. With a great deal of interest and zeal, I was able to order a variety of goods in large quantities, at excellent discounts, and all on credit. On my way back to the Land of Israel, I stopped off in Constantinople. There I visited with my father's acquaintances and with

---

167. Matalon (1872–1959) was born in Jaffa; his father, Yitzhak, had arrived from Baghdad in his childhood and became a money changer. Matalon studied with Chelouche at the Talmud Torah, and later he studied at Mikve Israel. Matalon was a lawyer as well as a land speculator and community figure.

one of the Greek merchants who traded wheat and flour with my father. They invited me to their homes, spent time with me, and showed me around the city. I returned home safely after a long trip that lasted three months, healthy and refreshed, my feeling of youth restored. I went back to being the driving force in all my businesses and strove to raise them up to their former heights. After a short time, the number of transactions in my business increased and became larger than before. Yet I did not forget my public pursuits and continued to dedicate myself to them, as I was accustomed, body and soul.

In 1902, a cholera plague broke out in Jaffa, alarming all the residents, many of whom fled for their lives.[168] Several of the wealthier Jewish and Christian residents pleaded with my father to leave the city, but he refused and responded emotionally: "I will not move from here; God will have mercy." Because they were unable to convince him to leave, they left their assets under his management and traveled far away.

After a short time, the epidemic grew more intense and began to claim many victims. The Muslims suffered the worst. The city took on a very melancholy air. The number of victims increased daily, and the city was hermetically sealed, with no one entering or leaving. The Jews gathered in the synagogues, where they recited prayers and supplications, and "poured out their complaints"[169] before the living God, begging for compassion for the sheep of his flock.

During this period, I had a sense of the bleak gravity of the situation, and driven by an attack of bitter despair, I approached several leaders of our community, seeking their advice on the possible actions that we might take without delay. I conferred with the late Shim'on Rokach, and he expressed the idea that Neve Tzedek should be isolated from the city, that no stranger should be allowed to enter the neighborhood, and also that we should forbid the entry of the Arab washerwomen who worked in the Jewish homes. Besides that, a special room should be set aside at some distance from the houses, with a supply of cognac and various medications as well as an aide who would be on call at all times.

---

168. The plague arrived from Port Said and broke out in Jaffa in October. The plague quickly spread to many of the surrounding villages and towns, and Ottoman officials rushed to deal with the contagion, sending doctors and supplies to the local hospitals. Officially 430 cases and 272 deaths were registered in Jaffa, although British reports suggested this was an undercount by as much as half.

169. Psalms 142:3.

If, Heaven forbid, a catastrophe occurred in a Jewish home, the family would be able to go to this address and receive urgent help for free from the aide.

Upon hearing this suggestion by the late Rokach, we drew up a complete plan and summoned a group of seven public figures. We proposed that we take immediate action to save our fellow Jews from this dreadful disease by setting up three rooms in three different areas—the Old City, Neve Shalom, and Neve Tzedek—and in this manner care for all the city's Jews. Aside from the medications and the cognac, we gave instructions that a bed or two be placed in each room, so that the sick could be brought to the room and could rest in bed as much as needed, and that strong young men be enlisted to care for the patient in accordance with the doctor's instructions.

We drew up a detailed roster of the young men capable of handling this work, the names of the physicians, and central locations where the rooms ought to be rented. The plan would come at great expense: purchasing medications and cognac; tea, sugar, and food for the helpers who would work day and night; clean bed gowns; lighting for the rented rooms; and lime to pour on all the diseased and dirty areas in the Jewish neighborhoods.

In order to organize the procurement of these items, we invited to our home the late Mr. Rokach, Dr. Stein, and others. The plan was unanimously approved, and we started to consult on how to raise the funds. The late Mr. Rokach proposed that those in attendance immediately contribute sums of money toward this objective, each according to his ability, and that money also be collected from others in the city. In the meantime, a telegram was drafted and was sent to Baron Rothschild. On the spot, a sum of 50 napoleons was collected and three people were chosen to go around and gather donations at the homes of other benefactors. Two days later, the sum of 500 napoleons was received from the Baron and we set down to work, following the plan that had been devised. Our strenuous labors proved effective, thanks to the wise and devoted actions taken by the late Shim'on Rokach. The dreadful disease did not affect a single one of the Jews, and our rescue stations were active day and night. One elderly Jewish woman and one pregnant woman died of the disease, even though there were more than forty deaths in the city each day.

The Christians, having heard of the actions we took, organized themselves along the same lines, although they took a different direction, as they purchased coffins and shrouds with the money that they collected, and in so doing they committed a fundamental mistake, and they had many victims. The epidemic lasted for three months straight, sowing cruel and catastrophic destruction among the residents, until God had mercy on his people, and the cholera loosened its grip on the city.[170]

All those who left the city returned, those who had deposited their assets with my father received them back, and the city went back to living its normal life, as in days past.

---

170. The Jerusalem governor blamed the Jaffa *kaymakam* for negligence and wrote to Istanbul asking for his removal. BOA, BEO Dosya 1954, Gömlek 146482, 24 November 1902. The outbreak finally ended in early January 1903. Dispatch Nr 3, dated 10 January 1903, from the French consul in Jerusalem Auguste Boppe to the French minister of foreign affairs Théophile Delcassé. French Consulate General in Jerusalem, Archives of the Ministry of Foreign Affairs in France, La Courneuve. (Open Jerusalem project.)

CHAPTER 8 *Visits to Our Home by Famous People*

The prince from Ethiopia | A descendant of King Solomon | His visit to the Land of Israel | The finest goods of the land shipped to Ethiopia | His visit to our home | His escorts, always on their feet | Getting acquainted with our family | Showing his battlefront wounds | The visit by M. Ussishkin to my father's home in 1903 | The preparatory gathering in my father's home | Establishment of the General Federation of the Jews of the Land of Israel | Our family's involvement in the barley trade of Gaza | Resolving a Protest among the Bedouin

One of the most important events that happened to my family in 1900 and that left a strong impression on me was a visit by the prince of Ethiopia, the son of the king of Abyssinia,[171] who visited our home in Neve Tzedek one Saturday with his entire entourage.

It was with great deference that we received the king's son, a descendant of the queen of Sheba, who, according to legend, visited the wisest of all kings in Jerusalem. According to the folklore of their people and in their land, the royal family of Ethiopia proudly maintains their direct line of descent from King Solomon down to the present day. As we saw not long ago following the bloody events of the year 1929, the delegate of the Ethiopian government to the League of Nations in Geneva lodged a protest in the name of his king, the descendant of King Solomon, against

---

171. Royal visits to the Holy Land were not uncommon, and there is documentation that an Ethiopian prince visited Palestine in October 1900. A British consular report identifies him as Prince Likamakoas Nado, prince of Shewa in Abyssinia, but we have been unable to find more information about him. However, the king of Abyssinia, Menelik II, did not have any sons with similar names, so this prince's exact position in the extensive Ethiopian royal family is unclear. It seems he held a monarchic title (*liqe mekwas*), perhaps through clan belonging or patronage, rather than being a direct descendant of the king. 27 October 1900, letter from J. H. Monahan, acting consul to Maurice de Bunsen, chargé d'affaires. GB-NAPRO/FO195/2084, pp. 178–80. (Open Jerusalem Project.)

the spilling of pure Jewish blood in the streets of Jerusalem and in the Holy Land.

The prince had heard about our family in Jaffa even before his visit from a wealthy and notable merchant in Aden, Banin Menahem Messa,[172] a major trader with the entire East, with India, Ethiopia, Persia, Arabia and other lands of the east, who traded also with our family in Jaffa for many years prior.

Prior to the prince's visit to the Land of Israel, Banin Menahem Messa informed our family that in the near future the prince of Ethiopia would be visiting our country, and he asked if our family would represent him and offer our services to the prince, and also offer to him a book of bank checks with which he would be able to draw funds if needed.

When the prince arrived with his entourage in Jaffa, he was received with great honor by the government and the army and was housed at the Hotel du Parc in the American neighborhood.[173] When one of our family members appeared before him with the letter from Banin Menahem Messa and with the checkbook in our name, he was very grateful, but he did not use many of the checks. He only asked my late brother Avraham Haim to accompany him on his travels throughout the country, that he travel with him to Jerusalem and throughout the entire region, indeed, wherever he went. The prince appointed my brother to look after the preparation and shipping of the goods that he purchased in the country in order to transfer them to the Jaffa port and from there on board a ship to the port closest to Ethiopia.

And what was the nature of these goods? Water stored in tin cans, collected from all the springs in the country on both sides of the Jordan River, as well as all sorts of soil and stones from the holy sites in the country. I still remember the hundreds of trunks and cans that we received in Jaffa for shipment to Ethiopia.

Once he returned from having toured the land, the prince came to visit us along with his entire entourage at our home in Neve Tzedek. I can recall a characteristic scene from his visit to our home: all eight escorts of the prince remained on their feet during their visit to our home,

---

172. The Messa family set up commercial branches in Port Said and Alexandria. They profited extensively from their ties to the British raj and were popularly known as the "Rothschilds of Arabia."

173. He is referring to the German colony, which was first settled by Americans.

which extended for over an hour. No matter how much we asked them to sit down using sign language, for aside from the Ethiopian language they understood no other language, nothing we did would persuade them. They persisted in standing the whole time without taking their eyes off their prince for even a moment, watching over him with utmost attention.

The prince wanted to be introduced to the entire family and asked for details about each and every one of us.

During the hour or more of his visit, he felt so intimately friendly that he even showed us two wounds on his leg and on his neck, which he received in a war fought by his people and his country and at which the prince, as the head of the army, fought on the battlefront.

I also recall the visit in 1903 to my late father's house in Neve Tzedek by Mr. M. Ussishkin[174] and Ze'ev Gluskin,[175] who had arrived from Russia to organize for the first time all the Jews in the Land of Israel from all communities, from the cities and from the colonies, into one unified national general federation.

Prior to the opening of a major conference in Zikhron Ya'akov, all the preliminary organizational work and all the preparatory sessions were held in Jaffa, which at the time was the center of the new *yishuv*.[176] And one of this organization's most important gatherings took place in our late father's home, with Mr. M. Ussishkin serving as the president.

My late father was—as the reader has already perceived from previous chapters—a Lover of Zion not only in name but also in practice, who believed that a strong organization of all the Jews of the Land of Israel into a unified and steadfast general federation would greatly benefit the building and expansion of the *yishuv*. He joined Mr. Ussishkin and his deputies in this effort and helped him significantly through his own influence on the Sephardi Jewish notables and common people, who also naturally joined the general federation of the Jews of the Land of Israel.

174. Menachem Ussishkin (1864–1941) was a Russian engineer and member of the Bilu and Hovevei Zion organizations. He immigrated to Palestine in 1919, after which he served as president of the Jewish National Fund from 1923 until his death.

175. Gluskin (1859–1949) was an early member of Zionist societies in Russia and worked to market and export wine from the Jewish settlements in Palestine. In 1904 he helped found a private land purchase society called Ge'ula (Redemption).

176. This is a highly ideological term that differentiated the new Zionist community of settlers from the older preexisting religious communities.

For numerous various reasons, and this is not the suitable place to detail them, this general federation did not endure. It existed for only a few years, and due to conflicts and suspicions it fell apart, but the idea of a general union of all the Jews in the Land of Israel into a single association that had the sole purpose of speedier and more effective establishment of the Land of Israel remained. In this matter our family has always followed the path of our father, and we supported and continue to support every idea of a true union of the Jews of the Land of Israel, a union without distinction between ethnic community, religious denomination, social status, or political party, to this very day.

From 1902 onward, at which time our family and in particular my late brother Avraham Haim began trading in the Gaza grain market on a major scale, I assisted him in the business venture through the handling and receiving of funds and more, which at the time was not an easy feat.

My brother would spend approximately three to four months in Gaza each year, in the season that follows the barley harvest. He would purchase barley from small merchants from the Gaza and Be'er Sheva district who traded with the Bedouins in the Negev, which was practically the majority share of all their barley. We would ship the barley abroad each year on three or four ships that were fully stocked.[177]

I have a strong memory of one particular trip in which I carried a large sum of money from Jaffa to Gaza via the desert road, which was considered to have a constant risk of robbers and thieves. However, I succeeded in transferring, safe and sound, the large amount of silver and gold, which totaled thousands upon thousands of Turkish liras and napoleons. And there is something else I recollect from that trip: when I brought the money to my brother in Gaza, he then distributed it to the merchants and the Bedouins with whom he traded, practically without even counting it. And when I commented on this to him, asking how he could do such a thing, and even more so without any receipts being issued, he responded that he could always rely on the honesty of the Arabs in this regard, since after each one counted his own packet, he would tell him the correct amount.

And so it was, with complete trust in the Arabs and the Bedouins with whom we traded for several years, it never happened that the Arabs or Bedouins cheated or deceived us in a business deal. Furthermore, it

---

177. Barley was by far the most important export from the Gaza district.

never once happened in our business dealings in Gaza that a commitment or a promissory note of an Arab or a Bedouin would result in a "Protest."[178] And this may be the appropriate place to recount an interesting and typical fact concerning the attitude of the Bedouins of the Negev, the Gaza district, and Be'er Sheva to the matter of the "Protest."

Whenever it happened on rare occasions that one of the residents of Gaza or Be'er Sheva would arrive at his repayment of a promissory note to the Protest, then the beautiful custom observed by these people of the Orient was such: if someone experienced a tragedy and could not repay his obligation of the promissory note on time, the owner of the debt would erect a tent at the crossroads before the entrance to his home. On this tent they would hang a black handkerchief that from a distance looked like a black flag bearing a terrible omen. Everyone who passed by the tent would ask, "Who is being declared 'black'?"[179] When the passersby learned that it was so-and-so who had not paid his debts in time, his acquaintances would gather right away and would redeem him from this time of trouble. An Eastern custom, but one with a beautiful outcome. If only this custom were standard practice in the business world and among us! Our trade in barley from Gaza continued in this vein for over a decade, until the outbreak of the war.

178. An official notice of the nonpayment of a promissory note on time, which constitutes grounds for a legal claim against the borrower.

179. This "blackening" (*taswid*) form of public denunciation was used among the Negev and Sinai Bedouin to highlight the treachery and lack of honor of the debtor and his clan, which was considered among the most significant offenses and character flaws.

CHAPTER 9 *Between Building and Destruction*

A few quiet years | Construction of the Feingold Houses in Jaffa | My trip to Port Said | Remains of the English ship are put up for auction | The swindler | The swindler's end | My trip to Egypt, as my father's emissary | Meeting my school friend Barukh Cohen | My business success | Building the Girls' School in Jaffa | Hebrew carpenters who did not know their profession | My warnings about dangerous building techniques | The collapse | Opinion of the engineering experts from Jerusalem | Who is to blame? | I build the Alliance Israélite Universelle School in Jaffa

In 1903, aside from forming a partnership for the import of lumber from Rhodes and elsewhere on sailing ships, there was fairly little news to report about my personal and business life. The lumber business involved three individuals who practiced three different religions: Jurji 'Abd al-Nur,[180] a Christian; Khalil al-Dumyati,[181] a Muslim; and me, a Jew. My two partners were well known as leading merchants specializing in the lumber trade. I worked together with them for several years in the business, which was profitable. We also constructed several buildings over the years, including government buildings such as the customs house, the quarantine house, etc. Nevertheless, after completion of the buildings that we built together, we were compelled to break up the partnership.

180. Jurji 'Abd al-Nur is listed as a household items merchant in a 1923 French commercial directory, as is Chelouche. 'Abd al-Nur's earlier lumber business constructed export crates for the orange industry.

181. No information has yet been found about him other than that the family emigrated from Dumyat, Egypt, and settled in the 'Ajami neighborhood. Khalil's son Salim Khalil was an Austrian-trained chemical engineer in Jaffa; after the 1948 war he lived in exile in Riyadh.

In 1904, I carried out the construction of the Feingold Houses[182] along the beach, thanks to my good relationship with Mrs. Palmer,[183] who placed her trust in me, both in word and in deed. At the time, I received a telegram from my acquaintance Avraham Tov to come to Port Said and take part in the purchase of the scrap remnants of a ship that had sunk at sea. I took a few hundred English pounds with me and made my way to Port Said. There I found several other merchants from various cities, all of whom had come to take part in the auction of the ship.

One clever Greek merchant gathered together all of the merchants, twenty-eight in total, and convinced them to form a partnership. One member of the group was the well-known Arab merchant Muhammad al-Hita.[184] A cooperative was formed, and each of the merchants signed a binding agreement. Then each member of the cooperative wrote a letter to the Suez Canal Company, requesting to buy a certain part of the ship, and enclosed a check for a specified amount in accordance with the company's request. Three days later, the merchants all gathered in the company's hall and waited for the letters to be opened. It became clear that each merchant had faithfully fulfilled his commitment as assigned to him by the cooperative. I myself proposed to the company to purchase all of the copper on the ship, a total of three and a half tons, at the price that the cooperative had set.

But when the letters were opened, a new face appeared—an Arab merchant from Egypt whom we had not seen when the cooperative was formed. It turned out that he had sent a series of letters to the shipping company for each and every lot that was up for sale, offering slightly higher prices than what our organization had set—between 2 and 5 percent higher on every listing. Of course, in accordance with the auction rules, the Arab merchant won all the bids.

We were all astonished that the details of this cooperative had been

182. Shlomo Feingold (1865–1935) was a Russian-born businessman and journalist who moved to Jerusalem after spending years in London and Paris. The beach area around his luxury houses was the new neighborhood of Yefe Nof; the two-story, thirty-room Bella Vista hotel (the Italian translation of Yefe Nof) was adjacent, and a new institute for hydrotherapy and sea bathing was located within the hotel.

183. Margaret Palmer was the adoptive mother of Feingold's first wife. She was a member of the British Israelites Christian society, and she provided many of the funds for Feingold's land purchases.

184. No information has been found about this individual.

discovered. The other partners and I walked around in a daze, like madmen, as we had now been deprived of the opportunity to gain thousands of pounds in profit, if not more. Eventually, it became clear that the Arab merchant from Port Said, Muhammad al-Hita, had betrayed the cooperative. He had apparently summoned this Arab merchant from Egypt, informed him of all the details of the cooperative and the conditions we had set, and then instructed him how to place the bids quoted in his letters. In this manner, the Arab merchant raised the bids—slightly—and won the auctions. Muhammad al-Hita had thought to enrich himself through this act of deception, affecting the all-inclusive purchase of the entire ship for a total of 30,000 liras.

But what did the Holy One Blessed Be He do? According to the regulations, each buyer was obligated to move his purchased goods off-site within seven days; otherwise, he would have to pay a specific amount in penalty fees, and if two weeks passed from the time of purchase, the fine would double. After three weeks, the fine was three times as high, and after four weeks, the purchaser would pay a sizable fine and the goods would return to the company. Al-Hita, the swindler, went into hiding and in his place sent a proxy to arrange for the purchase to be moved off-site. However, the Arab merchant from Egypt was a stranger to Port Said and did not know how to arrange for porters to move all the auction lots. Some three weeks passed by, and the goods remained where they were.

Meanwhile, day by day the leaders of the cooperative thoroughly investigated the affair and spied in order to ascertain who was behind the betrayal. Once it was discovered that al-Hita was behind the outrageous scheme, the members of the cooperative convened in order to formulate a strategy. It was determined that according to the law we could not do a thing, because the swindler al-Hita's name was not specified in the purchase bond. But the members of the cooperative were not prepared to simply ignore the insult done to them, and they made public announcements throughout the city about this act of treachery.

The facts of the matter spread far and wide, to the porters and to the company. The company did not find fault with members of the cooperative, only with the swindler. And the porters and freight handlers organized themselves and swore not to transport the parts of the ship and thereby enrich a man who was a swindler. The company dealt with the purchaser with all due severity of the law, not conceding a single penny of the penalties and punishments available to it. The leaders of our cooperative told us not to leave the city before an outcome was reached. And the outcome was, indeed, quite interesting.

The treacherous al-Hita was compelled to sell all of his large houses in Port Said in order to pay off the penalties, with three weeks having passed and the purchased goods having remained in place. In addition, al-Hita had to repay the loans he had received from banks, and so it turned out that from this act of deception he emerged without the goods, having failed in his attempt, and with all his wealth gone. "So may all your enemies perish, O God."[185]

After having spent over three weeks in Port Said, I did not wish to return home without having achieved any tangible accomplishment, and I therefore decided to continue to Egypt to seek merchandise there. As I walked down the street, I met Mr. Ben-Zion Amzalak. I told him about what had happened, and that I now wished to purchase some merchandise. He told me about an elderly man who sold enameled iron and tin items, cauldrons, dishes, cups, etc., and who now wished to liquidate his business due to his advanced age. We immediately visited his store and appraised the quality of the merchandise. Amzalak and I then bought the merchandise in partnership, loaded it into crates, and shipped it to Jaffa. Upon our arrival in Jaffa, we rented a special storeroom and set up the merchandise for sale, but even before we had a chance to put it up for sale, a dealer named Ya'akov Tajer[186] came in from Jerusalem, and we sold all the merchandise to him, at a profit of 200 napoleons.

A few days later, my father called me into his office and showed me a strand of expensive pearls and a diamond that he had bought during the previous month. Because there are no good customers in Palestine for these items, he asked me to go to Alexandria to sell the items there at a price that he would set for me. I traveled to Alexandria, where I noted the range of prices set by the merchants there. Then I showed them my items, but after great difficulty I could barely find merchants who offered a price almost the same as what my father had set. I decided not to be hasty and traveled on to Cairo.

The following day, walking through the streets of Cairo, I happened

---

185. Judges 5:31.

186. Tajer emigrated from Sofia to Jerusalem in 1880; he imported furniture and building supplies together with his brother Shmu'el, who settled in Jaffa and later became one of the founders of Tel Aviv.

to pass a fine jewelry shop, and above it a sign with the words "Barukh Cohen." Reading that name stirred my memory, and I was reminded that I had gone to school in Beirut with this same person. I walked into the shop and asked for the manager and was immediately led to his office. We recognized one another and then hugged each other. We began recalling our old memories of the days of our youth, and we spent quite a while engaged in a heartfelt and friendly conversation. I showed him the jewelry and told him about the prices quoted by the dealers and expressed to him my complete trust in whatever price he quoted. Mr. Barukh Cohen called for his assistant and asked him to carry out an exact calculation based on the prices at which his shop would have to sell the items. The assistant went to work, holding the jewelry in his hand, and Barukh Cohen and I continued our conversation over coffee and cigarettes. Half an hour later, the assistant walked in and announced that his calculated price was even higher than the prices that my father had quoted, by a total of 112 pounds greater.

"The total amount for the jewelry is 738 pounds," Mr. Cohen said to me, and asked if I agreed to the offer. "I already told you at the start that I hereby agree to any price that you would set," I replied, and without thinking too much, he added on to the total amount another 50 pounds, and with that he ordered his assistant to pay me 788 pounds. At my request, he paid me in English pounds. He then implored me to stay with him for a few days, and I was compelled to stay at his home for a day, which I greatly enjoyed. I returned to Jaffa with a balance of 180 English pounds more than the price that my father had set. I gave him the money and told him all about my trip.

In 1908, a Jew by the name of Mr. Feinberg,[187] from Irkutsk in Siberia, volunteered to build a school for girls at his own expense, to be situated on a piece of land that was purchased in partnership with the Alliance Israélite Universelle association. The plot adjoined our own land, where our factory and our home now stand. The committee that oversaw the construction of the school included the honorable gentlemen Zalman David Levontin, M. Dizengoff,[188] and Dr. H. His-

---

187. Yitzhak Feinberg was a member of Hovevei Zion; he donated almost 80 percent of the funds needed to build the school, with the remainder paid by Hovevei Zion.

188. Me'ir Dizengoff (1861–1936) was a Russian Zionist chemical engineer who initially immigrated to Palestine with the Hovevei Zion movement in the 1890s; he

sin,[189] acting as the agent for Hovevei Zion. The committee formulated the program and commissioned me to construct the building. The building plans, sketched by an architect who was new to the country and was not yet knowledgeable about conditions here, encountered numerous difficulties throughout its execution, since at the time our country did not have Jewish craftsmen and other professionals, but only Arabs who knew how to build according to the construction methods employed in the East. Nevertheless, I hired expert Arab craftsmen and set down to work on construction of the building, including all ornamentation and decoration noted in the building plans.

As I was about to begin building the tile roof, a group of Jews arrived from Russia and was looking for work. Since the construction was complete and the carpentry work had already been carried out by Jewish craftsmen, all that was left to do was the roofing work, which I had promised to two local Jews who were well skilled in this type of work. Yet at the building committee's request, I was compelled to give the work to the new arrivals, who were then in dire economic straits.

I invited the members of the group to my office and asked them to select the most proficient craftsmen among themselves, so that they could sit down without delay and compile an exact list of the quantity of required wooden boards, its nature, quality, and measurements. "All of us are experts," replied the members of the group. Nevertheless, at my request, three men were chosen. We sat down to make the specifications. I wrote down the numbers, took measurements and wrote them down, and they nodded in a sign of agreement. This raised my suspicion that perhaps they were not proficient in carpentry, but I gave them the benefit of the doubt. Maybe they did not yet quite understand the plans. I gave them the building plans and asked them to study them overnight, and to respond to me the next day with an exact specification sheet.

The next day they came in, accompanied by a local carpenter, who produced a list of items and numbers. I reviewed the list and found several mistakes in it. Once again, I gave them the benefit of the doubt.

---

returned to Europe for a few years and then re-immigrated to Palestine in 1905. He was involved in Tel Aviv from the beginning, and with the exception of a couple of years, he was its communal leader and then mayor until his death.

189. Haim Hissin (1865–1932) was a Russian Zionist active in the early Bilu movement. A doctor, he immigrated to Palestine in the 1880s and spent a few years in Gedera, returned to Europe for twenty years, and then returned to Palestine.

Maybe these men really were good carpenters but did not know how to put together a specification sheet. I sent them to the elderly Litwinsky,[190] who at the time was a lumber supplier, to bring wooden boards based on my order. They began working, but then, watching the carpenters as they sawed the wooden boards, particularly at the joints, I started objecting and warned them. But the carpenters shouted at me: "Are you actually going to teach us how to work?" and went on working, using their own methods.

I could see that there was no value to their work, and that they might even cause damage and monetary loss. I then called an urgent meeting of the building committee and explained to them the danger that was liable to develop due to the members of the group not knowing how to work. But the latter then spoke, in Russian, with the members of the committee and slandered me, claiming that I did not know how to work and that they were master carpenters from Russia. The committee assumed that since I was a contractor I had no idea about carpentry work, and they asked me to permit them to go on working as they saw fit. The carpentry work was then completed, the boards were placed in position, and the workers began to lay the roof tiles in place. That same night, after midnight, I heard the noise of something collapsing. I rushed outside and saw that the entire roof was ruined. That night, my sorrow was too difficult to bear, as I thought just how irresponsible these men had been to besmirch my good name and the quality of my work in public.

The following day, a huge crowd of people came to see the collapsed roof, including the committee and the carpenters. I was dismayed to hear the slanderous statements made against me, that I had skimped on expenses and cut back on materials, and that was why the walls were unable to hold up the wooden boards, which were too heavy. I bore all these defamatory statements in silence, waiting for the truth and my own integrity to come to light, as I knew that I was innocent of all guilt and misdeed.

The committee decided to commission several experts and engineers from Jerusalem to render their opinion on the situation and submit a report that would clarify who was to blame, me or the carpenters. Among the engineers was a German engineer who had built the German castle

---

190. Ya'akov Elhanan Litwinsky (1852–1916) immigrated from Russia to Palestine in 1879–1880. After failed ventures in Gaza and Rishon LeZion, he found commercial success in the lumber industry. He was among the original founders of Ahuzat Bayit.

in Jerusalem[191] on the Mount of Olives and also the building in which Herbert Samuel[192] lived; the second was the chief engineer of the Russian institutions in Jerusalem; and the third was a Jew who was then building a hospital. This committee of engineers visited the site, closely examined the wooden boards and the building construction, and then sat down in the office to consult together. The German engineer found on my desk the page on which I had sketched my method for constructing the trusses of the roof, and he asked the members of the building committee whose sketch it was. They told him that this was the contractor's notebook, and he immediately asked for me to be summoned. I walked into the office and the engineer posed the question to me: "Is it you who drafted this sketch?" I answered, "Yes, and about two weeks ago I approached the building committee with this sketch and warned them of the danger inherent in the carpentry work with respect to technique, dimensions, and quantity."

The team of engineers ordered me to leave and sat down to draft its report. After a while, the door opened, the members of the committee walked in, and the protocol was read aloud, in German. I turned to the committee members and asked them to explain the contents of the report to me, but I got the feeling that it was too hard for them to do. Then I spoke with Messrs. Dizengoff and Hissin and explained to them that I did not care at all about the collapse, and that I was even willing to rebuild the roof at my own expense, but that I wanted to know who was at fault. When the committee members heard these words, they came into the office with me and translated the entire report for me, which was in my favor and to the detriment of the carpenters, for they were the reason for the collapse.

In the end, I rebuilt the building according to my own method, with the help of the expert workers who I brought in. I built the Girls' School, with certain adaptations made by the team of engineers, and it stands to this very day on the street of the school buildings in Neve Tzedek, which is named after the late author E. L. Lewinsky.

191. He is referring to the Augusta Victoria complex, which included a cathedral, hospice, and hostel for German travelers. This housed the British high commissioner from 1920–1927.

192. Sir Herbert Samuel (1870–1963) was a prominent British Jewish politician who served as the wartime home secretary and then the first British high commissioner in Palestine, its chief colonial official, from 1920–1925.

FIGURE 9.1. *Yosef Eliyahu (R), his wife Freha (L), and their children Moshe, Me'ir, Avner, Zadoc, Hillel, and Yehudit, 1907. Missing from the photo is their younger son, Yoram, who was born in 1910. Photo by Da'ud Sabunji. Chelouche Family Collection.*

A few months later, when construction of the school had been completed, the then-headmaster of the Alliance school, Mr. Lupo,[193] asked that I take upon myself the construction of a new school building for the Alliance. He gave me the building plans that had been sketched by the director of the Austrian post office in Jaffa, and we adapted them based on the budget available for building the school. After we reached an agreement on the revised plan, it was dispatched to Paris for approval by the Alliance Israélite Universelle organization. I oversaw the work with great precision and without any disruptions. There were no complaints from any party regarding the quality of the work or the materials, and so I was able to deliver the completed two-story building within four months, including the adjacent house for the school's headmaster, who was himself quite satisfied. I recall that as a sign of affection, we were then photographed together. This is the Alliance school in Jaffa that now stands on Kol Israel Haverim Street, opposite the Girls' School.

---

193. Shmu'el Lupo (1860–1940) was born in Ottoman Ruşçuk and educated at the AIU's ENIO in Paris. He served as director of the Mikve Israel school from 1902–1915, and then later as the director of the vocational school of the AIU in Jerusalem.

CHAPTER 10 *Founding of Tel Aviv and Construction of the Gymnasium*

The Ahuzat Bayit Association, established for the purpose of building Tel Aviv | The unusual wealthy man from Bradford | Construction of the Gymnasium | Adventures in building the Gymnasium | The role played by the Zionist bank | A loan from the Jewish National Fund | M. Dizengoff at the head | Architect Barsky makes experimental building plans | Construction of the Gymnasium goes to arbitration | The Ahuzat Bayit Tel Aviv quarter blossoms overnight | The name "Tel Aviv" | My remarks on the occasion of the twentieth anniversary of the founding of the city

In 1906, the idea of founding a new settlement next to Jaffa was revived. The man behind the initiative was 'Akiva Weiss,[194] who gathered several members together, including the writer of this memoir, in order to chart a path for turning the words into deeds. Some sixty members embraced the idea, and over the course of a full year we would occasionally convene at Cafe Lifschitz in Neve Shalom, under the leadership of Mr. A. Weiss. We produced a variety of master plans for the construction of a magnificent neighborhood, on which the roads, sidewalks, and decent buildings were all marked off. There was a proposal that we should be applying for a loan from the Jewish National Fund[195] in the amount of 250,000 francs. In the end, it was decided to go ahead and purchase the land.

The duty of handling the purchase of the requisite land was assigned to Mr. A. Weiss. The land that the committee had decided upon belonged to a family with numerous heirs who had a contract with a Jew

---

194. 'Akiva Arieh Weiss (1868–1947) was a jeweler and watchmaker who immigrated to Palestine from Poland in 1906.

195. The Jewish National Fund (JNF) (Keren kayamet leIsrael) was established at the Fifth Zionist Congress in Basel in 1901 with the aim of purchasing land in Palestine for the Zionist project.

from Jerusalem, Mr. Israel Tannenbaum.[196] Mr. A. Weiss conducted negotiations in the name of all the members of the society and with whom he reached a compromise on the price, with the stipulation that the *kushan*s be awarded to the society once the payment of the purchase price had been completed. Following the signing of the contract, a general assembly was called, and after a great deal of consideration, it was decided to call the new neighborhood Ahuzat Bayit.

Numerous disputes broke out between the Jerusalemite Jew with whom the contract had been signed and the other heirs. To make things even more complicated, many Arabs put up tents on the plot of land, claiming it belonged to them.[197] In order to settle these disputes such that they would not unduly affect the purchasing procedure, Mr. Tannenbaum was compelled to grant the Arab claimants an additional sum of money, which came at our expense. In the end, the entire purchase was registered in the names of three society members and a price was then set for each member, amounting to eighty-five cents for the land. This land was parceled off among the sixty members, but another tract of land—which was twice as large—still remained; it was earmarked for new members.

Around this time, a wealthy tourist from England arrived in the country. His name was Moser.[198] He toured the institutions of the Jewish community in Jaffa, including the Gymnasium, which at the time occupied a rented building that was owned by an Arab. Moser paid a visit to the offices of the Anglo-Palestine Company (APC),[199] where he

---

196. Israel Tannenbaum, an immigrant who arrived in the early 1860s from Slovakia, was a real estate agent. His fifteen-year-old daughter Leah famously caught the eye of the wartime commander Cemal Pasha, about whom Chelouche writes a great deal in part 2 of his memoir, through her volunteer work in the Red Crescent.

197. Land sales in the Ottoman era were complicated by customary land use rights exercised by tenant farmers, by collective ownership rights of villages, and by inheritance laws that could leave dozens of heirs to a property.

198. Jacob Moser (1839–1922) was a German-born Jew who spent most of his life in Bradford, England, making a fortune in the textile business. A philanthropist, he became the lord mayor of Bradford in 1910.

199. The Anglo-Palestine Company (APC) was founded in 1902 as part of the Jewish Colonial Trust to raise funds for the Zionist movement. The APC opened its first bank in Jaffa in 1903 with the aim of assisting the "practical Zionist" work on the ground through land purchases, loans, and industrial concessions.

struck up a conversation with Mr. Z. D. Levontin, expressing his desire to build a building for the Gymnasium. Mr. Moser asked Mr. Z. D. Levontin to produce a list for him of five important men from among the residents of the city who would be of help to him in realizing this enterprise. Together, they would constitute the committee for the construction of the Gymnasium, which also included Rabbi Gaster[200] from England.

Mr. Z. D. Levontin submitted to Mr. Moser the list of these five people, namely Z. D. Levontin, the late M. Sheinkin,[201] E. Berlin,[202] Dr. Matmon-Cohen,[203] and me. He then added Dr. Levontin and Rabbi Gaster to this list and asked Levontin to call a meeting of this committee for four o'clock that same day in the offices of the APC. We received an invitation for three o'clock to attend a preliminary meeting at which Mr. Z. D. Levontin explained to us the objective of the committee. Mr. Moser appeared at four o'clock and was introduced to the members of the committee. He began speaking about the project he wished to undertake and expressed regret that he had to return abroad the following day, because of which he therefore commissioned us with drafting a plan that would cost up to approximately 100,000 francs. Moser then handed a check in that amount to Mr. Z. D. Levontin.

After Mr. Moser set sail, the committee convened for several more sessions, after which a detailed program was completed. But once it was completed, in consultation with the directors of the Gymnasium, it became clear that the sum of money that Moser had left with us was suf-

---

200. Moses Gaster (1856–1939), born in Bucharest, became a prominent linguist and Zionist figure.

201. Menachem Sheinkin (1871–1924) was a Russian Zionist and rabbi; he immigrated to Jaffa in 1906 and worked for the Hovevei Zion's information and immigration office there. Together with his wife, he was one of the founding members of Tel Aviv.

202. A member of Hovevei Zion, Eliyahu Me'ir Berlin (1866–1959) immigrated to Jaffa from Belarus in 1907 and was among the original founders of Tel Aviv. His daughter Nina was the second wife of Chelouche's eldest son, Moshe.

203. Yehuda Leib Matmon-Cohen (1869–1939) immigrated to Palestine in 1904 from the Ukraine. A year later, he and his wife Fania founded the Hebrew Gymnasium in Jaffa, and Matmon-Cohen served as its headmaster until 1910. Together with his wife, he was also among the founders of Tel Aviv.

ficient to cover only construction itself. We put our heads together to consider the purchase of a suitable lot and where the funds for this objective might come from. A proposal was raised to purchase a lot in Ahuzat Bayit—an area that would soon be expanding into a new settlement—where the construction of the Gymnasium would in return strengthen it and imbibe it with a living spirit. And this in turn would help to ensure the institution's existence.

The proposal was considered very favorably, and since a majority of the members of the Ahuzat Bayit committee were also members of the committee for the building of the Gymnasium, the proposal to purchase a suitable plot for the Gymnasium on land belonging to Ahuzat Bayit easily passed. Following an on-site visit by the two committees to view all the plots of land available in Ahuzat Bayit, and having carefully reviewed the general building plan, the two committees found that the most suitable site for the Gymnasium would be the site where Herzl Street would start, and in consideration of this fact, the institution itself would subsequently be known as the Herzliya Gymnasium.

It should be said that there were already concerns about money. The price for the lot was set by the Ahuzat Bayit committee—as a not-for-profit transaction—at 35,000 francs, but it had to be paid up front all at once, due to the fact that the Ahuzat Bayit committee members lacked the financial capacity to wait for the repayment in installments.

The committee members did commit a fundamental error: at the time, they imagined that the plot that was earmarked for the Gymnasium building would be at the far end of the neighborhood; they could not imagine that in the future, the neighborhood would expand and spread out along its length and breadth and become an important city. So it is a source of some dismay that this specific plot was selected. The plot where the Gymnasium currently stands blocks off Herzl Street.

The plot was duly marked and fenced off. Several members of the Gymnasium committee suggested issuing an appeal to a well-known institution abroad requesting an allocation of funds for the purchase of the lot. This proposal was accepted, a letter was sent to the institution, and a positive response was received. However, once Mr. Moser was informed of this development, he wrote a letter filled with grievances over the fact that he had not been informed about the money required for the purchase of the lot. He then sent us another check, in the amount of

35,000 francs, and so the lot was purchased in his name. Preparations for construction ensued, and the building plan was finalized by the architect Barsky.[204]

The proponents of the new residential settlement encountered numerous hardships along the way, with obstacle after obstacle frequently preventing them from executing the decisions that had been adopted. A group formed within the membership of the society that complained about the actions of Mr. A. Weiss, over him having remitted additional sums of money to Tannenbaum, a fellow Jew, and over the contract that had been signed and that did not adequately ensure the interests of the members. Other claims were made, as well as gossip that spread among the Ahuzat Bayit members.

I recall well the general assembly that was held and that was chaired by a man other than Weiss. Some of the members asked for permission to speak, and several individuals complained about the actions of the committee and its president, Mr. A. Weiss. However, Mr. Weiss then stood up and without showing any signs of being flustered by the inaccurate complaints, defended himself in the face of all the accusations directed at him, speaking in a calm and collected voice. He explained exactly why he had remitted the additional sums. The audience calmed down and ultimately expressed its confidence in Mr. Weiss.

At the same assembly, Mr. A. Weiss informed the membership of the size of the loan that had been received from the Anglo-Palestine Bank. Handling of this matter was entrusted to Mr. Weiss, who would oversee the distribution. In the meantime, a dispute broke out between the late E. Sapir,[205] a clerk at the APC, and Mr. Weiss, which caused delays in the construction of the houses of the new neighborhood. All the efforts made by various well-meaning individuals to make peace between the two sides proved ineffective. And it was the public that suffered from this feud, at a time when all the members of the group were completing their plans for construction and all they wished for was to simply begin building without delay. The members refused to continue waiting for

---

204. Yosef Barsky (1876–1943) was trained in architecture in Russia before immigrating to Palestine in 1907.

205. Before he was a clerk at the APB, Eliyahu Sapir (1869–1911) taught Hebrew and Arabic in Petah Tikva and worked at the Jewish Colonization Association arranging land sales to Jews.

peace to be made between the two sides and pleaded for a lottery to take place so that each member could be assigned his specific plot. Amid much celebration, the lottery was held in 1909.

Much time was spent attempting to bridge the gap between the two sides, but in vain. Mr. Levontin personally intervened, as well, but without success, and the entire matter of the loan was therefore at a standstill, without any action or deed, even though the members impatiently waited to receive the loan and start to build. At that time, seeing how the situation had become complicated, and in awareness of the distress of the members that touched my heart, I had a discussion with Mr. Weiss and asked him to accompany me to the home of Mr. Sapir. He promptly agreed but claimed that Mr. Sapir would not welcome him into his home. We walked together, and near Mr. Sapir's home, Mr. Weiss waited outside while I entered on my own. I then spoke with Mr. Sapir from the heart and shared my intense feelings. I pointed out all the suffering of the members until my words had the desired impact and Mr. Sapir consented to see Mr. Weiss.

I walked out of his house and called over to Mr. Weiss, and peace was restored. Word spread through the city about the reconciliation, and joy overtook the members. That evening, Mr. Levontin invited me to dinner at his home in recognition of my success in making peace, and this is how the loan issue was finally resolved. Each member received a sum of 250 napoleons in installments to be paid throughout the period of the construction work. There was a stipulation that half of the amount required for construction of the building would have to come from the members' own funds, and he would receive the other half as a loan. Each member had the option of investing more of his own money.

It was agreed between the bank and the committee that the bank would appoint a representative who would be responsible for issuing notes to each member each week, based on which he would receive the amount to which he was entitled in accordance with the proportion and with the amount of his own funds that he was investing. The APC chose me as supervisor, to the satisfaction of the members, and despite the fact that it allocated only a minuscule wage disproportionate to the work and responsibility that it entailed, I accepted the position.

Over time, complaints among the members were once again voiced, and at their request a general assembly was held at which a new committee was elected, with Mr. M. Dizengoff chosen as president. The new committee drafted bylaws for the society and for the buildings, which were approved at the general assembly by all the members.

The Gymnasium committee was also preoccupied with working on the plans that had been proposed for construction of the Gymnasium, and eventually one of the plans was chosen, a copy of which was forwarded to Mr. Moser. The committee proposed that I take upon myself the construction of the school building and asked me to calculate the budget. Because I agreed to the offer, I was thus forced to submit my resignation as a member of the committee.

The committee considered my resignation to be a logical step to take, for it was unreasonable for the building's contractor to simultaneously serve as a member of the committee. Negotiations between the committee and myself ensued. I was not particularly exacting about the costs and the conditions, for rooted deep in my heart was the clear recognition that I was building this for myself and that I did not even care if I was working for free. Rather, I was working solely for the privilege that the committee had given me to be the person building the Gymnasium school building, rather than some other contractor. We began to work, and the obstacles placed along my path were numerous.

On the one hand, they commissioned for the project a group of Jews from Jerusalem who were expert craftsmen, but whose lust for money was enormous. On the other hand, it seemed that this was the first time architect Barsky received a building project since completing his professional training in Russia, and the Gymnasium building was to be his first-ever practical work experience. This is why he produced so many construction plans, until at long last a final plan was approved. However, even this final plan was not executed as it was drafted, since over the course of the construction work the architect would come up with new inventions [that] required numerous added expenditures on labor —which the construction crews very painstakingly recorded—and also entailed greater use of materials.

These sorts of inventions were a frequent occurrence. I personally suffered from them greatly, as I did not want to burden the committee members nor was I accustomed to making new demands for every individual item. And so it happened that I bore it all in silence and simply executed all of the ideas that hatched in the architect's mind, even though more than once the workers refused to continue working and threatened to sue me when they saw that the work was not being done in accordance with the plans. The workers never ceased their demands for added payment for every single change, and it was up to me to comply and to pay. Nevertheless, the workers sued me in court, demanding that I pay them for all the changes made throughout the construction, from beginning to end, based on the modifications made by the architect. The judges ruled that I had to increase their wages in accordance with these changes.

But when I saw that the architect's new ideas were continuing nonstop, I went to the members of the committee and revealed my troubles to them. Several committee members promised me that they would reach a compromise with me and would repay all the extra wages that I paid the workers, so long as I completed the building quickly, and more specifically, by the day on which Mr. Moser was scheduled to come and lay the final stone. Upon hearing these words, I made the extra effort and gave in to all sorts of demands and ideas just to be done with this building. I brought in additional construction materials beyond what was in the plan, I handed out my money left and right, all in order to satisfy the committee and finish the building by the scheduled day.

When I made an exact calculation of how much money I had received from the committee and how much I had spent, it turned out that I was 50,000 francs short even just to cover my costs without any profit for myself. At this same time, I was also contracted to build thirty-two houses for Ahuzat Bayit members. I was using a quarry that I had leased from Iskandar Rock, which was close to Ahuzat Bayit (the quarry was located on the site where the Ramat HaSharon neighborhood now stands).[206] About two hundred workers worked at the quarry every day and even a few hours every night in order to supply the stones needed by the Arab masons that I employed (there were not yet any expert Jewish masons in the country), who performed their labors without making demands for added pay but rather in peace and quiet. At some point it became clear to me that all the profits I was gaining from the labor of the Arab masons I was then losing by paying added wages to the Jewish builders from the Jerusalem group who were working on building the Gymnasium. On several occasions, I considered discussing the situation with the Gymnasium committee, but I was too embarrassed to do so, since they had assured me that they would work out the final bill with me once the building was completed.

206. Today's Levontin Street in Tel Aviv and its neighboring streets.

When the work was completed, I submitted a detailed invoice to the building committee. I participated in a few meetings with the committee in which I explained the invoice line by line. My world turned dark following some very strident statements that were made by several committee members regarding the high expenses. My sorrow was greater than I could bear, not only in regard to the money I had spent on the building but also because of the unmerited stinging criticism. I was faced with the question of what to do—should I sue them? I could not come to terms with taking this step.

But on the other hand, they were well aware of the hardships I had endured during the building's construction, the numerous modifications made by the architect, the workers' demands for extra wages, etc. Despite all this the committee was rebuffing me with negative responses that were beneath my dignity, and all my requests that they not force me to bring a suit against them were disregarded. I proposed to them that we go to arbitration. The committee chose the late elderly Shertok,[207] and I chose Ben-Zion Amzalak. I served as my own advocate, and the late Sheinkin took up the side of the committee and fought with me not because I was not right, but simply because they did not have money.

The arbitration continued for several evenings, and in the end the arbitrators could not reach a compromise and added a third individual to decide on the case. Following lengthy negotiations, they ruled that I was to be paid 15,000 francs, in accordance with my righteous claim, but with no regard for the fact that I suffered so tremendously from this difficult job, nor did they take into account that I did not make any profit at all but actually lost about 35,000 francs. All of this will be written down and recorded in this book, not because I was not skilled in my work, but because I believed in people without insisting on receiving documentation for every item, large or small.

I had the honor of serving on the executive committee of the Ahuzat Bayit committee under the presidency of the honorable Mr. Dizengoff. Under his management, the small neighborhood called Ahuzat Bayit became Tel Aviv, the first Hebrew city in the world. After completing work on the well and the small water tower, the pipes were laid above the sand dunes in order to give members an opportunity to build. Several build-

---

207. Ya'akov Shertok (1860–1913) was a member of the Bilu who immigrated to Palestine twice before permanently relocating to Jaffa in 1910.

ings had already gone up, and new people were interested in buying land. The cost of land doubled, from two francs to four francs. Profits were earmarked for upgrading the neighborhood.

Meetings of the executive committee were held nearly every evening; it was the custom of the committee members to come directly to the meeting right after dinner. Mr. Dizengoff, the chairman of the committee, did not give himself or the others any time off. He worked diligently to build up Tel Aviv and he devoted the best of his strength and energy to its prosperity. Even the most daunting proposals, which in the opinion of the committee members were impossible to accomplish, were accomplished in reality by Mr. Dizengoff due to his indefatigability and his inability to give rest to his soul. It was clear to the committee members that Tel Aviv was his favored child of joy to which he was devoted body and soul for his entire life.

Laying down the infrastructure for the water supply system and the roadways, making sure the area was properly guarded, etc., all the things that were extremely hard to put into place in those days, were all carried out in spite of the hardships and obstacles. In addition to the paid Arab guards, all the members took turns in performing guard duty in the neighborhood, including Mr. Dizengoff himself.

Hectic work moved ahead at an inhuman pace. It was as if the neighborhood was blooming overnight, like a fairy tale of the *Thousand and One Nights*. Day by day, new buildings were added, which in turn created demand for new roads. I was awarded the contract to build these roads: I would bring stones from the quarry and lay down a long layer of them, on which I would then pour crushed *kurkar* sandstone mixed with water. After the steamroller rolled over and flattened them out, I poured about ten centimeters of Jerusalem gravel and then another layer of *kurkar* and water, and then another pass of the steamroller. All of this was done at a low cost of 2.25 francs per square meter because I had a great affection for the young colony and I knew that it did not have the ability to spend more money than that.

I took it upon myself also to level the sand dunes. Hills of sand formed from the storms coming in from the sea, and therefore there was a need to level the sand and prepare it for construction. At first, I used wooden planks, but later on I used a small trolley and tracks that I ordered from Port Said. I was truly drowning under the various jobs that I had taken on, constructing houses, building roads, leveling the sand dunes, and all

FIGURE 10.1. *Members of the first Tel Aviv municipal council meeting in front of Me'ir Dizengoff's house at 16 Rothschild Boulevard, 1911. Ya'akov Chelouche is the first man on the left, and Yosef Eliyahu Chelouche is on the far right; both are wearing a fez. Almost all the other members are mentioned in Chelouche's memoir (L to R): Moshe Goldberg, Eliyahu Berlin, Betzal'el Yaffe, Meir Dizengoff (the longtime mayor), Mordechai Ben Hillel Hacohen, Nissim Korkidi (the only other Sephardi Jew on the council), Yitzhak Genel, Yehuda Lev, and Dr. Yehuda Leib Pochovsky. Standing below are the neighborhood guards. Photo by Abraham Soskin. Betsy Frenkel Collection, Amsterdam Jewish Museum, F000520.*

of it under my own supervision. Aside from that, I took part in various projects and committee meetings to the point that I no longer had any set time for eating or sleeping. This situation went on for a few years; I was busy day and night. Aside from the work I've described above, there were numerous meetings and assemblies of the Tel Aviv committee, the city council, and the assemblies of the workers, who would often invite me to attend.

There was a great deal of work to be done on the Ahuzat Bayit committee. The head of the committee, Mr. Dizengoff, who worked with exemplary energy, would constantly come up with all sorts of ideas for upgrading and improving the neighborhood, which was truly an integral part of his life. Not only did he carry out the tasks that he assigned to himself, but he diligently oversaw the tasks assigned to the rest of the members of the committee, urging them to carry them out speedily. I myself punctiliously endeavored to carry out all the jobs assigned to me. For the most part, I was asked to handle affairs having to do with public figures in the city or Turkish government officials, since I had close relations with these circles, and if there was any obstacle that cast a shadow over the progress of our colony I would remove it, through a variety of means, so that there would be no impediment in the development of Ahuzat Bayit.

When the committee members and their chairman, Mr. Dizengoff, became aware of the developed state of the neighborhood, Mr. Sheinkin and others drafted a proposal to change the name of the colony to the beautiful name Tel Aviv in place of Ahuzat Bayit, and so it was.[208] The committee adopted the proposal with much delight. The general assembly that was held in the year 1909 unanimously approved the new name, and ever since then Ahuzat Bayit has been known by the charming name Tel Aviv, which gave truest expression to the feelings of the devoted builders who constructed its magnificent buildings on the desolate sand dunes. For this is Tel Aviv, which is today gaining fame as the first Hebrew city on earth, toward which the eyes of Jews in every land of the Diaspora are cast, a delightful city, the "city of miracles" of the national home of the Jews in the land of their forefathers. It is only through Jewish hardiness, through the power and energy of a people aspiring to rebuild its homeland, that it was possible to establish such a magnificent Tel Aviv, which now serves as an exemplary symbol, through its sumptuous houses, its well-arranged streets, and which is the center of our cultural lives.

These words are drawn from what I wrote at the behest of the city's leaders in honor of the twentieth anniversary of the founding of the first Hebrew city, a few of which I would like to say in this book of reminiscences on my life, to complete this important chapter of my life.

---

208. "Tel Aviv" (Hill of Spring) was the Hebrew translation of Theodor Herzl's utopian Zionist novella *Altneuland*.

We must not think, even for a moment, that the establishment of a glorious city such as Tel Aviv was an easy thing to do, along the lines of the building of other cities. The establishment of the first Hebrew city, which went through a few trials and tribulations, from the garden city "Ahuzat Bayit" to "Tel Aviv," a name that was given to it before it reached maturity, has three unique attributes that distinguish and symbolize the form and character in which the city was built, seemingly through superhuman and supernatural forces . . .

a. Tel Aviv, which is now marking its twentieth birthday, was built only twelve years ago, if we deduct the five years of the World War and the three years of crisis,[209] but it has nevertheless achieved its present state of development.
b. Tel Aviv is a 100 percent Hebrew city.[210]
c. It earned its fame as the first Hebrew city in the entire world.

These three attributes, which have been such significant factors in the pace of Tel Aviv's progress, are not to be found in the building of other cities. In all the enlightened world as we know it, it is not possible to build such a city in such a brief span of time without assistance from the government or from financial companies, and our beloved city Tel Aviv was built thanks to God, with frantic vigor and the powers of its owners themselves. Not only did the government not help one iota to establish the city, but the clerks of the Turkish government threw up obstacles at every juncture and at every opportunity to thwart the progress of its establishment, and it was only through demands and requests and at times also through "under-the-table payments" that they permitted us to pursue the labor of creating a new city in the land of our forefathers. Tel Aviv was built, then, from its foundations up to its rafters, through the inherent strength of its owners, and through their vigor and their vitality, except for the small loan that its first sixty members received from the Jewish National Fund.

We must not forget that only twenty years ago, Tel Aviv was a wilderness of sandy soil, not unlike a desolate desert of mountains and hills

---

209. Chelouche probably is alluding to the economic crisis of 1926–1928 in Palestine, during which construction works in Tel Aviv significantly decreased.

210. This was a central element of the Zionist movement that advocated for the separate development of Jewish communal life in Palestine.

filled with prowling jackals. It was sandy soil, bereft of grass and green vegetation, aside from a few withered grape vines sparsely planted here and there, neglected and abandoned. And today, Tel Aviv is blooming, in its trees, in its gorgeous vistas, and in its private and public gardens.

If we were to write down all the adventures that this young city has experienced, we would fill a large volume, therefore a few of the more significant facts will suffice.

The sixty or so members of the original group of settlers still recall the many meetings held at the Lifschitz coffee house in Jaffa, for the purpose of realizing the idea of creating a new settlement, which was the brainchild of the eminent 'Akiva Weiss. At this coffee house, the fate of these ideas was set in motion based on our mood, in joy or in sadness. It was no simple thing to purchase a plot of land from our neighbors, even after all the payments, the compensation, the receipt of the *kushan*, etc. Because all of a sudden, truly like mushrooms, new owners appeared on the scene staking claims of ownership to the site even after the purchase of the land of Tel Aviv had been concluded. They set up their tents and lived in them, armed with swords and ready for war, claiming that the land was their land. And only after compensation and conflicts that persisted for quite a while was the land freed.[211]

The path to protecting the security of the young neighborhood was no bed of roses; the area around Ahuzat Bayit was a den of thieves. These thieves were mainly found in the city, hiding in the walls of the old buildings along the road from Jaffa to Petah Tikva. Seeking to protect the neighborhood, the committee hired armed Arab guards who were able to track the movements of the thieves. There were numerous incidents of theft and there were no Jewish guards to hire,[212] and what's more, at

---

211. Chelouche is referring to the series of conflicts that emerged surrounding Zionist land purchases in Palestine. Traditionally, land use (*usufruct*) went undisturbed after its sale from one property owner to another, with tenant farmers continuing to live and farm on the land as before. In contrast, the property sold for Zionist settlement was conditioned on the eviction of tenant farmers in order to make room for Jewish settlers.

212. In fact, Jewish guards comprised primarily of new Russian immigrants organized themselves into a unit called Hashomer (The Guard) in 1909. However, their tactics, insensitivities, and in some cases provocative violence led to significant criticism against them by the officials of the Palestine Office of the WZO and by some of the leaders of the Jewish colonies themselves.

the time guarding was considered genuinely life-threatening. Left with no choice, the committee was compelled to obligate each of the members to guard the neighborhood as part of a regular rotation alongside the Arab guards, while keeping an eye on them as well. When it was my turn to guard, the nights would pass quickly and comfortably because it was also, coincidentally, Mr. Dizengoff's turn to guard. And in spite of the wind and the rain, I would spend the time engaged in conversations that were filled with hope and encouragement about the near future of Ahuzat Bayit, together with my fellow watchman Mr. Dizengoff.

The committee's level of dedication to the neighborhood was exemplary. Everything was done with extraordinary enthusiasm and through superhuman power; there was some inexplicable force that made things happen. The committee worked relentlessly, day and night. Plans were drawn up to extend the boundaries, new roads were paved; this fresh settlement was cared for with great vigilance. The founders of the settlement understood and sensed its future and value for the Israelite Diaspora, as well as the degree of its sympathetic and excited awareness to the conquest of any additional piece of land in the Land of Israel. Dizengoff devotedly kept watch over the enterprise, encouraging his fellow members to take action. He imposed on the writer of this memoir the task of resolving any conflicts that might develop between the neighborhood and the government, or with the Jaffa municipality, or with *effendi*s or neighbors staking claims of land ownership. In nearly every case, I can thank God that I was able to mediate between the sides, employing a variety of means.

One of the firmer foundations on which Tel Aviv was built is discipline, a symbolic discipline that existed within the committee and among the residents of the neighborhood. All of us were united as one when it came to valuing the objective of Jewish settlement on the land of the forefathers; members of the committee served the homeland out of a profound emotional love. All the internal differences were pushed aside, the greater good of the neighborhood and its development were always the primary focus of all. There was no privilege of individual interests or narrow and petty partisanship. Everyone served a single goal with love and idealism. It was with true joy that members of the neighborhood would carry out the decisions of the committee, as if they were holy writ from Heaven, even though there was no legal obligation to do so at the time. The members themselves meticulously observed the bylaws of the committee without needing to be reminded. All of this led to what Tel Aviv is today. This discipline should serve as a living example to all the Hebrew settlements that are now taking shape in the Land of Israel.

As the neighborhood started to develop and to slowly but surely take on the appearance of a city, through additional buildings, paved roads and sidewalks and water pipelines, cleaning, and shutting of the gate to the neighborhood with steel chains on Sabbaths and holidays (so that carts could not enter and disturb the sanctity of the Jewish holidays), the wrath of government officials and of the neighbors increasingly rose up against us. Out of their sheer envy of a clean and modern city, they started to make denunciations and accusations, spread baseless slander, and besmirch our reputation in the eyes of the government. Day after day there were new complaints about this or that, without any logic or basis. Our enemies were too narrow-minded to allow us to build an exemplary city in peace and creativity, such that we had no rest from them.

It is worthwhile to relate a single account, one among many: one night, a thief was caught in Ahuzat Bayit and the guards escorted him to Mr. Dizengoff's home. He ordered that the thief be taken to the committee building, along with the stolen items, and kept there under guard. In the meantime, notice was sent to the Jaffa police about the incident, and the police and the general investigator appeared shortly afterward. At seeing them arrive on the scene so quickly, we assumed that this could only be for our benefit, but we were mistaken. Instead of interrogating the thief who was caught red-handed, the investigator began interrogating us: Who caught the thief? Who ordered that he be placed in the neighborhood jail? Why did you put him on trial? And so on and so forth. They wrote up a police report filled with poison and rancor, based on fabrications without one iota of truth, by virtue of which the authorities threw up obstacles to the settlement's further development and regular way of life.[213]

Even before the end of Turkish rule, Tel Aviv became a municipality in its own right. At the time, there was a municipality only in Jaffa, and it issued the permits to construct the first buildings. There were no special

---

213. This incident received significant attention both in the local Arabic newspaper, *Falastin*, and in Ottoman government reports. Both the local press and local officials were alarmed at what they viewed as the security and legal autonomy flaunted by residents of Tel Aviv.

ordinances related to construction; the Jaffa municipality was barely interested in the shape or size of any building to be built, particularly if it was outside the city. The only thing the municipality cared about was the tax that the builder had to pay, which was based on the floor space of the building, with additional charges based on the dimensions of the facade and whether the building had balconies or not.

There was no particular supervision of a building under construction, except at the onset of construction—on the day that the foundations were laid, the municipality would send its designated construction commissioner to observe the builder and make sure he did not cross over the building line into the street. We received our first permits from the Jaffa municipality after having composed a detailed breakdown with total square footage of building plots, number of houses, their dimensions, measurements of length and width, plans of the facades, etc. The permit was issued on a single sheet of official stationery, which stated: Permission is granted to construct twenty houses in the neighborhood of the Jews, Ahuzat Bayit, on a plot measuring such-and-such square cubits, of such-and-such length and width of the facade, the balcony, etc., and the managers of this neighborhood are held responsible that the builders do not build over the street boundary lines, and such-and-such an amount has been received. The permit included the date, and the signatures of the treasurer and head of the municipality and three members of the municipality, and that is all.

Based on that first experience, we learned the routine. For the second and the third building permits, we did not submit any plans. We were issued general permits for two thousand cubits per building or five thousand square cubits, a certain length of the facade, so many cubits for the second floor, and the customary payments. Subsequently, we ourselves were granted the authority to levy a tax on each building proportionately. We became an independent municipality—without having received any concession even from Constantinople.

As for our current great government, instead of granting us municipality status, it has awarded us "borough" status,[214] leaving us in a

---

214. Officially, Tel Aviv was declared a "township" by the British Mandate authorities in May 1921. In this regard, Tel Aviv became a subsection of Jaffa, with limited autonomous authorities. Only in 1934 did Tel Aviv become a municipality in its own right, independent and separate from Jaffa.

pit,²¹⁵ even though we know well that there is not a single municipality in this land that compares to ours in beauty and splendor. Nevertheless, our neighbors in various cities were awarded independent municipality status even though they cannot compete with our city named Tel Aviv. But what are we complaining about? Such is the fate of every good and lofty enterprise that has a stellar future awaiting it. In spite of all the obstacles and hardships, Tel Aviv will march ahead in courage and with pride along the path charted for it by its builders.

After the episode that I referred to above regarding the thief and the police report written by the general inspector that was full of poison and hatred, we had an opportunity to explain our case to the local government and emerged with honor and dignity from the affair. This episode led us to demand that the government provide our district with special police protection. The government agreed to our demand and instructed the Jaffa municipality to purchase a lot for the purpose of building a police station on it at the Tel Aviv gate. However, the Jaffa municipal treasury was unable to cover the budget required for this objective, and we were therefore compelled to apply for a new permit from the municipality to construct buildings on another two thousand square cubits. We exploited the opportunity and set the condition that if within one year we did not manage to fill this plot of land with new buildings, we would have the right to complete them even if it took several years. But thanks to the fact that the settlement only continued to grow and we had to file for yet another permit before the year was over, it became possible for the Jaffa municipality, through the taxes it collected from us, to purchase a suitable plot of land for the construction of a police station.

Time passed and there was a change of personnel at the municipality, after which the plan to construct the new police station was canceled. It decided that due to a lack of funds it would auction off the plot and use the proceeds for other, more important objectives. Our neighborhood committee decided to buy the plot, lest it be purchased by a "stranger" among us. To this end, the committee assigned the purchase of the plot to Mr. Dizengoff and me at a price determined by the committee. But when I was invited together with Dizengoff to the Jaffa municipality on the scheduled day—which was the last day of the sale—we came up

215. In Hebrew, a pit is *bor*, thus a play on words.

against a difficult rival, an *effendi* who was among the most notable.²¹⁶ When we placed a bid that was a few piastres higher, he raised it by a few napoleons, and in the end he won the auction with a very high bid and the plot of land went to him. Early on, we thought that the *effendi* had bought the plot with the intention of reselling it to us at a high profit. But it became clear to us that he had actually purchased the plot for himself out of feelings of jealousy and hatred against Jews.

There was a very narrow and neglected alley that stretched between the plot and the entrance to Tel Aviv. He intended to seize it by brute force, aided by a law that forbids construction on such a narrow alley, in this case, the alley that separated our land and the main road. The *effendi*, who wanted to gain control of this alley, began building shops along the Jaffa–Tel Aviv road with doorways that also opened toward the Herzl Street side bordering the alley in our neighborhood, such that the alley would not be noticeable as a result of the shops being wide open also to the side of Herzl Street. All our attempts to reach a mediated solution between the two sides proved fruitless, and he remained stubborn.

The neighborhood committee could not bear to accept such an insult, and the committee decided to prevent this villain from accomplishing his foul scheme to steal part of our land by building a series of shops with one long facade but very shallow interiors. We knew that the construction work would take some time, and until it was completed, the municipality and the local government would continue to interfere with us. Disputes and lawsuits would proliferate since the *effendi* had considerable influence in the city. We considered how to outsmart him by executing a plan covertly and cautiously. And so, we devised something extraordinary.

We drafted a plan for the construction of four shops and prepared all the required building materials, stockpiled on a plot of land that was not far from the alleyway. We erected two long poles and hung kerosene lanterns from them. We hired four groups of masons and construction

---

216. A protocol from the Tel Aviv committee from 1914–1916 identified purchase of the parcel of the municipality from Sheikh Suleiman al-Taji (al-Faruqi) (1882–1958) from Ramle. A graduate of al-Azhar (in Cairo) and the Imperial Law School (in Istanbul), al-Taji returned to Palestine before World War I and wrote anti-Zionist articles for *Falastin* newspaper.

workers and then, an hour after sunset, the construction work commenced by the light of the kerosene lanterns. By daybreak, four stores had been built, from the foundations to the rafters, complete with a solid concrete roof. The residents of the neighborhood awakened to what they considered nothing short of a miracle: how could these shops have been built overnight without them knowing about it beforehand or having sensed it? After a while, the *effendi* was forced to send a message to Mr. Dizengoff, begging him to buy his plot, which was indeed purchased by the committee, not at the price he was asking but only after all the expenditures and the losses incurred to us had been deducted.

Similar incidents occurred elsewhere in Tel Aviv; several of our neighbors whose land bordered our own, ironically enough next to the more central and more nicely laid out streets, would not allow us to extend the streets and refused to sell the land at acceptable prices. The committee therefore erected barns and stables on these roads, blocking off the borders until, after a while, left with no other choice, some of the neighbors sold their land to us. At that point the barns would be demolished, and thus the city continued to expand in the four directions of the compass.

Tel Aviv gained a good reputation among Jews all over the Diaspora who heard talk about it far and wide. It became the favored son of the Hebrew people in the land of their future. Like a lighthouse, it cast its beams of light into the darkness of the Diaspora and portended the steps of redemption. By the time it was four or five years old, it already represented the center of Judaism in the country, the heart of our national-public life, a significant cause and catalyst of the movement of our people's revival. All the national institutions and cultural enterprises made their permanent homes in young and invigorating Tel Aviv: writers, teachers, education, culture, public institutions and Hebrew jurisprudence, the Palestine Land Development Company (PLDC),[217] etc. The convergence of all these institutions and enterprises into one location introduced a majestic spirit, imbuing Tel Aviv with the air of a modern city that aspires to ascend higher and higher all the way to the summit. People streamed to Tel Aviv from all the cities and colonies in the country, to relax and take a respite from their usual lives, to enjoy its

---

217. The Palestine Land Development Company (known as Hakhsharat hayishuv in Hebrew) was established in 1908 by the World Zionist Organization to direct land purchases in Palestine.

FIGURE 10.2. *The founders of Tel Aviv, 1929 celebration gathering. Yosef Eliyahu Chelouche is seated in the first row, fifth from the right. Photograph by Abraham Soskin. Soskin Collection at MUZA Eretz Israel Museum, Tel Aviv, #MHH2400.2017.*

fresh air and its unique charms. The numerous assemblies and the frequent meetings, both for the city's own institutions and enterprises and for the colonies (which also took place in Tel Aviv since their managers and leaders lived there), ensured that the settlement would never be lifeless or static.

Tel Aviv did a great deal to disseminate the Hebrew language through its network of schools. At home and in the street, its children did not utter from their lips a single foreign-language word. The immigrants whose feet stepped upon the Jaffa shore immediately felt as they walked through the gates of Tel Aviv that they had arrived in their homeland. The Hebrew language, with all its sweet pleasantness, resounded through every Hebrew home, in the street and in the places of business.[218] If we now see cultural and charitable institutions existing in other cities, it is

---

218. In fact, Diasporic languages continued to be widely spoken, in particular Yiddish, which led to the establishment of a youth organization to "defend Hebrew" in Tel Aviv, in which several of Yosef Eliyahu's sons were active.

only a living example that was taken from Tel Aviv, which excelled in all of this.

Tel Aviv, despite being conceived from the purest motives and cleanest conscience, was viewed with suspicion and concealed envy and fear by both the local government and our neighbors throughout the country. There was an unfounded dread of the Hebrew *yishuv* that was putting down deep roots in the homeland, and they therefore began to denounce the Jews, overtly and covertly, and poured insults and scorn on our heads and on our leadership in the pages of their newspapers. The sin of poison and the suppressed hatred delayed the normal progress of the construction and the creative flowering of Tel Aviv. This led to a suffocating atmosphere, which prevented us from fulfillment of the important tasks that we had assigned ourselves: promoting progress and prosperity in the city in the years before the outbreak of the World War, when it was under Turkish rule.

At this time, approximately a year before the outbreak of the World War, some of the founders of Tel Aviv, all natives of the country, decided to establish The Shield [Hamagen] association, in an effort to repudiate the defamatory reports appearing in the Arabic press and other media. Details about the activities of The Shield will be related in the next chapter.

All of this was before the war. But in the years that followed the World War and the Balfour Declaration, Tel Aviv advanced with such rapid and delightful and magnificent strides that it was a cause for wonder and amazement around the world.

The celebration of its twentieth anniversary in 1929 was a major Hebrew national holiday. On that occasion, the sixty first founders of Tel Aviv took the opportunity to pose for a group photograph, as a memento to the history of the settlement's building [figure 10.2].

CHAPTER 11 *New Company and The Shield Association*

M. Sheinkin and the founding of the New Company | New Company and the idea of a university | Purchase of Tal al-Shammam and Jaida | The Palestine Land Development Company | Slander | What Dizengoff said to me | N. Sokolow and L. Motzkin as mediators | Aftermath of the purchase | New Company breaks up | Accusations made in the Christian Arab press against the yishuv *| The Shield association | Objective and role of the association | Hafez Bek al-Sa'id | The Decentralization leadership from Syria | Their meeting with our association | Sentenced to hanging as traitors to the homeland | The death of Hafez Bek al-Sa'id while in custody*

In 1913, the late Sheinkin set up a company to purchase land in the environs of Tel Aviv and then sell it on easy payment terms, with the objective of developing the *yishuv*. Some forty people bought shares in the company and then selected an executive board, on which I had the honor of serving as a member; it was called New Company [Hevra hadasha]. The founding articles of the company stipulated that each share would cost 3,000 francs, of which 1,000 would be paid in cash, 1,000 as a promissory note payable one year later, and 1,000 as a note payable two years later. By 1914, the company had bought six vineyards and other plots of land, all in the environs of Tel Aviv.

The company had a wide range of operations and soon had to open a special office and hire more employees. The committee tasked me with land purchases, for which I was responsible. Since I was a native of the country and fluent in its language, I was adept at finding the easiest way to execute large-scale purchases on satisfactory terms. I endeavored to be exact when it came to the quality of the land, proposing the terms, and the drafting of contracts with the Arabs, and I exercised extreme caution in all these matters. My colleagues included

Lev,[219] Aboab,[220] Sheinkin, and Goldfarb,[221] all of whom have passed away, and Messrs. Ashkenazi and Hayat, may they live long lives.

In the continuation of our important work, the late Sheinkin proposed that we purchase a large tract of land in Jerusalem in the vicinity of the Temple Mount, in order to allocate within it a plot of land that would be suited to the construction of a Hebrew college, with the remainder to be divided into plots and sold at ten times the amount we paid, and then to dedicate these profits to the construction of the university.[222] We were certain that every Jew would wish to purchase a plot of land near the Temple Mount, even at high prices, given the sublime objective toward which the money would be earmarked. We traveled to Jerusalem, inspected various properties around the Temple Mount, and having seen them, we approached the honorable gentleman Malki'el Mani, with whom we consulted regarding the purchase.

We requested that Mani take upon himself the consummation of this purchase, and he agreed. A few weeks later, he sent us a detailed plan of several tracts in the vicinity of the Temple Mount along with their prices. We informed him that he could sign the contracts in our name, based on the conditions that we had stipulated. And so, Mr. Mani executed the desired purchase, and there was no limit to our great joy and contentment. We could envision the magnificent university to be built not far from the Temple Mount, with thousands of young Jewish immigrants converging on Jerusalem from every corner of the globe, to receive an education in our own language, with the prophetic mission, "For instruction shall come forth from Zion, the word of God from Jerusalem"[223] practically being fulfilled before our very eyes.

219. Israel Avraham Lev (1845–1921) was a wealthy gas and oil industrialist from Russia who immigrated to Palestine and settled in Tel Aviv in 1911.

220. Yehuda Leib Aboab (or Abohab) (1848–1921) was a wealthy timber merchant in Russia before immigrating to Palestine in 1907. He was one of the early founders of Tel Aviv and Nahalat Benyamin, and he served on a variety of local councils.

221. Yehoshu'a Goldfarb (1867–1920) was a member of Hovevei Zion and a banker in Poland. He immigrated to Palestine in 1909 and settled in Rehovot before buying property in Tel Aviv. He was involved in land purchases through the Kidmat haaretz land company, together with Aboab and Mani.

222. The decision to establish a Hebrew university was adopted in September 1913 at the Eleventh Zionist Congress in Vienna.

223. Isaiah 2:3.

It was then that we received a letter from Dr. Ruppin and Dr. Thon, appointed officials of the Zionist Office,[224] in which they asked us to come to their office. When we arrived, these gentlemen informed us of their request: they had heard of the excellent plan that we were soon about to fulfill, and in consideration of the fact that it related to the entire Jewish people and therefore could not belong to private individuals, we would have to transfer to the Zionist Office (which was the official local representative of the Zionist movement) the properties as well as all the documents and protocols relating to the fulfillment of the plan. They themselves would handle this important matter directly, and they would repay us the money that we had invested with the addition of some profit.

We happily transferred everything to the Zionist Office, and we also wrote to Mr. Malki'el Mani, saying that from that point on he should deal with Messrs. Ruppin and Thon as the purchasing party in the agreement. We ourselves refused to accept any profit, but our invested capital was returned to us two months later. What has happened with the building of the university from then and to the present day is well known to all.[225]

Seventeen years have passed since that time, and no one remembers who the first person was to come up with this "holy" idea and who the people who so devotedly saw it into fruition were; it was the members of the New Company who facilitated the purchase of land for the sake of realizing the goal of building the college on a firm foundation.

Around this time the Association of Settlers (Agudat hamitnahalim) approached us with a request to purchase agricultural land in the Jezreel Valley on behalf of the association. They told us that there was an opportunity to buy the villages of Tal al-Shammam and Jaida, both of which belonged to a Christian family.[226] We traveled to the area and

224. Arthur Ruppin and Ya'akov Thon served in the Palestine Office (Palästina Amt) of the World Zionist Organization, established in 1908. Ruppin (1876–1943) studied law and economics in Germany and directed the Berlin Office for Jewish Statistics from 1904–1907. He arrived in Palestine in 1908 to head up the newly formed Palestine Office, and over the years he authored a number of sociological and demographic studies on the Jewish community in Palestine. Thon (1880–1950) was a lawyer who worked with Ruppin first in Berlin before his own arrival in Palestine in 1907.

225. The sale, a protracted and conflictual process, was completed in March 1914, the cornerstone was laid in 1918, and the Hebrew University was officially opened in 1925.

226. British records show the family name as Twsiny, partners of the Sursock large landholding family in Beirut.

carried out an investigation, and it became clear that the family was interested in selling the two villages at the same time. Since the aforementioned association did not have the resources to buy the villages on its own, we consented to buy the two villages, which included some sixteen thousand *dunams* [four thousand acres], and to apportion one-third of the property to the Association of Settlers. As we were handling this important purchase, after having toured the area several times, we conducted research on the nature of the neighbors, and so on and so forth. We then received a letter from the Zionist Office, signed by Dr. Ruppin and Dr. Thon, who warned us not to buy these villages since they had been working on the completion of this purchase for some time.

As we did not wish to argue with the Zionist Office on the matter, we reported the state of affairs to the Association of Settlers, which in turn independently approached the Zionist Office asking it to purchase the land on their behalf, [and the office] promised to fulfill their request. A few months later, with the promise still not honored, the Association of Settlers again applied to the Zionist Office requesting that it make good on its commitment, but then it received a negative response from the Palestine Land Development Company (PLDC) informing them that the company was not going to complete the purchase. At that point, the association approached us again and asked us to handle the purchase.

We wrote to the PLDC and asked them either to reconsider the request of the Association of Settlers and go through with the purchase of the aforementioned villages, or to authorize us to execute the purchase. The PLDC responded that it would let us handle the purchase, since they were relinquishing the ties they had made with the local residents the previous year. Based on this authorization, we went back to Haifa and to Beirut and conducted negotiations for the purchase of the villages. I myself inserted a fundamental change in the contract that had been drawn up between Mr. Hankin,[227] representative of the PLDC, and Mr. Abela,[228] the British vice-consul in Haifa who was negotiating the sale.

---

227. Yehoshuʻa Hankin (1864–1945) emigrated from Russia to Rishon LeZion in 1882. Starting in 1890 he began working in land purchases on behalf of Zionist colonies under the Jewish Colonization Association, and then later in the various WZO land purchase societies.

228. Other than his first initial, P., no information has been located about him.

The contract had been voided since Mr. Hankin had not made a payment and violated the contract.

Almost every clause in the contract took on a new shape: instead of fifty-two francs per *dunam*, as the Hankin contract agreed to, I insisted on forty-five francs per *dunam*. Instead of the appraisal of the buildings and olive trees being completed by just any expert, I insisted that the appraisal be conducted by the director of the APB in Haifa, Mr. Kaiserman.[229] Likewise, I demanded that while the commissions were to be paid by the buyer (as usual), the repayment would go from three years to five years, and on the condition that the *kushan* would be issued immediately and in the name of a Jew of our choosing. In the contract Hankin had written that the owners would help the buyers clear out the peasants living on the land, [but instead] I demanded that immediately after the signing of the contract, half of the purchased land area would be cleared of peasants, with the other half cleared the following year.[230]

These changes made by me enabled us to complete the transaction under the best possible terms. But while I was in Beirut for the signing of the contract, I suddenly received a telegram instructing me to return to Tel Aviv immediately. I informed the landowner that I had to return home and asked him to preserve the conditions of the contract. When I arrived at our offices in Tel Aviv, I learned that an assembly called by the PLDC had taken place the previous day, at which a slanderous tale had been spread about the soil being tainted by malaria and full of swamps and that the New Company was deceiving the people in the Association of Settlers. At this assembly, it was decided that if the New Company purchased the land, the assembly would appeal to public opinion by means of posters and coverage in the press. All of this is why they were compelled to send me the telegram telling me to return immediately.

After hearing this news, I also found out that Mr. Dizengoff had fallen ill and that he had asked about me the previous night, whereupon he was told that I was in Beirut. I immediately went to Mr. Dizengoff's home. After I inquired about his health, he began complaining about

---

229. The Odessa-born Natan Kaiserman (1863–1945) immigrated to Palestine in 1890–1891. He worked as an agronomist for the early Jewish colonies; in 1908 he was appointed as director of the new Haifa branch of the APB.

230. Chelouche uses the Hebrew word *lefanot*, which also means to evacuate or, in this case, to forcibly evict the peasants farming the lands.

me, asking how it was that I had been swept up into the New Company and was now doing disreputable things with them. Since I had a respectable reputation in the city, he advised me to leave the company and not go through with this purchase, since the land was filled with swamps and was not worth the price we had agreed on with the sellers. It would be shameful to have the settlers settle on this swamp only for the handful of piastres that the New Company might earn.

I listened attentively to what Mr. Dizengoff said, from which it became entirely clear to me the extent to which the PLDC had managed to manipulate public opinion against the New Company. I then described the entire course of events to Mr. Dizengoff, and his eyes widened as he began to understand the situation and how it came to be. He immediately sent for the late Betzal'el Yaffe,[231] and then in my presence, relayed to him all the details I had related pertaining to the price and the conditions of the contract, as well as all the differences between Hankin's contract and the contract that I drafted. He also told Yaffe about the written permission from the PLDC. Both men were astonished to hear about the scheming of the PLDC, which they found unseemly. That same day, I was at the Tel Aviv committee and learned that our leaders, Messrs. Sokolow[232] and Motzkin,[233] had come to Tel Aviv in order to arbitrate between two important national institutions. I immediately issued a proposition to the management of the New Company that they write a letter to Mr. Sokolow and ask him to intervene in the matter of the conflict between us and the PLDC.

A letter sent by the New Company noted that in the event that Mr. Sokolow did not agree to our request, he would bear all of the responsibility for the situation. That same day, we were asked by Mr. Sokolow to come to the PLDC office at eight o'clock that evening. We arrived at the designated time along with all the documents in our possession

231. Yaffe (1868–1925) was a member of Hovevei Zion in the Russian Empire; he immigrated to Palestine in 1909 and settled in Tel Aviv. From 1910 until his death, he managed the Ge'ula land purchase society.

232. The Warsaw-based Nahum Sokolow (1859–1936) was a prominent journalist in the European Hebrew press as well as a leading Zionist figure before World War I, at which point he moved to London and worked with Chaim Weizmann in the WZO. Sokolow headed the Zionist delegation to the Paris Peace Accords in 1919.

233. Leo Motzkin (1867–1933) was a prominent Russian intellectual, cofounder of Berlin's Jüdischer Verlag, and Zionist activist.

related to the purchase, the correspondence between us and the PLDC, a copy of Hankin's contract, and a copy of the new contract that we had drafted. The New Company was represented at this meeting by the late Sheinkin, Aboab, and me; representing the PLDC were Dr. Ruppin, Dr. Thon, and Hankin.

I spoke for our side, as I had a very clear understanding of the entire matter. My principal words of appeal and words of caution to the judges before they rendered their verdict: since the PLDC had committed an act of slander regarding the nature of the land about to be purchased, the New Company could no longer purchase the land on its own. It could do so only in partnership with the PLDC, because the statement that the latter company had issued—after all the money that we had invested—had created a diminished supply of buyers, at the very same time as we were about to complete several other purchases within the city proper. Only by means of a directive issued by the PLDC company leadership to purchase the land in partnership with the New Company would it be possible to weaken the impression made on the audience present at the assembly convened by the PLDC. Only then would the public understand that the PLDC was not prepared to agree to the land being purchased solely by the New Company.

I explained this statement in depth and clearly proved that once they had a chance to review the paperwork in our possession and the permit granted us by the PLDC, their own leadership would see how justified our actions had been. The late Sheinkin also spoke and further explained the situation. The first speaker for the PLDC was Dr. Ruppin, and he was followed by Mr. Hankin, who had a clearer picture of the matter than his colleagues. After the claims of both sides were voiced, Mr. Motzkin addressed Dr. Ruppin and admonished him, saying that the PLDC had authorized the New Company to purchase the villages of Tal al-Shammam and Jaida and had no permission to convene an assembly that might cause undue harm to the purchase. Secondly, Hankin's contract was signed between the PLDC and the middleman, whereas the New Company's contract was made between it and the owner himself. Thirdly, there were colossal differences in all the sections of the contract that had been revised by the New Company, which had the effect of making its conditions more desirable.

A fifteen-minute recess was called, during which the leaders consulted among themselves and, at the end, they reentered the room and turned to us, saying: "You, the members of the New Company, are permitted to finalize the purchase as you have started." I then appealed to the leaders and once again explained that given the slanders that the PLDC had spread, the New Company would be unable to purchase the land on its own. And so it was that the leaders directed the parties to purchase the land together. Dr. Thon invited me to come into the PLDC office the next day to clarify the situation so that I could return to Beirut and complete the purchase. The following day, I made my way to the office of Dr. Ruppin, and he proposed that I go to Beirut and complete the purchase. But I refused, demanding that the partnership agreement be registered solely in the name of the New Company, and so it was.

I drafted a contract based on the now well-known conditions and bought the villages. Nevertheless, we did not receive money from the PLDC; it came from the New Company and from the Association of Settlers, which made a down payment of 3,000 napoleons. I then traveled with the late Sheinkin to complete the purchase, and along the way we talked and were pleased with the success of the transaction, after which we returned, safe and sound, to Tel Aviv.

Shocking rumors began to spread through the *yishuv* about the imminent declaration of a World War. Everyone was beset by depression and despair, the signs of which were easily discernible even in our daily comings and goings. People could no longer think about doing business, commercial development, new purchases and sales, and the like. Day and night, the only thing on people's minds was the war. In the chapters to come, in the second part of this book, I will be writing about the days of war itself. I now wish to complete the story about the outcome of the purchase of these aforementioned villages.

During the war, we were compelled to notify the owners of the villages to fulfill all the conditions of the contract, just as we ourselves were obliged to try and fulfill these conditions on our side. The outbreak of the war required us to safeguard our own position, and, of course, the owners of the villages also issued a warning to us regarding our need to uphold the conditions. If truth be told, both we and they failed to meet the conditions, owing to the World War. When the World War ended, we returned from [our internal] exile. A full year passed, but business volume was not yet back to its normal level. We were unable to think about the future of the New Company.

Some members of the Association of Settlers were not in the country, and some were still scattered and had not yet returned to the city, and those who were in the city did not have the financial means to pay their debts. Moreover, about a year after the conquest, the new government issued an order that no company had permission to purchase the land for settlement without government approval. And so it was that year after year passed; we were idle and did not take any action. Our company's situation was unchanged, and the owners of the villages were silent for some reason unknown to us. It was a source of dismay, for all the energy that had been invested in this purchase, for it all to come to naught, particularly in view of the fact that our company and the Association of Settlers had invested a total of some 60,000 francs in down payments, a drainage system, part of the middleman commissions, etc. The contract explicitly stated that if either side did not fulfill the conditions, they would have to pay damages of 60,000 francs, which in our case meant that all the money we had invested would be lost.

All this explains why I had to go to see the middleman, the owners' associates, and, eventually, the owners themselves, to get a proper sense of the situation and to learn what they were thinking. It became obvious that they refused to hand over the land at the price as stated in the contract conditions, and that they were even ready to pay damages in the event it went to trial and we won. This piece of information gave us some relief. We consulted with an attorney. He studied all the documents and considered the status of the contract we had in our possession, as well as our own liability that due to the war, we had not fulfilled all the conditions of the contract. But on the other hand, he found that the warnings that we had sent to the owners of the villages during the war would be beneficial to us if the case went to trial, if we would issue another warning now.

Following extensive consultations with more attorneys, we did just that, in order to reinforce our position and avoid losing our money. Meanwhile, the cost of real estate doubled and then tripled, but we had no members and no money. Regardless, we resumed talks with the villages' owners and aggressively demanded that they transfer the land in accordance with the conditions of the contract, but the sellers unanimously declared that they would not sell the land according to the conditions of the contract. Eventually, we realized that we would be able to complete the purchase not at the price of 45 francs, but at 3.5 Egyptian liras per *dunam*. And so in order that we could recover our capital as well as the land from their hands—fearing that they could sell it, even at as much as 5 Egyptian liras—we approached the PLDC and asked them to purchase the land in accordance with the conditions of the contract, on condition that they repay us the funds we had already invested, as well as the profits.

After a great deal of pleading, the PLDC consented to execute the purchase itself. We gave them all the documents in our possession and received from them a letter in which the PLDC committed to pay us once the purchase was completed, in accordance with the conditions agreed upon between us. The transaction dragged on for a long time, but the PLDC eventually purchased the two villages, and we finally received from it the share to which the New Company was entitled, as well as the share to which the Association of Settlers was entitled.

This is the story of the Tal al-Shammam and Jaida affair. Moshav Kfar Yehoshuʻa [was] situated on a portion of this land.

Three years passed from the time of the occupation, and the company was still unable to initiate any real activity. We deliberated over the question of the difficult state of the company. A majority of the shareholder-members were absent; even those who had purchased lots from us and owed us money were absent. The company was in substantial debt to banks and to numerous individuals, and we did not even have a government-approved license that recognized the transaction. In the meantime, a few of the directors of the New Company passed away, which left us facing a major complication and in a state of distress. The debtors began to pester us, and particularly me, and the company's situation worsened.

As time went by, the shareholders began returning to the country. We convened a general assembly attended by all of the members but three, which was a source of great joy for us, as we finally reconvened in the country. After several assemblies and a thorough review of the situation, we decided on liquidation of the company. Each member received 1,000 francs in cash and the remainder in the form of their own promissory notes (nearly everyone was in possession of these notes, for the date of their repayment had passed and they could no longer be used). All the land owned by the association was sold, and the debts of the company were repaid.

Nevertheless, the New Company still owed a fairly large amount of money to the APC, and we consulted over how to be released from this debt. It was discovered that there were buyers of lots in the Tel Aviv district who were not in the country, and their fees had not yet been paid. We therefore approached the Tel Aviv committee with a proposal: since our company had seventy-two plots in the Tel Aviv area, in order to transfer those plots with absentee owners into trusted hands, and since these absentees were still in arrears to the APC and we did not have a government permit to act even in the foreseeable future, we therefore asked the Tel Aviv committee to repay the APC the entire debt it owed, and in exchange, to mortgage all of the plots under its name. The Tel Aviv committee happily and willingly endorsed the proposal. We drafted the contract, in which it was stipulated that if the owners of the plots did not repay the sums they owed by the end of one year, the Tel Aviv committee was authorized to sell the lots and repay the debts. Once the contract was signed between us and the Tel Aviv committee, and between Tel Aviv and APC, the days of operations by the New Company came to an end.

Having described this financial affair in full, which began about one year before the World War began, I will proceed to address the political activity that year. From the current perspective, given the very complex and bitter relations between the neighboring peoples, it would be very worthwhile to dwell on the matter and tell the story, because aside from its political value, the story also sheds light on a significant event in my own public life.

In 1913, there was a proliferation of slander and accusation in the Arabic press and primarily the Christian press against the Jews in the Land of Israel in general, and against Tel Aviv specifically, as I have previously mentioned.[234]

We natives of the country who knew Arabic would read these libelous statements each day and very much took them to heart. About ten of us gathered one day at the home of Dr. Shim'on Moyal, who was also a noteworthy Arabic-language journalist. The participants at this gathering included Messrs. Avraham Elmaleh,[235] Nissim Malul,[236] David

234. Chelouche is referring here to *Falastin* and *al-Karmil*, prominent anti-Zionist newspapers published in Jaffa and Haifa, respectively.

235. Elmaleh (also written as Elmaliach) (1885–1967) was a prominent Hebrew and Judeo-Spanish language journalist in Jerusalem. He also taught Hebrew for a while in Istanbul and Damascus before the war. After World War I, he became an important communal leader in Jerusalem, and he published several dictionaries (Hebrew-Arabic and Hebrew-French) and translations of books from Arabic.

236. Nissim Malul (1892–1959) was an Arabic and Hebrew language journalist.

Moyal, Moshe Matalon, my brother Ya'akov and myself, and a few others whose names I cannot recall. The objective of our meeting was to create a secret association to be called The Shield. We collected a certain amount of money right then and there from all those who were present, and we agreed among ourselves that each of us would contribute a monthly payment. It would be our sacred obligation to work diligently and be vigilant with regard to the Arabic press. In those first few months of our association's existence, we used to get together almost every evening in the offices of the attorney Moyal.[237]

Our association, The Shield, saw it as its goal and objective to explain to the Arab world—in the pages of the Arabic press—the motivations and aspirations of the Jews of the Land of Israel, who not only were not opposed to the aspirations of the Arabs but, on the contrary, were bringing great benefits to the Arabs, economically and culturally.[238] With that purpose in mind, we wrote articles for the local Arabic newspapers on a variety of subjects, and also for Arabic newspapers in Syria and Egypt. Our main task was to prevent disaster by producing responses in the press that countered all the articles that defamed and libeled Zionism in general and the Jewish *yishuv* in the Land of Israel in particular.

Through our actions, we earned the approbation of several important Arab figures who issued responses to our articles under their own names, all in counterpoint to the defamatory articles against us in the Arab press.

Our association's initiatives were also meant to attract many of the more important and respected Arabs in the land in general, and Jaffa in particular, to our objectives. On one occasion, my colleague Moshe Matalon and I were tasked with paying a call to one of the most important

---

Starting in 1911, he began translating the Arabic press into Hebrew for the Jaffa-based Palestine Office, and he also wrote articles "explaining" Zionism to Arab audiences.

237. Dr. Shim'on Moyal and attorney David Moyal were the two sons of Yosef (Bek) Moyal mentioned earlier (footnote no. 96).

238. Hamagen's efforts were among the first organized public relations campaigns published in Arabic. However, this was a private initiative and was separate from the initiatives of the Palestine Office of the WZO in Jaffa, which paid subventions to the Arabic press for articles friendly to the Zionist movement. This line of "benefits to the Arabs" would remain a key tenet of Zionist public relations throughout Chelouche's lifetime and far beyond. *Haherut* covered Hamagen enthusiastically on 22 April 1914 and 24 April 1914.

elders of the Arab community in Jaffa, Hafez Bek al-Sa'id,[239] a man with whom the two of us were close and were personally acquainted. He had considerable influence on the Arabs of Jaffa. I considered him to be "righteous among the nations"; he was the uncle of 'Asim Bek al-Sa'id, the mayor of Jaffa to this very day.

We called on Hafez Bek al-Sa'id. I explained to him, along with my colleague Moshe Matalon, that the objective of our visit was ensuring peaceful relations with our neighbors, an objective that was close and dear to his heart. He received us with all due honor and assured us that he would use all his influence to promote this matter, to calm down the incited and angry voices found in Arab circles within the country and in neighboring lands, where he maintained both spiritual and political links with the Arab notables. Hafez Bek al-Sa'id published an important article on this subject that had a considerable impact.

During this period, an extremely nationalistic movement was arising among the Arab youth. It led to the founding in several Arab countries of a political association called the Decentralization Party (al-Lamarkaziya).[240] The main tenet of this association was a demand for local self-rule, an autonomy of sorts from the Turkish regime in Constantinople.

It was only sometime later that we learned that the important personage Hafez Bek al-Sa'id had also teamed up with this covert Decentralization association after our visit with him. In his desire to bring the leaders of the group, who lived in Syria, closer to important members of the Jewish community in the Land of Israel—so that they, too, could be acquainted with the aims of the association and help to accomplish its goals—he wrote to them about the objective of our visit to him, and he asked them to use all of the means and influence at their disposal to soothe the turbulent anti-Jewish tensions found in the Syrian press.

A short time later, a delegation of the Decentralization leadership ar-

239. Al-Sa'id (1843–1916) served in several Ottoman administrative positions before being appointed as the head of the Jaffa commercial court and a member of the Jaffa municipality. In 1908, al-Sa'id was elected as one of the Jerusalem district's three parliamentary representatives in Istanbul; he returned to Jaffa in 1912 and was later arrested and imprisoned during the war.

240. The Ottoman Party for Administrative Decentralization was an Arab political party established in 1912 in Cairo with the aim of promoting a federal system in the Ottoman Empire.

rived in Jaffa, seeking an interview and meeting with members of The Shield association. The meeting at which we were to conduct this conversation between us was held at the home of my brother Ya'akov, for the reason that one of the Syrian emissaries was an Arabic poet who was acquainted with my brother Ya'akov, who also wrote poetry in Arabic. Ya'akov was very active in our association. The guests arrived at exactly the time that had been set. We conducted an extensive political discussion with them, on all the issues that were of greatest concern to us, mainly pertaining to the relations between us neighbors, which needed to be better and more peaceful.

This visit was especially beneficial in terms of our objectives, as a short while after their visit, the views expressed in the Syrian press toward the Jews in Palestine shifted from bad to good, in our favor.[241]

Upon the outbreak of the World War, during the first year of the war, the Turkish minister of war Djemal [Cemal] Pasha assumed the position of military commander in Syria. He arrested and imprisoned all the Arab dignitaries belonging to the Decentralization association, having accused them of treason against the regime. Several of these imprisoned Arab notables had been exchanging letters with our colleagues in The Shield association, and since all these letters and documents were in the possession of Nisim Malul, he wasted no time in burning the papers before he himself fled the country. From that day on, The Shield association disappeared from our public life.

In early 1915, a military court under the command of Djemal Pasha tried and convicted these Arab notables and sentenced them to death. Several dozen were hanged on Mount Lebanon, on his orders.[242]

Our friend Hafez Bek al-Sa'id, who was incarcerated in Jaffa and was shipped to Lebanon as a political prisoner on the orders of Djemal Pasha, was not hanged like his comrades due to his age and his prominent social standing. Instead, he was placed under confinement in Lebanon, where he died in prison. The reason for his sudden death has never been determined.

241. The Palestine Office was also paying subventions to various Arabic newspapers and placing favorable articles for anonymous republication.

242. The 'Aley trial became a rallying cry for anti-Ottoman Arab nationalist mobilization during the war.

CHAPTER 12 *The Silicate Initiative, My Dream — and Those for Whom It Came True*

The simple stone | Problems and limitations in the construction trade | The start of Tel Aviv's development | My arguments in favor of Hebrew labor | The Egyptian red brick | Its unsuitability to our buildings | Searching for the right stone | The European silicate brick | My association with a factory in Stuttgart | Working as a menial laborer in a factory in Egypt | Dizengoff and Johann Kremenezky get involved | Purchase of land for the silicate factory — without my knowledge | My proposal to the Tel Aviv committee | Purchase of the sand dunes up to the banks of the Yarkon River | My trip with Dizengoff and Tolkowsky to tour the site | Tolkowsky refers to "their" project | Dizengoff talks | Tolkowsky is amazed to hear about it | The gathering in this matter at the home of Betzal'el Yaffe | They offer me a partnership | My warning to them

Around one year before the outbreak of the World War, in 1913, four years since the founding of Tel Aviv, having built most of the houses and also the Gymnasium building, I came to realize that the simple local stone impedes and hinders an accelerated building of the city.

Once I realized that the scale of construction of the city was about to take on a quicker tempo than even the optimists among us had imagined, I began considering and searching for all sorts of ways to procure a different material for construction to replace the local stone that was all sand and that crumbled easily. Another important consideration I had for searching for a different construction material instead of regular stone was the employment of Hebrew workers in construction works, since only Arabs knew how to handle the stone in construction.

Following my first experience of employing only Hebrew workers in the construction of the Gymnasium, I came to the realization that Hebrew workers can be employed as builders, but that a material for manufacturing bricks or a certain type of bricks must be adopted to facilitate their work in construction. As I began contemplating another building material like a stronger stone, I also examined the fired red brick and was obliged to take clay from here to Egypt, where similar bricks are produced in factories in Upper Egypt.

After seeing the red bricks being manufactured at a large factory in Egypt owned by a Jew named Sornaga,[243] I realized that it would be difficult to make this brick in our country due to the numerous machines required merely to prepare the raw material prior to actual production, and then the threshing machine needed to prepare the "dough" by repeatedly grinding the smaller particles of lime found in it, otherwise the product was liable to burst apart inside the kiln. Once I realized that this brick would be too difficult for us, I abandoned the issue, even after I had gone to contract and purchased for this purpose, together with others, a large plot of land in Hadera that was well suited for extraction of the clay, and after we had built a kiln for this purpose. We were forced to abandon it all.

Nevertheless, I did not abandon my search for a stone-brick that would be suitable for construction, and after my arduous search, I found the solution. I learned that in Europe they had long ago invented a means of producing a strong brick out of sand found on the seashore, which contained only 6 percent lime. The brick was strong and very good and nice-looking. The name of this brick was "silicate."

Based on this discovery, I began working as hard as I could, contacting factories that produced these bricks in Europe, and particularly a factory in the city of Stuttgart, in the state of Württemberg in Germany. Following an extensive exchange of correspondence with the factory and having received all the details, big and small, regarding how to manufacture this silicate brick, I learned, based on accurate estimates, that in order to establish a suitable factory for the scale of our construction we would need no less than 600,000 gold francs to build and equip a factory of this type.

Once I had nearly made the decision to move ahead and build the factory, I asked the factory in Stuttgart if they would explain to me not

---

243. Samuel Sornaga, of Italian-Jewish origins, opened his brick and tile factory in Cairo in 1895; at its height it reportedly employed two hundred workers. The factory still exists today.

only the theoretical process of how to manufacture the brick, but also the practical process of how the brick was actually made in the factory. I realized that I needed to see it with my own eyes. From Stuttgart they advised me that it was not worthwhile for me to travel all the way to Europe. There was a factory much closer to the Land of Israel that manufactured that brick, in Egypt, and which was owned by a Greek.

I learned that this Greek belonged to the Masons, and so I paid a visit to Iskandar Fi'uni,[244] the head of the Masonic lodge in Jaffa. He gave me a letter of introduction addressed to his Greek comrade, in which he requested that he show me his factory.

Upon arriving in Egypt, the Greek received me warmly, and with all due respect, but he was by no means willing to let me see the brick production line in his factory due to the industrial secrets involved. This harsh ban and the intense level of secrecy proved to be a great challenge to me and aroused my curiosity even further to see firsthand, to know and understand how this brick is made. But how could I achieve this difficult task?

It was then that an Egyptian friend of mine offered me some advice. He said that I had no other choice but to dress up as a simple laborer asking for a menial job. Then, he would bring me as a common laborer into such a factory in Egypt. Spurred by my intense desire to learn the inner workings of this industry, I accepted my friend's advice, and one fine day, early in the morning, he took his own courtyard servant's clothes and gave them to me to put on. Then, wearing the clothing of a laborer looking for work, I managed to get a job at such a factory in Heliopolis, which is in Egypt.

I "worked" for ten days or so as a common laborer in this silicate factory. And in order to observe everything that was going on there and so that no one would suspect me, I proposed to the factory foreman that I would be willing to give up a slight portion of my daily wages if he would assign me to a different type of work each day, because the initial work assigned to me was too hard for me. In addition, I bought him some fruit, thereby gaining his affection. Consequently, the foreman gave me

---

244. Fi'uni (Alexander Fiani) (1865–?), a Greek Orthodox Christian born in Beirut, was the first grand master of the Barkai/Shafaq Freemasons lodge in Jaffa established in 1906. As elite civil society organizations, Masonic lodges played an important economic, social, and political role in the late Ottoman Empire.

freedom of movement in my work in the factory. Thanks to this mobility, I had an excellent opportunity to see everything I needed to see in order to acquire the secrets of this industry.

Once I had acquired a good and broad understanding of the entire manufacturing process, theoretical as well as practical, I left Egypt and returned to Tel Aviv. At that point I reached the conclusion that if I were to go about building such a factory in Tel Aviv I would need a partner, both for the input of financial resources for a large-scale enterprise of this sort and for the sake of its management.

Only then did I approach Mr. Dizengoff and told him all about the matter, beginning with my theoretical idea and what I had experienced in practice. I showed him the paperwork and documentation and the calculations related to realization of such an enterprise in the Land of Israel. I spent half a day together with Dizengoff in his office in Jaffa discussing the subject. He reviewed all the paperwork, closely studied the numbers, and was happy and overjoyed at the notion of such an enterprise being realized in Tel Aviv, in aid of its building.

In the end, Dizengoff told me that he had an excellent partner for me, a man named Johann Kremenezky,[245] a wealthy merchant from Vienna and a good Zionist ever since the days of Theodor Herzl.[246] During this visit to his office in Jaffa, Dizengoff told me that this Kremenezky had already approached him several times in regard to building a factory in Tel Aviv but that he did not know how to answer him. But now, Dizengoff told me, he would be sailing to Europe in two weeks' time, and he would make sure to interest Kremenezky in this important project; he was certain that the enterprise would come to fruition. Dizengoff left for Europe two weeks later, taking all the relevant documents with him. Upon his return from Europe, Dizengoff informed me that he had almost finalized

---

245. Kremenezky (1850–1934) was a noted scientist-industrialist with a light bulb and battery factory in Vienna; he also helped to electrify a number of towns in the Austro-Hungarian Empire. A committed Zionist, he served as a cofounder and first director of the Jewish National Fund. In 1922 he established a small battery factory in Tel Aviv.

246. A Budapest-born lawyer and journalist, Theodor Herzl (1860–1904) is credited with being the father of institutionalized political Zionism; Herzl's published works *Der Judenstaat* (1896) and *Altneuland* (1902) were foundational texts envisioning the Zionist project. He served as president of the World Zionist Organization and presided over the first six congresses held before his death.

the matter, and that Kremenezky would arrive in the near future to arrange the matter altogether.

A couple of months later, a rumor spread through the city that the Anglo-Palestine Bank, together with the PLDC, had purchased a large property in the Tel Aviv sand dunes, not far from the neighborhood, for the purpose of building a silicate factory in Tel Aviv.

Once I had a chance to verify the rumor, I went to Dizengoff to ask him the meaning of this development. Dizengoff then went to the bank to find out whether the rumor was true or not and learned that it was indeed true. He calmed me down, saying, "It meant nothing: let them buy the land, and then Kremenezky will come here, at which point we will settle the matter for the best." And Dizengoff believed that the issue would certainly be arranged with me included.

When the war had finally ended and it was finally possible to move ahead and build up the land again, I noticed the large machines that were being brought in, senior engineers coming in from Germany, as well as a great number of managers and clerks and instructors. They began building the silicate factory building on a very grand scale, which clearly entailed exorbitant expenditures.

Seeing all this, watching how my one life's dream to build up the country was being realized—in unwanted fashion, by others—I remained quiet and kept my feelings bottled up inside, in a still inner voice.

At the time, I proposed to the Tel Aviv committee that the committee purchase all of the sandy land stretching from the shore of the Tel Aviv neighborhood to the Yarkon River, for I was absolutely certain that it could be acquired at a very low price and then it could be held in reserve until needed, at which time the land would cost much more than its current cost.

My suggestion was in part based on the notion that after purchasing this land, the committee would offer each homeowner in Tel Aviv an opportunity to fence off five hundred square cubits and then build handsome, painted summer cottages like the summer cottages often seen along the beaches in Europe. And I also thought that this would initiate more widespread activity in Tel Aviv all the way up to the Yarkon, and that this would generate great benefit to the building and development of Tel Aviv.

My proposal was unanimously accepted by the committee, and it was decided to dispatch a delegation to inspect the area and consider what might be done there. The committee appointed Dizengoff, Tolkowsky,[247] and me to this delegation, and on the day after the decision was passed, we set out on horseback to the site.

Riding through the dunes, we arrived at a spot not far from the still-under-construction silicate factory. Tolkowsky pointed toward the spot and said to me: "Look at what a great project we are realizing here for building up the country." At hearing these words, at that moment I recalled all those days and months that I had wasted dedicated to the realization of this project. I was filled with anger and wrath, and then I shouted angrily at the top of my voice at Mr. Dizengoff, who was riding on his mare some distance in front of us. I shouted, calling out: "Mr. Dizengoff! Mr. Dizengoff!" When Dizengoff heard me shouting, he was slightly alarmed as he thought something bad had happened, perhaps having to do with the riding, so he quickly rode back toward us. "Mr. Dizengoff," I asked him, as I pointed at the construction site of the silicate factory, "who owns this project that is under construction?" Without even thinking, for the issue was well known and quite familiar to him, Dizengoff replied: "You own it, Mr. Chelouche."

Tolkowsky, having heard the question that I asked Dizengoff and also his response, and without being familiar with the background to the question or to the answer, was simply astonished and amazed at what he had heard. And then Dizengoff told him the entire saga, from the beginning, and about all my adventures and the energy I had invested in the affair over quite some time, and also the expenses, about the days I had spent working as a menial laborer in Egypt—all toward achieving this objective.

That very same evening, I was invited to Mr. Betzal'el Yaffe's home for a cup of tea. I arrived at his home at the appointed time and found there Messrs. Tolkowsky and Boris Goldberg,[248] and another few people

247. Shmu'el Tolkowsky (1886–1965) was a Belgian-born agronomist who settled in Palestine in 1911, where he worked in the citrus industry. After his service in the Belgian army during World War I, Tolkowsky served as assistant to Weizmann and Sokolow at the WZO. Upon his return to Palestine, he served in the Tel Aviv communal council and authored several books on the Zionist project.

248. Goldberg was a chemical engineer and an early member of Hovevei Zion who published numerous articles on Zionism and Jewish life in the Russian and Yiddish language press. In 1920, he was appointed director of the commerce and finance department in the WZO; he immigrated to Palestine the following year but was injured in the 1921 riots and died months later, in 1922.

whom I did not know. The conversation turned to the founding of the silicate project, and it was clear that that is why I had been summoned. They told me that since they had learned that very day that I was the first person to conceive the idea of creating such a factory, they were therefore willing to bring me in as a partner. I then answered them, in these words: "Gentlemen! I thank you for your offer, but I cannot accept it. Your offer is coming a bit late, particularly because the scale of the work that you have taken on with the construction of this factory is in my opinion unsuited to the construction needs in our country. And the large sums that have already been invested, and which you are continuing to invest, can by no means be recovered by the income that you may derive."

And now, eleven years after I spoke these words at that meeting, I see how very accurate my words of warning were in regard to realizing a highly expensive project compared with its meager income. The fact that the factory continues to exist is itself truly a miracle.

II

CHAPTER 13 *Beginning of the World War*

*In the days of the Hassan Bek regime in Jaffa |
His demand for money, and the "receipts" he provided |
His demand for weapons from the Jewish* yishuv *| His cruelty
and tyranny | Baha al-Din | His iron fist | His governing style |
The arrival of my son Me'ir, a French subject | His return to the ship |
The residents' state of distress | Construction of the mosque in Neve
Shalom | Releasing the Yemenites from compulsory military
service | Steel beams from our warehouse for construction
of the Arab mosque | Between Baha al-Din and
Hassan Bek | My attempt to drive a wedge
between the two men | Outcome of the
division for the benefit of the* yishuv

The World War was declared in August 1914 and lasted approximately six years.[249] Many countries suffered from the war, including our own, where the Turkish army battled the Allied armies. More than any other city, Jaffa suffered notoriously under the rule of the tyrant Hassan Bek,[250] whose arbitrariness and cruelty knew no bounds. During his regime, the *yishuv* groaned in agony from his unbearable burdens, which aggravated

---

249. The Ottoman Empire did not officially join the war until 29 October 1914, when it joined on the German and Austro-Hungarian side, turning down the likely disingenuous offers of territorial protection given by the Entente powers in exchange for its neutrality. British troops occupied Palestine starting in late 1917 and completed their occupation in late 1918. Chelouche seems to be counting the period of the British military government of OETA as part of the wartime experience. In 1920, the British established civilian authority in Palestine.

250. Hassan Bek (al-Jabi) was military commander of Jaffa from August 1914–May 1916. He was an Arab officer, possibly from Basra or Damascus. 'Issa al-'Issa, the editor of *Falastin* newspaper, also referred to Hassan Bek as a "diabolical" "despot" and complained about his oppression of Jaffa's Christians. Khalaf, *Les mémoires de 'Issa al-'Issa*, 142. For his part, the Spanish consul in Jerusalem called Hassan Bek "terrible, although nice." De Ballobar, *Jerusalem in World War I*, 29. De Ballobar recounted the Jerusalem civilian governor's attempts to obtain his help in getting Hassan Bek fired, before he himself resigned abruptly in December 1914.

an already challenging situation. Before long, the Turkish regime exiled the residents of Jaffa to the south and the north of the country. The abominable actions of this governor and his savage attitude toward the *yishuv* in Jaffa will remain an eternal stain on the chronicle of the city of Jaffa. I will note here a few of the episodes as they happened, which are preserved in my memory and which shed much light on the inhumane behavior of this cruel governor.

A few days after his arrival in Jaffa, Hassan Bek called for a gathering of the city's notables, Muslims, Christians, and Jews; there were approximately forty individuals in attendance. From among the Jews, Rabbi B. Z. 'Uziel,[251] Dizengoff, and I were invited. He addressed the gathered audience with a speech, the essence of which I have recorded here.

> As you know, a World War between powerful countries has been declared, and our country is on the front lines of that war. As you have seen, the army is making its way, day after day, to the front, and not long from now the city will no longer have the army corps that has been guarding over it. And since it is not possible to leave an entire city without military guard, in particular during wartime, I came here to serve you and to ensure the safety of the residents. It is my wish that all will take place in an orderly fashion for the sake of public safety, and I propose that you organize groups of young people from among the residents of the city to safeguard the city and its people. I am certain you will agree with this step. My only question to you is, then, should clothing be prepared for these youths similar to the uniforms of soldiers, or should we let each one wear his own clothes, and only have them wear a sash, with his position noted on it?

A few of the meeting attendees responded that it would be better to make special uniforms for the youth so that everyone would be able

---

251. Ben Zion 'Uziel (1880–1953) was from a prominent Jerusalem rabbinical family; he was the *hahambaşı* (chief rabbi) for Jaffa's Jews from 1911–1920. Although the Ottoman authorities only recognized one chief rabbi, 'Uziel, Rabbi Kook served as the unofficial chief rabbi of the Ashkenazi Jews in the city. After three years as the chief rabbi of Salonica, 'Uziel returned to Palestine and served as the Sephardi chief rabbi of Tel Aviv from 1923–1939; later he was appointed as Sephardi chief rabbi of the Land—and later State—of Israel, where he served until his death. 'Uziel was a prolific scholar, publishing his *responsa* collections and other religious treatises.

to recognize them as belonging to the guard corps, because otherwise there would be neither order nor discipline. To this Hassan Bek replied: "I am pleased to hear such an accurate presentation of the facts from you, but unfortunately the government does not have the money. Neither can we request a budgetary allocation for this from the government, as it is expending immense amounts each day on maintaining the army. So, it would be a great honor for the residents if they themselves dealt with this issue."

When he finished speaking, one of the Arab leaders, the mayor of Jaffa, 'Umar al-Bitar,[252] stood up and spoke: "Mr. Commandant, please calculate how many youth are needed for guarding and then divide the expense of the uniforms they need between the three parts of the community in the country, the Muslims, Christians, and Jews."

And that is what happened. The commandant estimated the total amount required for the uniforms to be 500 liras. This amount was divided into three, and Mr. Dizengoff and the writer of this account had to come up with one-third of the total by the following day. Mr. Beiruti,[253] on behalf of the Christians, Mr. 'Umar al-Bitar, on behalf of the Muslims, and Mr. Dizengoff, on behalf of the Jews, all responded in the affirmative to the commandant's request.

The following day, we collected the money from our own financial institutions and then went to deliver the sum to Hassan Bek, and presumably to receive an official receipt. But he took the money without expressing any gratitude and without offering any receipt. I requested a receipt from him, so he took his calling card out of his pocket and wrote words on it that I still cannot clearly understand: "I received this amount, which you owed." He was in a furious mood. We failed to receive any official receipt from him and as we were about to leave, he called us back inside and asked us to sit and listen to what he had to say.

---

252. Al-Bitar (1880–1948) was a merchant and a member of the Jaffa municipality for many years. He was also a member of the Freemason lodge Barkai/Shafaq in the years before the war, and in the 1920s he served as the head of the Jaffa branch of the Muslim-Christian Association.

253. This was likely Michel Effendi Beiruti, who later served on the first High Commissioner's Advisory Council in 1920 and was a member of the Muslim-Christian Association in the 1920s. His brother Najib was a citrus merchant who in 1910 joined together with other Arab and Jewish merchants to form a citrus export cooperative.

He was pleased, thank God, that we were organizing the guard corps, but then he asked us to provide him with pistols and binoculars, which, he said, "you would be able to acquire from the Jews, and then deliver to us in order to arm the militia." We told him that the Jews did not possess weapons, and therefore we would not be able to deliver any, but we might be able to provide him binoculars if we could find any. At that, he jumped up as if bitten by a snake and shouted: "I am asking you not only for binoculars but also for weapons, which are most necessary for the youth of our militia." We repeated that we had no weapons and therefore would not be able to deliver them. Hassan Bek became enraged and responded furiously: "Oh, you will find them. You have until tomorrow to bring me the types that I am assigning to you," and then he left us alone, pretending to be occupied with something else.

We left him and went to see a few fellow Jews, and we asked them to help us fulfill the commandant's command. Two days passed and we had not yet acquired what he wanted. A policeman was sent to look for us and he demanded an affirmative response, so we began searching more seriously. With great difficulty, we managed to collect a few rifles and a dozen pistols of different types, and also a few binoculars that we received as gifts from our brethren, aside from a few excellent binoculars donated by Mr. Berlin, which were worth hundreds of francs. We were pleased at our success in having met the demands of the government and the commandant; we just wanted to be over and done with his excessive demands. We placed all the objects we had collected into a suitcase and went to the commandant.

When we appeared at the office of the governor, we found that Yusuf 'Ashur,[254] the respected Arab merchant, was with him. Hassan Bek called in a policeman and told him to open the suitcase and arrange the contents on his desk. Hassan Bek himself inspected the pistols and found among them two pistols of a simple type, which in a fit of rage he threw into a corner of the room, shouting: "You have come here to ridicule me. You have turned this into a children's game. You have brought me the kind of pistols that babies play with, while all along you have hidden the high-quality pistols and kept them for yourselves." Dizengoff and I were very alarmed at this venting of his rage and were not sure how to respond to this tyrant.

254. 'Ashur owned a large orchard in Jaffa.

I gestured to the respectable Arab sitting alongside him who understood my intention and then intervened, saying to Hassan Bek: "These are respectable and important men, and perhaps they did not understand what you wanted," as well as other words of persuasion and appeasement.

At this, Hassan Bek calmed down slightly and then addressed the Arab: "I know that these men are respectable and honest, but I will not allow them to make fun of me." And to us he said: "I am asking you to announce to all the Jews in Jaffa and Tel Aviv that anyone in possession of a pistol is obligated to bring it to you. You have twenty-four hours to bring the pistols here to this room, and if anyone does not obey the order, the government will conduct searches. Anyone found to be in possession of a pistol will be punished with all due severity of the law."

Based on this demand, we issued an official declaration to the entire Hebrew *yishuv* in Jaffa and Tel Aviv and informed our Jewish brethren of the order issued by the cruel tyrant. That evening, about 150 pistols of all types were collected at Mr. Dizengoff's home. Mr. Dizengoff summoned me to his home the following morning. When I arrived, I found him sorting the pistols into different types, in an orderly fashion. I registered my objections to what he was doing. After all, Hassan Bek would end up thinking that we had a factory for weapons and that we had brought him only a few of each type. I contended that we had to present him the pistols all mixed up, just as we had received them. Mr. Dizengoff saw the truth in what I was saying and stopped sorting the pistols. We stuffed them into sacks in no particular order and loaded these onto a cart and then rode to the *kishle* [the army headquarters]. The military commander gave the authorization to receive us.

When we entered his office, we found it was full of people and Hassan Bek was busy. We waited a few hours and in the meantime our hair stood on end upon seeing how tyrannically Hassan Bek treated the public. He gave orders to summon Mr. Beiruti. When he appeared before him, [Mr. Beiruti] trembled as he spoke, and Hassan Bek assaulted him with curses and abuse like a tiger tearing into its prey; even the pasha of Jerusalem never dared to speak this way to Mr. Beiruti, since he respected him. Hassan Bek addressed other notables present with the same sort of audacity and arrogance.

As we witnessed this display, we understood the kind of person we were dealing with. We started thinking about how to handle the situation, and a powerful sense of despair overcame us. We wished to consult with one another on how to behave, how to talk to him in a brave tone without any fear or without recoiling from him. We looked at each other but we could not get a word out of our mouths. When I decided by myself that the best tactic would be to address him bravely without any subservience, I hinted to Mr. Dizengoff what I was thinking, and he encouraged me in a low whisper.

Hassan Bek left us for last, and since it was already midday, he said to us: "I'm leaving you until the afternoon, so wait for me." We answered him:

> We did not ask you for a thing; instead, it was you who asked us for pistols and we brought them to you. We have been waiting here since the morning. If the honorable *bek* is hungry and wishes to eat, we are also hungry, for is it not noontime for every human being? Here in these sacks are the pistols that we found in the possession of the Jews, and therefore we will leave as you have no further need for us, since we completed the task that you assigned to us.

He listened to our statement and replied, "I will do as you wish, and I will not dine before you. We will sit for a while longer and see what you have brought, and afterward we will go to eat." He opened the sacks and when he found six pistols of a single type, he shouted angrily: "But didn't you say the Jews do not have any pistols? Here I see that you have a factory for pistols—I found six pistols of the same model."

Then I stood up and said in a raised voice: "The *bek* must understand once and for all that Dizengoff and I speak words of truth, and it is not our custom to tell lies. Nor are we so afraid that we would need to lie. We speak the truth, and from here on out the *bek* must know this."

I told him everything that I had seen that morning when I walked into Dizengoff's home and saw him sorting the pistols, when I complained to him that afterward the *bek* would suspect us. At this, the tyrant laughed and said: "And so you are saying that your words are the truth?" We replied: "We know no other way." "If so," the governor said, "tell me the truth: the large storerooms downstairs from the Anglo-Palestine Company offices, and the storerooms that are located at such-and-such place—to whom do they belong?" We answered: "To the APC, except for the empty storerooms, including the keys to them, which are owned by landlords and are mortgaged by the APC." He then handed us a set of keys and asked us to deliver them to the APC. And we parted on good terms and with smiles on our faces.

From that time on, Hassan Bek would pester us with any matter that concerned Jews, calling for us day and night. There were rainy nights with a strong wind blowing and rain pouring down, but it made no difference. We would have to walk on foot from Tel Aviv to Hassan Bek's office, because sometimes there were no available coaches, and the soldier would escort us riding on his horse. On several occasions we were summoned in the middle of the night by the emissaries of this tyrant who was incapable of treating us humanely.

Around that same year, a young *kaymakam* arrived in Jaffa, a product of the educated elite of Constantinople named Baha al-Din,[255] who was aggressive and cruel and a fanatic nationalist. He wore a lighthearted expression, but his heart was evil and as cunning as a snake. He showed up in Jaffa as a dictator, issuing orders on his own accord without obeying even the pasha in Jerusalem, who was of higher rank. He received most of his orders directly from Constantinople. His first step was to endear himself to the local clerks, from the lowest ranking to the most senior, as well as to the residents. He got close to them, received them hospitably, and frequently invited them to dine with him. All of this made the impression that before us was a kind, educated, and good-hearted young man.

He conducted a tour of all the offices and saw the dilapidated furnishings and the lack of required instruments. He approached each and every clerk and exhorted him: "How can you work at a broken desk, on a chair that is on the verge of falling apart?" The clerk would listen and then complain: "The government has not arranged any such budget, and we have to pay out of our own pockets for even the paltriest office necessities." Then the *kaymakam* commanded the clerk to compile a budget of everything needed to furnish his office; he issued orders to the government treasury, and the government offices were reorganized with new furnishings. The residents of the city were astonished. Not a single member of the government, not even the pasha, permitted himself to issue orders to the government treasury to allocate funds for such purposes. [The *kaymakam*] became everyone's friend, and through his

---

255. Baha al-Din was appointed to Jaffa from the Eighth Branch Directorate in late September/October 1914.

friendships with the notables of the city, he got to know the residents and their lives and deeds.

Four months passed and the *kaymakam* began to reveal the full extent of his power and his pride, which knew no bounds. He fired most of the clerks and in their place appointed a few individuals whom he liked. He also removed from office some of the higher-ranking government officials, including the mayor, 'Umar al-Bitar; the residents became incensed. Telegrams were dispatched to the pasha in Jerusalem and to Constantinople, but there was no response from either. A delegation was selected to appeal to the pasha, but it returned without calming the spirits of the residents, since it concealed something from the public. The public began whispering that the *kaymakam* had the stamp of approval from the central Turkish government to do as he wished, and the secret was also disclosed that the aforementioned pasha had told the delegation that the *kaymakam* was higher ranking than he, and that he in fact had the authority to dismiss the pasha. [The pasha also told them] that the residents should not appeal to anyone by telegram so that the residents' representatives would not be arrested.

The *kaymakam* ruled with a heavy hand, forcing all the residents of the city to pay their taxes regularly; the wealthy who owed [back] taxes to the government from different periods were forced to pay them off all at once. He even imprisoned one of them, which caused a great commotion among the residents, but nothing helped, and his family was forced to bail him out. Baha al-Din's absolute rule cast terror and fear over all the residents. When I fulfilled the tasks imposed on me by his clerks by serving on the *'ushr*[256] and the Food Staples Price Control committee, I witnessed Baha al-Din's heavy hand and the extent to which the masses, from the weak to the most noble, all feared and trembled before him.

He also oversaw the cleaning of the courtyards and the streets, and he ordered that the shop signs be painted white with red letters. I carried out my assigned tasks faithfully, and therefore the *kaymakam* respected me. At times, he would consult with me about matters within the committees to which he had appointed me as a member. One day, as I toured the villages on behalf of the government in connection to the *'ushr* tax, a ship arrived in Jaffa with my son Me'ir on board, whom I had

---

256. In Arabic, *'ushr* literally means "tithing"; this was a local tax on agricultural products.

not seen in some two years. The *kaymakam* happened to be standing on the shore, personally supervising the arrival of the passengers, inspecting their passports, and so forth. When he opened my son's passport and read in it "Me'ir son of Yosef Chelouche," he asked him, "Which Chelouche are you?"

My son answered him: "I am Me'ir, the son of Yosef Chelouche, a resident of Jaffa."

"Where have you been all this time?" the *kaymakam* asked him.

"I have been completing my studies in Cairo," my son replied.

"And what does your father do?" The *kaymakam* continued to pose question after question, and based on the answers, he understood that this was my son. Now he faced the question of what to do, since I was an Ottoman subject and my son was a French subject, and how could he be permitted to enter the country.

He thought about it long and hard, and said to my son: "You are a French subject and it is forbidden for a foreign subject to enter the country, especially since the French are fighting against our government." My son was silent and did not utter a word. The *kaymakam* continued, "If you promise me that in a few days' time you will submit a request to the government asking to become an Ottoman citizen and forfeit your French citizenship, then I will permit you to enter the country."

"I cannot do that," my son responded bravely. The *kaymakam* got very angry and ordered the boatmen to return him to the ship. Nevertheless, out of his affection for me he sent word to my office about the whole matter and permitted clothing, food, and money up to ten liras to be sent to my son. But since I was not in the city, my [other] sons went to the *kaymakam* to clarify the details. He recounted to them the entire conversation between him and my son Me'ir and added: "Due to the fact that I respect and esteem your father, I desired to act beyond the letter of the law, and I proposed to your brother to accept Ottoman citizenship so that I could take him off the ship. But now even if he promised to become Ottoman, I do not trust him. I wanted to do everything possible for your father, who is not in the city and who is working on government affairs, but as you can see, you no longer have any other choice but to send clothing and food to your brother on the ship, but the money only in accordance with the law, up to ten liras. If you send more than that, even by a single lira, you will be punished with all due severity of the law." Following these crystal-clear statements, my sons went to the ship and delivered to my son Me'ir[257] clothing, food, and ten liras, and then they returned home in misery and sorrow.

That same day, I returned to Jaffa without knowing anything that had occurred with my family. When I met with the general prosecutor, he told me about the matter of my son Me'ir and his response to the *kaymakam*. The matter caused me great sorrow. I immediately entered the *kaymakam*'s office, where he received me cordially and told me himself about the incident. I began to implore him: "Don't you know that this is my son and that he depends on me, and I promise you that I will make him an Ottoman subject even this very day." But the *kaymakam* refused, saying: "What is the use if your son is forced to become an Ottoman citizen instead of [becoming one] out of his own free will and self-determination?"

I asked him to permit me and my wife to visit our son and continued to beg him: "As you know, the ship is returning to Italy, a place where my son has no acquaintance and no redeemer, and what will be his fate without sufficient money in his possession? Permit me to pass along to him a reasonable sum of money." "The law does not permit this," replied the *kaymakam*. I rose from my seat depressed, and as I was about to leave he called after me: "If you want to see your son, go to the ship in an hour."

I said to him: "And what use will it be if I see my son and I am not able to help him?" He thought about this for a while and then replied: "I myself will give an order to the military that you are boarding the ship as an emissary of the government on a secret matter, and no one has the authority to touch you." I parted from him with gratitude and walked down to my house. I took my wife with me and sufficient money, and after an hour I went to the ship where the military received me honorably, as if I were a high-ranking official.

The war weighed heavier on the lives of the city residents from day to day. Businesses nearly collapsed completely due to a lack of customers. The government seized merchandise without consideration and without payment. Very infrequently the government assessed the value of the goods, using a very minimal evaluation, and then it would repay this

---

257. Me'ir Chelouche (1895–1960) returned to Palestine only in 1922. He studied law in Toulouse (according to his son Yossi) but never worked as a lawyer. He made his living from trade, brokerage, managing property, and assessment.

meager amount in Turkish notes, which had a notoriously low value, as its worth was dropping from one day to the next. In this manner the merchants had to provide their merchandise to the government not only without earning profit, but even at half of their own wholesale cost. The government transferred these goods to the army base.

With the passing of time, the government became smarter and did not set any prices for the goods that it took. Rather, it forced the merchants in the city to supply whatever the army needed at their own expense, until the residents sagged under the weight of their suffering and poverty. All of the army's needs, from uniforms to empty tin cans, became the responsibility of Mr. Dizengoff and myself, in our capacity as the representatives of the Jewish community. We had to weigh every option to find the sources to cover these expenses, which were more than the city residents could bear. We wasted entire days sewing uniforms for the soldiers, measuring each soldier, purchasing cloth in the correct size in order to sew uniforms for them. All of these expenses were borne by our financial institutions as well as by some individuals of means. Our work on all the committees kept us very busy and left us no rest, and yet we suffered in silence, for who would dare stand up to this tyrannical governor?

The arbitrariness of the governor knew no bounds. Not a day passed that he did not issue new decrees that the *yishuv* could not bear. When he decided to improve the city's appearance, he ordered the demolition of buildings without advance warning. He would call for the property owner and command him to evacuate the building within twenty-four hours, in order to demolish it and widen the street. His sheer maliciousness was primarily known from when he set down to plant the city's boulevard (now called King George Boulevard).[258] Financial ruin befell

---

258. Jerusalem Boulevard in present-day Jaffa. However, the road was originally named for Djemal Pasha, the Ottoman governor of Syria and Palestine and the commander of the Fourth Army. According to 'Issa al-'Issa, the road was originally planned to be one kilometer long, stretching from the end of Bustrus Street at the southern end of Manshiya and then heading south in a straight line to link up with the Jerusalem road. Because the proposed street would have passed through his family's orchard, al-'Issa suggested changing the route to start at the end of Bustrus Street heading west to the Manshiya beach, going south through town and then curving east to the Jerusalem road, resembling a semicircle. He argued that this would connect the boulevard with the heart of the inhabited center of the city, while the

several owners through whose properties the boulevard had to pass. Their buildings were demolished suddenly without any compassion or compensation.[259]

That boulevard took shape in a very short period. The *kaymakam* commanded that all the city's residents be conscripted to perform this work.[260] The army grabbed the young and old walking down the street and forced them to work. They took no notice of the sick or infirm or those unable to perform hard labor; they also did not differentiate between the masses and the notables of the city. The cries of the residents and their distress were heartbreaking.

When we saw the fate of the residents, we complained to the commandant that the army was not differentiating between the residents and was also conscripting the city's notables and respected citizenry. At this, the commandant lost his temper and demanded to send all the Jewish workers to government work. We did not know what to do. How could we with our own hands send workers to labor for the government for free at a time when they were sinking under the worry of finding bread for their families? We proposed to the commandant [that we would supply] a certain number of workers, if only he would order the army to stop grabbing people off the street. After much hard work and numerous complications, he accepted our proposal. We began to search for workers who would agree to work for the government for wages as opposed to them having to work for free. We came to terms with these workers and arranged a work schedule, and the plight of the residents of the city was somewhat eased. But these days did not last for long. The governor was never satisfied, and day after day, he would concoct new plans. His insane caprices intensified, and the residents shuddered at whatever came out of his mouth but stoically accepted all that he imposed upon

---

new portion of the Jerusalem road still would allow for luxury buildings to be constructed on both sides of the street and would offer residents a promenade. Khalaf, *Les mémoires de 'Issa al-'Issa*, 156–57. In the end, both streets were built; al-'Issa's proposed coastal corniche did not come to life, but al-Salahi road was built to offer a straight and wide connection between the port and the Jerusalem road. Djemal Pasha Boulevard connected the train station and the Jerusalem road.

259. 'Issa al-'Issa recounted his meeting with Hassan Bek in which he was told that the street would run through his family *waqf*, including its large *bayyara*, as well as several other large orange orchards. Khalaf, *Les mémoires de 'Issa al-'Issa*, 156.

260. The labor battalions, or *amele taburu*, were used widely in Jerusalem as well.

them. He exploited the city and its residents; their situation deteriorated considerably until poverty and disease spread.

While the entire *yishuv* was in great distress and was buckling under the weight of the heavy burden, and instead of the function of government being to concern itself with improvement of the residents' situation, the cruel Hassan Bek sought new ways to harm the well-being of the city of Jaffa and strike it with a mortal blow, such that it would be unable to ever rise again.

One of his plans that was executed and that sucked mercilessly at the life force of the residents was certainly the construction of the mosque in Neve Shalom.[261] He selected one of the plots of land along the beach, summoned its Christian owner, and informed him that the government had expropriated the land, but it did not have the capital for the construction of the mosque. That same day, Hassan Bek transferred the property to his own name and issued an order to requisition camels, donkeys, and wagons to haul stones from every part of the city, from demolished building sites to the plot on which the house of worship for Muslims would be built. A few days passed, and construction work began in full force. Naturally, Jewish and Christian workers were exempt from this work.[262] Conversely, Arab[263] workers volunteered en masse for the sacred labor. All the lime that peasants used to haul from distant areas into the city was seized by the government for the erection of the mosque, which was built for free using the resources of the residents, which Hassan Bek extricated from them by force.

The lime ran out and Hassan Bek began considering where he could acquire more. Through his loyal deputies he learned about Tel Aviv and the lime pits that were dug into the sand, which were prepared for buildings even before the outbreak of the war. He dispatched spies, who discovered the pits, and then Hassan Bek issued orders for the lime to be hauled in barrels by donkeys and camels to the mosque plot.

Of course, the Jews did not dare to object. Instead, they would hide the lime in such a manner that it would be impossible to recognize the

---

261. Chelouche is describing the Hassan Bek Mosque, designed by the Jewish engineer Ben Zion Gini, that is still in use as a mosque.

262. This is due to a custom that non-Muslims could not be employed on sacred projects.

263. Here Chelouche conflates "Arab" and "Muslim," a common feature in Hebrew language writing.

pits, or they would move the lime to another site using Yemenite workers.²⁶⁴ But one day, as they were busy with their labor, about seventy men were arrested and imprisoned.

When they came to me and asked me to lobby for their release, I began to think of the reason for their imprisonment. The matter of the lime was not known to anyone. They must have been taken by the army. I asked if there were any elderly among them and I was told that they were all young people, the oldest one being about forty years old. I knew that my hypothesis was correct. I traveled to Jerusalem immediately, where I found out the home address of the chief official in whose hands lay the fate of those who are taken into the army. I learned that this chief official was one of the Turks.²⁶⁵

I recalled that among the close acquaintances of this official was Mr. Isma'il Bek al-Husseini²⁶⁶ of Jerusalem, who was a man of great influence. I went to his home and consulted with him; he promised to help. After spending some time together, he said to me: "My friend, the chief official is accustomed to going to his office at the third hour. I myself will be there at that time. After one hour, you will arrive and will ask for me; I will greet you happily and introduce you to the official. While we drink the coffee, you will ask in passing if, according to the law, Bedouins, who do not have any permanent home and are nomads, are obligated to serve in the army or not. And at the same time, you will direct a question to me: 'In your opinion, aren't the Yemenites like the Bedouins?'—and I will respond to you in the affirmative: 'Of course, the Yemenites are nomads just like the Bedouins and do not have a permanent place of residence.'"

On this basis I arrived in the fourth hour at the official's office,

---

264. Yemenite Jewish immigrants had arrived in Palestine starting in the 1880s. In the 1910s, Yemenite Jewish laborers were used as a replacement for Arab labor, as they were cheaper to employ than European Jewish laborers.

265. Government officials were drawn from among the local notables as well as from the civil service ranks of the empire. While all government officials were fluent in Ottoman Turkish, their native tongues varied depending on their provincial and ethnic origin.

266. Al-Husseini (1860–1945) was the son of the mufti of Jerusalem and a member of one of the most prominent families in the city. He served as director of the education department of the local government, and for a while his duties included monitoring the press as a government censor.

knocked on the door, and entered, asking for Isma'il Bek. When I saw him, I greeted him joyfully: "You are here? I asked for you, and I was told that you were here."

He received me cordially and with all due respect, and then he introduced me to the official. Coffee and cigarettes were brought. "Perhaps you would like a water pipe?" the official asked me. I replied to him that cigarettes were sufficient. Isma'il Bek fixed his expression on me and I responded with a look, until we both understood one another well. He initiated a conversation with me about the welfare of my family and praised me and my family to the official. He spoke in such exaggerated terms that it must have seemed to the official that I truly was one of the most prominent Jews in the land. The official's initial conversation with me was the following: "It is your good fortune that you live in Tel Aviv, not far from Rishon LeZion, where you can drink fine cognac . . ." I asked him if he was fond of this beverage, and he replied: "And who does not like the fine beverages of Rishon LeZion?" I informed him that by the next day he would receive a wooden chest filled with an assortment of fine drinks, and he thanked me with a bow and with pleasure.[267]

We became friendly and discussed a variety of subjects, until I posed to him the requisite questions and was given the answer that the Yemenites really are like Bedouins, who wander from place to place and are not taken into the army. Even the sultan himself would not be able to coerce them, as that would be against the law.

Then I related the affair to him and asked him for a letter to the official in Jaffa, [ordering] that he should not touch them and also to give every Yemenite a certificate issued in his name, which no soldier would dare to challenge (at the time, any soldier had the authority to stop individuals walking on the street to demand a passport, and anyone who was without a document could be incarcerated and sent to the front). I received the requisite orders from the official, and I returned to Jaffa. I summoned the Yemenite leaders, and they informed me that the imprisoned Yemenites were to be taken to the army. I told them about the written orders in my possession and I instructed them to register the names of all the Yemenites, so that the military office could give each individual a certificate attesting to the fact that they could not be disturbed.

---

267. Indeed, Ottoman officials regularly received cognac and other products as "gifts" from the colonies.

I went to the commandant Hassan Bek and asked him the reason for the incarceration of the Yemenites. He replied that they were thieves, as the soldiers had captured them while they were stealing lime. I told him: "Your Honor does not know these people who wander from place to place and have no permanent residence, and they can barely feed their families. They engage in hard work that exhausts the body and live a life of hard and arduous labor. They did not steal the lime but rather they were working as porters, because in the past few days different people came with their camels and donkeys and took the lime without asking the owners. As a result, these Yemenites were hired as porters to move the lime from place to place. I can vouch for them, sir, that they are honest people."

Hassan Bek smiled: "If so, I will send them to the army, since they are healthy men." I told him that the law does not permit it, since they have the same legal standing as Bedouins. "I will try to write to Jerusalem," he angrily replied. "Your letter is superfluous since the matter is well known and clear to the government," I responded. Then he asked me: "Why haven't I seen you in the past two days?" I responded that I had been in Jerusalem on business, and I asked him to release the wretched people. Hassan Bek was silent and did not say a word. When he was aroused from his silence, he asked me: "Don't you know that now we are building a house of prayer? Have you seen it?" I replied that I had heard about it but not yet seen it. "Oh, you must see it." I replied, "I am ready to see it with all due respect." "If so," he continued, "you must take part and share in the sacred work." "I am willing," I answered, "if you ask this of me."

Hassan Bek chuckled and spoke to me coldly: "As far as I know, there are steel beams in your warehouse that are needed for the sacred building that I am constructing, and it is my wish that you hand over some of them to me for this purpose." "I am willing to send you such beams," I said, "if you inform me of the quantity and size that you require." He removed from his briefcase a list of seventy-two pieces, measuring between nine and twelve meters. "How is it," I asked, "that there are so many Christian merchants who have warehouses that stock these steel beams, but you are asking only me to supply you with such a large amount? And how will I bear all these expenses alone?"

He listened to what I said and then smiled. "I will not take anything that I need for construction of the house of prayer from the Christians, but taking from the Jews is permissible." I saw that I had no other choice and agreed. As soon as he heard me say that he could send word to my storeroom to take possession of the beams, he thrust a blank piece of paper into my hand and told me to write up an order to my warehouse to deliver seventy-two beams to the house of prayer. Naturally, I wrote the note against my will and handed it to him. And then he turned to me: "I believe that you came to me with the objective of freeing the Yemenites, so what can we do but fulfill your request."

He rang a bell, a soldier entered, and Hassan Bek ordered him to bring the Yemenites to him. "I am going to order each of them to be beaten with sticks, so that they will never steal again," he muttered through his teeth. At this, I jumped out of my seat: "Please do not beat these miserable souls, for I myself have already been beaten by you on behalf of all of them . . ." He understood the meaning behind my words, chuckled loudly, and said: "I will merely issue a warning to them, never to repeat their actions." A few moments passed and the Yemenites were brought in, each one shaking with fear. Hassan Bek told them that he was freeing them solely thanks to me, he warned them, and then he sent them to freedom. The following day, I distributed to all of these Yemenites the documents that had been signed by the military office in Jerusalem, according to which they were free from any military obligation and that no soldier or government representative had the authority to harm them.

One clear day, the *kaymakam* of Jaffa, Baha al-Din Bek, summoned Dizengoff and me. Also in attendance were the Armenian priest and the general prosecutor, and he demanded that we shut down the schools due to it being wartime. We failed to understand his plot with regard to this decree, which was solely meant to harm the Jews, to the children of the Jews, to neglect the Torah. We vehemently opposed this edict, and begged him not to enact the decree, which was to the detriment of the *yishuv*.

During this conversation, for some unknown reason, Baha al-Din began to speak ill of the commandant, Hassan Bek, telling us: "You think Hassan Bek is your friend and is seeking your benefit, but that is not the case; he is undermining you, and the militia that he is organizing is not for your benefit, either, but for your detriment," and so forth.

As I listened to the *kaymakam*'s indictment of the commandant, I had the idea that we should use these statements by the *kaymakam* to drive a wedge between the two officials. Such a division would only be to our benefit, for the good of the Jewish *yishuv*. I expressed this idea to Dizengoff. Dizengoff smiled in response, but he did not answer clearly if he was for or against.

Immediately after, I walked into Hassan Bek's office on some pretext and began telling him some of what Baha al-Din had said about him. Hassan Bek, as sly as a snake, pretended not to hear what I said, as if it had nothing to do with him, and all the while he sent out notes summoning this [person] or another. In the middle of our conversation, the Armenian priest, who had also taken part in the conversation with the *kaymakam*, entered his office after being summoned.

Hassan Bek asked him, "What did the *kaymakam* say to you about me?" The priest, who was afraid of conveying the *kaymakam*'s words, began stuttering and would not answer clearly. Hassan Bek sent him away with all sorts of derogatory expressions on his lips, such as "dog" and more. After expelling the priest, he called for the general prosecutor, who realized that I had without doubt shared with Hassan Bek at least some of what the *kaymakam* had said, and he too relayed what had been said. Hassan Bek did not make do with these two accounts, but he also summoned Dizengoff. When Dizengoff entered, I hinted to him that he should repeat what he had heard, and Dizengoff corroborated my account.

Once the commandant was convinced that I had spoken truthfully and accurately, he actually became, for a while, the best friend of the Hebrew *yishuv* in Jaffa and the district. Through the goal I had set for myself to sow division between the two men who governed over us, I achieved many benefits for the Hebrew *yishuv*, which otherwise would have collapsed in agony at the hands of this cruel, tyrannical commandant.

CHAPTER 14 *The Days of Ottomanization and the Cruel Expulsion of the Foreign Subjects*

The slogan "Jews, Be Ottomans" | M. Dizengoff and I act together | The question of Ottomanization | I forfeit my French citizenship | The military order for all Ottomans and those who have Ottomanized | The arrest of foreign citizens on the streets of Jaffa | Jaffa's kaymakam, *Baha al-Din | The telegram to Djemal Pasha | The savage expulsion | Stealing from the citizens | Dividing families — children without parents and vice versa | Acts of barbarism on the Jaffa coast on the night of the expulsions | I rescue the young men from military conscription | Late at night in 'Ajami | Finding the passports of the newly Ottomanized in my home | The last Italian ship on the Jaffa coast*

In the midst of the turbulent days of the World War, the issue of Ottomanization[268] arose with a fury. Turkey had expelled all foreign citizens from its land,[269] leaving only its own citizens. The worry of our own community leaders grew considerably that the foreign Jews would leave the Land of Israel after settling it, living and suffering in it, which would cause great harm to the idea of Jewish settlement in the Land of the Patriarchs. As a result, [our leaders] initiated a broad and comprehensive propaganda campaign to influence these Jews with all their strength to accept Ottoman citizenship.

Rabbi Haim Nahum Effendi,[270] the chief rabbi of Turkey who was

---

268. This was naturalization to adopt Ottoman citizenship, which required forfeiting one's previous citizenship.

269. Expulsions of enemy citizens began in December 1914, beginning with foreign clergy residing in the monasteries and convents, then moving on to civilians. French Jews were issued an expulsion order in early January 1915 if they refused to Ottomanize.

270. Haim Nahum (1872–1960) was selected as chief rabbi after the 1908 Ottoman

in Constantinople at the time, sent a telegram to the Jews of the Land of Israel asking them to become Ottomans. The late editor of *Hazvi*, Eli'ezer Ben Yehuda,[271] the father of spoken Hebrew and the reviver of our language, conducted a journalistic propaganda campaign employing the slogan: "Jews, Be Ottomans." Because it was clear that these leaders were concerned with the people's welfare and that they felt the pain of the *yishuv*, all the public figures agreed to take part in promoting this propaganda, materially and in spirit. Mr. Dizengoff and I took it upon ourselves to address this issue in Jaffa. We turned to the *kaymakam* and told him of the Jews' desire to Ottomanize and to remain in the country. The *kaymakam* gladly accepted our proposal and issued an order to the Ottomanization office to Ottomanize any Jews who submitted such requests.

Knowing the state of affairs in Turkish government offices, we were afraid it would take them a great deal of time to Ottomanize all the Jews wishing to do so, and in the meantime these people would be in danger of expulsion from the country. We therefore influenced the government, which authorized us to act for this purpose in the Jaffa municipality itself. We commissioned for this task several Jewish secretaries in addition to the government clerks and office manager. We printed notepads, forms, and receipts, we prepared stamps and the taxes required, and in doing so, we eased the burden of work borne by the office manager, who now only had to approve each request with his signature. In the course of a few days, we succeeded in Ottomanizing some of the Jews, even ahead of the deadline set by the government, after which the government would not accept any more requests for Ottomanization.

I will confess that as we ourselves were French citizens, our family was opposed to forfeiting our citizenship and replacing it with Ottoman citizenship. We decided to leave the country for Egypt until the storm blew over. But our plans did not materialize, and public demands and the good of the *yishuv* compelled us to give up on our desire in favor of the wishes and the welfare of the residents who had Ottomanized

---

revolution. He was the first Alliance-educated "modern" chief rabbi of the empire. After World War I, he relocated to Egypt to serve as chief rabbi there.

271. Ben Yehuda (1858–1922) was a Russian-Jewish linguist and journalist who immigrated to Jerusalem in 1881 and is considered the main driving force behind the revival of Hebrew as a spoken language. He taught Hebrew at the AIU school and was the publisher and editor of the Hebrew language newspapers *Hazvi* and *Hashkafa*.

and those who remained in Jaffa. At a general assembly held in Tel Aviv, where the situation was debated with serious consideration, it was unanimously decided to ask our family not to leave the country in order that the writer of these lines would also remain on duty and continue to work side by side with Mr. Dizengoff as the representatives of the Hebrew *yishuv* of Jaffa and Tel Aviv.

I will never forget the immense joy of my brethren, the Jews of Jaffa and Tel Aviv, when I informed them of my family's agreement to remain in the country and to continue to serve the community and not leave at this time of distress. Given that I was fluent in Arabic and was familiar with and knowledgeable about the practices and customs of the state, my services were very much needed by the Hebrew *yishuv*, in whose name I would appear at all the events and appointments before the district administration, protecting the critical interests to the best of my ability. On the day after the assembly, our family paid all the taxes and was Ottomanized together with all the other Jews.

About three months later, an order was received from Constantinople that all Ottomans from eighteen years to sixty years were to be taken into the army. You can imagine the magnitude of our sorrow. After all the propaganda and the investment of energy and effort so that the Jews would Ottomanize, now they would have to take leave of their homes and families and go to the battlefront. We hesitated, unsure how to proceed; the Ottoman laws stated that every Ottomanized citizen is exempt from compulsory military service during his first year. Those not wishing to serve in the army could offer "monetary redemption"[272] and thereby free himself. We therefore devoted deep thought to the issue to see how we should act in this case. Several days later, we were informed that everyone was to be taken to the army, without exception; the government would not take any special circumstances into account, nor would it accept monetary redemptions.

The entire city of Jaffa was struck down by this terrible decree. Many Jews were captured and placed in detention in order to be sent to the army. I was extremely concerned about the fate of the *yishuv* of Jaffa and Tel Aviv, for fear that it might shrivel up. I understood that I would have

---

272. *Bedel-i askeri*, "in exchange for military service." Before the universal conscription law passed by the Ottoman parliament in 1909, Christians and Jews were collectively exempted from conscription in exchange for paying the *bedel*.

to send my own sons to the army, and in the event that the government did consent to accept a ransom for them, then I would need huge sums of money for that. Why, then, did Rabbi Haim Nahum Effendi and the late Eli'ezer Ben Yehuda wage such a comprehensive propaganda campaign so that the Jews would Ottomanize, only to place them in such distress? And what would the Jewish public of Jaffa and Tel Aviv say about me and Mr. Dizengoff, who implemented this campaign?

I worried a great deal and could not find a solution to my worries, as the commandant and the *kaymakam* continued to make new demands on us practically every day. We could not endure these tribulations, and it exhausted us completely. For the tiniest of matters and for meaningless questions, soldiers were dispatched to our home day and night solely to disturb our rest, sometimes because of the commandant, sometimes because of the *kaymakam*; we were at our wit's end. Whenever any trouble befell a Jew, I was compelled to appear before those two tyrants.

When Baha al-Din received a telegram from Constantinople to expel all the foreign citizens from the country, he did not call in the representatives of the Hebrew public to consult with them on the fate of the deportees. Instead, on a clear day at two o'clock in the afternoon, he dispatched of his own accord a large military force to spread out over the streets of Jaffa and Tel Aviv, and they arrested all Jews who held foreign citizenship, without distinction between the unimportant and the important, and incarcerated them at the Armenian monastery, close to the customs house.[273]

Many Jews asked me and Mr. Dizengoff to intervene to help the Jews who were liable to be expelled on the Italian ship that was anchored off the coast of Jaffa and was to set sail that evening. We hurried to the *kaymakam* and asked him the reason for the matter. The *kaymakam* chuckled and replied: "I received an urgent order from Djemal Pasha to immediately expel the foreign citizens, so I issued a command to immediately incarcerate them and to send them out of the country tonight." We complained to him, how could Djemal Pasha issue a decree like this without giving advance notice to the public, so that those upon whom this forced exile is being inflicted could prepare for the journey? He advised us to telegram Djemal Pasha and request an extension. We asked

---

273. This was on 17 December 1914. A ledger recording the names of over five hundred foreign nationals who were deported survives in the Central Zionist Archives.

him for the telegraph address, which he provided, but he in fact deceived us. Instead of giving us the address of Djemal Pasha, the commander of the Fourth Army who had issued the order, he gave us the address of Djemal Pasha,[274] the commander of the Eighth Army, a lower-ranking official who had no knowledge about the order. As we did not yet know both men, we could not, of course, differentiate between the two. We hurried to send a telegram according to the address provided by Baha al-Din and paid a handsome sum. We had to explain the full depth of the situation and implored him to show mercy on these miserable individuals and nullify the edict, but we received no response.

In the meantime, we gathered a group of public figures to discuss the situation, and we decided to arrange for food to be brought to the prisoners, to bring them the most essential belongings, and also to reunite the families, because by grabbing people off the street, which triggered a wave of panic, they had separated parents from children and husbands from wives, and vice versa. The sun had already set and the darkness of night began to spread in the Armenian monastery until the poor wretches could not see one another. We ordered for lanterns to be brought and we illuminated the monastery, we sent food and clothing, and Mr. Dizengoff and I spent the entire evening at the monastery together with other public servants in order to watch over the imprisoned Jews and to be prepared to help them with anything they needed.

At nine o'clock that night, as we composed a list of all the passengers, we found army personnel at the monastery who began inspecting each and every prisoner. From some of them they began taking all their money and gold, and they emptied their luggage. We heard that the army had already stolen from fifteen people who had been separated from the others, and everything they had was confiscated and handed over to the commissar. I approached the commissar and complained about what he was doing. The commissar justified himself and said that he was not to blame, as it was the *kaymakam* Baha al-Din who ordered him to do it on the grounds that he had to pay the ship's agent for the cost of passage for all the prisoners. I told him that if that was the reason they took the Jews'

---

274. Merslinli Cemal was also known as "little Cemal," as compared to (Ahmad) Djemal of the triumvirate. In contrast to the collective memory of "big" Djemal as violent and cruel, memoirs stated that little Cemal had a clean record and honorable intentions. He was commander of the Eighth Army Corps from April 1914 to February 1918, when he took over for Djemal Pasha as the Fourth Army commander.

money, then please return it to them, and Mr. Dizengoff and I promised to pay the ship's agent for the cost of passage of these wretched deportees.

The commissar went to consult with the *kaymakam* and after a few minutes he returned and told us, "If you commit to pay the agent for the travel costs, then I will return to you the money and gold jewelry that we took from the Jews." And he gave an order to the army to bring a chain and gather all the prisoners so that no one would be able to escape, and it was found that there were about 750 prisoners. Given the degree of panic, we did not have a chance to find the fifteen people whose money and jewelry had been returned to us, since they were already mixed in with the rest of the passengers. I asked Mr. Dizengoff what to do with the money and the jewelry, and he answered that I should not worry about it at the moment. I turned it over to him, and he hid it.

We went down to the shore with all the migrants, where we found the *kaymakam* standing with the officers all around him, with him issuing commands. We waited until all the migrants had been lowered into the boats,[275] and then asked the *kaymakam* for permission to go out to the ship in order to return the money and jewelry to the people from whom they were taken. We also wished to speak with the ship's agent and ask him to reduce the cost of passage to Alexandria by one lira per person. The *kaymakam* consented, and we went to the ship on a special boat. In the middle of the sea, we heard cries for help and calls of despair that grew increasingly louder. We hurried to the site and found that the boatmen were harassing the passengers with their poor treatment, throwing bundles over the heads of the men, women, and children. Some were crying because of their injuries, some because families were being separated, children from parents and vice versa. We berated the boatmen for their actions and approached the ship.

In front of the ship, we found dozens of boats clustered together in place, not approaching the ship. We immediately climbed out of our boat and climbed from one boat to another until we finally arrived at the gangplank leading up to the ship. There we learned that the military was taking advantage of the Jews prior to their boarding the ship and was taking their money from them. When the military saw us, they were embarrassed and ceased harassing their prey. We boarded the ship and

---

275. As discussed earlier, Jaffa did not have a deep-water port, so small boats carried passengers from the dock to the anchored ships offshore.

appeared before the captain and the ship's agent and complained bitterly to them for not lowering all the gangplanks except for one through which 750 people had to board. As we were speaking with the captain, the shouts from the people on the boats rose up to Heaven. I looked out at the sea but it was pitch dark, a great black void covering the surface of the sea, and one could not see a thing. The cries of the children and women were heartbreaking.

I climbed up on some sacks of flour that were lying on the deck of the ship and pointed the lantern to the east, where I saw the sorrows done to my brethren by the boatmen who were plundering their possessions and harassing my sisters, the daughters of Israel. I was filled with rage, almost to the point of losing my senses, and in order to disturb them from their terrible deeds I left my position, sinking into a deep misery, and I descended to the boat. Many of the prisoners surrounded me and told me that the military had plundered their warm clothing, pillows, and blankets after not finding money in their possession. I asked where the plundered goods were hidden. One Arab sailor whispered to me that the plunder was concealed on the boat that was the furthest away, which was separated from the other boats. I hastened to that boat and searched it and behold—all the items were found there. I transferred them to my boat and gave instructions to go to the shore and show the *kaymakam* what his soldiers had done. But then I changed my mind, and I realized that it would be better to return the items to their owners. I headed back to the ship and returned the items.

I immediately went to the city to meet with the *kaymakam* and to inform him of the deeds of the boatmen and soldiers and to ask him to issue an order to the ship to lower all the gangplanks. I brought with me the chief boatman, 'Ali Khamis,[276] an honest and courteous fellow, to help me describe the situation to the *kaymakam*. I went down to the shore to look for the *kaymakam*, but I was told that he was not there, he had already left. I searched for him everywhere in vain. Along the way, I ran into Hassan Bek and asked him to have compassion on the wretched and ease their plight as much as possible. But he responded that the order had been given to the civil governor, not the military one, and therefore there was nothing he could do.

---

276. Khamis was indeed listed as one of the head boatmen in Jaffa in the 1920s in Bawwab, *Mawsu'at Yafa al-jamila*, 896.

I went to the government house to ask for the *kaymakam* but did not find him there. I sought him at his home, but did not find him there, either. I went back to the *saraya* to ask for the commissar's help, and it was there that one of the guards with whom I was friends informed me that the *kaymakam* was sitting in his coach behind the *saraya* building, eating, since he had been busy all day long with the matter of the deportees and just now he had asked for food to be brought from his home. I left the *saraya* and asked the commissar to accompany us. We approached the coach and found the *kaymakam* eating. We told him all about the tribulations of our expelled brethren on their way to the ship and all around the ship, and that most of them were still on boats but the ship would not board them. I spoke to him with strong emotions, thinking that he, too, would be moved by the plight of my fellow Jews and would then issue his sharp commands, as was his custom. However, he listened to my words coldly and continued eating as if nothing had happened. I understood that he had arranged all of this and that it was done on his instruction; otherwise, the boatmen and soldiers would not have dared to do such a thing given the fear cast on them by the *kaymakam*. Moreover, the *kaymakam* had changed, and he wore a different expression than that of a few days ago.

At this, I filled with despair, and I told the *kaymakam*: "If it is the government's wish to torture the non-Ottoman Jews, then it would be better to drown them at sea rather than cause them prolonged torture and torment." He became angry with me, saying that I had lost my mind talking about the government this way. I told him: "Mr. *Kaymakam*! Would any other sane man who had seen what I have seen these past ten hours not go insane? I am even prepared to say these same words before a military tribunal." At that, the *kaymakam* became silent and did not say another word to me. He turned to the chief boatman and asked him if it was true that not all of the people had boarded the ship yet, and the chief boatman responded that as of half an hour ago, there were still about thirty boats full of people, and Dizengoff had remained on board the ship to ask the captain to lower all the gangplanks.

The *kaymakam* issued an order to the commissar to go to the ship and arrange for the passengers to board as soon as possible. The order was given in the most indifferent manner, and in reality it had no meaning; however, along the way I asked the commissar, as a friend, to take advantage of the order and to have compassion on the poor wretches by ensuring that they lower all of the gangplanks, and by asking the captain to set sail that very night before the weather turned stormy. On the way, we ran into Dizengoff. I told him about my actions and about my conversations with the *kaymakam*. From him, I learned that the ship had already lowered around three gangplanks and the people were boarding at a vigorous pace. The ship would set sail tonight, although it would not be able to contain all of the Jews, because it was filled to capacity with goods and passengers. We ourselves felt broken and shattered and wanted only to rest, but how could we abandon our brethren in the hands of the soldiers and the army, in the event that not all of them could board the ship? We immediately told our friends in Tel Aviv to send others in our place as soon as possible, to stand guard on the shore, and we went to our homes, depressed and discouraged, our hearts in distress.

I entered my house and fell helplessly onto my bed without even removing my clothes, and I fell asleep fully dressed in order to be ready for any call that might come from those on watch on the shore. My family, thinking that I would soon get up to dine with them, let me rest, even though they, too, suffered from the aggravating situation and the bleak panic of that day, and they also went to sleep without having anything to eat. Just as I was on the verge of falling asleep, I heard sounds of shouting and crying from the street. I got up from bed and went out to the balcony, and there were the public figures from the shore, and trudging right behind them were the remaining refugees—men, women, and children—who were unable to board the ship. My eyes beheld a scene of horror. Small children were left behind as living orphans, with their parents having been exiled to Egypt, and vice versa, parents bereft of their children who were left aboard the ship in all the panic.

The screams of these poor wretches rose to the heavens and broke every man's heart. Who would not have been shocked and disheartened by this awful scene? My entire family and I went out into the street to comfort these wretches, and how much greater was our sorrow at seeing young children of seven or eight years old who had been savagely separated from their parents, crying and sobbing and asking for their fathers. My daughter-in-law of blessed memory, Rahel, the daughter of Rabbi Mednitzky, the first wife of my eldest son, Moshe, did her best to persuade them to come into our home. But all of them kept on crying and begging to be brought to their parents. Nevertheless, I took the children and brought them into my home and immediately ran to the home of my friend Mr. M. Dizengoff,[277] where I found him with his wife and Dr. Hissin. I burst into tears and told him of the awful sights I had just witnessed, and which stemmed from the tyranny and cruelty of Baha al-Din. I spoke with him about our need to travel to Jerusalem immediately to meet with the American consul, [to ask him to] telegraph people in all the high places in order to ease the suffering and tribulations of our brethren.

Speaking of this expulsion, I am reminded of another expulsion of twenty-seven young people that occurred sometime later, whom I rescued from the jaws of the Turks and helped to leave the country and thus avoid being taken to the army. This is what happened:

One evening when I arrived home late, tired and weary, broken and shattered, and desiring rest, I walked out onto the balcony of my home and asked my wife, may she live a long life, to serve me dinner. Before I even had a chance to bring the food to my lips, the late Sheinkin entered my house in an agitated state, handing me a list of young Jewish men who were at risk of being taken to the army and who it was necessary to save. I told him that it is out of our hands to save them after their passports are confiscated, and in their place, they are given *nufus* documents[278] and are registered in the government ledgers with their full names. He told me: "These young men are standing downstairs in front of your house and waiting to hear what you have to say." I replied to him that to my regret it was not in my power to help them in any way. Nevertheless, deep down, the idea of rescuing these young men did creep into my mind, although it would be dangerous and difficult to put into place, so I was afraid to disclose it. I also decided not to show any interest, lest these poor youth depend on me, but I hid the list of names that remained with me. The late Sheinkin left me in great sorrow, and all the young men followed him, anticipating his response.

Once I was alone, I got up from my seat and asked my wife to permit me to leave for a few minutes, and that I would go without dinner. Of course, so that she would permit me to leave the house in the middle of my dinner, I did not tell her where I was planning to go. I went to see

---

277. Dizengoff lived two houses down and across the street from Chelouche, whose home was at the corner of Rothschild Boulevard and Herzl Street.

278. Chelouche is referring to the *nüfus tezkeresi*, an Ottoman identity card, derived from the name of the Ottoman population registry office.

Mr. Efraim Halperin,[279] who put at my disposal Menashke the coachman with the horse-drawn carriage, and I rode straight to 'Ajami. It was then nine o'clock at night. I knocked at the door, and the owner of the house came out. He was very happy to see me and asked me in astonishment, "What are you doing here at such a late hour?" I asked him to permit me an urgent conversation. He lit the lantern and we entered a side room and closed the door. When we were alone, I pulled out the list and told him: "My friend! I have a request to make to you, as the director of the *nufus* office, to erase all these names from the government records." "How could I do such a thing?" he asked me in astonishment. "It is possible to erase two or three persons, but not twenty-seven."

"So what would you advise?" I asked him. He thought for a while and then replied: "I only have one piece of advice. If these young men were Ottomanized within the past month or two, then all or most of them are registered in a single ledger, so I will copy all their names from that ledger into another ledger." I was pleased with this idea, and we agreed that if in the morning he finds out that all or most of these young men were indeed registered in a single ledger, then he will inform me immediately and will begin to work. I asked how long it would take him to complete the work, and he said it would take some time. Before parting, he requested from me that if these young men had good fortune and if he would be able to copy the ledger of the Ottomanized, then it would be incumbent on me to somehow retrieve their passports from the possession of a government clerk. I calmed him and told him not to worry, and then I drove off, not yet to my own house but to one of the dark alleys. I knocked at the door; it was ten o'clock at night. After knocking at the door several more times, I was invited inside. I asked for the clerk whom I needed and was told that he was already asleep. I asked them to awaken him, and a few minutes later, the clerk appeared wrapped up in an *abaya*.[280] He was surprised to see me, and said: "What's with you, Mr. Chelouche, showing up so late in my house? You must surely have a serious matter. Tell me, for I am prepared to do you a service, in light of the favors you have done for my family. Tell me and I will do it with pleasure."

279. Halperin emigrated from Russia in the late 1890s and established a transportation business offering "diligence" carriage rides between Petah Tikva colony and Jaffa.

280. This is a traditional cloak.

I pulled out the list, copied it into Arabic, and handed it to him. "My request to you is to find and place in my possession the passports of these persons, who Ottomanized a month or two ago." "I am willing," he replied to me affirmatively, "to come to your service even if it is the most difficult service for me, just so long as I do not send you away empty-handed." "I am asking you," I added, at which he stopped me: "Say, 'I hereby command you,'" and then chuckled. I parted from him with affection and admiration and rode home.

Upon my return home, I found my poor wife sitting and worrying about me; it was nearly midnight. I had told her I was stepping out for a few minutes, and I was delayed for hours. Every hour that passed felt like an entire day to her. That same night I did not eat a bite of food; I was too nervous and I waited impatiently for dawn, to be able to go down to the city and ascertain whether the clerk had found what he was looking for. The following day, at seven o'clock, I entered the *nufus* office and found him sitting alone in the director's office, writing. When he saw me, he called me over to him and whispered into my ear that all had gone as we had hoped, and by this time tomorrow all the work would be completed. I left the *nufus* office with a happy heart that my role had succeeded. I began to wonder whether I should tell the late Sheinkin about the matter, but in the end, I decided that it would be best to keep it a secret until I had the documents in my hands.

The following day, as I sat in my office, a clerk from the *nufus* office came in and told me that the work had been completed. That evening, at nine o'clock, he came to my home. My wife received him cordially, as at that same hour I was at an assembly of the Assistance Council, which had asked me to distribute to the needy the assistance funds that had been sent from America.[281] After sitting for a few moments, he handed her a package for me and went on his way. When I returned home from the meeting and walked into my bedroom, I found a package with my name on it on the small bedside table. I opened it and was filled with emotion at seeing the requested passports along with a list of their owners. I could not restrain my emotions, and my joy knew no bounds. I wanted to run to Mr. Sheinkin's home and tell him the good news, but it

---

281. This was the Joint Distribution Committee, which distributed close to 1 million US dollars for relief in Palestine during World War I.

was two in the morning, and how could I knock on his door so very late at night? I waited impatiently for the morning.

When I knocked at the door of Mr. Sheinkin's home in the morning, his wife informed me that he had gone to Petah Tikva. I asked when he would return, but she did not know any details. I was very sorry about the late Sheinkin's absence from the city. I knew for certain that the last Italian ship would be arriving the next day to transport the foreign citizens abroad; who knew if all my work had been for nothing? For I did not know the addresses of the passport owners, and I dared not expose the secret to anyone, for my life was at stake. As I came to appreciate the urgency of the situation and realizing I had no other choice, I sent a special messenger to Petah Tikva to look for Mr. Sheinkin, who returned to Tel Aviv that same evening and made his way to my home. I gave him the good news and then asked him to comply with my request in order to facilitate the departure from the country of these young men: in two days at an appointed time, the young men should be divided up [and sent to] three different locations. Although Mr. Sheinkin did not understand my perplexing request at that moment, he nevertheless agreed, and in the special message he sent me, only [a few] words were written: "The table is set." I understood that the young men were ready for the journey and were located at the three locations I had specified.

I then sent a note to the commissar in which I informed him of the following: "I have learned that tomorrow the last Italian ship for transport of the foreign citizens will be arriving at the Jaffa coast. After reviewing your list and my list of the foreign citizens, I found another list with the names of twenty-seven persons who are evidently trying to hide from the government in order to remain in the country even though they have not Ottomanized. It may also be that these people do not know that this is the last ship. Since neither of us wishes to be held responsible for this, the responsibility falls on you to search for these men and to send them out of the country. In order to make it easier for you to find them, as far as I know these men can be found in such-and-such locations. I am certain that you will take advantage of all the means at your disposal to search for them and to send them out of the country as soon as possible."

Toward the evening, I was informed that soldiers were arresting people and placing them in military custody. I immediately went to the place and verified that these were the young men who wanted to leave the country. I immediately went to the commissar and asked him to come to the place of their incarceration. When they saw me, they began to shout and complain about their imprisonment. I said to them: "Are you not non-Ottoman subjects, because of which the government will send you [away] aboard the last ship tomorrow?" When the prisoners heard about their voyage, they calmed down and asked if they could be released until the morning in order to prepare for the trip. We compiled a list of the men, and they were released on my own bond on condition that the following morning at ten o'clock they all would report to the *saraya*. Some of them tried to shake my hand in front of the soldiers, but I gestured to them to go on their way without saying a single word to me.

In the meantime, I sent my son Moshe, who always helped me in such matters and had befriended the commandant Hassan Bek for this purpose, to stand next to him and keep him busy. This way, Hassan Bek would not have a chance to conduct his usual harsh inspection of those departing the country. The commandant Hassan Bek was very meticulous about this; he would look through the ledger of the Ottomanized and would carefully inspect the papers to verify that those departing were not in fact Ottomanized. He carried this out with the precision of a needle being threaded. Being aware of this, I implored Moshe to engage Hassan Bek in conversation and all kinds of other stratagems, and that he should not leave his side until the news was received that the travelers had boarded the ship safely. I was not calm and could not relax until my son brought me the news from the deportees that all was well.

And through my hands God succeeded in saving these young men from a state of degradation under the cruel rule of the tyrant Hassan Bek.

CHAPTER 15 *The Final Days in Power of Baha al-Din and the Audience with Djemal Pasha*

*Dizengoff's trip to Jerusalem | The American consul
Dr. Otis Glazebrook | His generous assistance to the yishuv |
Hassan Bek's comments about his colleague Baha al-Din Bek |
The call to Djemal Pasha | On the road from Jaffa to Jerusalem |
The audience with Djemal Pasha | The sentence to leave the country |
We were shocked | The decision what to do | The late Antébi and
Dizengoff's mission to Djemal Pasha | Days of wandering |
In Tiberias | Our return to Jaffa | The new road to Gaza |
I am appointed to the council of the American fund |
The weapons incident at government house and
the resolution of the situation*

We decided that a trip to Jerusalem was essential, but the times demanded that only one of us would travel so that we would not leave our brethren in the hands of the cruel officials without a protector. Mr. Dizengoff traveled to Jerusalem and succeeded in his mission. The American consul, Dr. Otis Glazebrook,[282] a righteous gentile and a friend of the Jews, was astounded at what he heard and immediately telegraphed the American representative in Constantinople, Mr. Morgenthau.[283] Glazebrook asked him to use every possible means to persuade the central government to ease the suffering of the *yishuv* in the country, which stood on the brink of disaster under the weight of Baha al-Din's edicts. Not many days passed before the government in Constantinople sent an order of dismissal of the cruel *kaymakam*.

282. A retired pastor and personal friend of President Woodrow Wilson, Glazebrook served as US consul in Jerusalem from 1914–1920, with two years spent back in the United States after it joined the war effort in February 1917 and was considered an enemy state by the Ottomans.

283. Henry Morgenthau, a prominent Jewish businessman, served as US ambassador to the Ottoman Empire from 1913–1916.

When the news spread in the city about Baha al-Din's dismissal, there was great rejoicing and happiness among the residents. Everyone felt that before long the shackles would be removed, the yoke of suffering would be eased, and relief would come to the lives of the residents.

That same day, Mr. Dizengoff and I were summoned to see Hassan Bek. There we met with the representatives of the other religions, and among them was seated Baha al-Din himself. Hassan Bek informed us that he was demanding that we pay the [shipping] agent Alonzo[284] the government's cost of passage for the deportees, which totaled more than 700 napoleons. I explained to the commandant that while it was true that we had guaranteed to repay the amount, and that toward this goal, we as the representatives of the Jews, had started to collect the required funds from the deportees, and we have in our hands some money and watches. However, to our sorrow, the deportees were robbed on their way to the ship by the military and the boatmen, leaving them destitute and penniless. Therefore, we [were] unable to give a sum larger than what we [had] in our hands together with the different items that we [had] collected.

Hassan Bek became enraged and came at us with his club, raising his voice rudely: "If you do not repay this money by tomorrow, I will immediately telegraph Djemal Pasha to say that you are inciting the Jewish residents against the government; you will be considered rebels against the regime and will be expelled to Angora."[285] I jumped out of my seat and, gritting my teeth, dared to say: "It would be better if we were exiled to some faraway land, just so we would not have to put up with your excessive daily demands." Hassan Bek was extremely angered and went to his desk, hastily wrote a report, and then commanded us to leave his presence.

That same evening, the general prosecutor and 'Umar al-Bitar came to my home, happy and excited. They told me that a telegram had al-

284. It is unclear which Alonzo Chelouche is referring to, but the Roman Catholic Alonzo family traced their descent from Crusaders who arrived in Palestine. Members of the family worked as *dragomen*, bankers, and shipping agents, and they were also intellectuals. Martin Alonzo published the Arabic-language newspaper *al-Taraqqi* (Progress) in 1909, while his relative Alfonse Alonzo published *al-Akhbar* (The news) in 1909. Alonso Alonzo was the Italian vice-consul in Jaffa until he left the country in June 1915, so it is possible he was also the Italian shipping agent.

285. An older name for current-day Ankara, the capital of Turkey.

ready been received from Constantinople about the removal of Baha al-Din and his replacement by the "ras al-mina," the director of the port. All of Jaffa's residents, without distinction of race or religion, had already suffered tremendously, so these glad tidings came as a relief and a balm to all the blows struck by Baha al-Din. Nevertheless, the joy was incomplete, as various rumors circulated in the city that Baha al-Din had been appointed as private secretary to Djemal Pasha. The city residents discussed the matter among themselves in whispers and great secrecy, and the heart trembled in anticipation of the coming days.

Baha al-Din was removed from office and in his place came another. But he still, as at the beginning of his term, walked the streets with his head held high and a poisonous laughter on his lips. A few days later, we were summoned again to Hassan Bek. This time, he spoke to us as friends. He asked us to be aware of the fact that Baha al-Din did not have the financial means to pay out of his own pocket for the travel costs and the government treasury was empty, so it would be up to us as the representatives of the Jews to bear this burden as well. He coaxed us in the softest tones and most flowery language and attempted to persuade us to fulfill his request. Mr. Dizengoff informed him that we did not have the money in cash but that we would give him a check for 350 liras (that is to say, half a lira per passenger), that would be paid to the ship's agency by our people in Alexandria. He was extremely happy, and we parted from him with satisfaction.

A few days passed and we had not yet given the check to Hassan Bek. He sent for us, and we knew that the objective of this summons was to pay for the cost of the passage. Mr. Dizengoff gave me the check and asked me to pass it on to Hassan Bek. When I entered his office, I found him quite agitated. He told me that he had refused to receive visitors that day and had ordered the doors of his office shut so no one would disturb his rest. Then he commanded me to sit next to him. "Look," he explained to me, "you know how I treat the other groups here, and it is only toward you Jews that I have shown a good attitude and behave as I would with friends . . . But that is not how that scoundrel Baha al-Din behaved with you, with his tyranny and steely heart. I was informed that yesterday, as he left the city, he said bad things about me on the train, and he sullied my reputation. Now I want to take my revenge on him —as well as yours. I am going to write a report revealing his misdeeds and evil actions, his cruel behavior toward the Jewish community, and all the distress and tribulations that were caused to the community by Baha al-Din. In order to corroborate my report, it would be best if for your part a special delegation would go to Djemal Pasha, to fully explain to him the suffering of the Jewish community. Then Baha al-Din will be ostracized."

I replied to him: "Neither you nor Baha al-Din ever gave us a moment of rest, but the difference between you two is that you act openly, while he acts covertly and deceptively." He interrupted me, "That's enough. It is better to be openly bad than to pretend to be good. I must warn you that Baha al-Din is about to be appointed as Djemal Pasha's secretary, and who knows if it will not be worse for you than up to now—unless you complain to the pasha before it's too late. You should go to Jerusalem this very day."

When I reminded him of the purpose of my coming to him at this time, to bring him the check for the travel costs, he replied: "There is no need. The *kaymakam* is the one who is responsible for paying for the ship."

In those days, every resident was forbidden to leave his city and travel to the village or another city without a special permit.[286] Because of this, he asked me for the names of the delegation members, and when I wrote out the names for him—Dizengoff, Mossinsohn,[287] Berlin, and myself—he immediately wrote out the permits and gave them to me. As I left the commandant's office, I met a policeman who took me to report to the new *kaymakam*. The *kaymakam* told me that on the orders of Djemal Pasha, I was to take the first train to Jerusalem the following day to report to [the pasha] together with the other representatives of the *yishuv*, whose names he read to me.

From the *kaymakam*'s office, I went to the home of Mr. Dizengoff and told him about my conversations with the commandant and the *kaymakam*. He showed me a list of twenty-eight people who had been summoned to Djemal Pasha, among them many public figures from Jaffa and the surrounding district. The reason for the summons was unknown to us, and we therefore decided to call a gathering that same evening of all the invitees, and to get advice. Dizengoff suggested that we order a spe-

---

286. This was the *murur tezkeresi*, a travel document required of all Ottomans for intercity travel.

287. A Bible teacher who emigrated from Russia, Benzion Mossinsohn (1878–1942) was at that time the director of the Hebrew Gymnasium in Tel Aviv.

cial car on the train so that the invitees could be together at all times of the trip and could consult with each other.

We gathered at eight o'clock that evening at the home of Mrs. Moskowitz,[288] and we discussed our grave concerns about the situation. We decided to submit to the summons and to go the following day on the first train to Jerusalem. The next day on Friday, we had already arrived at the train station at six in the morning, and the railway clerks issued us a special car. Through the windows of the car, we saw the acting *kaymakam* escorted by policemen circling the car. He got on board the car, counted us, and found that all the invitees had come in their expected number. Once he got off the train, it began to move, heading for Jerusalem. As the train departed, one of us opened the door of the railway car and found a unit of gendarmes blocking our way. We tried to open the other door and found a similar scene. Only then did we feel that we were imprisoned and that there was something going on. We began to talk among ourselves, and all sorts of murky thoughts shook us. What was the reason for this summons for which we were being transported as criminals or rebels against the empire? What was our sin, really? On what grounds were we being transported under military guard? Only God knew. None of us had met Djemal Pasha face to face, and only the mention of this tyrant's name was enough to shock every person . . .

The train stopped at the Deir Aban (Har Tuv) station[289] due to a problem with the locomotive, and we waited until the afternoon for another locomotive to arrive. Many Jews saw us [treated] like prisoners and asked us with great concern the meaning of the matter, although we calmed them, saying: "We are fine!" We were hungry, not having prepared any provisions for the journey, and here it was already afternoon, and we had nothing to eat. Some of the Jews took pity on us and hurried to Har Tuv, the colony close to the station, and brought us bread, cheese, *leben*,[290] butter, and even fruit to eat. The food was happily served to us,

288. Frieda Moskowitz (1883–1955) was the widow of Dr. Herman Moskowitz from Rehovot, and a pension owner in Tel Aviv. Local Ottoman authorities monitored and reported on Moskowitz's close ties to Zionists in Jaffa. BOA, Ministry of Interior. DH.ŞFR., 533/62, 14 Eylul 1332/27 September 1916; DH.ŞFR., 68/60, 21 Zillkade 1334/19 September 1916.

289. According to the Spanish consul Conde de Ballobar, the Deir Aban station was destroyed by the retreating Ottoman troops later in the war.

290. *Leben* is a fermented yogurt.

and we felt the warmhearted concern of our brethren, who saw to our well-being and peered deep into our eyes to determine whether we were sad or happy. We ate and gave thanks to God; we drank a toast to them and to all Israel. During all the hours of waiting for the new locomotive to arrive, these good Jews did not leave our railway car, and when the train began to move they parted from us with wishes that we would return quickly to our city, free and liberated.

We arrived at the station in Jerusalem at two o'clock in the afternoon, where we found many soldiers and cavalrymen surrounding and guarding us from all sides. An order was given to the carriages that were used to carry passengers to Jerusalem to return to collect us. After about a quarter-hour, the carriages returned, we were escorted off the car of the train, and then we boarded the carriages, closely guarded on all sides. Before reaching Bab al-Khalil, we encountered two other coaches. Seated in one was Djemal Pasha's chief military officer and seated in the other coach were Messrs. Ruppin and the late Antébi.[291] In the middle of the road, the officer dismissed the army escort, and we were immediately released. On his instruction, we made our way to the Kaminitz Hotel.

Upon entering the hotel, Messrs. Ruppin and Antébi told us that Djemal Pasha wished to see us at four o'clock that afternoon at the main government palace located at the large Jerusalem Hotel, seized by order of Djemal Pasha to serve as the military headquarters. Among those summoned to the meeting were four men from Jerusalem, including Antébi himself.

At four o'clock, we were escorted by a high-ranking military official to the designated spot. We entered the large hall and waited. Several high-ranking officers and senior government officials passed in front of us, and at the sight of each one our hearts skipped a beat, wondering if he was Djemal Pasha. After about an hour, a military official of about forty-five years of age walked in. He had a moustache, a clipped beard, and

291. Albert Antébi (1873–1919) was born in Damascus to a rabbinical family, and he was educated there and in France. He was sent to Jerusalem by the AIU in 1896 to teach at its vocational school, and the following year he became the director. Antébi was fluent in Arabic as well as French, and as a result he played an important mediating role with local government officials, notables, peasants, and foreign consuls. He worked for the Jewish Colonization Association and also privately helped out with Jewish land purchases.

black hair, and was of medium height. His black eyes were bright and wore an expression that pierced the kidneys and the heart, penetrating the thoughts of any man. It was the honorable Djemal Pasha himself, whose mere mention sent shock waves through the entire *yishuv* and disturbed its peace. He approached us in the company of the pasha of Jerusalem, Ekrem Bek,[292] as well as several other high-ranking officers. The pasha came toward us, and we all stood up on our feet with reverence and awe. He spoke in French: "Are all those summoned from Jerusalem and Jaffa present?" We replied, "Yes, we are here at your command." "Are there twenty-eight men present?" "All of us are here," replied the late Antébi. He came closer to us and began asking a few of us for our names. And then he said: "Prepare yourselves. In ten days' time you are to be exiled to Constantinople."

The harsh order pieced our hearts like a sudden clap of thunder. We looked at the ground and were utterly speechless.

"Do you understand?" he asked forcefully. "Yes," we responded feebly, with a nod of the head, in a state of sorrow and dejection. Then he called in Turkish, "Hayde!"[293] and gestured with his hand for us to leave. At that moment, I looked at the face of the pasha of Jerusalem, who had been standing the whole time right behind Djemal Pasha, and I saw his face go white at hearing Djemal Pasha's harsh edict, since he was acquainted and friends with nearly all of us . . .

We walked out deeply disappointed and made our way to the Kaminitz Hotel. All the Jewish residents of Jerusalem were preparing to welcome the Sabbath, while we, overcome with sadness and dejection, prepared to accept the harsh edict. It was difficult to come to terms with the fact that all of us would soon be deported to Constantinople. Who would look after our suffering and tortured public, left without shepherds or defenders? It was astounding that a great vizier could issue such a harsh verdict without any wrongdoing and without trial, grounds, or basis. This was the situation in Turkey, where the fate of innocent and honest people was decreed by tyrannical and ill-tempered people. Low, melancholy thoughts gave us no respite. Who knew if we would even reach Constantinople or if this cruel despot would not issue a warrant to

---

292. It is unclear whether Chelouche confused him with Ertuğrul Bek, who was the governor of Jerusalem at the time.

293. "Move along," in Turkish.

his minions to kill us along the way? And who would even object to his doing so, particularly during wartime?

Once we returned to the hotel, Dr. Ruppin, who was a German citizen and was close to the German regime that was allied with the Turkish government in the World War, came to see us. We filled him in on all the details of the audience, and he was astounded to hear the bad news. He expressed the view that it was probably the handiwork of Baha al-Din, who was now the personal secretary to Djemal Pasha and was a sworn enemy of the Jews. Apparently, he must have spread his slanderous lies about the Jews and informed on them until this terrible edict was issued. Djemal Pasha intended by this to distance the Jewish leaders in order to constrain [the Jewish community] even more; there would be no one left to stand up for them and protect them. We were in a very agitated state, and our nerves were frayed. Dr. Ruppin encouraged and comforted us, lest our spirits flag.

We decided not to miss the opportunity and composed a detailed memorandum to Djemal Pasha in which we asked why we were being sent to Constantinople, what sin had been found among us, had we rebelled against the government? Was it because we submitted to the government and paid taxes to it, that we sent our sons to the army, that we helped the government with everything it demanded of us, did we deserve all this? Was it because we were Zionist Jews, that we had sinned in some way against the government? We hoped that by means of this memorandum we would succeed in easing or canceling the edict. We hired two attorneys and gave them the general format in which the memorandum was to be written, and a few of our members convened with them in a separate room and drafted the memorandum. The memorandum was twelve pages long, and in it we expressed everything that weighed so heavily on our hearts.

It was ten o'clock at night, and all of us felt in the depths of our hearts the violation of the Sabbath evening. None of us had eaten anything, nor had we recited the *kiddush* over wine. Each of us was engaged in our own melancholy thoughts, ruminating on the catastrophic consequence of this edict, his heart filled with fierce yearning for his home and his family. It is precisely in times of trouble, when a person is facing calamity, that the only thing he wants is to be close to his family.

Meanwhile, the memorandum was completed, a final draft was written, and a few copies of it were made. All the members gathered together, and the memorandum was read out loud to us, with everyone in unanimous agreement over its contents. Nevertheless, one of our members commented that he did not believe Djemal Pasha, who was preoccupied with his own affairs, would want to read such a lengthy memorandum; therefore, he suggested that we write him a short letter stating that we had heard his edict that in ten days' time we should be ready to travel to Constantinople, and at his command, we were willing to leave even today. Our only request to His Excellency was that he would be willing to receive two of our members for a few minutes' [audience]. And [if] Djemal Pasha consented to that proposal, our members would present themselves to him and would start a conversation with him. If it was shown from the pasha's words that he was in a conciliatory mood, they would submit to him the memorandum and perhaps he would read part of it and feel remorse for the evil that he was committing against us. The proposal was adopted. Immediately, two attorneys sat down to write a short letter to the pasha. The letter was signed by all the members and was immediately dispatched to the pasha.

It was decided among us that in the event that the pasha agreed to an audience, Messrs. Dizengoff and Antébi would be sent to represent us. At midnight, the messenger returned and announced that the pasha was prepared to meet with the two members that we proposed. What a great tumult and commotion arose in the hotel; all of us got up out of our beds, we awakened Mr. Dizengoff and sent word to inform Mr. Antébi to be ready to appear before the pasha. A quarter-hour later, they left to see the pasha, and we again gathered in the hotel hall, waiting impatiently for our emissaries to return. A full hour passed, and our emissaries had not yet returned; the heart was beating and throbbing for their fates and our fates. Some of us prayed for their success, [and] Hakham Korkidi[294] recited Psalms in front of us; some of us were hungry and dulled their hunger with a cup of tea, while others, out of a lack of patience, went to wait for the emissaries out on the main road near the pasha's office, but then, out of their fear of being stopped by the Turkish soldiers and asked what they were doing there in the middle of the night, and in the middle of a war, they returned to the hotel.

294. Nissim Korkidi (1872–1937) arrived with his family from Bergama (Anatolia) to Jerusalem in the early 1880s. After completing his religious studies there, he relocated to Jaffa, where he worked as a communal leader and member of the chamber of commerce. Korkidi and his wife were among the original founding families of Tel Aviv.

Another hour passed, and our emissaries returned with wide smiles on their faces. Djemal Pasha received them and was in a reasonable mood. Our representatives asked what the crime was for which he was deporting us from the country, and over the course of the conversation they submitted the memorandum to him. He read the memorandum to the end and smiled: "Indeed, I pardon you, but in consideration of the fact that the army is in the near future going to attack Egypt and I suspect some of you, but do not wish to exile you to a distant land, I would advise these individuals to leave Palestine of their own accord and go to Syria for a couple of weeks."

Mr. Antébi replied: "We are at your command, O Pasha! But who is it that you suspect?" He removed from his cabinet a list of fourteen names and showed it to Antébi. Mr. Antébi asked that the pasha issue an order that all these men receive travel permits to Syria. Djemal Pasha informed them that the pasha in Jerusalem would give them the permits, and they parted from him in peace. The list of men considered dangerous to the government at that time included: Dizengoff, Dr. Mossinsohn, Eliyahu Berlin, Meerovitch,[295] David Yellin,[296] Dr. Bograshov,[297] me, and another few whose names I cannot recall. What amazes me to no end was that I was deemed the most dangerous to the government, for as the late Antébi conveyed to me, I was first on the list, and aside from that, there were special symbols made alongside the names of those considered most dangerous. Nevertheless, I was not alone as such, because among the most dangerous the names of Dizengoff and David Yellin were also listed. And so it was that the edict was rescinded. Instead of being expelled to a distant land, we would travel to nearby Syria on an excursion.

295. Menashe Meerovitch (1860–1949) was an early Hovevei Zion activist and member of the Rishon LeZion settlement. Meerovitch was a technical advisor to other Jewish colonies, and he published a short-lived newspaper for farmers called *Der Kolonist* (*Ha'ikar*); he also published anonymous letters in the Arabic newspaper *Falastin* pretending to be a Palestinian peasant farmer, "Abu Ibrahim."

296. David Yellin (1864–1941) was the son of a Polish Jewish father and Baghdadi Jewish mother; he was multilingual in Hebrew, Yiddish, Arabic, and French. Yellin wrote in the Hebrew press and taught Hebrew at the local AIU school in Jerusalem and then at the German Laemel school. Yellin was elected to the Jerusalem municipality in 1910, and then to the *meclis-i umumi* (general council) in 1913.

297. An immigrant from Russia, Haim Bograshov (1876–1963) was a Hebrew educator at the Herzliya Gymnasium, later becoming headmaster for two short terms.

The following day, Saturday morning, each of us returned home, united by the thought that fourteen of us, ostensibly a "danger to the government," would be prepared to set out on our way on Monday. On Monday, we received the *vesikot*[298] from the pasha in Jerusalem through Antébi. We immediately convened at the home of Mr. Dizengoff to make the arrangements for the trip; it was unanimously decided that since it was permitted for us to be in Syria, we would travel to Tiberias and stay there, as at the time it was considered to be on the border with Syria. We appointed a treasurer, transferred money to him in order to arrange some provisions and everything that was needed for this trip, and we departed Jaffa to Tiberias, via Haifa. Mikve Israel and Rishon LeZion both sent us wines produced by the colony as a goodwill offering.

There were numerous army camps along our route, as at the time they were multiplying from day to day. At every station we were forced to stand up while our *vesikot* were inspected and our belongings were checked to see if we had any weapons or any other forbidden items. After every thorough inspection, we continued on our way to the next station, where the whole procedure repeated itself. We arrived at the police station along the Haifa-Nazareth road toward evening. The soldiers stood us up and asked for our *vesikot*, inspected our belongings, and all was found to be in good order. They immediately began speaking to each other in Arabic, assuming that we did not understand their language: "Walla, mush nafi'," meaning, "It's no good . . ." said one to another. The meaning was that there was no pretext on which they could take *baksheesh*[299] from these people, everything is in order with them. Even now, whenever I meet Mr. Meerovitch, he reminds me of these words: "Walla, mush nafi' . . ."

After many bumps along the road, we arrived at our desired destination, Tiberias, where we lodged at a German hotel — this was before there was a Jewish-owned hotel — and we ordered kosher food. During our first meal there, we met a respectable gentleman who sat and gave orders to the policemen who were coming in and out. We learned from the

---

298. *Vesika* (Tur.) or *wathiqa* (Ara.) means "document" — in this case he is referring to the travel pass, or *murur tezkeresi*. Chelouche added a Hebrew plural ending to the singular Turkish/Arabic term.

299. A bribe to government officials. Ottoman officials at all levels were notorious for demanding bribes for both everyday and extraordinary requests.

hotel owner that this was the *kaymakam* of Tiberias, who permanently lodged at this hotel.

He entered into a conversation with us that did not revolve around the war, but rather was about various things, and we endeavored to be cautious and to offer laconic answers. And so it was that we conversed for several days about life, the nature sites around Tiberias, the weather, the Sea of Galilee, and so on, and the *kaymakam* did not ask us who we were or for what purpose we had come here.

A week after our arrival, he received a telegram instructing him to send Mr. David Yellin to Jerusalem immediately, under military guard. He was taken aback by the request. As far as he knew, Mr. Yellin was a notable, so how could he be sent to Jerusalem under military guard? The *kaymakam* looked for various ways to interpret the telegram: perhaps it was possible to just inform Yellin that he was to present himself before the central government in Jerusalem.

He sent word to Mr. Yellin to present himself before the *kaymakam* at the government house in Tiberias. When Mr. Yellin arrived, he asked him:

"Your name is David Yellin?"

"Yes, that is my name."

"What is the nature of the relationship between you and the government?"

"I am a member of the General Council[300] in the government..."

At that, the *kaymakam* understood the situation and said, with a gentle chuckle: "I received a telegram from Jerusalem to send you to Jerusalem immediately. As you, sir, know well, it is wartime, and I must carry this out as soon as possible. However, given that during the days that you have been lodging at this hotel with me I have come to know you, sir, as an important individual, I cannot permit myself to send you under military guard, and so I am hereby informing you and asking you, to travel to Jerusalem tomorrow."

Mr. Yellin thanked the *kaymakam* for his kindheartedness and asked him for a *vesika*. When Mr. Yellin returned to the hotel and told us about what had happened, we were very surprised—perhaps there was a new development regarding our own fate. We were very concerned about Mr. Yellin's fate and were also worried for our own welfare; perhaps

---

300. He is referring to the *meclis-i umumi*.

others among us would also be summoned to Jerusalem the following day. With that in mind, we considered it best to leave Tiberias immediately, since here we encountered the *kaymakam* several times per day, and now he would certainly watch us with some suspicion. It would be better for us to move on to the colonies[301] to spend the remainder of our time there, but how could we go without any *vesika*? The *vesikot* that we had received authorized us to travel to Syria but not back, and in those days the Turkish authorities were very meticulous about these matters.

I went to consult with one of my friends, Avraham 'Abadi,[302] who had a great influence in government circles in Tiberias. I asked him to procure permits for us, and we made our way to the colonies in the Lower Galilee. At noon we arrived at one colony, and in the evening at another, and wherever we went we were received with affection. They gave speeches welcoming us to the colony and we responded in kind. These feelings of loyal brotherhood encouraged us and gave us strength and energy to bear the fate of our wanderings in silence.

In the meantime, we heard that the late Betzal'el Yaffe had been arrested in Jaffa and the ledgers of the "Ge'ula" were searched. We realized that the government was harboring new suspicions against our community, and we were extremely concerned about the fate of the Hebrew *yishuv*. In the meantime, fourteen days had passed since we left Jaffa, and we began to think about our return. There were two versions. First: that Djemal Pasha had expelled us for only two weeks. The second: that he had expelled us for an unlimited length of time. At the time, we were in Zikhron Ya'akov and we began to consult about what to do. I proposed to my friends that I would travel alone to Jaffa right away, I would consult with my friends who were government clerks, and then I would ascertain if it was permitted for them to return to Jaffa and would immediately inform my friends. If not, I would return to Zikhron Ya'akov myself, where we would stay until God took mercy on us.

Early the next morning I traveled to Petah Tikva, where I remained until the day grew dark, and then I traveled to Tel Aviv. As soon as I ar-

---

301. At the time there were half a dozen Zionist colonies in the area of Tiberias.

302. From a rabbinical family in Tiberias, 'Abadi was a candidate for the position of *hahambaşı* in 1910, although he withdrew his candidacy. He reportedly worked in the government finance department for seven years.

rived home, I sent my son to invite the general prosecutor. He arrived about an hour later. To my question regarding the arrest of Mr. Yaffe and the searches, he answered that all had passed uneventfully. I told him about the situation in which my friends and I found ourselves, and he said that I could write to my friends to return to their homes. On the basis of his words, I wrote to Mr. Dizengoff, and the following day, everyone returned home safely.

We returned to prepare ourselves again to—together with the *yishuv*—grapple with whatever fate lay in store for us, to care for it, and to lighten the burden placed on it as much as possible.

A few months later, the government announced a contract for paving the road from Gaza via Julis, close to Gaza, all the way to Latrun, whose length would be 37.5 kilometers.[303] The road would pass through numerous villages on mountainous and hilly terrain, which would require the investment of a great deal of labor in order to straighten it. In spite of all the difficulties of paving a road through this terrain, the Turkish government nevertheless decided on the new route because it would be the shortest route and it would be well suited to the tactics of the war, whenever the army would be forced to flee from the south northward.

Due to the Turkish law that every contractor working on a public or government-military project was authorized to issue his employees certificates releasing them from army service, and in consideration of the fact that humanitarian conditions in the Turkish army camps were horrific and beyond human power to bear them, Dizengoff and I decided to take upon ourselves this contract, even though we were certain that we would make no profit on it at all. It was clear to all that entering into this sort of business transaction with the Turkish government was liable not only to suck your blood but your life force as well. Still, given that we would be in a position to exempt so many Jews from the "inferno" that was the Turkish army, saving our people from degeneration and decline, we agreed to take on this work.

We began an all-out effort to win the government contract. We paid a few visits to the government contracting office in Jerusalem and also toured the site where the road was to pass, and with the help of the

---

303. The Latrun–Julis road is still in use, integrating current-day Route 3 and a small part of Route 40. Julis was an Arab village later destroyed in the 1948 War; the nearby Moshav Hodiya, founded in 1949, was built on some of the village's lands.

late Antébi we succeeded in receiving the contract from the government, with two additional partners from the colonies.

All of the cars of the French railway company were at the time standing unused at the central train station known as Wadi al-Sarrar.[304] The government was not using the cars, since they had lost all value when the narrow-gauge tracks were replaced by the wide-gauge tracks. The government transferred a large number of these cars over for our use. We arranged in them an office and dormitories for the engineers and the laborers. Aside from that, we built a few huts for a kitchen and dining room for the laborers, a large stable for horses, and numerous tents, which were erected all over the expansive and desolate square. The entire work area was divided into different stations, and tents were put up in each one, but the main station was at Wadi al-Sarrar.

Mr. Dizengoff and the author of this memoir were the project supervisors, each one responsible for his own work zone, and from time to time we would meet to decide on the next stage of work. In order for the project to be completed as quickly as possible, the government transferred to us five hundred camels, two hundred soldiers and officers, and a commandant to supervise them all. For our part, we built strong wooden chests to strap onto the camels, in which the gravel would be placed. The work was divided up between all the groups of laborers and was carried out at a quick tempo and in cooperative harmony. Each group took upon itself a portion of the road measuring between half a kilometer and two kilometers. We appointed inspectors who would ride on horseback through the areas where the work was underway in order to supervise the quality of the work. As we expected, the planned route had to surmount a difficult obstacle—a high rocky mountain that required us to employ expert workers from among the Arabs of the villages who knew how to explode hard stones.

In some places, we would dig down as much as three meters below the surface, and vice versa—there were places that we had to fill with three or four meters of sand, and there was no sand in the area. The army officers who were assigned to the project in general as well as those [working with] the five hundred camels were feeble and lazy and would

---

304. Wadi al-Sarrar railway station, which was later named Nahal Sorek, is currently abandoned and dilapidated, situated between Beit Shemesh and the Na'an intersection, close to the spot where the railroad tracks cross Route 3.

not work until they were first given some money and enough cognac to get them drunk. Nevertheless, in spite of all these obstacles, the work proceeded at a feverish pace. My son Moshe would camp at Latrun and supervise the work up to Wadi al-Sarrar. My late brother Avraham Haim and Mr. Dizengoff managed the affairs from the office in Wadi al-Sarrar, from which their instructions were relayed to all the stations. My station was actually in two different sites, the villages of Masmiya and Qastina,[305] and I would ride a donkey or horse the six or seven kilometers between them, one time to the northern side and another time to the southern side. About two months passed and the work proceeded with great vigor, to the point that we did not have a spare moment to go down to the city and see the family.

One day, I received a letter in English from America (on which was inscribed on the stationery in Hebrew letters, "The voice of your brother's blood cries out to you") from the members of the Joint in America, in which they informed me that they were appointing me as a member of the Joint's council in Tel Aviv and Jaffa.[306] They asked me to assist the other members of the council in this sacred work, to ensure that there be no differences between one Jew and another. The letter touched me profoundly and I was overwhelmed with compassion, and I decided that despite my many troubles, I would take on this sacred work. I immediately wrote home to ask them to find out when the council meeting was to be held, and to inform me so that I could attend. A few days later, I received word from home that a letter arrived from the late Betzal'el Yaffe in which he wrote that the gathering would take place on Thursday at the Tel Aviv community council hall. I wrote down the date and time to remind myself, and a few hours before the meeting time, I rode a donkey to Tel Aviv.

At the gathering, I learned the meaning of the initiative, since money had been received from America in the name of the council that they had appointed in order to distribute funds among the poor of Jaffa and Tel Aviv. They had declared that they were prepared to send sizable amounts on a regular basis. The discussion continued until midnight.

305. Masmiya was thirty-eight kilometers southwest of Jaffa. Qastina was another five kilometers to the south.

306. Chelouche was the only Sephardi representative on the committee. *Haherut*, 13 March 1916 and 14 April 1916.

We scheduled the next meetings, and the following day I returned to my road-building work.

Nearly all the wagons belonging to the farmers of the Gedera and Qastina[307] colonies were employed by us, hauling materials. Work on the road continued for approximately four months, and when it was done, we completed the project just as we imagined in advance that we would — without any monetary profit. But we did have the spiritual satisfaction of knowing that we had saved the finest of our young men from degeneration in the Turkish army camps. To this very day we are still owed a total of 1,800 Turkish liras by the Turkish government.

Shortly before all this, the following episode took place.

When the *kaymakam* Fu'ad Bek Shihab,[308] who was my friend and advisor on the project distributing wheat to residents, was reassigned from Jaffa, a new *kaymakam* was appointed in Jaffa, named 'Arif Bek.[309] He was from a Damascene family and had been educated and lived for many years in Constantinople. During his tenure, the prosecutor was Ali Bek the Turk, and it was during their rule that 'Umar al-Bitar rose to prominence. They brought him closer to the empire, and they would spend every evening together. They also brought me in as a trusted friend in their company.

During those days it was the days of Ramadan. The plaza next to the government palace was lit up, and the Muslims gathered at the coffee houses to spend the night eating and drinking, because they would be fasting the following day. The government palace was also lit up, with the clerks working until midnight because throughout the month of Ramadan they were exempt from work in the afternoons.

On one of these nights as I was sitting at home, the late Sheinkin entered and told me that the government had seized two wagons with weapons that Jews had transported to Petah Tikva. The Jews had been arrested pending investigation, and therefore I was to go immediately to

---

307. Chelouche is referring here to Be'er Tuvia, not to be confused with the nearby Arab village of Qastina.

308. Fu'ad Bek was formerly the *kaymakam* in Haifa before he was appointed to serve as Jaffa's *kaymakam* in May 1916. Al-'Issa writes that he was originally from Lebanon. Khalaf, *Les mémoires de 'Issa al-'Issa*, 159.

309. 'Arif Bek was appointed in September 1914. According to Mordechai Ben Hillel Hacohen's diaries, *Milhemet ha'amim*, 'Arif Bek took significant bribes from the Jewish community in Petah Tikva throughout the war.

the city, as perhaps I might be able to help out the detained men. It was wartime, and possession of a weapon was considered a crime, but the Jews feared the army that had raided the colonies and destroyed all their labors over many years. In addition, there were plenty of thieves and robbers who carried out their crimes in broad daylight, who went into the vineyards and orchards and treated them as if they were their own. Only through self-defense was it possible to protect Jewish property so that it would not be lost entirely.

I immediately rushed to the city. I entered the *kaymakam*'s room and found him meeting with the prosecutor, talking about the wagons and preparing to conduct the investigations. I asked them: "What are you busy with, my friends?"

They told me the whole story, and added:

It's a good thing you showed up right now. The situation is serious. The public was gathered in the plaza and they saw with their own eyes the wagons with the weapons being brought in, so concealing it is not an option. Our advice is that you go down to the arrested men and tell them to say when they are under investigation that they have nothing to do with the goods that were conveyed in the wagons. And the coachmen should claim that they did not know what they were hauling, since the sacks were tied up, and there aren't any weapons in them, anyhow.

And that is what happened. The investigations were conducted, everyone was declared innocent, all without monetary payment.

CHAPTER 16 *Days of Hunger in the Land*

The Wheat Committee | The Turkish lira | My work on the Wheat Committee | A thank you from Djemal Pasha | The new commandant in Jaffa | Exchanging banknotes | The "Austrian submarines" and the sacks of flour | The commandant sells the bread | The crime I committed on behalf of the twenty-seven subjects that I saved comes to light | The Turkish oversight committee | Accusations made against me and against the kaymakam *| Djemal Pasha, our protector | The Wheat Committee is liquidated*

In the year 1917, hunger spread throughout the country. Djemal Pasha arrived in Jaffa and convened a general committee of the city's Muslim, Christian, and Jewish leadership; the Jewish appointees were Dizengoff and me. The object of the committee was to accept delivery of twenty-thousand kilograms of wheat each day from the army's warehouse in Ramle, and then to distribute it to all the residents of Jaffa and Tel Aviv: half a kilo per person for half a *quruş*. The chairman of the committee was the *kaymakam* of Jaffa, Fu'ad Bek Shihab.

We rented two large apartments on Iskandar 'Awad Street (where Dizengoff's office was located) as our offices. We divided the city into eight districts and carried out a general census of all the residents.[310] Clerks were appointed to keep records and manage the finances. It was hard work, managed in a cumbersome and erratic manner. A smaller executive committee, of which I was part, was appointed. For many days I fought against the lack of order that characterized the operations of the committee. The *kaymakam* always understood my perspective, which

---

310. 'Issa al-'Issa, who also served on the Wheat Committee, wrote that the city was divided into three major sections: Manshiya, the old city, and 'Ajami/al-Jabaliyya. Each section conducted a population census and delivered the wheat to each head of household, two or three times per week depending on need and supply. Khalaf, *Les mémoires de 'Issa al-'Issa*, 155.

FIGURE 16.1 *Yosef Eliyahu Chelouche during his service on the Wheat Committee, 1917. Chelouche Family Collection.*

resonated with his own, and he related to all my suggestions and proposals with all due gravity; eventually, he put me in charge of managing the affairs. I brought about a total revolution in the work methods. I researched the names of the residents, particularly among the Muslims, and discovered several Bedouin names that did not even exist. I fired all the clerks who were suspicious in my view, and I appointed in their place Jewish clerks. I managed the ledgers in French so that I could review them myself whenever required.[311] I appointed one special and loyal clerk to take charge of the register, and I appointed my son Moshe as general manager of the wheat, to help at my side.

311. It is evident that Chelouche did not know Ottoman Turkish.

After finding that the residents' registry was incorrect and changing the method of districts, I created additional districts and reduced the number of residents in each one, as a means of simplifying control. Even after these corrections were implemented, I was conscious of many improprieties and instances of theft and evasion. I resolved not to show any favoritism. I announced to all the workers that if anyone discerned even the slightest impropriety or anything that was out of order, the transgressor would be arrested immediately and put on trial. In this way, the situation changed completely, and matters were administered in a uniform fashion and with exacting precision.

Only one obstacle stood in my way, and that was the Turkish lira. The lira was issued in one lira, a half-lira, and a quarter-lira. How could anything happen when we did not have the ability to offer change? It was a taboo to speak in public about this drawback, in particular when we were in a government office. We had to show respect for the Turkish lira, which was in fact losing value. I began to consult with others. I printed up special pieces of paper in different bold colors that would be difficult to forge so that they would serve as the smaller denominations. I went to show them to the *kaymakam* and to receive his approval. When I arrived, he closed the door to his office and said to me,

> Although you've done something smart here, did it occur to you that you took this action without receiving any special governmental order, and for that they are allowed to hang you? It would be best for us to burn these right away. However, to find a way, I hereby suggest that you place an advertisement signed by us in which we inform the public that anyone coming to buy wheat should bring small change with him. Every month, we will exchange all the liras that they bring with them.

Naturally, my papers were burned, the advertisement was published, and the matter was resolved. The committee members rarely came into the office, and they found that the work was proceeding apace and with precision. The Arab members of the committee were angry at me because I had reduced the number of Muslim families, following an inspection that revealed that several families were not to be found. Nevertheless, they did not dare express their anger publicly, because they knew that I was guided by a strong desire to enforce order. They also knew that the *kaymakam* was on my side.

When Djemal Pasha and his men paid a visit to the Wheat Committee office and inspected the documents, they checked the accounting and found that everything was conducted appropriately. Before leaving, he asked the *kaymakam* what my monthly salary was for this work, to which the *kaymakam* replied: "The committee offered him a salary but he refuses to accept it. Not only is he busy with this responsible work, but he also employs his son, who has the keys to the grain warehouses, without expecting a reward." As a sign of his gratitude, Djemal Pasha shook my hand, and left us with a sense of satisfaction. All this encouraged my spirit, and I continued to improve the work by means of double inspections. I oversaw the work in the office as best as I could. I was there at all times. Lunch for me and my son was brought from our home, and those clerks whom we trusted were always there to help us.

At the same time, Commandant Hassan Bek was transferred elsewhere, and his place was taken by a new commandant by the name of Ahmad Shukri Bek,[312] who was from Damascus. Three weeks after his assumption of the office, I was introduced to him by the *kaymakam*. We used to meet in the street and would inquire as to the other's well-being. I always tried to maintain good relations with high-ranking government officials, as I knew that the day would come when I would have to ask them for a favor for the Jews.

One day, this commandant sent his officer to get change for a 10-lira banknote. I understood that he was testing me. It was commonly known that this note was then worth only 2 liras, and since he was aware that we kept small denominations in our register—it was taking in 600 or 700 liras a day or more—he was asking to make a profit of 8 liras. From that income we had daily expenses to pay to the Bedouin camel drivers who hauled the wheat, who refused to accept banknotes and only wanted coins, for why should they accept a lira that was worth 100 *quruş*?[313] It was not feasible to take measures against them, for fear that they would stop hauling the wheat. As a result, I did not know what to do about the commandant, who knew the true situation. In the end, I decided to sign

---

312. Al-'Issa writes that he was named Hassan Shukri Bek. Khalaf, *Les mémoires de 'Issa al-'Issa*, 158–59.

313. As Chelouche explained earlier, the banknotes had only 20 percent of their face value at the time.

a voucher to the register, and give him change for the banknote, which the officer took and left.

A few days later, the same officer returned, this time with a fifty-lira banknote in his hand. Without thinking too much, I took the fifty liras, tucked it in my pocket, and told the officer to relay to the commandant that I would come up to his office in another few minutes. The officer left and I sent [word] to my own private office to send me fifty gold napoleons. I put the coins in my pocket and went to the commandant's office. When I arrived at the office, I found it was closed. The guard at the door told me that there were two *effendi*s inside. I sat in the waiting room until the commandant would become available. The officer, who was aware of my presence, immediately informed the commandant that I was waiting for him. In the meantime, the *effendi*s left, and I entered the commandant's office. He received me with all the enthusiasm that one is accustomed to in Eastern hospitality and asked me to sit down next to him. I told him that to my regret I could not afford to exchange the banknote with public funds, but I was prepared to do so with my own private money. The commandant, who listened carefully to what I was saying, responded clearly: "Do as you wish, as long as you exchange the banknote."

I took both the banknote and the fifty gold napoleons out of my pocket and pressed both of them into his hand, since wasn't it obvious to the commandant that the banknote was worth only ten liras, and what would be the use if [I] exchanged it for fifty liras [in coins]? Better that I give them to him as a gift, in order to buy his favor for an hour of need. The commandant took the money and thanked me. We parted in peace, and he escorted me to the door.

Two weeks passed from the time of this episode, and the commandant walked into my office. As soon as I was informed of his arrival, I hurried to greet him. He showed me two telegrams that had been received from Jerusalem, in which he was informed that sometime in the coming days two Austrian submarines would arrive on the Jaffa coast, and the government was to prepare provisions for their journey. The commandant's request to me was that I issue an order to Gelat,[314] the

---

314. Antoine (Anton) and Francis Gelat founded the National Palestinian Flour Mills company in 1914; Francis was expelled from Jaffa to Istanbul in 1917. The Gelat family were successful merchants; the Sandel map illustrates the houses of Jibran

owner of the mill, to provide him with eight sacks of fine flour, for which he would pay into our register three liras per sack. I explained to him that I had no authority to do so, because according to the contract between us, we were to receive coarse flour and not fine flour, and certainly not at such a low price. I asked him to meet Gelat himself and speak with him. The commandant refused, saying that since the matter was secret, he himself could not discuss the matter with Gelat. but only with me, as the manager of a government office. I informed him that I would give him my answer in an hour, and I went to consult with the *kaymakam*.

As is known, after I revised the contract between us and Mr. Gelat, he no longer produced twelve sacks a day of fine flour. Instead, he would mill only a few sacks a day, which he sold to well-known and prominent individuals, at a price of six liras per sack. How could we ask Gelat to give us sacks of fine flour at the price of a three-lira banknote each?

The *kaymakam*, who listened intently to my account, agreed, seeing as the wheat was required for covert military operations. On that basis, I informed the commandant that he should send me a note stating: "In accordance with secret military order number such-and-such, dated such-and-such, I hereby request from the director of the government office for wheat to remit to my subordinates a total of eight sacks of top-grade flour, and I hereby enclose payment for their value." Once I received this order, I gave the commandant a letter addressed to Gelat, in which I told him to provide eight sacks of top-grade flour at the price of a three-lira banknote per sack. The matter was carried out, although none of this was entered into my ledgers, because the money was paid directly to Mr. Gelat by the commandant. Incidentally, the order of the commandant, complete with his signature and a government stamp, is preserved in the archive.

Interestingly, the commandant sent the sacks of flour to a bakery to bake bread, and by the following day all of the flour had been used. However, the submarines did not arrive. Fearing that the bread and the rest of the food that he prepared might spoil, the commandant put it all up for sale through special brokers, and the bread was sold for full price, for two reasons: first, because no one dared to buy a single loaf with a banknote and then ask for change, but instead, he purchased the bread

---

Gelat (which he spells as "Dschellad") and Francis Gelat; the Gelats were connected by marriage to other prominent Christian merchant families that Chelouche mentions in his memoir—including 'Akkawi, Beiruti, and Farwaji.

with very small coins. Primarily, though, it was a time of hunger, and for a long time the public had not seen such fresh bread baked with fine flour, clean without any waste in it. The commandant made a tidy profit from the bread sale.

Once the sale was completed, the commandant turned to me with another request: "As you know, the submarines did not arrive, but I am nervous—what if they come today or tomorrow? I ask you to give an order to Mr. Gelat to provide me with eight new sacks of top-grade flour, in order to prepare provisions for the submarine crews." I told him once again, as on the previous occasion, that I would give him an answer in an hour. As was my custom, I presented myself to the *kaymakam* and consulted with him. The *kaymakam* agreed this time, as well, to honor the commandant's request, since it did not incur any loss to the public treasury. I informed the commandant that he should send me a note stating: "Due to the fact that the submarines did not arrive at the specified time and we were then compelled to sell all the bread, I hereby request from the manager of the government office for wheat to give the appropriate instructions to Gelat, that he provide a total of eight sacks of top-grade flour." I received the note in question, and the matter was carried out. The submarines did not arrive this time either, and the bread was sold once again. This scenario was repeated several times, and the commandant grew wealthy at the expense of others.

When I became interested in learning who the purchasers of this bread were at a time of financial distress when most residents relied on our assistance, I learned that the bread was being sold to the monasteries and the European hospitals.

One day, the commandant sent a special messenger who summoned me to his office. When I walked into his office, he shut the door behind us. "Are you aware," he turned to me, "that today I saved you from disaster?" I became overwhelmed and wished to learn more about the reason for this disaster, but he continued: "As you know, a special policeman brings me mail every day from the central government in Jerusalem, which I then confirm by giving a receipt with the serial number of the letter and the date on which it was written. This morning, I felt like going to the bathhouse, and from there I did not return home, but instead came to my office. On the desk, I found seven letters. I opened one of them and found various documents, the subject of which was you, sir. After reading all the documents with great interest, I put them back in the envelope and hid it in my coat pocket. When the policeman came, I signed a receipt for six letters, and he left."

"So what is this all about?" I asked him impatiently.

He half-smiled and answered: "The central government has discovered that you committed a great sin. Through your efforts, twenty-seven people who were Turkish citizens fled the country, and you arranged forged passports for them. The matter came to light due to the passengers themselves, who were talking with one another on the ship and praising you, without whom they would not have been liberated from the yoke of the Turkish government. Our spies reported this to the central government. A decisive order has now been received to investigate the matter and to try you to the full extent of the law." Listening to this serious accusation against me, I struggled to maintain an air of calm, and I told him: "These people were foreign citizens. As a matter of fact, when I found out that this was to be the last ship to set sail abroad with foreign citizens, I hurried to inform the commissar of the location of these men's living quarters. So what is my guilt, exactly?"

The commandant sensed how pale I had become and rang for a servant. He ordered the man to heat the small stove, as it was a cold winter day, and to make coffee. Turning to me, he said: "Here is the envelope that contains all of the protocols, papers, and documents on the basis of which a terrible tragedy is liable to befall you. I am ripping them into shreds and burning them." And that is what he did. All the documents went up in flames before my eyes. I parted from the commandant with a handshake, and I thanked him from the depths of my heart.

The wheat office continued to exist for some six or seven months. Meanwhile, the storeroom in Ramle was gradually emptied of its wheat. The government began to be stingier about wheat distribution, in spite of complaints made by the local residents to the *kaymakam* and to Djemal Pasha himself. In the meantime, rumors spread that the residents would soon be deported from the country to Angora and to the Hawran. The worry was evident on each and every face.

Around that same time, there was an oversight committee composed of officers who went throughout the country conducting searches in every governmental and private institution. This committee came to my office as well one day and requested to inspect all the papers and documents. Once they showed me a certificate from the central government in Jerusalem, I did not refuse and led them to the accounting room. I asked Yitzhak Amzalak,[315] our treasurer, to show them all the vouchers and to open the register for them. As I was preoccupied with work, I asked for their permission and went to my office. They counted the money and the banknotes and audited the register account book. When they completed the audit, they entered my room and asked to conduct a search of the archive. In the meantime, the *kaymakam* sent a special messenger to inform me that the oversight committee would be coming to my office today to conduct an inspection and that I should raise no objections, and that I should receive them politely and offer them cigarettes and coffee. I responded to the *kaymakam* that the committee had already arrived and was already at work. I immediately ordered cigarettes and coffee and served the guests.

The committee left to have lunch and returned to resume its work. They went through the entire archive, reviewed the contract with Gelat, and paid close attention to the revisions made to it. The audit continued for about three days, and in the end, the committee came into my office. Since they only spoke Turkish and did not know Arabic, I asked the *kaymakam* to come over, and he spoke with them and translated into Arabic for me. The committee posed a few questions to me. Why was I distributing a bulk quantity of wheat to the Jews, while to the Muslims and Christians based on districts, with each resident receiving his individual portion? Why did I pay fair wages to clerks, when I could be saving public funds?

I responded to the committee members that if the Muslims and the Christians had been organized by an elected committee of respected members of the community who could be relied on to be trustworthy, I would also be giving them a set amount of wheat in bulk for them to distribute to members of their communities. The Ottoman government had to bear in mind that due to the organization of the Jews and their respected community committee that was composed of honest and reliable individuals, the government was saving a great deal of expense, because when it came to the Jews, I had no need for districts, nor did I have need for extra clerks. As for the clerks, as the manager of this office, I treated them as I did private clerks, so that they would be able to support themselves with an adequate salary and would not consider the idea of earning money on the side.

315. Amzalak was married to Chelouche's sister-in-law, Rahel (née Moyal).

The committee members listened to what I had to say and opened an argument, in which all of them took part. I did not understand what they were saying as it was in Turkish, although I did sense that it was directed against me. When they left, the *kaymakam* told me that they suspected me of working hand in hand with the Jews, and that I was no doubt earning a tidy profit from this business. But the *kaymakam* had responded to them: "I know this man very well, and he comes from a very respectable family. He is a man of means and has his own private businesses. Both he and his son have left all his businesses, and they now work for the good of the city, not in order to win any rewards. How could you even think of suspecting this man? For if your suspicions were justified, this man would not have turned down a monthly salary that could be as much as sixty or seventy liras."

A few days later, I was informed by the *kaymakam* that the committee had submitted a report accusing me and the *kaymakam* of working hand in hand with the Jews and making money from the business. I heard this from the *kaymakam*, who heard it from the private secretary of Djemal Pasha.

After reviewing the report, Djemal Pasha summoned the committee to his office and asked them to withdraw it. He told the committee: "I know this man and the *kaymakam* of Jaffa very well. I am familiar with the office. He is most assuredly an honest man and his loyalty can be relied upon. I request that you withdraw the report, for I am not capable of suspecting him or the *kaymakam*." The report was canceled.

Following this event, the wheat stored in the warehouses began to dwindle; very little wheat remained. I asked the *kaymakam* to permit me to make the arrangements to liquidate the office. And with the *kaymakam*'s permission, I arranged a final balance sheet of the office accounts, and I dismissed the clerks and paid them their salaries. At the end of the day, there was still money and banknotes left in the cashbox totaling about 170 liras. I gave all of it to the *kaymakam* and received from him an official receipt and a letter full of thanks for my dedication and loyalty to this labor.

CHAPTER 17 *The Expulsion of Jaffa and Tel Aviv*

The commandant ʿAbd al-Hadi Bek | The military commission that depleted merchants | The expulsion edict | Tel Aviv and Jaffa in exile | On the road | Stops from Ras al-ʿAyn to Samakh | Petah Tikva, the first stop of the exiles | My son Moshe is drafted | Forty sacks of wheat as ransom | ʿAbd al-Rahman al-Taji comes to my aid | The camels with the wheat | Hauling my possessions to Petah Tikva | The attitude of the Petah Tikva colonists toward the exiles | My relative David Hayoun | My family settles down in the colony | Back to work on behalf of the exiles | My brother Yaʿakov and the branch of the Anglo-Palestine Company in his home

At a time of deep worry and agitation, in the days when the *yishuv* prepared for a harsh and terrifying edict to be expelled from Jaffa to either the far edges of the country or to Angora, the commandant Ahmad Shukri Bek was posted elsewhere, and in his place arrived Commandant ʿAbd al-Hadi Bek, a native of western Tunisia. He was tall and erect, an honest and kindhearted man who shunned bribery and who always tried to put a human face on the dry laws in spite of his high position, which demanded adherence to the orders issued by his superiors even if they ran counter to his own feelings, logic, and common sense. In short, ʿAbd al-Hadi Bek was a righteous gentile.

Nevertheless, all the most heinous edicts were issued during his term in office. Martial law was declared in the city. Pursuant to an order issued by Djemal Pasha, a military commission circulated in the city, seizing goods of all sorts—for free—from the merchants for the army. No merchant dared to prevent it from taking whatever goods it wanted, nor did he utter a word or voice any complaints about his fate. When the commission entered his store, the merchant was forced to put on a happy face and receive these bloodsuckers generously. He would stand there helplessly, watching as they plundered his property in broad daylight, looking with his eyes as the light in them flickered out . . . Anyone who dared express opposition was harshly punished, and all of his merchandise was confiscated by the government. More than anything else, the government was in need of construction material. The commission would walk into our warehouses and simply select whatever it wanted, take it, and in exchange would give us signed receipts for whatever amount that they deemed reasonable. These piled up in our archives for a long time without a human hand bothering to touch them. It goes without saying that all of this was done in the name of our honest and beloved commandant. Only in recent days did we receive, through the French government, a small percentage in exchange.[316]

Those were days of hunger. There was no grain and no wheat. The peasants stopped bringing their grain to the city, for fear of the army seizing it. For its part, the government ceased to concern itself with the welfare of its citizens and securing a supply of wheat. Only the Jews suffered less than the others. Through the efforts of Mr. Dizengoff, our leader in the city, emissaries were dispatched to bring in abundant supplies of wheat. Still, bread was a very expensive commodity.

Most of the wheat was brought in from Transjordan, from the Hawran, to which Mr. Shmu'el Moyal was dispatched several times. He succeeded in his mission and fulfilled his duty faithfully despite all the difficulties and obstacles inherent to such a dangerous trip during wartime, and in such a wild location.

In the meantime, an edict of expulsion from Jaffa was issued—an irrevocable edict.[317] The Muslims were expelled by the hundreds and the thousands deep into the hinterland. The fate of the Jews was extremely distressing. Mr. Dizengoff, who did not rest or relax for even a moment in his efforts to safeguard his brethren, marshalled his strength once again and gathered together all of the public figures in the city, among them the writer of these lines. He set up ad hoc committees of different types, to arrange for an adequate number of railway cars, to register the passengers, to collect personal belongings, and to prepare provisions for

316. Through the postwar treaties signed at Versailles, Sèvres, and Lausanne.

317. The expulsion order was issued on 28 March 1917. Peasants were permitted to remain behind to work their fields, and the citizens of Germany, Austria, and Bulgaria were exempted from the order, but all other Ottoman and neutral power citizens were to relocate to anywhere but Jerusalem or Haifa.

the trip. One special committee was appointed to collect heavy possessions from individuals, and then to seal and preserve them.

In those days, there was a major shortage of camels, horses, and donkeys in Jaffa, for most of them had perished in the famine,[318] and the few animals that remained were busy moving the Arabs. The leaders of the *yishuv* were greatly concerned about the fate of the Jews and how they would be moved, and they issued a heartrending appeal for help to the nearby Hebrew colonies, asking them to send as many wagons as they could spare. Thanks to the help of our brother farmers, wagons and coaches came in from the colonies, with each one sending in accordance with its ability.

We sent families to Tiberias. We set up a station at Ras al-'Ayn,[319] up until which the wagons would arrive, and from which passengers would ride trains that reached the Samakh station, and from there they traveled by wagons to Tiberias. Pairs of central committee members were sent on ahead to the two railway stations—Ras al-'Ayn and Samakh—to maintain order and oversee the wagon traffic. They were supplied with money and provisions to assist those in need, and they distributed aid to the poor and indigent. The families suffered less thanks to this excellent supervision. Over the course of two to three weeks, numerous Jewish families left in this fashion, with their possessions and furniture remaining behind in Tel Aviv, protected in the committee's warehouses. All merchandise and objects that had commercial value were stored in warehouses until Tel Aviv was emptied of human beings; subsequently, we transferred them to Petah Tikva, where they were stored in special warehouses under the supervision of the central committee appointed for this purpose.

My family was among the last to remain in Jaffa. As a public servant on the committee, I could not leave the city. I prepared to close up all our warehouses and to prepare provisions for the journey as well as sufficient food for the period of our emigration,[320] at least three months. Meanwhile, my son Moshe was captured. When I arrived in the city, I learned that he had been called up by the army. At the time, the gov-

---

318. In addition, several weeks prior beasts of burden were requisitioned from the surrounding villages and were sent to Gaza to help evacuate the residents before the British attack, where they then died from hunger.

319. Present-day Rosh Ha'Ayin.

320. Chelouche uses the word *hagira* (emigration); we have retained his original word choice throughout.

ernment would accept a "ransom," and it wanted from me forty sacks of wheat, stipulating that the sacks be new and the wheat fresh. Where would I be able to acquire forty such sacks and such wheat? When I traveled to Ramle, I was able to acquire eight sacks of flour with great difficulty, but how could I rest when my firstborn son Moshe was in prison? Sources within the government informed me secretly that I would have to pay a similar ransom for my son Avner, as well, and that I too would also probably be arrested.

My heart was filled with tremendous sorrow, and I felt humiliated. I did not have any cash in my possession aside from the 300 liras that I set aside to support the entire family during the days of our emigration. The banks were sealed shut. Our merchandise was stored in warehouses, with no one to purchase it. That night, we also saw to the needs of our clerks who were also emigrating, giving them sufficient sums of money for two or three months. At this difficult time, I met with one of my Arab friends, a truly righteous gentile, 'Abd al-Rahman al-Taji.[321] He became emotional when he saw my sad and troubled face and asked what the reason was. I told him all about the troubles I was facing, and how I did not know where I could get my hands on eight thousand kilograms of clean wheat and new sacks, in order to offer them as a ransom to the government for my two sons, one of whom, Moshe, was imprisoned. His sense of compassion was aroused, and he requested that I accompany him to the city.

[Al-Taji] brought me to the army offices to meet the manager responsible for accepting ransom payments. As we walked in, 'Abd al-Rahman asked him to whom one remits ransom payments, and he responded that the ransom was to be remitted at the government warehouses in Ramle. Then 'Abd al-Rahman said, "Write down that I hereby commit that within three days from today I will deposit at the government warehouses the ransom for the two sons of Mr. Chelouche, Moshe and Avner." At the request of the manager, 'Abd al-Rahman put this commitment in writing and signed the stamps in accordance with the law. The commitment was sent to the commandant and was approved, and an order was issued to free my son Moshe from his imprisonment.

321. Al-Taji was a prominent landowner and citrus merchant in the Jaffa-Ramle region. In the 1920s he served on the Supreme Muslim Council. Al-Taji was recalled favorably in the diaries of Yitzhak Rokach, a prominent Jewish citrus merchant in Jaffa.

I was given two receipts for payment of the ransom of my two sons. I shook ['Abd al-Rahman's] hand and asked him to calculate how much I owed him. He replied: "I don't need any money right now. You can pay me another time." And then he added, "When do you think you will be leaving with the family?" I replied that I would be able to leave Jaffa in another few days, "now that I have been freed, thanks to God and thanks to you, from the ransom which weighed so heavily on me."

"Where are you thinking of going?"

"To Petah Tikva, for now."

"Have you set aside a sufficient quantity of wheat?"

"I bought eight sacks of wheat in Ramle."

'Abd al-Rahman paused and said: "That quantity of wheat will not suffice for a large family like yours, and once you are at the colony, you won't be able to acquire more wheat later. I am sending you ten sacks of wheat tomorrow."

"And where will I get hold of the animals to haul all this cargo?" I wailed before him.

"When I send you the five camels with the wheat tomorrow, keep them until you have moved all your possessions to Petah Tikva," replied 'Abd al-Rahman obligingly. I thanked him and parted from him, with much affection.

The camels arrived the following day. I loaded all of our essential possessions and valuable papers on them, and we traveled to Petah Tikva. I arrived there on Thursday before noon, innocently believing that we had come to live among our people, in a Jewish colony, and that they would make our time spent there as comfortable as possible. Every homeowner would surely vacate some of his rooms for the émigrés[322] at such a time of distress. So how astounded I was when I found the exact opposite to be the case! I found many of the émigrés living on the streets in the open air and under the shade of the trees, sitting on their possessions for the past two or three days. I asked them, aren't there any empty apartments in Petah Tikva to live in, had they already been filled with our émigrés? How shocked I was to hear that there were plenty of vacant apartments, except that the owners were demanding high rents. Some of the owners

---

322. Throughout this episode, Chelouche uses "émigrés" (*mehagrim*), although in other places he refers to them as "exiles" or "expelled." We have retained his original word choice throughout.

simply did not know how much rent to ask for, so they would ask for an excessive amount and then were dissatisfied with what they were being paid, because they were getting everything they asked for, and the rents were climbing higher and higher. These émigrés were unable to rent apartments, so what would they do? The Emigration Committee would be meeting [that night] with the Petah Tikva committee to discuss the situation.

I unloaded my possessions beneath the shade of the trees and arranged them in a stack, leaving my family there. I sent the camels and wagons back to Jaffa to bring the rest of our possessions, and I went myself to find us an apartment. When Mr. David Hayoun[323] found out that we had arrived in Petah Tikva, he sent for me and complained, why hadn't I informed him of our arrival, for then he would have had sufficient time to prepare apartments for us. In the meantime, he implored us to come live in his home for a few days, until we could rent an apartment. Meanwhile, I learned that right across from where we were parked were three homes for rent, although the owners were asking for high rents. I sent for my relative David Hayoun and asked him to negotiate with them over the rent, without insisting too much on the price. We rented the homes, which belonged to Cohen and Dankner.[324] My family and I moved into Cohen's house, my late brother Avraham Haim moved into Dankner's house, and my dear late father and his family moved into the house in the middle. My brother Ya'akov rented a home far away from these houses, and so we settled into our new homes in Petah Tikva.

The following day, Friday, I went back to work together with all the other public figures of Jaffa. The Tel Aviv committee temporarily gathered at the colony's committee building, but later it rented an apartment and began frantic labors on behalf of the Jaffa émigrés. It also maintained contact with émigrés who relocated to many other places in the country. A branch of the APC operated in my brother Ya'akov's house, secretly providing banking services to customers in Petah Tikva.

323. Hayoun (1881–1958) was born in Damascus and educated at ENIO in Paris. He briefly taught in Tunis, and in 1904 he arrived in Palestine to teach at the JCA school in Petah Tikva. He married Rivka, a third daughter of Avraham Moyal, in other words, the second sister-in-law of Chelouche.

324. Haim Cohen-Reiss (1861–1932) was born in Jerusalem and trained as an agronomist in Europe; he worked for the JCA in Petah Tikva. Me'ir Dankner (1869–1932) lived in Petah Tikva.

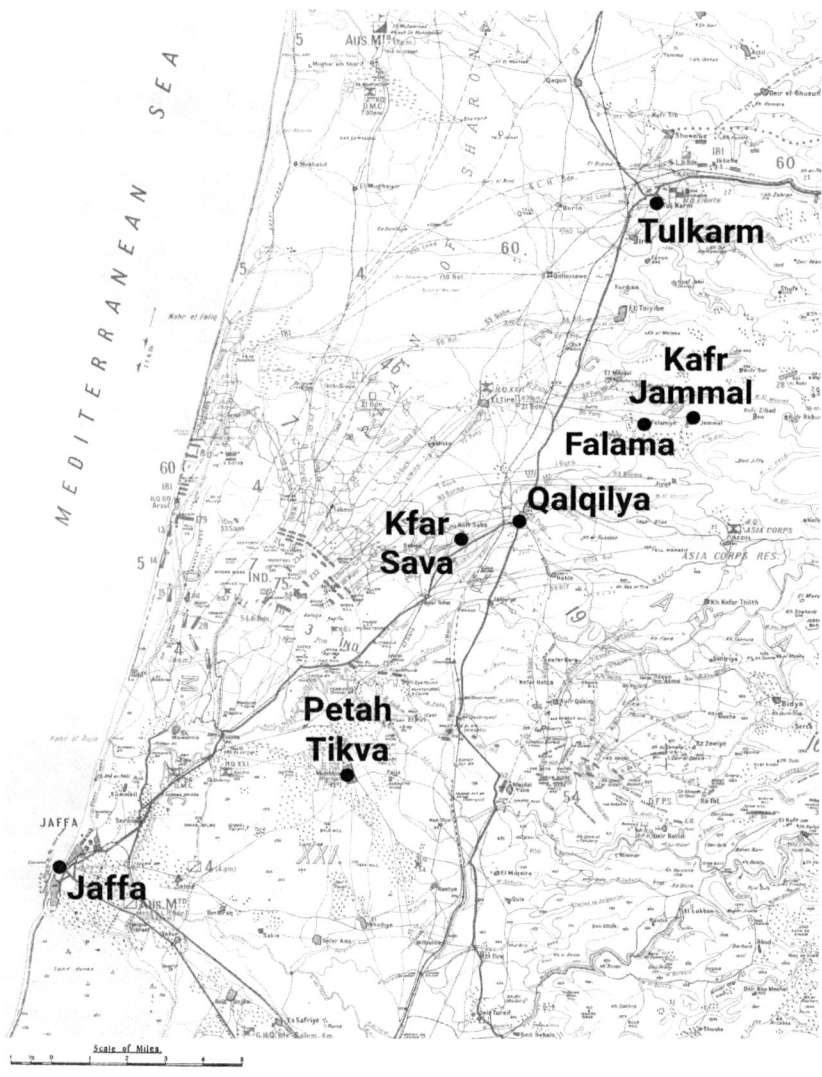

MAP 17.1. The Chelouche family's inland travels
after the deportation from Jaffa in April 1917.

The front lines between British and Ottoman-German troops kept shifting between late 1917 and late 1918. As Chelouche describes, even after British troops occupied Jaffa and Petah Tikva, his family remained on the opposite, northern side of the front until late in 1918. The background map is taken from Megiddo, 1918: The Battles of Sharon and Nablus, 19 September 1918, Ordnance Survey, 1929. Laor Collection, National Library of Israel, 990023677100205171.

CHAPTER 18 *A Terrifying Night in Deserted Jaffa and More . . .*

Pipes from my warehouse to the battlefront | I'm in deserted Jaffa, as a houseguest of the commandant | The commandant at work | Looking for cigarettes | Noise of the airplanes | Shouts of the military | Jaffa faces the enemy | My conversation with the commandant at night | I leave abandoned Jaffa | My return to Petah Tikva | Yitzhak Cohen's help | The edict of expulsion from Petah Tikva is canceled | My journey to Jerusalem on the eve of Rosh Hashanah | With the director of the Manzil *| A high-ranking official visits Petah Tikva | The welcome he was given | The edict as act of revenge | With the pasha | Cancellation of the edict | At the colony's well | Improper distribution of financial aid | Discrimination between ethnic communities*

One day, the commandant of Jaffa arrived in Petah Tikva searching for pipes. I invited him to lunch at my house and he arrived at the scheduled time along with his escorts. I introduced him to a few members of the colony committee. During our conversation, I understood that this time the government had instructions to pay in full for the merchandise. I informed him that we had pipes in our warehouse in Jaffa, and I was prepared to place some of them at his disposal. The commandant was very pleased and asked me to ride back to Jaffa with him. "I am willing to pay you both in gold and in banknotes according to the value of the gold, as long as you give me the pipes required for the battlefront without delay."

I knew that after taking possession of the pipes, the commandant would issue me a government receipt and that I would have to go to Jerusalem to collect what I was owed. But in consideration of the fact that the commandant was an honest and amiable man, I rode with him to Jaffa. I unlocked the warehouses, and the soldiers began taking inventory of the pipes. The sun was setting as we finished the work. The commandant implored me to remain in Jaffa until the following day and invited me to stay with him. When I arrived at his office, he asked his butler Ahmad to prepare a nice dinner for us. "You should know," he told Ahmad, "that I have an important guest with me today, so you should prepare the finest foods you can." I then told him that to my regret I would not be able to eat with him unless it was an all-dairy menu. The commandant smiled, apologized, and said: "I completely forgot that Mr. Chelouche is Jewish. Based on my own experience from my hometown, I most assuredly know that the Jews of Tunisia are good and loyal. Ahmad," he called to his butler, "on tonight's menu are dairy foods. Bring butter, cheese, *zebda*,[325] cream, and eggs, and fruits, too. This evening, I will dine with my guest and will share his meal with him."

Meanwhile, he was extremely busy. He signed papers and answered the army messengers, who gave him no respite.

An extraordinary volume of army traffic ensued. Messengers entered in a state of alarm and urgency. The commandant's face was filled with worry. His eyes sank in their sockets and his forehead creased from excessive worry and concern. Meanwhile, I sat off to the side as if forgotten and anxiously looked around. He woke up and said to me: "Excuse me, my guest, for having diverted my attention from you. I'm so preoccupied; it is wartime and there is a lot of work to be done. I do not believe that I will be able to sit down and dine with you at the same table. It would be best if you would go to my house, eat, and go to sleep." He rang and Ahmad entered. "Go and escort my honored guest to my house, see him into the dining room, show him the bedroom. Provide him with the hospitality that he deserves. Take the key and lock up the house and then bring it to me." And then he turned to me and said: "Later on I will come back and we'll talk."

I parted from him with affection and left with Ahmad. I walked through the streets of the city, which were desolate and abandoned. I did not come across a single civilian, only soldiers. The entire city was abandoned by its residents. When I walked up to the commandant's house, Ahmad ushered me into the dining room and also showed me the bedroom. I asked him about the commandant's room, and he showed me the room across from mine. He told me that the commandant had this entire upper story of the house to himself, because his family had stayed in Tunis; downstairs, on the ground floor, lived his servants and his coachman.

---

325. This is a raw, fermented butter.

I was left alone. Ahmad shut the door behind him, and I remained in this large house, which had several furnished rooms but without another soul to speak with. I became sad and very despondent. I could not eat and only nibbled at a piece of cheese in order to dull my hunger. I took out the box of cigarettes and saw that there were only five left, which saddened me greatly. I certainly would not sleep tonight; what would I do without anything to smoke? I went to one of the windows and yelled downstairs, "Listen!" without knowing whom I might be calling to, and a voice answered without me being able to see who was speaking to me: "What would you like, Mr. Chelouche?"

I asked him, "Do you know where it is possible to buy cigarettes?" He replied: "Have you forgotten that this city is deserted? Go into the commandant's room and you will find cigarettes and tobacco of the finest type." I went into the commandant's room and found what I was looking for. I left him a note, saying that I had taken a box of cigarettes, and then went to my room. All the lanterns in the house were turned off, and only my room was lit by a large lantern. I did not dare to undress, and I lay down on my bed, eyes open wide, smoking cigarette after cigarette. My melancholy thoughts merged with the rising smoke.

I heard an unusual commotion from outside the house, wagons coming and going. The army was on its feet, moving in both directions. I also heard the sound of airplanes overhead. Dear God! Were they aiming for the commandant's home in order to destroy it? And if so, what would be my fate? Would there be at least a memory of me that remains? Tears poured from my eyes. Who knew what my family was feeling at this moment in time? My heart began pounding like a stormy sea. I felt a sense of distress such as I had never felt before. The army's shouts in Turkish, its harried movement, and the turmoil shocked me.

All of a sudden, I became aware of someone walking through the rooms. I looked up and saw that it was the commandant. It was midnight.

"Why haven't you fallen asleep?" he said to me.

"I won't be able to fall asleep. I have too many thoughts troubling me. You probably haven't had anything to eat yet. His Honor the Commandant is so preoccupied and busy."

"True, my friend," he answered. "I haven't eaten a thing all day. It is wartime and I have so much work. I just came to have a bit to eat and change my clothes, which are soaked, and then return to my office . . . Duty calls."

He had something to eat, changed his clothes, locked the door behind him, and left. Once again, a mute silence settled in the house. My kerosene lantern ran out of fuel, and I would have to sit in the dark. My melancholy thoughts cast fear into my heart, so I walked into the adjoining rooms to find some kerosene. All of the other lanterns were empty, and none was to be found in the commandant's room either. I entered the kitchen looking for the primus stove, but it had no kerosene left either. I kept on looking until at last I found some kerosene in one of the small lanterns, which I poured into my own. I also managed to light the primus stove and made myself coffee. I drank and I smoked. The many clocks in the house were ticking, this one sluggishly and this one briskly, this one less and this one more. I imagined that the sun would be rising in another three hours.

Outside the noise was getting louder. Through the windows I could hear the shouts and cries of the army. I looked out toward the sea and could see various lights. In the skies the airplanes were thundering. My whole body was shaking, and like a prisoner in his jail cell, I lay down on my bed. In the morning, Ahmad came in and awakened me. I walked in to see the commandant, who again asked for my forgiveness. The previous night had been abnormal. They were preparing for the enemy's arrival. There was a concern of war breaking out overseas. But for now, the Turks and the Germans had rebuffed the enemy last night.

When we said goodbye, the commandant gave me 60 Turkish liras in gold, and he was very sorry that he had no more gold coins to give me just then. As for the remainder, he gave me promissory notes amounting to 2,700 liras for the main *Manzil-Stab*[326] in Jerusalem. He placed at my disposal a donkey and a soldier to escort me back to Petah Tikva. When I parted from him, I shook his hand and expressed my gratitude for his kind treatment. I left a city that only days earlier had been teeming with people and was now seemingly frozen in time, abandoned by humankind. All the homes were sealed shut, there was no commerce, bargaining, or selling, truly a dead city. I rode out to my family, who was extremely anxious for my well-being. In Petah Tikva, as well, they had felt that that night passed like a nightmare, an extraordinary night.

---

326. This was the commissariat of the Fourth Army, garrisoned in the Notre Dame church in Jerusalem. Since the allied German and Austrian armies were present and active in Jerusalem, it was known by the Turkish and German names.

As I have mentioned, I received promissory notes from the government for a sum of 2,700 liras and therefore had to go to Jerusalem to receive the money from the *Manzil*. As I was planning my trip, Mr. P.[327] came to see me and said: "I have heard that you have these promissory notes. On more than one occasion, I myself have sent them to my brother in Jerusalem, who is the personal friend of the finance minister, and I received the entire amount to which I was entitled. If you intend to easily receive your money, I will give you a letter of recommendation to my brother, and he will help you to easily obtain it."

It goes without saying that I was extremely pleased, and I thanked him from the bottom of my heart. Immediately after receiving the letter, I traveled to Jerusalem. I went to P.'s store and showed him the letter, and when he had finished reading it, he asked me for what amount I had received promissory notes. I answered him that I was holding such notes for a sum of over 2,700 liras. When he heard that, he became furious and said: "To hell with these evil people! With every passing day they grow more and more wicked. Now even the bribes they demand aren't enough to satisfy them!" He turned to a man who was in the store at the time, and said: "Listen to this, Mr. S.,[328] Mr. Chelouche here also has promissory notes addressed to the *Manzil* in the amount of 2,700 liras. And now I have received a letter from my brother, asking me to help him, but what will I be able to do, dealing with these people who skin you alive?"

Mr. S. responded to him, "You know how it works. If someone wants to make some money, he also has to allow others to make some money. Without a doubt, the finance minister will demand a sum of 500 liras in exchange for paying such an amount."

I listened to their words and considered them to be serious. After all, who was not aware of the thirst for money of Turkish government clerks? I therefore told them that if indeed there was no other advice and that was the custom, then I could not refuse to do the same. The two of them consulted with one another, and one of them said to his friend: "It

---

327. In the original manuscript, the full name is given, but it was omitted in the published book. We are preserving the anonymity of the individual in line with Chelouche's own editorial and ethical decision to withhold it from publication.

328. In the original manuscript, the full name is given, but it was omitted in the published book.

would be best if you would go tonight in my name to the director of the *Manzil*—to his home, not to the government house—so that no one else learns about it, and then you can settle on a price with him. After all, we have the moral obligation to help Mr. Chelouche." I spent the rest of the day in the city, waiting for the following morning. Most of the time I was at the clothing store of my acquaintance Mr. Yitzhak Cohen,[329] but I did not say a word to him about the promissory notes.

The following day, I met with Mr. S., who told me, "I have practically completed all the arrangements, except that his servant, through whom all of this passes, is delaying the transaction unless I buy him as a gift a small rug of good quality for his prayers." I asked him how much such a rug would cost, and he answered that it would be about fifteen liras. I naturally agreed to pay the amount. "If that's the case," he said, "then come to P.'s store in two hours' time and we will conclude the matter." I walked back to Mr. Yitzhak Cohen's shop and waited there. Mr. Cohen wasn't in his shop, so I talked with his clerks.

About half an hour later, Mr. Cohen entered, walked up to the register and hastily removed some documents, and said, "What can I do? We must help fellow Jews," and in the most natural fashion, started telling me that some Jews had come to him seeking his assistance. They had received promissory notes for the director of the *Manzil* in Jerusalem, and since he was friends with the director and met him every evening, they were asking him to do them a favor. "In the evening, when I spend time with the director of the *Manzil*, I hand him all the promissory notes for signature, and as soon as he signs them, the register pays out the entire sum immediately." I asked if he could help me as well. I gave him the promissory notes and asked him if he would be gone for long. He replied: "If you would like, come with me," and so I went with him. When we arrived at the *Manzil*, he entered the director's office and had the papers signed, and then he handed them to me to go to the register. Within minutes, I received everything to which I was entitled.

From there I went back to Mr. Cohen and thanked him for his help. I tried to offer him a commission for his efforts, but he insisted: "Heaven forbid I should take a commission from you. Aren't we Jews, who are

---

329. We have been unable to locate more specific information about this person, but a Yitzhak Yehuda Cohen is listed as renting a store owned by the Jerusalem municipality in 1897.

obliged to help one another? Today I helped you and tomorrow you will help someone else. And in what way are you any worse than other people? Hasn't Mr. P. come to me on more than one occasion with his own and other people's promissory notes like these, and I get them signed by the director of the *Manzil*." After hearing this, I became very angry and proceeded to tell him the entire story. He instructed me to take a seat behind a mirror in his store and told me to listen to what was about to happen. And then he sent for Mr. P.

When Mr. P. arrived, Mr. Cohen engaged him in conversation: "Tell me, Mr. P., how many times have I helped you get your money and that of others from the *Manzil*?" And he replied: "Many times, and I thank you very much for the actions you have taken on behalf of myself and others."

"Have I ever taken from you a commission? If so, please specify when that was and what the sum was."

"Heaven forbid. You have not taken any commission."

"That being the case, aren't you ashamed—you, who are so strictly religious—together with your friend Mr. S., when an important Jew from Jaffa comes to you, in possession of a promissory note to *Manzil*, to ask him for 500 liras?"

Mr. P. began to justify himself: "We did not make any deal with Mr. Chelouche. He came to us and asked us to arrange the promissory notes, but then he left and we haven't seen him since. We didn't ask him for any payment." Mr. P. began to stutter. It was at that point that Mr. Cohen moved the mirror, and I appeared. In a moment, P.'s face went white. I did not say a single word about the matter, and they, too, were silent for several minutes. Eventually, Mr. Cohen said to Mr. P.: "As punishment for what you've done, go and bring me fifty banknotes for the Greek Jews who were deported from Jerusalem and to whom we must send the money this week." Then he left and sent fifty liras back with his clerk. I made note of this entire event to the credit of Mr. Yitzhak Cohen and to condemn both P. and S. To this very day I still cannot bring myself to meet them face to face, and conversely, to Mr. Cohen I have since become a true lifelong friend.

I returned to Petah Tikva and continued to work with the other members of the committee in public works. The situation of the émigrés became increasingly worse. Even the wealthy Jews were greatly impoverished. Although they owned merchandise in Jaffa, what use were these goods to them now? Because of this, aid was given to three types [of persons]: Type A—wealthy individuals who did not have their assets with them and who could not sustain themselves or their families who received assistance in exchange for promissory notes; Type B—the middle class, who were given assistance against their assurance that if their situation improved they would return what they had received; and Type C—the wretched poor who received assistance as usual.

The High Holy Days were drawing near. Soon the winter months would arrive, and the committee was concerned for the fate of the émigrés in Kfar Sava, who were living outdoors, in tents and huts made of eucalyptus. What would they do in the rainy season? Mr. Dizengoff was compelled to go to Damascus and present himself to Djemal Pasha and ask him for the means to build huts and barracks for the émigrés to shelter them from the rain.

In the meantime, officers arrived at the colony and conducted searches of the homes. They entered the house where my brother Ya'akov and my son Moshe were living and arrested them, evidently by mistake, since they were looking for other men who happened to have similar names. I rushed to see the *kaymakam*. I asked him to come to my aid and release my brother and son from their prison cell, but he said he was powerless to help me, since the order was a military and political one and he was forbidden to intervene in the matter. I was in great anguish and asked him: "Where will they be sent?" The *kaymakam* told me that a telegram had been received from Jerusalem, according to which several people had been sentenced to be exiled to Damascus.[330]

I arrived home brokenhearted and went about preparing provisions for their journey. I wrote letters to a friend in Damascus asking him to help them out in any way possible and to save them from their imprisonment. They were sent to Damascus, and from that day on officers began coming around more frequently, harassing the colony with harsh edicts and new troubles.

On the eve of Rosh Hashanah, policemen arrived and delivered an

---

330. On 27 October 1917, Ottoman officers searched the houses in which the Chelouche family were staying looking for a man named Cherour; not finding him, they conducted a short interrogation after which they arrested Ya'akov Chelouche and Moshe Chelouche. The men arrived in Damascus almost a month later. Evyatar (Tari) Chelouche, "Hahayim be'et hamilhama."

order to our *mukhtars*[331] to sign, which they did, as usual. When they read the order, they nearly fainted. It was a decree expelling all of the émigrés from Petah Tikva within twenty-four hours. There were only two hours before the start of the sacred holiday, and the residents were thrown into a state of utter confusion and tumult. The rabbis and public figures in the colony gathered together to consider our options; what should we do? Who could possibly revoke this terrible edict? From the camp of the émigrés the cries grew louder, and signs of great worry could be discerned on every forehead. A crowd of the émigrés gathered in front of the committee house, wanting to know what their fate would be, awaiting the last word from the shepherds of the community.

It was unanimously decided that I should ride to Jerusalem, since Dizengoff was in Damascus, and strive to have the evil decree revoked. And how would I get there? In just a few more minutes, the Jews would be converging on the house of prayer, and how could I violate the sanctity of Rosh Hashanah? Inside, my heart was weeping, but this was a matter of saving human life, and the rabbis, and particularly the late Rabbi Citron,[332] encouraged me, saying that I was obligated to go, that saving lives—and in this case, saving the life of our people—supersedes the religious laws of rest. I parted from everyone in the colony and rode in my wagon to Jerusalem. By the next morning, I arrived at the home of Mr. Yitzhak Cohen, meeting him just as he was preparing to leave for synagogue. I told him what had happened and implored him to help me to carry out my plan without delay, in order to free our brethren from the evil of this edict. How could we move them within twenty-four hours? Where would we lead them?

Mr. Cohen grew emotional and said, "We must see the director of the *Manzil*. I will invite him to my home for lunch and will introduce him to you. You will say your piece, and he will surely help you." "My friend," I replied, "how can I wait until lunchtime when this matter is so pressing? If we delay, we will miss the opportunity. It would be better if we go immediately to the director of the *Manzil* and speak with him. The good of the nation demands it." "But," my friend said to me naively, "the director of the *Manzil* only arrives at his office at half past eight or nine."

331. *Mukhtar*s were official representatives of villages, neighborhoods, and religious denominations who served as intermediaries between the government and their population.

332. Israel Abba Citron (1881–1927) was the chief rabbi of Petah Tikva.

"Then we'll go to his house!" I cried out from the depth of my heart. "We'll speak with him at his house."

It was a very great distance to the house of the director of the *Manzil*,³³³ but nevertheless, we walked due to the sanctity of the holiday. We arrived at his home and were given a very warm welcome. Mr. Cohen introduced me, and the director said: "I have already heard all about Mr. Chelouche, he is one of the leaders of the Jewish community." His comments encouraged and strengthened me, and I explained to him the reason for our visit. He smiled and said:

> It was I who issued this harsh edict, because the residents of the Petah Tikva colony sinned before me. When I made an inquiry with them in regard to purchasing pipes for the sake of the battlefront, I found out that they were taking old pipes out from under the ground and selling them at full price. I got angry and rode out to the colony myself to see if it was true. Aside from that, they did not receive me with the dignity that is customary for high government officials. They ushered me into a small inn, where they fed me dishes that I found unappetizing and unappealing. I asked the proprietor of the inn to prepare me a dish with meat and dairy together, but he refused. "Among the Jews," he said, "we do not cook meat with milk." I asked him to prepare a dish for me with dairy products, cheese and eggs, and this, too, he cooked with no flavor. I nearly vomited that night, and why? I have always liked the dishes of the Jews. I have eaten several times at the home of Mr. Yitzhak Cohen and at the homes of other Jews. I spent a full day and night at the colony, and its directors paid no attention to me. So I decided to teach them a lesson about my strong hand, and I issued the edict for both the émigrés and the residents of the colony, that they be expelled within twenty-four hours. And now you are going to have to appeal the matter directly to the pasha here in Jerusalem.

I told him that I was very sorry about what happened, and that the directors of the colony were not to blame, as they obviously did not recognize His Excellency. [I said:]

---

333. According to numerous sources, this was Ali Ruşen Bek. According to the Spanish consul de Ballobar, with whom he was on friendly terms, Ruşen Bek was promoted to colonel in December 1915.

Another time, His Excellency should inform the colony that he will be arriving for a visit, and they will welcome him as befits a great man. He will dine at the table of the committee chairman, and he will not stay at inns. After all, high government officials pay regular visits and are always received in the most dignified manner. And I have no doubt that had the colony been aware that His Excellency was the director of the *Manzil*, they would have received him with all due dignity.

My words had an effect on him and calmed his fiery spirit. He turned to Mr. Cohen and said: "Only on your behalf, you, my friend, and on behalf of your guest Mr. Chelouche, who will from now on be my friend, as well, would I cancel the edict, but the matter is out of my hands. You will have to appeal to the civilian pasha in Jerusalem." "And what will happen if he does not believe us?" we asked. "Time is of the essence."

He considered this for a moment and replied: "Go to the pasha's office, and I will come in half an hour." When we got to the pasha's office, we found he was busy. Many priests were waiting and asking to speak with the pasha. We were left to wait, unable to enter to see the pasha. We waited for half an hour or so, and in the meantime, the director of the *Manzil* walked in. The pasha immediately came out of his office, and they greeted one another warmly, and he turned to us: "Honorable guests, how is it that you have not yet gone in to see the pasha? Please, I beg of you, to enter," and we followed right behind them. We told the pasha the whole story and requested that he issue the appropriate directive to cancel the awful edict. "I believe," I added, "that the honorable director of the *Manzil* would not object, either."

The director of the *Manzil*, who was sitting to the side looking at a Turkish newspaper, now intervened in the conversation and said: "As far as I am concerned, there is no reason at present not to cancel the edict, since it is still early. Only in another month or two will I be obliged to carry out this edict." The pasha, upon hearing the director's words, said, "If there is no objection from the honorable director of the *Manzil*, then I, too, agree to cancel this edict." I asked them to inform the *kaymakam* in Jaffa by telegram that the edict had been canceled. The telegram was sent immediately, and I received a copy of it as well. I immediately sent a telegram to the late Betzal'el Yaffe, who was filling in for Mr. Dizengoff, and informed him of the good news, asking him to calm the colony residents. I remained in Jerusalem that day, and the following day, when I returned to Petah Tikva, the colony was waiting for me with bated breath. Everyone wanted to hear from my own mouth how I had managed to solve everything.

After this event, we celebrated our holiday in joy and happiness. On the eve of Sukkot, it so happened that the "water machine" at the colony's well to the south, right above Dankner's house, broke down. It was three thirty. The émigrés arrived—men, women, and children, each one with a bucket in hand to draw water from the well for cooking and bathing. I observed this scene and was astounded to see two local residents arrive and push aside the émigrés, to allow the local residents a chance to draw water first, without forming a line for everyone without differentiation. When an émigré finally succeeded in reaching the well, they blocked him and gave preference to the local resident, until I intervened and did not allow them to do so. That matter will remain an eternal disgrace, a symbol of the deplorable attitude exhibited by these people toward the wretched émigrés.

Around those same days, I entered the offices of the committee at the hour when the aid was distributed. I was greatly disturbed at seeing the discrimination between the different ethnic communities. Based on the method of allocation, the Sephardim were second place, and the Yemenites were last. This matter pained me greatly, for it was quite logical to distribute the aid as we had done in the past, based on the three types: well-to-do, middle class, and impoverished. I entered the office of the secretary and demanded that he immediately summon Mr. Betzal'el Yaffe, peace be upon him. When the late Yaffe arrived, I vehemently protested against the new arrangement, and asked for an immediate general assembly. My principal claim was: Is this what the American Jews appointed us for, to discriminate between different people and to differentiate between them? Is the Yemenite Jew not like the Sephardi Jew and the Ashkenazi Jew? Why should he be deprived of his rights, and why are the Easterners viewed as superfluous? And so it was that the following evening, a general assembly was held, and my opinion was adopted unanimously, and order and peace were restored. One thing became clear to me—and to my sorrow I must emphasize things here as they occurred—but the late Yaffe had acted of his own accord without consulting with other members of the committee.

CHAPTER 19 *The Entry of the English into Petah Tikva, and Their Departure*

The English enter Petah Tikva for the first time | Joy in the Jewish camp | The Jews' fear of being termed "deserters" passes | My decision to return to Jaffa | I returned to Petah Tikva to spend the Sabbath | On Saturday night at midnight | The English withdraw from Petah Tikva | Misery and sadness among the colony residents | Turkish forces enter | Tyranny of the Turkish army | The Germans and Turks dig in on Napoleon Hill | Firing on Jaffa | Bombing the colony | We hide in the cellar | My son Avner is wounded by the airplanes | The order for the émigrés to leave the colony | "And a new king arose, who did not know Joseph" | We leave Petah Tikva | At the head of the exiles to the village of Qalqilya

While the *yishuv* was brought to its knees, crumpling under the weight of suffering and hardship, the first buds of redemption began to appear. With the entry of the English, it seemed as if salvation for our tortured brethren was at hand. Now they would get a respite from the fury of their cruel fate. However, the *yishuv*'s joy was temporary, for the English disappointed us. In the middle of a clear day, we saw the English enter Petah Tikva. They arrived slowly, wagon by wagon, tethered to four horses, riders and cavalrymen escorting all the gear, and the joy in the Jewish camp was enormous. A new world was revealed to the tormented émigrés, and how great was the wonder in their eyes when the English soldiers paid for their food with their own good money in gold and in silver, at a time when the Turks never paid for anything they took from the Jews. The fact in itself that a savage regime would be replaced by a civilized regime brought comfort to the hearts of our brethren, instead of their troubles and tribulations. A majority of the Hebrew youth awakened to a rebirth. There was no end to their happiness at their liberation from the yoke of the Turks, and with the joy of freedom, they went to

Jaffa. From now on, they would no longer have to hide in vineyards and orchards, attics and cellars, for fear of the "firar."[334] Instead, they would walk the streets of the city freely, like everyone else. In their mind's eye, they could already see the English ruling there, for they had in fact captured all the strategic positions and government buildings.

The entry of the English into Petah Tikva reinforced my own realization that the time had come for us to return to Jaffa. I decided to move our household to Tel Aviv, all our possessions, and after spending one more Sabbath in Petah Tikva, we would all return to our city. How great were our feelings of jubilation! We would return to our hometown and would no longer have to wander around the country. We spent two days in Jaffa, preparing everything for the return of our family, and then we went to Petah Tikva to spend the Sabbath, except for my son Zadoc,[335] who remained in Jaffa with the intention of returning, as well, later that evening. Many other residents of Tel Aviv did as we did, bringing their possessions back to the city and then returning to the colony for the Sabbath. We gathered together with a joyous heart to return to the colony, only to find that the English army had blocked our way. We were compelled to go to the military headquarters. My son Zadoc, who was fluent in English, arrived and negotiated on our behalf; eventually, we were given a permit to travel to Petah Tikva. At several other points along the way, the army stopped us and interrogated us. We felt that the military authorities did not allow our return to Petah Tikva out of goodwill, but only because we had left our families alone there without anyone to look after them.

The émigrés' community went to the synagogue feeling a sense of holiness, rejoicing, and happiness. It appeared as if redemption had arrived in every respect. On Sunday, everyone would return to the city and revive it from its state of abandonment, and its streets would no longer grieve, for its sons would return to it.

Sabbath eve. Midnight. Extraordinary commotion. Incessant shooting.

---

334. "Desertion" in Ottoman Turkish. As the war dragged on, Ottoman officials conducted searches for people escaping conscription or fleeing military service. Desertion was punishable by death.

335. Zadoc Chelouche (1900–1948) was seventeen years old when these events took place. After the war, in 1920, he was appointed deputy director of the Department of Immigration & Travel of the Government of Palestine. In 1926 he became an entrepreneur and founded a private enterprise for export of citrus fruit to Europe.

Military shouts and cries. We understood that something major is happening here. Who knows if it will not be to our detriment. The heart is pounding, and the shock is throbbing. All of us listened with deep anxiety, unable to utter a single word.

The next day, we went to the house of prayer. Sadness and misery are visible on every face. We learn that during the night the English withdrew from the colony, and the Germans and Turks have returned in their place. The Jews who sold animal feed to the English have gone into hiding and left no trace. Trembling overtook everyone. The only concern was: how will the Turks choose to avenge the short-lived joy of the tormented émigrés?

While we are still praying, through the windows horses pass by laden with crates of weapons being hauled from the north southward. We look closely at the faces of the soldiers and are disappointed—we are not mistaken; they are from the Turkish army.

We began to feel the bitterness of our fate. Those who hauled all their possessions to the city are particularly disappointed, as they remain naked and lacking everything. The Turkish army was acting brutally this time: beating, stealing, trampling, and savagely attacking the residents. A great sorrow overcame us. Our holy Sabbath has been violated. No one touched the Sabbath food, all of us have lost our appetites, and we walked around in bitterness and rage. What can we do? We did not leave any of our belongings, only the clothes on our backs, and who can say how much longer we will continue to suffer the tribulations of exile in the Holy Land?

The shooting never stopped that day or that night. The Germans dug in at Napoleon Hill. They were shooting at Jaffa, and Jaffa was shooting back. Airplanes flew overhead and dropped bombs. Bits of lead shrapnel were falling into the colony, and we were in danger. Panic set in. People began to hide in cellars. My son Avner took care to gather our family in the cellar closest to our home, but while he was leading the elderly and the children to safety, they came and informed us that he was injured by an airplane. I nearly went out of my mind. My wife and I ran to look for him and found him lying on the ground, bleeding profusely. We picked him up and carried him to the pharmacy. Hearing our cries and entreaties, Dr. Cohen arrived. He examined the injured man and found a serious wound on his left arm. He bandaged the wound and calmed us down, so that we would not worry.

In our fear that the airplanes would return, we stayed in a cellar that was somewhat closer, beneath the home of Mr. David Hayoun. After clearing away the logs for the fireplace and the empty bottles, the entire extended family crowded into the cellar, without a bit of air to breathe. We brought the patient, my dear son Avner, to us on a stretcher. The doctor came and examined him again; he changed the bandages and found nothing. But [Avner's] temperature began to rise, and the patient suffered excruciating pain. He tossed and turned in misery all night long. Early the next morning, we summoned Dr. Cohen again. As he began to examine him, he found a piece of shrapnel still lodged in his arm; it would have to be removed immediately. And so, with great trouble and with the noise of the sobbing of our family, the doctor removed the shrapnel. It was a sizable piece of lead which to this day we have saved.

Meanwhile, an order was issued for the émigrés to leave the colony. We began to worry about the fate of our wounded patient. How could we transport with us such a large family that required a great deal of care: the family of my brother Ya'akov,[336] imprisoned and exiled to Damascus; the family of my son Moshe,[337] who also had been sent to Damascus, with no news about either one of them; the family of my late brother Avraham Haim,[338] who was then ill with a variety of maladies; and the family of my sister,[339] whose husband had remained in Egypt. How could I haul, by myself, all this baggage, when we did not even have anything to cover ourselves with, since all our belongings had been sent to Jaffa? No possessions and no money, and what despair! All our possessions were two hours away, but we were here and would be left to starve to death. We were in dread of what the future held for us.

---

336. The family of Ya'akov Chelouche included his wife, Perla, and their children Margalit (age 15), Gavri'el (11), Me'ira (9), Lea (4), and Shlomo (1).

337. The family of Moshe Chelouche included his wife, Rahel, and their daughter, Lea (age 3).

338. The family of Avraham Haim Chelouche included his wife, Sara, and their younger children Simha (age 20), Riquetta-Rivka (18), and Shimshon (16). Their older sons Marco (28), Zaky (26), and David (24) were in France and Egypt throughout the war.

339. The sister was Jamila Fedida (1882–1952), the second of Yosef Eliyahu Chelouche's four sisters. Jamila was expelled together with her four children. Her husband, Me'ir Fedida, was in Egypt on business at the outbreak of the war, and he could not return.

The expulsion order loomed larger. The people of Petah Tikva tried to wait and send the émigrés from Tel Aviv out of the colony first, [hoping that] perhaps the government would be satisfied only with them. We also received a note from the leaders of Petah Tikva [instructing us] to leave the colony. However, my son Avner's illness compelled me to ask them to wait until he recovered; as long as the doctor would not allow him to be moved, we would be unable to travel. Dr. Cohen came on behalf of the committee to examine my son, to determine if he was permitted to travel, and his answer to the committee was that it would be possible to move the patient in another two days.

The pressure from the committee on my family was quite unpleasant for me, and I was filled with great sorrow. Was this what I got in return for my devoted labors on behalf of the Hebrew *yishuv*? I freed prisoners from their jail cells, and now there was no one to free me? And they are even harassing me to travel with the elderly and the infirm? I went to see the army commanders and the administrators who were dealing with the expulsion, but I was disappointed to realize that all of the soldiers were strangers to me, and I did not know a single one of the military commanders. It was as if the verse had come true: "And a new king arose who did not know Joseph."[340] Left with no choice, I informed the committee that I would agree to travel to Qalqilya. Two days later, government wagons were sent for us, and we left for Qalqilya. Some of the other émigrés rode right behind us.

---

340. Exodus 1:8.

CHAPTER 20 *And They Journeyed and Encamped in the Village of Qalqilya*

Our little community in the village of Qalqilya | Our request for a Torah scroll from Kfar Sava | Good relations with the village residents and the government | Our money runs out | Worry about the day after | I appeal to the "Head of the Exile" Mr. Dizengoff in Damascus | His assistance, and his request for my own help with his work | My visit to the center of the exiles in Kfar Sava | The heartrending situation of the Jews of Kfar Sava | I purchase wheat and sorghum for baking bread | The government threatens me | A point of light in the darkness | Sheikh Ibrahim Samara | His generous assistance | My work to improve the lives of the exiles in Qalqilya | On the front lines of the war | Destruction and ruin | Between life and death | Prayers from the heart | Mr. Dizengoff's visit to Qalqilya | A joyous reunion between brothers | Our visit to Kfar Sava

Around 115 souls settled in Qalqilya in addition to our family. We got off at a wide square in the middle of the village. I went off to look for apartments. To my great happiness, I found several acquaintances among the Arabs who assisted me, and within a few hours we found rooms for all the émigrés. Our Jews scattered all around with each living in his new home. Our family was also scattered throughout the village, since we were unable to find rooms near one another.

Our initial welcome to Qalqilya by the military government was not an especially warm one, but the wrongs were soon righted by the acting *kaymakam*, who recognized me among the men who were detained for the *sukhra*.[341] This is what happened:

The day after we arrived in the village, as we were walking through the

---

341. Forced labor.

Qalqilya market, army personnel began to grab everyone who passed by for the *sukhra*, meaning work for the military government. On that occasion, it was for the purpose of clearing weapons out of the station. We were captured and thrown into jail.

After approximately an hour, the commandant of the city, a Circassian named Sadiq Bek, together with the acting *kaymakam*, 'Umar Shihab al-Din,[342] came to the jail to inspect the prisoners prior to their being sent out to work.

When the door opened and I saw the commandant enter accompanied by 'Umar Shihab al-Din, who was wearing civilian clothes, I knew nothing about his position in the government, and when our eyes met, I wondered why this civilian had not been seized along with us for the *sukhra*.

As I was thinking that thought, and since he was beginning to recognize me, he hurriedly and with great emotion asked me, before anything else, to leave the other prisoners and led me away from there. He had me stand next to him and the commandant, and then he introduced me to the commandant after telling him who I was and what my worth was in his eyes.

After he freed me, he wished to know the reason for my having come to the village of Qalqilya, and in what other way he might be able to help me. I told him of the hardships of the expulsion, about the situation of our small community that was with us.

He expressed great interest in the situation of my family and of our community, and thanks to him and to Commandant Sadiq Bek, the Circassian, who was a kindhearted and honest man and who also became friendly with me, right then and there they released all the Jews from the *sukhra*. They continued to do favors for my family and for our community throughout our stay in exile in Qalqilya.

The following day, I began to concern myself with the fate of our small community. I made a request for a Torah scroll from Kfar Sava and I set up a house of prayer. I appointed Pisanti to serve as the *shochet*[343]

---

342. As Chelouche clarified below, Shihab al-Din (1885–?) was a native of Jaffa who recognized him. He worked as an Ottoman official in the *tabu* (land registry) office before the war, and he was also a Freemason.

343. This is the ritual slaughterer who carries out the religious dietary laws of *kashrut*.

and Mr. Segal as a medic. I ordered all sorts of prescriptions, medicines, and cotton. I made contact with the Arab butchers, who permitted us to slaughter in accordance with our unique customs, and our community did not lack for kosher meat. Relations between me and the commandant were good. He received me warmly and fulfilled most of my requests. When young Jewish men were seized for the purpose of government labor, he would release them at my request. I also had friendly relations with the acting *kaymakam*, 'Umar Shihab al-Din. He was a Jaffan and knew me well. We spent every evening together with the commandant at the Arab coffee house that was set up on the wide square.

I drafted a plan to plant a garden on the square and proposed it to the commandant. He was in favor of the idea and gave an order that it be carried out. They began bringing in stones collected from the abandoned piles in the village, and they erected a fence around the town square. Seedlings and flowers were gathered and planted by workers, and within a couple of weeks, a beautiful garden came into being, where all the government officials visited.

A serious concern began to worry me—a concern for my family's existence. I had run out of money. The gates to Tel Aviv were shut, with no one entering or exiting, and all my property was there, far away, and I had no means to extricate myself from my distress. I felt that within a few days I would be left altogether penniless and would have nothing left to give my household. I could not go to another city and seek a loan, since it would require a permit. The government was watching every step you took, and without a special permit there was no way to move from place to place. It was also difficult for me to leave my little community in Qalqilya for even a single day, now that I had become its guide. People would turn to me for matters small and large, and whenever any difficulty occurred, I was the only one whose responsibility it was to struggle to overcome it.

Meanwhile, I remembered Mr. Dizengoff in Damascus, and I wrote him a letter describing my situation and asking if he could arrange a loan for me. A few days later I received a response along with a bundle of banknotes amounting to 500 paper Turkish liras. In the letter, he expressed his happiness that I had come to Qalqilya. As he saw it, it was God's will that I be sent there, to help him and assist him in his work. Dizengoff asked me to go to Kfar Sava and meet with the committee of émigrés and ascertain how I might be of help. And so on that very same day I traveled to Kfar Sava. I met there with the honorable gentlemen Shmu'el Ashkenazi, M. Hayat, and Dr. Slor.[344] We discussed the situation and I learned that the government was considering removing the Jews from Kfar Sava, but in the meantime Djemal Pasha had received a reprimand from the central government in Turkey for having expelled the Jews from Tel Aviv,[345] because of which Djemal would not be able to fulfill his wishes on this occasion.

Only, Djemal Pasha had chosen another way to persecute the Jews; he held back from them that most essential food of all, bread. The only bakery was in Qalqilya, and Jews did not have permission to go there, and the Arabs of Qalqilya were forbidden to enter Kfar Sava. There were attempts to bring in wheat from Tulkarm, Nablus, and Haifa, but the government would delay its arrival on the train until half of it was always stolen, and only a paltry, limited quantity reached the Kfar Sava Jews. Eventually, even this incurred the wrath of Djemal Pasha, who issued an order that no individual had permission to haul wheat by train, only the army had the sole right to do so. Thus, the Jews of Kfar Sava were left without any wheat. There was no bread and they had not tasted meat for a long while. In general, they were at the end of their rope. As a result of the lack of wheat, there was an upsurge in disease in Kfar Sava, typhus in particular. Djemal Pasha was laughing in secret at the misfortune befalling the starving Jews.

The situation of the Kfar Sava Jews affected me greatly, and I returned to Qalqilya with an aching heart. I immediately bought a substantial supply of wheat and sorghum at a high price, even compared to the prices of that time. The grain was delivered to my home, and I asked the Jewish women in Qalqilya to come in their free time to assist my wife in cleaning the wheat from the chaff. The women cleaned and my sons Avner[346] and

---

344. Zvi Arye Slor (1875-1959) was born in Jerusalem, studied medicine in Hamburg, and joined the French Foreign Legion, during which he was deployed to Mauritania. In Africa he had a colorful life: after he deserted the army, he was enslaved by tribes in southern Morocco for one year. He finally escaped before returning to Palestine in 1899. He served as doctor to the Jewish colonies in Petah Tikva and Kfar Sava.

345. In fact, Ottoman telegrams from Istanbul revealed concern about the European and American diplomatic and media response to these reports.

346. Avner Chelouche (1898-1950) was about twenty years old when the family arrived in Qalqilya. During his youth, Avner was active in the "Protectors of the

Hillel[347] devoted themselves to this with abundant dedication, working together with other young people to separate and weigh out every five *rotl*s,[348] which were then distributed among the peasant women to be ground up for a relatively low price. I borrowed mills from the notable Arabs, which I brought home so that the Jewish women could learn and become accustomed to milling wheat. The flour was collected and weighed every few hours by my sons. I calculated that I would be able to mill six sacks a day, but if needed, I could do even more. I sent the flour to Kfar Sava by camel, guarded by two Jews who were sent along for this purpose, and at other times by local Jews. I also slaughtered a few cows and sent the meat to Kfar Sava, and for a few weeks, welfare came into the lives of the Jews who had been weakened in their starvation.

One day, the government caught the camels laden with wheat on their way to Kfar Sava, and the commandant ordered that the camel drivers be savagely beaten until their blood flowed. When I heard about it, I rushed to the commandant and shouted: "What have you done? After all, this is my wheat!" Straightaway, he led me into his private room and whispered in my ear: "How dare you transgress the laws of the government? I have orders to treat any such instance with the full force of the law. But because of my love for you, I will take mercy on you, and I will have these camel drivers brought here and I will grant them a pardon on your behalf, just so long as they will never be seen again and will haul your wheat secretly at night. I will turn a blind eye to all this, as if I knew nothing of your deeds." I thanked him for his kindness, and from then on, I delivered the wheat to Kfar Sava in a secure manner, and no one said a thing.

One day I was sitting in the village garden, reading a second letter

---

[Hebrew] Language Battalion," which promoted the usage of Hebrew in the public sphere. He founded the Mizrahi Youth association and the Young Hebrew association and was one of the founders and chairman of the Maccabi sports association. Later, he was active publicly as a municipal judge in Tel Aviv and deputy chairman of the Tel Aviv community.

347. Hillel Chelouche (1904–1971) was around fourteen years old when the family arrived in Qalqilya. After the war, in 1919, he moved to Paris to study, graduating as an architect of the École des Travaux Publics in 1925, and later as an engineer-surveyor in 1927. Hillel returned to Palestine in 1933 and worked as a self-employed architect.

348. A weight used in Ottoman times; approximately three kilograms.

from Dizengoff in Damascus that arrived together with 500 liras in new banknotes. As I was reading it, I apparently let out a deep and heartfelt sigh. At that moment I became aware of someone some distance away from me, who asked: "Why are you sighing, Mr. Chelouche?" And as he asked this, he moved his chair close to my own chair. I chuckled and replied:

"Perhaps you imagined it. For I did not sigh."

"But I did hear you sigh, and from some distance away."

"No, that is but a figment of your imagination . . ."

"But," the man implored me once more, "my imagination will not lead me astray. I distinctly heard you sigh. Pray, tell me, what is it that ails you? Perhaps I can help you."

"You do not know me. How could you help me?"

"I know you very well, but clearly you do not recognize me. It has been quite a while since I have been to Jaffa, and I haven't had the opportunity to see your late father and kiss his hands. That was my custom whenever I came to that city. Several years ago I got married, and I now live in the village of Danaba, which is near Tulkarm, a village of which I was one of the founders. And here is my home and my family, which I come to visit very frequently. Alas, your dear father of blessed memory, what a cherished person he was. Whatever wealth I have is thanks to him."

"And why would you imagine that my father is no longer alive?"

"Is he really alive?" He became overjoyed at my words.

"He is with us today."

The man implored me to go with him to his family home in Qalqilya, but now that I informed him that my father was alive, he went with me. Along the way, I told him the secret of my sigh, and he listened very intently to what I said. As we entered my home, he found my father lying in bed. He walked up to him and kissed his hands.

"Do you not recognize me, my friend?"

My father looked long and hard at the man's face, and then said his name: "Sheikh Ibrahim Samara," and the two friends hugged one another.

When I arrived at the home of Sheikh Ibrahim, he introduced me to his family and I was received very warmly. He referred to me as the son of his friend who was responsible for his fortune.

While I was spending time with the family, Sheikh Ibrahim went out to the yard and he came back in with an ax and a rope. He measured off the length of the wall and then struck at the plaster; the plaster fell to the floor, exposing a plate. Then he opened it, exposing a hole in the wall. Sheikh Ibrahim then pulled out of the hole a red handkerchief that had a total of 500 gold liras wrapped inside, and he placed it in my hands. "You can return this money to me after the war," he called to me happily.

"Thank you so much, but I have no need for money right now. Indeed, I have just now received banknotes from Damascus."

"That does not matter. I would be humiliated if you do not take the money right now . . ."

"But I have no safe or anywhere to hide the gold. Thieves would no doubt come and steal the money," I claimed, hoping that he would leave me be.

None of my arguments helped. Sheikh Ibrahim was adamant: "If you do not take the money, you humiliate me."

I told him that I was inclined to accept the money from him and give him the satisfaction, but only in order to repay my debts. Sheikh Ibrahim agreed to this condition. Before parting from him, I asked him to accept a promissory note for the sum of money. He chuckled: "Ha! How could I take a promissory note from you?" I commented, "But what will be if—Heaven forbid—we die during this war?" "If we die," he replied simply, "then neither of us will need money."

I used the money to buy 2,000 Turkish banknotes in exchange for 400 gold liras and transferred them to Mr. Shim'on Rokach in Tulkarm; it was through him that I had received the loans from Damascus. I asked him to transfer 500 liras to Mr. Dizengoff and 1,500 to another Jew. I was left with approximately 100 gold liras to sustain my family, and when my own situation was eased, I began to do what I could to improve the lives of the Jews in Qalqilya. I made efforts to focus my attention on them. I brought in sewing machines from Kfar Sava for the young women who sewed undergarments and such items for the Arabs. I advised one family to bake cakes and then secured a permit so the family could sell them in the village garden. The Arabs were very fond of these cakes and the family earned a respectable living. In these sorts of ways I helped several other families, who rose from the depths of their dire situations and saw some light in their lives.

At the same time as I was enlisting my entire family in the service of the Jews of Kfar Sava, milling wheat and transporting it by camel, my son Avner came down with typhus. He suffered terribly, in addition to the agony he went through when he was wounded. When the commandant heard of my son's illness, he came to see him in the company of the respected Jewish army physician, Dr. Krieger, and ordered him to examine the patient.[349] Dr. Krieger thoroughly examined the patient and began to keep an eye on his illness. Following the commandant's request, Dr. Krieger visited the patient twice a day and gave him medications from the German military hospital pharmacy.

One night, during the crisis of my son's illness, I went out into the street. At that time, shells were flying overhead in an attempt to destroy the station that was near my home. One shell fell on the house next door to ours, destroying its walls, and right in front of my eyes, houses were reduced to heaps of debris with people buried alive beneath them. I stood there in the moonlight beneath the barrage of fire, my eyes cast heavenward. My heart could not contain the agony and pain, and I stretched out my hands, a prayer forming on my lips. I prayed in my innocence for everything that came to my mind, yet the prayer came from the heart, filled with the trembling of my soul and with holiness. The pain of the world filled my soul, and my spirit became deeply depressed. I saw myself all alone, within the intense agony that surrounded me. My son Avner was critically ill, my son Moshe was imprisoned in Damascus, my brother Ya'akov was in exile there as well, and his family was now my responsibility. My wife had grown ill from fear and worry, and my elderly parents were on their deathbeds, and I was responsible for their care. I faced these tribulations alone, and I beseeched God: "Please, O Lord. If I have any virtue before you, I ask that you not leave it for the world to come but redeem me on its behalf immediately. Release me from my troubles, which have grown numerous. May the shooting cease and send a full recovery to my sick child."

I finished my prayer and sensed relief. A heavy stone was lifted from my heart. A benevolent spirit pulsed within me, invigorating me. The moment of spiritual elevation pierced through the still quiet of grief and

---

349. Moshe Krieger (1885–1975) was born in Russia, trained in Europe, and immigrated to Palestine in 1912. He served as an Ottoman medical officer first in the Balkan wars, and again during World War I.

sadness. Little by little, my tears flowed, and I began to feel that I had been saved.

A few moments later, the shelling ended. My son's symptoms eased and with God's help after some time the rest of my family members improved, and they slowly but surely regained their strength. And I know that God listened to my prayer, which had burst from the depths of my suffering heart. To this day, that night is etched onto the chambers of my heart, having left an intensely profound impression on me.

A significant event in our dark lives, when I and the other exiles sat in our exile in Qalqilya village, one that brought a bit of light and joy in our time of distress, was the sudden visit of the "Head of the Exile,"[350] Mr. M. Dizengoff, who came to see the fate of the exiles.

It was on a winter day, as our entire family along with our community was busy milling wheat for the flour that we sent daily to the Kfar Sava exiles. While we were busy with that work, which was a matter of life and death for the exiles of Kfar Sava, he appeared quite suddenly, without us knowing anything about it beforehand.

[Dizengoff] arrived in a plain wagon together with his escort, Mr. Yehuda Grazowski.[351] He arrived on his long journey between all the exiles, beginning in Damascus, where he himself was residing, to appraise the situation of all the exiles wherever they were, and particularly the main—and most dreadful and terrifying—site where the exiles resided, Kfar Sava.

M. Dizengoff and Grazowski immediately entered my large room—our only room where all the members of my family lived. They were our guests for the night and slept together with us on the floor.

I simply do not have the words to describe the strong impression left on me and my entire family by this sudden visit of my great friend, and the friend of our family, after we had been torn apart by fate and by the times in which we were living, and after having not seen each other for several months in the midst of such a fateful time of colossal disaster.

Both Dizengoff and we—even though the meeting was held in

---

350. Chelouche uses the Aramaic term *reish galuta*, which referred to the leader of the Jewish community during the Babylonian exile.

351. Grazowski (1862–1950), later Hebraized to Gur, was a linguist, writer, and editor, who also worked as an assistant manager at the Jaffa branch of the Anglo-Palestine Bank.

FIGURE 20.1. *Yosef Eliyahu Chelouche and Me'ir Dizengoff, longtime mayor of Tel Aviv, late 1920s. Chelouche Family Collection.*

strained conditions due to our wanderings in exile—nevertheless felt a boundless sense of joy, and we spent the evening in conversation until midnight.

We ate some bread with salt, which tasted as if we were feasting on royal delicacies. We slept on straw mats on the floor, but it felt like we were sleeping on golden beds in the king's palace.

The following day after the visit, I traveled with them to Kfar Sava to assess the situation of our exiled brethren there in their sorrowful state, and to better learn how it might be corrected.

It was the rainy season, and the roads were full of water, mud, and mire. Our wagon sank deep into the mud and the water, which came all the way up to the passengers' legs.

We spent the entire day together in Kfar Sava. We visited the exiles, assessed their situation, and considered ways to correct it. During the day, we held several assemblies and meetings and adopted decisions on several urgent matters. We parted ways that same evening, me returning to my family and our little community in Qalqilya, and he, the head of the exiles, continuing on to all of the places of the expelled and the exiles, visiting them once more on his return trip to Damascus, where he devotedly stood watch over the situation of the exiles, with total devotion truly up to the point of self-sacrifice.

CHAPTER 21 *From Qalqilya to Kafr Jammal*

*The edict to expel the Jews from Qalqilya |
With the exiles to Kafr Jammal | The village elders
receive us warmly | We settle in | A visit from the village
leaders and* sheikhs *in my home | They welcome our arrival |
A rainwater cistern for our community | Arranging for kosher slaughter |
The villagers' preference for kosher slaughter | Business in an army
commissary | In Kafr Falama | A letter without an envelope | The
German commandant | Funcke, among other firms | Funcke's son,
the commandant | The generous assistance of the commandant |
Setting up the commissary | The peasants' barley | Letter from
the mayor of Tulkarm | Wheat for the exiles | My daughter
Yehudit | My son Yoram and his longing for Tel Aviv*

One day Commandant Sadiq Bek approached me and informed [me] that about a month earlier he had received a decisive order to expel the Jews from Qalqilya and send them further inland, although he had not yet carried it out due to his fondness for me. He had just received a telegram instructing him to expel the Jews immediately, and he could no longer prevent the fulfillment of this order, even though he himself could not see any danger in the Jews remaining in Qalqilya. The commandant suggested that I send away the exiles from Qalqilya along with part of my family, and that the rest remain in Qalqilya, although we should rent a different house further away from the center of the village. I informed him that to my regret I would not be able to accept this generous offer, as I could not possibly reconcile myself to the fact that my brother and sisters would leave for exile while I would stay behind, all alone. My words made a strong impression on him.

I asked him to ease the burden of the émigrés, and to place beasts of burden at our disposal to carry our belongings, and wagons to convey us. I also asked for permission to take with us several sacks of wheat and sorghum, at a fair price. I also sought his advice on where it might be best to go, which village did he think would be most comfortable for our settlement? The commandant apologized: "You know, my friend, I am a stranger here, and I am not very familiar with the surroundings. But I promise to investigate the matter and to let you know the results."

The commandant returned that afternoon and told me that the best village for our relocation would be Kafr Jammal, which is located on an attractive hilltop. "I will send a messenger there to inform the people of the village that they should prepare houses for you and should treat you fairly. In addition, I have dispatched a special messenger to acquire for you wheat and sorghum at fair prices to take with you for your food supply. And one other thing that I wish to inform you," the commandant said, "I have fifty gold liras here. Since you are no doubt in need of money, please accept them as a loan, and when you are able, you can repay me." I thanked him from the bottom of my heart for his generosity of spirit, and I showed him that I had an ample amount of money for my upkeep.

On Passover Eve, we moved—by camel, donkey, and horse—to Kafr Jammal. Aside from our own family, there were another 115 souls. With us were six sacks of wheat and one sack of sorghum. The village elders, including the *mukhtar*s and *sheikh*s, received us warmly. We found prepared apartments and a kind attitude. For me they prepared the special guesthouse for visitors passing through the village.[352] The house was built of Ternolit[353] and surrounded by a fence. I settled my family into the house, and in the house next door were my parents and my brother's family. As it would soon be summertime and there would be no particular need to receive guests in the house, the village leaders prepared the square near the guesthouse to receive their guests, paving it and surrounding it with a fence. They put down straw mats, and the guests slept under the stars.

I passed through the village and saw that all of the Jewish families were settled. I immediately sent my sons Avner and Hillel to locate bakeries and instructed them to clean the oven with the help of the other young people, make it kosher with fire,[354] and prepare it for baking

352. The village guesthouse (*mudayfa*) hosted visitors and travelers and also served as a public space for village meetings and celebrations.

353. A brand name of asbestos cement plates, also commonly known under different brand names as Eternit and Salonit.

354. Fire is used to ritually purify the oven and any dishes or utensils that previously cooked nonkosher food, or in this case, leavened bread.

matzah.³⁵⁵ I obtained three stone mills for grinding wheat, and I sent word to all the women to come to my house the next day to help mill the wheat and knead the dough to bake *matzot*.

In the meantime, I learned that the *sheikh*s, elders, and *mukhtar*s of the village were planning to visit me at home. I rushed home and prepared cigarettes, coffee, and several types of sweets. At five o'clock that afternoon the guests appeared at my home, each of them shaking my hand before being invited to take a seat. We all sat on the ground, on rugs that were spread out. The eldest in the group began, with these words:

> In my own name, and in the name of the residents of the village, we welcome you and our Jewish guests who came with you to dwell among us. Aside from the recommendations of the commandant of Qalqilya in regard to you, we are pleased to say that we have known about you for a long time and are ready to be at your service for whatever you might need.
>
> At our own meeting earlier today, we made a decision to welcome you, and also to inform you that in our village there are no freshwater springs, and we depend on rainwater that is collected in cisterns. We have these both inside and outside the village, although the military government has been using them constantly, in particular the ones outside the village, and has been taking all of the water for the soldiers. It goes without saying that none of us dare raise any objection. But within the village itself we have closed wells the government does not know about. We leave those cisterns for our drinking water in the summer.
>
> However, now, as we are welcoming respected guests such as yourselves, we must take into account that you will also be drinking water like us. We know that there are still five months until winter comes, and we nevertheless have a quantity of jugs of water.
>
> Based on the number of residents, and now, adding to them the number of our guests, we think that we should distribute the water each day, such that each family of approximately five persons will receive two jugs, or two canisters per day, both for you and for us. We are certain that we will be able to distribute even more than that,

---

355. Singular; plural *matzot*. The unleavened bread baked during Passover to commemorate the Jews' hasty departure from ancient Egypt.

but in case there is a drought, we should be extremely precise, for your benefit and for ours. Therefore, would it be possible for Your Honor to inform the other guests of this, in order so they come every morning to the well that we will open up in your honor, and take the water, which will be allocated equally to all of us?

I thanked them for their kindheartedness and emphasized that this was evidence of their affection for us, by putting all of us on an equal footing. Before their departure, I asked them if it was possible if, whenever they were about to slaughter sheep, they would permit us to slaughter, and if the animal turned out to be kosher, then we would buy the meat from them, and if not—they would buy the meat. The *sheikhs* wondered at this request and said: "But we ourselves eat only slaughtered meat." I explained to them that there was something different about our slaughter, but they had difficulty understanding. I sent for the *shochet*, and he arrived with his knife and explained the difference to them.

The following day, all the sons of the village assembled at the square where animal slaughter took place. Our *shochet* made his preparations, the butchers held the sheep, and he slaughtered them. The butchers looked in wonder at the *shochet*, who slaughtered the sheep with a single cut, unlike them, who were accustomed to passing their knife several times across the sheep's throat. They watched carefully and saw how the *shochet* examined the sheep to see if it was infected, by inflating its lungs with a small pipe to see if they were injured or punctured. The *sheikhs* were amazed and said, "Based on what we just saw, we understand that a sick sheep is *treif*, and a sheep that is healthy is kosher." That day, one sheep turned out to be *treif*, and the butchers sold it to another village, because the villagers refused to eat its meat because the sheep was sick. Seeing that an argument might eventually break out between the butchers and us, I secretly added to their wages, without the people of the village knowing about it, another five piastres for every *rotl* of meat, and that pacified them. They sold the *treif* meat to other villages or to their poorer villagers, at a lower price.

We spent a quiet month in Kafr Jammal, far from the world and its troubles. We did not see even the shadow of a single soldier, and at times we forgot that there was a war going on. Gradually, group after group of soldiers began to appear, passing through the village. Fear prevailed among the émigrés, for many of them were young men who had been ransomed from the army but whose certificates of exemption from army service had expired. I, too, was worried for my sons Avner and Hillel, for although I had paid a ransom for Avner, a year had passed and I had not yet paid a ransom for the current year. I was greatly concerned about my nephews as well.

In the meantime, individual Jews had been coming to our village to hide, also out of fear of the army. The camp of émigrés was joined by the late Bekhor Gagin,[356] Me'ir Matalon,[357] and Giladi, for whom Kafr Jammal provided asylum. My money was running out—I had only thirty-five napoleons left, and I began to think of my friend Sheikh Ibrahim Samara, who lived a good distance away from this village. I could have traveled to him to ask for a loan, except that I was too embarrassed to do so. There was no option of sending word to Damascus about getting a loan—the nearest post office was too far from the village. As for asking for a loan from the *sheikh*s of the village, I deemed it to be degrading to my own dignity and honor, as they viewed me as the leader of the émigrés.

The issue caused me to lose sleep. I was also very concerned about my son Avner, who constantly complained about a life of idleness and boredom, since it was hard for him to sit and do nothing. I was greatly disturbed by my son's state of depression and began to consider ways to keep him occupied and to develop a livelihood for him.

My son heard from the villagers that a German army contingent was camped out in Falama, the neighboring village. The young people of our village were trading with them and making a nice profit. So he asked if I would allow him and his brother Hillel to go to the village and do business there, too. I refused, telling him: "My son! We have not yet sunk to the level of being peddlers and circulating among soldiers. It would be better if we go there together tomorrow to see what can be done there in a different manner, better suited to our dignity." The following day, we walked for about half an hour until we arrived at Kafr Falama. There were many tents and huts scattered around the field, and a major German army base had been established on the site. I walked around with

356. Although we have not found information on this individual, the Gagin family was an important rabbinical family in Jerusalem with origins in Morocco.

357. Me'ir Matalon, a brother of Chelouche's childhood friend Moshe, was listed as a money changer in Jaffa's *shari'a* courts; in the early 1920s he is listed in a French commercial directory as owning a textile shop.

my son and we carefully observed the situation. We stopped one officer whom we saw there, and I asked him if we might be permitted to open a small commissary. His response was to make a written request to the staff commandant. I asked him to show me where the commandant's quarters were, and we approached his residence. Soldiers were patrolling around the hut, making entry to the commandant impossible.

We decided to return home and draft a written request to the commandant in French, and to present it to him in person. And that is what happened. We returned home. We could not find ink or paper. We could only find a few blank pages in my daughter Yehudit's notebook. And my son Avner wrote the following letter in French in pencil, which I dictated to him:

> We, the undersigned, are a well-known family from Jaffa who due to the World War was expelled with other residents of the city to the interior of the country. For the past year or so, we have been wandering from place to place, and we are currently residing in Kafr Jammal. As merchants and active members of society, it has been difficult to accustom ourselves to a life of inactivity. The money that we had has dried up and we are left but a paltry amount to maintain a family of about thirty-seven people.[358] We would therefore ask His Excellency to permit us to open a commissary to sell the army anything that it needs.
>
> Based on what the soldiers told us, we should apply in writing to His Excellency and present a detailed list of the items for sale with their prices. Regrettably, we cannot anticipate what items are needed for the army, and at any rate it is difficult for us to set prices in advance. Nevertheless, we ask His Excellency to permit us to open a commissary, and we commit to bring all the things that the army requires, in order that we will be able to work and earn a living.
>
> We do not aspire to grow wealthy, but rather to work — and not "to eat the bread of idleness" — until the end of the war. To our regret, we are unable to give His Excellency the addresses of the honorable people who know us personally, for we have been exiled from our

---

358. There were thirty-seven members of the extended Chelouche family when they left Tel Aviv. However, by the time Yosef Eliyahu met the commandant, the number of family members had declined by nine due to imprisonment, separation, and death.

city and all our acquaintances have scattered to the four corners of the country; if there are some of the German residents of Jaffa within the army, they certainly will know us and without doubt will vouch for our good character. It is our hope that His Excellency will take note of our situation and fulfill our request. We are his loyal servants who are awaiting his positive response. Signed: Chelouche Brothers.

When we finished writing the letter, we could not find an envelope and had to give up on one. We hurried to Kafr Falama. When we reached the office of the commandant, we encountered many people amassing in front of the office, with only a single soldier guarding the gate. I handed the letter, folded into a square, to the soldier and asked him to give it to the commandant. I apologized to him for not finding an envelope. About ten minutes later, a person emerged from the office and stood at the doorway, looking at the people standing around the office. Then he turned to the soldier: "Who is it that gave you this letter?" The soldier pointed his finger at me. He immediately turned to me: "Are you Mr. Chelouche?" I answered in the affirmative. He asked me to enter his office. Once I was in the room, I realized that I was standing before the commandant himself. "Which one of the Chelouche brothers are you? What is your name?" the commandant asked me. "Yosef Eliyahu Chelouche," I answered him. "My brother Avraham stayed with the rest of the family in Kafr Jammal, and my brother Ya'akov is in Damascus."

"What do you work with in Jaffa?" he continued to ask.

"Construction materials," I answered him.

"From which countries do you import your goods?"

"From Europe. Mainly from Germany, but also from Belgium and elsewhere."

As I answered, a tremor passed through my entire body. I thought to myself, "Who knows if the commandant is not angry with me for daring to submit a letter to him on notebook paper, written in pencil, and without an envelope?" Perhaps there was some hidden purpose behind the questions he was asking. I was afraid of saying the wrong thing, but nevertheless, I made an effort to answer all his questions.

Finally, the commandant asked me, "With which firms in Germany do you have a business relationship?" I told him the names of the firms with which we had commercial ties, and the names of the cities where these firms were based.

"When were you in Germany?" he asked me.

"I was in Germany in 1900," I replied, "in the city of Remscheid."

"Were you really in Remscheid?"

"Yes, I was there on a business trip."

"With which company did you do business in Remscheid?"

"I did business with a firm called Wirminghaus & Funcke, and others."

The commandant got up from his seat, took my hand, pulled me closer to him, and asked me to sit down, as he said full of emotion: "I must inform you that I am the son of Funcke."

I was astounded at this unpleasant surprise; I felt so very wretched. Here I was, wearing filthy clothes, without even a collar on my shirt; I had not changed my clothes since the day of our expulsion to the Arab village. I had a *tarbush*[359] on my head and my shoes were dusty and dirty. Due to the sorrow, pain, humiliation, and disgrace that I felt over the low point at which I found myself, tears began flowing silently, without me even noticing. A large firm with which we had conducted a significant volume of business and from which we had purchased large quantities of goods—here I am standing like a pauper at the door, torn and worn, before one of the owners of the firm, and he is seeing me in my low station. The tears ran down my face, and I did not even have a handkerchief in my pocket to dry my face.

The commandant sensed my state of misery, and he was overwhelmed by compassion. He brought me into his private room and comforted me. He gave me water, soap, and a towel and asked me to wash up. When I had done so, we went back to the other room and he sat me down next to him and added, to comfort me: "Tell me, Mr. Chelouche, how is your family?" "All of them are healthy, thank God," I answered him. Then he said: "I am very happy to hear that you all are healthy; do not forget that given the times, the most important thing is our health. The war will end soon, maybe in another six months, and if you are healthy, you will be happy and you will be content because you will be able to overcome all of the troubles and hardships that you are now going through."

The commandant rang a bell and asked that a glass of warm milk be brought for me. He implored me to drink it, and he also offered me cigarettes. "In these days, whenever I pass through Kafr Jammal, I will stop

---

359. The rimless headwear of the Ottoman Empire, also known as the *fez*.

by to see you. And now I will arrange your request." He called in a tall Turkish clerk named Fayiz Bek[360] and asked him to find a building suitable for the needs of a commissary as soon as possible. After ten minutes Fayiz Bek returned to announce that the most suitable building for a commissary was the one that now housed the sanitation office. Then the commandant gave an order to erect tents around the building and to set up the sanitation office in them, and then to evacuate the building within a few hours in order to set up a commissary. Fayiz Bek went off to carry out the order.

In the meantime, [the commandant] telephoned someone and spoke in German. Five minutes later, a young man walked in, holding a list in his hand. "This is the list of items the army needs, and the prices at which you can sell them," the commandant happily relayed to me. I thanked him profusely for his benevolence. He arranged travel permits to Nablus, Haifa, Zikhron Ya'akov, Tulkarm, and Hadera, for me or my representatives, as well as a special permit to establish a commissary in the building that had just now become available. Moreover, he issued an order to put at my disposal three delivery wagons, complete with soldiers who would be at my service and accompany me on all my travels. When I parted from him, he shook my hand with great affection, wished me luck, and did not permit me to go empty-handed to the village without a gift for my family—and he gave me small sacks filled with coffee, sugar, cigarettes, tea, and boxes of various sweets. Aside from that, he ordered a Turkish soldier to escort me to the village and guard me. I emerged from the commandant's office astonished by everything that had just happened; once outside, I raised my eyes toward the heavens and thanked God for his kindness to me. I went home, elated and with a full heart.

Now that I had acquired the permit to establish the commissary, a new worry arose. I only had a total of 30 napoleons; how could I build up the commissary with this sum? After all, in a large commissary such as this, I could not sell inconsequential items. In the meantime, word had gotten out in the village that I had acquired a permit to establish a commissary; two people showed up, an Arab and a Jew—Al-Shanti[361]

---

360. No information has been found about this individual.

361. Chelouche does not specify the first name, but this was likely a relative of Muhammad al-Shanti, a native of Qalqilya who moved to Jaffa and edited the news-

and Eliyahu Matalon[362]—who agreed to go into this business with me and to invest 50 napoleons each. I thought about it and calculated that the sum of 130 napoleons would suffice in the meantime to establish the commissary. I agreed to my partners' proposal that they set out right away on a trip to buy merchandise. I showed them the permit I had received from the commandant and also the list, and we drew up a list of the items they would bring.

The following day I went with my son Avner to the commissary, where I received all the keys as well as the wagons and the soldiers. I gave Matalon my 30 liras, and my partners set out on their way. A week later they returned, at night, and told me that they had brought the merchandise and that it was loaded in the wagons that were now next to the commissary building, under the supervision of the soldiers. They told me what they had bought and gave me a detailed list of their purchases. I reviewed the list and was surprised at the high costs that they had expended; I also noticed that they had not brought the more essential goods. Without even considering profit and loss, I started thinking about how I could even stock this merchandise, which consisted of vegetables, etc. Wouldn't I be a laughingstock in the eyes of the commandant, in the event that he ever visited the commissary?

The next morning, we went together to unload the merchandise from the wagons and arrange it in the commissary. We found that the vegetables had rotted, and we were forced to throw half out. I suppressed the humiliation on my face and dejectedly returned to the village, leaving my partners with my sons Avner and Hillel to arrange the rest of the merchandise. I made arrangements with one of the wealthier residents of the village to come to my aid with a loan of 250 napoleons, without delay. Happily, I succeeded and immediately received the requested loan. I returned to Falama and paid back each of my two partners all their money, including their expenses, and I absorbed the expense of the rotten produce myself. I sent my son Avner to Tulkarm to purchase at the Jewish commissary run by S. everything that the army needed, in exchange for all the money that I had left. A day and a half later he returned with the

---

paper *al-Iqdam*. That al-Shanti was a member of the Decentralization Party and was executed in Beirut in 1916.

362. Matalon (1887–1953) was a cousin of Chelouche's childhood friend Moshe Matalon.

required merchandise, we organized the commissary, and opened for business.

My son Avner ran the commissary while I visited occasionally in order to pass the time. Over the course of ten days, my son Avner learned which goods were needed most by the army. He would send a special emissary to bring them from Haifa and Zikhron, and at times also from Tulkarm. The accounts indicated that the commissary was making a profit of between twenty and twenty-five *mejidi*s a day.

We were satisfied: on the one hand, we were busy and the time passed, no longer full of indolence and boredom; on the other hand, we were turning a profit. Once the commissary grew and the work increased, and it was difficult for my son Avner to manage it all on his own, I added on my son Hillel as well as my two nephews, Shimshon[363] and Gavri'el,[364] to help him out. The business expanded, and my son Avner learned German, which he speaks well, and he also learned some Turkish. All the soldiers and officers liked him and got along very well with him, and nearly all of them cared for him and helped him in expanding the commissary.

Meanwhile, our financial situation greatly improved. I could afford to buy clothes for the family and also new clothing for myself, to replace the clothes that I wore during the week and on the Sabbath. Perhaps I would have to meet with the good commandant, whom God placed on my path to save me in my time of trouble, and it would be best if I were dressed like a human being. I ordered clothes from Zikhron Ya'akov and also a few essential items for the family, and only then did I replace my old clothes with the new ones and also wore a collar on my shirt.

About a month passed, and we received goods from Nablus, too, which included a canister filled with a selection of candies made of honey, nuts, and butter. I saw fit to pack up a large box with these candies and sent it to the commandant as a gift, as a token of appreciation for the kindness he had shown me. When the commandant received my gift, he tasted them and liked them very much. He summoned me to his

---

363. Shimshon Chelouche (1901–1984) was the youngest son of Avraham Haim, Yosef Eliyahu Chelouche's older brother.

364. Gavri'el Chelouche (1906–1938) was the son of Ya'akov Chelouche, Yosef Eliyahu Chelouche's younger brother. A civil engineer, Gavri'el was assassinated by an Arab gunman in 1938 during the Great Revolt.

office. At the appointed hour, I entered his office. He received me very hospitably and asked about my family and how the business was faring. I answered that we are healthy and that the business is going well. Then the commandant asked me: "Do you have any idea how much profit the commissary generates?" I replied, "Yes. It is approximately thirty *mejidi*s a day."

The commandant considered this for a moment and then cried out: "That is definitely not enough to support a family of thirty-seven persons." I thanked him for his extreme sensitivity and told him that it was more than enough. After all, we did not aspire to become wealthy, but rather to earn a minimal subsistence through honest labor. "But my friend, Mr. Chelouche, your family also needs clothes to wear! I can see that you are wearing winter clothes, even though it is summer now. I am guessing that you are unable to buy anything else, and I imagine the same is true for the rest of your family." The commandant rose from his seat and asked me to lunch with him. I thanked him from the bottom of my heart but turned him down: "I am a Jew, and as you know, I am forbidden to eat meat dishes." "That is of no consequence," the commandant said, smiling. "For the past two months, no meat has touched my lips due to a stomach illness, so I have become a vegetarian; now we are on an equal footing."

We had lunch together and ate kosher food, and we conversed, as friends do. Over lunch, the commandant informed me that they needed barley and straw for the horses every day. They bought these supplies each day from the peasants who sold it to them for 4 piastres per kilo. However, since there was no oversight of the quality of the merchandise, the peasants were cheating them and mixing sand in with the barley. "Therefore, I am ordering all of the commissaries to stop buying from the peasants directly. Instead, the peasants will send their barley and straw to your commissary, and since you are fluent in their language, customs, and character traits, you will stand firm on a price and on the quality of the merchandise, and in so doing you will be doing us a favor and will make a profit for yourself as well."

I responded that although it was an important proposal, to my regret I did not have the means to be able to pay the peasants for their goods in the meantime. At this, the commandant announced that he would be able to arrange it; the most important thing was for the barley to be clean without any pollutants. I said to him: "It would be best to conduct a trial run." That same day, he issued an order to all of the commissaries not to purchase their barley and straw from the peasants, but to send them to our commissary. Indeed, the next morning peasant barley merchants gathered at my commissary. I asked them to tie up their camels some distance away from the commissary in the broad square opposite it, and I invited them to come in. Since I was experienced in purchasing barley, having learned in Gaza from my late brother Avraham Haim as the reader saw in a previous chapter, this is what I did: I asked them for a few samples of barley. They went out and came back with four samples each. Of course, the samples were clean and unpolluted. I therefore asked each peasant to bring me a single kilogram of barley from his harvest. They went out and weighed it and then brought it to me. I placed each sample in its own separate place, and after the weighing I recorded the names of the sellers. Of course, each merchant praised his own grain and showed me how clean and unpolluted it was.

I informed them that I would not agree to buy the barley at a cost of 4 piastres per kilo. They left and returned several times. I inspected the samples once more and sorted out the good samples among them. I informed them that I was willing to purchase the good samples at a price of 3.75 piastres, and that I could not buy the other samples. At the outset they refused, but once they realized how adamant I was and that I would not be dissuaded, they eventually agreed to my conditions: I would purchase good-quality barley at a price of 3.75 piastres, and standard quality at a cost of 3.5 piastres per kilo, on condition that I be given one or two sacks in advance from each seller in order to make my selection. They would have to have been cleaned already, and afterward they would be weighed, and then, based on the net weight of those sacks, we would then multiply the amount by the total number of sacks.

The peasants began unloading the sacks from the camels. I asked them to wait a while, to give me a chance to mark off the area where they would place the barley. I then went to the commandant and explained to him the conditions based on which I had purchased the barley. He was extremely pleased, especially with the stipulation that the sacks would be calculated according to the weight of a sack that was clean and free of all pollutants. As for the price, he ordered that I write down 4 piastres per kilo, and that I should take the difference for myself. The commandant sent a policeman with me to show where the sacks should be unloaded. He was accompanied by a few other policemen who would handle accepting delivery of the merchandise, according to my instructions. In addition, the commandant sent with me the man who handled the weighing and the treasurer, with a supply of gold coins, in order to finalize the bills together with me and pay each peasant individually—and at the end of the workday, to pay me the difference.

We finished the work in a few hours and paid the peasants for their merchandise, although they were not pleased, particularly at the amount of money they received, which was based on the weight of the clean barley. In fact, many of them declared that it was no longer worthwhile for them to sell their grain, and they took their money and left. I stayed with the treasurer, who finalized the accounts and paid me the difference, which came to forty-six liras and a few *mejidi*s. I believed that this figure was excessive and told him to make sure he had not made a mistake in his calculations. He calculated again and found that his accounting was precise, so he paid me the sum and left.

The peasants did not keep their word, and the following morning they were back again to sell their barley, along with a few new peasants. I was wary of being cheated and became even more exacting about the quality of the merchandise. Indeed, I discovered that some of them were cheating, selling me barley mixed with sand, and not the natural sand found in the soil in which the barley grows, but sand from the beach, which is harder to spot. I was not interested in accepting this merchandise, and I agreed with the others on the same conditions as the previous day. The day's work was a near repeat of the previous day, and the treasurer paid me the difference, which came to the same amount that I had received the day before. This went on for some days, and I earned a tidy profit. I purchased more clothes for myself and my family, and I made an effort to help my Jewish neighbors, doing what I could to ease the burden of their difficult lives.

While I was in Kafr Jammal, I received a letter from the mayor of Tulkarm, Abu Salim 'Abd al-Rahman, who wrote: "As I have heard that you and your family are staying in Kafr Jammal, and as I am appointed as the government's wheat supervisor, tasked with distribution of wheat to the needy against payment of a token sum, it is therefore incumbent on me to ask you to inform me how many persons there are in your family. Perhaps you are in need of a quantity of wheat, a one-month supply."

I responded to the letter, thanking him for his interest in my family's situation, but in truth thanks to the fact that I had recently received wheat from our friend Sheikh Ibrahim Samara, I had no need right then for any additional wheat. However, I wrote to him, aside from our family, there were 115 others in my company in Kafr Jammal, and I therefore asked him to put the wheat at their disposal, and I enclosed a list of these persons. However, I did not send him any money for the wheat, choosing to wait for his affirmative response.

Only two days later, the wheat arrived, in a quantity sufficient for all 115 individuals. Enclosed was a bill for a paltry sum—about seventeen Turkish liras in banknotes, which had very little value. I immediately distributed the wheat among the exiles, and I sent him the cash, along with a letter of thanks for his interest on our behalf.

All through our stay in Kafr Jammal, my family expressed a powerful longing to return to Tel Aviv. I remember just how much my then-young children, my daughter Yehudit[365] and my youngest son Yoram,[366] longed for Tel Aviv, their birthplace, which was expressed such.

My daughter Yehudit was once sitting and reading a Hebrew book. When she finished reading, she began to sing a sad Hebrew song full of longing for the homeland, a melancholy song full of longing, which she sang with feeling and baring her soul.

When Yoram, my youngest son, heard this sad song, his little heart was also filled with longing for Tel Aviv, the city of his birth, and he asked us, with tears streaming down his cheeks, "Father! Mother! When will we return to Tel Aviv? When will we return?" And he went on and on in this manner, crying, asking the same questions over and over again.

When I heard his crying and his questions, I began to reminisce and a smile formed on my lips; surely the boy missed returning to climb on the fences that lined Rothschild Boulevard, with Dizengoff yelling at him, as he did back then: "Yoram, get down from there! Yoram, get down! Now!"

365. Yehudit Chelouche (1905–1965) was twelve years old when the family settled in Kafr Jammal. After the war she began her studies at the Herzliya Gymnasium. She was later sent to Paris to study piano and composition in the music conservatory next to the Sorbonne.

366. Yoram Chelouche (1910–1986) was eight years old when the family settled in Kafr Jammal. After the war he was sent to study at the American University in Beirut, and then Nancy, France, where he acquired a diploma in agronomy. After obtaining his master's degree in agriculture in California, he returned to Palestine and worked in agricultural consulting.

We comforted him and we did our best to calm him down, urging him to stop crying and to relax, because in another week, in another month, we would return from our exile to Tel Aviv. He accepted our answer, in full faith. But a week and a month passed, and we were still in Kafr Jammal. Then our youngest would occasionally awaken and ask his questions yet again. "Father! Mother! When will we return to Tel Aviv? When will we return home to Tel Aviv?"

CHAPTER 22 *Informers, the Turkish Government, and Kindly Arabs*

The informant from Tulkarm | Our community and our family are at risk of expulsion | A sleepless night | My visit to the German commandant | The kaymakam *of Tulkarm visits my home | Dining in the sheikh's home | Relations between the Arab village and my family and the Jews | My mother's death | The question of burial | We purchase a plot of land for the grave | The negotiations | Tribulations of my brother Ya'akov and son Moshe | The story of their exile in their words | Their life in a Damascus prison | Their release*

Some two weeks after establishing the commissary, an Arab who was one of the more prominent notables of the village came to my house and shared a secret with me. That day he had visited Tulkarm on private business, and he was summoned to the government house as well. When he entered the office of the *kaymakam*, he asked him, "Are there any Jewish émigrés in your village?" When he answered in the affirmative, the *kaymakam* lost his temper: "How is it that you did not inform me of this before today? After all, it is wartime, and the government must know about every single movement. Tomorrow or the day after tomorrow I will travel to your village, and I will see for myself."

"In my opinion," added the Arab notable, "this is the result of an informant. According to what I heard from the *kaymakam*'s secretary, the informant comes from among the Jews living in Tulkarm who own the commissary there and who are motivated by envy, because their commissary's business has been diverted to the commissary operated by Jews in Falama. This group of Jews understood that only by informing [to the government] would the Jews be expelled from Falama, and the commissary business would revert to them alone, just like before. And since I am your loyal friend, as you know, I have now come here to inform you about it, so that you can take steps to protect yourselves in anticipation of the edict." When he finished, I thanked him, and we parted affectionately.

I could not fall asleep that night and lay awake in bed thinking about what to do. I was particularly bothered by the thought that if it was true that the informers were motivated by the commissary, then all the Jews in Kafr Jammal would suffer because of me. I decided to present myself the next morning before the German commandant and beg him for mercy, and that is what I did.

Early that morning, before the commandant left for his office, I went to his house. I told him everything I had heard from the Arab notable. He told me: "Two days earlier, I received a letter from Kazim Pasha,[367] the acting pasha in place of Djemal Pasha, asking if it was true that Jews were living in Kafr Jammal and that they operate a commissary in Falama. And he asked who it was that gave them permission to do so. I replied that there is indeed an upstanding Jewish family that I have known for many years through commercial ties between us that date back to well before the war, and since they are émigrés in the area, they made an official application to me to permit them to establish a commissary, and I approved the request. I am extremely pleased with the help they have given us, and with their honesty and loyalty. I sent this answer a few hours after receiving his letter, but nevertheless, as soon as I finish eating breakfast, I will be going to Tulkarm to see the *kaymakam*, and if there is a need, I will go see the pasha, too."

I thanked him and said goodbye, hoping to hear an encouraging response from him that afternoon. At the appointed hour, I went to his office. The commandant greeted me inside with a weary smile: "While the matter has been settled, the *kaymakam* will nevertheless be coming for a visit to the village, and it would be best that you will be there in case he asks for you. But don't worry, he assured me that he will not harm you in any way." I went home and invited all the Jews to my house, and I related the whole saga to them and asked them to stop off at the homes of all our fellow émigré brothers to tell them not to leave their homes tomorrow, so that the *kaymakam* will not sense a flurry of Jews moving about the village.

At ten o'clock the next day, when I sat in front of my house looking through a book (as is known, my house was at the top of the village, since

---

367. No information has been found about him.

it served the villagers as a guesthouse for visitors), I saw the *kaymakam* ride in on horseback, with two cavalrymen accompanying him. As he drew closer to me, I stood up and greeted him with the proper show of respect.

"Who are you?" the *kaymakam* asked me.

"My name is Yosef Eliyahu Chelouche, an émigré from Jaffa who is now a resident of Kafr Jammal."

He smiled.

"Look over there," he said, pointing with his finger to the house opposite my own, "I am going into that house as a guest of the *sheikh* of the village. In another half hour, come over and visit me."

Half an hour later, I walked up to the *sheikh*'s house. When the *kaymakam* saw me from a distance, he called out to me to enter. He stood up in a show of respect, and so did all the others who were lounging there, including the Arab notable who had revealed the secret to me. [The *kaymakam*] invited me to sit down next to him. The Arab notable was astounded, for it had been so clear to him that the *kaymakam* had come to the village specifically to expel the Jews, and yet here he was treating the representative of the émigrés with extreme courtesy. The *kaymakam* inquired as to my and my family's well-being and asked if we were content with our residence in this village. I answered in the affirmative. He then turned to the leaders and notables of the Arab community and asked them if they were treating these good émigrés who had settled in their midst with sympathy, and they responded, somewhat meekly, "Yes," as they could not understand his intent.

Then the *kaymakam* said to them, "You should know that only a few days ago I found out that there were strangers living in your village. I, as the civilian government official responsible for everything that happens in the villages in my district. Therefore, I was very surprised to learn that I did not know at all about the settling of émigré Jews in your village. I therefore decided to come and see them with my own eyes, and to reprimand you. But just yesterday I was told that your guests are good and honest people, and I am also in the possession of an order from Kazim Pasha, warning you to live in peace with these guests, and make the time they spend living among you as easy as possible for them."

Upon hearing this statement by the *kaymakam*, almost all of the men gathered in the room cried out from their seats: "His Honor the *Kaymakam* can ask Mr. Chelouche how the residents of the village treat their guests. We placed the guesthouse at the disposal of Mr. Chelouche, and each and every evening we spend time with him and endeavor to make the days of his stay in our village pleasant." In the meantime, the servant entered and whispered something into our host's ear. He turned to the *kaymakam* and invited him into the dining room. When the *kaymakam* stood up, all the other guests did, as well, and took their leave, as did I. But the *kaymakam* grabbed my hand and said to me: "Do not leave, Mr. Chelouche. You shall dine together with me, at the honorable *sheikh*'s table."

I answered him: "While it is true that I have visited the very important owner of this home several times, as a Jew I am nevertheless forbidden to eat foreign foods." At this point, the owner of the house interrupted the conversation and said: "But you yourself taught us to eat only kosher meat," and then he went on to tell the *kaymakam* all about Jewish slaughtering customs. I asked the *kaymakam* if he might permit me to bring over my own food, to eat it together with him at the table. He agreed. I walked to my home, along with his servant. They prepared my lunch, and the servant carried it to the *sheikh*'s house. And then only three men sat down to eat at the table: the *kaymakam*, the *sheikh*, and me.

After the meal, we spent a long time engaged in conversation over coffee and cigarettes. The *kaymakam*, a good-hearted fellow, told me: "If you wish to bring things from your home in Jaffa, I can arrange it, because we have spies who go to Jaffa and return to us." I thanked him very much but told him that I was not lacking anything. I left out the fact that my son Zadoc was in fact in Jaffa, since I suspected that his question was intended to interrogate and test me. He lay down to rest and asked me to return an hour later.

I went home and told my parents that God's grace was with me that day. My mother smiled and said: "Yes, my son, you are over there, while your father is here, praying for your success." "Mother," I replied, "you should know that Father's prayers have indeed been accepted. The *kaymakam* arrived here intending to expel us, and now he has become our advocate, praising our virtues to the village notables." "The Lord's salvation comes in the blink of an eye," shouted my elderly father, hugging me tightly and kissing me on the forehead.

I did not have a watch with me, but nevertheless I was on time returning to the *kaymakam*. He was then washing his face. And once again all the men who had previously congregated there reassembled, and the conversation revolved around planting the fields and the tithe tax. They asked him for various concessions in paying the tithe tax, and he listened to their requests attentively. Eventually, he got up to leave, and all the guests accompanied him out to the main road. While holding onto my hand and squeezing it, he turned to the gathered men and said, "I warn you once more: Be sure to treat the respectable Chelouche family well and pay attention to them. And I wish all of you well." And then the *kaymakam* went on his way.

The days that we resided in Kafr Jammal were good ones. The village residents treated us with great respect. Bonds of affection prevailed between the Jews and the residents. There were no disturbing incidents at all, save for a few minor squabbles between the Arab and Jewish children. In such instances, I would help reconcile between them by handing out various candies. The Arab residents were accustomed to scolding and beating their children. As for the children of the Jews, I cautioned their parents to force their children to live in peace and harmony with the Arab children. Indeed, the order and peace in the village were exemplary.

In Tammuz 5678 (1918),[368] my mother grew gravely ill and took to bed, never to rise again. All my efforts to restore her health failed, and her soul departed in a state of purity. Her entire family and several from among the Jews gathered at her bedside, and she blessed them before her death. Her only question was: "Where is my son Ya'akov? Has he not yet returned from Damascus?" And with those words our dear mother departed from us forever. All the émigré Jews came to our house to mourn her alongside us.

My late brother and I were at a loss, and we did not know where to dig her grave. The closest colony was Hadera, a distance of five hours on foot, and without a permit it was forbidden to go from one place to another, and it was especially prohibited to transport a corpse. For now, we decided to have a coffin made. We made inquiries among the Arabs and found a man who had some wooden boards and nails. We bought them from him, and then my late brother Avraham and I built the coffin.

Meanwhile, the three *sheikh*s of the village made their way over to offer us comfort, and said: "Why should you move the deceased woman

---

368. According to the inscription on her tombstone, Chelouche's mother Sara actually passed away on 5 Sivan 5678 (14 May 1918).

somewhere else? After all, our cemetery is at your disposal. Bury her in whichever plot you wish." We thanked them for their kindness, and I asked them to sell me a small plot of land near the home in which our parents lived, in order to bury her next to the house. The *sheikh*s thought about it for a while and responded: "You have our permission to bury your mother next to the house, even without purchasing the land. Because that land is ownerless and is the joint property of the village." "We have a custom," I attempted to explain to them, "to pay for all burial costs, and we are not permitted to bury our dead on foreign land.[369] It would be preferable if you sold it to us, and then you could use the money for the needs of the village." "Do as you wish," replied the village *sheikh*s. "We will make things as easy for you as possible." I walked with them to the place I had in mind and chose a suitable spot. I paid them forty *mejidi*s and we wrote up a contract, which noted that they sold me this plot of land, and they signed that they had received the fair price for it. Only then was my mind able to rest, and I went with my brother to sit together and mourn her.

The Jewish men went to the synagogue and read Psalms for the ascent of her soul, and the women dealt with the purification [of the body itself]. When that was done, we placed her in the coffin and sealed it. We gathered around her along with the rest of the community, to mourn and eulogize her. After an hour or so, we moved her toward the burial plot that our younger émigré brothers had dug.

At that moment, an Arab neighbor approached me and asked if it was permissible for residents of the Arab village to take part in the funeral. I responded that it was most certainly permitted. The Arab then relayed what I said to the village residents. Evidently, they had all been standing right behind my house waiting for my permission, for all of them came, young and old.

We accompanied her to her grave, amid the crying of the Jews and the Arabs alike. Alongside the grave we recited *kaddish*, and the cantor Pisanti recited the prayer that is chanted as a body is laid to rest, and then we buried her. That same day, I built a memorial on her grave, for fear of the animals in the area. We sat *shiva*, in keeping with Jewish law, and throughout the days of mourning, group after group of Arabs from the village came to comfort us. The heartfelt sentiments of the local

---

369. Meaning, on land not owned by Jews.

residents encouraged us in our time of misery, and we repressed our feelings of sorrow—aside from my sister Jamila, who could not stop mourning for a very long time following our mother's death.

Thus, our mother passed away in expulsion, far from our home and far from her son Ya'akov, the youngest of her sons, who had been exiled to Damascus. She was the most cherished woman, who throughout her life loved to serve learned religious scholars and enjoy the light of their Torah. May her memory be blessed, and may her soul be bound up in the bond of the life of the nation.

Once the days of mourning had passed, an Arab acquaintance of ours from Jaffa came to see us. We invited him in to sit and we offered him coffee and cigarettes, but he was disoriented and it was difficult for him to speak. Apparently, he had been running quickly and was having difficulty breathing.

"What happened, Sa'id Muhammad Sha'aban?[370] What news do you bring, is it good news or bad news?"

He was encouraged and chuckled: "I am a man who brings news to you today. I bring you very glad tidings. Your brother Ya'akov and your son Moshe have arrived—and are already on the outskirts of the village." We all jumped up from our seats and went out to greet them. When we saw them, we burst into tears. We ushered them in to see our elderly father, who hugged them and blessed them. And when they heard about my mother's death, they both cried so much, and we cried with them as well. They told us that they had heard from the Arabs that we were living in Kafr Jammal, but they did not know the road to here, and then God brought before them Mr. Sa'id Muhammad Sha'aban, who found them in Tulkarm, and then he left his shop there and led them to our village.

That evening, we gathered around my father and heard all about the hardships suffered by those who were exiled to Damascus but were now sitting among us, healthy and whole. The entire chapter—the episode of exile—is deeply saddening, but it is worthwhile to record it for memory of the extent to which the Jews suffered from the rule of the Turks.

When the officers captured my son Moshe and my brother Ya'akov in Petah Tikva, they transferred them to Jaffa and later that same day

---

370. The Sha'aban family were orchard owners in Jaffa.

sent them to Jerusalem.[371] There they were imprisoned for a week, and afterward, together with fifty other Jews with their hands cuffed to one another, they were marched on foot to Nablus. The seven days they spent in the jail were especially depressing. Hundreds of Arabs were jailed, and they were densely packed together, standing without being able to move a limb, all of them starving for bread, torn apart and worn thin, barefoot and naked. The stench and the putrid odor were horrific, and the filth and scum came up to their necks. In such conditions the Jews had to suffer their fate in silence. My son Moshe managed to make acquaintance with the officer in charge, and through a bribe given secretly, was able to acquire two donkeys to ride on, and so the sick and weaker Jews took turns and rode on the donkeys for part of the time. In this fashion, they walked for six days until ultimately reaching Samakh, camping at every station along the way. At the Samakh station, they were transferred to Damascus in sealed freight cars that had only small windows for air to breathe.

When they were taken off the railway cars, they were moved into the prison in Damascus. Once again, more filth and scum. Many imprisoned soldiers who looked like the walking dead, gaunt near-skeletons, their faces terrifying. Protruding bones, sunken cheeks, eyes burrowed deep in their sockets. No longer human beings, they were dark shadows milling about helplessly. When they saw this, Ya'akov and Moshe approached the officer in charge of the prison, and by granting a sizable reward, they were assigned a separate room in the prison. They cleaned the room extremely well, and afterward they moved in. At the time, my sister Rahel Mehoudar[372] lived in Damascus, and she had connections with the prison administration. Whenever a relative or an acquaintance was brought to the prison, she would rush to the prison and through her efforts, as well as those of her late son Rafa'el Mehoudar[373]—who

371. The dossier of the Deportees' Council of Damascus kept in the Central Zionist Archives holds a document that lists all the deportees who were imprisoned in Damascus.

372. Rahel Mehoudar (1869–1933) was Aharon Chelouche's second child and Yosef Eliyahu's older sister. She married Binyamin Mehoudar and had four children: Sarina, Rafa'el, Simha (Sim), and Emile. Sarina married Ben-Zion Rizo-Levi, and they are listed as one of the founding families of Tel Aviv.

373. After his father's death, Rafa'el Mehoudar (1888–1924) moved with his mother to Beirut, where he studied at the Alliance school before earning his pharmacy

wielded influence in government circles—they were able to bring them food and books to read. Due to her efforts, their suffering was less than that of the other prisoners. Yet in spite of all these relief efforts, my son Moshe became ill with typhus.

As is known, the government would actually poison those ill [with typhus], for fear of the disease spreading. My sister was therefore very frightened of the government finding out that my son Moshe had typhus, at which point they would transfer him to the hospital, and then who knows what his fate might be. She therefore bribed the officer and the army doctor, and my son Moshe was left to lie in his room, where he was treated by my brother Ya'akov, my sister Rahel, and her son, who came to see him daily and sat and watched over him. Medications and prescriptions were passed to him through a small window, and the army doctor would walk into the room as if Moshe were merely an acquaintance. Officially, no one knew he was ill.

When my son Moshe recovered, my brother Ya'akov collapsed from exhaustion, but he was afraid to remain in his room and turned himself in to the hospital. My son Moshe, who had recovered but was still weak, also asked the doctor to admit him to the hospital. He was in need of good air and nutritious food, neither of which they had in the cell. When my brother Ya'akov recovered, they both remained in the hospital thanks to a steep *baksheesh* payment that amounted to a significant sum of money. Even as healthy individuals, it was better for them to remain in the hospital than to return to prison. My sister cooked for them and brought their food to the hospital, and she frequently stayed overnight along with her son to help ensure their health.

In the meantime, the officer announced that he would not be able to keep them in the hospital any longer due to his fear of the government; they would have to return to prison. My brother Ya'akov and my son Moshe decided to draft a letter to the government, requesting transfer to another prison that would be cleaner, explaining that they had been ill and they were now extremely weak, and that they feared becoming ill

---

degree at St. Joseph's. He returned to Jaffa to establish a pharmacy in 1914. On the eve of World War I, Mehoudar served as vice-consul of Spain in Jaffa. He joined the Jewish exiles from Jaffa in the Galilee, and later in Damascus, and supplied them with various medicaments. Rafa'el was also a public figure. After the war, he was elected as a representative of the Jewish community in Jaffa to the first convention of Knesset Israel (1920).

yet again. The government accepted their request and transferred them to another prison. While they found the new prison to be cleaner, all of the inmates were statesmen and political prisoners, so it was constantly surrounded by a new military guard. It was difficult for anyone to enter the prison and visit them, since it was as closed as the walls of Jericho, and no one could get in or out.

Imprisoned in this prison were six *effendi*s and Pasha Salim al-Ayoubi,[374] who was well acquainted with my family, as well as two Jews who were accused of spying.[375] They passed their time with this pasha, reading books that were brought in for him and conversing with him. But then, when the two Jews were executed by hanging, my brother and son were so greatly anguished that they determined that they could not bear to remain in prison. They managed to send notes to my sister Rahel and her acquaintances, asking to be ransomed from the prison. Mr. Dizengoff, who was in Damascus at the time, found out that my brother Ya'akov and my son Moshe were imprisoned there, and he attempted to have them released. Through his efforts, they were brought to a tribunal in order to ascertain what were their sins and crimes against the government that imprisoned them. The judges were high-ranking army officers, approximately seven in number, including the commissar who had been in Jerusalem and who was not only a family friend but also a personal friend of my son Moshe.

When the judges entered the courtroom, they both burst into tears, and spoke quite forcefully to the commissar: "It has been a full year that we have been sitting in prison, even though we committed no crime. We have suffered terrible torments and perils, and we do not even know the reason for our imprisonment." The judges listened to their statements and issued an order to search for [the] case file. They reviewed the papers, asked them various questions, and then announced that they were innocent.

As they walked out of the military court, jubilant and uplifted and planning to go to my sister Rahel's house, they were captured along the

---

374. Salim al-Ayoubi was a large orchard and property owner in the Jaffa area.

375. These men were Na'aman Belkind and Yosef Lishansky, active in the anti-Ottoman NILI spy ring based in Zikhron Ya'akov during World War I. Belkind was born in the Jewish settlement of Gedera while Lishansky emigrated from Kiev. They were both executed on 16 December 1917.

way by the army and were taken to an army barracks. There they were informed of a new edict: they were to prepare themselves to be sent with the army to the front. Of course, they were extremely distressed and immediately wrote to my sister Rahel to tell her about their situation. My sister immediately went to the home of the *vali*[376] and broke down in tears before him. She described to him the suffering and tribulations of my brother Ya'akov and my son Moshe. Her words touched his heart, and he promised to look into the matter. Then she said that she would not be able to leave the *vali*'s house until he told her that they had been released, since it had been a full year that they had been suffering for no reason, that they were delicate men who had never before walked on foot. How could they possibly go into the army, since back in Jaffa hadn't the family paid a ransom against their lives? If it was required, the family would pay once more, but why imprison them now after the judges had exonerated them?

The *vali* went off to investigate the matter and ascertained that they had been imprisoned mistakenly. He immediately returned home and gave my sister a letter for the army commander, sending her with a police escort. On the basis of the letter, they were released. They arrived at my sister's home, and the joy was immense.

My son Moshe found it too difficult to wait for the passenger train to leave Damascus, so he boarded a cargo train carrying food supplies and rode it to Nablus, and from there to Tulkarm. He searched for me in Tulkarm but could not find me. So, he had to spend a few days there; in the meantime, my brother Ya'akov arrived, and the two of them then ran into Muhammad Sha'aban, who led them to us in Kafr Jammal.

This is a brief summary of their life in prison, which was so heartrending to us. Their release cost a great deal of money, which we borrowed from our acquaintances in Damascus and which we repaid immediately after the British conquest.

Following their return to us, my son Moshe and his family settled in Hadera,[377] and my brother Ya'akov in Zikhron Ya'akov.

---

376. The governor of a provincial *vilayet*, in this case of Syria; this was the equivalent rank to the *mutasarrif* of the Jerusalem region.

377. During the war over seven hundred Jewish refugees from Jaffa, Tel Aviv, and Petah Tikva settled in Hadera, far beyond the capacity of the small settlement.

CHAPTER 23 *Imprisoned in Tulkarm, and Once Again in Kafr Jammal*

The army heads to the front | Liquidation of the commissary | Under military guard to Tulkarm | My son Moshe comes to my aid along the way | My statement to the commandant | My imprisonment in accordance with the law | In the prison | The officer Hassan Abu 'Ali comes to my aid | A worker from our floor tile factory | My son Moshe visits me | My imprisonment among spies | Interrogated by the military | False accusations against me | The suspicions | "What is your relationship with Dizengoff?" | My response | The intervention of slanderers | Facing the military interrogators again | Their attitude toward me improves | The women campaign for our release | Release from prison | A night wandering through Tulkarm | We return to Kafr Jammal | Prayers emanating from broken hearts | The soldiers who heard our prayers | Joyous reunion of brothers | Yom Kippur | My father's illness | The days before our redemption

Little by little, the soldiers in Falama began to disperse to different places. One morning when we arrived at the commissary as usual, we did not find a single soldier; the entire village was already abandoned and empty. In a single night, the army had left, and even our friend the German commandant did not inform us that he was being sent to the front. We were greatly disheartened. We were left with a commissary stocked with merchandise, and what would we do with it? To whom could we sell the goods? Aside from that, we would now have to guard it well to prevent thefts from taking place. I had the idea of immediately hiring wagons and hauling the merchandise to Tulkarm, but my son Avner was against the idea, contending it would be better to liquidate the commissary and sell all our merchandise to the army that was camped nearby.

The following day, which happened to be an extremely hot *khamsin* day,[378] my son persuaded me—although I was not in complete agreement—and he traveled with most of the inventory to sell it to the army. My son Avner spent about two days away at the army camp, and I grew extremely concerned about him. I regretted that I had let him travel on such a hot day, and when he finally came back alive and well, I thanked the Lord and resolved not to let him travel anymore, come what may.

Two days after my son's return, a policeman came to me and informed me that I was being summoned to Tulkarm. I was very surprised by the summons and told the policeman that I would go on my own, but the policeman refused to leave me alone and said that I was to go to Tulkarm on foot, under military guard. This surprised me even more. After all, only a few days earlier the same policeman had acted deferentially toward me, so how was it that he now dared speak to me in such a manner? No doubt there must be an order given from above, so I yielded. I noticed some of my Arab acquaintances standing at a distance, watching and listening to everything that was happening to me; I called out to one of them, asking him to inform my family. I set off on the way, surrounded by soldiers with drawn swords, with the policeman riding on his horse alongside us.

When we were about halfway there, not far from Kafr Falama, my son Moshe caught up to us riding on his horse. He was simply shocked—how could it be that I was being led on foot, surrounded by soldiers? He came up to the policeman and spoke with him courteously, requesting that they permit me to ride, but the policeman refused, saying that I was no better than the soldiers who were also walking on foot.

"But," my son added, "my father is not accustomed to this. He is tired and soaked through with sweat." This had an effect, and he permitted me to ride on the condition that when we got to Tulkarm, I would enter on foot. And so I rode on the horse and my son went on foot. Along the way, he hired a horse from an Arab, and so he rode as well. Just before reaching Tulkarm, I descended from the horse and then proceeded on foot. I was extremely humiliated by such a journey, as well as looking at the faces of the residents of Tulkarm who knew me.

They led me into the army office, where a German clerk asked for my name. When I answered that my name is Yosef Eliyahu Chelouche, he

---

378. The *khamsin* are the hot, dry, and strong summer winds.

wrote a note and issued an order to put me in jail. I was shocked. How could they arrest me without any preliminary investigation? I asked the clerk if before I was imprisoned, I might be permitted to present myself before the director of the office, but he informed me that the director of the office was very busy and preoccupied. I pleaded with him that I only wanted to say a few words to him. The clerk went into the director's office, and then emerged, and he informed me that I was permitted to enter.

I went into the commandant's office, and he, too, was German. I spoke with him in French: "Mr. Commandant," I said to him. "I have been brought here for no good reason. I know that I have not committed any sin against the government, and it is certainly only by mistake that I have been arrested without preliminary investigation. If I enter the jail, I will be forsaken there. Would you be so kind to order that a preliminary investigation be conducted? Perhaps I am not the person that you are looking for."

The commandant then asked me: "Is your name Yosef son of Aharon Chelouche?"

"Yes," I said. "That is my name."

"You are hereby arrested in accordance with the law," the commandant declared. He then explained that he could not issue an order to interrogate me yet because my papers were not ready. However, he would do what he could to make sure the investigation would begin within three days. I thanked him and went with the soldiers to the prison. They led me into a large courtyard that was filled with different prisoners. I sat down in a corner, overcome with sorrow and anguish.

My son Moshe knew where I was being imprisoned, and his sorrow knew no bounds. How could they arrest Father? Would the same fate befall him to taste the bitter taste of prison? Was the long imprisonment of his own brother and son not enough? Not knowing what else to do, my son Moshe said to me, "Father, I'm going to go and bring you something to eat."

"I have no appetite at all, my son," I said. "Better yet, bring me some water."

He brought me water. I drank it, and my spirits returned. When my son Moshe went out to buy me something to eat, two policemen came up to me and told me to go with them. I asked them: "Where are you taking me?" At which the policemen reprimanded me, saying, "Wherever you are ordered to go, you must obey."

Naturally I started walking, like a lamb to the slaughter. I was led outside the city, all the while surrounded by a large group of gendarmes, all with drawn swords. I was filled with sorrow; once again, I had to walk down the street like one of the common thieves under arrest. As we walked past the commissary owned by the Jews in Tulkarm, I asked the soldiers to permit me to walk over and tell them that if my son Moshe should happen to come by, they should inform him that I was being taken somewhere else. The gendarmes agreed to my request. When I entered the commissary and asked them to do so, the owners of the commissary answered me rudely and did not express any interest in my situation.

I was led to a new prison with a very large courtyard with a building in the center, surrounded by a wall and a large number of soldiers. I was told that this was the political prison. I was placed in a prison cell where I found approximately forty men, all of them sitting on the floor and talking with one another. I was exhausted and my legs buckled under me, but what could I sit on? There was no chair. I saw a bundle of blankets and walked over and leaned on it. Another prisoner warned me to stay away from it because the bundle belonged to an officer who was the prison supervisor, and if he saw me leaning on his bundle I would be beaten mercilessly. I walked away from the bundle and squatted on the floor, but when my strength finally failed me, I was compelled to sit on the ground.

I was completely powerless. My eyelids slowly closed, and I leaned against the wall and fell asleep. Then I felt a hand shaking me, rousing me compassionately from my slumber, and I heard a voice calling out to me in a friendly tone: "Abu Musa! Abu Musa! Why are you sleeping on the floor? Get up and lie down on the bed." I opened my eyes, and there before me was the officer, who was now arranging a bed for me. He helped me take off my coat and shoes and urged me to sleep comfortably.

"You must recognize me, Abu Musa," he said.

I looked at his face, dumbfounded.

"Don't you know who I am? That being the case," the officer replied, "I can tell you that my name is Hassan Abu 'Ali. I worked for you for two years, in your floor tile factory."

"Oh, Abu 'Ali! Now I remember you!" I shouted with glee. "Do not abandon me in my time of trouble."

"Rest assured, I will not leave you," the officer answered with deep emotion. "I will see to it that you will be able to sleep comfortably in a bed for as long as you are in this prison under my supervision. I will now go into the city to secure a bed for you."

I told the officer that I would write out a note for Mr. S.,[379] one of the owners of the commissary, asking him to send me a bed. He took the note from me and left.

After the officer departed, my son Moshe arrived at the prison. The soldiers permitted him to enter, as they had seen the officer showing me such respect. He asked for me, and they let him into my cell. He told me that he had searched for me for four hours and that he had been to the commissary, but they had not told him a thing. Only through a miracle had he found out that I was here. My son Moshe implored me to eat, but I could not take a bite of anything.

I told him all about the officer Abu 'Ali, whom God had placed on my path, and how this man was treating me so kindly in this imprisonment. All of this made my son very glad, as he was worried about me and troubled by my incarceration. I myself felt bad; this imprisonment, which had come upon me so suddenly, was so very shocking to me. I asked my son if he could bring me some food in order to revive my spirits. In the meantime, the officer returned with a porter who was carrying a bed for me. He was extremely pleased to see my son Moshe and shook his hand with great affection. Then he turned to me and asked, "Who is this terrible person Mr. S. to whom you sent me? After reading your note, he tore it to pieces and became angry. 'I have no bed,' he shouted, 'and I do not know this person who wrote this note to me.'" I listened to these words from the officer and bottled up my disgrace.

The sun began to set, and I asked my son to return to the village to be with the family. I implored him not to tell my father anything about what had happened to me, so as to not trouble him. My son Moshe parted from me, and again I remained alone and deserted in the prison. Although my mind was at ease thanks to the officer's attitude toward me, I was unable to fall asleep all that night. My thoughts were strange, and they intruded on my rest. I was in a bad state. This was my first-ever taste of imprisonment, but I had committed no crime or transgression.

Toward morning I fell asleep, exhausted from my sleepless night, and I woke up only at nine o'clock. I looked all around in a state of confu-

---

379. In the original manuscript, Chelouche indicated the family name of the commissary owner, but it was omitted in the published book.

sion. Am I really not in my home, but in a prison instead? Where were the prisoners who were with me last night? Why had the room been cleared out, with all the other items removed, the floor scrubbed and the cleanliness so exemplary?

I walked up to the door of the cell and saw that all the prisoners were cleaning the courtyard, under the excellent protection of the policemen. When the officer saw me, he rushed over and asked, "How did you sleep, Mr. Chelouche? I tried to ensure that your sleep would be pleasant. I ordered that the room be cleaned and the floors scrubbed. For you are a dear guest of mine, and I was concerned that the filth might be damaging to your health. Now you will come with me, and we'll sit in the shade beneath a tree to dine together." When we sat down under the tree, I found a table nicely set, with butter, cheese, eggs, olives, oil, and honey. My heart was gladdened, and we spoke at length.

I asked the officer to send someone to purchase, at my expense, underwear and soap for every prisoner, so they would be able to wash themselves and so that they would all be clean. They then took off their clothes and washed them; they dried in the afternoon sun for hours, at which point they put them back on. Over the course of days, I became acquainted with the prisoners. I learned that they were for the most part natives of distant lands, while some were natives of our own country, but most of them were from Tunisia and Morocco.[380] All of them had been accused of spying. Among them was also a young Jew from Zikhron Ya'akov, who was accused of being a spy for England, although in truth he had nothing to do with espionage, particularly because he was not in his right mind. This young man had already suffered in the prison approximately a year and a half before my own arrival.

One day, this young man approached me and thanked me sincerely for the improvements that had been made to the general condition of the prison: "All of these Arab prisoners who are detained here with us are so thankful that you were brought here." Prior to my own incarceration in the prison, they had never cleaned the building or the courtyard, and the filth was horrendous. There also were instances of diseases that spread as a result of the filth.

380. As discussed earlier, throughout the nineteenth century, immigrants from North Africa lived and worked in Palestine. Many of them maintained their French protection as colonial subjects, rendering them "enemy aliens" during the war.

Although I wholeheartedly wished to enjoy the company of this young man, due to the fact that he was accused of such a serious offense —espionage, which was punishable by death—I was wary of becoming friendly with him, for the government officers would look at this with a suspicious eye. I asked him to leave me alone, as it was a matter of life and death for me. He understood my intention and complied with my request. This whole matter, of course, caused me great sorrow, for other than myself he was the only Jew with whom I could spend time together. Even though he had opinions that were strange to my spirit, and the signs of insanity were evident from his gestures and his speech, nevertheless he was a Jew and a brother in sorrow. Still, the fear of being accused of espionage was at the time a great fear.

One day, several gendarmes escorted by two officers entered my prison cell and told me to accompany them to the interrogation hall. I was extremely humiliated that I would have to walk down the street escorted by policemen and asked the officers to lead me through the alleyways instead. The officers agreed to my request and led me through the side streets, and thus I arrived at the interrogation hall without encountering any acquaintance or friend who would have seen me in my state of disgrace.

As I entered the interrogation hall, I was seated in the courtroom before two military judges, one German and the other Turkish, who spoke Arabic between themselves. The German judge turned to me and asked for my name, age, and address. Among the other questions I was asked: What was my connection with the English? How did I dare slaughter cows in Qalqilya and Kafr Jammal, secretly at night, and then send the butchered meat to the English front? I was astonished to hear these sorts of questions and immediately realized that someone had slandered me and falsely accused me of serious and contemptible crimes.

I gathered my strength and responded: "It is true that I slaughtered cows in Qalqilya and also in Kafr Jammal. Every two or three days, I would slaughter a cow and send the meat to Kfar Sava, to the émigrés' committee. The meat would be distributed among the Jews living there, most of whom were sick and weak, and their committee had asked me to assist it in its efforts. Is that a sin in your eyes?"

I began to list before them the names of the owners of the cows I had purchased, as well as names of the camel owners who had transported the meat to Kfar Sava. Likewise, I informed them that at my home in

Kafr Jammal I had an account ledger that contained a detailed listing of the dates on which I shipped the meat, and the weight of each shipment, and all in all I had slaughtered only fifteen cows. How was it that anyone could level such a foul accusation at me? Furthermore, I added, in the event that it became clear to the government that I had any connection whatsoever with the English, I would turn myself in to be hanged.

The judges, who listened intently to my statement, again asked me why, at the time of the English army's entry in Petah Tikva, I was among the first to leave the colony and traveled to the English, and "you returned to Petah Tikva that Friday, but with the intention to move your family, as well, on Sunday, over to the English."

"Yes," I said. "I will not deny that I traveled to Jaffa. I naively thought that the war was over and that the émigrés could now return to their hometown. I, too, wanted to return to the city where I was born, to the place where all of my assets and property is located and neglected, without the care of their owner—and even the most patriotic individual would choose to do so in such a situation, at a time when the road back to his own house and garden was reopened to him, without having to wander any longer and to no longer live a transitory life filled with hardship and tribulation."

And then again I was asked: "For what reason, when you were expelled from Jaffa, did you not travel further inland, to cities such as Nablus and Damascus? Instead, you lived in Qalqilya and now in Kafr Jammal, so close to the front." Questions like this were upsetting to me. I realized that my situation was grave, and who knew if I would ever be able to see my family again as a result of this slander? A passion for life suddenly awakened within me, a desire to be able to once again embrace my family and friends, and I was encouraged, and my spirit did not fail.

I responded: "That is indeed true. We did not travel very far because, as you may know, our family is well known and respectable, and how could we live like paupers and as impoverished persons in cities where many of our acquaintances and other people we know were residing? For if we must live a life of limited means such as this, in deplorable economic conditions, it is preferable for us to live in villages among peasants, among whom there would be no sense of embarrassment."

The judges wrote down my answers, and continued to ask: "What is the connection between you and Mr. Dizengoff, the Zionist?"

My heart tightened with pain at these questions, in which I saw the hand of people who personally knew me. How strong their feelings of envy must have been to lead them to tell the military government about all sorts of chapters of my life and my work. But I regained my composure and responded: "Mr. Dizengoff is my friend, and he is an honest and respectable man, one who is extremely devoted to the émigré Jews and who works hard to ease their plight as much as possible. Engaging in Zionist work does not constitute betrayal against the government. We have already explained more than once to Djemal Pasha the essence of Zionism and he knows us well. He absolutely relied on us and trusted us. He entrusted us with building the road to Gaza and appointed me director of the flour supply office. More than once he praised my devotion and loyalty. How is it that the government can now forget all of my service on its behalf and listen to despicable slander spread by people who have come to lie with an obvious agenda?"

These words came directly from my heart, with strong emotion, and tears flowed from my eyes. But the judges did not perceive my despondent spirit and continued to interrogate me: "Why did you go to Kafr Bidya, to a place where the German army is camped out next to the front? Didn't you know it was forbidden for anyone apart from the army to stay there even for a moment?"

This question opened my eyes, and I understood exactly who the slanderers were. I explained to the judges that thanks to the German commandant, I had received a permit to establish a commissary in Kafr Falama. "When the army moved to Kafr Bidya and I was left with all the merchandise in my commissary, the Germans advised us to transfer the merchandise to Kafr Bidya and sell it there. My young son Avner transported the merchandise to the site where the German army was encamped—to my chagrin. It was an extremely hot *khamsin* day and I was concerned about his health, but he didn't listen to me and traveled because he was so worried about the merchandise spoiling, [leading to] a substantial financial loss. I was very nervous that whole entire day and waited impatiently for my son to return home safe and sound. Overall, I have a hard time understanding why the German soldiers didn't warn my son it was forbidden to travel there. On the contrary, they even advised him to do so. They asked him to bring the merchandise to Kafr Bidya, and if there really were a military prohibition to do so, then it was their duty to inform my son, so that he would not violate the law."

There were many more questions, and I answered all of them openly and completely. When the interrogation was over, I was led back to the prison.

I did not find the officer at the prison, and I was told that he had left right after I was taken to the interrogation hall. I waited for him impatiently, as I wanted to ask him to find out what sort of impression my answers had left on the military judges. About half an hour later the officer appeared, and with words of encouragement on his lips, he told me that he had just then come from the coffee house where he often sat and spent time with his fellow officers. When his friends asked him why they had not seen him in the past few days, he told them the entire story of my incarceration and about me and my family.

One of the officers there said that he had heard of me before and that he was surprised that I had been placed in a political prison. As this man was speaking, the secretary of the court, who was in their company, joined in the conversation and said: "You are surely talking about the imprisonment of the Jew Yosef Eliyahu Chelouche. As far as I know, they have not found him guilty on any count. Some Jews who own the commissary in Tulkarm slandered him due to their envy. The investigation was conducted today, and I am certain that he will be found innocent. The government knows the accusations are baseless. These Jews wanted to slander [him] to the government long ago, but as long as the German commandant helped Mr. Chelouche, they were afraid to make these accusations. Because the commandant was transferred elsewhere that day, they decided to proceed with their plot."

I began to contemplate the actions of these Jews. How much humiliation and embarrassment must cover their faces until this very day. I do not wish to spend much time on this, because what's done is done. But even today I cannot understand what motivated these people to have me subjected to a military trial as a result of disgraceful acts of slander. After all, when I opened the commissary, I opened it in Falama, not in Tulkarm. And as it is known, I did not open it in order to compete with anyone, but solely to keep ourselves busy with something, particularly as we were not accustomed to sitting around, crossing our arms, and doing nothing. Secondly, we were in dire straits and had to secure a livelihood for a family as large as ours.

On more than one occasion, I had an inkling that conspiracies were being woven against me. There was the time that an *effendi* paid a visit to me in Kafr Jammal and told me that the *kaymakam* had asked him how it was that we were permitted to settle in Kafr Jammal. It was perfectly obvious that someone had informed on us, but thanks to the German commandant, everything worked out for the best.

What pains me most is that we had a close relationship with these people. When we first learned about them, we purchased merchandise from them in quite a significant amount and we made an effort to become regular customers of their commissary. Nevertheless, due to envy, as our commissary was expanding at a faster rate than theirs, they saw fit to inform on me and hand me over to the authorities. The evil they did to me was palpable. Although I always gave them the benefit of the doubt, telling myself that it was wartime and that takes people out of their right mind, these latest facts came as a slap in the face, and I was very let down by them. I hope and believe that if at this time these people still remember their evil actions, they must certainly regret what they did and their faces must turn red with shame, and it is my prayer that God will forgive them.[381]

On one of the days of my incarceration, my nerves were stretched very thin, and I was irritable. That entire day, I was extremely bored, gloomy, and dejected. My late brother Avraham Haim came to visit me, and I shared with him my bitter state of mind. How many people had been imprisoned, and I had always done everything I could to secure their release. Yet on the day when I myself am in prison, there is no one to lobby for my release. I felt entirely alone and isolated. The charges against me were serious—military charges—and who knows what fate might await me if my Lord does not take mercy on me and send his redeemer to me.

We sat together and considered what could be done. My brother told me that the late Mr. Rokach had received a telegram from Mr. Dizengoff in Damascus saying that he would make efforts to have me released, but since I was in a political prison, he was wary of showing too much interest in me due to the heavy charge that had been made against me.

I sought the means by which I might rescue myself from the prison. By my nature, I loved to be a man of action, and here I was, enclosed for ten days with nothing to do. As I was considering my situation, I remembered my friend the commandant, who had stood by me in times of

---

381. Because of these sentiments we have decided to maintain the anonymity of this and other private parties about whom Chelouche complained.

trouble and whose sincere attitude had encouraged me during my time of exile. I implored my brother to draft a letter to our friend the German commandant as soon as he arrived back in Kafr Jammal to inform him of my situation.

I parted from my brother with his promise to me to fulfill my request, and then I passed another three days in prison—days of boredom and isolation. But God took notice of my low state and sent me a rescuer and savior. On the morning following the fourth day, gendarmes entered my cell and summoned me to the interrogation hall. Upon my arrival at the interrogation room, I found the same judges who had already interrogated me. They asked me to sit down next to them. I was astonished at their sudden change of attitude toward me. One of the judges offered me a cigarette, which I dared not accept and left on the table. The judge assumed this was because I must not have any matches, so he pulled out a match, lit it, and presented it to me. I accepted the match and lit the cigarette, but in my heart I wondered: what is the meaning of all this high esteem?

As I sat and smoked, cups of tea were brought in and the judges asked me to drink. I was astonished: who is the man who had caused their hearts to turn toward me for the good? Only recently I was a political criminal, and even now, I had not yet been released but was already being treated as an esteemed personage. I did not understand the meaning of what was going on.

The judges informed me that although they desired to interrogate me again and had a list of some questions to ask me, they were in fact dropping the matter, [saying]: "The main thing is that he goes far away from here." The government was willing to offer me a regular monthly stipend of 500 Turkish liras in banknotes, so long as I went to live with my family in one of the cities. I replied that although I wanted to live in the city, our financial situation was difficult and did not permit us to live in a city. Secondly, it was inappropriate for us to live off government stipends. Rather, I would suggest that the government repay us the amounts that were owed to us in exchange for the goods that were taken from us for the army.

In answer to the judges' question, I replied that the amount owed to us by the army came to nearly 13,000 liras, and that all of the relevant papers and documents were in Jaffa along with the rest of our property, but I believed that there were other government officials in Nablus, Tulkarm, or Damascus who would be able to prove the truth of my claims based on their memories and the ledgers they kept. The judges listened attentively to my words, and then asked me to return to the prison, saying that they would discuss the case with Nazim Pasha that very evening and decide what to do with me. I returned to prison, not depressed as I had been previously, but more elevated and revived in spirit, for I now felt that God had not forsaken me and would send a ray of his light into the darkness of my imprisonment.

After another day or two, my brother came to visit me in prison. He told me that he had sent a letter to the commandant the day after we had last met, but he had not been given a receipt for it, simply an authorization on the envelope. He was not certain if the signature was that of the German commandant. In addition, a notable Arab had come to him and proposed that he pay fifty liras as a redemption fee to redeem me from the prison, and my brother came here to ask me if I agreed to this. I opposed it very much. I was afraid of it becoming known that I had been freed by virtue of *baksheesh*,[382] and then my situation would be many times worse. In the meantime, I was informed that my wife and sister-in-law wanted to see me. I asked that they be admitted to my cell. As soon as they saw me, they burst into tears. I comforted them and asked them to cheer up.

"Take note," I told them. "Fourteen days have already passed since my arrest, and I don't see any movement toward my release from prison. I ask you to go immediately to Nazim Pasha and lodge a complaint before him. Perhaps you will influence him, and he will consent to release me."

And indeed, that very same day, the women went to see Nazim Pasha. They met his personal secretary at the door to his office and asked his permission to enter. When he understood that they had come to ask Nazim Pasha to release me, he told them to wait. "His Honor the Pasha is busy right now and is not receiving visitors. I do not know if I will be able to permit you to see the pasha today." They tried to wait, but the permission to enter [to see] Nazim Pasha was not granted to them.

Only after some time did I learn the reason why the secretary had not allowed the women to enter. The pasha had written a letter to release me two days earlier, but the secretary had held it up. He desired to extort

---

382. A financial bribe or "gift" to government officials, often used to grease the wheels of Ottoman bureaucracy.

money from me in exchange; it was he who had sent the Arab who proposed that my brother give him fifty Turkish liras for my release. But since my answer had been negative, and as he saw that the women had come to see Nazim Pasha to complain that he was not releasing me, the secretary was afraid that Nazim Pasha would discover his scheme, if not that same day, then perhaps the next, since the women were apt to meet the pasha somewhere else. Therefore, the secretary hastened to give the letter of release to the police station.

And so it happened at eight o'clock that night (which was a Friday night), while I was eating dinner, not even aware that it was the Sabbath, that I was hastened to the police station. When I appeared before the officer there, he asked for my full name, age, and parents' names. He then informed me that I was free to go.

That night was one of the nights at the end of the month. Darkness surrounded me, and when I walked out of the police station, I did not know which way to turn. I was a stranger in the city and where would I find a place to sleep that night? I decided to return to the prison and spend the night there, but I got lost on my way back to the prison and could not figure out how to get there. I searched on my own and I also asked passersby, until with great difficulty, I arrived at the prison. There I found new policemen guarding the entrance gate who did not know me and would not let me enter.

During the two hours I spent outside the prison, the guards changed their shift. I asked them to call the officer Abu 'Ali for me, but they answered in unison: "There is no such officer." I began shouting, "Send for the officer Abu Hassan," but again they said, "There is no such officer here." Suddenly there was a shout from inside: "Why won't you let him enter? He is a political prisoner here." The man shouting these words was the deputy officer. The policemen became alarmed and permitted me to enter. When I walked into my old prison cell, I found the officer Abu 'Ali lying on the bed and told him that I had been released. He was overjoyed to hear it and advised me to sleep in the prison that night and return to Kafr Jammal the following day.

I responded that it would be better if he accompanied me to the city, where I would search for my brother. After all, my wife and his wife had been at Nazim Pasha's office, and surely they had not yet returned to the village. He considered the idea for a moment and replied: "I agree to accompany you to the city." That night was a night of Ramadan, and the city was rejoicing and celebrating. When we arrived in the city, I found my brother in one of the shops, where he was sitting and talking with the shopkeepers. He was overjoyed to see that I had been released, and we embraced as only brothers can.

My brother told me that our wives were at the home of an Arab friend, where they were spending the night. We decided to go to them and deliver the good news about my release. After we arrived, they did not want to stay any longer at the Arab's home, so we all went together into the city. In the city there was a big pandemonium. The Arabs were celebrating the Ramadan holiday. We spent the whole night until dawn talking at a party among friends, and at sunrise, we set out to Kafr Jammal on foot, due to the sanctity of the Sabbath.

When we arrived in Kafr Jammal, the rejoicing was great. My father hugged and kissed me: "This time, your journey has been much longer, my son—all the way to Damascus," he said in a voice shaking due to his old age. I told him all about the episode, and he listened to my account and cried. Once again, I was surrounded by my family and my fellow émigrés, who received us with tears of joy upon seeing me released. I went out in the open, and my soul was free to enjoy the sunlight. But the days of war continued without stopping. The economic situation was growing worse with each passing day.

The festival season was upon us. I sent word to Zikhron Ya'akov to purchase prayer books for the migrants and ordered additional Torah scrolls. On Rosh Hashanah we gathered to pray at my late father's spacious residence. His home was on a pretty hill that overlooked its surroundings. Its windows faced the main road to the north. Our hearts were filled with suffering and tribulation. We all prayed from the depths of our hearts. The prayers went on longer than usual, and we prolonged our liturgical chanting and multiplied our hymns. Perhaps God would hear our voices and see our suffering and redeem us from the distresses of this terrible war that was causing us such great harm. We prayed like that with broken hearts, in a singsong melody as was our custom, and our voices carried in the wind to the desolate areas all around: until when would we remain here, abandoned in this barren desert, living a life of nomads, unable to return to our homes?

At the same time that our prayers were growing stronger, streaming forth from the heart, a group of Turkish soldiers entered the room. Instantly, my nerves tensed up and I filled with anger. They don't even allow us to pray. "How can you permit yourselves to disturb us in the midst of our prayers?" I shouted out, as loud as I could. "This is a holy day for us!" The soldiers looked at me with tears streaming from their eyes, and practically simultaneously, they all shouted out these heartfelt words: "We are your brethren! We are all Jews, from the Balkans, who just happened to be passing by with the army unit heading to the next village over. For four years we have been cut off from Judaism, but then we suddenly heard these pleasant melodies and were reminded that we are Jews. We came here following the echo of your voices. And now give us prayer books and we will pray together with you."

I was intensely moved by the entire scene; tears welled up in all our eyes. "Dear brothers," I said, "you will pray with us, and you will share the holiday meal with us." We gave them prayer books and they began to pray. We were overjoyed, for we had not yet read from the Torah, and I would be able to honor them by calling on them to read from the scroll. In the meantime, I sent word to arrange for a dozen chickens from the local Arabs and gave orders for the *shochet* to slaughter them. Then I sent the women to cook them. We commissioned an Arab woman to knead dough, and she baked pita. How endearing was the resulting scene as we sat down together to enjoy the holiday meal.

We will never forget that day. Brothers in time of trouble and suffering. Brothers to the sacrifices of that awful war, a war that was exacting a cruel revenge on all humanity. Brothers who have been cast so far away from their homes for several years, and who once again were granted an opportunity to be among brothers. I pleaded with them to remain with us until after the festival day ended. Some of them were compelled to leave, while a few remained until the following day, and they, too, parted from us with infinite affection and love. We invited them to come to us for Yom Kippur and spend the day with us in prayer and supplication on the greatest and holiest day for us.

Yom Kippur arrived, but the Jewish soldiers did not return. I understood that they were now far from our area and therefore could not come to pray with us. On this holy day, my father took ill and developed a fever. At his request, we brought him in his sickbed into the synagogue, and I sat next to him and cared for him. I prayed with a broken heart while I applied the cold compresses to his head. Only that evening did his condition improve, and his fever broke. Within a few days, he recovered his health and was walking again.

CHAPTER 24 *The Arrival of the Redeemers and Conquerors of Our Country*

The army's movement from Judea to Samaria and the Galilee | Our redemption is near | Return of the exiles on foot to Jaffa and Tel Aviv | Held up in Qalqilya | The English general sees my father | His special permit to return home | Simchat Torah in Tel Aviv | We return safely to Tel Aviv | The reception | A deserted Tel Aviv comes back to life | Back to my business | Facing the military administration | Adventures of my son Zadoc | Request for a travel permit | Wagons from Egypt | My meeting with a childhood friend in Alexandria | A meeting with Dr. Eder | Regarding the assistance not extended to the Jews of Sidon | The sugar that got wet | Exhuming my mother's remains

On one of the intermediate days of the Sukkot holiday redemption arrived for the suffering of the miserable émigrés who had been tormented by the tribulations of the World War. Cast far away from their permanent places of residence, they lived in tents and eucalyptus huts without shelter from the arid heat of day or the chill of night.

The propitious event unfolded on that day of rejoicing. Camps of soldiers set out in two long lines, one to the east, the other to the west. As if struck by fate, we stood near the village, looking into the distance and wondering: Which army is that? Had the end to the World War really come, and had the English army arrived to declare liberation to the tormented people? Or was this the Turkish army running for its life from the front and it most certainly would not show mercy to those encountered on its way.

We decided to enter our homes and shut ourselves in. Utter silence reigned in the village. Only Arab spies moved around outdoors to keep track of the situation. All day and all night the army was on the move, although its sound was coming from far away, beyond the hills, and we were unable to see its face clearly. But while we were still closed up in our homes, the people of the village called to us to come outside because the army was composed of English, French, Australian, and other soldiers.

When I went outside, I saw two officers approaching us on horseback, with two soldiers right behind. One of the officers spoke to me in Hebrew, to my utter joy. I asked him if we could return to Tel Aviv, but his response was negative because the roads were filled with military traffic and there was currently no passage for civilians.

One of the officers was holding a map and studying the road network. The officers called for the *mukhtar*s to come out and informed them that henceforth they were to comply with their orders: if any Turkish, Austrian, or German soldiers were hiding in the village, they were to immediately disclose their location. The *mukhtar*s replied that not a single man from the enemy army still remained in the village. Then they stretched out telephone wires and erected tents from each station to the telephone machine, and they warned the *mukhtar*s that anyone who dared cut a wire would be punished with death. That night, we could hear the sound of the army advancing beyond the hills. Our joy knew no bounds, for we knew that our redemption was at hand.

I began to concern myself with our return to Tel Aviv. It was difficult to secure pack animals to ride on, so we decided that everyone who was healthy would walk on foot, while the older men and women would ride. And so it was. The entire group of émigrés returned from its exile together. We the healthy walked on foot, the older men and women and the children rode, and the youth supervised the animals transporting the possessions.

When we reached Qalqilya, I kept all the baggage outside the city and entered the city alone in order to ascertain if it was possible to return to Jaffa. I presented myself to the military general there and requested that he permit us to return to the city of our residence. All of my pleading was useless. The general was adamant in his refusal and said that given the situation it was forbidden to go to Jaffa. Only in another two weeks would it be possible to open the roads to civilians. When I explained to him that all of the migrants were located right outside the city with their possessions, he dispatched the Egyptian officer who was translating between us to ascertain if I was telling the truth. When the officer returned and reported to the general what he had seen with his own eyes, the general commanded that all of us be brought into the old *saraya*, where we settled in, albeit in very crowded conditions with a family in almost every corner. In the meantime, Mr. Rabbi Yehuda Grazowski and other fellow Jews arrived from the north, and our temporary quarters became a way station.

We remained in Qalqilya in anticipation of the opening of the road to Tel Aviv. On the second day of our stay there, my late father sat on a chair on the balcony of the *saraya* building, reading a book.

Coincidentally, the English general of the staff based in Qalqilya walked past and saw a handsome, patriarchal gentleman with a white beard, engrossed in the book he was reading. The general paused next to him and asked those close by: "Who is this old man?" I immediately approached him, and through his Egyptian interpreter, I explained that he was my father, and the head of our family. I then explained to him about the tremendous suffering our father had gone through, along with our entire family, and what we had experienced from the time of our expulsion from Jaffa and in exile far from our home and possessions. I briefly told him about only a small portion of the adventures our family had experienced during the war. I begged the general to show mercy on our family and grant us permission to return home as soon as possible.

The general, who listened very attentively to my entire story, which evidently left a strong impression on him, nevertheless replied that due to military reasons, with the army still on the march, he could not issue a general permit to the entire family to return home. However, he would order that a permit be issued immediately exclusively to this handsome, elderly man, the head of the family, who could set out for home without interference to rest there in his old age. He would send him that very day in a military vehicle. With great difficulty, I was somehow able to persuade the general to also grant a permit to my two sons, his grandsons, who would accompany the elderly man on his way home to Tel Aviv. The general consented to my insistent request, and they were also given a permit.

The permit that he issued enabling the safe passage of the elderly man and the grandsons-escorts was written explicitly emphasizing that the military checkpoints along the road to Jaffa were not to obstruct his passage homeward in any way. And thanks to this permit the older man and his escorts were not delayed even by the military intelligence unit that operated out of the Feingold Houses near Jaffa, at which anyone entering

Jaffa or Tel Aviv was forced to spend a day until it became known who this person was and that there were no suspicions about him.

Upon his arrival in Tel Aviv—as my father later told the story, with joy—it was the eve of Simchat Torah. Given his fatigue from the exile, the journey, and his illness, he did not go to synagogue. On the day of Simchat Torah, when he saw the Jews of Jaffa and Tel Aviv marching in the streets in great joy with the Torah scrolls going from one synagogue to the next, he stood on the balcony of his home looking at them with joy and exuberance over both his return home and the joy of the holiday.

When his acquaintances from Tel Aviv and Jaffa saw him standing on the balcony, they came upstairs and actually lifted him in their arms, dancing and rejoicing with him for hours on end. And there was great rejoicing that my late father had returned from exile to his home in Tel Aviv.

But we ourselves spent another few days in Qalqilya. We did not stay long in the old *saraya*, but these few days of anticipation were more difficult for us than the whole period of exile, for we were impatiently waiting to return to our city. Every so often, the officer would come to count us and verify that all of us were still there. Finally, an automobile was sent for us, and the order was to send only the elderly in the car. The car filled with the elderly and two young men whom I sent to protect them.

A few days later, the remaining émigrés arrived safely in Tel Aviv. On a clear day at four o'clock in the afternoon in the year 1918, we entered our beloved city riding donkeys.[383] Our entrance was as a group, and the people of Tel Aviv received us with cheers and applause. This left a strong impression. Once again, we were in Tel Aviv, after much hardship and distress, suffering and torture. We encountered friends and acquaintances from every side, with warm handshakes and loyal brotherly blessings from every direction. Once again, we met with those close to us whom fate had cast so far away from us. On our way home, our hearts burst with happiness at seeing that Tel Aviv, so desolate and grieving only yesterday, was today noisy with its sons who had returned to it.

That same evening, I was invited to attend a meeting of the commu-

---

383. The deportation of the Chelouche family from Tel Aviv lasted seventeen months. They stayed in Petah Tikva for about eight months, in Qalqilya for about three and a half months, and in Kfar Jammal for about five and a half months.

nity council as one of the returning public servants for whom a warm reception was held. Heartfelt speeches were given, and refreshments and sweets were served. It was an hour of elation of the spirit and true satisfaction of the soul.

Immediately after I returned to Tel Aviv from exile, I began keeping track of the situation and I learned that the main business was in clothing and food supply. The émigrés had returned home naked, barefoot, and hungry, and they were buying clothes and food. It became clear to me that we would not be able to develop our building supply business for now, and I therefore decided to sell clothing and food staples.

The same day after the reception, I went into the city. I entered the government offices, and I found there my family friend Yusuf Farwaji[384] (Christian) and asked him to introduce me to the director of the Intelligence Office and translate for me. He fulfilled my request. I explained to the director that I was a native of Jaffa and had spent the past year and a half wandering around the country, and that we had suffered a great deal of hardship and misadventure. My request spoken to him was such:

"I have today arrived in Tel Aviv from expulsion and exile, along with the thirty-seven members of my family. I have in my possession a lira and a half. Being a merchant since my youth until this very day, I would like to conduct my business. I have heard that there is no business these days outside of food staples, and these items are found in Egypt. I have also learned that from the moment when a travel permit to Egypt is requested, the government issues it only after two months. I have also heard that in order to acquire wagons for transporting the merchandise you have to pay fifty-lira *baksheesh* for each wagon. If that is really the case, then I would say there is a real fear that we could die of starvation here. We suffered a great deal and we waited impatiently for the arrival of the English. We request our salvation right away."

I requested from him:

a. That he grant me a travel permit to Egypt;
b. That he place at my disposal fifty wagons for transporting merchandise.

---

384. The Farwaji family had an import-export company that was established in 1863. By the mid-1920s they were also working as shipping and insurance agents, citrus traders, and manufacturer agents.

I also used the opportunity to request a special permit for the transfer of my late mother's remains from Kafr Jammal, in order to give her a Jewish burial in our city.

The director listened to my words and took notes on my request. He asked me to wait there while he went into a second room. According to Farwaji, the director went to research details about our family in their books. After a while, he emerged, shook my hand, and asked me to accompany him to the government house. When we entered, the governor was speaking on the telephone. I waited a few minutes until he finished, and then the director started speaking with the governor. The interpreter Mr. Tamari[385] (from one of the respected Christian families in Jaffa) was called in. As soon as he crossed the threshold of the governor's room and saw me, he became very excited, and called out, "How are you, Mr. Chelouche? Thank God we are again seeing each other, alive and well!" and proceeded to embrace and kiss me. On seeing this, the governor asked Tamari for more details about me. He informed the governor that our family was one of the old families in Jaffa, and "this Mr. Chelouche is the father of Zadoc, who worked with us."

And how had my son Zadoc come to be a clerk working with the English in Jaffa? This story, and what my son went through before arriving at that point, are worthy of inclusion in this memoir of my life and the life of my family.

As I already mentioned, upon the initial entry of the English to Petah Tikva, when we went with our possessions to Tel Aviv and returned to Petah Tikva only intending to spend a final Sabbath there, but because of the sudden exit of the English we were compelled to remain there and could no longer return to Jaffa, at the time, the only member of our family who remained in Jaffa was my son Zadoc. He was forced to remain in Jaffa and Tel Aviv because the lines of the battlefront were then drawn between Jaffa and Tel Aviv, and Petah Tikva.[386] And so it happened that we were torn apart from our son for over five months, fearing for his

---

385. This was possibly Emile Tamari (1891–?), who was a tourist *dragoman* (translator) before the war. Tamari was also a member of the Barkai/Shafaq Masonic lodge.

386. The British army occupied Jaffa in late November 1917, crossing into the southern parts of Palestine from the Sinai. In December 1917, Jerusalem also surrendered to the British. Yet after these successes, the British offensive came to a standstill until the second half of 1918.

well-being, as we did not know a thing about his condition throughout this entire period.

Our son was also in the situation of not knowing of the status of his parents and family, as he did not know of their fate behind the Turkish lines. Were they alive or had they all been killed, Heaven forbid, by the Turkish army? This state of not knowing about the situation of his family and his parents was of even greater concern to him than his own life. He was completely isolated, living in a deserted city, with nothing to do and no livelihood through which he might support himself. As for my son Zadoc's life during those months in Jaffa and the reason for his incarceration until he became a clerk in the government house, my son told us the following details:

After wandering without a source of income in the militarized city of Jaffa, and since he had all the keys to all of our warehouses and homes in Jaffa and Tel Aviv, he would open up one of the houses or warehouses and find in it a few items that he could then sell to sustain himself.

The English army, which was on guard, noticed this young man walking around with many keys in his hands, unlocking this house and that warehouse here and there, and taking some items out to sell. This was extremely suspicious behavior in their eyes. They suspected him of being a thief who was stealing the merchandise of others by means of keys he had made especially for this purpose, and they arrested him and threw him into prison.

In prison, my son asked the soldiers to bring him before the governor of the city to whom he would explain his situation. His request was fulfilled, and they brought him before the governor of the city. He explained to the governor who he was, and how it came about that he was living alone in Jaffa, without any source of livelihood, and how he was compelled to enter his family's homes and warehouses and remove different items from them in order to sell them and live off the proceeds.

The governor stopped him with his question, wondering about the large number of keys in Zadoc's possession, which was the source of their suspicion. My son responded that he had even more keys in his possession—that these were only the keys to our family's homes and warehouses, and our possessions in them, all of which belonged to our family. Zadoc went on to explain to the governor about our family's expulsion into exile and our terrible suffering there, and how a long time had passed without him knowing if they were alive or dead. He became so emotional in his retelling of these matters regarding the fate of his beloved family that he began to cry and his throat choked up, and it became difficult for him to speak before the governor, due to the tears that burst forth from his heart to his eyes—the tears of a son devoted to his family.

When the governor saw his state, and upon listening very closely to this very moving rendering of his family's fate on the other side of the Turkish front lines, he immediately ordered to summon a few residents from Jaffa in order to confirm the truth of his testimony. Once the governor had heard from the notables of Jaffa (who had by then already returned from exile) that my son was speaking the truth, the governor did two important things for my son. The second thing was even more important than the first, because by doing so he truly revived my son's soul. The first thing was to appoint him as a secretary in the military government headquarters, on the clerical staff. This position came with a monthly salary with which he would be able to support himself respectably. But the second thing the governor did for him, the bigger and more important one, was to bring him periodic news and updates about his parents and the rest of his family in exile on the other side of the Turkish front lines, that they were alive and healthy and well. In doing so, the governor brought my son a genuine sign of life.

And just how did the governor, on the English front, know about our situation on the Turkish front? It was by means of a spy, a Turk. And this is how it unfolded: The English army had captured a Muslim Turkish spy named Darwish, who had crossed the Turkish lines in order to spy on the English. When this spy was being interrogated by the governor, he mentioned the Chelouche family, whom he had seen on the other side of the front in several places, conveying that they were healthy and well. As the governor was aware of my son Zadoc's great concern for his family's fate, after the spy was convicted and given a death sentence, he did not carry out the sentence until after the spy could be brought to my son Zadoc's office, giving Zadoc an opportunity to question him and learn more details. Thus, my son was updated on the situation of his family, whom the spy had seen alive only a short while beforehand, healthy and well.

When the governor heard my request for fifty wagons, he smiled and chuckled, and said to me: "If that is the case, Mr. Chelouche, the lira and a half you have in your possession will not be enough to fill fifty wagons with merchandise."

I replied that the governor should not be worried about that, for I was known in Egypt and I would be able to fill all the wagons.

The governor informed me that he was prepared to fulfill my request. But in regard to my petition to transfer my mother's body, he advised me to wait until after my return from Egypt. In the meantime, the government would consult with its department of health and would issue a directive to the *mukhtar*s of the village to look after the grave and ensure that no damage would come to it.

"But now," the governor told me regarding my remaining requests, "it is half past nine, today's train to Egypt left at eight o'clock, and you must wait until tomorrow." He asked me to wait, and after a few minutes I was issued a permit to travel to Egypt, as well as an order for fifty wagons to be placed at my disposal, exactly as I had requested. I expressed my gratitude to the governor and to the director and parted, giving thanks.

The journey by train was extremely difficult. The tracks had not been repaired and there were no lights on the trains, so we traveled in the dark and with a great deal of jolting. I arrived in Egypt extremely tired. I entered the home of my sister Sultana, the wife of Yesha'ayahu Louria,[387] and her joy was immeasurable, as she believed that I had perished. I comforted Sultana on the death of our mother. After eating to my heart's content followed by a nap, some friends of mine from before the war visited me, among them Mr. Yosef 'Antebi.[388] He had been a clerk at the Anglo-Palestine Company. During the war he made a good living in Egypt and had amassed some savings.

After telling him how our family was doing, he informed me that he wanted to contact me and consult with me about commercial ties. I told him that I had come to Egypt with the aim of purchasing merchandise. [He asked,] "But how will you transport the goods when the government does not provide wagons?" I responded that I was in possession of a letter addressed to the central military office in Egypt. He was astounded that I had been able to procure such a letter.

387. Sultana Louria (1889–1943) was deported to Egypt in 1915 together with her husband, Yesha'ayahu, and their son, Yeroham (age 1).

388. 'Antebi had served as an assistant to the British vice-consul in Jaffa, Haim Amzalak, for some years. We have transliterated his name precisely rather than writing it in the latinized form used by Albert Antébi; it is unclear what the men's relationship was, if any.

The following day, we went together to the military office. A huge crowd of people was waiting outside, and so as not to waste any time I presented my letter to a soldier, who then handed it to its intended recipient. A few minutes later, he emerged and called out: "Who here is Yosef Eliyahu Chelouche?"

I walked in with Mr. 'Antebi, and the director of the office asked me if we wanted to use all fifty wagons all at the same time. We told him that we did want all fifty wagons but preferred to receive them a few at a time.

The following day we received twelve wagons, in which we shipped rice, sugar, onions, and matches.

For my business I traveled to Alexandria, where I met with my childhood friend Mr. Hazan, with whom I had attended Zaki Cohen's school back in 1886. I cannot describe how happy we were to be together again after the days of rage of the World War.

In Alexandria, I met with Senator Joseph Bek Picciotto.[389] He invited me to a meeting attended by Dr. Eder,[390] who at the time was the chairman of the Zionist Commission,[391] but due to my numerous appointments I was unable to accept the invitation. Mr. Joseph Bek Picciotto asked me if it was true that the Jews of Sidon had been left to fend for themselves without any assistance from the Immigration Committee, even though the community had issued a call for help on more than one occasion. I replied that to our embarrassment, that was the case. The Jews of Sidon had been left without assistance, despite having requested help from the Immigration Committee on more than one occasion. They had also sent a delegation, but their voice was a voice calling

---

389. Picciotto (1872–1938) was appointed senator by King Fuad in 1924. He was a leading businessman in the trading and textile import industry, and he served as a key Jewish communal leader in Alexandria.

390. David Eder (1865–1936) was a British psychoanalyst who was invited to serve on the Zionist Commission established in 1918. Eder spent four years in Palestine and sat on the Zionist Executive from 1921–1927, first in Jerusalem and then in London. He was acting chairman of the Executive at the time of the 1921 riots, and he was criticized in the Haycraft report for his maximalist Zionist vision.

391. The Zionist Commission was established in early 1918 by Chaim Weizmann, president of the Zionist Federation of Great Britain and the key party responsible for securing the Balfour Declaration. Over three years the semiofficial ZC played an instrumental role advising the British government over the terms and policies of the Mandate for Palestine.

in the desert. I spoke up on behalf of the Sidon Jews more than once, but my battle was ineffective.

When Mr. Picciotto heard that, his heart filled with bitterness, and he asked me if it was still possible to do something on behalf of our brethren. I responded that it was not only a duty, but it was a necessity that we help them immediately. And when I returned to Tel Aviv from Egypt, I learned that a delegation had been sent to Sidon to distribute funds to the Jews there. The members of the delegation included Rabbi 'Uziel and Jacques Bek Mosseri.[392]

In the meantime, a telegram arrived from my late brother Mr. Avraham of blessed memory, announcing that all the goods that I had sent had been received and had already been sold. He asked me to send him other goods: pistachios, seeds of the sort sold by the Yemenites and others, all kinds of thread for sewing, and pepper and cinnamon of the type sold by the Arabs in the city. I decided to consult with Mr. 'Antebi.

From time to time, various merchants called on me to make me all sorts of offers. The middlemen began to disturb my peace, asking me to sell them my rights to the government wagons, but I was firm on this point: I would not cheat the government that had shown such compassion to me and awarded me this right.

One textile merchant in particular began to pay me visits, one of my best friends named Bigio. He proposed that I become his agent for the export of manufactured textile goods, or that I be his partner. I informed him that I would have to consult with my brother. The following day, just as I was sitting down to write my brother about the merchant Bigio's offer, the merchant Toledano came to me and told me: "I have learned that you are going into the textile business. You are obliged to trade with me. I am willing to set you the same conditions that others have offered."

I offered him the same response that I had given to Mr. Bigio. When we left, I began to wonder what I would do if my brother answered me in the affirmative. Both these businessmen were my friends to the same degree, and both of them were honest and fair, and if we purchased from one of them we would be sinning against the other. I therefore decided not to enter into any arrangement with either man, and I dropped the matter without even informing my brother.

---

392. Mosseri (1884–1934) was a member of an influential Sephardi family in Cairo. He was a banker and communal leader, as well as a Zionist activist.

I was invited to lunch at the 'Antebi home. As we sat down to eat, I voiced my complaint that the food prepared in Egypt did not taste as good to me as in the Land of Israel, due to there being no olive oil in Egypt, where the food was fried or cooked in oil prepared from cotton or flaxseed. And then I had the idea that it might be worthwhile importing a quantity of olive oil to Egypt and selling it there at a good price. And that is what I did. I sent a telegram to my brother, who then shipped me 1,600 cans of oil. Many of the cans were damaged and the oil spilled, but some of them arrived whole and were sold immediately. I ordered a second shipment, and this time I cautioned my brother to stack the cans better, and they arrived whole. The oil was sold in its entirety at a profit to landlords from Damascus, Aleppo, Mesopotamia, etc., who were living in Egypt but had never grown accustomed to the artificial oil.

After some time, I left Egypt and returned to the Land of Israel. I had to consult with my brother on the future development of our business. In the meantime, changes were taking place in the government. The government had appointed a special officer as a commissioner of trade, Mr. Williamson.[393] Now it was simply impossible to take a single step without receiving a license from the government.

Nevertheless, all the requests that we submitted to him were approved. I received affirmative responses to our requests, even as many requests filed by other entrepreneurs were disregarded.[394]

One day, we received a shipment of eight wagonloads of sugar. It was pouring rain, and the sugar got wet. The porters carried the 1,600 sacks of sugar into three warehouses, and my heart tightened out of sorrow to see how severely the rain had damaged the sugar. Most of the sacks were wet, and the sugar had either melted or solidified into chunks. I could not take my mind off this catastrophe, but I could think of no possible solution. I knew the government would not take any responsibility for the disaster, because it was a military train, it was still wartime, and we were living under a military regime.

But then a respected Arab merchant from Syria approached me and

---

393. G. W. Williamson was a judge in the Sudan courts of justice and the former head of the land registry in the Sudan. In 1919, he was placed in charge of Palestine's land registry issues.

394. The Haycraft report (1921) identified disproportionate benefits (permits, travel passes) issued to Jewish merchants over Arab merchants in this period, much like Chelouche benefited from.

offered that I sell him all of the sugar at full price based on the original weight—on condition that I secure a permit for him to ship the sugar to the cities in Syria. I hesitated, unsure if this was even in my power, since the government was forbidding small packages of food staples from being shipped to Syria and was confiscating them. So how would it permit such a large shipment of merchandise? Nevertheless, the Arab merchant insisted: "What do you have to lose? Try petitioning the government, and maybe you'll succeed . . ."

Left with no other choice, I entered Officer Williamson's office. Many people waited outside his door. I, too, stood outside looking at his face, until he noticed me and called me into his office. I told him what had happened. He smiled at hearing my request and said: "The government will by no means be able to consent to your request." Nevertheless, he did express a wish to see the merchandise with his own eyes. We walked over to the warehouses together, and he counted the sacks of sugar. He was shocked to realize the tremendous loss I was liable to suffer and then walked with me over to the governor's office, where he said some favorable things about me. I was then granted the permit on an exceptional basis—on condition that I not reveal it to anyone. I drew up the list of cities in Syria to which the merchandise was to be shipped, submitted it to the government, and received the sought-after permit. I handed the permit over to the Arab merchant, who then paid me the full cost of the sugar, without me losing a single cent.

Once I had an opportunity to rest from all these business dealings, I began to apply my energies to moving my mother's remains from Kafr Jammal to Tel Aviv. The governor with whom I had previously conducted negotiations on this matter had left the city, and a new governor had arrived in his place. I therefore decided to appeal to Mr. Tamari, the secretary to the governor, who was fully aware of the details related to the issue. When I visited him, he informed me that throughout the period of my stay in Egypt, negotiations had taken place between the government and the Ministry of Health. There had been an exchange of correspondence, issues arose, and answers were addressed to those issues. The permit was eventually issued, with some conditions.

I went to the Ministry of Health and received directives from the government physician there. The following day, we traveled to Kafr Jammal, two doctors and I, one a civilian and the other an army doctor. I brought along a zinc coffin and a wooden coffin. Also with us were a blacksmith and ten men for the *minyan*.³⁹⁵ We spent the night in Kafr Jammal. In the morning, we opened the grave and were astounded to see that my mother's remains were well preserved, even though ten months had passed. The body was placed in the zinc coffin and then into the wooden coffin. Then the blacksmith sealed it well, but only after all of the requisite markings had been placed on it. We set out on our way. The residents of the village, from young to old, accompanied us all the way to Qalqilya. When we arrived in Tel Aviv, the entire family as well as many of our friends and acquaintances were waiting by our house, having come to bestow this final honor on the departed. We unloaded the coffin by the house, and after reciting the *kaddish*,³⁹⁶ we conveyed the coffin in a religious ceremony to the cemetery. I was finally able to rest easy, knowing that my mother had found her perfect rest. "May her soul be bound up in the everlasting life of the nation."³⁹⁷ Amen.

---

395. The required quorum of adult Jewish men necessary for some religious rituals, such as funerals.

396. The mourners' prayer.

397. This phrase originated in 1 Samuel 25:29.

CHAPTER 25 *Following the Balfour Declaration, Days of Light and Shadow*

Days of work and creativity | Sweeping plans to rebuild | Me'ir Dizengoff's role in the rebuilding | The visit to the Land of Israel by Louis Brandeis | His interest in the Arab question | His questions and our answers | What Brandeis said to us | The Arabs awaken against us | An unseen hand | Preparations for a major countrywide demonstration against us | The demonstration in Jaffa is canceled | Disturbances in Jerusalem during Passover | The disturbances leave a strong impression on my father | His heart is broken by the disaster | My father's death | Residents of the city and the Arab villages come to mourn him | My father's will | Obtaining kushans *for the property owners | The government's stumbling blocks | My father's will comes to my assistance | I obtain the desired* kushans

The days of work and creativity had arrived. The Balfour Declaration struck deep roots in the hearts of our people and began to chart a new line of action for us. A national reawakening was beginning. Efforts were made to expand the scope of work underway in the city and in the village, building and creating, with all due vigor and strength as befits a period of creative endeavor. Indeed, these public figures began to work as energetically as possible. A constant flurry of meetings was held, new committees were elected for education, health, social welfare, and so forth. A concentrated effort was made to build and broaden the power base of the Tel Aviv council, and the organization of the local communal council.

I, too, was drawn to all these positions that were on the horizon and would be brought to fruition. The trailblazer in all these efforts was the trusted public figure of the Hebrew *yishuv* and the builder of Tel Aviv, Mr. Me'ir Dizengoff.

In those days Louis Brandeis[398] arrived from America to visit the Land of Israel. He invited a few public figures to meet with him, including Mr. Yehoshuʻa Abrevaya[399] and the author of this memoir. He asked us, what did we know about the natives of the land, including their lifestyle, character, and any other traits? We explained to him that the Muslims in Palestine constituted a people unlike any other. They did not harbor any hatred for us. The simple Arab masses were extremely innocent. One needed to know how to act with them and how to live with them.

Over the course of half an hour we told him a number of facts, through his interpreter de Sola Pool,[400] about the life of the *yishuv* and the attitude of the neighbors since its beginning, which strengthened our ambitions. But our new Jewish brothers who arrived from Europe did not know how to act with them, and as a result [the Arabs'] attitude toward us changed.

When we parted ways, Brandeis said the following: "I'm very pleased to have heard from you such accurate and true statements, which I have been hoping to hear. They have found their way into my heart, and I am therefore grateful to you. I must tell you that I am inclined to embrace your accurate vision, one that I have not yet heard from others. I hope that we will have an opportunity to see one another again."

Some hidden hand was busy weaving plots and intrigue. The same days that Brandeis was visiting our country, he found that the nerves of the Jewish community here were quite stressed, their spirits were inflamed, and it was a time of worry. You could feel that something was happening and rising to the surface. The spokesmen for the Arab people were the *effendi*s, who themselves felt that the ground of their ruling over the enslaved and submissive peasants was being pulled out from

---

398. Brandeis was an associate justice on the US Supreme Court from 1916–1939. He visited Palestine in July 1919; en route, he stopped in Paris at the peace talks to firmly advocate on behalf of the Zionist demands for turning Palestine into the Jewish national home.

399. Abrevaya (1878–1933) was born in the Dardanelles and educated in the AIU school there, after which he taught in Gallipoli. In 1904, he immigrated to Jaffa to work for the JCA. He was fluent in Turkish and French.

400. David de Sola Pool (1885–1970) was an American rabbi from a prominent British Sephardi family. De Sola Pool and his wife went to Palestine in 1919 to carry out relief work for the JDC and the WZO.

under them. These *effendi*s incited the masses to demonstrate against the Balfour Declaration, and to protest that it gave the right to establish a national home for the Jews in Palestine. And the Arab masses were open to these ideas and decided to hold demonstrations all over the country. This effort was aided by the Arab press, and especially the newspaper *Falastin*, which spread lies and libel.[401]

One of those days, the Zionist Commission telephoned from Jerusalem and informed the provisional council in Tel Aviv that the Arabs had decided to demonstrate throughout the country, and that we should ensure that the Jews were far from any potentially dangerous places. The provisional council convened an urgent meeting that same evening, to which I myself was invited in order to give advice. In the middle of the numerous debates, which stretched late into the night, I decided to accede to the request of a few of my friends, and I went into the city. I went to the necessary places, and I asked one of the Arab leaders in Jaffa to persuade his friends not to hold the demonstration the next day. But he said that it would not be possible to cancel the demonstration, which was to be held all across the country. He did promise me, however, that nothing bad would happen to the Jews; they would demonstrate quietly and peacefully.

I said to him, "Prove your bravery to me. Even if they have declared that the demonstrations should be held throughout the country, do what you can to ensure that no demonstration is held in Jaffa. Remember that it is your friends who are asking this of you."

The Arab leader thought for a moment and then said to me: "If that is what you want, I will immediately send my brother and brother-in-law in your coach to some of my friends, and I will invite them to come to my house tomorrow morning before they begin organizing the demonstration." We rode into the heart of the city; they set out on their mission, and I returned to Tel Aviv. By then, the assembly had ended and there was no one around. I was forced to go home, and in the morning, I informed Mr. Dizengoff and the rest of the leaders that the demonstration in Jaffa would not take place, and it was not worth saying anything to the

---

401. Both the Arabic and Hebrew press played critical roles among their respective nationalist movements during this time; both occasionally published misinformation and false reports, whether due to journalistic negligence or to a politically motivated intention of misleading their readers.

Jewish public, in order to avoid alarming them for no reason. However, the public who heard was full of worry.

No one went down into the city that morning before ten o'clock, but when it became evident that the Arabs were carrying out their lives as usual, their shops were open and they were bringing their merchandise for sale to Tel Aviv, the Jews began to go down into the city, each one to his work. No demonstration took place. And even those demonstrations that were held elsewhere in the country went off in an orderly and peaceable fashion, and no incident occurred against the Hebrew *yishuv*.

Nevertheless, the open incitement against the Jews by our true haters did strike roots in the hearts of the Arab masses: during the intermediate days of Passover in 1920, the rumors spread about the pogrom that had been perpetrated in Jerusalem.[402] My late father, who was a broken and shattered man following the World War, was unable to restrain himself in view of the terrible tragedy that occurred to our brothers in the city that was the capital of our glory. What happened there was so very heart-wrenching to him that it simply brought about his death. Returning home from a visit to my sister Jamila who was mourning her late husband, he learned about the bloody riots in Jerusalem, and before he could even open the front door, he crumpled to the floor and died.

None of us was at home. By the time we did arrive, it was too late, and his soul rose up to the heavens in a state of purity. Jews and non-Jews from all over the country attended our father's funeral, and all through the seven days of mourning they did not cease to come and comfort me, in particular the sons of the Arab villages who came to mourn our father.

These were difficult and bitter days for the Hebrew *yishuv*. The Arabs were incited and agitated, and my heart told me that any day now, a terrible catastrophe would befall us. For that reason, I felt compelled to desecrate the days of mourning, and on the basis of an exemption granted by the chief rabbinate that was brought to me by Mr. Dizengoff, I went into the city to act on behalf of the *yishuv*, partly in consideration of the fact that the situation called for a consolidation of forces.

402. Demonstrations in favor of Faysal, king of Syria, and against the Balfour Declaration in April 1920 coincided with the annual Nebi Musa pilgrimage, when thousands of villagers from around the country convened in Jerusalem. The demonstration on 4 April 1920 turned into a riot, over the course of which 9 people were killed (5 of them Jews), and almost 250 people were wounded (the vast majority Jews).

FIGURE 25.1. *Aharon Chelouche on the balcony of his son Ya'akov's home in Tel Aviv on 11 Rothschild Boulevard, shortly before his death in 1920. Chelouche Family Collection.*

Following the death of my father of blessed memory, in the year 1920, as well as the following year, our family—and mainly myself—worked energetically to fulfill the will of our late father in regard to acquiring *kushan*s for residents of the neighborhoods that he founded.

The veteran residents of Jaffa knew well that my late father was an enthusiastic Lover of Zion in practice, who always aspired to expand the Hebrew *yishuv* of Jaffa as much as possible. My late father had purchased several large plots of land and divided them into hundreds of individual plots. He sold these plots at low cost, at affordable monthly payments, to poor people who settled the land and built the various neighborhoods in Jaffa. These individuals, who belonged to the lower economic class, built themselves small homes in which they lived. Most of them, none of them, never even considered the idea of acquiring a *kushan* in their own name. Some of them had never even completed paying the low purchase price for the land.

My late father, who dedicated heart and soul to the *yishuv* and to the sons of the *yishuv*, and who concerned himself in particular with the poorer members of our people, made a special, and sacred, request to us in his will. In one section of the will, he asked his sons to endeavor with all our power to acquire *kushan*s, approximately 740 in number, for all those who had purchased plots of land from him, even if they still owed us money for the land, which was the case in a few instances.

We, his children, began doing everything to realize this final wish of our late father, which we considered sacred to us. Because I was closer to these sorts of matters, it fell upon me to fulfill our father's wish as quickly as possible.

Previously, none of us had been aware of the enormous difficulty of realizing this task; we could not have imagined how difficult it would be to achieve. We were certain that the matter would be easily resolved. But in the course of the great deal of work we devoted to the matter, we realized that we would have to start from scratch: measuring the plots again, reproducing the parcellation plans, drawing up new maps and lists from various lists, which made it more difficult to complete the task. We prepared a complete dossier devoted to the matter, which with every passing day grew thicker with various papers and documents according to the demands of the *tabu*.

I also made the effort of assembling all the contracts that were made at different times between my late father and the purchasers, by means of which I hoped to calculate the exact amounts that my father received for the land, and on the basis of this cost to calculate the tax assessment, which had been much lower than they were now.

My tireless efforts on this matter persisted for over a year. Throughout this entire period, I adhered to the instructions of the director of the *tabu* in Jaffa, Mr. 'Araman,[403] who always listened to me and explained to me which additional papers and documents I needed to produce. I complied with all the requests based on his instructions.

One year later, after I had completed preparation and filing of all the papers and certificates, I asked this clerk when we might be finished with the whole procedure. He replied that only now would he send all the papers and documents to Jerusalem, and only after he received an order from the main office would he be able to approve the matter.

And then, only a week later, the *tabu* clerk in Jaffa summoned me to the office and informed me that he had received an order from Jerusalem on the basis of which he could move ahead with the entire matter, but only if I agreed to these conditions:

a. Assess the plots based on their present-day value.
b. Assess the buildings constructed on the plots based on their present-day value.
c. Have all the buyers and sellers come to the *tabu* office together.

When I heard the *tabu* clerk explaining the harsh conditions stipulated by the government in Jerusalem, I truly panicked, as I knew it would be impossible to meet these conditions. I knew that if the government assessed the plots and buildings at their present-day values, then the tax assessments would be immeasurably higher—truly shocking amounts that the residents of these poor neighborhoods would by no means be able to pay. Then, all the work that I had put into the initiative for over a year would be wasted.

I was also aware of the great difficulty presented by condition C, which called for all the buyers to appear together with the sellers at the *tabu*

---

403. Michel 'Araman (1887–?) was a 1908 graduate of the American University in Beirut and member of the Barkai/Shafaq Masonic lodge who worked as a fruit importer (probably oranges) and merchant in Liverpool before the World War. A relative, Georges 'Araman, helped form a joint Arab-Jewish orange export cooperative in Jaffa in 1910. In 1920, Michel 'Araman was appointed as a land registry officer.

office. Most of the buyers had died long ago, and it would not be easy to gather together all of their heirs. Not knowing what to do, I asked the director of the *tabu* office in Jaffa for his advice. He said that he would be going up to Jerusalem in a few days' time and suggested that I go with him. There, at the government offices, we might get an idea of how the issue could be resolved. I listened to his advice and went to Jerusalem.

On the same day that 'Araman went there, I paid a visit to the chief director of the *tabu* office.[404] I complained to him about how long the process had taken and explained that I had already done everything a human being is capable of doing, and that there was nothing more that could possibly be done. I emphasized and explained to him that in the event that the matter was not resolved, all of us would lose. People would not have *kushan*s for their landholdings and their homes, and neither would the government be able to levy taxes on them. The director responded to my claims and explained that that was the law, and that he could not diverge even one inch from the law.

At that point, I stood up and said to him, "Sir! I understand that law is law, but the dry law was passed by a human being who has a brain in his skull and a heart in his chest, in order to interpret the law according to his reason, and the need to apply the law in the real world. These dry laws were not meant to be applied by someone who does not know how to interpret them in a normal manner, blankly, and not for my benefit, sir, who must understand how to interpret the law in real life."

I concluded by pointing out in regard to the third condition that according to Turkish law it was only necessary for the seller to come to the *tabu* office and testify that he had sold the property in accordance with such-and-such conditions; the buyer did not have to appear.

Apparently, my brazen remarks about his duty influenced him against me and against the entire matter, and he replied angrily and irritably in order to insult me: "I would like to know what you hope to gain in this whole affair. Are you an agent or a middleman? Are you trying to profit from this whole business? And why are you dealing with this matter all alone? Why aren't the buyers handling their own affairs themselves?"

---

404. This was the land registry office in Jerusalem; land registration had been suspended by the Occupied Enemy Territory Administration (OETA) between summer 1918 and summer 1919. The head of the land registry office in 1919–1921 was Frederick Oliver Jones Ongley, a former colonial land official in Cyprus.

I answered without irritation or anger. "Sir! Your question is a good one, and I will tell you why I am the only person handling this complicated matter. I am not an agent and I am not working on commission, nor do I wish to make any profit. In fact, I will almost certainly lose money in this matter. I am simply doing this to fulfill my late father's will, his last wish, which is sacred to his sons, was to acquire the *kushan*s for the buyers, and it is for this sublime and sacred goal that I have been indefatigably working for over a year—in order to fulfill our father's wish, which he made prior to his death."

When the director heard these words, he asked in disbelief and with great curiosity: "Was such a will really left by your father?" I replied, "Yes!" Then the director said to me, "I would like to see it." I asked him to allow me to use his telephone to call without delay the government house in Jaffa, to ask them to have the will sent from my house while I remained here to wait for it. He permitted me to do so. I telephoned my office, and two and a half hours later, the will was brought to Jerusalem by a clerk from our office.

When I brought the will to the director, he called and asked that the Hebrew-speaking clerk from the head *tabu* office, Mr. Moshe Dukhan,[405] the director of land registration, be summoned.

The director asked Dukhan to read aloud the relevant section in my late father's will. And even though the will was handwritten in Hebrew in the Rashi script, Dukhan was nevertheless able to correctly read the relevant section of the will. Among other things, this section included the statement: "My beloved sons, my final request of you is to secure *kushan*s for all those who purchased land from us, even for those who have not yet completed their payment."

When Dukhan finished reading this section of my father's will to the director, the latter rose to his feet and shook my hand and said, with deep feelings of respect: "Now, this whole affair of yours is going to end according to your wishes." He called for 'Araman, who was in his office, and gave him an order to immediately conclude this matter based on the existing certificates and papers, and to do it exactly as Chelouche wants, for now he had great faith in me. And in fact, within a short while after

---

405. Dukhan (1884–1958) was a Russian lawyer who immigrated to Palestine in 1920. From 1921–1936 he worked in the government land office. Dukhan also published books on land law, and he taught law at the Hebrew University.

my return to Jaffa, I concluded all of the details in the Jaffa *tabu*, and with that, I fulfilled our late father's will, each and every word of which was sacred to us.

The government maintained its profound trust in me and used me at several other junctures, including during the term of Samuel as high commissioner,[406] as well as during the days of Lord Plumer.[407] And it is only to avoid an excessive reference to "me" in these events that I choose to skip over these episodes without dwelling on them.

---

406. Samuel served as high commissioner from 1920–1925.

407. Viscount Herbert Plumer (1857–1932) was the second high commissioner in Palestine, serving from 1925–1928.

CHAPTER 26 *Bloody Clashes in Jaffa, May 1921*

*The demonstration of the Hebrew laborers |
May Day | The Arab attack | Helpless | Dizengoff
and I confer with Governor Stirling | An urgent meeting is
called in Tel Aviv | What Nachum Sokolow said to me | Regarding
peace with the Arabs | Who will conduct the negotiations? | I risk
my life going to Jaffa | My meeting with 'Asim Bek, the mayor of
Jaffa | My forceful shouts | A joint meeting with the Arabs |
General Deedes heads the talks | The Arab "leaders" and
the good of the nation | Banin Menahem Messa, the Jew
from Aden | His activity on behalf of building Tel Aviv*

The bloody riots on 1 May 1921 shocked the Hebrew *yishuv* due to the terror and violence of the rioters. The Jewish laborers were celebrating May Day, as per their custom.[408]

The Arabs, who had been incited and riled up with repressed hatred toward the Jews since the Balfour Declaration, barbarously attacked the Jewish laborers and began beating them and shooting at them. News spread throughout the city, and the wounded and dead began arriving in Tel Aviv. The Gymnasium turned into a hospital. Doctors and nurses immediately volunteered to treat the wounded.

I was stunned that the Arabs, with whom we had lived in peace for centuries, dared to brutally attack an entire community, whose sole interest was creation and building. I was completely bewildered and did not know where to turn. Dizengoff and I decided to ride into the city and

---

408. Since 1905, socialist Jews immigrating to Palestine had advocated for workers' rights and a segregated labor market that privileged Jewish workers. A similar May Day parade in 1908 had led to localized clashes in Jaffa. Chelouche was a harsh critic of socialism and the increased role of the socialist parties in the Zionist movement in Palestine, as he writes in the epilogue. The Palestinian press was similarly hostile to the socialist and "Bolshevist" immigrants, as was the British regime.

see Governor Stirling.[409] When we arrived, we found him pacing in the street with a military escort. We asked him to put an end to the bloodshed, and he replied that he had called in reinforcements from Sarafand.

We returned to Tel Aviv. In the meantime, new wounded and dead were brought in. The Gymnasium filled up with victims. At our request to the governor, guards were placed near the homes of Jews living in Arab neighborhoods.[410]

On the second day of the riots, Mr. N. Sokolow passed by my house and saw me standing on the balcony in a state of profound sorrow. He asked what I thought of the disturbances and asked me to go with him to the home of Mr. Dizengoff. From there, we summoned the late Shim'on Rokach and Messrs. Bril,[411] Franck,[412] and Rutenberg[413] to a meeting. They all came.

At the beginning of the meeting N. Sokolow turned to me and asked: "As a native of the land, please tell us your opinion of the situation."

Before answering, I asked him, as a representative of the Zionist Ex-

---

409. Lt. Col. Walter Francis Stirling (1880–1958) served as the colonial governor of the Jaffa district from 1920–1923. Previously he had been a company commander at Gallipoli and served with T. E. Lawrence as a military advisor to Faysal in Damascus from 1918–1919.

410. The British government commission of inquiry report details that there were two sites of rioting and violence in Jaffa: Manshiya, in the north between Jaffa's old city and Tel Aviv, which was the site of the initial demonstration and scuffle that grew into wider violence and looting; and 'Ajami, further south, where a large Jewish immigrants' hostel became a second locus of violence. Jews were the disproportionate victims in the Jaffa riots, with 43 killed and 134 wounded, versus 14 Arabs who were killed and 49 wounded. The British report detailed evidence of acts of indiscriminate violence carried out by both sides, including the murder of women and children (pp. 26–29).

411. Avraham Bril (1866–1925) emigrated from Romania to Zikhron Ya'akov. He studied agronomy in Europe and oversaw several colonies for the JCA and PICA.

412. Henri (Zvi) Franck (1878–1937) was a French engineer who in 1903 began working as the JCA representative in Beirut. After his military service during the war, Franck relocated to Palestine and continued to oversee the Jewish agricultural colonies.

413. Pinhas Rutenberg (1879–1942) was a Russian hydraulic engineer and industrialist who immigrated to Palestine after World War I. During the riots he served as the main Hagana ("Defense" force, an unsanctioned Jewish militia) official in Tel Aviv. That year he won the British concession to electrify Jaffa and Tel Aviv.

ecutive, to report what he knew about the government's position on the disturbances.[414]

N. Sokolow replied: "The local government is against us. The telephone wires have been cut, and it is impossible to make contact with the government."[415]

I then answered him candidly, and said that in my opinion, there was no other way than to make peace with the Arabs. "Then," replied Sokolow, "if that is the case, which of us will go to conduct negotiations with the Arabs?" I suggested myself and announced that I was willing to immediately go down to the city, even though this constituted a danger. Then Mr. N. Sokolow asked me: "How can you go to the city? Don't you fear for your life?" I answered him: "How can I sit here in peace and tranquility when the blood of my brother is spilling like water?"

I immediately left for the city without even stopping at home to inform them, for certainly they would not have permitted me to do such a dangerous thing. I went on foot.

The streets were extremely agitated. A mob of Arabs wandered around the street with clubs in their hands. When I reached the corner of Bustrus and King George streets, an Arab tried to attack me. He was a villager who did not know me. To my relief, an[other] Arab came to my rescue who shouted as loud as he could: "Leave this man alone; he is a native of the land." I asked him to accompany me to the Jaffa municipality. My idea was to meet with three *effendi*s who were the heads of three different tribes. Each of them had his own personal stage and his own special interests, and each of them was, deep down, opposed to

---

414. Later that fall at the Twelfth Zionist Congress in Karlsbad, Sokolow was elected chairman of the Zionist Executive, the successor to the Zionist Commission.

415. The British government's so-called Haycraft report refutes this and criticizes the role of the Tel Aviv committee, stating that "the telephone at Tel Aviv Town Hall was a fount of perpetual false rumours, and the military were kept in continual movement, inquiring into unfounded reports" on the third day of the riots. *Palestine: Disturbances in May, 1921*, 34. One anonymous Jewish reader who was directly involved in the Tel Aviv–Jaffa leadership during the riots wrote to *Palestine* journal to object to the report's censure of the Tel Aviv town council's actions as "utterly unfair," although he acknowledged that based on the chaos of the situation, they inadvertently forwarded incorrect messages. "The Jaffa Riots," *Palestine*, vol. 10, no. 13 (28 January 1922).

the others; in addition, each of them aspired to gain leadership over the masses. Their influence over the Arab public was immense.

I had planned to arrange a joint meeting with all of them, even though I knew in advance that each of them had his own particular interests, but for the purpose of quieting down the incensed mobs it would be better if they appeared united before the masses. But as soon as I entered the municipality, I could see that my entire plan had been turned upside down.

I found the three of them sitting and relaxing and talking amicably among themselves after the lunch meal.[416] On this bitter and wretched day, these three men, who had always hated one another, had now united forces for the sole purpose of hatching schemes against the Jews.

Upon seeing them sitting there, I momentarily stood still. I looked at their serene faces and said: "Oh, now I understand everything. I understand your unity today—you have united at our expense, with your shared intention to destroy us."

I was so agitated at seeing their carefree composure that I exploded from repressed rage: "How can you sit here like this after such a brutal massacre? Don't you bear the human obligation to prevent a disaster and stop the mob from this drunkenness? Tell them: 'Stop the spilling of blood.' Do you think the government is not going to hold you all responsible for this? After all, you, as leaders, had the power in your hands to prevent these sad events. Peace existed between us for many years. My brother has not done you any wrong. How could you incite this wild and bloodthirsty mob against them?"[417]

One of them stood up, agitated, and began screaming at me in a mur-

---

416. In the manuscript, Chelouche identified the three as 'Asim Bek al-Sa'id, Jaffa's mayor, 'Umar al-Bitar, and 'Abdallah al-Dajani. Al-Sa'id was exiled to Anatolia during the war; upon his return to Jaffa, he served as mayor and was also active in the Muslim-Christian Association. Al-Dajani (1871–1927) was a graduate of the Frères school in Jaffa, served as a judge in the Jaffa court, and was a member of the General Council in Jerusalem. In the 1920s, he was a member of the Muslim-Christian Association in Jaffa as well as of the Supreme Muslim Council. Al-Dajani was also briefly a Freemason in the Jaffa lodge, Barkai/Shafaq.

417. According to the British report, the day prior (the first day of the riots) the three men had "offered their services to quieten the people" and had accompanied Lt. Col. Stirling to Manshiya. *Palestine: Disturbances in May, 1921*, 25. The report rejected the claim that the masses were incited to violence by their leaders, and instead listed the longer-term political and economic causes of the violence.

derous tone of voice: "Why did you come to us? For what reason did you come here? You came here to antagonize us; you came here to defend your Bolsheviks. Ah! If you weren't Yosef Chelouche, the son of Aharon Chelouche, a man who is highly respected by all of us, I would kill you right now."

At hearing these words spoken with such intense anger, I cut him off and responded with even greater anger and shouting: "Yes, I have risked my life to come to you. If you want to, kill me, but I came here to show you, the leaders of the people, what you have done to us—as well as to yourselves—through this incitement of neighbor against neighbor." I spoke harshly to them, but they were words of truth—bitter things that were difficult for them to hear from me.

I spoke with pride and in a tone of voice that they would not have thought possible to hear. I exposed all their terrible schemes against us, and how much they themselves would suffer for it. I spoke for a long time, admonishing them, shouting as my blood boiled until I almost felt that I had lost my mind. I shouted with all my might, and they sat there turning pale, their faces completely white.

One of the three men[418] silenced me. He led me outside and said to me: "Don't you know that 'U. A. is ill-tempered? If he wasn't your friend and admirer, he would have killed you. It would be best for you to settle down and calmly conduct negotiations toward peace." I told him: "How can I calm down when with every passing moment more pure and innocent victims are being struck down?"

When I went back in, all three began shouting all at once: "Who is to blame for all the disturbances if not your Bolsheviks, whom you brought here from Moscow?" I told them: "My new brothers who are arriving from abroad have come to build the country and not destroy it. You have not yet had a chance to understand them."

In the end, it was decided that we would set up a joint meeting of Muslims, Christians, and Jews; the leaders of these communities would issue a proclamation requesting that the public remain quiet and calm down, and that peace between the inhabitants should be restored without any threats to life. I proposed to them that before drafting the list of notables who would take part in this gathering, I would go to Tel Aviv to invite my four colleagues who would help compose the list. They agreed

---

418. In the manuscript, Chelouche identified him as al-Dajani.

to this idea. They sent an escort with me to the Tel Aviv border, which would also escort the delegation from Tel Aviv.

When I returned to the meeting and told the others about the idea of a joint meeting, they were all in favor; Dizengoff, Rutenberg, and Bril immediately rode with me into the city. We composed a list of eighty notables from all the communities. We were again escorted back to the border, and we asked them to quiet the Muslim public while they asked us to calm the tempers of the Jews.

Since I was afraid the Arabs would make extreme demands that we would not be able to meet, I asked Mr. N. Sokolow to telegraph General Deedes,[419] the civilian secretary, to ask him to take part in the gathering. The following day, Deedes came to the gathering and chaired the meeting. He thanked the gathering for their common desire to foster peace and brotherhood. However, he added, the government would not turn its cheek from the guilty, and it would try them with the full severity of the law; anyone found guilty would meet his punishment. He reported that in a few days' time Chief Justice Haycraft would arrive and would carry out the investigations, and the trials would be carried out swiftly so that all the guilty parties would be found and would receive the punishments they deserve.[420]

---

419. Wyndham Deedes (1883–1956) was a decorated British army officer and colonial official. He served as chief secretary to the high commissioner, Herbert Samuel, from 1920–1922. Deedes was known for his Christian Zionist sympathies.

420. The Haycraft Commission was appointed on 7 May and worked from 12 May to 26 July; over the course of the summer, it heard 291 witnesses. In addition to the chief justice, the commission included two other colonial officials, and it was "assisted" by a Muslim, Christian, and Jewish "assessor."

The commission's final report was presented to the British parliament in October 1921. The report detailed Jewish socialist activism in Jaffa in the months preceding the riot, including pamphlets distributed in Arabic advocating a revolution to establish a "Soviet Palestine." The report found that the spontaneous riots had been instigated by the Arabs, but it found fault with the Zionist Commission for not being more proactive in allaying Arab concerns. It concluded that "the general belief that the aims of the Zionists and Jewish immigration are a danger to the national and material interests of the Arabs in Palestine is well nigh universal amongst the Arabs, and is not confined to any particular class," contrary to the attempts of the Zionist leadership (and Chelouche, as shown above) to dismiss these concerns as fabricated by Palestinian elites. The Zionist leadership vigorously objected to the commission's report.

These words made a strong impression on them. It was decided that religious leaders in mosques and synagogues would give sermons about the value of peace, and a petition calling for peace and unity between the races would be signed by all of the community leaders.

Gradually, the situation calmed down.[421] Life resumed its ordinary routine. But the invisible hand soon reappeared and began to organize. The Arabs and the Christians united and formed a Muslim-Christian association, although the government kept close watch over them.[422] For the sake of appearances, they conducted a fundraising campaign for the victims of the disturbances. Initially, some of the Arabs contributed to it, but subsequently these donations ceased because it was learned that the leaders were benefiting from the money and were doing nothing for the benefit of the people.

Among the important activities of the wealthy Jews of the East on behalf of the establishment and development of Tel Aviv in which our family played a part, one may include the visit and the subsequent results of the great and wealthy merchant from Aden, Banin Menahem Messa, who had a business relationship with our family over decades.

A few years after the Balfour Declaration, in 1921, the late Banin Menahem Messa came to see our country. He stayed at the home of my late brother Avraham Haim, with the intention of seeing the country at the dawn of its reawakening. However, as he saw the country still in great ruin, he decided to do something toward its rebuilding. He wished to purchase tracts and plots of land for the construction of colonies and cities.

However, due to the law still in effect in the country at the time that

---

421. The Haycraft report detailed lingering tensions and sporadic violence through July 1921, including an anti-Jewish economic boycott, the refusal of some Arab boatmen to land Jewish immigrants at the port, and random stabbings. For their part, the Hebrew and Arabic press continued to incite their respective publics.

422. The Muslim-Christian Associations were established in early 1919 and had local chapters throughout the country; 'Umar al-Bitar was president of the Jaffa branch. It maintained firm opposition to the Balfour Declaration, the pro-Zionist British policy, and unchecked Jewish immigration to Palestine; as a result, the British refused to grant it official recognition. In June 1921 the MCA held its fourth congress in Jerusalem, which is likely what Chelouche is referring to here. An executive council traveled to London that fall to unsuccessfully petition the colonial secretary, Winston Churchill, to change British policy in Palestine.

forbade land purchases and all other real estate transactions by foreign citizens, while permitting these purchases only to residents of the country within certain boundaries,[423] he encountered hurdles along the way to realization of his decision to carry out significant purchases in the Land of Israel.

However, as he was unwilling to leave the country without taking any steps to make it bloom economically, Messa utilized his close relationships within the central government in London, in the hopes of perhaps receiving the permit to purchase land, outside of the letter of the law.

He wrote a letter addressed to the high commissioner, Sir Herbert Samuel, and asked us to submit it to him. In the letter, he briefly introduced himself as an English subject, complete with all the numerous and lofty honorary titles that he had received from the English government in recognition of the great service he had rendered to England in Aden generally and in the Near East specifically. The letter concluded with a request that the government of Palestine treat him according to the value of his service to the English government, and to permit him to fulfill his great desire to purchase lands and buildings in Tel Aviv.

Following the submission of this letter to our high commissioner and through the efforts of Mr. David Yellin, Sir Herbert Samuel, known for his strict adherence to the law, adopted a softer attitude. Based on Messa's notable and consequential services rendered to England in Aden, the high commissioner made an exception and authorized his purchase of tracts of land and buildings in Tel Aviv.

Having received this permit, Mr. Banin Menahem Messa purchased lots and buildings in Tel Aviv for a total of approximately 60,000 English pounds.

Thanks to the bonds that he forged with the country, not long afterward Messa's heirs and relatives came to the country as well. They purchased and continue to purchase, built and continue to build, several significant factories and buildings in Tel Aviv.

There is another characteristic of the Jews of the East that may be highlighted from this interesting fact. [Messa] had the idea and the capital to build a large and elaborate synagogue in Port Said for the Jewish community there, and he wanted to construct the synagogue exclusively with stones from Jerusalem, no matter the cost.

---

423. The 1920 Land Transfer Ordinance limited land sales to citizens of Palestine.

Eventually, when he learned through persons loyal to him that aside from the large amount of money such a building would cost, there were also serious technical difficulties in realizing the plan, he agreed to be satisfied with only parts of the synagogue built of Jerusalem stone, although this too was an exorbitant expense.[424]

[424]. Messa supported at least one synagogue and a school in Port Said; the Ohel Moshe synagogue was consecrated in 1911. In the late 1920s, the Jewish community there numbered approximately a thousand people, many of them originating in Aden; there was also a small Ladino-speaking Sephardi community with their own synagogue.

CHAPTER 27 *The Neighborly Relations That Broke Down*

Years of building and creative endeavor | Development of Tel Aviv | On the political council | On the Tel Aviv council | Between Tel Aviv and the Jaffa municipality | The hatred in the Arabs' hearts | The mayor of Jaffa and his entourage | Their political "excursion" to Egypt | A rumor about Emir ʿAbdallah's coronation over our country | We stand watch | My trip to Egypt | In Dizengoff's house | Slander against me | My decisive answer prior to my trip | Ahad Ha'am's words of comfort to me | In Egypt | Cancellation of the gathering | The effendis of Jaffa and Jerusalem return home empty-handed | Back to Egypt | Remembering the late Zaki Cohen in Beirut

These bitter days of bloodshed did not bring despair into the hearts of the Hebrew *yishuv*; on the contrary, they exponentially increased the community's efforts for the rebirth of our homeland. We knew well that it is impossible to establish a country without victims. The Jewish people sacrificed many victims on the fields of foreign homelands, and now it was sacrificing the most precious for its freedom and its liberty; this thought encouraged the sons of the Hebrew *yishuv* in the land. We had seen with our own eyes the prophetic statement "I said to you: Live, despite your blood"[425] being fulfilled through us. By our blood we will live and by our blood we will be redeemed!

Difficult and productive work ensued. I continued to carry the burden with greater exaltation and with greater vigor. We decided that our only response must be creative endeavor and construction. Indeed, after the riots of 1921, Tel Aviv began to be built at an accelerated tempo. There were numerous assemblies; the community council and the town council convened frequently. I was assigned to work on the political committee, which consisted of Mr. Dizengoff, the elderly Lewin-Epstein, who was a member of the Zionist Commission, and the writer of these lines.

425. Ezekiel 16:6.

FIGURE 27.1. *Members of the Jaffa municipal council, early 1920s. The mayor, 'Asim Bek al-Sa'id, is in the center. Chelouche is facing the camera, third from the right. Photo by Frank Scholten. Leiden University Libraries, NINO F Scholten Jaffa 24: 97.*

At the same time, I was appointed on behalf of the Jews to the Jaffa city council, and I also sat on Jaffa's municipal planning committee, which was chaired by the governor. Aside from that, I had the honor of being appointed by the high commissioner as an honorary judge on the municipal court. These tasks demanded a great deal of concentrated and active effort from me, and since it is in my nature to complete everything that is assigned to me, I took on a greater burden than I could handle. I neglected my business and did not pay attention to my health. My sons, may they live long, managed the business, while I dedicated myself entirely to the public work that I loved so dearly.

The days passed in this fashion until 1923, with me frequently in meetings, particularly of the Tel Aviv council. At the time there was a great deal of movement, with new immigrants arriving every day,[426] some of them people of means who purchased land and opened small industries and workshops in the Tel Aviv area. My work on the Tel Aviv council focused on fostering links between it and the Jaffa municipality, especially

---

426. Between 1920 and 1924, over forty-eight thousand Jews immigrated to Palestine.

FIGURE 27.2. *Members of the Jaffa municipal council, early 1920s. Chelouche is seated third from the right, while the mayor, 'Asim Bek al-Sa'id, is seated at the desk. To Chelouche's right is Yehoshu'a Abrevaya, and to his right Cesar 'Araktinji. All three men are mentioned by Chelouche in his memoir. Photo by Frank Scholten. Leiden University Libraries, NINO F Scholten Jaffa 17: 06.*

its town planning committee. It was my responsibility to carry out the decisions that required the approval of both of those bodies. Naturally, as Tel Aviv expanded, the scope of my work expanded as well, and there was a great deal to do. Nearly every day, I had to conduct negotiations with the Jaffa municipality, the town planning committee, or the Jaffa municipal courts, on all manner of issues related to them and that were critical to the prosperity of Tel Aviv.

I constantly came up against a brick wall; it was the suppressed hatred that took root deep in the hearts of the Arabs toward the Jews following the riots. This hatred was a constant stumbling block on the path of my efforts. Members of the Jaffa city council, and especially the Christians, would object to any proposal made by the Tel Aviv town committee, even if realization of the proposal would cause them no harm. Their opposition became natural, a simple objection without any sense or rationale, all because the proposal might promote the prosperity and progress of Tel Aviv. However, I would prepare the mayor and certain members of the council a few days before each meeting in the most tactical and prudent manner, and in this way, I overcame all those difficulties. My influence accomplished its goal, and Tel Aviv did not suffer, even though at the time it was still subordinate to the Jaffa municipality.

One day, I was present at a meeting of the Jaffa municipality together with my colleague on the city council, Mr. Yehoshu'a Abrevaya. I had requested from the mayor prior to the council meeting that he place on the agenda one of the urgent proposals of the Tel Aviv committee, but he smiled and replied: "Because the groundwork isn't ready yet for the introduction of this proposal, leave it for Monday when we will have another meeting, during which we will discuss the proposal. In the meantime, they will prepare the necessary paperwork." But only moments later, he declared that it would not be possible to discuss the proposal on Monday either, because he was traveling to Egypt, together with some colleagues whose names he mentioned.

I asked him: "Why are you all traveling together at the same time? What happened?" He replied without thinking: "It's just an excursion." That news robbed me of my relaxation; I thought that it was impossible that this whole group would travel for a mere excursion. Surely something was going on here, and we must be on our guard. There must be a large gathering of Muslims in Egypt for which they were traveling as the representatives of Palestine's Muslims. I revealed these suspicions to my friend Abrevaya, and we both agreed immediately to travel to Egypt to follow them and try as far as possible to monitor their trip.

As I was preparing for the trip, I remembered the existence of the political committee and my obligation to inform it of our decision. I went to Mr. Dizengoff's house and told him about my suspicions, and about our decision about our trip. He listened very attentively to my words, and in response to my request that he accompany us, he responded that his public work would not permit him to leave the country at that time. Dizengoff wished us every success.

On Saturday, when I was in synagogue, Mr. Dizengoff sent word asking me to come straight to his house after services for a critical emergency meeting. When I arrived at Mr. Dizengoff's house, I found respected public officials already there: Ahad Ha'am,[427] of blessed memory; Mr. Dizengoff, may he live long; Dr. Mossinsohn; and Hoofien.[428]

---

427. Asher Ginzburg (1856–1927) was a prominent Russian Zionist intellectual and journalist who published under the pen name Ahad Ha'am (One of the People).

428. Netherlands-born Eli'ezer Hoofien (1881–1957) was an accountant who, in 1912, was sent to Palestine to serve as the deputy director of the Anglo-Palestine Bank.

Mr. Dizengoff addressed the gathered men: "On Thursday evening, Mr. Chelouche came to me and told me about a conversation he had with the mayor of Jaffa, in the presence of Mr. Abrevaya, prior to the meeting of the Jaffa municipal council. They learned that he, as well as several of his friends, *effendi*s from Jaffa and Jerusalem, were taking a sudden trip to Egypt.

"Due to their suspicion regarding this trip as well as the identity of the travelers, namely that it is a political trip that would be to our detriment, Mr. Chelouche and Mr. Abrevaya decided to travel to Egypt together with them in order to keep track of their actions and to learn what develops there. I expressed my gratitude to Mr. Chelouche for taking this step.

"The next day, Friday, Dr. M. came to see me and informed me of rumors spreading in the city about crowning the *emir* [as king] of our country, and that many important *effendi*s from Jerusalem and Jaffa are traveling to a major assembly in Egypt, where this subject would be discussed.[429] And some say—Dr. M. added when he spoke to me—that the Sephardic Jews are also inclined toward this, and their representatives Mr. Chelouche and Mr. Abrevaya will be traveling together with the *effendi*s to this gathering in Egypt." In concluding, Dizengoff announced that he had received a report along these lines from the Zionist leadership in Jerusalem.

When I heard this, I nearly lost my mind. I could not restrain myself in the face of this insult to me and to my friend, in the face of the slander spread about us and about Sephardic Jews in general. To besmirch our names, to spill our blood, all this when the objective of our trip was to disrupt this meeting that we opposed!

My blood was boiling, and I answered harshly: "I was born in Zion and I have no other homeland, and these slanderers were born and

429. The *emir* 'Abdallah bin Hussein had participated in the Arab revolt led by his father, the *sharif* of Mecca, during World War I. British officials had promised the Hashemites that they could establish an Arab kingdom in greater Syria once the Ottomans were overthrown, but this proved to be only one of many wartime promises that the British would not honor. The Cairo Conference in March 1921 maintained the separation of Palestine from Transjordan, and 'Abdallah was crowned king of Transjordan (the East Bank of the Jordan River, today's Hashemite Kingdom of Jordan) in April 1921.

raised at the knees of exile.[430] I have property in this country and am connected to it, and I am unable to leave it even for a moment, even if I wanted to, while these slanderers have their suitcases packed and are ready to leave at a moment's notice. We Sephardic Jews have no part in this nonsensical idea, which has no possibility of happening. The idea of crowning the *emir* king of our country? While I am not overly enthusiastic about having a pure Israelite kingdom established at this time, I certainly would not want any other kingdom. For the moment, I certainly have enough with an English kingdom, until the time comes. We thought of traveling to Egypt in order to serve our people, out of the purest motivation, but now we are convinced that the *yishuv* would be unappreciative of our efforts and would only reward evil for good. I will by no means travel to Egypt."

Having finished what I had to say, I stood up and was about to leave the house, but Ahad Ha'am stopped me. He began speaking to my heart. "We know your value and your actions. We know what you do for our people. Slanderers exist all over the world, and even the most reputable persons are slandered. Among the Jewish people, slander was committed even against our prophets. That being the case, you mustn't pay attention to all these trifling matters; instead, you must pay attention to the sacred goal you have set for yourself. The good of the Jewish people demands that you travel, and [so] travel you must. May God bring you success in your efforts."

Ahad Ha'am's words calmed my agitated spirit. My devoted friend Mr. Dizengoff also pleaded with and encouraged me greatly, and he implored me to travel to Egypt immediately and to not listen to slanderous words. I was compelled to decide in favor of traveling, without even telling my friend Yehoshu'a Abrevaya anything about the incident, so that he would not regret traveling with me. On Monday we traveled to Egypt.

When the mayor of Jaffa and his *effendi* friends saw that we were traveling to Egypt as well, they were surprised. "What is this?" they asked. "You weren't thinking of traveling, and what do you have in Egypt?" We simply laughed, and replied that we, too, were taking an "excursion" to Egypt.

430. An important component of Zionism was the negation of the Diaspora, negatively framed as a state of exile.

In Egypt, we stayed at a hotel opposite the hotel in which the *effendi*s were staying. The first thing we did was to meet with a few of our fellow Jews who lived there. We visited C.,[431] who told us that he had received a telegram from the Zionist Commission in Jerusalem concerning us and asking him to keep an eye on us. I understood well that this was the handiwork of the slanderers.

"And what did Your Honor respond to the Zionist leadership?" I asked Mr. C., who had grown silent while looking at us.

"I responded," Mr. C. replied, "that there is no need to keep an eye on them, because as I understand it, they came here to keep an eye on others."

Our notable Jews hurried to arrange meetings with several individuals who wielded consequential political power in government circles in Egypt. This major gathering, which would not have been for our benefit, was canceled.

The dinner that was held at the home of the Bek M.[432] took place in accordance with our plan, and we had an opportunity to watch their every step and to track them and their movements on this occasion. We did not take our eyes off of them for even a moment. Our work was carried out quietly and in complete secrecy. We also took advantage of the assistance provided by others who helped us tremendously by keeping an eye on the visitors from Jaffa and Jerusalem, so that we knew of each and every step that they took. As if in a mirror, we saw even their slightest movement in Egypt. Their grand assembly never took place, and that is how their political journey ended, with each of them going back to the place from which they had come without achieving his dream.

I returned home sick. Already when I was in Egypt my health was failing. At home, I laid down in bed and the doctors ordered me to rest. Mr. Dizengoff's visit raised my spirits greatly. I decided to take a break

431. In the original manuscript, Chelouche related the story to "the late" Cicurel, "the head of the Zionist Organization in Egypt," referring to Solomon Cicurel, who was murdered in his home in 1927 at the age of forty-six. The Cicurel family owned one of the grandest department stores in Cairo, and Solomon's murder was considered a burglary gone awry.

432. According to the original manuscript, upon arriving in Egypt Chelouche and Abrevaya met Jacques Bek Mosseri, a local Jewish leader and a banker, who suggested inviting the Arab delegation for "a cup of tea" and to use the occasion to change their minds "to our side."

from public service, in order to regain my strength. The attitude of the slanderers depressed me greatly. I stopped believing in their Zionism and their nationalism. The only man who enchanted me in my work was Mr. Dizengoff. It was he who had brought me into public service and he was the only one whom I believed in, and still I believe with all my heart and soul in his work for the benefit of the people and the homeland, which were in turn enriched by the depth of his soul and genuine self-awareness.

I quit all of the meetings; I kept my distance from them. I only maintained my membership in what I deemed to be the more important councils, those whose work was most beneficial in my opinion.

One day in 1925, my health took a slight turn for the worse, and Dr. Hissin advised me to spend the winter in the Egyptian city of Helwan. I went there with my wife and after a while I felt a bit better. My brain was once again capable of dreaming of building enterprises and endeavors, which constitute my life plan.

Among the Egyptians who came to visit me in Helwan were many who had been students at the late Zaki Cohen's school in Beirut, which reminded me of the days of my youth, and of theirs.

Because of this, I had an idea that I proposed to these classmates from my youth, and I told them: "Gentlemen, friends of my youth! The time has come for us to create a great memorial to our teacher and principal Zaki Cohen. It will not be overly difficult for us to do it now. There is a well-organized Jewish community council in Beirut now, and important people there concern themselves with the public good. They are working to improve the cultural and spiritual situation of the Hebrew community in Beirut, and they have already done quite a bit in this regard.

"It would therefore be both thoughtful and appropriate to restore the crown to its former glory and erect a living memorial to one of the pioneers, the man who played a dominant role in fostering the spiritual and cultural development of the Jewish community in Beirut. Primarily and specifically, it falls upon us, the pupils of the late Zaki Cohen who attended his first Hebrew school in Beirut, to begin the blessed deed of memorializing this saintly figure. The most appropriate and exalted thing that we could do in the pursuit of this goal is to repurchase the building that held this first Jewish school in Beirut, which the late principal infused with his vitality and spirit. We would open a school in the original format and then hand it over to the local community as a gift, so that it might run the school as befits the good name of our exalted teacher."

After hearing my proposal, most of those present were inclined to agree to the realization of the idea but only suggested: since one of the late headmaster's sons, Dr. Israel Cohen, lived in Egypt and was an extremely wealthy man, we must first appeal to him as a son devoted to his father's memory. After he contributed the first 1,000 gold napoleons, we, too, would each contribute his portion. It was decided that we would begin work on this proposal and then see it through to completion by means of a committee to be selected that would disseminate the idea to all of the school alumni, wherever they might be. Among them were many affluent and wealthy individuals with significant social standing in the lands of the East as well as in Europe.

For now, they assigned me, the initiator of the idea, to meet with the son of the late principal, Dr. Israel Cohen, and present our proposal to him.

When I had recovered sufficiently that I could engage in such affairs, I first paid a visit to the second-eldest son of the deceased, Raphael Cohen, who was very enthusiastic about my proposal.

He accompanied me to the home of his brother, Dr. Israel Cohen. Although the wealthy man was extremely pleased with this wonderful idea, when he heard that our proposal was based on him being the first to contribute the sum of 1,000 napoleons, he immediately began to backtrack on his support for it. Nevertheless, once I had enthusiastically explained the immense value of this enterprise in honor of his late father, he agreed to take part in the initiative. It was difficult, but he agreed.

Meanwhile, I wrote a letter detailing my proposal to the council of the Jewish community in Beirut, addressed to the head of the community, Mr. Joseph Farhi,[433] as well as to Joseph Bek Dichy,[434] and to the publisher of the newspaper *al-'Alam al-Isra'ili*, Mr. Salim Mann.[435]

---

433. Farhi (1878–1945), born in Damascus, was educated in the AIU schools and served as a deputy director in three schools in the region. In 1908 he left education for business and settled permanently in Beirut. He was a prominent communal leader for forty years.

434. Dichy (1882–?) was born in Beirut but spent years working in business in Cairo; he was granted the honorific title *bek* by King Fuad. Dichy was a communal leader and prominent businessman in Beirut after he returned in 1920 until his death.

435. The Beirut-born Mann (1872–1969) was an Arabic teacher in the local AIU school, and he also published two books on Arabic. In 1921 Mann began publishing the pro-Zionist newspaper *al-'Alam al-Isra'ili*.

The community council was very happy to receive my letter and our proposal, but not in the form that we had proposed. They were opposed to purchasing the same building, which was too distant from the city and from the Jewish street. They were also opposed to the school being established in its previous format promoted by Zaki Cohen, in which the pupils also ate and slept there. Their proposal was the establishment of an ordinary school in the city, to be named after the late Zaki Cohen, in which the children would only study there.

After feeling unwell in Egypt, I returned home, but I did not neglect this matter. Through the correspondence that I carried out with the late principal's sons, I came to realize that the wealthy son, Dr. Israel Cohen, who was supposed to be the first donor to this blessed project, had altogether backed out of it.

Nevertheless, I did not despair over the idea. The community council of Beirut doggedly persisted to defend its request to the Beirut municipality to rename the Jews' street in Beirut, which had a different name, and in which all of the religious, social, and health institutions of the Jews were concentrated. That street would be named after our late teacher Zaki Cohen. The community council succeeded in this effort, and the street was renamed after our dear teacher. It is my greatest hope that more of his ex-pupils will be found who will actualize our initial proposal in its original form.

CHAPTER 28 *My Work on Behalf of Building and Expanding Tel Aviv*

My work on the Jaffa city council on behalf of Tel Aviv | Jaffa's envy of Tel Aviv | Extending Herzl Street to the Jaffa–Jerusalem road | Opposition from the Christian Arabs | My letter to Governor Stirling | My proposal is adopted | Across from the Hassan Bek Mosque, in the area of Tel Aviv | Paving a road to Tel Aviv across from the mosque | Opposition of the Christian Arabs | The excuse and explanation that I offered to the Muslim Arabs | My proposal is adopted | The editor of Falastin's *words about me | The Jaffa municipal council's objections to bringing Rutenberg's electricity to the city | I explain the benefits to my colleagues | The Jaffa municipal council | Signing the Rutenberg electricity protocol, with trembling hands | The question of building a joint slaughterhouse | A port in Jaffa and in Tel Aviv | The meeting with Mr. Gruenblat, builder of small ports | My trip to Tripoli | My tour of the Yarkon River area with Mr. Ussishkin | Ussishkin's words | The letter from the Jewish National Fund, and my reply | My article in the newspapers*

Following the slanderous accusations related to the crowning of 'Abdallah that were lodged against me by people in Dr. M.'s camp, my desire was to resign from all public activities. I avoided going to meetings to which I was invited. I only continued my work on behalf of Tel Aviv and the meetings of the Jaffa city council, to which I had been appointed as a member. I also continued in my position as a member of the municipal planning committee in Jaffa and in Tel Aviv, and I did not resign from my post as a judge on the Jaffa municipal court.

Thus, I continued my work on the Tel Aviv committee and in the Tel Aviv municipality until ultimately resigning from these positions at the

FIGURE 28.1. *Members of the Tel Aviv municipal council, early 1920s. Seated in the front row (L to R): Yosef Eliyahu Chelouche, Ben Zion Mossinsohn, Me'ir Dizengoff, and Ahad Ha'am. Standing in the rear (L to R): David Smilansky, Israel Rokach, Abraham Mibashan, David Izmojik, Arieh Leo Osterman, and Theodor Zlocisti. Photo by Frank Scholten. Leiden University Libraries, NINO F Scholten Tel Aviv 19: 38.*

time of the rise to power of the Workers [party] in the municipality,[436] due to reasons I detailed in the press at that time.

I continued to carry the burden of my work on the Jaffa city council until 1927. I played a dual role, as I was always assigned the duty of implementing decisions of the Tel Aviv municipality that called for close cooperation with the Jaffa municipality and which required mutual agreement. I fulfilled my position as best I could, as required in this or the other situation, according to my style in this work. Prior to the meetings I would brief the chairman and several members of the Jaffa

---

436. David Bloch (1884–1947), the head of the Jaffa Workers Council party in the municipality, became the mayor of Tel Aviv in early 1926 and remained in this position until early 1929, when Dizengoff resumed power following local elections.

city council, gaining their agreement to my proposals ahead of time. The expansion and development of Tel Aviv depended on this.

In spite of the thorny relationship that developed between us and our neighbors in the years following the Balfour Declaration and the riots in Jerusalem and in Jaffa, I nevertheless succeeded in carrying out nearly every task assigned to me by the Tel Aviv committee and the Tel Aviv municipality. I did this public work under conditions of envy by our neighbors, in particular the Christians, who from one year to the next saw the steady decline of the Jaffa municipality's annual budget, which decreased from 60,000 pounds to 30,000 pounds, and conversely, the increase of the Tel Aviv budget from 35,000 pounds to 116,000 pounds.

The envy and hatred of the Christian community's representatives on the Jaffa city council were exacerbated by some projects for the construction and development of Tel Aviv, which I had adamantly insisted that we approve, come what may. Upon their approval, one of the Christian members felt the need to resign, and his resignation was accepted. Two other members stopped attending the meetings of the Jaffa city council. These are but a few episodes relating to my city council activities, through which the hatred and envy of the Christians toward our national enterprise in our land became painfully and utterly obvious to me.

Episode A: Once, while I was an active member of the joint Jaffa/Tel Aviv municipal planning committee, I proposed to the committee and to the governor, who served as chairman of the committee, that we continue to extend Herzl Street and link it directly to the main road to Jerusalem, instead of it twisting around for three and a half kilometers for no reason. A Christian member of the Jaffa city council who also sat on the municipal planning committee, an owner of flour mills in Jaffa,[437] was vehemently opposed to my proposal. His objections were illogical and impractical, but they stemmed from his abiding hatred and envy, as he knew the road extension would be of tremendous benefit to Tel Aviv, which he greatly envied.

Nevertheless, Governor Stirling—even if he was not one of our greatest friends—considered my proposal to be quite logical, and to that end he appointed a committee to prepare a detailed plan before the next

---

437. Chelouche is referring to Antoine (Anton) Gelat, whom he identifies as A. G. below. Gelat served on the High Commissioner's Advisory Council in 1923.

meeting, which would include pros and cons of the proposal, and the feasibility of implementing the plan.

In addition to that, I asked the governor to give me an opportunity to appear before the committee to present my reasons and explanations in favor of the proposal. The governor appointed me as a member of the committee as well, but he also added A. G., who would appear before the committee in order to present his arguments and rationale opposing the proposal.

One clear day when I was called to appear before a session of this committee, I was sick in bed with kidney disease and could by no means participate in this important meeting on matters that involved my cherished Tel Aviv. I feared that my failure to attend the meeting would result in a negative decision. I called in my son Moshe, and asked him to write a letter in my name to the governor with these contents: I request from the governor, given that I am lying ill in bed and cannot take part in this important meeting, and in view of the fact that at this meeting my proposal will be discussed and which I strenuously wish to defend, and as I fear that my absence will be used against me and a decision counter to my desire will be adopted, therefore it would only be right and just for the governor to remove it from the agenda of the meeting until I recover.

I received a reply from the governor the following day, informing me that the municipal planning committee meeting had not even been held, since it had originally been called solely to discuss this consequential issue. Due to my just request, he had postponed the meeting indefinitely, until I recovered and could take part in it.

Sometime later, following my recovery, the meeting on this proposal took place. Since I had prepared the majority of the members of the council ahead of time to support my proposal, my proposal passed with a majority of votes in favor, against the votes of the Christian representatives. When my proposal passed, the Christian representative A. G. jumped to his feet and submitted his resignation from the municipal planning committee. I made an effort to have the resignation go into effect immediately, as I knew it was offered as a protest filled with hatred and envy of the building and blossoming of Tel Aviv.

The resolution in favor of the extension of Herzl Street up to the Jaffa–Jerusalem road really did bring great benefit to the transportation in Tel Aviv. All the inhabitants of the city were highly appreciative of the convenience and usefulness of this important matter.

A second episode in which the envy and hatred of the Christians for every facet of our national effort in the country stood out: In the municipal planning committee in Tel Aviv, they felt it was very important to orient the new road passing alongside the beach toward the left,[438] in the direction across from the Hassan Bek Mosque. The Tel Aviv town council resolved that it was highly important for this mosque to be seen all along the length of the street, as far as Allenby Street. So it was decided by the Tel Aviv city council, and the two Jews who sat on the Jaffa municipal planning committee, Dizengoff and I, resolved to defend this decision to the utmost.

Although, here too, the perpetual opponents to every proposal initiated by the Jews appeared and objected to this matter as well. They contrived all sorts of obstacles to disrupt the fulfillment of this plan, which was an insult to the Muslim mosque, particularly because they found that there was another plot of land there that belonged to the Arabs.

But I unequivocally defended my proposal before the chairman of the committee, Governor Campbell,[439] and explained to him that the exact opposite was the case—that the Tel Aviv town council was demanding this out of honor and respect for the Muslim mosque, as it would beautify the street and not, Heaven forbid, humiliate it. And through the words of warmth and logic that emanated from the heart, I persuaded the Muslim members, who agreed to the proposal. The proposal was on the verge of passing. Suddenly, a minor technical hurdle arose, which could have prevented the passage of the resolution. At the start of the meeting, the governor had announced that the matter had to be resolved in that day's meeting.

The editor of *Falastin*, 'Issa al-'Issa,[440] who also took part in this meeting as a representative of "his newspaper," used the governor's an-

---

438. Now known as HaYarkon Street, whose southern end was originally set at the center of the mosque's northern facade.

439. Major James Campbell served as assistant deputy governor of Jaffa. Previously he had served in the military secretary's department in Cairo.

440. The Greek Orthodox 'Issa al-'Issa (1878–1950) was a graduate of the Frères school and the American University in Beirut. Together with his cousin Yusuf, he cofounded and coedited *Falastin* from 1911–1914, during which time it published dozens of articles critical of the Zionist movement. Al-'Issa was expelled from Jaffa during the war, after which he was briefly allied with the pro-Faysal camp in Damascus. He returned to Jaffa in 1921 and resumed publication of *Falastin*.

nouncement, and said, "According to the governor's comments that this matter must be concluded today, and since the second Jewish member of the municipal planning committee, Dizengoff, who was supposed to appear at this meeting with the detailed plan, has still not arrived, we cannot accept Chelouche's proposal."

When I heard the editor of *Falastin*'s comments, whose strategic intention was solely to sabotage Tel Aviv's proposal, I saw that due to Dizengoff's failure to attend the meeting the whole proposal could fall apart. So I asked the governor for permission to telephone Dizengoff from [the] government house. I placed the call and spoke to Dizengoff very excitedly in the presence of the others, telling him to come immediately with the plan, for otherwise they wanted to sink the proposal.

While speaking with such excitement on the telephone, I heard the editor of *Falastin* commenting to the others seated: "Just look at Chelouche. 'May his house be destroyed.' See how devoted he is to Jewish affairs. A French subject, sitting on two chairs in Tel Aviv and in Jaffa, who works like the devil to promote the interests of his nation."

It didn't take more than fifteen minutes for Dizengoff to appear with the plan. Our proposal was adopted by a majority vote of the Muslims, against the opposition of a few of the Christians.

Among my labors on the Jaffa city council over the past few years was the passage of the contract between the Jaffa municipality and Rutenberg's electric company for the purpose of lighting the streets of Jaffa and of city hall. Everyone still remembers the vehement opposition of the Arabs of Jaffa to using Rutenberg's electricity plant.[441]

As I was then on the Jaffa city council, little by little I managed to quiet down the opposition. At one meeting, I came with a proposal that was based upon extremely well-founded numbers. I showed the city council a chart showing the darkness that prevailed in the city and the prodigious expense that this "illumination" was costing the municipality. I then compared these findings with Rutenberg's electrical light, which

---

441. Given his backing by the Zionist Executive, Rutenberg's electrification project was viewed by Palestinian nationalists as a deeply political project whose aim was to benefit the Zionist movement at the expense of Palestinians. The Arab Executive submitted a complaint along these lines to the British government in 1922. In 1923, a public demonstration against the electrification of Allenby Street featured chants, "Rutenberg's lampposts are the gallows of our nation!" Meiton, *Electrical Palestine*, 80.

would cost the municipality less than the previous amount. I explained the advantages of light over darkness, and I also mentioned the thefts carried out in the dark of night.

And so it was that my logical explanations were gradually accepted by the mayor, who then appointed a three-man committee, consisting of the Christian Mas'ad Sayegh,[442] the Muslim 'Ali Mustakim,[443] and me. After drawing up the proposal with them, they were forced to sign the protocol, although their hands were shaking as they signed, as if they considered it a true act of betrayal against the homeland. Immediately after the signings, the Jaffa municipality contracted with Rutenberg's electric company to illuminate the city of Jaffa.

One other minor accomplishment of mine from the period in which I was a member of the Jaffa city council, which happened a few years ago: At the time, the question of building a joint slaughterhouse for both Jaffa and Tel Aviv was on the Jaffa municipal council agenda. The Jaffa municipality agreed to it and demanded that the Tel Aviv town council participate in covering half of the building's cost. The Tel Aviv town council was not prepared to enter such a partnership, and neither did it have the necessary budget. Nevertheless, I, along with my Jewish colleagues on the Jaffa municipal council, made it known that the Jaffa municipal council committed to pay 40 percent of the income of the slaughterhouse to the Tel Aviv town council.

The natural aspiration of Tel Aviv, from the day it began to develop from a small neighborhood into a city and a mother in Israel,[444] was always to build a small port in the Tel Aviv area within the city limits, a port in the form of a maritime dock or a maritime bridge, of the sort that may be found in several coastal cities of Syria.

However, when the town council's leaders approached the government with this justifiable request, the government rebuffed them time and again, offering all sorts of pretexts and excuses, saying that the Arabs in Jaffa would never agree to building a port in Tel Aviv nor would they agree that the Jews ever leave the Jaffa port. The government already

---

442. Sayegh (1883–?) was a businessman, wholesale dealer, and member of the Freemason lodge Barkai/Shafaq. He owned a large warehouse, or *khan*.

443. Mustakim (?–1952) was a former government translator, orchard owner, and merchant.

444. 2 Samuel 20:19.

knew that if a major port were ever built [in Palestine], then it would certainly be in Haifa. In addition, the government's position was that it was not possible in such a small and poor country to have two ports, and so it continuously denied Tel Aviv's requests for a port through all manner of excuses and pretexts, even rejecting a large port to be shared by Tel Aviv and Jaffa.

Eventually, once the founders of Tel Aviv came to understand that a [new] port in Jaffa would not be built, they stood firm in their decision and demanded from the government a marine pier or a maritime bridge in the Tel Aviv area. In connection with this, we had an opportunity to meet with Mr. Gruenblat,[445] who was the contractor of maritime bridges of this type in several Syrian cities near Beirut, including the city of Tripoli. Together with the other colleagues on the Tel Aviv town council, I initiated a discussion with him on this matter, and found that his plans for construction of these sorts of maritime bridges were extremely close to the idea that the Tel Aviv town council was considering.

Gruenblat invited the chairman of the town council, Dizengoff, to tour the maritime bridge in Tripoli along with other members of the council, after which they would discuss the matter in greater detail. Dizengoff, Gruenblat, and I traveled there. After we arrived in Tripoli, we examined all aspects of the plan and construction of this maritime bridge and researched every detail on-site. We were extremely impressed. We held several meetings with the committee that had already been appointed for this specific project, headed by the director of the Anglo-Palestine Company, Mr. Hoofien, who was so enthusiastic that we went so far as to draft a provisional contract.

The only delay was the government's approval. The answers we received from the government were the usual, neither a yes nor a no, just to postpone and delay. In the meantime, time passed, and after the members of the committee understood that the government definitely would not permit the construction of even a small maritime bridge in Tel Aviv, they despaired of the entire matter and altogether ceased to engage in this important project.

However, I could not resign myself to [giving up on] the idea in my mind and in my heart. I knew that without ports in Jaffa and Tel Aviv,

---

445. Claude Gruenblat (?–1969), a French engineer, married Maxa Nordau, the daughter of the early Zionist leader Max Nordau.

both those cities would suffer economically once the port in Haifa was built. I wrote a detailed article on the issue for publication in the Arabic press in the newspaper *Falastin*, so that the Arabs would also have a clear understanding of the economic dangers facing Jaffa after the building of a port in Haifa, should a small port not also be built in Jaffa and Tel Aviv.

I believed all along that the government would surely approve the plan for a small port in the environs of Jaffa and Tel Aviv, and I was certain that this port would be built near the Yarkon River. To that end, I quietly and modestly purchased three plots in this area from the village of Sheikh Muwannis, with the intention of setting them aside in the meantime until the port would be built there. I did not rest and did not cease to work on the project. I asked Mr. Dizengoff to speak with the head of the Jewish National Fund, Mr. M. Ussishkin, to propose that the JNF purchase the entire area from Sheikh Muwannis at a low price. There was no doubt that the Jaffa and Tel Aviv port would someday be built on this site.

Mr. Dizengoff, who was always enthusiastic about the idea and was influenced by my strong belief in it, wrote to Ussishkin and brought him to Tel Aviv for this purpose. After I met with him and appealed to him on the matter, we took a coach and rode together to tour the entire area around the Yarkon River. On the way, I explained to him all of my reasoning and my strong belief that the Jaffa–Tel Aviv port, if built, would be built only along the Yarkon coastline. I told him that I had already purchased plots in the area, and I impressed upon him how supremely important it was that the JNF purchase land at the low price of five or six pounds per *dunam*, for which they would have to pay a much higher price a few years later.

Mr. M. Ussishkin took a good look at the site and then went back a second time, inspecting the entire area and perspective of the site, for an hour or more. Afterward, he said to me in a conclusive tone: "I have decided. Yes! Here there will be a port, just like in Riga, and first thing tomorrow I will give an order to begin taking care of the matter."

We returned to Tel Aviv and parted amicably. Ussishkin shook my hand with enthusiasm and promised once again that tomorrow he would issue instructions to handle the matter. But it wasn't until three months later, on 19 July 1925, that the Chelouche firm received a letter from the JNF along these lines: since the JNF is considering purchasing a tract of land in the area of the Yarkon River, and since we have heard that Mr. Chelouche is also negotiating to purchase lands in this area, we hereby request that he suspend these purchases there.

After receiving this ridiculous letter, we answered them in the name of our family, in a letter dated 25 July 1925, thus: We received your letter dated such-and-such, and according to our recollection, your interest in purchasing land in the village of Sheikh Muwannis only developed following a proposal made by one of us, Mr. Yosef E. Chelouche, to Mr. Ussishkin on the occasion of his visit with us here in Tel Aviv. At the time, we already owned various plots in the area in question.

At the end of the letter, we added that "there should be no doubt as to our devotion to the idea of redeeming the land, which has been our family's founding principle ever since we arrived in this land approximately eighty years ago."

In the end, until today, aside from the three plots that I purchased at this site, the JNF has not purchased a single square inch of land. We still firmly believe that if a small port is to be built for Jaffa and Tel Aviv, it will be located only in the environs of the Yarkon River.[446]

It is through such labors that I have occupied myself in the past few years. Although I had wanted to keep my distance from public service, it was in my nature and in my blood, and I have never liked being idle in my free time. Over the years, I also published a few columns on issues of the day.

I have already said that I am not a writer, and I certainly do not have a great deal of writing experience, but given the progression of events of the hopes of our people in our land—not all of which unfolded properly, according to my understanding and perspective—I wished to express my views on the mismanagement of several matters, in order to rescue what was possible to rescue and correct what needed to be corrected. From time to time, I was compelled to air my feelings openly in various newspapers, in my own name. In these columns, more or less, I expressed those thoughts and feelings most dear to me, words of truth that stemmed from the depths of my heart and soul.

---

446. The Tel Aviv port was eventually opened in 1936 west of this area along the coast, not at the mouth of the Yarkon River.

CHAPTER 29 *The Bloody Riots of August 1929, and Their Aftermath*

Outbreak of the bloody riots | In the Lebanon mountains | Terrifying news from the land [the Land of Israel][447] *| We link the land to the rest of the Jewish world | My wife's illness delays my return | Upon my return to the land | Status of the raised tempers | The changed expression on our neighbors' faces | My article "Words of Truth and Peace" in the Arabic press in Syria and in the land | The comments of the editor of* Alif Baa' *| The economic boycott | My efforts to cancel it | Minor actions that will become major*

In August 1929, that most bitter and explosive month in our *yishuv*, some weeks before the bloody riots that were suddenly unleashed on us without my having sensed what was happening nor even having discerned any prior signs of their arrival, in those dreadful and terrible days, I was, to my regret and to my great anguish, beyond the borders of our country, in the mountains of Lebanon.

Due to my illness that attacked me at the time, my doctor ordered me to go to a summer resort on Mount Lebanon. I traveled there with my wife in early August 1929. The situation in the country at the time we left was complex concerning the Western Wall question,[448] but by no means

---

447. Throughout this chapter, Chelouche's shorthand reference to Palestine as *haaretz*, "the land/country," might be confusing in translation, given that he was in Lebanon at the time; however, he was consistent in his usage of *haaretz* as only ever referring to the Land of Israel, given his typical terminology for the country.

448. Already in 1928 tensions between Jews and Arabs over the Western Wall, believed to be the retaining wall of the Second Temple and thus holy in Judaism—while also believed to be the wall where the prophet Muhammad tethered his horse "al-Burak," thus holy in Islam—had erupted with scuffles, protests, and increasing

FIGURE 29.1. *Members of the Chelouche family sharing a meal in their home in Tel Aviv, ca. 1927. Freha and Yosef Eliyahu Chelouche are seated at the head of the table. Chelouche Family Collection.*

could I have imagined that within a matter of weeks such violent and bloody riots would erupt.

One day during our stay at a summer resort in the city of 'Aley in Mount Lebanon, at a party with fellow Jews, terrible rumors began to spread about riots taking place all over the country, and about a dreadful massacre in Hebron in particular.[449]

I wanted to run, to fly as if on wings of eagles, to return to the country, but all of the roads were closed, and no one could leave or enter.

---

agitation in the Hebrew and Arabic press. At issue was the question of whether Jews could alter their use of the wall area in any way, namely by bringing a screen to separate male and female worshippers or chairs for the elderly. However, this religious question quickly took on a much more volatile political and nationalist symbolic value.

449. Demonstrations and low-level tensions had been simmering in Jerusalem since late July, but the riot broke out on 23 August 1929. The Hebron massacre took place on the second day, 24 August, in which almost 70 Jews were killed by rioters. Hundreds of others were saved by their neighbors. On 25 August the riot spread to Jaffa and Tel Aviv. Countrywide, almost 250 Jews and Arabs were killed and over 500 were injured.

We also did not have any clear news about what was happening in the country. I struggled with all my weak powers and made contact with trustworthy persons in both Syria and the Land of Israel in order to get clearer news of what was happening in the country in general, and with our family specifically. Important telegrams from the country were transmitted through us to Jewish leaders in exile[450] regarding the situation in the country and issuing calls for help, since it was not possible to send the telegrams to them directly from the country.

As I have already said, as soon as we received the first terrifying news from the country, I wanted to fly home as if on wings of eagles, but two important reasons prevented me from doing so. I have mentioned the first reason—that all the roads leading to our country were closed and sealed. The second reason was my wife. Upon hearing the news, she fell seriously ill and took to bed; I was compelled to be at her bedside for over a month. As soon as she was able to get out of bed, we immediately returned to the country.

Once I arrived home, having heard and seen what was happening in the country, I was shocked to see the significant change that I found among our neighbors following the riots.

I thought long and hard, helpless about what to do. Then I began to do whatever I could, speaking and writing, to show our neighbors and make them see what they had done to us—and to themselves—through these bloody riots.

I came out with an article titled "Words of Truth and Peace" that appealed to the Arabs of the Land of Israel. The article was published in a prominent place in the largest and most influential newspaper in Syria, the Damascus-based *Alif Baa'*,[451] alongside an important comment from the editor about our family's brave friendship with several of the most respected Arabs in the Land of Israel and Syria.

The article also appeared in other Arabic newspapers in Damascus and Beirut. Due to the importance of the situation, the value of these

---

450. Here Chelouche means the Diaspora.

451. *Alif Baa'* was edited by the Jaffa-born Yusuf al-'Issa, the prewar editor of *Falastin* and the cousin of its current editor, 'Issa al-'Issa. The al-'Issa cousins had arrived in Damascus after the war in the initial stages of euphoria in support of King Faysal; after his deposal by the French, 'Issa returned to Palestine, but Yusuf, banned by the British authorities from returning, remained in Syria.

matters, and the timing of the writing of my memoirs, I hereby present the contents of my article, which came out then as a shout from my aching heart aimed at my Arab brothers.[452]

> The majority of my Arab brothers in the country certainly know that our family has lived in the country for entire generations, and that the writer of these lines is one of their grandsons. Like you, I was born in this land, and now I am nearly sixty years of age. I have naturally inherited a legacy of love for my Arab brothers and have mixed with them, between the business world and in their times of sorrow and of joy, throughout these many years. I am therefore obliged to speak my mind, which is rooted in truth.
>
> Upon my word, I was shocked, and I still cannot understand the recent episode of attacks and disturbances that spread throughout every corner of the country, in a serious and alarming manner, the likes of which we have never seen, and for which there is no justification, for a variety of reasons, which I will detail now.
>
> I know for certain that the Arab Muslim does not bear a grudge in his heart to such a degree. I know their values and good attributes well, including the sense of hospitality that is an inheritance from our father Abraham, peace be upon him.
>
> I know well their celebrated behavior with their neighbor, which is one of the commandments of the great prophet, Muhammad. I know most of them, and their propensity toward peace because they are Muslims. It is due to all of these factors that I was so astounded and shocked over how they could have been drawn into committing such a grave error: neighbor killing his neighbor—someone who lives in the same house or in his neighborhood, who was with him in times of joy and in times of sorrow, someone he encountered nearly every day, morning and evening, greeting him as a neighbor—to kill him in the middle of the day, him and his family, within sight of the tomb of the father of these two peoples, the Jews and the Muslims?[453]
>
> Even if we suppose that they were incited by decisive orders

---

452. The original Arabic language article has not been found, nor is its date of publication known.

453. He is referring to the Tomb of the Patriarchs, believed to be the grave of the prophet Abraham (as well as Isaac and Jacob), in Hebron.

to carry out "holy riots"[454] to kill all the Jews, how is it that the murderer did not consider for one moment that after the massacre, once the country had grown quiet once more, there might still be Jews who remained alive through the protection of the Supreme Being? How would the murderer meet those who remained, and how would he not be ashamed to look in their faces?

The Arabic press, and surprisingly even the more moderate newspapers among them, transformed itself suddenly and printed baseless libels in order to incite the masses to riot in an insane fashion, as opposed to what they are meant to do, which should be to educate the people and quiet the spirits at such times, should they arise. These gentlemen published libels that have no basis in fact. In some instances, they themselves were compelled to retract their statements a day or two later.

And then comes the defense of the lawyers, whose defense of their clients is unjustified. They have debased themselves from the stage of law and justice, and a few of them even tried to turn black into white in the courtrooms. All of this leaves me astounded at the revolution that came into being.

Does the disseminator of fabricated stories not know that it won't take very long before the lies come to light and the truth emerges, at which point he will cover his face in shame?

Furthermore, those murderers and looters do not seem to understand that after the deed they will have to face interrogation and stand trial and will eventually pay the price for their actions.

---

454. Here Chelouche adopts the major discursive framing of the Zionist press, namely that the riot was the action of an "inflamed mob," and that the violence was carried out by neighbors. (Both themes were prominent, especially in the right-wing *Do'ar hayom* in which Chelouche often published his essays.) Hillel Cohen critiques the view that the "'inflamed mob' lacks any ideological motivation or judgment of its own," in Cohen, *Year Zero of the Arab-Israeli Conflict*, 11. Campos, "Remembering Jewish-Arab Contact and Conflict," critiques the framing of "neighbors" as only partially accurate and instrumentally used. While there were some documented cases of perpetrators of violence who were known to their victims, many of the instances of violence were committed by strangers, in many cases from villages or other towns. In addition, there were numerous documented cases of neighbors rescuing their neighbors from violence.

How was the murderer driven to kill the neighbor who lived safely alongside him since ancient times? As opposed to what has on more than one occasion been published by the Arab Executive, the Jews residing in the country have lived for centuries with them in peace and will continue to live with them in peace for eternity. Even though the massacre was particularly vicious, some of the lawyers are not even ashamed to deny in court that the killing in Hebron took place in a violent manner, as the Jews have testified. Is it permitted to kill and to spill innocent blood inside the victim's home even in a "simple" manner?

Upon my soul, those terrible acts are unimaginable and have no parallel in world history. They are particularly unbelievable to someone like me who has known the Arabs for such a long time. I would certainly never accuse the Arab people of Palestine in its entirety, in the same way that I am certain that all enlightened Muslims are completely opposed to what was done in these riots. But there are certain individuals and groups whose objective is to incite the masses periodically, and they use this in the name of nationalism as their symbol, although their aims and intentions differ—with each individual or group motivated by their own particular interests. The God of truth will most certainly judge them for their actions. He who digs a pit—will fall into it.[455]

I was extremely surprised that the entire press, including the fanatical, cheap press as well as some of the more moderate and respectable press, unanimously sang the same tune in their lead editorials: "Attack by the Jews in Palestine," "Attack by the Jews on the Muslims," "Attack by the Jews on the al-Aqsa Mosque," "Attack by the Jews on al-Buraq."

Is it true that the Jews attacked the al-Aqsa Mosque? Heaven forbid. Or that everyone attacked the Arab villages or the neighborhoods in the cities where the Muslims or Christians live? No, on the contrary. The Arabs attacked some of the Jewish colonies and the Jewish neighborhoods in the cities: Hebron, Jerusalem, Tel Aviv and Jaffa, Haifa and Safed—with the exception of Tiberias, which did not play any part in all this improper behavior, because

---

455. This is a paraphrase of Proverbs 26:27.

the vast majority of its inhabitants are Jews.[456] The overriding evidence will without doubt be recorded in world history.

As for the Jews' "attacks" on the Western Wall: the whole world knows that the Wall has for centuries been the Jews' place of prayer. Nevertheless, those who wish to stir up trouble have placed and continue to place numerous obstacles along the way, so that the Jews will stop coming to pray at the Wall, as is their custom. However, despite all the obstacles now found in their way, the Jews continued to pray at the site. And this is considered an attack!

In truth, the situation is altogether different. The primary motivation for all those who are looking to cause a rift is the Balfour Declaration. It is a political issue that concerns the Mandatory government, but any thinking person knows that the Balfour Declaration is intended so that the Jews will come with their money, knowledge, and energy in order to build up the country so that it will not be desolate, as it had been for centuries until now. What have our Arab brothers lost from the Jews' immigration to the country in order to build it? On the contrary, they have gained many benefits, in every sense. Many of them sold land to Jews, most of which is of the worst quality—rocky land that has not been touched by human hand since ancient times—for which they received sums they had never even hoped to get. With the money they received, they improved their own fertile lands.[457]

In those villages adjacent to the Jewish colonies, they learned from the Jews diligence and labor techniques, transforming those villages into the most fertile, and their financial situation vastly improved in comparison with other villages that are further away from the Jewish colonies, which remain as they had been, without progressing even in the slightest. Is this a loss for the Arabs?

Moreover, malaria persisted in this country for centuries and took its toll on its inhabitants without them even knowing how to

456. The various communal leaders in Tiberias issued calls to avoid violence, although one synagogue was torched by Arab demonstrators. Cohen, *Year Zero of the Arab-Israeli Conflict*, 181.

457. While Chelouche was likely sincere in this belief, as Cohen traces in "Zionism as a Blessing to the Arabs," the claim that Zionism posed a blessing to Palestinian Arabs had a long history of political instrumentalization within the Zionist movement.

conduct research and discover its causes. Now malaria has been practically eradicated, and thanks to whom? Who battled the swamps if not the Jews, through their energy and their funds?

And the Arabs still complain that Jews take most of the government clerkships, but that is simply a lie. The government's statistics are well known, and the numbers are quite clear. If you do the math, you will find that there aren't even as many Jewish officials in the government as they would be entitled to proportionally.

What else: mass immigration of Jews? Every Muslim knows that prior to the World War, there were 120,000 Jews in the country.[458] If we add 2 percent natural growth annually, over the ten years of the British Mandate, that adds 24,000 to the previous number, which together is 144,000. According to the most recent government census, there are 160,000 Jews. Thus, all of the immigration over these past ten years has produced an excess of only 16,000 beyond the natural increase. And yet you claim that you agree to limited immigration. So why all this noise? And if some of the Jews came to the land with their money and energy in order to settle here, but then after losing their money in the country, a large portion of them returned to the wider world after realizing that at this moment in time this country is not yet flowing with milk and honey. And who is it that profits from the money left behind in the country by that poor wretch if not the inhabitants of the land, most of whom are Arabs?

Therefore, my suggestion to our enlightened Arab brothers is that they take into account everything stated above, which is based on the reality of the situation and on clear economic trends, and then make an effort to sway the minds of those agitators and inciters, so they will cease their destructive activity so that the country and its inhabitants may to be brought back to life, and not brought to ruin and decay of its inhabitants.

Upon my return from Lebanon to the country, the economic boycott between the Arabs and the Jews began to develop in rapid strides.

458. This is a completely unsubstantiated figure; the prewar Jewish population was closer to 80,000. The actual size of Jewish immigration between 1919 and 1928 was 101,400 Jewish immigrants, according to the statistics submitted by the Zionist Organization to the Permanent Mandates Commission of the League of Nations. This was more than six times the number that Chelouche argued in his essay.

FIGURE 29.2. *Yosef Eliyahu Chelouche,*
late 1920s. Chelouche Family Collection.

As an experienced businessman for decades, I saw from the early signs that the boycott would cause grave damage to the economic situation of Jews throughout the country—and not only to the Jews but to the Arabs as well.

As I observed and watched the boycott and its outcomes, I could not rest or relax. Through the help of several important Jewish public figures, we succeeded in making contact with several Arab leaders and notables who had considerable influence among their people, as well as with publishers of their newspapers, in order to end the boycott that was damaging both sides. The boycott was canceled before it had a chance to strike damaging roots in our economic life, which was between us and our neighbors.

As we were handling these economic issues, I helped others to embrace the economic truth of our life in this country—that our shared economic lives in the country were linked by an unbreakable bond, and that we will not build our life in the country as a "people that dwells apart."[459]

459. Numbers 23:9.

By virtue of our quiet and modest work, and without calling attention to our activities, we relieved ourselves and from our economic life the harsh and damaging boycott. I arranged and coordinated the work of a team of friends, who helped me resolve additional issues pertaining to relations between neighbors in the country, to peaceful labor and commercial relationships that we hope will culminate in the desired solution and positive results.

In those activities and in the activities of my life over the past few years that I undertook in the arena of improving relations, I collaborated with Mr. Dizengoff, and at times with Mr. Tolkowsky as well. For understandable reasons, it is not yet possible to speak publicly of these actions and their value to the *yishuv*, although several of them have produced important results.

The initiatives toward which I have devoted all of my attention in the past few years may appear insignificant in the eyes of the reader, but I believe in them, and I know that these minor initiatives will sprout great outcomes that we in our generation cannot yet appreciate. Only the history of Israel and those who write the chronicles of the *yishuv* will, after the passage of some time, be able to judge these activities in the proper light and in a nonpartisan manner. At that point, our minor activities and initiatives will be viewed in a completely different light. Only our children and grandchildren after us will joyously reap the benefits of our having planted these seeds with tears, in the soil of our land, for the benefit of our entire people.

EPILOGUE

This chronicle of my life has come to an end, but my life has not come to an end. Now, in my twilight years, as a final chapter to my sixty years on this earth, I would like to add a bit of the perspective I have gained from my life experiences, which I have not expounded upon in the book.

I have held myself to the promise I made in the prologue of this book —that I would restrict myself to describing the story of my life and surroundings and telling the story as it happened. However, this memoir appears at such a gloomy period and such a sad and wretched time in the life of our people, both in exile and in our own land, during the year that the White Paper[460] was issued, at a time when the Jewish multitudes in exile find themselves at a crossroads and ask which way to turn. At a time when the pioneers of the rebirth and the builders of our land sadly ask in the gloom of night, Watchman, what of the night? Times like these compel every writer, public figure, and man of position to share what is in his heart.

We now face a fundamental shift in the Balfour Declaration in the aftermath of the publication of the White Paper by the Labour government in England, with Passfield's[461] reinterpretation of the declaration,

---

460. The White Paper referred to the formal statement of British policy in October 1930 that was issued in the aftermath of the Hope-Simpson report on the 1929 riots. The White Paper revised British policy in Palestine, severely curtailing its support for the Zionist movement. It was denounced by the Zionist movement and cautiously supported by the Palestinian nationalists. In early 1931, British prime minister Ramsay MacDonald backtracked on some of the White Paper's recommendations in a personal letter to WZO chairman Chaim Weizmann, in what became known as "the black letter."

461. Sidney James Webb, 1st Baron Passfield (1859–1947), was a British socialist who served as colonial secretary in 1929–1930 under the Labour government headed by Ramsay MacDonald. The White Paper he issued found that British obligations to Jews and Arabs in Palestine were equal, and that the rights of Arabs should not be negatively affected by the Jewish national home policy; as a result, new regulations

which cast despair into the hearts of many Jews around the world but in particular among the builders of our country. I am among those builders who retain our faith and hope in the building up of the land, no matter what happens along the way.

Despite the apathetic attitude of the English people and of the English government to our national enterprise, due to disputes with our neighbors and those who would instigate a feud between neighbors, I am nevertheless filled with hope and faith that peace between us and our Muslim neighbors will come to be. Our national home will be established, for there is no power on earth that can stop two neighbors from living in peace, for it is the elixir that bestows life on both of them.

I have a strong belief that by modifying the way we are building up the country and by changing the understanding and perception of the relationship between the neighbors, if we do those things, then we will repeat what happened during the Turkish era when the "Red Note"[462] became a "note" for construction and expansion because of our good relations with our neighbors. It is my abiding faith and hope that through a fundamental transformation of values in our work doctrine and in our relations with our neighbors, we will also transform the White Paper, which many people see as a Black Paper, into the building paper for our national home.

The relations with our neighbors in this country must now be the main thrust of our activities. This is the greatest issue of all, which must be the focus of all of our attention. The natives of this land, who have lived in this land for decades, are the ones who must work energetically and resolve this serious issue faced by the *yishuv*. And although this work has become so much more difficult since the days of the Balfour Declaration and the bloody events that ensued, it is nevertheless incumbent upon the native sons of this land, those who are most familiar with the issue, to carry out the task tactfully and quietly. There is genuinely a great deal of work to be done in this regard. I am not saying that I am in possession of an instant solution to a complicated and terribly painful issue in the

---

were set to limit Jewish immigration to Palestine and Jewish land acquisition from Palestinian Arabs.

462. A nickname for the temporary residency visa in Palestine issued by Ottoman authorities intermittently between the 1880s and 1913 that limited Jews to a three-month residence.

life of the *yishuv*, but we must consider every possible path to the solution, which is critical to our settlement work both now and in the future.

I am not misleading myself. I realize that maintaining the relationship between us and our neighbors demands much deliberation and effort, but we can no longer put off addressing this issue, which affects not only the present but the future as well. Like it or not, this pressing issue stands now very clearly on our personal and communal agendas, and we cannot be negligent and simply dismiss it because the issue is weighing so heavily upon us. It is the stumbling block, it is the obstacle that stands in the way of practically all of our settlement work in the country, and without us finding a solution to it, we will not be able to move ahead with our work.

In this epilogue, I would like to elaborate and go into a bit more detail about this important issue, which I was unable to expand upon due to the technical considerations of the book, even though this issue took up an important part during the course of my life. We should acknowledge at least now, in light of the events that have taken place, and we should acknowledge the truth that we natives of the land have been aware of ever since we made our first steps in the *yishuv*, that there is no greater danger than that which results from an incorrect appraisal of the forces at your and your allies' disposal, and the forces of the others and those of your opponents. We must fully comprehend our difficult situation in the land of our forefathers and appraise, at the very least now, our forces and the forces of those who oppose us.

Anyone even slightly familiar with the history of our *yishuv* from its earliest days knows that the principle of building a close relationship with our neighbors and living in peace with them was the primary obligation of the natives of this land. We fulfilled these principles as our guiding ideology. And if we succeeded in this work, our success was largely due to us having properly evaluated and taken into consideration our neighbors, as well, alongside whom we had to construct our building.

However—and here we will speak the bitter and terrible truth, but the truth, all the same—our managers, and many of the builders of the *yishuv* who arrived here from exile to manage us, did not acknowledge the tremendous value of neighborly relationships, this basic, simple principle. Perhaps they did not understand it or did not care enough to take it into account, but their failure to address it now bears a great deal of blame for the complication of the issue to the extent that it is now the most painful subject faced by the *yishuv*.

EPILOGUE

As many have already publicly written and commented, from the day that Herzl first conceived of the idea of political Zionism, Zionist propaganda in every country and in every language always described the land in which we are going to build our national settlement as a desert land, desolate and uninhabited. After such a description of the land, in print and in speech, always referring to it as virgin soil—this certainty was the basis for the shaping of Zionist doctrine and methods for building up the land, which considered all factors except for the one that they forgot: the attention to the inhabitants already residing in this land.

In order to understand the extent that this disdainful attitude has negatively affected the Zionist enterprise in the *yishuv*, it is sufficient to mention just a few anecdotes, among many. Throughout the entire period of our work on building up the country, we have not made the effort to even learn the language of the country, the language of our neighbors, while at the same time we have been happily learning other languages. Even now, in the new Hebrew *yishuv* in our cities and our colonies, precious few people are able to read and write their language.

Another important issue: [After] the years of our construction work next to our neighbors, what do we know about the lives of the Arab people and its movements, sects, and tribes? Its customs and manners? Its economic and cultural situation, and so forth? In the entire body of Zionist literature, there is not a single book that accurately and realistically describes the life of this people, or offers factual data on its situation, in every sense. A book that will concentrate all the important material about this question that is so important to our *yishuv*, a book that would shed light on the subject for those interested in it. There has long been a need for such a book, and in the wake of the riots and the White Paper, there is an even greater real-time need for it in the highest order, at a time when so many are stumbling around in the dark in the earnest search for a solution to the Arab question.

Based on these two illustrations, and we could have cited many more, one understands that throughout the entire period of building our new *yishuv*, our leaders have concealed this hidden question from the Jewish world. It is not only our neighbors who have turned their backs on us; our own managers are guilty of having always viewed them with a disdainful and patronizing attitude.

Those who newly arrived treated the local inhabitants, alongside whom they had to settle and live, with indifference. Because of this attitude, the neighbors did not want to appreciate the significant benefits accruing from our settlement work, even though they were significant for them as well. Certainly, in reaction to the indifference shown toward them by the managers of the building of the land, they are unhappy with our building, despite knowing that the lion's share of the immense capital that comes from the Jewish nation and from Jewish individuals has found its way into their own hands, in a variety of ways. It is solely due to this dismissive attitude that they are not content to recognize this important fact: that by virtue of our contributions and our settlement work, they have received numerous improvements and enhancements to their economic and cultural life.

For what did they see in us and our work, from the beginning of our settlement to this very day? Only cold indifference, alienation, and derision. On top of that, they also heard our spokesmen in the Zionist press expressing a lot of blather and nonsense that at times caused us a great deal of damage.

It is interesting to note that there were times in the past when the more enlightened Muslim Arabs sought ways and made attempts on several occasions to get closer to us. Because many of them knew—and still know—that the Jews are the only element capable of bringing progress to the development, in all aspects, of this neglected land, to the benefit of the entire country. And the more clever among them are conscious of the fact that the Arabs' current opposition is merely artificial, caused by external reasons, by inciters and incitement, and they, as well as us natives of this land, know this to be clearly the case—that it is possible, in fact very possible, to forge an attitude of mutual understanding between us and them. One needs only to employ tact and a slight understanding of psychology to prepare the groundwork for what has been broken, to prepare it by taking real steps, by speaking the truth, and mainly by means of proper actions and acts that will lead us to the target.

It is incumbent on us to build the bridge between us and them, for otherwise our work on expanding the *yishuv* will be impeded, as it relies solely on our own feeble forces and on the forces of the British bayonet, which changes according to the spirit of the times and the political situation of the empire, similar to the biblical formula dating to Israel's war against Amalek. "When Moses's hands grew heavy"[463] and they raised

---

463. Exodus 17:12.

his arms, Israel triumphed, and vice versa. One thing is for certain—we cannot and must not rely solely on the British bayonet.

We will be able to build this bridge if we can consider this truth, that *our London is here in this country*, that only here in this country can we find the solution to this problem. But only if we confront the situation with a purehearted and correct attitude, with a warmhearted and true attitude, without any insidious, partisan, or alien intentions that are at odds with the pathway of peace and truth.

This is something that we natives of the land understood a long time ago, even before the British occupation, and right after it. But our managers, who steered the storm-tossed ship of the *yishuv* over our heads and without our knowledge, who did so from Berlin before the war and from London after the war, had no interest in taking into consideration our opinions. For we natives of the land thought differently, and they always tried to silence our correct voice on this issue like "a voice ring[ing] out in the desert."[464]

I sincerely hope that the chapters of my book, in which I have described the genuine, warmhearted attitude of our Muslim neighbors, will arouse those who would engage in the question of neighborly relations, by employing different methods and tactics. They would be wise to adopt the methods and tactics of the natives of the land, who have a great deal of experience in neighborly relations, and to correct as much as possible that which was distorted.

Those who will take it upon themselves to address this issue, like the other issues in building the *yishuv*, the needs of the *yishuv* demand that they should not only be the enthusiastic Zionists who give speeches and attend congress after congress, but they should also be good Jews, aside from their Zionism and nationalism. I am fed up with those who choose their Zionism over their Judaism, as opposed to us locals, who see in Judaism also nationalism. It is therefore so much dearer to us, which is why we are Jews and we do not believe in dry nationalism and nothing more. The passage of time has proven to me that all those who were Zionists connected to their Judaism also remained connected to their nationalism. And the opposite [is also true]—all those who adopted nationalism as a monopoly for their pleasure and moved further away from their Judaism—their nationalism also grew further away from them. Because

---

464. Isaiah 40:3.

nationalism without Judaism is nationalism that is dependent on interest and cannot exist on its own. And the opposite [is true]—those whose Judaism and nationalism coexisted, continued to exist, to this very day.

At this juncture I will also express my opinion on the Zionist leaders who succeeded Herzl. I believe that they misinterpreted two fundamental principles in the beginning of their work in building the country, and by doing so they strayed from the path paved by Dr. Herzl.

The first fundamental principle concerning the building of the country from which they strayed: Dr. Herzl wrote and warned us in his Zionist speeches, and also made it happen in life—it is strictly forbidden to establish the Zionist movement and build up the country on a basis of *schnorrering* [begging] in every possible form: charity, donations, contributions, et al., for it is not possible to build a people or a country with *schnorrered* funds.

Herzl founded the Colonial Trust as a robust institution. And if not for all the public funds that were wasted so alarmingly, if all of the funds that were deposited in the Colonial Trust had been expended in a commercially constructive manner that would have provided yields and repaid the principle at low interest, we would now have a national bank that could compete with the sort of banks that you find among other healthy nations. Our people and land would have been further strengthened from it, and by it the land would really be built. The second principle we encountered while building up the country: the socialists of all types and all the "true believers" proliferated in our small and impoverished country under red flags from which the country will most certainly not be built, and one can only hope it will not come to ruin by their hands. Here, as well, one should only bear in mind what Herzl said on this subject—that it is forbidden to allow international socialism to penetrate political Zionism, because it is anti-nationalist and because Zionism is based solely on nationalism, and without it there is no justification for the existence of Zionism.

And what did our leaders, the heirs of Herzl, do with these principles? In my lifetime, they have carried out the complete opposite of Herzl's doctrine and in doing so have steered the building of the land to the edge of a slope and to a disaster for the Zionist movement.

I have come to the conclusion of what I have come to say. Although I am not a writer and I do not have a monopoly on the preaching of morality, I will nevertheless take the opportunity to offer the following comments. I make these comments as an individual who has watched and observed the actions of the past generation and the actions of our current panic-stricken generation. On the basis of these observations, I have come to the conclusion that "like father, not like son": if our fathers were like human beings, then it is hard to say what name you could give to our current generation. Because although in the previous generation we did not have a Balfour Declaration, and we did not have special councils for education and for culture, we nevertheless were a better community, both as a general public and as individuals:

   a. We were not divided into several extremist factions—religious extremism on the one hand and anti-religious extremism on the other. We were one single unit in the Land of Israel, and every single Jew ranked the concerns of the general public above any individual or partisan interests.
   b. In the past, there was no room within us for a political party that cries bitterly and unceasingly about exploitation and thievery, while at the same time it itself imposes its authority on the public, employing brute force—all in the name of nationalism.
   c. In the past, there was no such thing among us as this shocking waste and pursuit of luxury, because every Jew would behave modestly in his business dealings and never spent more than he was able to. Then, every Jew's spoken word was sacred, and it never occurred to anyone to waste the money of others for his own pleasure. In our neighbors' eyes, our moral status was very high. And these comparisons would tip the scales even further toward the side of our generation if we bear in mind that we are considered the first generation of the redemption.

I have offered here, at the conclusion of my memoir, a few main points that are based on my life experiences, and on my direct observation of the pitfalls of life—we lived our lives as individuals and as a part of one people. And I hope that these heartfelt words will find their way to an attentive ear, as I have not come merely to voice criticism, but also to seek a solution to correct the situation of our people and our land. As the honest reader can judge, having followed my life story as retold in this book, this has been my prayer each day of my life, and it remains my pure prayer in the twilight of my life.

APPENDIX
Family Tree of Yosef Eliyahu Chelouche

1ST GENERATION

Avraham Chelouche (1809*–1855*) and Simha (née Hacohen Alkalatz) (1811*–1886)

2ND GENERATION

Rika Rivka Chelouche (1829*–1898) and Nissim Carsenty (1825–1870)
Hana Chelouche (1831*–1916) and Alter Louria (1837*–1861*)
Eliyahu Chelouche (1833*–1842*)
Yosef Chelouche (1835*–1842*)
Aharon Chelouche (1840–1920) and Sara (née Barukh) (1849–1918)
Yosef Chelouche (1845–1865)

3RD GENERATION (CHILDREN OF AHARON CHELOUCHE)

Avraham Haim Chelouche (1864–1925) and Sarina Sara (née Elbaz) (1875–1967)
Rahel Chelouche (1869–1933) and Binyamin Mehoudar (1868–1898)
Yosef Eliyahu Chelouche (1870–1934) and Freha Simha (née Moyal) (1872–1934)
Ya'akov Chelouche (1875–1944) and Perla (née Barukh) (1877–1944)
Jamila Chelouche (1882–1952) and Me'ir Fedida (1878–1920)
Luna Chelouche (1883–1915)
Sultana Chelouche (1889–1943) and Yesha'ayahu Aba Louria (1885–1948)

4TH GENERATION

<u>Children of Avraham Haim Chelouche</u>
Marco Chelouche (1889–1965) and Paulette (née Banasiak) (1896–1932)
Zaky Chelouche (1891–1973) and Mafalda (née Abouchdid); and Mira
 (née Liebenson)

Notes:
1. Asterisks (*) indicate assumed date of birth/death (no supportive documentation exists).
2. Italics and bold indicate direct ancestors or descendants of Yosef Eliyahu Chelouche.

David Chelouche (1893–1948) and Julia (née Bohbut) (1899–1999)
Shlomo Chelouche (1896–1896)
Simha Chelouche (1897–1990) and Yosef Pomrock (1894–1942)
Riquetta Rahel Chelouche (1899–1940) and Shlomo Goverik (1903–1961)
Samson Chelouche (1901–1984) and Margueritha (née Baeschlin) (1914–1962)

Children of Rahel Mehoudar
Sarina Sara Mehoudar (1888–1947) and Ben-Zion Rizo-Levi (1885–1909);
    and Ya'akov Tschianouroff (1884–1962)
Rafa'el Mehoudar (1889–1924) and Hana Rose (née Bernstein) (1892–1977)
Simi Simha Mehoudar (1893–1941) and Ya'akov Gara (1889–1965)
Emile Mehoudar (1898–1973) and Esterina (née Cohen) (1910–1987)

Children of Yosef Eliyahu Chelouche
Moshe Chelouche (1891–1968) and Rahel Mednitzky (1893–1922);
    and Nina Berligne (1897–1963)
Me'ir Chelouche (1895–1960) and Zehuvit (née Saharov) (1905–1999)
Avner Chelouche (1898–1950) and Miriam (née Gorodenchik) (1898–1961)
Zadoc Chelouche (1898–1948) and Rose (née Apfelbaum) (1901–1995)
Hillel Chelouche (1904–1971)
Yehudit Chelouche (1906–1965) and Hiram Cohen (1895–1976)
Yoram Chelouche (1910–1986) and Alisa (née Kaplan) (1916–2008)

Children of Ya'akov Chelouche
Margarita Margalit Chelouche (1902–1984) and Moshe Havatselet (1904–1981)
Gavri'el Chelouche (1906–1938)
Me'ira Chelouche (1908–1966) and Walter Adam (1900–1996)
Lea Chelouche (1913–1978) and David Lubinsky (1911–1998)
Shlomo Chelouche (1916–2006) and Mary (née Hayoun) (1928–2024)

Children of Jamila Fedida
Shma'aya Caspi (1909–1979) and Rivka (née Abadi) (1917–2009)
Edmond Fedida (1910–1987) and Ida
Annette Fedida (1912–2015) and Ya'akov Arouh (1908–1967)
Pnina Fedida (1916–2000) and Eli'ezer Kassirer (1922–2015)

Children of Sultana Louria

Yeroham Louria (1914–1977) and Tikwah Weinstock (1925–2022)

Aharon Louria (1922–1999) and Regine Ethel (née Rabinovitz) (1924–1966); and Dalia (née Triber) (b. 1937)

Sarka Sara Louria (1927–2010) and Monya Avrahami (1928–2014)

BIBLIOGRAPHY

PRIMARY SOURCES

Archives
Central Zionist Archive, Jerusalem
    Chelouche Family Personal Archive (A488)
Devlet Arşivleri Başkanlığı Osmanlı Arşivi (BOA), Istanbul
French Ministry of Foreign Affairs, Nantes and Paris
Israel State Archives, Jerusalem
    Ottoman Government Notebooks
The Montefiore Endowment, London
    Montefiore Registers, www.montefioreendowment.org.uk/census-search
National Library of Israel, Jerusalem
    Shariʻa Court Registers of Jaffa

Published Primary Sources
Abramson, Glenda, ed. *Soldiers' Tales: Two Palestinian Jewish Soldiers in the Ottoman Army during the First World War*. London: Vallentine Mitchell, 2013.
Barron, J. B. *Palestine. Report and General Abstracts of the Census of 1922*. Jerusalem: Greek Convent Press, 1923.
Behar, Moshe, and Zvi Ben-Dor Benite, eds. *Modern Middle Eastern Jewish Thought: Writings on Identity, Politics, and Culture 1893–1958*. Waltham, MA: Brandeis University Press, 2013.
Bulletin de la chambre de commerce d'industrie et d'agriculture de Palestine, vol. 1, no. 2 (August 1909).
Chelouche, Aharon. *Migalabiyya lekovʻa tembel: Sipurah shel mishpacha* [From the Galabiyya to the Tembel Cap: Story of a family]. Tel Aviv: Bnei Sha'ul, 1991.
Chelouche, Julia Bohbut. *Haetz vehashoreshim* [The tree and the roots]. 1982.
Chelouche, Yosef Eliyahu. *Parashat Hayay, 1870–1930* [The story of my life]. Tel Aviv: Stroud, 1931.
———. *Parashat Hayay (1870–1930)*. Tel Aviv: Babel, 2005.
Chelouche-Havatzelet, Margalit. *Zikhronot leveit saba* [Memories from grandfather's house]. Tel Aviv, n.d.
Cohen, Amnon. *Yehudim beveit hamishpat haMuslimi: Hameʻah ha-19* [Jews in the Muslim court: The 19th century]. Jerusalem: Yad Ben Zvi, 2003.

Cohen, Israel. *The Turkish Persecution of the Jews*. United Kingdom: Alabaster, Passmore & Sons, 1918.

Cook's Tourists' Handbook for Palestine and Syria. London: Thomas Cook and Son, 1876.

de Ballobar, Conde. *Jerusalem in World War I: The Palestine Diary of a European Diplomat*. New York: Bloomsbury, 2011.

Dizengoff, Meir. *'Im Tel Aviv bagolah* [With Tel Aviv in exile]. Tel Aviv: Emunot Eretz Israel, 1930.

Druyanov, Alter. *Sefer Tel Aviv* [Tel Aviv book]. Tel Aviv: Va'adat Sefer Tel Aviv, 1936.

Eliav, Mordechai. *Österreich und das heilige Land: Ausgewählte Konsulatsdokumente aus Jerusalem, 1849–1917* [Austria and the Holy Land: Selected consular documents from Jerusalem, 1849–1917]. Wien: Österreichischen Akademie der Wissenschaften, 2000.

Elmaliach, Avraham. "Letoldot haMa'aravim beYerushalayim" [History of the Maghrebim in Jerusalem]. *Luah Eretz Israel* 14 (1908–1909): 53–88.

Elmaliach, A., and Y. A. 'Abadi. *R. Yosef Eliyahu Chelouche, Z"L: Sefer zikaron lemle'at shana leftirato* [Yosef Eliyahu Chelouche, z"l: Memorial book on the first anniversary of his death]. Jerusalem: Uriel Press, 1935.

Geddes, Patrick. *Town Planning Report Jaffa and Tel-Aviv*. Typescript, 1925.

Government of Palestine. *Commercial Bulletin of the Department of Customs and Trade*. Vol. 4. Jerusalem, 1924.

Grayevsky, Pinchas Ben Zvi. *Milhemet haYehudim bamisyon mishnat takpad 'ad hayom hazeh* [The war of the Jews against the missions]. Jerusalem: Histadrut, 1935.

Great Britain, Local Government Board, Medical. *Annual Report of the Medical Officer of the Local Government Board*. H. M. Stationery Office, 1904.

Great Britain Colonial Office. *Palestine: Disturbances in May, 1921; Reports of the Commission of Inquiry with Correspondence Relating Thereto*. London, 1921.

Hacohen, Mordechai Ben Hillel. *Milhemet ha'amim* [War of the nations]. Jerusalem: Yad Ben Zvi, 1985 reprint.

Howard, Alexander. *Howard's Guide to Jerusalem and Vicinity with Map of Palestine*. 1895.

L'Indicateur syrien: Annuaire de la Syrie et du Liban, de la Palestine et de l'Egypte [The Syrian indicator: Annual yearbook of Syria and Lebanon, Palestine and Egypt]. Beirut: 1923.

Khalaf, Noha Tadros. *Les mémoires de 'Issa al-'Issa: Journaliste et intellectuel palestinien (1878–1950)* [The memoirs of 'Issa al-'Issa: Palestinian journalist and intellectual]. Paris: Editions Karthala, 2009.

Kushner, David. *To Be Governor of Jerusalem: The City and District during the Time of Ali Ekrem Bey, 1906–1908*. Istanbul: Isis Press, 2010.

Luncz, A. M., ed. *Jerusalem Yearbook for the Diffusion of an Accurate Knowledge of Ancient and Modern Palestine*. Vienna: Buchdruckerei von Georg Broeg, 1881.

Mills, E. *Census of Palestine 1931. Part 1 Report*. 2 vols. Vol. 1. Alexandria: Whitehead Morris, 1933.

Musallam, Akram, ed. *Yawmiyaat Khalil al-Sakakini* [Diary of Khalil al-Sakakini]. Vol. 1. Ramallah: Khalil Sakakini Culture Centre and the Institute of Jerusalem Studies, 2003.

Palestine: Blue Book; 1926–1927. London: Waterlow and Sons, 1928.

Porter, Josias Leslie. *A Handbook for Travelers in Syria and Palestine*. London: John Murray, 1868.

Report of the Commission on the Palestine Disturbances of August 1929. London: His Majesty's Stationery Office, 1930.

Sâlnâme-yi Vilâyet-i Sûriye [Yearbook of the province of Syria]. Vol. 3. 1287/88 (1871/72).

Samuel, Sydney Montagu. *Jewish Life in the East*. London: CK Paul, 1881.

Sandel, Theodor. "Karte der Umgebung von Jafa." *Zeitschrift des Deutschen Palästina-Vereins*. Vol. 3. 1880.

Schick, Conrad. "Fortschritte der Civilisation in Palästina in den letzten 25 Jahren." *Österreichische Monatsschrift für den Orient* 6 (1880): 63–67.

Scholten, Frank. *Palestine Illustrated*. 2 vols. London: Longmans, Green, and Co., 1931.

Tamari, Salim. *Year of the Locust: A Soldier's Diary and the Erasure of Palestine's Ottoman Past*. Berkeley: University of California Press, 2011.

Tamari, Salim, and Issam Nassar, eds. *Al-Quds al-'Uthmaniyya fil-mudhakkirat al-Jawhariyya: Al-Kitab al-awwal min mudhakkirat al-musiqi Wasif Jawhariyya, 1904–1917* [Ottoman Jerusalem in the Jawhariyya memoirs]. Vol. 1. Beirut: Mu'assasat al-Dirasat al-Filastiniyya, 2003.

———, eds. *The Storyteller of Jerusalem: The Life and Times of Wasif Jawhariyyeh, 1904–1948*. Northampton, MA: Interlink, 2014.

Tolkowsky, Samuel. *The Gateway of Palestine: A History of Jaffa*. 1925.

———. *The Jewish Colonisation in Palestine, Its History and Its Prospects*. London: Zionist Organisation, 1918.

Weiss, Akiva Arieh. *Reshitah shel Tel-Aviv: Toldot yisod ha'ir ureshimot yoman* [The beginning of Tel Aviv: The history of the foundation of the city and diary notes]. Tel Aviv: Ayanot, 1956.

Yahuda, Avraham Shalom. "Lezikhron David Yellin" [In memory of David Yellin]. In *'Ever ve'Arav: Osef mekhkarim vema'amarim, shirat he'Aravim, zikhronot ureshamim* [Hebrew and Arab: Collection of research and articles, poetry of the Arabs, memoirs and impressions]. New York: HaHistadrut ha'Ivrit beAmerika/Shulsinger Bros., 1946.

Yellin, Yehoshuʻa. *Zikhronot leben Yerushalayim* [Memoirs of a son of Jerusalem]. Jerusalem, 1925.

BIOGRAPHICAL DICTIONARIES

al-Safi, ʻAbd al-Rida Muhammad, and Iftikhar Fahim al-Farakh Badran. *Muʻjam abnaʼ Yafa* [Encyclopedia of the sons of Jaffa]. ʻAmman, 1998.

Gaon, Moshe David. *Yehudei haMizrach beEretz Israel*. Vol. 2. Jerusalem: Ariel, 1937.

———. *Yehudei haMizrach beEretz Israel beʻavar uvehove*. Vol. 1. Jerusalem: Vaʻad ʻedat haSfaradit, 1928.

Mannaʼ, ʻAdel. *ʻAlam Falastin fi awakhir al-ʻahd al-ʻUthmani (1800–1918)* [Palestinian notables in the last days of the Ottoman era]. Jerusalem: Muʼassasat al-dirasat al-Falastiniyya, 1986.

Qalyubi, Taher Adib. *Aʼilat wa-shakhsiyyat min Yafa wa-qadaʼha* [Families and personalities from Jaffa and its province]. Beirut: Al-muʼassasa al-ʻArabiyya lil-dirasat wal-nashr, 2006.

Tidhar, David. *Entziklopediya lehalutzei hayishuv uvonav*. Multiple vols. Tel Aviv, 1947. https://www.tidhar.tourolib.org.

SECONDARY SOURCES

Abramson, Glenda. "Haunted by Jackals: The Expulsions of 1917." *Israel Affairs* 24, no. 2 (2018): 201–20.

———. "The 1914 Deportation of the Jaffa Jews: 'A Little Footnote of War'?" *Israel Affairs* 28, no. 5 (2022): 706–23.

Aharonson, Ran. *Rothschild and Early Jewish Colonization in Palestine*. New York: Rowman & Littlefield, 2000.

Akın, Yiğit. *When the War Came Home: The Ottomans' Great War and the Devastation of an Empire*. Stanford, CA: Stanford University Press, 2018.

Aksakal, Mustafa. *The Ottoman Road to War in 1914: The Ottoman Empire and the First World War*. Cambridge: Cambridge University Press, 2008.

al-Bawwab, ʻAli Hasan. *Mawsuʻat Yafa al-jamila*. Vols. 1–2. Beirut: Al-Muʼassasah al-Arabiyah lil-Diraasat wa-al-Nashr, 2003.

Aleksandrowicz, Or. "Forget and Rewrite: Unearthing the History of Manshiya/Neve Shalom." *Architectura* 51, no. 2 (2024): 202–23.

———. "A Journey in the Wake of a Forgotten Yesteryear." *Sharsheret Hadorot* 19, no. 3 (2005).

———. "A Wish for Destruction: The Life and Death of the Herzliya Gymnasium Building" [Hebrew]. In *Gymnasium Days: The Herzliya Hebrew Gymnasium, 1905–1959*, edited by Guy Raz, 26–47. Tel Aviv: Eretz Israel Museum, 2013.

Aleksandrowicz, Or, and Samuel Giler. "The New Gate of Jaffa during the Late Ottoman Period." *History and Archaeology of Jaffa* 2 (2017): 179–90.

BIBLIOGRAPHY

Aleksandrowicz, Or, and Yamu van Nes. "Spatio-Syntactical Analysis and Historical Spatial Potentials: The Case of Jaffa-Tel Aviv." *Journal of Interdisciplinary History* 49, no. 3 (2018): 445–72.

al-Tarawnah, Muhammad Salem Ghathiyan. *Qada' Yafa fi al-'ahd al-'Uthmani: Dirasah idariyah iqtisadiyah ijtima'iyah, 1281–1333 H/1864–1914 M* [The district of Jaffa in the Ottoman period: An administrative, economic, and social study, 1864–1914]. 'Amman: Ministry of Culture, 2000.

Amara, Ahmad. "The Ottoman Tanzimat in the Palestinian Frontier of Beersheba (1850–1917)." In *Living in the Ottoman Lands: Identities Administration and Warfare*, edited by Hasan Kılıçarslan, Ömer Faruk Can, and Burhan Çağlar, 126–55. Istanbul: Kronik, 2021.

Arbel, Yoav, and Baruch Rosen. "Concepts and Facts of Late Ottoman Jaffa: Cartographic Records and Archaeological Evidence." Paper presented at the Proceedings of the International Cartographic Association, 2021.

Arraf, Shukri. *Al-Saraya: Government Headquarters in Palestine during the Ottoman Era*. Ramallah: Riwaq, 2016.

Avcı, Yasemin. "Jerusalem and Jaffa in the Late Ottoman Period: The Concession-Hunting Struggle for Public Works Projects." In *Late Ottoman Palestine: The Period of Young Turk Rule*, edited by Yuval Ben-Bassat and Eyal Ginio, 81–102. London: IB Tauris, 2011.

Azaryahu, Maoz, and S. Ilan Troen. *Tel-Aviv, the First Century: Visions, Designs, Actualities*. Bloomington: Indiana University Press, 2011.

Bailey, Clinton. *Bedouin Law from Sinai and the Negev: Justice without Government*. New Haven: Yale University Press, 2009.

Bar-Gal, Yoram. "Naming City Streets—a Chapter in the History of Tel-Aviv, 1909–1947." *Contemporary Jewry* 10, no. 2 (1989): 39–50.

Bashkin, Orit. *The New Babylonians: A History of Jews in Modern Iraq*. Stanford, CA: Stanford University Press, 2012.

Beinin, Joel. "The Karaites in Modern Egypt." In *Karaite Judaism: A Guide to Its History and Literary Sources*, edited by Meira Polliack, 417–30. Leiden: Brill, 2003.

Ben-Arieh, Yehoshua. *Jerusalem in the 19th Century: The Old City*. New York: St. Martin's Press, 1984.

Benbassa, Esther. *Haim Nahum: A Sephardi Chief Rabbi in Politics, 1892–1923*. Tuscaloosa: University of Alabama Press, 1995.

Ben-Bassat, Yuval. "Local Feuds or Premonitions of a Bi-National Conflict? A Reexamination of the Early Jewish-Arab Encounter in Palestine at the End of the 19th Century." PhD diss., University of Chicago, 2007.

———. *Petitioning the Sultan: Protests and Justice in Late Ottoman Palestine, 1865–1908*. London: IB Tauris, 2014.

———. "Reconsidering the Role of a Maghrebi Family in the Yishuv in Late Ottoman

Palestine: The Case of the Moyal Family." *Journal of Modern Jewish Studies* 19, no. 4 (2020): 490–508.

Ben-Hanania, Yehoshuʻa (Yaʻakov Yehoshuʻa). "Dr. Shimʻon Moyal vehabeʻaya haYehudit-haʻAravit" [Dr. Shimon Moyal and the Jewish-Arab problem]. *Hed haMizrach* (Jerusalem), October 10, 1944.

———. "Hasoferet Ester Moyal utkufatah" [The author Esther Moyal and her era]. *Hed haMizrach* (Jerusalem), September 17, 1944.

Bensinger, Gad J. "Palestine in German Thought and Action 1871–1914." PhD diss., Loyola University, 1971.

Ben Yaʻakov, Michal. "Mifkadei Montefiore veheker haYehudim beagan hayam hatichon." *Peʻamim* 107 (2006): 117–49.

Beška, Emanuel. *From Ambivalence to Hostility: The Arabic Newspaper Filastin and Zionism, 1911–1914*. Studia Orientalia Monographica 6. Bratislava: Slovak Academic Press, 2016.

Betzalel, Yitzhak. *Noladatem Tziyoniyim: HaSefaradim beEretz Israel baTziyonut uvatchiya haʻIvrit batkufa haʻOtomanit* [You were born Zionists: The Sephardim in the Land of Israel in Zionism and the Hebrew revival during the Ottoman period]. Jerusalem: Ben Zvi Institute, 2007.

Buessow, Johann. *Hamidian Palestine: Politics and Society in the District of Jerusalem, 1872–1908*. Leiden: Brill, 2011.

Bunton, Martin. *Colonial Land Policies in Palestine, 1917–1936*. Oxford: Oxford University Press, 2007.

Campos, Michelle. "Mizrah umaarav (East and West): A Sephardi Cultural and Political Project in Post-Ottoman Jerusalem." *Journal of Modern Jewish Studies* 16, no. 2 (2017): 332–48.

———. *Ottoman Brothers: Muslims, Christians, and Jews in Early Twentieth-Century Palestine*. Stanford, CA: Stanford University Press, 2011.

———. "Remembering Jewish-Arab Contact and Conflict." In *Reapproaching the Border: New Perspectives on the Study of Israel/Palestine*, edited by Mark LeVine and Sandy Sufian, 41–65. Lanham, MD: Rowman and Littlefield, 2007.

Caplan, Neil. "Faisal Ibn Husain and the Zionists: A Re-examination with Documents." *International History Review* 5, no. 4 (1983): 561–614.

Chelouche, Evyatar (Tari). "Hahayim beʻet hamilhama: Yosef Eliyahu Chelouche uvnei-mishpachto bemahalach hamilhama" [Yosef Eliyahu Chelouche and his family during the first world war]. In *From the Sharon to Wadi Ara, the Battles of Megiddo 1918: The Cavalry Breakthrough to the North*, edited by Zvi Shilony and Eran Tearosh, 140–70. 14th Annual Conference of the Society for the Heritage of World War I in Israel. Jerusalem: Ariel, 2017.

———. "The Mystery of the Second Joseph Chelouche" [Hebrew]. *Sharsheret Hadorot* 24, no. 1 (2010): viii–xvii.

Cohen, Amnon. "Ottoman Rule and the Re-emergence of the Coast of Palestine (17th–18th Centuries)." *Revue des mondes musulmans et de la Méditerranée* 39, no. 1 (1985): 163–75.

Cohen, Hillel. *Year Zero of the Arab-Israeli Conflict: 1929*. Waltham, MA: Brandeis University Press, 2015.

———. "Zionism as a Blessing to the Arabs: History of an Argument." In *The British Mandate in Palestine: A Centenary Volume, 1920–2020*, edited by Michael J. Cohen, 157–71. London: Routledge, 2020.

Cohen, Julia Phillips. *Becoming Ottomans: Sephardi Jews and Imperial Citizenship in the Modern Era*. Oxford: Oxford University Press, 2014.

———. "Between Civic and Islamic Ottomanism: Jewish Imperial Citizenship in the Hamidian Era." *International Journal of Middle East Studies* 44, no. 2 (2012): 237–55.

Derri, Aviv. "The Construction of 'Native' Jews in Late Mandate Palestine: An Ongoing Nahda as a Political Project." *International Journal of Middle East Studies* 53, no. 2 (2021): 253–71.

Dierauff, Evelin. *Translating Late Ottoman Modernity in Palestine: Debates on Ethno-Confessional Relations and Identity in the Arab Palestinian Newspaper Filasṭīn (1911–1914)*. Vol. 2. Goettingen: Vandenhoeck & Ruprecht, 2020.

Dolbee, Samuel, and Shay Hazkani. "Impossible Is Not Ottoman: Menashe Meirovitch, ʿIsa al-ʿIsa, and Imperial Citizenship in Palestine." *International Journal of Middle East Studies* 47, no. 2 (2015): 241–62.

Eckfeldt, Jacob Reese, and William Ewing Du Bois. *A Manual of Gold and Silver Coins of All Nation, Struck within the Past Century: Showing Their History, and Legal Basis, and Their Actual Weight, Fineness, and Value, Chiefly from Original and Recent Assays*. Philadelphia: Assay Office of the Mint, 1842.

Eppel, Michael. "Note About the Term *Effendiyya* in the History of the Middle East." *International Journal of Middle East Studies* 41, no. 3 (2009): 535–39.

Even-Zohar, Itamar. "The Emergence of Native Hebrew Culture in Palestine, 1882–1948." *Studies in Zionism* 4 (1981): 167–84.

Evri, Yuval. *The Return to Al-Andalus: Disputes over Sephardic Culture and Identity between Arabic and Hebrew*. Jerusalem: Hebrew University Magnes Press, 2020.

Evri, Yuval, and Hagar Kotef. "When Does a Native Become a Settler? (with Apologies to Zreik and Mamdani)." *Constellations: An International Journal of Critical and Democratic Theory* 29, no. 1 (2020): 3–18.

Evri, Yuval, and Hillel Cohen. "Between Shared Homeland to National Home: The Balfour Declaration from a Native Sephardic Perspective." In *The Arab and Jewish Questions*, edited by Bashir Bashir and Leila Farsakh, 148–72. New York: Columbia University Press, 2020.

Fainholtz, Tzafrir. "Ville Blanche: Levantine Gentlemen, Architectural Modernism and the 'White City' of Tel Aviv, 1930-48." *Architectural Theory Review* 26, no. 3 (2022): 405-26.

Fishman, Louis A. *Jews and Palestinians in the Late Ottoman Era, 1908-1914: Claiming the Homeland*. Edinburgh: Edinburgh University Press, 2019.

Freitag, Ulrike, and Nora Lafi, eds. *Urban Governance under the Ottomans: Between Cosmopolitanism and Conflict*. London: Routledge, 2014.

Frey, Albert R. "A Dictionary of Numismatic Names: Their Official and Popular Designations." *American Journal of Numismatics (1897-1924)* 50 (1916): v-311.

Gavish, Dov. *The Survey of Palestine under the British Mandate, 1920-1948*. London: Routledge, 2005.

Glass, Joseph B., and Ruth Kark. *Sephardi Entrepreneurs in Eretz Israel: The Amzalak Family, 1816-1918*. Jerusalem: The Magnes Press, 1991.

———. *Sephardi Entrepreneurs in Jerusalem: The Valero Family 1800-1948*. Jerusalem: Gefen, 2007.

Goldberg, Harvey E. "From Sephardi to Mizrahi and Back Again: Changing Meanings of 'Sephardi' in Its Social Environments." *Jewish Social Studies: History, Culture, Society* 15, no. 1 (Fall 2008): 165-88.

Goren, Tamir. *Ge'ut veshefel: Hitpatchuta ha'ironit shel Yafo vemakoma be'imut haYehudi-ha'Aravi beEretz Israel 1917-1947* [The urban development of Jaffa and its place in the Jewish-Arab conflict in Eretz Israel]. Jerusalem: Yad Ben Zvi, 2016.

———. "Relations between Tel Aviv and Jaffa 1921-1936: A Reassessment." *Journal of Israeli History* 36, no. 1 (2017): 1-21.

Gribetz, Jonathan Marc. "An Arabic-Zionist Talmud: Shimon Moyal's at-Talmud." *Jewish Social Studies: History, Culture, Society* 17, no. 1 (2010): 1-30.

———. *Defining Neighbors: Religion, Race, and the Early Zionist-Arab Encounter*. Princeton, NJ: Princeton University Press, 2014.

Halperin, Liora. *Babel in Zion: Jews, Nationalism, and Language Diversity in Palestine, 1920-1948*. New Haven, CT: Yale University Press, 2015.

Hatuka, Tali, and Rachel Kallus, "Loose Ends: The Role of Architecture in Constructing Urban Borders in Tel Aviv-Jaffa since the 1920s." *Planning Perspectives* 21, no. 1 (2006): 23-44.

Helman, Anat. *Young Tel Aviv: A Tale of Two Cities*. Lebanon, NH: University Press of New England, 2010.

Hourani, Albert. "Ottoman Reform and the Politics of Notables." In *The Modern Middle East: A Reader*, edited by Albert Habib Hourani, Philip Shukry Khoury, and Mary Christina Wilson, 83-109. Berkeley: University of California, 1993.

Ichilov, Orit, and Andre Elias Mazawi. *Between State and Church: Life-History of a French-Catholic School in Jaffa*. Frankfurt: Peter Lang, 1996.

Issawi, Charles. *The Fertile Crescent, 1800-1914: A Documentary Economic History*. New York: Oxford University Press, 1988.

Jacobson, Abigail. "American 'Welfare Politics': American Involvement in Jerusalem during World War I." *Israel Studies* 18, no. 1 (2013): 56–76.

———. "Citizenship and Loyalty in Times of War: The Ottomanization Movement in Palestine during World War I." *Jewish Social Studies* 27, no. 2 (2022): 117–43.

———. *From Empire to Empire: Jerusalem between Ottoman and British Rule.* Syracuse, NY: Syracuse University Press, 2011.

Jacobson, Abigail, and Moshe Naor. *Oriental Neighbors: Middle Eastern Jews and Arabs in Mandatory Palestine.* Waltham, MA: Brandeis University Press, 2016.

Juhasz, Esther. "Trousseau Lists of Jewish Brides from Izmir: Between an Official Document and a Personal Narrative." In *Fashioning the Self in Transcultural Settings: The Uses and Significance of Dress in Self-Narratives*, edited by Claudia Ulbrich and Richard Wittman, 261–96. Würzburg: Ergon-Verlag, 2015.

Kabha, Mustafa, and Nahum Karlinsky. *The Lost Orchard: The Palestinian-Arab Citrus Industry, 1850–1950.* Syracuse, NY: Syracuse University Press, 2021.

Kanaʿan, Ruba. "Waqf, Architecture, and Political Self-Fashioning: The Construction of the Great Mosque of Jaffa by Muhammad Aga Abu Nabbut." *Muqarnas* (2001): 120–40.

Kark, Ruth. *American Consuls in the Holy Land, 1832–1914.* Detroit: Wayne State University Press, 1994.

———. "Cartographic Sources for the Study of Jaffa: From the Napoleonic Siege to the British Conquest." *Cartographic Journal* 25, no. 1 (1988): 37–49.

———. *Jaffa: A City in Evolution, 1799–1917.* Jerusalem: Yad Ben Zvi, 1990.

Katz, Yossi. "Ideology and Urban Development: Zionism and the Origins of Tel-Aviv, 1906–1914." *Journal of Historical Geography* 12, no. 4 (1986): 402–24.

———. *Zionism and Urban Settlement: The Jewish National Fund's Contribution to Urban Settlement Prior to World War I.* Jerusalem: Institute for the Research on the History of JNF, Land, and Settlement, 1992.

Kayalı, Hasan. "Jewish Representation in the Ottoman Parliaments." In *Jews of the Ottoman Empire*, edited by Avigdor Levy, 507–17. Princeton, NJ: Darwin Press, 1994.

Khalidi, Rashid. *The Iron Cage: The Story of the Palestinian Struggle for Statehood.* Boston: Beacon Press, 2007.

Khalidi, Walid, Sharif S. Elmusa, and Muhammad Ali Khalidi. *All That Remains: The Palestinian Villages Occupied and Depopulated by Israel in 1948.* Beirut: Institute for Palestine Studies, 1992.

Klein, Menachem. "Arab Jew in Palestine." *Israel Studies* 19, no. 3 (2014): 134–53.

———. *Lives in Common: Arabs and Jews in Jerusalem, Jaffa, and Hebron.* Translated by Haim Watzman. Oxford: Oxford University Press, 2014.

Kushner, David. "Ali Ekrem Bey, Governor of Jerusalem, 1906–1908." *International Journal of Middle East Studies* 28 (1996): 349–62.

Lang, Yosef, and Reut Green. "Hamohel Me'ir Hamburger vetzfunot pinkaso: Lahistoria hahevratit shel kehilat Yafo" [The circumciser Me'ir Hamburger and his notebook: Toward a social history of the Jaffa community]. *Katedra* 156 (2014): 71–100.

LeBor, Adam. *City of Oranges: An Intimate History of Arabs and Jews in Jaffa.* New York: W. W. Norton, 2007.

Lemire, Vincent. *La soif de Jérusalem: Essai d'hydrohistoire (1840–1948).* Paris: Publications de la Sorbonne, 2010.

Levi, Tomer. *The Jews of Beirut: The Rise of a Levantine Community, 1860s–1930s.* New York: Peter Lang, 2012.

LeVine, Mark. *Overthrowing Geography: Jaffa, Tel Aviv, and the Struggle for Palestine, 1880–1948.* Berkeley: University of California Press, 2005.

Levy, Lisa Lital. "Jewish Writers in the Arab East: Literature, History, and the Politics of Enlightenment, 1863–1914." PhD diss., University of California, Berkeley, 2007.

Levy, Lital. "The Arab Jew Debates: Media, Culture, Politics, History." *Journal of Levantine Studies* 7, no. 1 (2017): 79–103.

———. "Cohen, Zaki." In *Encyclopedia of Jews in the Islamic World*, edited by Norman A. Stillman. Leiden: Brill, 2010.

———. "Partitioned Pasts: Arab Jewish Intellectuals and the Case of Esther Azharī Moyal (1873–1948)." In *The Making of the Arab Intellectual*, edited by Dyala Hamza, 139–74. London: Routledge, 2012.

Lockman, Zachary. "Railway Workers and Relational History: Arabs and Jews in British-Ruled Palestine." *Comparative Studies in Society and History* 35, no. 3 (1993): 601–27.

Malak, Hana 'Isa. *Al-Judthur al-Yafiyya* [Jaffan roots]. Jerusalem: Al-Sharq al-'Arabi, 1996.

Mandel, Neville. "Ottoman Policy and Restrictions on Jewish Settlement in Palestine, 1881–1908." *Middle Eastern Studies* 10, no. 3 (1974): 312–32.

———. "Ottoman Practice as Regards Jewish Settlement in Palestine, 1881–1908." *Middle Eastern Studies* 11, no. 1 (1975): 33–46.

Marglin, Jessica. "The Two Lives of Mas'ud Amoyal: Pseudo-Algerians in Morocco, 1830–1912." *International Journal of Middle East Studies* 44, no. 4 (2014): 651–70.

Mazza, Roberto. "Transforming the Holy City: From Communal Clashes to Urban Violence: The Nebi Musa Riots in 1920." In *Urban Violence in the Middle East: Changing Cityscapes in the Transition from Empire to Nation State*, edited by Ulrike Freitag, Nelida Fuccaro, Claudia Ghrawi, and Nora Lafi, 179–94. New York: Berghan Books, 2015.

———. "'We Will Treat You Like the Armenians': Djemal Pasha, Zionism, and the Evacuation of Jaffa, April 1917." In *Syria in World War I: Politics, Economy, and Society*, edited by M. Talha Çiçek, 87–106. London: Routledge, 2015.

Meiton, Fredrik. *Electrical Palestine: Capital and Technology from Empire to Nation.* Berkeley: University of California Press, 2019.

Mitter, Sreemati. "A History of Money in Palestine: From the 1900s to the Present." PhD diss., Harvard University, 2014.

Morris, Benny. *The Birth of the Palestinian Refugee Problem Revisited.* Cambridge: Cambridge University Press, 2004.

Nassar, Issam, Stephen Sheehi, and Salim Tamari. *Camera Palaestina: Photography and Displaced Histories of Palestine.* Vol. 5. Berkeley: University of California Press, 2022.

Ram, Hanna. *Hayishuv haYehudi beYafo: Mikehila Sfaradit lemerkaz Tzioni, 1839–1939* [The Jewish settlement in Jaffa: From Sephardi community to Zionist center]. Jerusalem: Hotsa'at Carmel, 1996.

Rodrigue, Aron. *French Jews, Turkish Jews: The Alliance Israélite Universelle and the Politics of Jewish Schooling in Turkey, 1860–1925.* Bloomington: Indiana University Press, 1990.

Rubin, Avi. "Bahjat and Tamimi in Wilayat Beirut: A Journey into the Worldviews of Two Ottoman Travelers at the Turn of the 20th Century." Master's thesis, Ben Gurion University of the Negev, 2000.

Ryzova, Lucie. *The Age of the Efendiyya: Passages to Modernity in National-Colonial Egypt.* Oxford: Oxford Historical Monographs, 2014.

Saposnik, Arieh Bruce. *Becoming Hebrew: The Creation of a Jewish National Culture in Ottoman Palestine.* Oxford: Oxford University Press, 2008.

Schillo, Frédérique. "Les commerçants français en Palestine pendant la période ottomane (1842–1914)." In *De Bonaparte à Balfour: La France, l'Europe occidentale et la Palestine, 1799–1917*, edited by Ran Aaronsohn and Dominique Trimbur, 137–65. Paris: CNRS Éditions, 2008.

Schneer, Jonathan. *The Balfour Declaration: The Origins of the Arab-Israeli Conflict.* New York: Random House, 2010.

Schölch, Alexander. "The Demographic Development of Palestine, 1850–1882." *International Journal of Middle East Studies* 17, no. 4 (1985): 485–505.

———. "The Economic Development of Palestine." *Journal of Palestine Studies* 10, no. 3 (1981): 35–58.

———. *Palestine in Transformation, 1856–1882: Studies in Social, Economic, and Political Development.* Washington, DC: Institute for Palestine Studies, 1993.

Shacham, Tzvi. "Jaffa in Historical Maps (1799–1948)." *History and Archaeology of Jaffa* 1 (2011): 137–74.

Shafir, Gershon. *Land, Labor, and the Origins of the Israeli-Palestinian Conflict, 1882–1914.* Berkeley: University of California Press, 1996.

Shafir, Nir. "In an Ottoman Holy Land: The Hajj and the Road from Damascus, 1500–1800." *History of Religions* 60, no. 1 (2020): 1–36.

Shaham, Ron. "Christian and Jewish Waqf in Palestine during the Late Ottoman Period." *Bulletin of the School of Oriental and African Studies* 54, no. 3 (1991): 460–72.

Shar'abi, Rachel. "The Splitting of the Oriental Communities from the Sephardi Community, 1860–1914." *Pe'amim* 21 (1984): 31–49.

Sharim, Yehuda. "The Struggle for Sephardic-Mizrahi Autonomy: Racial Identities in Palestine-Israel, 1918–1948." PhD diss., University of California, 2013.

Shavit, Ya'akov, and Gid'on Biger. *Hahistoriya shel Tel Aviv* [The history of Tel Aviv]. Vol. 1, *The Birth of a Town (1909–1936)*. Tel Aviv: Ramot, 2001.

Shoham, Hizky. "'Buy Local' or 'Buy Jewish': Separatist Consumption in Interwar Palestine." *International Journal of Middle East Studies* 45 (2013): 469–89.

Soufan, Anas. "An Overview of Cement Tile Manufacturing and Importation in Syria and Lebanon: Damascus-Beirut, 1880s–1940s." *ABE Journal* 8 (2015).

Spiegel, Nina S. *Embodying Hebrew Culture: Aesthetics, Athletics, and Dance in the Jewish Community of Mandate Palestine*. Detroit: Wayne State University Press, 2013.

Stillman, Norman. *Sephardi Responses to Modernity*. Reading, UK: Harwood Academic, 1995.

Talbot, Michael. "'Jews, Be Ottomans!': Zionism, Ottomanism, and Ottomanisation in the Hebrew-Language Press, 1890–1914." *Die Welt des Islams* 56, no. 3–4 (2016): 359–87.

Toledano, Ehud R. "The Emergence of Ottoman-Local Elites (1700–1900): A Framework for Research." In *Middle Eastern Politics and Ideas: A History from Within*, edited by Ilan Pappe and Moshe Ma'oz, 145–62. London: Tauris, 1997.

Wasserstein, Bernard. *The British in Palestine: The Mandatory Government and the Arab-Jewish Conflict, 1917–1929*. London: Royal Historical Society, 1978.

Wheatley, Natasha. "Mandatory Interpretation: Legal Hermeneutics and the New International Order in Arab and Jewish Petitions to the League of Nations." *Past & Present* 227, no. 1 (2015): 205–48.

Yahav, Dan. *Hayei hatarbut vehakalkala beYafo shelifney haNakba (1948)* [Cultural and economic life in Jaffa before the Nakba]. Tel Aviv: Mabat, 2007.

Yazbak, Mahmoud. "Jaffa before the Nakba: Palestine's Thriving City, 1799–1948." In *The Social and Cultural History of Palestine: Essays in Honour of Salim Tamari*, edited by Sarah Irving, 8–25. Edinburgh: Edinburgh University Press, 2023.

———. *Madinat al-Burtuqal, Yafa: Hadara wa-mujtama'a, 1700–1840* [City of oranges, Jaffa: Civilization and society, 1700–1840]. Beirut: Institute for Palestine Studies, 2018.

———. "A Mamluk Household in Jaffa: The Case of Abu Nabbut (1805–1819)." In *From the Household to the Wider World: Local Perspectives on Urban*

Institutions in Late Ottoman Bilad al-Sham, edited by Yuval Ben-Bassat and Johann Büssow, 35–45. Tübingen: University of Tübingen Press, 2023.

———. "Penetration of Urban Capital into the Palestinian Countryside: The Beginnings, Jaffa in the 1830s." In *Life on the Ottoman Border: Essays in Honor of Nenad Moacanin*, edited by Vjeran Kursar, 251–63. Zaghreb: University of Zaghreb/FF Press, 2022.

Yehoshu'a, Ya'akov. "Sahifat 'Sawt al-'Uthmaniya': Al-sahafa al-'Arabiya fil-balad fi matl'a al-qurn al-hali" [The newspaper "Voice of Ottomanism": The Arab press in the country at the beginning of the current century]. *Al-Sharq* 3, no. 9.(1979)

———. "Tel Aviv in the Image of the Arab Press in the Five Years after Its Founding, 1909–1914" [Hebrew]. *HaMizrach hehadash* 19, no. 4 (1969).

Yinon, Ya'akov. *Saviv kikar hasha'on: Lesayer baYafo 'im Yad Ben Zvi* [Around the clock tower: Touring Jaffa with the Ben Zvi Institute]. Jerusalem: Ben Zvi Institute, 2001.

Zohar, Motti. "A Land without People? The GIScience Approach to Estimating the Population of Ottoman Palestine towards the End of the 19th Century." *Applied Geography* 141 (2022): 1–11.

INDEX

Italics indicate photographs in the text.

'Abadi, Avraham, 285
'Abadi, Yitzhak, 58
'Abd al-Hadi Bek, 301
'Abdallah bin Hussein (Hashemite king of Transjordan), 416
'Abd al-Nur, Jurji, 186
'Abd al-Rahman, Abu Salim, 349
Abdul Hamid II (Ottoman sultan), 33, 36
Abela, P., 221–22
Aberle, Paul, 151–56
Aboab, Yehuda Leib, 219, 224
Abrevaya, Yehoshu'a, 61, 394, *414*, 415–18
Abu 'Ali, Hassan, 366–67, 376–77
Abulafia, Shlomo, 70n73
Abu Nabbut, Muhammad Amin Agha, 4–5
Abushadid, Shlomo, 19, 61
Abutbul family, 21, 32, 67n42
Agnon, Shai, 1
Ahmad Shukri Bek, 294, 301
Ahuzat Bayit, 38–42, 77, 196–213. *See also* Tel Aviv
'Akkawi, Elias, 162
al-'Ajami (neighborhood), 48, 269
Al-Amrikan (colony), 118
Alchemister, Me'ir, 141
Aleksandrowicz, Or, 62
Alexandria, 7, 9, 26, 189, 264, 275, 388
Alif Baa' (newspaper), 56, 434
Ali Rusen Bek, 317–18
Alliance Israélite Universelle (AIU), Beirut, 1, 25, 190–95

al-Naqib (neighborhood), 15
Alonzo (shipping agent), 274
al-Qal'a (neighborhood), 13, 22
'Amiel, Maimon, 19, 87, 147
Amzalak, Ben-Zion, 150, 189, 204
Amzalak, Haim, 31, 68n53, 96–97, 104–5, 115, 147, 164, 169
Amzalak, Yitzhak, 299
Anglo-Palestine Bank, 200, 236
Anglo-Palestine Company (APC), 197–201, 227–28, 246–47, 306, 387
animal slaughter, 326–27, 329, 339, 355, 369–70, 378, 428
Antébi, Albert, 61–62, 73n118, 278–79, 281–83, 287
'Antebi, Yosef, 387–90
antiquities, 157–58
Arabic press, 42–43, 57, 63, 217, 228–29, 434–39. *See also Alif Baa'* (newspaper); *Falastin* (newspaper)
'Araktinji, As'ad, 153, 162
'Araktinji, Cesar, *414*
'Araman, Michel, 399–402
'Arif Bek, 289
Ashkenazi, Shmu'el, 219, 328
Ashkenazi Jews, 14, 30, 44, 53–54, 62, 63, 70n73
'Ashur, Yusuf, 244
Association of Settlers (Agudat hamitnahalim), 220–27. *See also* land purchases; Zionism
Assouline, Yitzhak, 111

'Awad, Iskandar, 11, 33, 150, 154
Ayoubi, Salim al-, 361
'Ayun Kara, 120. *See also* Rishon LeZion

Baha al-Din (Jaffa *kaymakam*), 247–50, 257–58, 262–63, 268, 273–76, 280
Balfour Declaration, 47, 52, 63–64, 71n83, 217, 393–96, 438, 442–43
Banat, Hana, 162
barley trade, 184–85, 347–49
Barnett, Zerah, 69n59, 96
Barrellet, Marius, 152–54
Barsky, Yosef, 200–204
Barukh, Avraham (uncle), 162
Barukh, Haim (maternal grandfather), 14, 67n43
Barukh, Yitzhak (cousin), 154, 160
Barukh family, 7–15
Barukhi'el, Ya'akov, 95–96
bazaars, 19–22
Bedouins, 23, 91, 94, 184–85, 254–56
Be'er Sheva, 184–85
Be'er Tuvia (Jewish settlement), 141–43, 289. *See also* Qastina (village)
Beirut, 5, 7, 9, 11, 28, 36, 93, 97, 145–46, 158–60, 173, 221–22, 225, 419–21. *See also* Alliance Israélite Universelle (AIU), Beirut; Tif'eret Israel School, Beirut
Beiruti, Michel Effendi, 243–45
Beit Midrash, 109–14
Belkind, Israel, 123
Belkind, Na'aman, 361
Ben Yehuda, Eli'ezer, 260–62
Berlin, Eliyahu Me'ir, 198, *206*, 244, 276, 282
Beška, Emanuel, 70n74
Bialik, Haim Nachman, 1
Bilu (society), 122–23. *See also* Zionism
Bitar, 'Umar al-, 60, 73n115, 243, 248, 274–75, 289, 406. *See also* Muslim-Christian Associations
Biton family, 141
Blattner, David, 121
Blattner, Robert (Reuven), 163
B'nai B'rith, 1, 64n3
Bograshov, Haim, 282
Bohbut, Shabtai, 98
Bohbut, Shlomo, 98, 110, 118
Bonnafous, Jean Louis, 171–72
Bouskila, Ya'akov, 86–87
Brandeis, Louis, 394
Brenner, Yitzhak Moshe, 120–22
Bril, Avraham, 404, 408
Brill, Yehi'el, 122
British Mandate, 47–48, 51–54, 393, 400–402, 408–10, 443, 447. *See also* Balfour Declaration; riots
British military, 321, 370, 379, 383–86. *See also* World War I
Bustrus, Najib, 33

Campbell, James, 426
Carsenty, Barukh, 87
Carsenty, Nissim, 14, 87
Carsenty, Yehuda, 87, 149–53
Cemal (Merslinli), 263
Cemal Pasha. *See* Djemal Pasha
Chelouche, Aharon (father): aiding the *Chikhachev* (Russian ship), 166–70; arrival in Jaffa, 7–16; death and will of, 396, 398–402; French protection, 16; government moneylending, 173–75; house robbery incident, 175–76; houses, 19, 22, 28–29, *82*, 85–86, 89–90, 147–48, 171–72; Jaffa-Jerusalem railroad contract, 171–72; kidnapping episode, 99, 107–15; *kushans* acquisition, 398–402; land purchases, 29–31, 95–97; money changing, 21–22,

90–94; Neve Tzedek, 30–31, 163–65; photograph, *84*, *397*; prince of Ethiopia, visit from, 181–83; Talmud Torah, 86–87

Chelouche, Aharon (grandson), 23, 43–44, 52, 60

Chelouche, Avner (son), 69n57, 71n93, 154, *194*, 304, 322–24, 328–29, 332–33, 337–38, 340–46, 363–64, 371

Chelouche, Avraham (grandfather), 14

Chelouche, Avraham Haim (brother), 15, 27, 30, 36, 112, 118–19, 123–25, 133, 145, 165, 175–76, 182, 184, 288, 306, 323, 348, 373, 409

Chelouche, Freha Simha (née Moyal) (wife), 28, 44, 138–40, *194*, 250, 268–71, 322, 328, 332, 375, 376, 419, *433*, 434

Chelouche, Gavri'el (nephew), 346

Chelouche, Hana (aunt), 14

Chelouche, Hillel (son), 69n57, *194*, 329, 337, 340, 345–46

Chelouche, Luna (sister), 172

Chelouche, Me'ir (son), 45, 69n57, *194*, 248–50

Chelouche, Moshe (son), 43, 59, 60, 69n57, 71n93, 157–58, *194*, 272, 288, 292, 303–4, 315, 323, 332, 358–62, 364–67, 425

Chelouche, Rahel (daughter-in-law), 267

Chelouche, Rika (Rivka) (aunt), 14

Chelouche, Riquetta (Rivka) (niece), 54

Chelouche, Sara (née Barukh) (mother), 7, 46, 90, 99, 112–15, 138–39, 355–58, 384, 387, 391–92

Chelouche, Shimshon (nephew), 346

Chelouche, Simha (paternal grandmother), 14

Chelouche, Ya'akov (brother), 27, 30, 38, 42, 43, 71n93, 173, 229–31, 306, 315, 323, 332, 342, 356, 358–62

Chelouche, Yehudit (daughter), *194*, 341, 350

Chelouche, Yoram (son), 69n57, *194*, 350–51

Chelouche, Yosef (uncle), 14

Chelouche, Yosef Eliyahu: Ahuzat Bayit, 38–42, 196–212; army commissary, 341–48, 352–53, 363–64, 371–73; arrest, 364–75; August 1929 riots, 432–34; business ventures, 160–63, 164–65, 177–78, 186, 187–89, 347–49; construction trade and supplies, 35–37, 150–57, 160–65, 186, 187, 190–95, 202–4, 205–6, 232–38; death and funeral, 58–60; Djemal Pasha, summons to meet with, 276–83; early life, 85–98; economic boycott between Arabs and Jews, 439–41; education, 27–28, 86–87, 118–19, 123–24, 126–36, 144–47; and Egypt, 189–90, 233–35, 383–90, 415–21; engagement and wedding, 137–40, 145, 149–50; expulsion of Jaffa and Tel Aviv, 301–7; forged passports, 268–72, 298; French protection, 45, 260–61; house robbery incident, 175–76; houses, 22, 28–29, 43–44, 82, 85–86, 89–90, 147–48, 171–72; intra-Jewish ethnic tensions and competition, 51–55, 319; on Jaffa city council, 260, 413–15, 422–28; to Jerusalem, 87–89, 155, 219, 254, 276–80; Kafr Jammal, relocation to, 337–58, 376–78; kidnapping episode, 99–117; land purchases, 165, 218–28, 430–31; May 1921 riots, 403–9; money changing, 151–52; mother's death, 356–58; New Company, 218–28; *Parashat Hayai*, reception of in Petah Tikva, 1–2, 62–63; in Petah

Tikva, 305–6, 308, 314–16, 319–24; photograph, *76*, *132*, *194*, *292*, *334*, *413*, *414*, *423*, *433*, *440*; press articles, 56, 431, 434–39; in Qalqilya, 325–35; return to Tel Aviv from exile, 321–24, 380–84; The Shield association, 229–31; silicate factory, 233–38; silver- and goldsmithing, 119–20; slander against, 222–25, 416–19; Tel Aviv Committee, 204–7, *206*, 223, 423–28; Tel Aviv development, 38–44, 204–17, 412–15, 422–31; Tiberias house arrest, 283–85; Tif'eret Israel School, Beirut, 27–28, 118–19, 126–36, 145–47, 158–60; Tulkarm imprisonment, 363–76; wartime economic ventures, 286–89, 301–3, 308–9, 390–91; Wheat Committee service, 291–300; World War I, 44–46, 225–26, 241–58, 276–83, 289–90, *307*, 308–11, 352–53

Chelouche, Zadoc (son), 69n57, *194*, 321, 355, 384–86

Chelouche Frères (firm), 36, 163

Chelouche-Havatzelet, Margalit (niece), 38

Christians, 16, 22, 25, 37, 38, 46, 47, 56, 64, 179–80, 242–43, 291, 299, 407, 409, 424–27. *See also* Palestinian Arabs

Cicurel, Solomon, 418

Citron, Israel Abba, 316

Cohen, Barukh, 129, 190

Cohen, Israel, 322–24, 420–21

Cohen, Mordekhai, 176

Cohen, Nissim Hanokh, 167

Cohen, Raphael, 420

Cohen, Yitzhak Yehuda, 313–18

Cohen, Yitzhak Zaki, 118–19, 126, 128, 136, 158, 388, 419–21. *See also* Tif'eret Israel School, Beirut

Cohen-Reiss, Haim, 306

Constantinople, 93, 142–43, 171, 173, 174–75, 177–78, 212, 230, 247–48, 260, 261–62, 273, 275, 279–81, 289 currencies, 91, 151–52, 172, 184, 226–27, 293–96

Dajani, 'Abdallah al-, 406

Damascus, 10–11, 13, 65n14, 162, 315–16, 323, 327–35, 358–62, 375, 434

Damiani, Hanna, 85

Dankner, Me'ir, 306

Deedes, Wyndham, 408

Deir Aban (train station), 277

de Sola Pool, David, 394

Dichy, Joseph Bek, 420

Dizengoff, Me'ir, 47–48, 51, 61, 73n120, 190–93, 201–7, 210, 213–15, 222–23, 235–37, 242–58, 260–68, 273–77, 281–83, 286–88, 291, 302–3, 315–16, 327–35, *334*, 36–, 370–71, 373, 393, 395–96, 403–8, 412, 415–19, *423*, 426–30, 441

Djemal Pasha, 231, 262–63, 273–85, 291, 294, 298, 300, 301–2, 315, 328, 371

Do'ar hayom (Daily Mail) (newspaper), 52, 54–55, 71n90. *See also* Hebrew press

Dukhan, Moshe, 401

Dumyati, Khalil al-, 186

Eder, David, 388. *See also* Zionist Commission

education: *Beit Midrash*, 109–14; Herzliya Hebrew Gymnasium, 28, 39, *40*, 43, 69n57, 197–204, 232, 403–4; Mikve Israel, 25, 100, 123, 283; Talmud Torah, 50, 86–87, 98, 99, 108, 118; Tif'eret Israel School, Beirut, 27–28, 118–19, 126–36, 145–47, 158–60

Egypt, 4–5, 13, 136, 189–90, 233–35, 383–90, 415–21
Ekrem Bek, 279
Elmaleh, Avraham, 228–29
Elyashar, Ya'akov Sha'ul, 157
English missionaries, 120–21
Eretz Israel (Land of Israel), 7–11, 39, 57, 120–21, 143–44, 161. *See also* land purchases; Zionism
espionage, 361, 368–69, 386. *See also* World War I
Ethiopia, prince from, 181–83

Falastin (newspaper), 43, 56, 59, 60, 395, 430. *See also* 'Issa, 'Issa al-
Farhi, Joseph, 420
Farwaji, Yusuf, 383–84
Fayiz Bek, 344
Faysal bin Hussein (Hashemite king of Syria and Iraq), 57, 72n103, 396
Fedida, Jamila (née Chelouche) (sister), 323, 358, 396
Feinberg, Yitzhak, 190
Feingold Houses, 96, 187, 381–82
Fi'uni, Iskandar (Alexander Fiani), 234
France, 4, 6, 8–9, 16, 45, 47, 143, 302. *See also* Alliance Israélite Universelle (AIU), Beirut
Franciscan Church of St. Peter, 89
Franck, Henri (Zvi), 404
Frankl, Ludwig August, 13
Freiman, Ya'akov Peretz, 120–22

Gagin, Bekhor, 340
Gaon, Moshe David, 55, 72n101
Gaster, Moses, 198
Gaza, 5, 23, 46, 175, 184–85, 286–89, 348, 371
Geddes, Patrick, 50

Gedera (Jewish settlement), 122–23, 169, 289
Gelat, Antoine (Anton), 295–97, 299, 424–25
George, Teodor, 115
German army, 311, 322, 340, 371. *See also* World War I
Ge'ula (society), 183, 223. *See also* Zionism
Giladi, 340
Ginzburg, Asher (Ahad Ha'am), 415–17, 423
Glazebrook, Otis, 273
Gluskin, Ze'ev, 183
Goldberg, Boris, 237–38
Goldberg, Moshe, 141, *206*
Goldfarb, Yehoshu'a, 219
Goldin, Shlomo, 157
Grazowski, Yehuda, 333, 381
Gruenblat, Claude, 429

Haaretz (newspaper), 54, 62. *See also* Hebrew press
Hacohen, Mas'ud, 111
Hadera (Jewish settlement), 233, 344, 356, 362
Haifa, 8, 221–22, 283, 328, 344, 346, 429–30
HaLevanon (newspaper), 68n51, 122. *See also* Hebrew press
Halevi, Yehuda, 105
Halperin, Efraim, 269
Hamburger, Me'ir, 68n52, 110–11
Hankin, Yehoshu'a, 221–24
Hassan Bek (military governor), 241–58, 265, 272, 274–76, 294
Havatzelet (newspaper), 68n51, 118. *See also* Hebrew press
Hayat, M., 219, 328
Haycraft Commission, 408. *See also* riots

Hayoun, David, 306, 323
Hazan, Haim, 156, 388
"Hebrew city" concept, 38, 40, 48–49, 51, 54, 81, 204, 207–8. *See also* Ahuzat Bayit; Tel Aviv; Zionism
"Hebrew labor" (*'avoda 'ivrit*), 42, 51, 232–33, 403. *See also* Zionism
Hebrew language, 216–17
Hebrew press, 26, 33, 51–52, 62, 68n51. See also *Do'ar hayom* (Daily Mail) (newspaper); *HaLevanon* (newspaper); *Havatzelet* (newspaper)
Hebron massacre, 433. *See also* riots
Helwan, Egypt, 419
Herzl, Theodor, 235, 448
Herzliya Hebrew Gymnasium, 28, 39, 40, 43, 69n57, 197–204, 232, 403–4
Hirsch, Shmu'el, 144
Hissin, Haim, 190–93, 268, 419
Hita, Muhammad al-, 187–89
Hoofien, Eli'ezer, 415, 429
Hovevei Zion (Lovers of Zion) (society), 55, 121–22, 138, 141–44, 169, 191. *See also* Zionism
Howard Hotel, 33–34
Husseini, Isma'il Bek al-, 254–55

Imam, Ragheb al-, 51
Iran, 8–10, 13
'Issa, 'Issa al-, 426–27. *See also* Arabic press; *Falastin* (newspaper)
'Issa, Yusuf al-, 56. See also *Alif Baa'* (newspaper); Arabic press
Izmojik, David, 423

Jaffa: agricultural hinterlands, 23–25; al-'Ajami (neighborhood), 48, 269; al-Auja river, 26; British army occupation of, 383–86; Bustrus-'Awad Street, 33–35; of Chelouche's childhood, 16–28; *Chikhachev* (ship), sinking of, 166–70; cholera epidemic, 178–80; citrus industry, 6, 24; clock tower square (*meidan al-sa'ah*), 32–33; commerce and industry, 160–63; destruction of, 68n44; development of, 4–5, 31–35, 48–50; European powers' interest in, 5–7; exports and trade, 6; expulsion from, 45–46, 301–7; *extramurous* construction, 28–29, 147–48; government house (*saraya*), 22, 32–34, 86, 116, 266, 272, 381–82; Great Mosque, 5, 19, 22, 29–30, 40; Hassan Bek Mosque, 253–57, 426; Jaffa–Jerusalem railroad, 32, 171–72; Jerusalem Boulevard, 251; Jerusalem Gate (Abu Nabbut Gate), 5; Jewish Girls' School, 190–95; Manshiya/Neve Shalom (neighborhood), 29–30, 48, 50, 69n59, 96, 157–58, 253; May 1921 riots, 48, 403–9; modern development of, 17, 28–38; municipality, 17, 42, 47–48, 58, 60, 210–14, 260, 413–15, 423–24, 427–28; al-Naqib (neighborhood), 15; Ottoman conquest of, 4–5; population, 16, 38–39, 47; port, 11–12, 428–31; public works, 17; al-Qal'a (neighborhood), 13, 22; relations with Tel Aviv, 213, 413–15, 432–38; religious endowments in, 30; return to, 320–23; Rutenberg's electricity plant, 427–28; Sandel's map, 18–25; separation of Tel Aviv from Jaffa, 47–51; Sheikh Ibrahim (neighborhood), 15, 22; Suq al-Khawajat (Khawajas's market), 21; Talmud Torah, 86–87, 97–98; and Tel Aviv development, 38–44, 412–15; urban size, 17, 28; World War I, 241–58, 291–300

Jaffa–Jerusalem road, 425
Jaida (village), 220–27. *See also* Tal al-Shammam
Jellat, Mitri, 123
Jerusalem: Bab al-Khalil (Jaffa Gate), 88, 278; Chelouche family's travel to, 87–89; Chelouche's trips to, 155–56, 219, 254–55, 273, 277–82, 286, 312–14, 316–19, 400–401; Jaffa–Jerusalem railroad, 32, 171–72; land purchases in, 219–20; *Manzil-Stab* (Ottoman military headquarters), 311–19; pasha in, 142–43, 174, 247–48, 282–83, 318
Jerusalem Hotel, 278
Jewish Colonial Trust, 448. *See also* Zionism
Jewish National Fund (JNF), 196, 208, 430–31. *See also* land purchases; Zionism
Jews: Arab incitement against, 394–96; Ashkenazi Jews, 14, 30, 44, 53–54, 62, 63, 70n73; expulsion from Jaffa, 302–3, 328; general federation of the Jews of the Land of Israel, 183–84; immigration/immigrants, 7–10, 13, 30–31, 37–38, 52, 438–39; intra-Jewish ethnic tensions and competition, 51–55, 319; Jaffa community council, 165–66; Jewish-Arab relations, 2–3, 26–27, 39, 48, 51–52, 56–58, 61–64, 77–79, 394–96, 403–9, 432–34, 439–41, 443–47; Jewish community council, Beirut, 419–21; Jewish guards, 209–10; justice system, 26–27; Kaminitz Hotel, 278–79; Knesset Israel, 53; land purchases, 14, 29–31, 37, 41–42, 141–42, 190; Maghrebi (North African) Jews, 7–9, 13, 16, 19, 21–22, 25, 66n26, 166–67; mobility of, 27; native Jews, 2–3, 38, 53–55, 57–58, 63, 443–44, 447;

Ottomanization, 259–62; Sephardi Jews, 14, 30, 42–44, 51–55, 57–58, 60–63, 65n8, 70n73, 71n92, 319, 416–17; Sidon Jews, 388–89; slander, 228–29; Yemenites, 54, 254–57, 319, 389. *See also* World War I; Zionism; *individual Jewish settlements*
Joint Distribution Committee, 270

Kafr Bidya (village), 371
Kafr Falama (village), 340–45, 352–53, 363–64, 371–72
Kafr Jammal (village), 46, 337–51, 353–56, 358, 362, 369–77, 384, 391–92
Kaiserman, Natan, 222
Karaite Judaism, 129
kaymakam of Jaffa, 27, 108–9, 113–16, 142–43, 167–68, 173–76. *See also specific Ottoman officials*
kaymakam of Tulkarm, 352–56
Kazim Pasha, 353–54
Kfar Sava (Jewish settlement), 315, 326–35, 369
Khamis, 'Ali, 265
Korkidi, Nissim, 58, 70n73, 72n110, 206, 281
Kremenezky, Johann, 235–36
Krieger, Moshe, 332

land purchases, 29–31, 37, 41–42, 95–97, 120–21, 141–44, 165, 196–200, 209, 213–15, 218–27, 236, 409–10; Association of Settlers (Agudat hamitnahalim), 220–27; in Jerusalem, 219–20; Jewish National Fund (JNF), 196–97, 208, 430–31; *kushans*, 104, 141, 197, 398–402; New Company, 218–28; Palestinian opposition to, 37–38, 52, 60, 209, 214–15. *See also* Zionism; *individual Jewish settlements*

Lev, Israel Avraham, 219
Levontin, Zalman David, 120–22, 190, 198, 201
Levy, Ben Zion Rizo, 70n73
Lewin-Epstein, Eliyahu Ze'ev haLevi, 157, 412
Lewinsky, E. L., 193
Lilienblum, Moshe Leib, 143
Lishansky, Yosef, 361
Litwinsky, Ya'akov Elhanan, 192
Louria, Alter, 14
Louria, Sultana (née Chelouche) (sister), 387
Louria, Yosef, 160–61
Louria, Zvi Yesh'ayahu (brother-in-law), 160–61, 387
Lupo, Shmu'el, 195

Maghrebi (North African) Jews, 7–9, 13, 16, 19, 21–22, 25, 66n26
Malka, Moshe, 137–39, 157
Malul, Nissim, 228–29, 231
Mani, Eliyahu, 110, 112–13
Mani, Yitzhak Malki'el, 110, 219–20
Mann, Salim, 420
Manshiya/Neve Shalom (neighborhood), 29–30, 48, 50, 69n59, 96, 157–58, 253
Manzil-Stab (Ottoman military headquarters), 311–19. *See also* World War I
Masmiya (village), 288
Matalon, Eliyahu, 345
Matalon, Me'ir, 340
Matalon, Moshe, 177, 229–30
Matmon-Cohen Yehuda Leib, 198
Meerovitch, Menashe, 282–83
Mehmet (Muhammad), Ali, 5
Mehoudar, Rafa'el, 359–60
Mehoudar, Rahel (née Chelouche) (sister), 359–62

Me'ir, Mercado, 110
Me'ir, Ya'akov, 110
Messa, Banin Menahem, 182, 409–11
Mibashan, Abraham, 423
Mikve Israel, 25, 100, 123, 283
Mizrahi, David, 70n73
Mizrahi, Yosef Nissim, 70n73
money changers, 21–22, 67n43, 91–92, 151–52
Montagu, Samuel, 93
Montefiore, Moses, 66n19, 104
Montefiore orchard, 104–7
Montefiore registers, 7, 10–11, 13–14
Morgenthau, Henry, 273
Moser, Jacob, 197–203
Moshe, Yosef, 167
Moskowitz, Frieda, 277
Mosseri, Jacques Bek, 389, 418
Mossinsohn, Benzion, 276, 282, 415–16, 422, 423
Motzkin, Leo, 223–24
Mount Lebanon, 231, 432–33
Moyal, Aharon, 19, 140, 149
Moyal, Avraham, 68n43, 69n58, 138, 140–44
Moyal, David, 41–42, 126, 136, 229
Moyal, Shim'on, 126, 136, 228
Moyal, Shmu'el, 140, 177, 302
Moyal, Yosef Bek, 31, 69n53, 96–97, 115, 126–27, 140, 147, 164, 167
mukhtars, 111, 115, 316, 337–38, 380, 387
Muslim-Christian Associations, 52, 409. *See also* British Mandate; Palestinian nationalism; Zionism
Mustakim, 'Ali, 428

Nahum, Haim, 259–60, 262
Nasr, Tanus, 69n58, 97, 147
Navon, Yosef Bek, 171
Nazim Pasha, 375–76

Neve Shalom. *See* Manshiya/Neve Shalom (neighborhood)
Neve Tzedek (neighborhood), 30–31, 36, 38, 44, 77, 160, 163, 164–65, 171–72, 175, 178–79, 181–83, 193
New Company, 218–28. *See also* land purchases; Zionism
North African Jews. *See* Maghrebi (North African) Jews

Ohel Moshe synagogue, 411
Oran, Algeria, 7
Oslo Accords, 62
Osterman, Arieh Leo, 423
Ottoman government officials. *See* 'Abd al-Hadi Bek; Ahmad Shukri Bek; Ali Rusen Bek; 'Arif Bek; Baha al-Din (Jaffa *kaymakam*); Djemal Pasha; Ekrem Bek; Fayiz Bek; Hassan Bek (military governor); *kaymakam* of Jaffa; Kazim Pasha; Nazim Pasha; Sadiq Bek; Shihab, Fu'ad Bek
Ottomanization, 45, 70n76, 259–62, 269–72
Ottoman Party for Administrative Decentralization, 230–31

Palestine Hotel, 34
Palestine Land Development Company (PLDC), 215, 221–27, 236. *See also* land purchases; Zionism
Palestinian Arabs: Ahuzat Bayit/Tel Aviv, relations with, 42–43, 47–51, 196–214, 426–30; economic boycott, 439–41; expulsion from Jaffa, 302–3; incitement against Jews, 394–96; Jaffa municipality, 47–48, 405–7; Jewish-Arab relations, 2–3, 26–27, 39, 51–52, 56–58, 61–64, 77–79, 394–96, 403–9, 432–34, 439–41, 443–47; May 1921 riots, 48, 403–9; nationalism, 46, 52, 230, 447–49
Palestinian nationalism, 37–38, 46, 52, 60, 230, 394–96, 447–49. *See also* Muslim-Christian Associations; Zionism
Palmer, Margaret, 187
Panijel, Raphael Me'ir, 157
Perlman, Elimelekh, 155–56, 162
Perlquart, Israel, 163
Petah Tikva (Jewish settlement), 46, 156, 209, 271, 285–86, 289, 303–7, 308–19, 320–24, 358, 370, 384
Picciotto, Joseph Bek, 388–89
pilgrims, 6–7, 13
Pines, Yehi'el Michal, 122
Pinsker, Yehuda Leib (Leon), 143
piracy, 9
Plumer, Herbert, 402
Port Said, 187–89, 205, 410–11

Qajar dynasty, 8, 10
Qalqilya, 46, 324, 325–35, 336, 369–70, 380–82, 392
Qarqash (architect), 164
Qastina (village), 141–42, 288. *See also* Be'er Tuvia (Jewish settlement)

Ras al-'Ayn (train station), 303
Red Note (temporary residency visa), 443
Rehovot (Jewish settlement), 157
Rihani, Amin al-, 56
riots: August 1929 riots, 432–34; Haycraft Commission, 408; Hebron massacre, 433; May 1921 riots, 48, 403–9
Rishon LeZion (Jewish settlement), 120, 123, 156–57, 255, 283. *See also* 'Ayun Kara
Rock, Iskandar, 161, 203
Rokach, El'azar, 30, 141

Rokach, Israel, 58, 72n109, *423*
Rokach, Shim'on, 30, 141, 162–63, 178–79, 331, 373, 404, *423*
Rothschild, Edmond de, 61, 144, 179
Ruppin, Arthur, 39, 220–21, 224–25, 278–80
Rutenberg, Pinhas, 404, 408, 427–28

Sabbagh, Najib, 154
Sabbah, Habib, 90
Sadiq Bek, 326–32, 336–49, 353, 363–65, 371–75
Sa'id, 'Asim Bek al-, 48, 60–61, 230, 406, *413–14*
Sa'id, Hafez Bek al-, 230–31
Salama (village), 107
Samakh (train station), 303, 359
Samara, Sheikh Ibrahim, 330–31, 340, 350
Samoury, Gabriel, 167–68
Samuel, Herbert, 47–48, 193, 402, 410
Sandel, Theodor, 18–26
Sapir, Eliyahu, 61, 200–201
Sarona (German colony), 105
Sasson, Reuven Yehezkel, 130–35, 146–47
Sayegh, Mas'ad, 428
Schick, Conrad, 17–18
Sephardi Jews, 14, 30, 42–44, 51–55, 57–58, 60–63, 65n8, 70n73, 71n92, 319, 416–17. *See also* Maghrebi (North African) Jews
Sha'ar Zion (Gate of Zion), 30
Shalabi, Ya'aqub, 158
Shanti (business partner), al-, 344–45
shari'a court, 4, 6, 8, 14, 15, 21, 68n50
Sheikh Ibrahim (neighborhood), 15, 22
Sheikh Muwannis (village), 430–31
Sheinkin, Menachem, 198, 204, 207, 218–19, 224–25, 268–71, 289–90
Shertok, Ya'akov, 204

Shield [Hamager] association, The, 217, 229–31. *See also* Arabic press; Zionism
Shihab, Fu'ad Bek, 289, 291
Shihab al-Din, 'Umar, 326–27
Shimol, Ya'akov, 105
Shmerling, Haim. 69n63
Simhon, Israel, 103–7, 113–14
Simhon, Ya'akov, 110
Simhon, Yosef, 110
Singer, Albert, 155–56
Slim, George Saliba, 89
Slor, Zvi Arye, 328
Smilansky, David, *423*
Sokolow, Nahum, 223, 404–5, 408
Sornaga, Samuel, 233
Stein, Marc, 163, 165, 179
Stirling, Walter Francis, 404, 424–25
Stughum, Hassan, 95
Suez Canal Company, 187
Syria, 11, 70n82, 229–31, 282–85, 390–91, 428–29, 434

Tajer, Shmuel, 70n73
Tajer, Ya'akov, 189
Taji, 'Abd al-Rahman al-, 304–5
Taji, Suleiman al-, 214–15
Tal al-Shammam (village), 220–27
Talmud Torah, 30, 86–87, 98, 99, 108, 118
Tamari, Emile, 384, 391
Tannenbaum, Israel, 197, 200
Tawil, Ya'akov Yosef, 131
Tel Aviv: afterlife of Chelouche, 60–64; cooperation with Jaffa municipality, 413–15, 423–28; development of, 38–44, 409–11, 412–15, 422–31; expulsion from, 45–46, 301–7; founding of, 70n73, 204–17; "Hebrew" city characteristics, 39–41; Herzl Street,

40–41, 199, 214, 424–26; May 1921 riots, 403–9; Messa visit, 409–11; mother's remains moved to, 391–92; New Company, 218–28; Palestinian opposition to, 42–43, 209, 211, 214–15; port proposal, 428–31; propaganda campaign, 261–62; return to from exile, 321–24, 380–84; separation of Tel Aviv from Jaffa, 47–51; silicate factory, 235–38; town council, 426–29; town planning, 50; Yosef Eliyahu (Chelouche) Street, 62

Temple Mount, 219

Thon, Ya'akov, 220–21, 224–25

Tiberias, 1, 8, 11, 13, 283–85, 303, 437–38

Tif'eret Israel School, Beirut, 27–28, 118–19, 126–36, 145–47, 158–60

Tiomkin, (Vladimir) Ze'ev, 169–70

Tolkowsky, Samuel (Shmu'el), 55, 236–37, 441

Tov, Avraham, 187

Tripoli, 429

Tulkarm, 352–56, 363–76

Turkey, 173, 259–60, 279, 328

typhus, 328, 332, 360–61

Tzeruya, Moshe, 111

Ussishkin, Menachem, 183, 430–31

'Uziel, Me'ir Ben Zion, 58, 72n107, 242, 389

Valero, Haim Aharon, 172

Vidal, E., 21

Wadi al-Sarrar (train station), 287–88

Webb, Sidney James, 442–43. *See also* White Paper

Weiss, 'Akiva Arieh, 196–201, 209

Weizmann, Chaim, 58, 72n103. *See also* Zionist Commission

Western Wall, 56, 432–33, 438

Wheat Committee, 291–300

wheat supply, 302–5, 328–29, 332–33, 337–38, 349–50

White Paper, 442–43. *See also* British Mandate

Williamson, G. W., 390–91

World Federation of Sephardi Jews, 53

World War I, 44–46, 231, 241–58, 379–80; British army occupation of Jaffa, 383–86; espionage, 361, 368–69, 386; expulsion of foreign nationals, 45, 262–72; expulsion of Jaffa and Tel Aviv, 46, 301–7; German army, 311, 322, 340, 371; Joint Distribution Committee, 270; labor battalions, 7, 46, 252; land purchases, 225–26; *Manzil Stab* (Ottoman military headquarters), 311–19; military conscription and exemption, 256, 261–62; promissory notes, 311–15; Wheat Committee, 291–300. *See also* Ottoman government officials

Yaffe, Betzal'el, *206*, 223, 237–38, 285–86, 288, 318–19

Yahuda, Avraham Shalom, 58

Yarkon River, 170, 236, 430–31

Yellin, David, 282–85, 410

Yesud HaMa'ala (society), 120. *See also* land purchases; Zionism

Zikhron Ya'akov (Jewish settlement), 183, 285, 344–46, 362, 377

Zionism, 2–3, 37–38, 39, 42–44, 46, 48, 51–55, 56–58, 62–64, 65n7, 141–44, 215, 219–20, 229, 370–71, 442–49; Association of Settlers (Agudat hamitnahalim), 220–27; Jewish Colonial Trust, 448; Judaism and, 447–49; land purchases, 37, 141–44, 215, 219–20; New Company, 218–28; Palestine Land Development Company (PLDC), 215, 221–27, 236; Palestinian opposition to, 37–38, 46, 52, 60, 230, 447–49; political Zionism, 445–49; practical Zionism, 2, 38, 42, 65n7; Zionist Office, 220–21. *See also* Ge'ula (society); Hovevei Zion (Lovers of Zion) (society); *individual Jewish settlements*

Zionist Commission, 395, 418. *See also* Eder, David; Weizmann, Chaim

Zlocisti, Theodor, *423*

THE TAUBER INSTITUTE SERIES FOR
THE STUDY OF EUROPEAN JEWRY

ChaeRan Y. Freeze, Series Editor
Sylvia Fuks Fried, Series Editor
Jehuda Reinharz, Series Editor
Eugene R. Sheppard, Series Editor

The Tauber Institute Series is dedicated to publishing compelling and innovative approaches to the study of modern European Jewish history, thought, culture, and society. The series features scholarly works related to the Enlightenment, modern Judaism and the struggle for emancipation, the rise of nationalism and the spread of antisemitism, the Holocaust and its aftermath, as well as the contemporary Jewish experience. The series is published under the auspices of the Tauber Institute for the Study of European Jewry—established by a gift to Brandeis University from Dr. Laszlo N. Tauber—and is supported, in part, by the Tauber Foundation and the Valya and Robert Shapiro Endowment.

For the complete list of books that are available in this series, please see
https://brandeisuniversitypress.com/series/tauber

Yosef Eliyahu Chelouche (Michelle U. Campos and Or Aleksandrowicz, editors)
Between Jaffa and Tel Aviv, 1870–1930: A Memoir

Sven-Erik Rose
Making and Unmaking Literature in the Warsaw, Lodz, and Vilna Ghettos

Amit Levy
A New Orient: From Jewish Scholarship to Middle Eastern Studies in Israel

Juliet Carey and Abigail Green, editors
Jewish Country Houses

Noa Shashar
The Marital Knot: Agunot in the Ashkenazi Realm, 1648–1850

Jehuda Reinharz and Motti Golani
Chaim Weizmann: A Biography

Blanche Bendahan (Yaëlle Azagury and Frances Malino, editors)
Mazaltob: A Novel

*Scott Ury and Guy Miron, editors
Antisemitism and the Politics of History

Jeremy Fogel
Jewish Universalisms: Mendelssohn, Cohen, and Humanity's Highest Good

Stefan Vogt, Derek Penslar, and Arieh Saposnik, editors
Unacknowledged Kinships: Postcolonial Studies and the Historiography of Zionism

Joseph A. Skloot
First Impressions: Sefer Hasidim and Early Modern Hebrew Printing

*A Sarnat Library Book